HISTORY OF
THE SECOND WORLD WAR
UNITED KINGDOM MILITARY SERIES
Edited by Sir James Butler

The authors of the Military Histories have been given full access to official documents. They and the editor are alone responsible for the statements made and the views expressed.

VICTORY IN THE WEST

VOLUME I

The Battle of Normandy

BY

MAJOR L. F. ELLIS
C.V.O., C.B.E., D.S.O., M.C.

WITH

CAPTAIN G. R. G. ALLEN, C.B.E., D.S.O., R.N.
LIEUT-COLONEL A. E. WARHURST
AIR CHIEF MARSHALL SIR JAMES ROBB,
G.C.B., K.B.E., D.S.O., D.F.C., A.F.C.

This edition of Victory in the West: Volume I
first published in 2004
by The Naval & Military Press Ltd

Published by
The Naval & Military Press Ltd
Unit 10 Ridgewood Industrial Park,
Uckfield, East Sussex,
TN22 5QE England
Tel: +44 (0) 1825 749494
Fax: +44 (0) 1825 765701
www.naval-military-press.com

Victory in the West: Volume I first published in 1962.
© Crown copyright. Reprinted with the permission of
the Controller of HMSO and Queen's Printer for Scotland.

In reprinting in facsimile from the original, any imperfections are inevitably reproduced and the quality may fall short of modern type and cartographic standards.

CONTENTS

	Page
FOREWORD	xvii

CHAPTER I. THE ORIGINS OF 'OVERLORD' . . 1

Dunkirk to Pearl Harbour	1
Anglo-American co-operation	3
Combined Chiefs of Staff	4
North Africa landings, November 1942	7
Development of the Combined Bomber Offensive	9
Appointment of Cossac	10
Cossac's outline plan approved, August 1943	17
Combined Bomber Offensive and Overlord	21
Appointment of Supreme Allied Commander, December 1943	24

CHAPTER II. THE SHAPING AND COMMAND OF OVERLORD . . 27

Allied build-up in Britain	28
Command and staff appointments	30
Enlargement of plan	32
Assault craft problems	34
Subsidiary landing in southern France?	36
Overlord's start postponed	36
Directive to General Eisenhower	39
Command of Allied Strategic Air Forces	40

CHAPTER III. THE SITUATION IN FRANCE . . 45

The Vichy régime	45
French Resistance and General de Gaulle	48
Allied help	50
Resistance in the Low Countries	51
Evolution of German defence policy	52
Appreciation by von Rundstedt, October 1943	54
Rommel to command an army group	56
Enemy situation, early 1944	56
German war production and new weapons	59

CONTENTS

	Page
CHAPTER IV. THE PLAN OF CAMPAIGN	63
Neptune Initial Joint Plan, February 1944	63
Naval, air and army plans	64
Review of plans, April 1944	80
Eisenhower's view of future strategy	82
Administration and maintenance	83
Artificial harbours ('Mulberries')	87
Conditions governing choice of H-hour and D-day	91
CHAPTER V. PREPARATORY OPERATIONS	93
New directive to strategic air forces	94
'Big Week' and air superiority	94
Attacks on airfields and radar	96
Transportation Plan	97
Assault on enemy railway system	98
On coastal defences and other military targets	102
Deception and reconnaissance	103
Counter-offensive against V-weapons	105
Effort expended and results achieved	109
CHAPTER VI. DEVELOPMENTS IN FRANCE	115
Hitler's 'Atlantic Wall'	115
German Army in the West	117
Anti-invasion measures redoubled	119
Von Rundstedt and Rommel differ	119
German air and naval forces in the West	120
Sabotage by the Resistance	121
Security and de Gaulle	125
Allied cover plans	127
German forecast of Allied intentions	128
CHAPTER VII. THE END OF THE BEGINNING	131
Naval preparations	131
Composition of Twenty-First Army Group	132
Final exercises and assembly of shipping	133
Briefing, maps and waterproofing	136
Rôle of airborne divisions	137
D-day provisionally 5th June	140
Naval movements begin and midget submarines leave	140
Postponement	141
D-day finally decided for 6th June	144
Assault forces sail	144

CONTENTS

vii

Page

Chapter VIII. D-DAY: AIRBORNE ASSAULT AND OPENING BOMBARDMENT 149

    The airborne divisions open assault 149
    Bomber Command attacks coastal defences . . 158
    Tactical surprise achieved 159
    Further measures to deceive 159
    Naval bombardment begins 161
    Allied fighters cover the fleets 161
    Assault forces reach lowering positions and deploy . 164
    American bombers attack beaches 166

Chapter IX. D-DAY: SEABORNE LANDINGS . 169

    Run-in and touch-down 169
    50th Division at Gold 173
    3rd Canadian Division at Juno 178
    3rd British Division at Sword 184
    Americans at Utah and Omaha 187
    Failure of German Air Force and Atlantic Wall . 193

Chapter X. D-DAY: ADVANCE INLAND . . 197

    German dispositions and reactions 197
    3rd British Division advance towards Caen . . 201
    6th Airborne Division reinforced 204
    3rd Canadian Division advance in centre . . 206
    50th Division close on Bayeux 209
    Allied air forces range the battlefield . . . 211
    American progress at Omaha and Utah . . 213
    Germans prepare counter-attack 216
    Beach organisation and anchorage defence . . 217
    Casualties and the day's effort 222

Chapter XI. CONSOLIDATING GAINS . . 225

    Army operations, 7th to 9th June 225
    Second Army repulses German armour . . 228
    First American Army's lodgements expanded . 232
    German Air Force impotent 233
    Allied air operations delay enemy reinforcements . 234
    Allied landings behind schedule 239
    Maritime operations, 6th to 16th June . . . 240

CONTENTS

	Page
CHAPTER XII. EXPANSION OF THE BRIDGEHEAD	247
Second Army to outflank Caen	247
Small gains east of the Orne	248
Right repulsed at Villers-Bocage	255
Americans take Caumont and cut Cotentin peninsula	256
Von Rundstedt and Rommel report situation dangerous	257
Hitler demands counter-attack	259
Mulberries, small harbours and build-up	263
Flying bombs start, 13th June	266
Hitler visits his commanders in France	268
CHAPTER XIII. THE STORM, 'EPSOM' AND CHERBOURG	271
Storm delays Caen operations	271
Second Army opens Epsom operation, 25th June	277
Heavy panzer counter-attacks beaten off	283
Americans capture Cherbourg	288
Maritime successes	289
Naval reorganisation	293
Neptune officially ended, 30th June	294
Von Rundstedt and Rommel visit Hitler in Germany	296
CHAPTER XIV. THE CAPTURE OF CAEN	299
Maritime operations	299
Effects of storm and loss of American Mulberry	301
Normandy base and build-up	302
Summary of Allied air operations since D-day	305
Opposing armies' strengths at end of June	307
Montgomery's policy unchanged	308
Second Army takes Caen, 9th July	311
Americans fight for St. Lô	318
Von Rundstedt replaced by von Kluge	321
Rommel injured and evacuated	326
CHAPTER XV. OPERATION 'GOODWOOD'	327
Evolution of the plan	327
Object to facilitate American break-out	330
Preliminary air bombardments	337
Progress of Second Army	340
Additional German tanks drawn to British front	347
Americans take St. Lô, 19th July	348

CONTENTS

	Page
Postponement of attempt to break out	348
Public concern and Shaef criticism	352

Chapter XVI. THE PLOT TO MURDER HITLER — 361

Earlier conspiracies	363
Attitude of German commanders in West	366
Plot misfires and Hitler reacts promptly	369
Events at von Kluge's headquarters and in Paris	370
Consequences for the German Army	373

Chapter XVII. THE AMERICAN BREAK-OUT — 377

First Canadian Army operational, 23rd July	377
American break-out succeeds	382
Enemy's left shattered and way to Brittany open	383
Germans start reinforcing from Pas de Calais	385
New British attack near Vire	386
German generals discuss withdrawal	395
Hitler admits its possibility, 31st July	395
Achievements of Allies' heavy bombers	399

Chapter XVIII. BEGINNING OF THE ENVELOPMENT — 401

British hold German counter-attacks	401
Third American Army operational, 1st August	402
One corps to clear Brittany	403
Main American forces to wheel left	403
Hitler orders counter-thrust to west coast	405
Montgomery orders advance to R. Seine	407
Allied armies push ahead	408
Hitler's counter-thrust defeated near Mortain	413
Explosive motor boats, 'human torpedoes' and U-boats	416

Chapter XIX. FALAISE — 419

Canadians attack towards Falaise, 7th August	419
Second Army progress	425
American corps turns north from le Mans	425
Bradley sends Third Army eastwards	429
Canadians capture Falaise	432
Hitler sanctions withdrawals	433
Model replaces von Kluge	434
Allies land in southern France, 15th August	437

CONTENTS

	Page
CHAPTER XX. ADVANCE TO THE SEINE	439
Germans in a shrinking pocket	439
Allied air attacks devastating	442
Gap finally closed, 21st August	447
Allied and German intentions	449
Americans at Seine wheel down left bank	453
British and Canadians close to Seine	454
Air attacks on enemy's escape routes	455
Paris liberated, 25th August	457
Eisenhower and Montgomery differ on future strategy	459
CHAPTER XXI. THE SEINE TO THE SOMME	465
Montgomery's objectives include Channel ports and Antwerp	465
Passage of the Seine	466
Second Army crosses the Somme	470
Americans abreast and Canadians in Dieppe	471
Le Havre blockaded from land and sea	471
U-boats lose heavily	471
Allied air operations	472
Supply problem of fast-moving armies	473
Eisenhower defines tasks	474
Assumes command in the field, 1st September	476
CHAPTER XXII. THE WINNING OF OVERLORD	477
Naval contribution to Overlord	477
Merchant Navy's part	478
Artificial harbours, petrol and supplies	479
Maintenance area and airfields	481
Army specialist corps and services	481
Contribution of the Air Forces	484
German generalship	489
Allied fighting efficiency	491
Montgomery's conduct of the battle	493
Allied progress on other European fronts	496

APPENDICES

		Page
I.	DIRECTIVE TO SUPREME COMMANDER, ALLIED EXPEDITIONARY FORCE	499
II.	ALLIED NAVAL FORCES IN OPERATION NEPTUNE	501
	Part I. Command	501
	II. Organisation of Task Forces showing associated Army formations	503
	III. Bombarding Forces	504
	IV. Summary of Forces assigned to Operation Neptune	507
	V. Landing ships and craft	511
III.	GERMAN NAVAL FORCES IN THE WEST, JUNE 1944	519
IV.	THE ALLIED ARMIES	521
	Part I. Forces engaged on the Continent	521
	II. Notes on British Army organisation	533
	III. Notes on American Army organisation	540
	IV. British Army weapons, vehicles and equipment	541
	V. Tanks and anti-tank guns	545
	VI. Measures to deal with the German mortar	550
V.	THE ENEMY	552
	Part I. German Command in the West	552
	II. German land forces encountered by the Allies	553
VI.	ALLIED AIR FORCES	556
	Part I. Forces engaged	556
	II. Notes on Allied aircraft employed	563
VII.	GERMAN AIR FORCE IN THE WEST	567
	Part I. Organisation and strength	567
	II. Notes on German aircraft employed	569
VIII.	CIVIL AFFAIRS IN FRANCE	571
IX.	OVERLORD AND FRENCH RESISTANCE	573
X.	CODE NAMES MENTIONED IN TEXT	575

GENERAL MAPS

	Page
Central Europe—At the outbreak of war, 3rd September 1939	15
The Normandy Battlefield	27
The British Assault Area	197
The Odon Battlefield	275
St. Lô to Falaise	389

SITUATION MAPS

German Army Dispositions, dawn 6th June 1944	120
The British Assault Area—Situation midnight 6th June	212
The American Assault Area—Situation midnight 6th June	222
Situation morning 10th June	248
Villers-Bocage, 11th to 15th June	256
Situation midnight 17th June	262
The Epsom Battle, 24th June to 1st July	286
Situation midnight 30th June	288
Capture of Caen, 7th to 9th July	312
The Goodwood Battle Plan	350
The Goodwood Battle, 18th to 20th July	352
Situation midnight 24th July	378
The Break-out, 24th to 31st July	380
Situation midnight 31st July	386
Caumont and Mt. Pinçon, 29th July to 6th August	410
Mortain Counter-Attack, 6th and 7th August	414
The Envelopment, 1st to 16th August	428
Capture of Falaise, 7th to 16th August	432
The Falaise Pocket, 16th to 20th August	448
The Crossing of the Seine and Advance to the Somme, 21st August to 1st September	470

DIAGRAMS AND SKETCH MAPS

	Page
Combined Chiefs of Staff Organisation	4
Supreme Headquarters Allied Expeditionary Force	38
German Armies in the West, June 1944	57
Assault Force—Naval organisation	67
Allied Air Forces—Outline order of battle, 6th June 1944	74
Operation 'Neptune'—Air cover for the assault on D-day	76
Assault Force—Army organisation	79
British Supply System	86
Mulberry Harbour at Arromanches, 4th September 1944—D+90 days.	89
Zerstörungskarte Mai 1944 (Railway Destruction)	112
Operation 'Neptune'—Convoy routes and naval covering forces.	136
Fly-in Routes of the American Airborne Divisions	157
Operation 'Neptune'—The naval bombardment.	168
Organisation of the Seaborne Assault—British Second Army.	172
'King' Beach in 'Gold' Area—Showing the German defences as known to Allied Intelligence, May 1944	176
Organisation of the Seaborne Assault—United States First Army.	189
Beach Organisation—British Sector	218
Seaward Defence System—Assault Area	220
British and German forces, July 1944.	333
Battle Forecast Diagrams—I, II and III	357, 359
Zerstörungskarte Juni, Juli 1944 (Railway Destruction).	400
The Rear Maintenance Area—Layout early August 1944	482
Europe, 5th June and 1st September 1944.	495
Overlord—Chain of Command.	500
German Naval Command Group West, June 1944	518
German Air Force in the West, June 1944—Location of headquarters	568

ILLUSTRATIONS

A majority of the illustrations are from copyright photographs supplied by the Imperial War Museum. In selecting the most suitable from its vast national collection the help of the Director and Staff of the Museum is gratefully acknowledged. Acknowledgements are also made of the help given by the U.S. Department of the Army, the Canadian Department of National Defence, the Air Ministry and the National Maritime Museum in supplying photographs which were not otherwise available.

1. General Paget	*Following page*	30
2. General Morgan		30
3. General Eisenhower		30
4. Air Marshal Tedder		30
5. Admiral Ramsay		80
6. Admiral Kirk		80
7. Admiral Vian		80
8. General Montgomery		80
9. General Bradley		80
10. General Dempsey		80
11. General Eisenhower, General Brereton, Air Marshal Coningham, General Vandenberg, Air Marshal Leigh-Mallory		96
12. *British Chiefs of Staff.* Admiral Cunningham, Field-Marshal Brooke, Air Marshal Portal, Field-Marshal Dill, General Ismay		96
13. The President with the British and Canadian Prime Ministers. Mr. Roosevelt, Mr. Churchill, Mr. Mackenzie King		96
14. Field-Marshal von Rundstedt		144
15. Field-Marshal Rommel		144
16. Field-Marshal von Kluge		144
17. Field-Marshal Model		144

Preparation for D-day

18. Aircraft for the British airborne assault		144
19. Landing craft for the naval assault		144
20. Enemy beach obstacles		160
21. Engineer tanks of the 79th Armoured Division		160
22. Mine-clearing (flail) tank		160

Airborne Assault

23. Gliders near Ranville		160
24. Bénouville bridge and gliders of *coup de main* party		160

ILLUSTRATIONS

Seaborne Approach

25.	British warships open fire	192
26.	Assault craft head for the beaches	192

Landings on D-day

27.	Infantry and amphibious (DD) tank	192
28.	Royal Marine Commandos	192
29.	Canadian troops	208
30.	Follow-up units	208
31.	Beach organisation taking shape	208
32.	Mulberry harbour under construction	208
33.	Rocket-firing Typhoon	280
34.	General de Gaulle returns to France	280
35.	Air Marshal Harris	280
36.	General Doolittle	280
37.	General Spaatz	280
38.	Lancasters of Bomber Command attack armoured divisions near Villers-Bocage	280

Air attacks on railways

39.	Near Paris	280
40.	At Vire in Normandy	280
41.	Spitfires in flight	320
42.	Air Marshal Sholto Douglas	320
43.	Air Marshal Hill	320
44 & 45.	In the Normandy *bocage*	320
46.	General Hodges	336
47.	General Patton	336
48.	General Crerar	336
49.	Lancaster bomber and Spitfire fighter	336
50.	Cromwell and Sherman tanks advance south of Caen	336
51.	Infantry with Churchill tanks attack in the cornfields	336
52.	German dual-purpose 88-mm gun	424
53.	Knocked-out German Tiger tank	424
54.	British medium (5·5-in.) gun	424
55.	Shermans in the Caumont country	424
56.	Rocket-firing Typhoons over the Falaise 'pocket'	424
57.	German transport destroyed by air attack	424
58.	Knocked-out German Panther tank	424
59.	Six-barrelled German mortar ('*nebelwerfer*')	424
60.	Mosquito of Coastal Command	476
61.	Seine bridges, old and new	476
62.	Trail of a beaten army at the Seine	476
63.	Advance of a victorious army from the Somme	476

FOREWORD

A CAMPAIGN which began with the greatest assault that has ever been made on a fortified and strongly defended coast by combined sea, land and air forces, and ended with the total defeat and unconditional surrender of Germany, must hold an outstanding position in military history. Such was the Allied campaign in North-West Europe in 1944 and 1945, of which the British operations in particular are the subject of these volumes.

Before describing how it was fought and won, the reader may be reminded of two under-lying considerations about which there can be no dispute.

This campaign could not have been fought at all if the Allies had not possessed the power to make full use of the sea and air.

All the Allied forces which defeated Germany in the West and all their material equipment reached the Continent from overseas. The combined maritime power expressed by the Allies' naval and air forces and their merchant shipping enabled them to control and use sea communications stretching thousands of miles across the oceans of the world. Had the Allies not been able to transport their strength overseas how little would it have availed them. Hitler or his successors might still be holding in thrall most of western Europe.

Moreover, the Allies' mastery in the air was not only a necessary ingredient of their maritime power but of all operations of war. The most significant revolution of warfare during the present century has been effected by the development of air power. The essential part it played in the war against Germany will appear as Allied operations are described.

Yet in spite of the Allies' maritime power, the strength of their armies, and their almost complete mastery in the air,

the campaign could hardly have been fought successfully in 1944–1945 if Germany had not at the same time been fighting for life against Russia.

To measure the relative strengths of armies it is usual to take a division as the yardstick, though divisions vary greatly in size, composition and fighting value. In June 1944, Germany had some sixty divisions with which to fight the Allies on the western front: at the same time she had over two hundred divisions fighting the Russian armies on the eastern front and about twenty divisions opposing the Allied armies in Italy. In the course of the war relative strengths changed, but it is certainly true that the western Allies defeated much less than half of the German forces and that much more than half were defeated by Russia—assisted by over £400,000,000 of war material provided by her western Allies. In appraising the conduct of the western operations these fundamental facts should not be forgotten.

Apart from its size, the dramatic completeness of the Allied victory, and the fact that it destroyed Hitler's Nazi régime and freed western Europe from German domination, the campaign has several distinctive features which add to its military significance.

In the first place Allied co-operation, built on a foundation of Anglo-American partnership, was closer and more effective than in any former war. This was indeed the key to success. In this history attention is focussed on operations under British command. That must not seem to imply under-valuation of Britain's allies; American forces were responsible for a major share of the fighting and of the Allied victory but it must also be remembered that French, Polish, Belgian, Dutch and Czechoslovak fighting men also contributed to the Allied victory, so far as they were able. The American history is being written by their own historians and several volumes are already published; we are greatly indebted for permission to use their historical studies and the results of their research. Here only enough is told of American operations to explain the conduct and progress of the fighting and the setting in which their operations took place. We also owe much to the work done by Canadian historians and gratefully acknowledge their help in describing Canadian operations under British command.

Another noteworthy feature of the campaign was the successful conjunction of sea, land and air forces in combined operations. The potential unity of military power was realised more fully than ever before and in planning, training and execution the three Services combined their distinctive skills to weave the final pattern of victory. The establishment of a British Combined Operations Headquarters was evidence of the new emphasis on inter-Service co-operation.

During the years that preceded the opening of the assault in the West the Allies had enlarged their experience of warfare with Germany in North Africa and Italy and had greatly developed their military strength. Science was called on increasingly to reinforce military knowledge and full use was made of technical skill and of organised industrial capacity. For their conclusive defeat of Germany's armed forces the Allies were equipped with advantages that no invading army had ever enjoyed before. As in every war human courage, character and skill were ultimately deciding factors, but in all three Services the human element was supported by unparalleled wealth of material power, scientifically developed and supplied on an unprecedented scale through the faithful and sustained labours of the civil population. The millions of men and women engaged in

FOREWORD

war production knew that they were indeed essential partners of those in the fighting Services, and the latter gained not only material but moral support from this knowledge of their common purpose.

Yet military success depends largely on leadership, as does the use in wartime of a nation's human and material resources. It is perhaps to the political leadership of the British and American peoples as well as to the quality of their respective military leaders and of the forces they commanded that history will largely attribute the Allied victory in the West.

This account of the British share in the campaign will be published in two volumes. The present volume contains the story up to the end of August 1944; the second will describe the remainder of the campaign which ended with victory in May 1945.

Our account is based mainly on the vast quantity of contemporary records of all three Services and of those captured from the enemy. References to published sources have been given but our far more numerous references to contemporary documents, which are not available for public inspection, are included only in a confidential edition. This should be available for use by students when the archives are opened.

We have had the advantage of personal advice and help from many of the leading commanders who were concerned and from members of the Editor's Advisory Panel. We are greatly indebted to them. We also wish to thank Mrs. R. Donald, Mrs. H. Southern, Miss D. J. Dawson and Lieut-Colonel G. W. Harris who at various stages have helped us in our researches; Mr. B. M. Melland, Mr. R. R. A. Wheatley and Mr. A. M. Sefi for the study and translation of captured German documents; and Mr. D. K. Purle who, under the guidance of Colonel T. M. Penney, has drawn all the maps and diagrams. We are deeply grateful to them and we acknowledge thankfully how much we owe to their work. We have learnt much from the criticism and counsel of Sir James Butler and we thank him for his unfailing kindness and help.

We have had unrestricted access to naval, army and air force records and to other relevant documents which are not available to the public, and complete freedom in using them; the Historical Sections of the Cabinet Office and the Service Ministries have been consistently helpful and we have never been asked to modify our text in order to conform to an 'official' view. What is written in the following chapters is our own view of the campaign, formed after very careful study. For any errors of fact or judgement we alone are responsible.

L. F. ELLIS

December 1960

CHAPTER I

THE ORIGINS OF 'OVERLORD'

'You will enter the continent of Europe and, in conjunction with other United Nations, undertake operations aimed at the heart of Germany and the destruction of her armed forces.'[1]

The simplicity and confidence of this order, given to General Eisenhower early in 1944, may not impress the reader who knows what happened afterwards but does not remember so clearly what had gone before. To English people who had lived through the torturing uncertainties of the four previous years it marked an amazing climax.

Nearly four years had passed since the British Expeditionary Force, which entered the Continent on the outbreak of war to combine with France against the armed forces of Germany, had been withdrawn to England leaving Hitler master not only of France but of Norway, Denmark, Holland, Belgium, Luxembourg, Austria, Czechoslovakia and western Poland. Eastern Poland, Finland and the smaller Baltic States had been absorbed by Russia with Germany's connivance; Hitler's ally, Italy, had overrun Albania. Alone in Europe, weakened by loss though backed by all the nations of the Commonwealth, Britain then confronted the massive strength of Germany and her associates. British confidence in ultimate victory was not shaken, but it was recognised that while the fight for existence continued at sea and in the air, action must be mainly defensive; economic blockade at sea and air attack on German centres of production were the chief weapons to employ till the armed strength of the nation and Commonwealth had been restored and expanded, and we could again take the offensive. The loss of any foothold on the Continent from which Germany could be attacked underlined the need of amphibious forces and gave impetus to the development of equipment for amphibious operations.[2]

Other volumes of this series tell of the years which passed before Britain could join with the United States of America in so confidently ordering General Eisenhower to re-enter Europe and

---

[1] Appendix I.

[2] Following common practice, the term 'amphibious' is used to describe operations which require the use of both sea and land forces, but it should be remembered that the term also covers the use of air forces which are an *essential* component of all 'amphibious' operations.

destroy the enemy's armed forces, yet the significance of that order and the story of how it was obeyed cannot be appreciated fully without remembrance of how our position had been revolutionised between 1940 and 1944.

There had been the threat of invasion and victory in the Battle of Britain as there had been continuous war in the air in succeeding years. There had been victories and defeats in Cyrenaica, Libya, Abyssinia and Somaliland, in Greece and Crete, Syria, Iraq and the Far East. There had been Germany's vicious onslaught on Russia in 1941, which alined a new and powerful ally with Britain and the Commonwealth though at the cost of material aid which could be ill spared. Later that year the United States, an even greater ally, had joined us in the war, when Japan attacked at Pearl Harbour and seized islands and territories in the Pacific and the Far East. It was not until late in 1942 that the tide turned. Then British and American troops who had landed in Algeria and Morocco struck eastwards to meet converging British forces driving the enemy westwards from Egypt, while Russia struck back successfully at Stalingrad and other points in her long front. Thereafter there had been no major setbacks. In 1943 Russia had renewed her counter-offensive and recovered more lost ground, while the western Allies had freed all North Africa, Sicily and southern Italy, destroying in their progress large enemy armies and forcing Italy to surrender. Meanwhile, in the Pacific, Japanese ambitions had been baulked effectively, and the Allies' position had been progressively improved.

Throughout these long and fluctuating fights, embracing every theatre and every front, the Anglo-American fighting capacity had been sustained by their navies' never-resting war at sea, despite its fearful toll of men and ships. The stern challenge of the U-boats, which had threatened our very existence, at length appeared to have been mastered, and from the middle of 1943 the security of the Allies' sea communications was comparatively assured. We no longer faced the question of survival but the task of building up strength for a decisive attack on Hitler's 'fortress'. The very fact that through those lean and dangerous years we had been able to move troops and supplies across the oceans of the world, though often through great dangers and with severe loss, was a measure of the significance of maritime power and of the debt we owe to the Royal Navy and the Merchant Navy and to their partner, the Royal Air Force.

When the pageant of those years is reviewed from a distance the outstanding changes which had taken place between 1940 and 1944 are easily distinguishable. A great national effort together with the passage of time, the fruits of experience, the moral support and material assistance of the United States (in the President's phrase, 'all aid short of war'), had already enabled Britain and the Commonwealth to make war more effectively by the end of 1941 when the entry of America into the war added her full resources of man-power, materials and industrial capacity to the forces matched against the Axis powers.[3] By the close of 1943 the advantages which Germany had won by force in 1940 were more than counter-balanced through the combination of the Allies' strength; thereafter the balance of power was progressively weighted in their favour and while their position was thus conspicuously improved the relative position of Germany was no less conspicuously worsened. In 1940 her armies had held in Europe what seemed to be a position of unchallengeable dominance; by the end of 1943 they were being driven back on two fronts and a third was threatened. So large a proportion of her army and air force was fighting a defensive war in Russia and Italy that, whereas in June 1940 there were 137 German divisions in France and the Low Countries, now less than half that number could be spared to meet the Allies' coming thrust. Moreover, Hitler's obstinate belief that he could strangle us at sea and wound us mortally from the air had proved to be as vain as his desire to dominate Europe, and by the end of 1943 Allied mastery in both elements was virtually assured. Germany had still great war-making capacity, but the Allies' capacity was even greater when General Eisenhower was given command of the forces which were to win for the Allies victory in the West.

Plans and preparations for the Allied campaign had already reached a penultimate stage when the Supreme Commander was chosen at the close of 1943. Two years before, that is a fortnight after Japan's attack on Pearl Harbour had brought America into the war, Mr. Winston Churchill and President Franklin D. Roosevelt, with their military advisers, had met in Washington to take counsel together. They had been in almost continuous consultation since the outbreak of war in Europe and as American aid to Britain increased they had agreed that the defeat of Germany would take precedence even if Japan should enter the war. They had met earlier in 1941 and had expressed the British and American unity of purpose in the Atlantic Charter.[4] But the meeting in Washington at the end of that year was the first of its kind, for now both America and Japan were at war. It was distinguished from those which were to follow by the code name 'Arcadia', though anything less arcadian than its purpose

---

[3] For the story of Anglo-American co-operation during 1940–1941 see the volumes of Grand Strategy in this series.

[4] The Atlantic Charter was an eight-point declaration of peace aims issued by Mr. Roosevelt and Mr. Churchill during their meeting at sea on 14th Aug. 1941. It was published in Great Britain as a White Paper (Cmd. 6321) on 31st Oct. 1941.

or than Washington in mid-winter would be hard to conceive. A decision was taken there which had immeasurable consequences, for it confirmed an agreement that the western Allies' war effort and use of resources in man-power and materials should be accepted as combined responsibilities—an arrangement which was certainly more nearly ideal than any other arrangement made by any other Allies, in any other war.[5]

To implement this resolution, subject to the direction of the Prime Minister and the President (whose close friendship and almost daily communication ensured their personal accord), the Chiefs of Staff of the three Services of each country were constituted as 'the Combined Chiefs of Staff', who were in practice to serve the Allies as the corporate, directing mind for all operations of war. The composition of this momentous conjunction is shown below.

COMBINED CHIEFS OF STAFF'S ORGANISATION

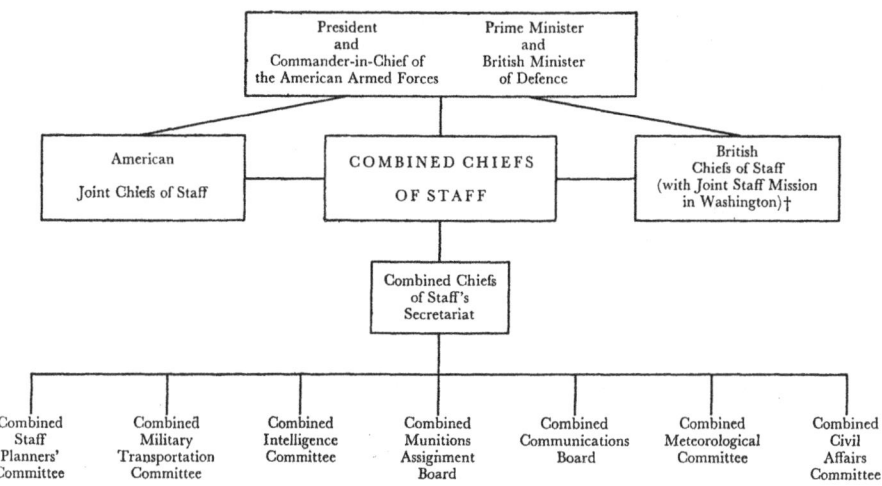

† The British Joint Staff Mission represented the British Chiefs of Staff at routine meetings of the Combined Chiefs of Staff and also acted as liaison between the British diplomatic and supply bodies in Washington and the Combined Chiefs of Staff organisation.

It will be remembered that Mr. Churchill was both Prime Minister and Minister of Defence, and under him the British Chiefs of Staff Committee were virtually responsible for the central direction of all British operations of war. Mr. Roosevelt was both President and Commander-in-Chief of all armed forces of the United States.

The original membership of the Combined Chiefs of Staff was as follows:

---

[5] *Biennial Report of the Chief of Staff of the United States Army to the Secretary of War, July 1, 1943 to June 30, 1945* (H.M.S.O., 1945), p. 8.

British Chiefs of Staff Committee
    General Sir Alan Brooke, Chief of the Imperial General Staff.
    Admiral of the Fleet Sir Dudley Pound, First Sea Lord and Chief of the Naval Staff.
    Air Chief Marshal Sir Charles Portal, Chief of Air Staff.
    Lieut-General Sir Hastings Ismay, Mr. Churchill's representative.

American Joint Chiefs of Staff
    Admiral W. D. Leahy, Chief of Staff to the President.
    General G. C. Marshall, Chief of Staff of the Army.
    Admiral H. R. Stark, Chief of Naval Operations.
    Admiral E. J. King, Commander-in-Chief of the United States Fleet.
    Lieut-General H. H. Arnold, Commanding General Army Air Forces and Deputy Chief of Staff for Air.

Later, Sir Dudley Pound was succeeded by Admiral of the Fleet Sir Andrew Cunningham; Admiral Stark left for London as Commander, United States Naval Forces in Europe, and Admiral King combined the offices of Commander-in-Chief of the U.S. Fleet and Chief of Naval Operations.

Since it was also decided that the headquarters of the Combined Chiefs of Staff should be in Washington, full meetings could only be held at intervals, so the members of a British Joint Staff Mission, which had succeeded an earlier military mission and was already stationed in Washington, were appointed to represent the British Chiefs of Staff at routine meetings held for the day-to-day conduct of business. Field-Marshal Sir John Dill, who had until recently been Chief of the Imperial General Staff and was at this time acting as personal adviser to Mr. Churchill in his capacity of Minister of Defence, was now appointed to remain as his personal representative in Washington and to head the Mission, whose other members were Admiral Sir Charles Little, General Sir Colville Wemyss and Air Marshal A. T. Harris.

Though the history of grand strategy is being written in other volumes of this series, any account of British operations in the final campaign in North-West Europe must take cognisance of such high-level decisions as directly affected the conduct of the campaign. Moreover, the first statement of Allied strategy has distinctive importance.

In confirmation of British and American agreements on strategic aims which had been reached before the United States was at war, it was reaffirmed at the Washington Conference that 'notwithstanding the entry of Japan into the war' the Atlantic and European theatre was still considered to be 'the decisive theatre', Germany 'the prime enemy', and her defeat 'the key to victory'; 'only the minimum of force necessary for the safe-guarding of vital interests in other theatres should be diverted from operations against Germany'. For the American public, traditionally sensitive to any threat of Japanese encroachment, this might well have proved an unpopular decision; it is the more notable as evidence that on this fundamental question British and American war leaders had at this stage reached a common conclusion.

It could hardly be expected that this would always be so. In the conduct of a world war the widely separated standpoints of two such differently circumstanced countries as Great Britain and the United States must inevitably make it difficult for their political and military leaders always to find a mutually acceptable policy, and it is neither surprising nor disturbing that British and American views did not always coincide, that, indeed, they differed radically at various times. What is more impressive is the fact that their leaders so often saw alike, and that even when prolonged discussion failed to reconcile opinions, agreed decisions were none the less arrived at and, once reached, were loyally observed. A characteristic illustration was provided during the ensuing months.

Having agreed that their first aim was to defeat Germany, the Allies defined the essential features of their strategy as requiring security of the main areas of British and American war industry and the maintenance of their essential sea and air communications; the closing and tightening of the ring round Germany; the wearing down and undermining of German resistance; and the continuous development of offensive action against Germany. While concentrating on these tasks, only such positions in the eastern theatre should be maintained as would safeguard vital interests and deny Japan access to raw materials needed for her continuance of the war.

They went on to enumerate the 'steps to be taken in 1942 to put into effect the above general policy'. Of these only three need be mentioned here. The 'ring round Germany' was to be strengthened and closed 'by sustaining the Russian front, by arming and supporting Turkey, by increasing our strength in the Middle East, and by gaining possession of the whole North African coast'. The 'wearing down of Germany' would be sought through 'ever-increasing air bombardment by British and American forces'; other means would be assistance to Russia, blockade and the maintenance of a spirit of revolt and the organisation of subversive movements in occupied countries. It did 'not seem likely' that in 1942 any large-scale land offensive against Germany would be possible except on the Russian front, but the Allies must be ready to take advantage of any opening that might result from the wearing down of German resistance 'to conduct limited land offensives'. 'In 1943 the way may be clear', they said, 'for a return to the Continent across the Mediterranean, from Turkey into the Balkans, or by landings in Western Europe.' That was as far as the Allies could foresee their long-term strategy at the beginning of 1942, but preliminary steps were taken to plan and prepare for the assembly in England of the Allied forces that would be needed for large-scale operations on the Continent.

And even as they reached these decisions the world situation was changing in ways which would modify their application. In the first half of 1942 the Allies' position went from bad to worse nearly everywhere. A Russian winter counter-offensive had regained ground, but a heavy German attack was renewed after the thaw and the Russians were driven back at crucial points. Japanese conquests in the Pacific and Far East (including our loss of Hong Kong and Singapore) threatened India, Australia and the remaining islands of the Pacific; Rommel's advance in North Africa threatened Egypt and the Middle East; while the continued loss of Allied merchant shipping threatened world-wide ocean routes and in particular the Atlantic communications on which any Allied offensive in Europe must depend. During this time much of the Allies' resources and shipping was inevitably absorbed by urgent measures to arrest the enemies' advances. A plan which had been discussed at Washington for British and American landings in North-West Africa, to close the ring round Germany on the southern front, had perforce to be laid aside, though the Joint Planning Committee of the Combined Chiefs of Staff (later called the Combined Staff Planners) had regarded it 'as of the first strategical importance in the Atlantic area'.

After the return from Washington in January 1942, British planning was intensified for the major operation envisaged in 1943—namely the launching of a full-scale attack by Allied forces landed in France—or, alternatively, an immediate landing in France by such forces as would be available at the time if circumstances required such an emergency operation in 1942. The first of these was known as 'Roundup', the second as 'Sledgehammer'.

In April, General Marshall and Mr. Harry Hopkins (the unofficial personal emissary of the President) came to England bringing a project in general terms for the major operation against Germany in 1943 and meanwhile for the opening of 'an active sector on this front by steadily increasing air operations and by raids and forays all along the coasts'. It also called for immediate preparations in readiness for an emergency operation in 1942 though this 'WOULD BE JUSTIFIED ONLY IN CASE (1) THE SITUATION ON THE RUSSIAN FRONT BECOMES DESPERATE ... (2) THE GERMAN SITUATION IN WESTERN EUROPE BECOMES CRITICALLY WEAKENED'.[6]

---

[6] Capitals in the original text.

These proposals were warmly welcomed. American participation in 1943 was promised on a scale which greatly enlarged the previous conception of Roundup and enhanced the prospect of an earlier German defeat. The comparatively small contribution which was all that America could provide in 1942 if the Allies were led by circumstances to embark on the emergency operation, Sledgehammer, was also defined.

It would be necessary to go far beyond the scope of this volume to trace events which, in the following months, led to a gradual divergence of British and American views on the policy to be pursued against Germany. The fact must be noted that American opinion moved away from the limitations of action in 1942 which had been stressed in the April text of the Marshall plan. By July, when, with Admiral King and Mr. Hopkins, General Marshall again came to London it was to urge 'that Sledgehammer be immediately adopted as a combined British-American operational plan for execution at the earliest possible date in 1942, not later than October 15th' and 'be regarded as the opening phase of Roundup with the consequent purpose not only of remaining on the Continent but of building up ground and air forces and logistic facilities, and expanding our foothold, to the limits of our capabilities'. The President had instructed them that he regarded it as 'of the highest importance that U.S. ground troops be brought into action against the enemy in 1942' and Sledgehammer 'of such grave importance' that they 'should strongly urge immediate all-out preparations for it'.[7]

In the discussions which had been pursued between April and July there had been no corresponding change in the British view. British leaders shared the desire of both the American and Russian leaders to open a 'second front' against Germany in the West as soon as possible, but anxious and prolonged study had only confirmed their conclusion that, except in emergency, to launch a cross-Channel operation in 1942, with the comparatively small forces and equipment, mostly British, which were all that could be available then, would be a grave mistake. It would offer little hope of success against unbroken German strength and might well result in costly failure; it would but 'eat up the seed corn' from which a later and larger harvest must be won. In the British view the only favourable opportunity for action against Germany in 1942 was in North Africa, and they reverted to the plan discussed at Washington for Allied landings there 'to close the ring round Germany'.

When General Marshall and his colleagues were at length con-

---

[7] Presidential memorandum, 'Instructions for the London Conference, July 16th, 1942' (quoted in Robert E. Sherwood, *White House Papers of Harry L. Hopkins* (London, 1949), vol. II, p. 605).

vinced that these opposed views could not be reconciled they reported this to President Roosevelt and on his instructions agreed to the North African operation; but although this might delay the major cross-Channel assault in 1943, preparations for such an assault were to continue vigorously. A plan, 'Bolero', for the movement of American forces, supplies and equipment to Great Britain and for their reception, accommodation and maintenance there, was already in operation under the direction of combined staffs, constituting 'Bolero' committees, in Washington and London.

It was characteristic of both British and American leaders that when once a plan which they had opposed strongly was finally adopted by mutual consent, they threw themselves whole-heartedly into preparations for its achievement. The agreement which had been reached so slowly in July was quickly put into effect. British and American forces landed in French North Africa that autumn and by January 1943 their action was already yielding good results when a further meeting at the highest level was held near Casablanca, in Morocco. This meeting was more appropriately christened 'Symbol', for it was indeed symbolic of Allied unity in action and it marked a crucial turning-point in the war with Germany. When the meeting was in progress, converging attacks from east and west were visibly loosening the enemy's grip on North Africa. In Europe, Russia was regaining more lost ground and had in turn surrounded a German army besieging Stalingrad. In both theatres the enemy had been forced on to the defensive. The ring round Germany was being closed.

At Casablanca it was agreed, among much else which does not directly concern this volume, that when North Africa was cleared pressure on the enemy must be maintained by a follow-up attack on Sicily, though this would mean that the Allies could not also stage in 1943 a large-scale invasion of Europe from the west against unbroken opposition. They would develop the Combined Bomber Offensive aimed at the enemy's war-making capacity and morale; they would continue to assemble the strongest possible forces in readiness to re-enter the Continent as soon as German resistance was sufficiently weakened; and meantime they would undertake such limited cross-Channel operations as might be practicable with the forces and material available. One other decision was taken which indirectly bore heavily on Overlord. The battle of the Atlantic was in its most critical stage and it was agreed that this must be given priority over all else; production of landing craft was cut down to make way for more escort vessels and other warships. The difficulty of mounting 'a large-scale invasion of Europe' was correspondingly increased. The Combined Chiefs of Staff went on to define the operations to be undertaken in 1943 and, in considering the question of command, they now envisaged an invasion in force in 1944. The President had suggested that the supreme commander should be British, but Mr. Churchill felt that this could be determined later, on the principle that command should be held by an officer of the nation which furnished the majority of the forces employed.[8] In order to prepare plans for the operation it was, however, decided to set up at once a combined allied staff, under a British chief of staff with an American deputy. Subsequently Lieut-General F. E. Morgan was appointed 'Chief of Staff to the Supreme Allied Commander (designate)' with Major-General Ray W. Barker, of the United States Army, as his deputy. Other members of the staff were drawn from all three Services of both nations and the organisation became known as C.O.S.S.A.C. from the initials of General Morgan's designation.

Some little time elapsed while the Combined Chiefs of Staff settled the terms of General Morgan's directive, so that he only received it on the 26th of April, 1943. It declared that 'our object is to defeat the German fighting forces in North-West Europe' and it instructed him not only to prepare plans for a full-scale assault against the Continent as early as possible in 1944 but also for 'an elaborate camouflage and deception scheme' extending over the coming summer and designed to pin the enemy in the West and keep alive German expectation of large cross-Channel operations in 1943. He was also to prepare plans for an immediate return to the Continent, with whatever forces might be available at the time, in the event of German disintegration.

At the next full meeting ('Trident'), held in Washington in May 1943, the shape of a large-scale assault in 1944 was given further definition. Its aim would be to secure a lodgement on the Continent from which further offensive operations could be carried out. The target date was to be May the 1st, 1944, and forces and equipment for the operation would be established in the United Kingdom as rapidly as possible. Subsequently General Morgan was given a supplementary directive and a list of forces which were expected to be available. These would comprise an assault force of nine divisions (that is, five infantry divisions simultaneously loaded in assault vessels, two infantry divisions as follow-up and two airborne divisions) and twenty divisions for movement into the lodgement area. Provision was to be made for the seizure and development of ports that would enable these forces to be augmented by further divisions, shipped direct from America or elsewhere at the rate of from three to five a month. Naval forces would include about 3,300 assault ships and landing craft; air forces were expected to consist of about

---

[8] See W. S. Churchill, *The Second World War*, vol. IV (1951), pp. 393–407, 827.

11,400 aircraft which would include 632 transport planes for airborne operations.

General Morgan was to submit an outline plan for the operation—now renamed 'Overlord'—by August the 1st, and as it was already the first week of June this allowed him very little time.

Fortunately Cossac inherited a mass of material from those who had been planning Roundup and Sledgehammer, and on this his staff had begun work immediately on appointment. Staff studies, appreciations and plans for cross-Channel operations, of various kinds and on increasing scale, had indeed been prepared almost without pause since the British Expeditionary Force had returned from France in 1940; for even before evacuation from Dunkirk was completed and though the country was threatened with invasion, Mr. Churchill had ordered the adoption of an offensive policy by raids on enemy-held coasts and had instituted a small organisation to give effect to it under the command of General A. G. B. Bourne, Royal Marines. The day when we should be able to return to France in force to fight the German Army seemed then to be remote indeed, but while building up our strength we could do something immediately to trouble the enemy's occupation of the shores which faced us across the Channel and the North Sea.

In the years which followed, many raids of varying size and importance had been carried out in order to damage or destroy German installations or equipment and to disturb the enemy's peace of mind. As our raiding experience accumulated the small organisation which Mr. Churchill had instituted was gradually expanded, first under the direction of Admiral of the Fleet Sir Roger Keyes and later under Commodore Lord Louis Mountbatten, into a Combined Operations Headquarters, separate alike from the Admiralty, the War Office and the Air Ministry, though with close affiliations to all three. This was an innovation in British military organisation, and partly because, in its adolescence, its functions in relation to the Services and other Ministries were shaped by the needs of the moment rather than to any previously-designed pattern, and partly because the seed which it grew bore fruit in the operations of others, the importance of the part which Combined Operations Headquarters played in the final campaign is often not sufficiently recognised. Yet by 1943 its work had had three results of far-reaching consequence.

First, the Chief of Combined Operations, Lord Louis Mountbatten, had been promoted Vice-Admiral with equivalent ranks in the Army and Royal Air Force; he had been given the status of a Chief of Staff and, when major issues or matters affecting combined operations were under consideration, he sat as a member of the Chiefs of Staff Committee.

Secondly, the Chief of Combined Operations and his staff had acquired recognised authority as indispensable advisers on the planning and equipment of all seaborne assaults; in collaboration with the Service Ministries they had prepared and published a comprehensive series of training manuals which were in use by the Services; and they had acquired, and furnished with expert instructors and special equipment, a number of training areas, on which the necessary instruction in the new assault technique was being practised under skilled guidance and in realistic conditions.

Thirdly, experiment and concentrated study of the special requirements of a seaborne assault, based at first on experience gained in raids and more recently in Mediterranean landings, had been joined with the Royal Navy's long experience and skill to produce a variety of specially designed assault shipping and landing craft which were to play a decisive part in the coming assault on the French coast, and indeed in seaborne assaults in every theatre of war.

The Chief of Combined Operations had one other task of a different nature. He was responsible for the organisation, training, and control of 'Commandos'—small formations of troops drawn from the Army and the Royal Marines (one was also found from the Allied contingents in Britain) who were specially trained for employment on expeditions which called for a high degree of disciplined daring and initiative, such as the raiding of an enemy coast or the quick seizure of a threatening strongpoint. Eight Commandos were among the first of the Allied troops to reach France as were the closely corresponding American 'Ranger' battalions.

But the contribution of Combined Operations Headquarters to the success of the coming campaign cannot be measured only by these and other easily distinguishable achievements. The doctrine preached by Combined Operations Headquarters, with its emphasis on unified staff-work and control, affected the outlook and permeated the thought of all three Services and influenced action in many unrecognised ways. It was indeed fortunate that so much imagination and energy had been available for the propagation of its faith and the proof of its works before the Allies were to launch the biggest combined operation yet known. Especially in that formative period it owed a great deal to the ability and zeal of Lord Louis Mountbatten.

The climax of our raiding policy was reached in August 1942 with a so-called 'reconnaissance in force' at Dieppe in which the land forces engaged consisted mainly of Canadian troops. It was on a much bigger scale than any previous raid, and though carried out with great gallantry the main tactical object was not achieved and the raid involved heavy losses. But it provided experience of great value and its lessons had far-reaching influence on the planning and conduct of the final cross-Channel assault, for tactical failure may be more instructive than success if the lessons are duly learnt. It not only re-emphasised the need for meticulous inter-Service planning and training to ensure exact but flexible performance, smooth co-operation and the effective use of available means, but exposed the necessity for improved technique, organisation and equipment, and for a higher standard of arrangements for communications and control. Outstanding among the lessons learnt was the importance of overwhelming fire-support in the initial stages of a seaborne landing. This led to the evolution of a new technique of bombardment, in which all types of naval, air and army weapons were combined. Special types of craft were designed to provide close support inshore and to enable the Army's field guns to fire while still afloat. These developments and the advent of the amphibious tank and other specialised armoured fighting vehicles combined to establish the fire power of the Army during the initial stages of a landing.[9]

Dieppe taught that the association of considerable naval and army forces for combined operations involved complex problems of organisation which had not been fully mastered. The naval forces which had been engaged at Dieppe were therefore retained as the embryo of 'Force J' which served for the continuous study of amphibious problems and was developed as the prototype of the other naval 'forces' to be used in the assault. Eventually Force J bore the Canadian component of our assaulting armies to the initial landing in Normandy.

The long-range striking power of modern armaments and air forces, scientific apparatus to give the enemy early warning of our approach, and concrete and other coastal defences would constitute difficulties against which no seaborne force had ever before been matched. Yet the pregnant importance of specially designed assault ships and landing craft may not at first sight be obvious, for it derived from another special characteristic of the Second World War. During this war highly mechanised armies were being engaged for the first time, and these were employing a variety, size and weight of equipment hitherto unknown. Seaborne assault was no longer mainly an affair of landing men but of also landing the vast scale of artillery, tanks, vehicles, mechanical plant, ammunition, stores, supplies and petrol on which a mechanised army is dependent in battle, and of landing them not in ports but on open beaches and in the face of modern ground and air defences. In every seaborne attack assault ships and landing craft in sufficient numbers had

---

[9] Notes on these and other weapons used in the Overlord campaign are given in Appendix IV.

become a prerequisite of success. An account of these essential instruments of seaborne invasion is given in Appendix II, but as the subject will recur constantly in this history it may be helpful to explain here what is involved. Assault *ships* comprise passenger liners equipped to carry both assaulting troops and small landing craft for putting them ashore; specially built naval vessels to carry tanks or vehicles and to discharge them on the shore over ramps; and a wide range of merchant ships adapted to perform various functions in the assault area. All these were capable of making ocean voyages. Landing *craft* were designed to land troops, vehicles or stores on open beaches during an assault, or to give them fire support from close inshore. They varied in size and function from small craft holding thirty-six men which could be carried at davits by infantry landing *ships*, to craft designed to land heavy vehicles or any close fire support weapons. Landing craft are open-decked for use in comparatively sheltered water and are not capable of making ocean voyages.[10] It will be found that as the war progressed shortage of certain categories, notably tank landing ships (L.S.T.s), at times had a marked influence on strategy. Why this shortage persisted, why, as General Marshall wrote, it 'was to plague us to the final day of the war in Europe', why in Mr. Churchill's phrase 'the plans of two great Empires like Britain and the United States should be so much hamstrung and limited by . . . these particular vessels',[11] is discussed in Appendix II and in the volumes dealing with grand strategy. It will be seen later how it affected the campaign to be described.

When the Cossac staff were appointed they entered into a rich inheritance not only of experience focussed in Combined Operations Headquarters but also of work done by the group known as the Combined Commanders, who throughout the previous year had been studying conditions to be met in a seaborne attack on Germany under various conditions—that is in Sledgehammer or Roundup. The Combined Commanders were General Sir Bernard Paget, Commander-in-Chief Home Forces, with, at different times, Air

---

[10] The principal types of assault ships and landing craft, and the initials by which they are commonly known are as follows:

Landing Ship Headquarters	(L.S.H.)
,, ,, Infantry	(L.S.I.)
,, ,, Tank	(L.S.T.)
Landing Craft Infantry	(L.C.I.)
,, ,, Assault	(L.C.A.)
,, ,, Tank	(L.C.T.)

There were in all nineteen different types of assault ships and landing craft.

[11] *The War Reports of General Marshall, Admiral King and General Arnold*, ed. Millis Walter and J. B. Lippincott (New York, 1947), p. 154; Churchill, *The Second World War*, vol. V, p. 454.

Marshal Sir Sholto Douglas succeeded by Air Marshal Sir Trafford Leigh-Mallory as Air Officer Commanding-in-Chief, Fighter Command, and Vice-Admiral Sir Bertram Ramsay (who had at this time been appointed as Naval Commander (Designate) of the Expeditionary Force for Sledgehammer) or other naval representatives. General Dwight D. Eisenhower and later Lieut-General Frank M. Andrews, Commanding General, European Theatre of Operations of United States Army (known as E.T.O.U.S.A.), were associated with them, while Vice-Admiral Lord Louis Mountbatten, as Chief of Combined Operations, joined them when required. Their planners had summarised among other things an exhaustive collection of information on the nature of the whole seaboard from Holland to the Bay of Biscay. In this they had examined the respective advantages and demerits of every beach on which a landing might be made, of every port which might be captured and every locality from which operations could then be developed. In each case they took into account the sea approaches, the prevailing winds and tides; the nature of the beaches, their exits, hinterlands and possible inundations; the prospect of an early seizure of one or more major ports; the availability of airfields or land suitable for their early construction; the volume of fighter protection that could be afforded from British airfields in the opening phase; the enemy's coastal and beach defences, and the strength of the troops holding them; the location of enemy naval forces and minefields; the nature and strength of the naval support required; and, finally, the capacity of the assault area for a build-up of forces to compete with the enemy's reserves. Taking all these into consideration the Combined Commanders agreed that the most favourable place for a large-scale landing was the Caen sector of Normandy provided that the eastern beaches of the Cotentin peninsula were *included* in the assault area so as to facilitate the early capture of Cherbourg. They regarded this condition as essential.

The Cossac staff re-examined all this material and quickly narrowed the choice to two areas, namely the Pas de Calais coast or the Caen sector of Normandy. At first sight it would seem obvious that the cross-Channel assault should be made where the French coast lies within sight of the cliffs of Dover and air cover for the assaulting forces could most easily be provided; moreover, a landing there would open to the Allies the shortest route to Germany. But just because this was so obvious the German defences of the Pas de Calais coast were the most formidable; this was indeed the pivotal area of their defence system. Moreover, the ports in the Dover area were far too small to accommodate the invasion shipping which would have to assemble at many ports along the south coast and in the Thames estuary. Apart from this there were other disadvantages. The conformation of the Pas de Calais coast with its high cliffs,

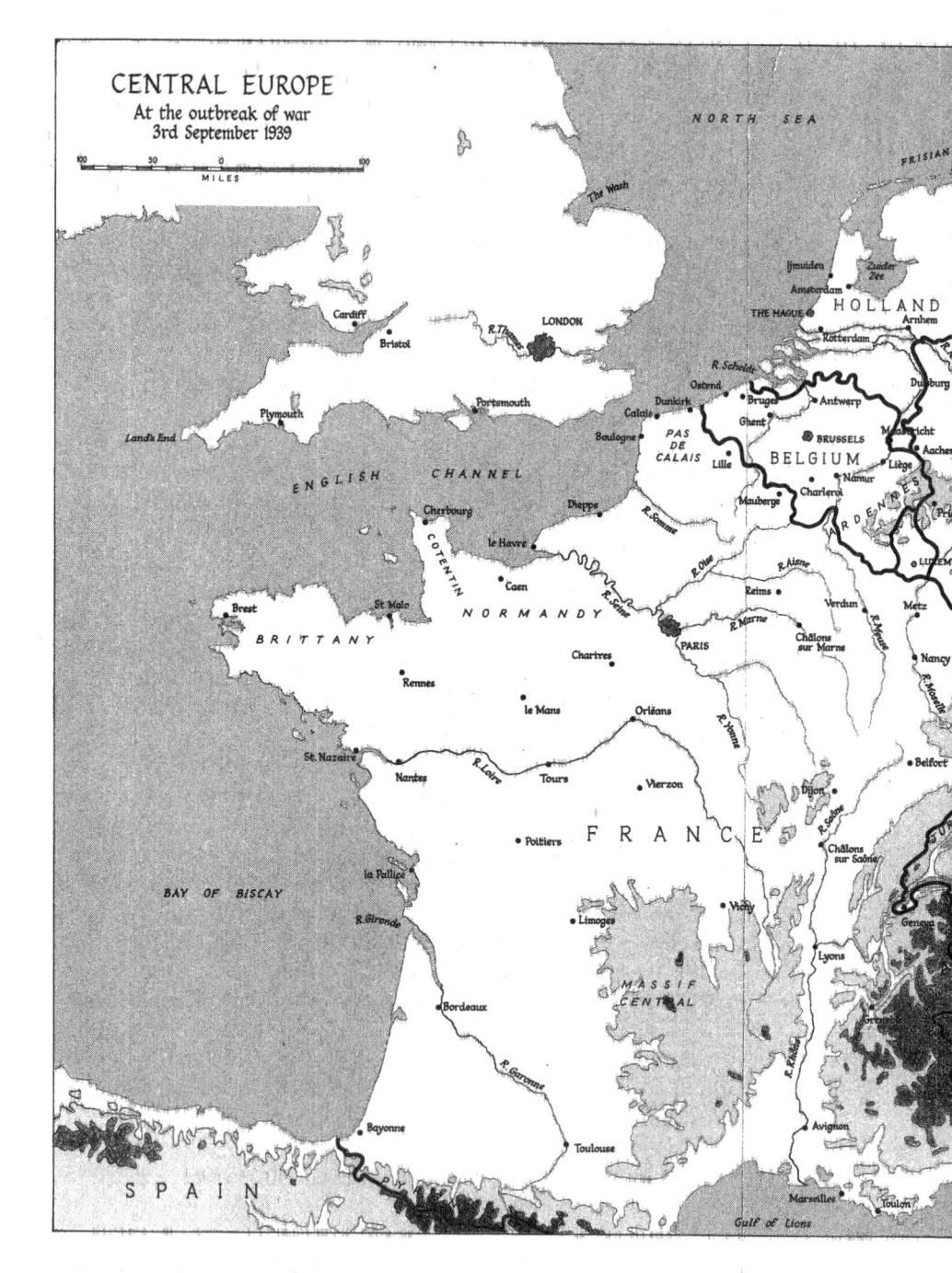

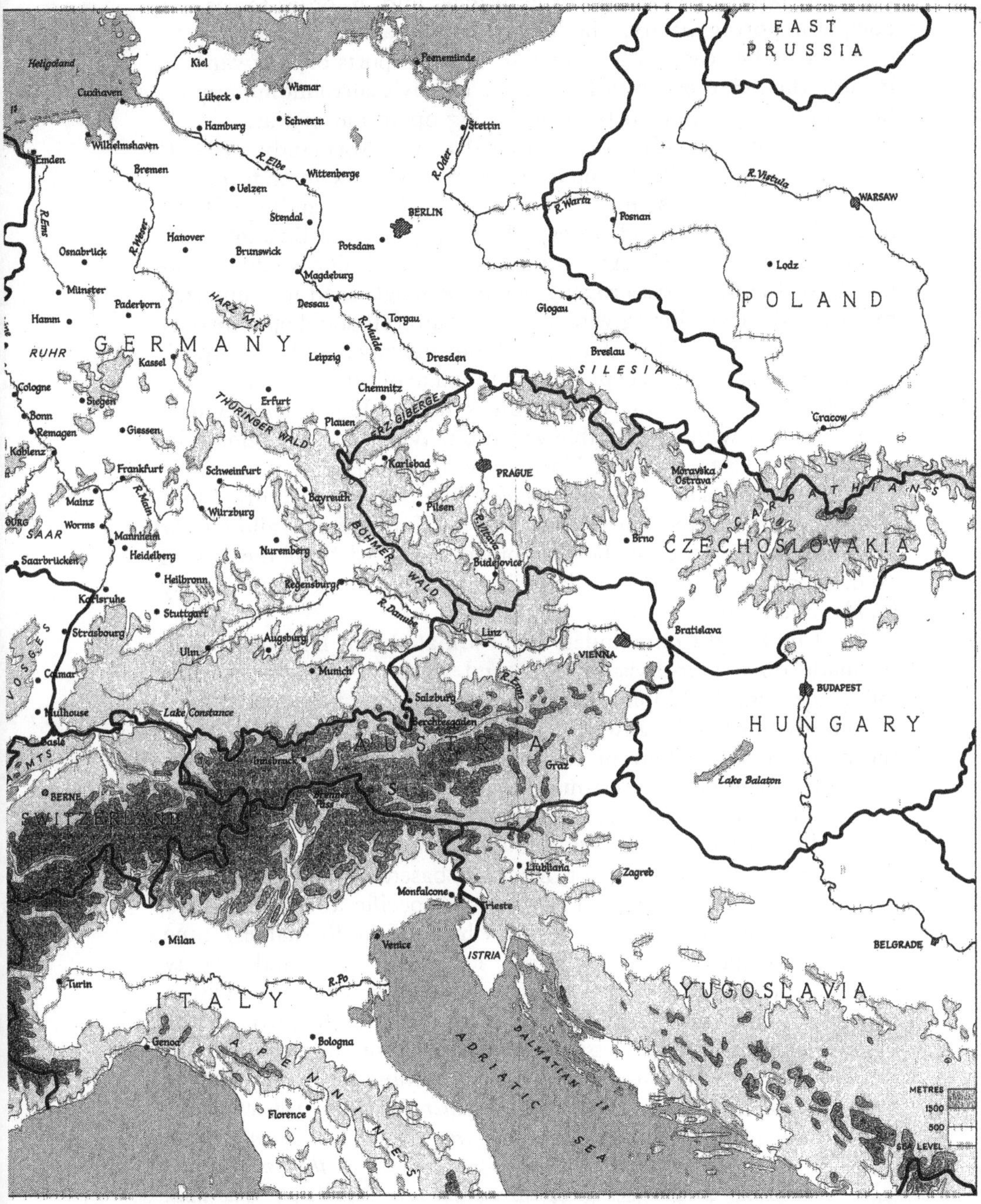
EAST PRUSSIA
Heligoland
Kiel
Swinemünde
Cuxhaven
Lübeck
Wismar
Schwerin
Hamburg
Stettin
Wilhelmshaven
Emden
Bremen
R. Elbe
Wittenberge
R. Oder
R. Vistula
WARSAW
Uelzen
R. Ems
R. Weser
Stendal
BERLIN
R. Warta
Posnan
Osnabrück
Hanover
Brunswick
Potsdam
Lodz
Magdeburg
Münster
Paderborn
HARZ MTS
Dessau
Glogau
POLAND
Hamm
R. Mulde
Torgau
GERMANY
RUHR
Kassel
Leipzig
Dresden
Breslau
SILESIA
Cologne
Siegen
Erfurt
Chemnitz
Bonn
THÜRINGER WALD
ERZ GEBIRGE
Cracow
Remagen
Giessen
Plauen
Koblenz
Frankfurt
Schweinfurt
Karlsbad
PRAGUE
Moravska Ostrava
CARPATHIANS
Mainz
R. Main
Bayreuth
Pilsen
Worms
Würzburg
R. Vltava
SAAR
Mannheim
Brno
CZECHOSLOVAKIA
Saarbrücken
Heidelberg
Nuremberg
BÖHMER WALD
Budejovice
Heilbronn
Regensburg
Karlsruhe
R. Danube
Stuttgart
VOSGES
Strasbourg
Linz
Bratislava
Augsburg
Ulm
VIENNA
Colmar
Munich
R. Enns
BUDAPEST
Salzburg
Mulhouse
Lake Constance
Berchtesgaden
HUNGARY
Basle
AUSTRIA
Innsbruck
Graz
Lake Balaton
BERNE
Brenner Pass
SWITZERLAND
Ljubliana
Zagreb
Monfalcone
Trieste
Milan
Venice
BELGRADE
ISTRIA
Turin
R. Po
YUGOSLAVIA
ITALY
Genoa
Bologna
APENNINES
ADRIATIC SEA
DALMATIAN IS
Florence
METRES
1500
500
SEA LEVEL

narrow beaches, and restricted exits would make it very difficult to maintain large forces through the beaches and, in order to capture adequate port capacity, the lodgement area would have to be extended either eastwards to include Belgian ports or westwards to include the Seine ports; in face of the enemy's surrounding opposition neither appeared to be a promising operation of war.

None of these disadvantages applied to the Normandy coast. It was less strongly fortified. The beaches are partly sheltered from prevailing westerly winds and are more suitable for the landing of large quantities of vehicles and stores; Cherbourg and the Brittany ports are within closer reach. Any advantage of proximity would be forfeited, for the direct sea crossing would be lengthened to a hundred miles and the time during which a fighter aircraft could operate over the assault area would be diminished, but the naval and air authorities were prepared to accept this for the sake of other gains.

Cossac came to the same conclusion as the Combined Commanders had done, but with one notable variation. While landings should be made in the Caen sector of Normandy, the eastern beaches of the Cotentin peninsula should be *excluded*. The need to capture Cherbourg quickly was recognised, but with the limited forces allotted for the Overlord assault by the Combined Chiefs of Staff the risk of landing troops on the peninsula while its narrow neck was in enemy hands should not be taken.

The Combined Commanders had estimated that landings should be made on a four-division front and that, for this and for the follow-up, assault shipping and landing craft must be available to lift ten divisions and eighteen commandos; they had also envisaged the employment of four or five airborne divisions. That was the Combined Commanders' estimate of the forces needed for a successful assault under conditions which then obtained.

The 'Appreciation and Outline Plan' which Cossac duly submitted in August 1943 was not, however, based on this or any other estimate of what was needed but on the specific allocation which had been made by the Combined Chiefs of Staff—namely nine divisions (including two airborne) for the assault and twenty divisions for the subsequent build-up of the lodgement area, with a defined amount of assault vessels and transport aircraft. Governed by these limited means the Cossac plan provided for the initial assault to be made on a three-division front in conjunction with airborne troops and commandos. *If the enemy's fighter forces were reduced; if his reserve troops in France and the Low Countries as a whole did not exceed twelve full-strength, first-quality divisions on the day of the assault; and (since maintenance would have to be carried out over beaches for some three months) if improvised sheltered waters were provided for use till adequate ports were available,* it was thought that an Allied assault on the lines of this outline plan should have 'a reasonable prospect of success'. At the same time it was urged that if possible the resources to be employed should be strengthened so as to increase the weight of the follow-up and possibly to extend the assault frontage.

The Cossac outline plan was considered in turn by the British Chiefs of Staff, the American Joint Chiefs of Staff and, finally, by the Combined Chiefs of Staff, all of whom recommended its adoption to Mr. Churchill and President Roosevelt at a meeting in Quebec in August 1943 known as 'Quadrant'. Both accepted the plan, but in doing so Mr. Churchill urged that the forces to be employed should be strengthened by at least twenty-five per cent and that the assault front should be extended to *include* the eastern shores of the Cherbourg peninsula. The Combined Chiefs of Staff agreed that stronger forces should be made available 'if possible', but they did not then increase the allocation of assault shipping and craft on which the Cossac plan was based. While, therefore, it was satisfactory to General Morgan that his outline plan had been approved and that he was now ordered to proceed with detailed planning and full preparations and was given authority 'for taking the necessary executive action to implement those plans approved by the Combined Chiefs of Staff', he still held the anomalous position of chief of staff to an unknown commander, with orders to continue planning for the use of forces which *might* be increased and, as he considered, with insufficient assault shipping and transport aircraft even for the comparatively limited forces allotted. His position was not eased by the knowledge that, on Mr. Churchill's suggestion, it was now agreed to appoint an American soldier as Supreme Commander. American staff procedure differs in many respects from the British, so that General Morgan's other uncertainties were increased by the knowledge that he was planning for a supreme commander who would be accustomed to the use of a different idiom.

Throughout the months which followed the meeting at Quebec these unanswered questions as to who would be the supreme commander and what forces and assault craft would in fact be made available were continuing subjects of debate at high level, for with them were involved other questions of grand strategy. The Allied resources of men and material were mounting steadily, but they were not yet sufficient for all the tasks the Allies had in hand in the several theatres of war. The number of American troops assembling in Britain under the Bolero plan was increasing but not so quickly as had been forecast.

The supply of assault shipping and landing craft was large and growing but it was being claimed for operations in the Pacific, the Mediterranean and in South-East Asia as well as for the coming cross-Channel assault. Moreover, a proposal had been made at

Quebec that this main attack, Overlord, should be backed by a synchronised assault on the French Mediterranean coast, later to be known as 'Anvil'. If so this would add yet another claimant to the competition for assault shipping and landing craft. The positive shortage of shipping owing to U-boat sinkings and the relative shortage for the operations envisaged were factors which influenced both strategic and tactical planning during these years.

Debate on the means to be made available for Overlord turned largely on what was to happen in Italy and on the course to be pursued there. The conduct of the Italian campaign, which had followed the defeat of the enemy in North Africa and Sicily and the Italian surrender, had been influenced since its inception by two considerations which were not easily reconcilable. On one hand was the Allies' desire to engage and hold in Italy as many German divisions as possible, so as to reduce correspondingly the number that could be employed on the Russian front or be used to oppose an Allied assault in the West, and to have air bases from which to bomb the aircraft industry in southern Germany. To this end General Sir Harold Alexander's armies must be strong enough to maintain unrelenting pressure on German forces in Italy. On the other hand was the Allies' intention to launch a major cross-Channel offensive in the coming spring; to that end the strongest possible forces must be assembled and trained and none that were wanted for the major campaign should be tied up in Italy or elsewhere. The proposal to launch a synchronised assault on the south coast of France had been made before any effort to decide an appropriate share-out of resources which would be available in the European theatre at the time concerned.

Thus considerations of grand strategy bore directly on the planning and preparations for Overlord and, while there was agreement that Germany must be finally defeated by assault from the west, there were stubborn differences of opinion as to how the success of that assault could best be assured. Put shortly, the British Chiefs of Staff thought (in the autumn of 1943) that the success of Overlord, *on the limited scale on which it was being planned*, would be jeopardised unless diversionary operations in Italy or elsewhere occupied substantial German forces in south Europe and so prevented their transfer to the western front. The American Joint Chiefs of Staff feared, on the other hand, that such diversionary operations might absorb too large a share of Allied resources, and, if so, Overlord might fail through starvation. The justice of these contrasted arguments is examined very fully by Mr. Ehrman in his account of grand strategy during this period.[12] The difficulty of resolving them was increased by the fact that there was as yet no supreme commander for Overlord

---

[12] John Ehrman, *Grand Strategy*, vol. V (H.M.S.O., 1956), chap. II *passim*.

to say with authority what forces and equipment he must have to ensure its success.

Delay in deciding whether the strength of Overlord could be increased was due partly to the difficulty of foreseeing the course of events in Italy and of reaching agreement on the requirements of the Italian campaign, and partly to the demands of other theatres of war; in particular for American operations against Japan on which the British were not fully informed. But it was also attributable largely to delay in the appointment of a supreme commander for Overlord, and this procrastination affected both planning and preparations and had ultimate bearing on the conduct of the campaign.

At times American leaders suspected that, notwithstanding formal agreement on the priority of Overlord, British leaders were half-hearted about the pledge to launch it in the spring of 1944. There was indeed some justification for this American uneasiness for, though British leaders *never* contemplated the abandonment of Overlord and *never* for a moment allowed the work of preparation to slacken, they did at times consider advocating its deferment. It is not necessary for an understanding of Overlord to trace all the tangled causes for high-level embarrassment in 1943, but it is right to notice that British hesitation on strategic grounds was fostered by a suspicion on their part that American leaders still under-estimated the difficulties of Overlord as they had done of Sledgehammer when they urged its launching in 1942, and British leaders had better reasons for their uneasiness. To them it seemed that American protestations of belief in the prime importance of Overlord did not square with their apparent unwillingness to settle matters which must have decisive influence on the success of the campaign. At Casablanca American leaders had pressed for the immediate appointment of a chief of staff to the supreme commander (designate) in order that planning might begin without delay. But the Combined Chiefs of Staff did not at first give General Morgan any executive authority and only in September was he authorised to proceed with detailed plans and preparations. In May they had agreed to a preliminary allocation of forces and equipment for the assault phase of the campaign but, although in August they agreed that these should be increased 'if possible', no specific measures were taken to increase them. They agreed in August to approve the nomination of Admiral Sir Charles Little (Commander-in-Chief, Portsmouth) and Air Marshal Sir Trafford Leigh-Mallory (Commander-in-Chief, Fighter Command) as, respectively, Naval and Air Commanders-in-Chief for Overlord, yet did not think it desirable to define their authority, pending the selection of a supreme commander. In October it was recognised that the Portsmouth Command must be separated from Overlord and Admiral Sir Bertram Ramsay succeeded to the Naval

Command of Overlord, but still no directive was given him. Although in November Sir Trafford Leigh-Mallory was given a directive which defined his command of the tactical air forces allotted to Overlord, it left undecided his authority in regard to strategic bomber forces which constituted a major part of Allied air power.

On these and some other crucial issues British and American leaders held divergent views and it was consequently difficult to reach an agreed decision. To Americans it seemed wise to postpone major decisions till the supreme commander was appointed and able to state his requirements. British representatives urged in October that the appointment should therefore not be deferred any longer, but since it had meanwhile been agreed that an American should be given supreme command the nomination would be made by the President and he had not yet made up his mind. It was widely believed in the autumn that General Marshall would probably be his choice and General Morgan visited Washington in order to discuss matters with him in person. While there he urged a more adequate provision of assault craft, but although he was met with great understanding, in this regard he had no success. Neither then nor after his return was his importunity rewarded and planning and preparations continued to be seriously handicapped by these uncertainties.

It will be seen later that all, and more than all, that General Morgan was arguing for so tirelessly in 1943 was provided in 1944 in response to demands of the supreme commander; but it will also be found that, at such a late date, it could only be done by a postponement of the opening attack.

The recital of these divergent views and minor misunderstandings must not give a warped impression of British-American co-operation in 1943. It must not be allowed to appear that between the periodical conferences, when the Combined Chiefs of Staff were joined by the Prime Minister and the President and a common policy was sought on world-wide issues affecting both nations and every theatre of war, there was any pause in combined staff work or any less successful pursuit of agreement on the day-to-day conduct of Allied affairs. Only five of the major conferences had been held, but during 1943 there had been over a hundred meetings of the Combined Chiefs of Staff. At these a huge mass of business affecting both nations had been transacted without unresolved difficulty. Normally the British view was expressed by Sir John Dill and his colleagues on behalf of the British Chiefs of Staff and it would be difficult to over-estimate the value of their part in this extraordinary and hitherto unique example of international combination.

The next full conference for the determination of outstanding questions was held at Cairo ('Sextant') and Teheran ('Eureka') in November and early December 1943. As before, they were attended by Mr. Churchill and President Roosevelt. During part of the early meetings in Cairo, General Chiang Kai-shek and his advisers from China were present at the President's request and for some days subsequently the conference adjourned in order to confer with Marshal Stalin and his advisers in Teheran before returning to complete its business in Cairo. After the conference a *communiqué* was agreed by the Prime Minister, the President and Marshal Stalin which read: 'The military staffs of the three Powers concerted their plans for the final destruction of the German forces. They reached complete agreement as to the scope and timing of the operations which will be undertaken from East, West, and South, and arrangements were made to ensure ultimate and continuous co-operation.'

The main decision reached was 'that "Overlord" would be launched in May in conjunction with a supporting operation against the south of France on the largest scale that is permitted by the landing craft available at that time'.

At the conclusion of these meetings the Allied programme for the defeat of the Axis in Europe was restated. First, they said, 'the progressive destruction and dislocation of the German military, industrial and economic system, the disruption of vital elements of lines of communication, and the material reduction of German air combat strength by the successful prosecution of the Combined Bomber Offensive from all convenient bases is a prerequisite of Overlord'; it must continue to have 'the highest strategic priority'. In stating this the Combined Chiefs of Staff were reaffirming the primary object of the Combined Bomber Offensive which had been defined during the Casablanca meeting a year previously in a directive, and subsequently amplified in another known as 'Pointblank', issued in June 1943. It had been in progress ever since.

Nothing has yet been said of this offensive, though it had been steadily mounting in violence, for the time had not yet come when its operations were directly related to the coming land campaign; up to this point their description belongs rather to other volumes in this series.[13] Yet in order to appreciate the significance of the Cairo decision recorded above it is necessary to understand the position of the Allies' strategic bomber forces at the turn of the year 1943–1944, for air power had become a predominant factor in all operations of war. No longer could the Navy be masters at sea, no longer could an army advance to victory unless their sister service had such air superiority that the enemy's air forces could not interfere effectively

---

[13] See Sir Charles Webster and Noble Frankland, *The Strategic Air Offensive* (H.M.S.O., 1961).

with their operations. Not only did the older services need such negative protection from air attack, they also needed the positive and distinctive assistance which could only be made by the striking power of air forces. So much was proved beyond all question. Whether in addition to their complementary rôle in actions by land or at sea there was also an independent, strategic rôle which air forces could fulfil was a matter about which there had been long-held differences of opinion.

The concept of independent strategic air power had seemingly not been appreciated by German war leaders. The German air force had been designed mainly for co-operation with land forces. It had fought the Battle of Britain as a preliminary aid to invasion by land forces and the subsequent sporadic bombing of Great Britain and the attacks on shipping were not based on any coherent strategic plan. In Britain and the United States, on the other hand, those who were responsible for shaping air policy had long studied not only the complementary rôle of air forces to operations by land and sea but also their ability to play a distinct, strategic rôle, by independent attack on an enemy's war-making capacity. Protagonists of this view argued that air forces enjoy signal advantages for such a task. From widely dispersed bases their massed power of attack can quickly be focussed on vital targets, deep in the heart of the enemy's country, without first having to break through any 'front' or to expend strength on intermediate targets; and they can hit incomparably hard.

But while British air leaders had recognised the potentialities of strategic bombing they had had insufficient opportunity to prove its value during the opening years of the war. The limited range, power and number of available aircraft had restricted their operations; diversion for other imperative tasks had interrupted their programme; insupportable losses in daylight attacks on defended targets had led to the adoption of night bombing, and in those early years difficulties of navigation and bomb-aiming on dark or cloudy nights had largely vitiated results. Ever since 1940 high priority had been given to the production of more powerful, four-engined bombers and new aids to navigation and bomb-aiming, but it would take time to provide these in large numbers. At the close of 1941 evidence of the effect of bombing on Germany's war-making capacity, by the comparatively small number of less powerful aircraft which was all we then had, was inconclusive and for a time such operations were slowed down while a more powerful force was building.

The entry of the United States brought weighty reinforcement of the view that strategic bombing might have decisive influence on the course of the war and, although some considerable time would elapse before American bombers could be based in England and join in active operations against Germany, it was decided that the Royal Air Force should meanwhile resume its offensive with a new directive. By a decision formally approved by the War Cabinet on the 14th of February, 1942, their attacks were 'to be focused on the morale of the enemy's civil population and, in particular, of the industrial workers' in cities within the range of a new aid to navigation (known as 'Gee') just coming into use. Cologne and Essen, Duisburg, Düsseldorf and other places in the Ruhr were named. Shortly after the issue of this new directive Air Marshal Sir Arthur Harris was appointed as the new Air Officer Commanding-in-Chief, Bomber Command.

It has been wittily said that while 'some men make a noise and some men make a difference' Sir Arthur Harris did both. The directive he inherited was not of his making but from the date of his appointment he made it his own. From then on he was an unshakable advocate of 'area' bombing on the largest practicable scale, holding that this was the quickest, surest and most economical way to destroy the enemy's morale and war-making capacity. He backed his opinion by energetic action, and although during 1942 his force could not be numerically increased, reorganisation with the new four-engined bombers and new navigational aids greatly increased its striking power. Improved techniques, which included the employment of specially trained 'pathfinders' and greater use of incendiary bombs, were developed and the organisation of the first thousand-bomber raid, on Cologne on May the 30th, gave impressive, if not conclusive, evidence of what strategic bombing might effect.

Meantime American bomber forces—organised as the United States Eighth Air Force commanded by Lieut-General Ira C. Eaker—assembled in Britain and began active operations. Their bombers had been designed and equipped for precision bombing of targets by day rather than for area bombing of towns by night, and they soon found (as the Royal Air Force had found in 1940) that when their objective lay in Germany, beyond the range of their own fighter cover, their losses were prohibitive. They had calculated that their more heavily armed bombers, flying in close formation, would be able to ward off attacks by the enemy's fighters; they learned by bitter experience that this was not so. But instead of changing over to night bombing, as Bomber Command had done, they set out to develop long-range fighters and with these, and by attack on the enemy's fighter production centres, to weaken German air defence and obtain the air superiority needed for effective daylight bombing.

Both of these powerful bomber forces were operating under the direction of the Combined Chiefs of Staff. For unlike the tactical air forces which were being prepared under the control of Sir Trafford Leigh-Mallory for co-operation with naval and land forces largely dependent on air support, the strategic bombers were carrying on an offensive which, though a 'pre-requisite to Overlord', was independent of other arms so long as their bases were safeguarded. The time was soon coming when their operations would be more directly related to the cross-Channel assault and the subsequent campaign, but that time had not yet come when the Cairo meetings confirmed the position of the Combined Bomber Offensive at the head of the Allies' programme for the defeat of the Axis in Europe.

Next on the Cairo programme came Overlord which, since the Quadrant meeting in Quebec, had been regarded as 'the primary ground and air effort against the Axis' for 1944 and was to be carried out 'during May' of that year. It was recognised that Overlord as at present planned was 'on a narrow margin' and that 'everything practicable should be done to increase its strength'. The examination of the proposed supporting operation against the south of France—Anvil—(now regarded as an essential complement to Overlord) was to be pressed forward on the basis of not less than a two-division assault, and if it should prove that greater strength was needed the provision of additional resources 'would be considered'. It had been recognised at the August meeting in Quebec that 'a shortage of vehicle lift for "Overlord" and the necessity of additional landing craft therefore' would also have to be made good from the Mediterranean. Craft were to be returned to the United Kingdom in January for use in Overlord and 'every effort was to be made' by accelerated building and conversion to provide essential additional landing craft for the European theatre of operations.

All this was satisfactory as far as it went but for those who were planning and preparing for Overlord it did not go very far. General Morgan was no wiser as to the scale on which to complete detailed plans for he still did not know what forces and assault craft would in fact be made available—yet the campaign was due to be launched in four months' time.

But one momentous decision was announced at the close of the Cairo Conference. Marshal Stalin had raised the question of the supreme command at Teheran, urging strongly that the appointment should be made without further delay, and President Roosevelt had promised an early decision. A few days later, at the last meeting of the resumed conference in Cairo on December the 6th, it was announced that he had decided to nominate General Dwight D. Eisenhower to be the Supreme Allied Commander for Overlord.

At last there would be someone to state requirements with authority, someone who could insist that outstanding questions must be answered without delay. In place of the limited power of a staff officer there would henceforth be substituted the full authority of a supreme commander.

It may be well at this point to review what Cossac had achieved before General Eisenhower took up his appointment.

Aided by the studies and material of the Combined Commanders, Cossac had outlined a plan for launching the Overlord campaign with the forces and equipment allocated. Once that was approved the Cossac staff had been reorganised as the nucleus of an operational staff for the future Supreme Commander, in which the three Services of two nations were fully represented, all imbued with unity of purpose and employing a single method. Cossac headquarters had become the source from which both Service and Civil Ministries derived impetus and guidance on the co-ordination of all tasks related to Overlord. Much progress had been made by those directly responsible for the organisation of supply and communications and the design and production of special equipment, including the preparation of embarkation facilities along our own coasts, of artificial harbours for erection off the far shore, and of pipe-lines for the submarine delivery of petrol to the armies and air forces in France. Formations to be employed in the opening phases of the campaign were being given intensive special training, and, among much else, measures were being rapidly developed for the quartering, supply and movement of the large number of aircraft and troops that would be involved, for the allocation and adaptation of shipping, and for the all-important requirements of security. There were, too, many other matters for which Cossac was responsible. These included the co-ordination of air, land and sea reconnaissance related to Overlord; Intelligence; camouflage and deception plans; meteorological organisation; measures to animate and aid subversive action by resistance movements in the occupied countries of North-West Europe; organisation for dealing with the legal, fiscal, economic and other aspects of Civil Affairs which would be met in the countries to be liberated from German control. Foundations on which the structure of Overlord was based were thus already well laid before the Supreme Commander took charge.

In his review of the campaign when all was over General Eisenhower wrote that General Morgan's work before he arrived on the scene 'made D-day possible'.[14]

---

[14] Dwight D. Eisenhower, *Crusade in Europe* (London, 1948), p. 253.

THE NORMANDY BATTLEFIELD

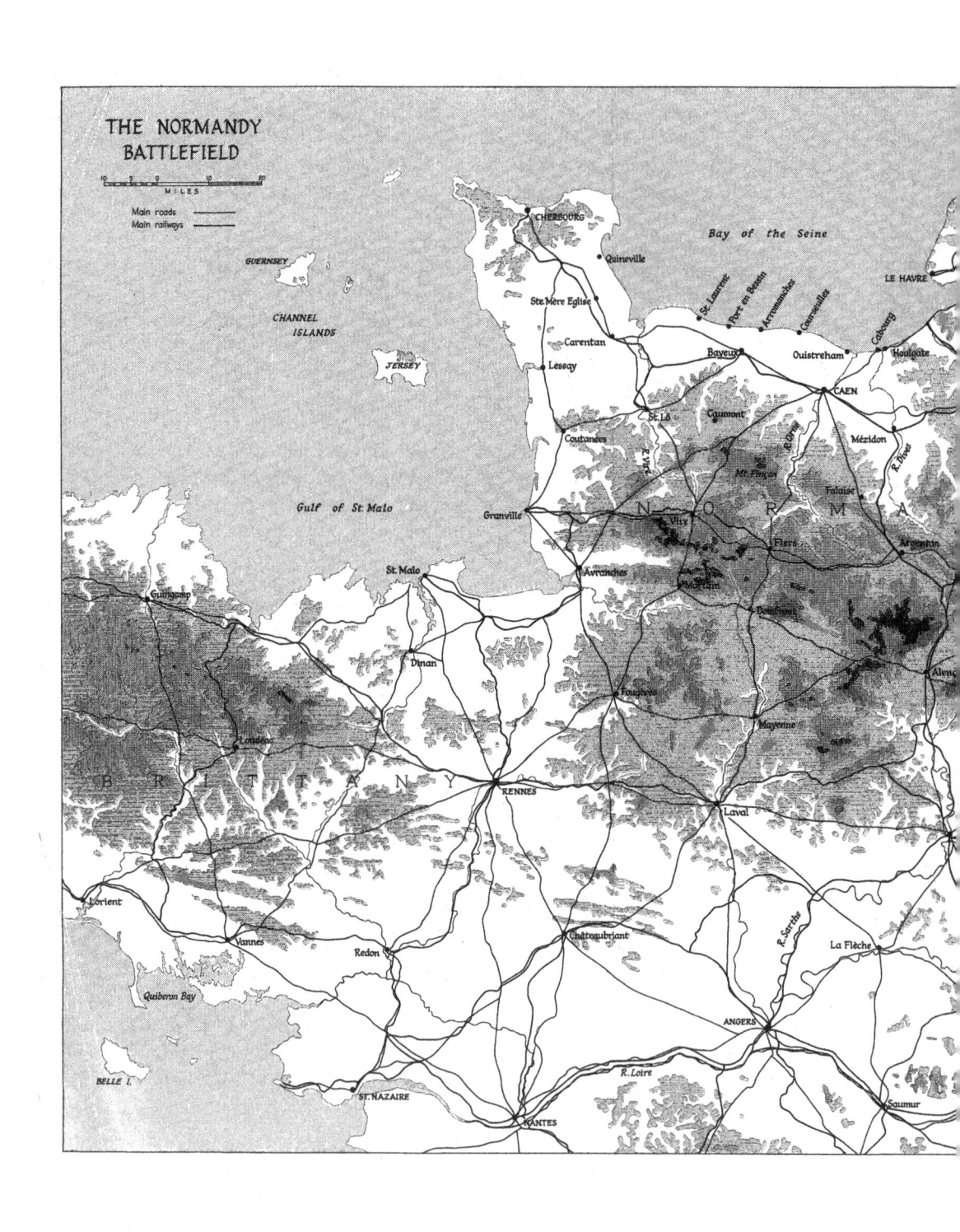

Main roads
Main railways

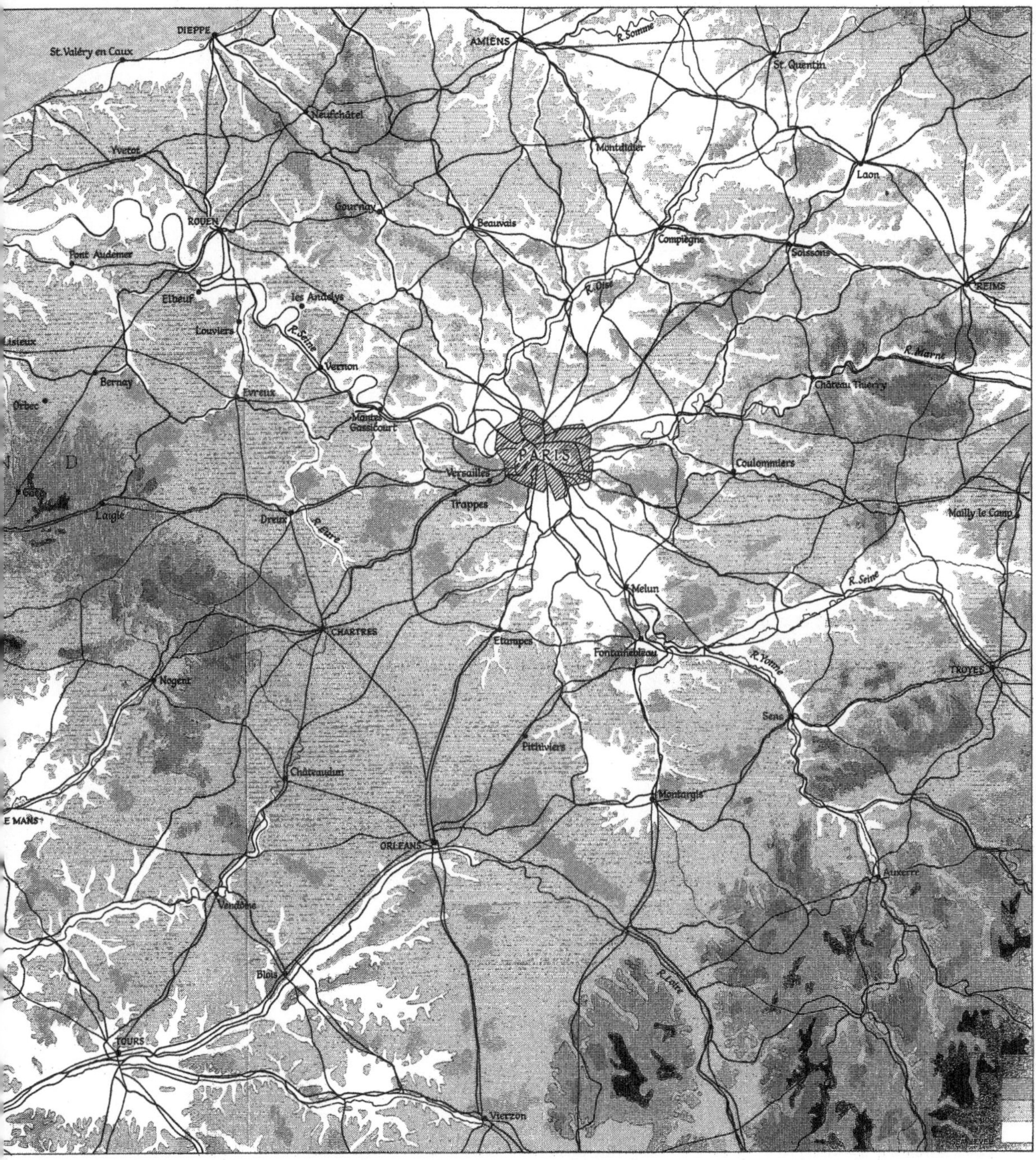

DIEPPE
St. Valéry en Caux
AMIENS
R. Somme
St. Quentin
Neufchâtel
Yvetot
Montdidier
Laon
Gournay
ROUEN
Beauvais
Compiègne
Soissons
Pont Audemer
R. Oise
REIMS
Elbeuf
les Andelys
Louviers
R. Seine
Vernon
R. Marne
Bernay
Evreux
Château Thierry
Mantes Gassicourt
PARIS
Versailles
Coulommiers
Trappes
Laigle
Dreux
R. Eure
Mailly le Camp
Melun
R. Seine
CHARTRES
Etampes
Fontainebleau
R. Yonne
TROYES
Nogent
Sens
Pithiviers
Châteaudun
Montargis
ORLEANS
Auxerre
Vendôme
Blois
R. Loire
TOURS
Vierzon

CHAPTER II

THE SHAPING AND COMMAND OF OVERLORD

WITH the turn of the year and the appointment of a supreme commander, preparations for the coming campaign enter their final phase and it will be well to reflect for a moment on what was involved, before our vision is affected 'by the dust of conflict or the glamour of success'. The opening cross-Channel assault tends to pre-occupy attention, for it involves the mastery of a first tremendous obstacle on which all else depends. Yet this will be only a beginning, and its absorbing interest should not be allowed to dull the apprehension of what must follow if the Allies' ambitions are to be fulfilled. After the seizure of a bridgehead in France and its expansion as a base for further operations, the enemy must be driven out of France, Belgium, Luxembourg, Holland, Denmark and Norway; Germany must be conquered and her armed forces destroyed, so that the world might be purged of the evil she had bred and had diffused like a canker among the nations of Europe.

In order to realise their intention the Allies were organising the mightiest fighting forces they could muster. They were also to pledge a large proportion of their shipping to the transport of men and materials, and a major share of their industrial plant and population to the equipment and sustenance of the campaign. During the war the convenience of civilians and their standards of life were of secondary concern.

At the very outset of their enterprise Allied forces must engage in combined operations which were unique in difficulty and danger. Germany had held an almost unchallenged position in France for four years. To resist the approach of seaborne foes she held at readiness round the coast considerable numbers of U-boats and light surface-craft and a few destroyers, to dispute the passage of the Channel, as well as an extensive organisation for mine-laying by ships and aircraft. Parts of the French coast had been fortified by the exploitation of modern engineering skill and a large concentration of labour and materials. Within these defences were numerous batteries, many sited in almost indestructible emplacements to cover beaches thickly sown with ingeniously destructive obstacles, and behind them considerable armies were waiting to repel an invader, with air forces to assist them and direction-finding appliances, radar, to give early warning of his approach. In 1942 the Dieppe raid had shown that a high price might have to be paid before this coastal crust could be broken through—and since then it had been continuously strengthened. As an additional hindrance the enemy would be sure to destroy port facilities and render them unusable for weeks if not for months; during that time attacking armies and immediate reinforcements must be landed and sustained over open beaches, exposed alike to the vagaries of the Channel weather and to German malice. To force such defences had never been attempted before.

Fortunately on this occasion the Allies held advantages usually enjoyed only by an aggressor nation. They had time to prepare for the coming campaign with care and forethought which matched its difficulty; they held the initiative and could attack when and where they chose; and the combination of all Allied Services, supported by abundant material, would enable them to attack, this time, in preponderant strength.

In the final months of preparation the greatest strain must fall inevitably on Great Britain as the main base of Allied operations. Within her relatively confined shores millions of her own and Allied forces were already assembling, while ammunition, stores, equipment and food were being amassed in unprecedented quantities. Shipyards were working at high pressure building, repairing and fitting out ships and craft for many special duties and landing craft production was at its peak, often in unusual places and by unorthodox means. Special equipments were being developed to overcome foreseeable difficulties.

Never before had Britain sent into battle large forces which were so well equipped, well balanced and elaborately trained. The war had been in progress for over four years and experience from many seas and many battlefields had been brought to bear on the task that lay ahead. The armada which was to put the armies ashore and to sustain them on the Continent included over twelve hundred fighting vessels of all kinds, over four thousand assault ships and craft and about sixteen hundred merchant ships and ancillary vessels. The armies too had a variety of arms and equipments never previously conceived and the air forces a strength, power and mobility never before attained. By the time the campaign opened there would be gathered in the United Kingdom Allied armies totalling over three and a half million men. The British army would number nearly one and threequarter millions, Dominion forces a hundred and seventy-five thousand, the United States army and air forces a million and a half and other national contingents nearly forty-four thousand. There would be some thirteen thousand aircraft in the country, including over four thousand bombers and some five thousand fighters, apart from thousands in use for training or held for replacements, and about three thousand five hundred gliders.

Britain had become a huge storehouse, workshop, arsenal, armed camp, and aircraft carrier. 'It was claimed facetiously at the time that only the great number of barrage balloons floating constantly in British skies kept the islands from sinking under the seas.'[1] In all this accumulation of strength the United States authorities were associated, and indeed it was only made possible by the addition of their great resources of energy and power; but the fact that they were pouring fighting men, munitions and supplies into a country where with our own forces large contingents of many other Allied nations were now serving—Canadians, Australians, New Zealanders, Frenchmen, Norwegians, Belgians, Dutch, Poles, and Czechs—augmented day by day the congestion on English soil, and added to the strain on British shipping, material resources and manpower. By the end of May 1944 over a million and a half men had been brought from America across the threatened waters of the Atlantic. Nearly sixty per cent came in normal escorted convoys but over thirty per cent in unescorted passenger ships, all British or British-controlled, which relied for safety on their speed. The British liners *Queen Mary* and *Queen Elizabeth*, each adapted to hold fifteen thousand men, together brought over four hundred and twenty-five thousand troops and during all this movement not a man was lost at sea. About sixty per cent of the accommodation needed for American troops was found by the requisition or transfer of existing facilities, but about forty per cent had to be newly constructed and of this additional accommodation twenty-seven per cent was British built. A hundred and thirty-three airfields were provided for the American air forces; eighty-three of these were transferred from the Royal Air Force, but fifty new airfields were built for their use, thirty-six by British, fourteen by American labour. Moreover, of the vast amount of supplies and equipment required for the American forces in Great Britain, by the end of May over two-thirds, five and a quarter million tons, was brought in by sea, forty per cent of it in the five months before D-day; but approximately thirty-one per cent of all supplies for the American forces in Europe (apart from Italy) was provided from British sources.[2] Moreover, tension was increased by awareness of the fact that on Britain, if anywhere, all German counter-measures would certainly be spent. By the end of May nearly fifty-two thousand civilians had been killed and sixty-three thousand seriously injured in German air raids, and the fact that Germany was preparing to attack with new long-range weapons was known in high quarters though not yet to the public.

---

[1] Eisenhower, op. cit., p. 63.
[2] See R. G. Ruppenthal, *Logistical Support of the Armies*, vol. I (Dept. of the Army, Washington, D.C., 1953), pp. 231, 237, 258.

With movement severely restricted and large areas of the country reserved for military use, the civilian population saw comparatively little of what was going on and knew nothing definite about impending operations; yet sober confidence, tempered by anxiety, grew with the belief that the main attack on Germany was soon to be opened. This sense of approaching crisis was quickened when the appointment of a supreme commander was publicly announced early in the new year.

General Eisenhower had already many friends in England, for he had come there to command all the United States' forces in the European theatre in June 1942. In the autumn of that year he had left to serve as Commander-in-Chief, Allied Expeditionary Force, in the landings in North Africa and in the subsequent campaigns in Tunisia, Sicily and Italy. He had been outstandingly successful in emphasising the Allies' unity of aim and in overriding the petty rivalries and mistrust which spring all too easily from national divergencies of outlook, method and manners, and have so often marred the conduct of Allies in arms. He had been equally successful in securing the co-operation of all three Services of both nations—a co-operation which was fostered by the fully integrated character of his own headquarters. In his conduct of the Mediterranean campaigns he had shown ability to take decisions yet a notable willingness to trust subordinate commanders, and he was liked and respected by all who came in contact with him. In British Service circles and with the public his reputation stood high and his new appointment was welcomed on both sides of the Atlantic.

At the same time Air Chief Marshal Sir Arthur Tedder was appointed Deputy Supreme Commander—a significant recognition of the importance of the air arm in the coming campaign. Sir Arthur Tedder had commanded our air forces in the Middle East and the co-operation of army and air forces during his command had been markedly effective. From February 1943 he had been Commander-in-Chief, Mediterranean Allied Air Forces, and as such had been responsible for the planning and execution of Allied air operations in Tunisia and against Sicily and Italy. He had thus been closely associated with General Eisenhower and his staff, with whom he had worked in complete harmony.

At General Eisenhower's request Lieut-General W. Bedell Smith, his chief of staff throughout the North African and Mediterranean campaigns (and previously first American secretary of the Combined Chiefs of Staff), was appointed as his chief of staff for Overlord. General Eisenhower's desire to retain an American chief of staff who had been with him so long was not unnatural, for not only did the two men use the same Service idiom but they were accustomed to working together and were familiar with each other's idiosyncrasies.

1. General Paget

2. General Morgan

3. General Eisenhower

4. Air Marshal Tedder

General Morgan now became a deputy chief of staff and his knowledge of all that had gone before in the development of the Cossac plan, and his intimate contacts with the British ministries and organisations concerned in the preparations for the coming campaign, would indeed have been irreplaceable.

The British and Canadian armies which were to be employed comprised the British Twenty-First Army Group. Its headquarters had formed in July 1943 in evacuated premises of St. Paul's School in west London and General Sir Bernard Paget had then been appointed to the command. In the ill-fated expedition to Norway in 1940 General Paget had experienced the futility of engaging in combined operations which were inadequately planned, insufficiently manned and unsuitably equipped. Later, as Commander-in-Chief, Home Forces, he had proved to be a modern Sir John Moore, and by his influence and energy had raised the standard and quickened the spirit of training throughout the Army. As chairman of the Combined Commanders (page 14) he had been intimately associated with leaders of the other Services and with the Chief of Combined Operations in the study of factors involved in a cross-Channel assault and in the earlier planning for a return to the Continent, which was later taken over by Cossac and developed as Overlord. In command of the Twenty-First Army Group he had laid firm foundations on which its waxing strength was eventually built up. General Paget's distinctive contribution to final victory should always be recognised.

In the autumn of 1943 it had been decided that the Commander-in-Chief of the Twenty-First Army Group should be 'jointly responsible with the Allied Naval Commander-in-Chief and the Air Commander-in-Chief, Allied Expeditionary Air Force, for planning the operation (Overlord), and when so ordered, for its execution, until such time as the Supreme Allied Commander allocated an area of responsibility to the First American Army Group'. Thus General Paget would command both the British and American ground forces employed during the first phase of Overlord.

When, however, General Eisenhower was selected for the supreme allied command of Overlord, General Sir Henry Maitland Wilson took his place as Supreme Allied Commander in the Mediterranean, General Paget succeeded Sir Henry Wilson as Commander-in-Chief, Middle East, and General Sir Bernard Montgomery was appointed to take over from General Paget the command of the Twenty-First Army Group and with it the command of all ground forces to be engaged in the first phase of Overlord.

General Montgomery had proved his military skill and fine qualities of leadership in the 1940 campaign in France and Flanders, in his notable defeat of Rommel in North Africa, in the campaign in

Sicily and in early operations in Italy. In the last phase of the North African campaign, and in the Sicilian and Italian fighting, his Eighth Army had been part of General Eisenhower's command; the latter had thus had ample opportunity to appreciate General Montgomery's soldierly gifts and to evaluate the fighting experience in which they had been signally displayed.

At home the appointment was popular. As one of Britain's best known and most successful soldiers he had become 'Monty' to the man in the street as well as to the troops of the Eighth Army. His personality inspired confidence and his picturesque figure was easily distinguishable; for although he was an infantryman, he wore when in battle-dress the black beret of the Royal Armoured Corps and with it the badge of the Royal Tank Regiment set beside the badge of his own rank.

Both the other Commanders-in-Chief had special qualifications. Admiral Ramsay had organised the evacuation of the British Expeditionary Force from Dunkirk in 1940; he had helped to plan the Allied landings in North Africa in 1942 and, in 1943, had commanded the British naval task force in the assault on Sicily. Air Marshal Leigh-Mallory had commanded 12 Group in the Battle of Britain, had been Air Force commander in the Dieppe raid, had been Commandant of the Royal Air Force School of Army Cooperation, and Air Officer Commanding-in-Chief, Fighter Command. Since his appointment for Overlord he had been responsible for the build-up and training of the British element of the Allied Expeditionary Air Force.

The Supreme Commander was to pay a short visit to America before taking up his command. On setting out for Washington he first saw General Montgomery and told him that, in his view, the scale on which Overlord was being planned was too small and the front to be attacked was too narrow; the plan did not provide effectively for a quick capture of Cherbourg or emphasise sufficiently the early need for the use of major ports and for a rapid build-up of forces. He instructed General Montgomery and General Bedell Smith to act for him in England, pending his return from America, and to examine the Cossac plan in detail with the Naval and Air Commanders-in-Chief with a view to its revision on lines which would obviate these weaknesses. General Eisenhower then saw the Prime Minister in Marrakesh and expressed the same dissatisfaction with the width and weight of the opening assault as at present planned.

On his way to England General Montgomery also visited Marrakesh, where the Prime Minister was convalescing after the sharp attack of pneumonia which had overtaken him towards the end of the Cairo and Teheran conferences. There Mr. Churchill gave him a copy of the Cossac Outline Plan and told him that from the first he, Mr. Churchill, had considered that the assault was designed to employ too small a force on too narrow a front. General Montgomery expressed emphatically the same opinion and, knowing that the Prime Minister and the Supreme Allied Commander both held this view, he was on sure ground when he reached England on January the 2nd, and at once took up the matter with the Naval and Air Commanders-in-Chief and with the planning staffs and Ministries concerned.

When General Eisenhower arrived in England on January the 15th to assume his new command General Montgomery was ready to submit proposals for the enlargement of the Cossac Outline Plan. These were considered at a meeting with his principal commanders which General Eisenhower held on January the 21st. The principal changes proposed were, first, an increase of the number of seaborne divisions for the initial assault from three to five (the Combined Commanders had advocated four and Cossac had been restricted to three by the limitation of forces and equipment allocated by the Combined Chiefs of Staff); and, secondly, an expansion of the assault front from twenty-five to nearly fifty miles, including part of the eastern shore of the Cotentin peninsula, so as to facilitate the early capture of Cherbourg. General Eisenhower was satisfied that both the requirements he had stated to General Montgomery before going to Washington were met by the new plan and his approval of the plan was quickly endorsed by the Combined Chiefs of Staff; but it took much longer to decide whether and how the necessary additional resources could be found.

Air Marshal Leigh-Mallory explained that an additional eight fighter squadrons would be required to cover the extended assault area and wider shipping lanes, and some two hundred more troop carrier aircraft in order that three airborne divisions could be dropped within twenty-four hours. These air forces should be available in Britain two months before D-day to allow for the training of glider and troop carriers crews.

Admiral Ramsay showed that two more naval assault forces (one British and one American) would be required to lift the two additional assault divisions, while the proposed attack on a wider front would also involve a considerable increase in naval strength, particularly in bombarding ships, escorts and minesweepers. A large increase of merchant shipping must be found to match the increased scale of attack and accelerate the rate of build-up. The existing insufficiency of landing craft would also be greatly accentuated.

Hitherto naval support and cover for Overlord had been accepted as a British responsibility 'with some augmentation from the United States', and the Admiralty at once promised to meet as much as possible of the increased requirement by cutting commitments elsewhere. They did so eventually only by seriously weakening the Atlantic convoy escorts, reducing the destroyer strength of Home commands and the Home Fleet, stopping reinforcements to the Far East and recalling ships from the Mediterranean. Even so they could not meet all Admiral Ramsay's new 'bill' for Overlord and the Americans were at first unwilling to make up the balance. It was not until April the 15th, when it had been made clear to them that without additional help General Eisenhower's requirements could not be fully satisfied, that Admiral King undertook to meet the outstanding requests. Then three American battleships, two cruisers and twenty-two destroyers were promised for bombardment duties —more than had been asked for.

As for merchant shipping, for the new scale of the assault 224 ocean-going cargo ships and roughly half of the British coastal shipping—about 625,000 tons—normally engaged in the distribution of coal and other essential commodities would be needed to discharge over the beaches or in artificial harbours. Though these could be found only with great difficulty and inconvenience to the civil population this was accepted as inevitable.

But the problem of assault craft, which had so long troubled Cossac, was now greatly aggravated by the new demands. Inherent difficulties were complicated by long and firmly-held differences of opinion between those preparing in London and the American Chiefs of Staff in Washington. The latter were not easily convinced by British calculations nor wholly satisfied that Britain was unable to supply more from her own resources. The far greater shipbuilding capacity, and almost boundless room for expansion in America, doubtless made it hard for them to believe that British effort had already been stretched to the limit. Yet not only was our potential capacity very much smaller but our circumstances were very much harder; our industries and our very life depended largely on imports. We had already been at war for over four years. In that time we had lost over eleven and a half million tons of shipping, and had suffered much other damage at sea. Besides meeting the overriding requirements of the Navy we had built in the United Kingdom in the same period over four and a half million tons of merchant shipping while about half a million tons had each year been salved, repaired and brought back into service; another one and a half million had been built in the British Commonwealth overseas. The expansion of British shipbuilding in these years had been without precedent; in order to achieve it every yard had long been working continuously at high pressure and there was no room for further expansion.

We had already postponed for three months the completion of a fleet carrier, four destroyers and fourteen frigates which were urgently needed by the Navy, in order to build seventy-five additional tank landing craft (L.C.T.) for Overlord. By simplified methods of construction and the employment of some seventy thousand men who were not shipyard workers we had vigorously stepped up the production and repair of landing craft. We could not do more at this juncture and, without disturbing their commitments for other theatres, the American Chiefs of Staff also were unwilling to supply what was now required for Overlord.[3]

Moreover, it did not prove easy to agree on what was really necessary. There was a stated lifting capacity in men and equipment for each of the many types of landing ships and craft and it might be supposed that from these data requirements could be readily calculated. Unfortunately there were a number of data incapable of precise assessment. How many of the allotted craft could be expected to be serviceable on the day of the assault, having regard to casualties through wear and tear in training, the limited facilities for repair, enemy action, or the hazards of the sea? How many should be committed to the opening attack and how many held back for the early build-up? How many should be allocated to close fire support at the expense of 'lift'? What allowance should be made for loss or damage? In any given operation the length of the voyage from the base to the scene of operations has great significance. In the cross-Channel attack craft would be able to make several voyages in the time required for a single voyage in many of the Pacific actions. On the other hand, the known strength of enemy defence was incomparably greater in north-western France than elsewhere and, therefore, prudence demanded a higher rate of build-up and a higher scale of insurance against loss to counter-balance the enemy's inherent advantages.

Finally, how many men or vehicles could be loaded into a particular craft? The Washington planners calculated this figure largely on the designed maximum lift, whereas in London there was a clearer recognition of the need to allow a margin for the fickleness of the Channel weather. The two staffs using different data thus arrived at different conclusions and decision was further complicated as detailed planning proceeded by a tendency of the Army to increase their demands for space, so as to include more men and equipment in the assault formations. It became necessary to limit the number of vehicles accompanying each division in the assault to 1,450, instead of the 3,000 originally planned and, even so, in the event many craft were greatly overloaded and a few foundered at sea.

---

[3] Comparative figures for British and American production of assault shipping and craft are given in Appendix II.

Thus disagreement as to the number of landing craft required sprang from technical questions.

But a second and more serious disagreement, which involved problems of high strategy, reached its climax when the difficulty of finding additional resources for Overlord (especially landing craft) *had* to be overcome without further delay. It sprang from a difference of opinion as to whether, in the circumstances then obtaining, the success of Overlord should be buttressed by a complementary attack on the French Mediterranean coast—operation Anvil. At Quebec in August 1943 it had been easy to agree that the possibility of Anvil should be explored. At Teheran and Cairo in December it had been more difficult to agree that 'Overlord and Anvil are the Supreme Operations for 1944. They must be carried out during May . . .' By January, when the scale of Overlord was increased and General Eisenhower got to grips with the struggle to find the necessary resources, it was soon clear that the Cairo decision could not be implemented; for there would not be adequate resources for both Overlord and Anvil to be 'carried out during May'. At this point rival views on the conduct of the campaign in Italy complicated the decision of what, then, should be done.

Differences between the British and American approaches to the conduct of war perhaps explain the vehemence with which opposed views were pressed and account for the heat which was generated in protracted argument, but it is not necessary here to examine in detail either the technical considerations or the strategic issues which combined to bedevil the progress of planning and preparation; they are dealt with very fully by Mr. Ehrman in his history of grand strategy for this period.[4] But it is necessary to realise that all this argument and delay greatly added to the anxieties which beset General Eisenhower and his commanders. Although by compromise and goodwill the gap between what they required and what appeared to be available was gradually reduced, it was finally closed at long last only by two cardinal variations of the Allies' plans.

The first, agreed by the Combined Chiefs of Staff on February the 1st, was a postponement of the target date for Overlord from May the 1st till the 31st. This would make available for Overlord a further month's production of assault craft and have other advantages—and disadvantages—which will be assessed when the campaign is reviewed. The second was arrived at more tardily. On the 25th of February the Combined Chiefs of Staff agreed that Anvil *might* have to be postponed in order that resources in the Mediterranean could be used to nourish the battle in Italy and assault shipping and craft in the Mediterranean (which would be needed

---

[4] Ehrman, op. cit., chap. VI *passim*.

SUPREME HEADQUARTERS STAFF

for Anvil) could be transferred to the Channel and used first for Overlord; but not until March the 24th did they finally agree that use of these craft was essential to Overlord, and that therefore Anvil *must* be deferred until the progress of Overlord justified the retransference of assault craft for subsequent use in Anvil. It was well that planning and preparations had meanwhile been pressed forward on the assumption, but with no certainty, that the necessary resources would be forthcoming, for when doubt was at last resolved only ten weeks remained for the completion of final arrangements. Subsequently the British Chiefs of Staff supported Mr. Churchill in arguing that because of changed circumstances Anvil should be abandoned. But the American leaders remained equally convinced that reasons which had led to the earlier agreement on the importance of Anvil as a contribution to the success of Overlord still held good and should be implemented without regard to changed circumstances or other considerations. The dispute continued with growing asperity till well after Overlord had been launched; how it was eventually settled will be seen when a decision was at last reached.

Soon after General Eisenhower landed back in England he set up his headquarters in Bushey Park near Hampton Court Palace. They were officially named 'Supreme Headquarters, Allied Expeditionary Force' but fortunately the initials make a pronounceable word; they became known as S.H.A.E.F., and will be referred to as Shaef in this history. Most of General Morgan's Cossac staff were assimilated in the much larger organisation which was necessary to mount and conduct the operations which lay ahead, but many key appointments were filled by men who had served with General Eisenhower in the campaigns in North Africa and the Mediterranean. The layout and principal appointments are shown in the diagram overleaf.

The Shaef staff was modelled on a pattern that General Eisenhower had evolved for the North African and Mediterranean campaigns. The outstanding feature was its inclusive character. Men of all three Services and of both nations were closely associated at every level of its complex structure. In no previous war had any comparable provision for unity of direction been made by allied nations. The overriding authority with which Marshal Foch was charged during the closing phases of the First World War was limited to coordination of the actions of the Allied armies on the western front.[5] No attempt was made to form an Allied general staff or to unify control of conduct below the level of high strategy. Similarly in the 1940 campaign, when the small British Expeditionary Force served as one

---

[5] See *Military Operations in France and Belgium, 1918*, vol. I (H.M.S.O., 1935), p. 542.

SUPREME HEADQUARTERS ALLIED EXPEDITIONARY FORCE

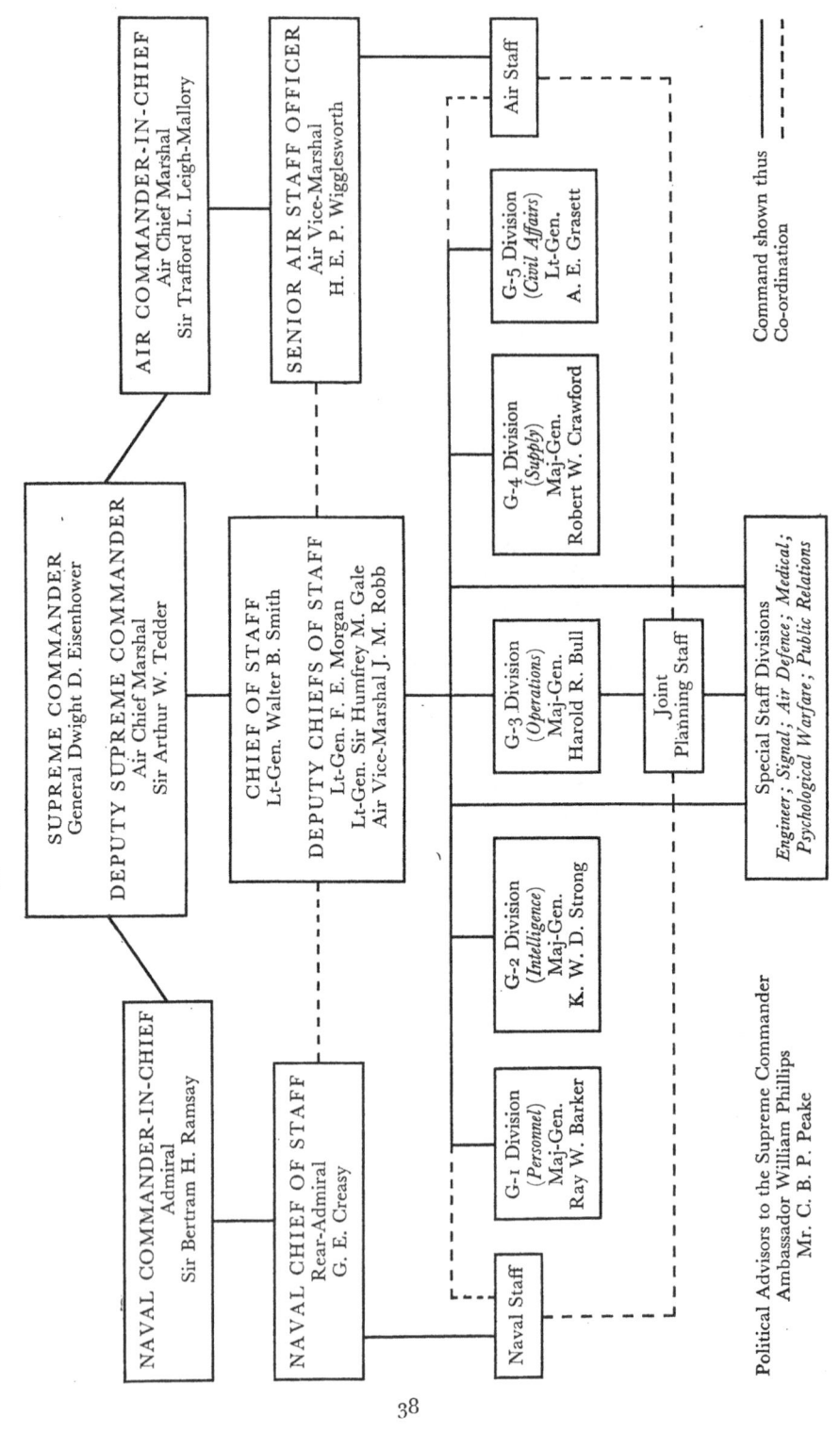

- **SUPREME COMMANDER**
  General Dwight D. Eisenhower
- **DEPUTY SUPREME COMMANDER**
  Air Chief Marshal Sir Arthur W. Tedder

- **NAVAL COMMANDER-IN-CHIEF**
  Admiral Sir Bertram H. Ramsay
- **NAVAL CHIEF OF STAFF**
  Rear-Admiral G. E. Creasy

- **AIR COMMANDER-IN-CHIEF**
  Air Chief Marshal Sir Trafford L. Leigh-Mallory
- **SENIOR AIR STAFF OFFICER**
  Air Vice-Marshal H. E. P. Wigglesworth

- **CHIEF OF STAFF**
  Lt-Gen. Walter B. Smith
- **DEPUTY CHIEFS OF STAFF**
  Lt-Gen. F. E. Morgan
  Lt-Gen. Sir Humfrey M. Gale
  Air Vice-Marshal J. M. Robb

Divisions:
- **G-1 Division** (*Personnel*) — Maj-Gen. Ray W. Barker
- **G-2 Division** (*Intelligence*) — Maj-Gen. K. W. D. Strong
- **G-3 Division** (*Operations*) — Maj-Gen. Harold R. Bull
- **G-4 Division** (*Supply*) — Maj-Gen. Robert W. Crawford
- **G-5 Division** (*Civil Affairs*) — Lt-Gen. A. E. Grasett

- Naval Staff
- Air Staff
- Joint Planning Staff

Special Staff Divisions
Engineer; Signal; Air Defence; Medical; Psychological Warfare; Public Relations

Political Advisors to the Supreme Commander
Ambassador William Phillips
Mr. C. B. P. Peake

Command shown thus ———
Co-ordination - - - - -

OVERLORD DIRECTIVE

of the armies under a French supreme commander, there had been no allied general staff. Both cases were explained by the circumstances of their times, but when nations combine for extensive operations, unification of direction and execution requires something more than the appointment of a supreme allied commander. A combined allied staff is no less necessary if mutual understanding and confidence are to be maintained.

On February the 12th, 1944, General Eisenhower received his directive from the Combined Chiefs of Staff. The overriding order, quoted at the opening of this history, was to enter the Continent of Europe, and 'undertake operations aimed at the heart of Germany and the destruction of her armed forces'. The target date was 'the month of May', but he was to be prepared at any time to take advantage of favourable circumstances, such as withdrawal by the enemy from the western front, to effect re-entry to the Continent 'with such forces as you have available at the time'. It will be recalled that a similar order had been given to General Morgan (page 10) and plans for such an eventuality (operation 'Rankin') had been prepared. As they were never used it is needless to do more here than to note that the burden of this additional planning was also borne by Cossac.

The directive instructed General Eisenhower that while he would be responsible to the Combined Chiefs of Staff he should communicate direct with the United States or British Chiefs of Staff when this would facilitate operations and secure the needed logistical support.

The concentration, quartering, movement and supply of forces, in short 'logistics', were to rest with British Service Ministries and with the United States War and Navy Departments so far as British and United States forces were respectively concerned; but logistical arrangements on the Continent and the co-ordination of all requirements would be the Supreme Commander's responsibility. He was also empowered to recommend any variation of the action which was being taken, by various agencies of sabotage, subversion and propaganda, in preparation for the Allied campaign.

Finally he was told that Russia would so time her coming offensive that it should prevent the transference of German forces to the western front; and that the Allied Commander-in-Chief of the Mediterranean theatre would launch operations, including an attack against the south of France, 'at about the same time'. General Eisenhower would be given command of forces landed in southern France as soon as he was in a position to assume it. The subsequent deferment of Anvil and its occasion have already been told.

The full directive, given in Appendix I, laid down the arrangements for command. It will be noticed that while, under the Supreme

Commander, there are Commanders-in-Chief of the Allied naval forces and of the Allied Expeditionary Air Force, there is no corresponding Commander-in-Chief of the Allied ground forces. It had been decided by the Combined Chiefs of Staff in the previous autumn that in the coming campaign the respective United States and British army group commanders should each report directly to the Supreme Allied Commander and that no intermediate commander-in-chief of ground forces was necessary or desirable; in the opening assault phase, however, (as already noted) when only two armies would at first be involved, the commander of the British Twenty-First Army Group (at that time General Paget) would be responsible for planning and for the command of all ground forces engaged in the operation until such time as the Supreme Allied Commander allocated an area of responsibility to the commander of the United States First Army Group. In a directive issued by General Eisenhower to Admiral Ramsay, General Montgomery and Air Marshal Leigh-Mallory on the 10th of March this arrangement was confirmed, General Montgomery's name being substituted for that of General Paget.

As already explained, General Montgomery had meanwhile been acting for General Eisenhower, in co-operation with the Naval and Air Commanders-in-Chief, in remodelling the plan of assault, and in directing preparations for the conduct of initial operations so far as all ground forces were concerned. It will be seen later that he held command of these during the first three critical months' fighting, by the end of which the German armies in France had received a first sound beating and were in full retreat.

There is a second gloss which needs adding to the diagrammatical statement of the chain of command, for it alone does not fully explain the command arrangements for Allied air forces. The tactical air forces are shown but not the mighty strategic forces which were already engaged in an awesome bombing offensive against Germany. It has been explained (page 21) that since 1943 these had been working under a directive of the Combined Chiefs of Staff (Pointblank), and when the directive to General Eisenhower was issued in February 1944 it had still not been decided when, or in what measure, the strategic air forces should be brought under the control of the Supreme Commander.

The original purpose of the Combined Bomber Offensive was 'the progressive destruction and dislocation of the German military, industrial and economic system and the undermining of the morale of the German people to a point where their capacity for armed resistance is fatally weakened'. Had it succeeded fully there might have been little armed resistance to overcome. How far it succeeded may best be judged when the story of the land campaign has shown what resistance was in fact encountered. It would be out of place here to trace the course of its progress, or the controversies which it occasioned before and when it was related organically to Overlord in 1944, for its history during that period is fully recorded in other volumes of this series.[6]

But the directive issued by the Combined Chiefs of Staff in January 1943, after Casablanca, had concluded its specific instructions with the following general order to the strategic air force commanders: 'When the Allied armies re-enter the continent you will afford them all possible support in the manner most effective'. That time was now rapidly approaching and there was good reason for General Eisenhower to look to the strategic air forces for help. It had been one of the Allies' aims when they embarked on the Italian campaign to prevent Germany from transferring substantial reinforcements to France by engaging as many divisions as possible in Italy. Their aim had been partially, but only partially, achieved. Early in 1944 twenty-two German divisions were engaged in Italy, where there had been only six early in July 1943; but though Germany had thus been forced to increase the number of her divisions in Italy the German High Command had managed, during the same period, also to increase the number of divisions stationed in France to resist the expected assault. When the Cossac outline plan was considered in August 1943 there were believed to be some forty divisions in France and the Low Countries; by March 1944 there were known to be at least fifty-one. The Allies could do nothing further to induce the withdrawal of these divisions, but their combined air forces could do four things to minimise their effective use and so to ease the way for the coming campaign—four things of great importance and growing urgency. They could weaken if not destroy the power of the German air force to hinder our operations, by obtaining mastery of the air; they could make it difficult for the enemy to concentrate his land forces quickly when battle was joined, by disrupting his communications and destroying his means of transportation; they could weaken his coastal defences; and they could induce him to disperse or misplace his forces before the battle, by deceiving him as to the point of our attack. Some of the tasks in which both tactical and strategic air forces were already engaged would indirectly facilitate Overlord, but the time was coming when the help of heavy bombers in strength would be needed, acting in co-ordination with the tactical air forces, for tasks of immediate concern to the forthcoming assault and subsequent campaign. Who then was to determine priorities if the strategic air forces remained outside General Eisenhower's control?

---

[6] See Ehrman, op. cit., pp. 286–304; Webster and Frankland, *The Strategic Air Offensive*. vols. II and III.

To him, it appeared, the only satisfactory answer was that (excepting only Coastal Command) all Allied air forces in Britain, if not in Europe, should now come under his command. But this was not the British view and it was because an agreed answer had not been found that the diagram which accompanied General Eisenhower's directive did not show the command arrangements for strategic air forces.

Looked at from General Eisenhower's point of view or in Washington (where the American point of view naturally tended to predominate in the counsels of the Combined Chiefs of Staff), his proposal appeared to offer the logical answer; but from the British point of view the matter did not seem so simple. Overlord and the Pointblank bomber offensive were distinct though related operations. The latter was a strategic affair with implications for all European fronts including the Russian. In the British view control of strategic air forces should therefore be retained by the Combined Chiefs of Staff who should allocate part or all of them to Overlord as and when they might decide.

Personalities and labels further complicated the issue. It will be recalled that months before General Eisenhower was appointed, Sir Trafford Leigh-Mallory was appointed 'Air Commander-in-Chief, Allied Expeditionary Air Force' for Overlord. As, however, the future control of strategic air forces had not then been decided only tactical air forces were included in his command. That was still the position when the directive to General Eisenhower was issued. General Eisenhower had had no voice in the appointment of the Air Commander-in-Chief and when he arrived in England it soon became clear that he did not contemplate any enlargement of Air Marshal Leigh-Mallory's existing command. Air Marshal Sir Arthur Harris and General Carl Spaatz, who commanded respectively the British and United States strategic air forces and derived their authority for the Pointblank campaign directly from the Combined Chiefs of Staff (with Sir Charles Portal as the latter's representative in Britain), were both opposed to the suggestion that the Supreme Commander for Overlord and, even more strongly, that the latter's Air Commander-in-Chief should now be interposed between them and the body in Washington which directed Allied strategy. Remote control from far-away Washington had left them happily free to interpret the general terms of Pointblank in their own ways; they did not welcome an interruption of the courses they desired ardently to pursue, or a change of control that would inevitably curb their freedom of action.

The question was eventually settled by a compromise. Bomber Command and the United States Eighth Air Force were not, as such, brought under General Eisenhower's command but, by decision of the Combined Chiefs of Staff, the direction of all air operations out of England 'engaged in an approved air programme in preparation for and in support of "Overlord" and incorporating Pointblank would pass to the Supreme Commander on April the 14th . . . until Overlord is established on the Continent'; thereafter their employment and the method of their direction was to be reviewed by the Combined Chiefs of Staff. On April the 15th an approved air programme was issued and the Deputy Supreme Commander (Sir Arthur Tedder) was made responsible by General Eisenhower for the co-ordination of all air operations—tactical and strategic—under his command; from that date the story of strategic bombing becomes inseparably interwoven with that of other operations of the campaign, although the control of strategic forces was changed as Overlord developed. An account of the new air programme and the active operations which followed its adoption will be given in later chapters.

By April the Supreme Commander had thus established his headquarters and formed his staff, the scale of operations had been enlarged and the difficulty of obtaining adequate resources was being overcome. Planning of the assault and seizure of a bridgehead in Normandy and its enlargement into a lodgement area from which further operations could be developed had been entrusted to Admiral Ramsay, General Montgomery and Air Marshal Leigh-Mallory; their 'Initial Joint Plan' had been issued in February and, under their direction, the detailed plans based on it were being elaborated by the three Services.

Before describing these, however, it will be well to know something of the conditions which the Allies expected to find in France, on whose soil the opening battle was to be fought—to know something of how German occupation had affected the French nation and how the Germans were preparing to defend their position.

CHAPTER III

THE SITUATION IN FRANCE

'Gallia est omnis divisa in partes tres.'
Julius Caesar—*De Bello Gallico*.

THE country through which a mighty attack was soon to be 'aimed at the heart of Germany' belonged to our first ally; it was also the country of the only nation at war with Germany whose government had concluded an armistice with Hitler. Through this France had secured, at the time, freedom from military occupation for rather less than half of the country; by 1944, however, all France was occupied. For the Allies, about to embark on her liberation, it was important to know what conditions they would encounter and fortunately they were well informed. Their intelligence was both full and accurate, and although the account that follows has been clarified here and there by the light of after-knowledge, most of its important features and a great many additional details were known to the Allied commanders when Overlord was being planned.[1]

On July the 10th, 1940, the French parliament, the Chamber of Deputies and the Senate, sitting as the National Assembly, had voted itself out of existence. The Third Republic was dead; the Vichy régime was born. All power was vested in Marshal Pétain in order that he might promulgate a new constitution, to be ratified by the nation and applied by the political organs it would create. At the time when he was given this position of supreme personal authority he was Premier under the old régime and it was his government that had accepted Hitler's armistice terms. By the nation he had long been held in high honour as the hero of Verdun in the First World War; now he was regarded by many as the saviour of France from further useless bloodshed. By politicians he was known to hold authoritarian and reactionary views.

The Marshal was not slow to assume the trappings of power—or in any hurry to share them. He took no steps to frame a new constitution. In the meantime Ministers of State, civil servants, soldiers, magistrates and officials of all kinds were required to swear fealty to him in person and were made responsible to him alone. All representative elements in the state were eradicated or reduced to

---
[1] The first half of this chapter is based largely on a volume of *The Survey of International Affairs 1943–1946*, entitled *Hitler's Europe* (O.U.P., 1954), and an unpublished study by Susan Passant (Mrs. R. Donald) of sources referred to in that volume.

impotence. The Senate and Chamber were suspended and their offices abolished; local elections were done away with and the old representative institutions of local government were superseded by organs deriving their authority from Pétain, and centrally controlled. He 'governed' through a Council of Ministers, with an inner cabinet council, but authority for all laws derived from '*Nous, Phillipe Pétain...*'

Yet although the old Marshal of France—he was 84—had achieved this appearance of power and was in fact able to modify German demands considerably, and although it suited Hitler to accept him as the figurehead of French government, real power, in so far as there was any in the Vichy régime, was exercised to a large extent by the chairman of his inner council of ministers, known at first as Vice-President of the Council and later as Chief of Government. For the first six months that position was occupied by the ex-Socialist germanophile Pierre Laval; after a short interregnum it was held for fourteen months by Admiral Darlan, hardly less anti-British though less pro-German than Laval. Then in April 1942 Laval obtained reinstatement and he was still in office when the Allies began landing in 1944.

It is unnecessary to trace here the chequered history of the Vichy régime. It is less a history of government by Pétain, or anyone else, than of competing factions who, with various motives, fought for power over what remained of stricken France—of a long struggle constrained by the conditions of a world-wide war and by the dominant force of German authority. Leadership in this struggle was held by men whose rise and fall was determined by their success or failure in out-manœuvring rival claimants for Hitler's approval and for Pétain's acquiescence. The former required a policy of collaboration with Germany: the latter required a cunning restraint in its application. Most of 'the men of Vichy' came from the conservative, Catholic, anti-republican right, who before the war had argued the desirability of authoritarian measures to curb the growth of proletarian power. Pétain's repression of representative institutions and his policy of centralised administration had the ready support of such men; and since these measures would facilitate German control of politics, administration, industry and finance, his policy in this regard was also acceptable to Hitler. The fact that Vichy could effect such changes without destroying the good-will widely accorded to Pétain disposed Hitler to support the régime, for it was no part of German policy to alienate French opinion needlessly; his support required the inclusion of a leader in the régime—a Laval or a Darlan—who could secure the measure of collaboration which he demanded.

Centred in Paris there was indeed an anomalous collection of dissident groups who were dissatisfied with Pétain's policy and were frankly anxious to associate France with Germany on a National Socialist basis. Some had little political importance, others represented parties which had been alive before the war. All denounced fervently their particular bogies—Britain, America, Jewish financiers, Wall Street—while advocating various and often internecine policies. In German eyes their pro-German zest had its disadvantages, for whereas Pétain made collaboration seem respectable the Paris partisans made it look discreditable. The Germans, in this instance, preferred to look respectable. They could use Paris when need be as a stick with which to beat a hesitant Vichy but so long as Pétain let himself be guided by Lavals or Darlans there was no need to include more troublesome Déats or Doriots in the Vichy régime.

Except in Alsace and Lorraine, which were promptly annexed by Germany and assimilated in the Reich, civil administration throughout the whole of France remained under the Vichy régime but, in varying degrees, it was everywhere subject to German supervision and was required to conform to German demands. In the occupied zone German establishments for military government and civil control were interlaced at every stage and although in the unoccupied zone control was less obvious and exploitation less severe the difference was one of degree rather than of principle; in both areas there was enough to ensure the fulfilment of German requirements. After the military occupation of all France in the autumn of 1942 differences were progressively evened out, the German stranglehold on industry was everywhere tightened and economic exploitation intensified.

Certainly France suffered grievously in these years, when German officials supervised the French civil service and German troops and police supervised, or tried to, the behaviour of French citizens; when banking, business and industry were under German regulation and the rules and orders of German authorities had the force of law and took precedence over the law of the land. Demands for positive co-operation were accompanied by a multitude of repressive measures; strikes and 'agitations' were punishable by hard labour or even death; and equally severe punishments might be inflicted on those who failed to make any contribution of goods and services which was levied by the Military Commander. In these years the strength of France was sapped by a steady drain of men, materials and money. Nearly a million Frenchmen, prisoners of war taken in 1940, were retained in Germany and nearly half a million more were transferred from France to work for German industry. The equivalent of at least five hundred million pounds was taken for the 'costs' of occupation and some calculations put the total far higher. Raw materials and manufactured stocks were requisitioned on a considerable scale. By the beginning of 1944 France was short of men, short of money, short of materials, short of food, and commerce was at a standstill.

The conflict of individual interest and patriotic duty, the haunting sense of national shame and personal danger, sorrow for the loss or unknown fate of absent kin, and hatred of Germany's arrogant assurance, were joined, often, to physical strain and economic uncertainty and were interwoven in the texture of French life. As frequently happens in times of national calamity, they brought out, in many, inherent qualities of self-sacrifice, endurance and courage, but in others greed and self-seeking, cowardice and even treachery.

Any generalisations about the mood and attitude of the French people can be only partially true and must be subject to many qualifications. Yet it may perhaps be said with justice that after the armistice had signified the national defeat a mood of half-stunned acquiescence was widely prevalent, in which grief was tempered by thankfulness that a hopeless fight was ended. A belief that Britain was also virtually beaten made the acceptance of Hitler's 'new order' seem inevitable.

But before long this passive mood began to be less common. As Britain fought on and first Russia and then America joined the war on Germany, French hearts were lifted by a dawning hope that Hitler might yet be beaten in the end and that France might yet become herself again—that all was not yet lost. Whereas in 1940 the nation lay bemused by defeat, by 1944 large numbers worked and waited for liberation from their odious bonds with growing confidence.

While Overlord was being planned the Vichy régime was rocked by intrigue and at last representatives of the Paris extremists progressively gained influence. Pétain's authority had waned and Laval only held what power he had by leave of Germany. German demands increased in severity and outwardly the condition of France was worsened, but in the soul of France a braver spirit was reviving. Beneath the surface tiny fires of resistance which had been lit in 1940 had been smouldering and spreading ever since. Now they burned hotly, bursting into flame with increasing frequency and in places blazing openly in spite of all German efforts to subdue them. 'Resistance' had become a factor of military and political importance not only to France but to the Allies preparing for her liberation. Its implications for General Eisenhower—and indeed for the Allied governments—are explainable only by some knowledge of its origins and evolution.

Respect for constitutional authority is a characteristic of the French people, and Pétain had been vested with authority by constitutional process. When he accepted Hitler's terms there was then no figure in France of comparable standing to rally opposition; yet from the first a spirit of resistance stirred beneath the surface, in groups which had often little in common except the determination to thwart the enemy's will and to stultify his purpose. The story of these early resistance groups and their gradual burgeoning is a long and tangled one, revealing a 'blend of courage and patriotism, ambition, faction and treachery'. Many French men and many French women lost their lives in brave attempts to win freedom for France, and although the German authorities succeeded in the discovery of much secret activity which they ruthlessly repressed, they failed, in spite of all their power, to prevent a steady growth of organised resistance, though it was fostered in groups which were themselves handicapped by internal rivalries and the pursuit of opposed policies. By 1944 the resistance movement had reached both a measure of unity and a substantial strength. It had done so to a large extent under the influence of General Charles de Gaulle.

On June the 17th, 1940, when Marshal Pétain announced that he had applied to the Germans for armistice terms, General de Gaulle flew to England. The next evening he broadcast a memorable exhortation and appeal to his countrymen.

From that day he began to rally members of the French forces in England and Frenchmen everywhere who shared his faith in French recovery. He claimed that though France was for the time being conquered the French Empire was not; that though the Vichy government was subservient to Germany it did not represent the French nation. Such leadership as Vichy gave was not the true leadership of a great people and, with the support of the British Government, de Gaulle set out to provide it from a headquarters in London. He had a long and stormy passage through the years which followed but by the autumn of 1943 his uncompromising hostility to Germany, his unshakable faith in the greatness of France, his equally firm confidence in his own leadership, and the moral and material backing of the Allies, had won for him a position of military and political ascendancy as the protagonist of French revival.

The Allied landings and subsequent victory in North Africa in 1942 and the simultaneous extension of German occupation to the whole of France, had convinced even the constitutionally-minded that de Gaulle rather than Vichy spoke with the true voice of France and throughout the French possessions overseas his leadership was at last fully established. His relations with resistance movements in metropolitan France were not quite so clearly defined for reasons that are explainable only by reference to their development.

From among the many earliest resistance groups which came into being, were suppressed by the Germans, succumbed to internal difficulties, or survived and grew, five principal groups could be distinguished by 1941. In the occupied zone the *Parti des Fusillés*, organised by the French communist party, attracted much sympathy and support in the absence of any effective alternative. The party had also some organisation in the unoccupied zone, but there three others exercised between them a wider influence. These were the *Libération Nationale, Liberté* and *Libération,* whose members ranged from the Catholic right to supporters of the old *Front Populaire.* These three soon came together, while a fourth, the *Carte,* held aloof. In July 1941 M. Jean Pierre Moulin, a leading representative of the three linked organisations, came to London to seek aid from de Gaulle. Till then the latter had been chiefly useful to resistance groups as a symbol; now he began to be thought of as a source of supply and a focus of more effective organisation. Following this and subsequent visits closer relationships developed and by the autumn of 1942 a central organisation with both military and political objects had been formed in France, relying largely for its unity on the leadership of de Gaulle. He was less successful with the communist groups, partly because a mission which he sent to them was quickly captured by the Germans and partly because they were not in sympathy with his political aims or those of the associated movements which he now led. The latter were organising a 'secret army' to join with the Allies on the day of deliverance and meanwhile to carry on a programme of sabotage and subversive action; but they were also planning to form an administration which would take charge on the disappearance of the Vichy régime. It was on this political ground that not only the French Communists but the Allied governments had difficulty in accepting de Gaulle's full claims. As the architect of military recovery and the head of a reconstituted French army the Allies were ready to give him their whole-hearted backing provided that in military action he recognised General Eisenhower as Supreme Commander; they were less ready to give unqualified support to his political design for government and his desire to return to France as the political head of the French people. Indeed, even the associated resistance movements were not wholehearted in their agreement with his political programme, or ready to surrender to him all the authority he claimed.

It will be necessary to examine more fully the Allies' relations with de Gaulle during the last few months of preparation for Overlord, but in this outline of conditions which the Allied armies would meet in France there is, first, more to be said about internal resistance movements. By far the largest were the associated movements already noted, organised now under a National Council of the Resistance in France, which was in turn represented on a committee of National Liberation over which de Gaulle presided in Algiers. But there were other *foci* of resistance which must be explained.

First there were the 'Maquis' who differed radically from other resistance movements in their origin, aims and methods. During 1942 German demands induced Vichy to impose a scheme—the *relève*—to conscript labour for work in Germany on the understanding that Germany would gradually release French prisoners of war. By this means over four hundred thousand Frenchmen were transferred but when, in April 1943, a further four hundred thousand were demanded there was widespread and spontaneous refusal by the younger men affected. Thousands disappeared from their homes and made their way to the mountains. There they gathered gradually into camps and in time developed an uneven measure of discipline and command. By 1944 there were some hundred thousand of these Maquisards, more or less effectively organised and in relation with, but only partially controlled by, the Council of the Resistance and de Gaulle's organisation—good material for guerrilla warfare but needing arms.

And here an Allied organisation must be included in the picture—a conjunction of the British 'Special Operations Executive' and of the American 'Office of Strategic Services'. The Special Operations Executive (known in short as S.O.E.) was formed in 1940, by a reorganisation of earlier agencies, to stimulate and assist subversive elements in enemy-held countries. The S.O.E. did not concern itself with the political aspirations of resistance movements in France but sought to establish communications with individual resistance groups and to help them by supplying arms and sabotage equipment. In those early days the limitations of personnel, equipment and above all of transport aircraft restricted severely what could be done but throughout the years which followed direct links with resistance groups in France were slowly but progressively strengthened. The part played by the British Broadcasting Corporation in stimulating French resistance movements was also considerable. They started broadcasting messages to the French people from the moment France fell and continued them throughout the years that followed. The growth of all resistance movements in 1943, their association with the National Council of the Resistance and their recognition of de Gaulle's leadership, greatly increased the opportunities and occasion for S.O.E.'s help; and towards the end of that year the representatives in England of the American Office of Strategic Services joined forces with S.O.E. in a single organisation which was to come under the Supreme Command of General Eisenhower and work in future under his directive.

Special Force Headquarters, as this joint organisation within Shaef came to be called, concerned itself not only with French Resistance but, in time, with all resistance movements in North-West Europe. The Belgian Resistance consisted of the Secret Army (with some 45,000 effectives), and the civilian organisations combined as the

Comité National de Co-ordination, which were co-ordinated under M. Ganshof van der Meersch at the end of 1943; in the second quarter of 1944 there were fifty-five air operations to supply them with arms. The Dutch Resistance had a less fortunate history because from March 1942 until May 1943 S.O.E. had unwittingly dropped forty-three agents into the arms of two able German officers of the *Abwehr*. After this disaster had been discovered by S.O.E. in the autumn of 1943, a ban was laid on air operations to Holland until the end of March 1944, and even then priority was low and there were only nine sorties before August. Thus the three main Dutch Resistance movements with para-military branches, *Orde Dienst*, *Raad Van Verzet* and *Landelijke Knokploegen*, were still poorly equipped by D-day.

Allied leaders differed in their estimates of the military value which ought to be attached to these resistance movements, and indeed it was not possible to obtain the data for an accurate assessment. Actual and potential strength could only be estimated; control of resistance activities would be difficult and incomplete; requirements of security made it undesirable to inform resistance leaders of Allied plans; and at the last minute the effectiveness of resistance measures might be ruined by German discovery and suppression. The Cossac view had been that military reliance should not be placed on resistance activities and therefore that any success in their operations should be treated as a bonus. In the early months of 1944 this view was shared by General Eisenhower's staff, but all agreed that it was desirable to help resistance forces both in continuous sabotage activities and in armed risings when the time came. An account of the steps taken to this end belongs, however, to the story of preliminary operations rather than to this review of conditions in France which were taken into account in planning the assault. And of these the most important factor of all has yet to be described—namely the strength and nature of the enemy's defences and of the armies which must be beaten in France.

The fluctuating course of the war since 1940 had been reflected in the evolution of German policy for western defence. At first, when there seemed no possibility of any serious danger from Great Britain, the High Command regarded coast defence merely as a precaution against enemy raids, but by the close of 1941 the situation had changed. Russia and America now had to be reckoned with. A long war was inevitable and the risk of war on two fronts threatened, for eventually attack from the west appeared probable. The development of coastal defences was ordered by OKW (the High Command of the Armed Forces) and Hitler's conception of an 'Atlantic Wall' began to take shape. At this juncture Field-Marshal von Brauchitsch, Commander-in-Chief of the German Army, was retired and Hitler himself assumed that office. In the following March, that is in March

1942, Field-Marshal von Rundstedt was for a second time recalled from retirement and was appointed Commander-in-Chief, West. Subordinate only to Hitler, von Rundstedt thus became responsible for the defence of France, Belgium, and Holland. The probability that Britain and the United States would launch an attack through one or more of these countries as soon as they were able to do so had now to be faced, and on March the 23rd Hitler propounded a policy of defence designed to thwart any attempted landing. Coastal sectors liable to assault were to be turned into fortified areas and provision was to be made for the immediate counter-attack of any troops which effected a landing so that they might be quickly destroyed or driven back into the sea.

Five days later, on March the 28th, a British raid on the German naval base of St. Nazaire which put the great dock out of action stung Hitler to order yet more and stronger defences and his belief in the efficacy of coastal fortifications was strengthened by what happened later in the summer at Dieppe. For German Intelligence, largely based on deceptive rumours initiated by the Allies, together with German estimates of probable Allied strategy, had led them to expect a large-scale British landing operation during the summer. The British and Canadian raid on Dieppe seemed to justify this foresight and its repulse to confirm the value of coastal defence works. Self-satisfaction reinforced a wilful misreading of events (for they captured orders clearly indicating the true nature and limited aim of the Dieppe raid) and had a lasting influence on German defence policy.

The Allied landings in North Africa during the following November convinced Hitler that there was, however, no immediate likelihood of a further large-scale operation in the West during the coming winter and, with the war going badly for Germany in both Russia and North Africa, the forces under von Rundstedt's command began to be drained away and ever greater reliance to be placed on the virtues of steel and concrete. As Allied operations in the Mediterranean underlined the probable postponement of any major attack in the West, the draining of trained troops from France continued. From April to December 1943 twenty-seven divisions were transferred from the West. In their place the number of divisions in course of formation and training was increased and additional reserve divisions were brought in from Germany's 'replacement army' (*Ersatzheer*) responsible, among other things, for providing trained divisions for the field force. The immediate fighting value of these heterogeneous forces was not comparable with the five armoured, two motorised and twenty infantry divisions which had been taken from von Rundstedt's command.

Von Rundstedt repeatedly represented to the High Command the danger of thus reducing his armies, but events in Russia and Allied landings in Sicily were held to justify reductions in the West, which was not thought to be in immediate danger of invasion; the main threat of invasion lay in the Mediterranean. In any case the removal of von Rundstedt's troops was 'only possible because the Atlantic Wall had meantime attained a considerable degree of strength'.

In September 1943 the Allies staged the large-scale feint attack in the Straits of Dover which Cossac had been instructed to plan (Operation 'Starkey'). It was designed to provoke an air battle over the area, to stop the further transfer of troops to Russia or Italy, and to encourage the enemy to believe that the Pas de Calais was where the Allies' main assault would eventually be made. The German air force appears to have thought that discretion was the better part of valour and refused to be drawn, and von Rundstedt had not moved his forces when our demonstration ended. But it strengthened Hitler's opinion that the Pas de Calais would be the scene of the Allies' main assault when the time came. Here, therefore, coastal fortifications were to be strongest. For this there was additional reason. Hitler had laid it down that top priority of development should be given to those portions of the Atlantic Wall where the projected new 'V'-weapons would be committed. The chief of these was the Pas de Calais.

Troubled by the continual bleeding of his best troops and unsatisfied with the progress of defence works, von Rundstedt had ordered, in May, a searching enquiry into all aspects of the defence. On the results he based his own estimate of the situation on the western front. His report is dated October 28th, 1943. It is a sober assessment of the Allies' opportunity, of the value of coastal fortifications and of the adequacy of the coastal defence troops under his command. He saw three courses of action open to the Allies, namely, an attack 'in the Channel, probably combined with an attack from the south against the French Mediterranean coast'; or 'attacks against Normandy and Brittany to establish bridgeheads with good harbours and to eliminate submarine bases'; or co-ordinated attack 'from the south against the French southern coast and from the Bay of Biscay . . .' 'Because of our inadequate means of reconnaissance, the enemy is in a position to ensure surprise to its full extent', but it was 'probable that for military and political reasons the enemy does not yet consider the attack as timely and has postponed it (Moscow Conference). Many indications, however, point to the fact that he is preparing for it.'

Reviewing the length of coast to be defended he concluded that many parts of the front could not be defended (*Verteidigung*) in the true sense of the word; they could only be covered (*Sicherung*); and on the west coast south of the Loire no more than an armed watch (*verstärkte Beobachtung*) was possible. Although the permanent fortifications of the Atlantic Wall were 'indispensable and valuable for battle as well as for propaganda', yet 'in spite of all fortifications a "rigid defence" of the long stretch of coast for any considerable length of time is impossible.' Defence must therefore be based ultimately on a general reserve 'especially of tanks and motorised units'.

Before arriving at these conclusions he had made a detailed evaluation of the troops provided for coastal defence, and his report sets out the composition, armament, and state of training of each division, with his own conclusion as to its capabilities. Of the twenty-three divisions on the coast between the Scheldt and Spain seventeen were fit for defence, but of little or no value for any offensive action; five were only partially fit for defence; one was not mentioned. Many were insufficiently supplied with artillery and heavy infantry weapons. Many were armed with captured weapons—he names French, Belgian, Dutch, Polish, Russian and Italian—and in one army there were ten types of artillery. 'This situation causes difficulty in ammunition supply.' He found that the morale and discipline of the German troops were 'gratifyingly good', but he had only accepted the 'Turk Battalions' (a name used to describe battalions of anti-Bolshevik soldiers, mostly taken as prisoners of war on the Russian front) 'in order to have some "men" to show on the thin fronts'. He added that they 'will only be of assistance if they hold out; otherwise they will be a burden'. His final conclusion was that if the High Command expect 'offensive operations by the Anglo-Americans seeking decision against the heart of Europe', then it was not only necessary to increase the inherent value of coastal defence forces and troops capable of immediate counter-attack, but also to constitute a centrally-located and completely mobile army at the disposal of the commander of the western front for counter-offensive action. At this date his reserves consisted of twenty-three divisions; eleven of these were only in the process of formation; two more were arriving.

On November the 3rd Hitler issued his directive No. 51: 'All signs point to an offensive against the Western Front of Europe not later than the spring, and perhaps earlier . . . I have therefore decided to strengthen the defences in the West, particularly at places from which we shall launch our long-range operations against England . . . there, unless all indications are misleading, will be fought the decisive invasion battle.' A schedule of arms, tanks, assault guns, motor vehicles and ammunition to be allocated to the western front and Denmark within the next three months was to be submitted as soon as possible and 'only an unsurpassed effort in the construction of fortifications, enlisting all available man-power and physical resources of Germany and the occupied areas, will enable us to strengthen our defences along the coast within the short time that in all probability remains'.

In November 1943, Army Group B, which Field-Marshal Rommel had commanded in Italy, had been transformed into 'an army group for special employment' directly under Hitler. It consisted only of a headquarters staff and was to study defence preparedness of the occupied coasts and to submit proposals; and it was to 'arrange operational studies for offensive operations against an enemy landing force'. Rommel was to report direct to Hitler without any reference to von Rundstedt, who was not only his senior but as Commander-in-Chief was already responsible for the defence of the West. This arrangement, so typical of Hitler's policy of 'divide and rule', was however short-lived. On December the 13th Rommel submitted his report on Denmark, which was not within von Rundstedt's command. Then the latter intervened and Rommel's position was regularised.

On December the 31st the war diary of the Armed Forces High Command (OKW) Operations Staff included an entry to the effect that, acting on the previous day's request by C-in-C West (that is by von Rundstedt), Rommel's command, now known as Army Group B, would be integrated in the western command machinery. It would cease to be directly under Hitler and in future Rommel would submit his proposals and receive orders through von Rundstedt. His command, Army Group B, would now consist of the Netherlands Command and the Fifteenth and Seventh Armies whose position is shown on the map facing this page.

On paper the rôles and relationship of the two dominant commanders in France seemed to have been settled, but differences of age and outlook remained and were not so easily reconcilable. The old and sober strategist foresaw that the coastal crust would be broken, however strongly it was fortified; only strong mobile forces held in reserve and available for use as the situation required could defeat an invading army whose point of main attack could not be foreseen with certainty. The young and ardent tactician accepted the Hitler view that invading forces must be defeated on the coast, made up his mind where the main attack would come, and wanted to dispose available forces, ready for prompt counter-attack, near the threatened coastal sectors. The result of divided counsels will be seen later.

During the first three months of 1944 Germany's deteriorating position on the Russian and Italian fronts handicapped, and at times reversed, the last-minute attempt to bolster up the defence against the Allied attack in the West which now appeared imminent. Some new formations were created, others were re-graded, re-equipped and brought up to strength. But orders for the transfer of armoured

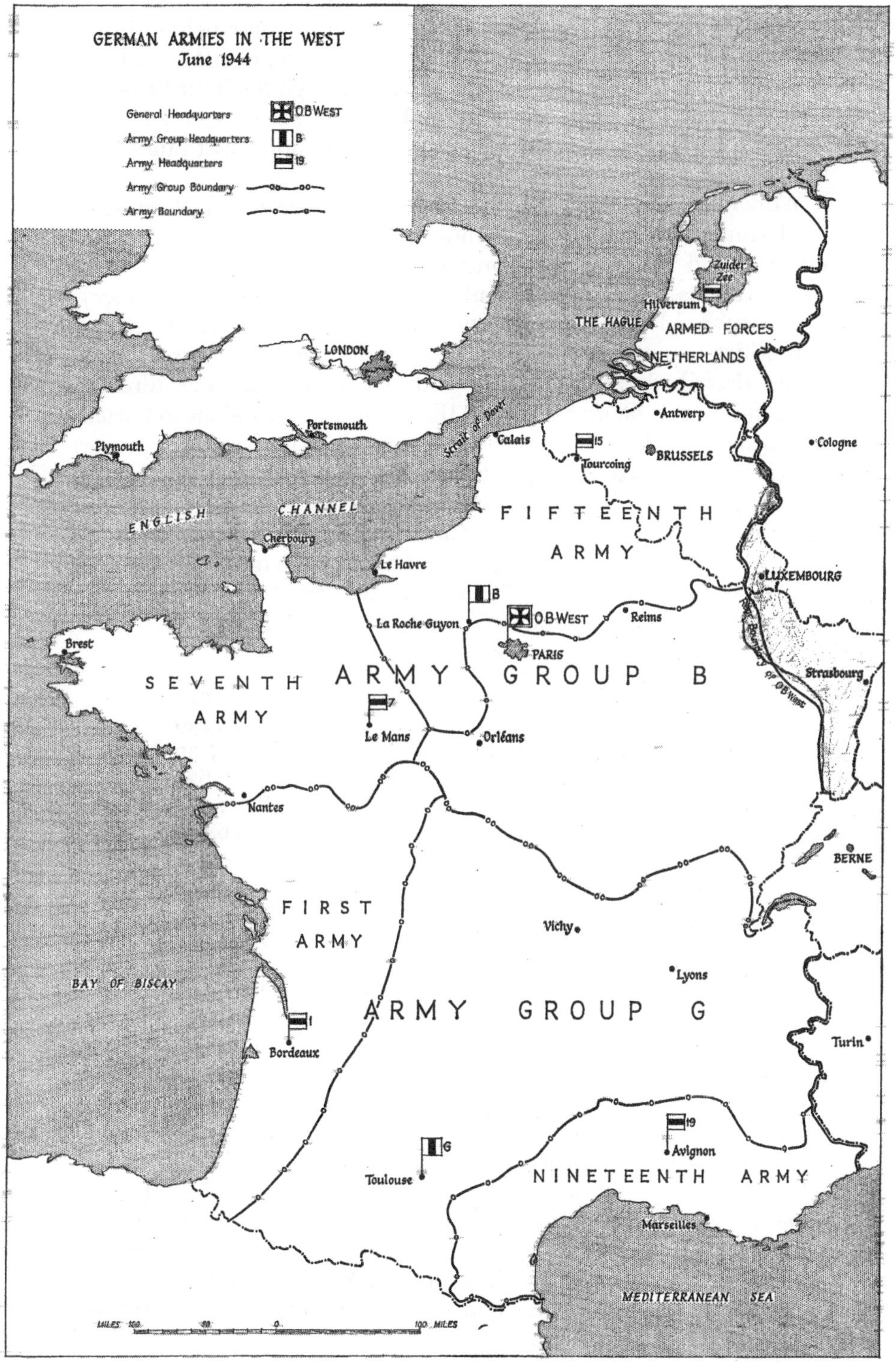
GERMAN ARMIES IN THE WEST
June 1944
General Headquarters
OB WEST
Army Group Headquarters
B
Army Headquarters
19
Army Group Boundary
Army Boundary
Zuider Zee
Hilversum
THE HAGUE
ARMED FORCES
NETHERLANDS
LONDON
Antwerp
Portsmouth
Plymouth
Calais
15
Tourcoing
BRUSSELS
Cologne
Strait of Dover
ENGLISH CHANNEL
FIFTEENTH ARMY
Cherbourg
Le Havre
LUXEMBOURG
B
La Roche Guyon
OB WEST
Reims
PARIS
Brest
SEVENTH ARMY
ARMY GROUP B
Strasbourg
7
Le Mans
Orléans
Nantes
BERNE
FIRST ARMY
Vichy
Lyons
BAY OF BISCAY
1
Bordeaux
ARMY GROUP G
Turin
19
Avignon
G
Toulouse
NINETEENTH ARMY
Marseilles
MEDITERRANEAN SEA
MILES 100
0
100 MILES

divisions from Russia and Italy were cancelled because neither front could spare them. More armour and infantry were, in fact, sent East in the latter half of March, as well as the assault guns of four first-line divisions; new divisions supplied to the West were less good than those which had been taken away though the number of tanks had been increased.

Work on fortifications, too, though pushed forward with Rommel's newly-imported energy, was handicapped both by insufficiency of material and by a steadily worsening transport system. The Allied air operations (and to a less extent sabotage by the French Resistance) were responsible for a deterioration of the German means of transport which was a most important part of the preparatory operations to be described later, but one indication of what was already happening may be given here. Military formations alone reported the loss of one hundred and twenty-nine locomotives through air attack and sabotage during the first ten days of March—not yet a crippling affliction but a gnawing sore.

Before leaving for the time being this outline of conditions in France which those planning Overlord had to take into account in so far as it was known to them, the numerical strength of the occupying forces on March the 1st may be noted. The German ration strength recorded for that day was as follows:

Army	806,927
SS and Police	85,230
Volunteers (Foreigners)	61,439
Allies	13,631
Air Force	337,140
Navy	96,084
Total Armed Forces	1,400,451
Armed Force Auxiliaries	145,611

The air force figures, unless explained, are liable to give a false impression of the German air strength in France at this time. For over a hundred thousand of the personnel shown above were in anti-aircraft artillery (flak) formations, designed for air defence but liable also to be used against land forces; and over thirty thousand were 'paratroops'.

The German air forces stationed in France were known as the Third Air Fleet and were commanded by Field-Marshal Sperrle. They consisted of miscellaneous squadrons of bombers and torpedo bombers, long and short-range reconnaissance aircraft, and of day and night fighter squadrons. The approximate numbers of aircraft available for operations were 890 and of these some 150 were reconnaissance or transport aircraft.

The German naval defence of France at the date of the Allied assault will be described in detail later. Here it need only be noted that it consisted of a number of heavy naval coastal batteries, with radar equipment, situated at key points on shore; and at sea, one weak flotilla of destroyers, a few torpedo-boats, five flotillas of motor torpedo-boats and a considerable number of small patrol craft and minelayers; the main sea-going defence consisted of U-boats based on Brest and other Brittany and Biscay ports. All except the U-boats were under the command of Vice-Admiral Krancke, commander of 'Naval Group West'. The fact that some coastal artillery was thus under naval control and some under army command complicated defence policy.

It will be found later that the strength of the coastal defences and of the garrison was increased during the time which remained before the Allies launched their assault. The 'unsurpassed effort' for which Hitler had called bore some fruit, but a description of the position when the Allied campaign opened may be deferred till that point in the story is reached.

This review of conditions which the Allies were to meet in France may be left here for the time being, though it may be well to look for a moment beyond France, in order to see how far Germany's war-making capacity at this date appeared likely to affect the coming campaign.

At the beginning of 1944 Germany had over 300 divisions in the field, outside of the Reich. Of these, 179 were on the Russian front, 26 in the Balkan States, 22 in Italy, 53 in France and the Low Countries, 16 in Scandinavia and 8 in Finland. In various occupied countries 24 of these divisions were in process of formation. There was no general reserve in Germany. All Hitler's huge land forces were committed, and without denuding other fronts there could be no substantial increase of the armies in the West.

With the sinking of the *Scharnhorst* in Arctic waters on December the 26th, 1943, Germany could offer no effective challenge to Allied seapower except with U-boats. 'Small battle units' made up of such unorthodox craft as midget submarines, radio-controlled explosive motor boats and other ingenious devices which might achieve tactical surprise were still in course of development. In the air, the enemy's 1,700 long range bombers and 2,420 fighters which constituted half his total air force had to face attack in Russia, Italy and the West; and the growing menace of the Allied bombing of Germany entailed such a concentration of fighters for the defence of the Reich that there could be no material expansion of air fleets on any of the threatened fronts.

The maintenance, armament and renewal of the enemy's forces was of course dependent on German industry, supported by contributions from conquered countries; and nowhere was German ability more strikingly evident than in this field. In 1942, Albert Speer, a young architect (he was 36) who had worked with Hitler on the design of various public buildings, was appointed Reich Minister of Arms and Munitions. He had little or no knowledge of industrial production, but he brought to his new task an acute mind, imagination, energy and a gift for improvisation. His quickening influence on the industrial machine is reflected in the following astonishing figures in his production survey for 1940–1944:

	1941	1942	1943
Ammunition—metric tons	540,000	1,270,000	2,558,000
Automatic weapons	324,800	316,691	435,400
Artillery—including anti-aircraft		7,092	11,988	26,904
Armour—including tanks and self-propelled guns	2,875	5,673	11,897
Aircraft—all operational types	9,540	12,950	22,050

And production was still increasing in 1944. The question was whether it could be maintained in face of the rising scale of Allied bombing. This had already created much havoc and had at times slowed down production, but so far Speer's countervailing measures had made good the loss. The Allied air leaders believed that the time was near when this would cease to be possible, but it had not yet come at the opening of 1944.

During these war years German scientists and engineers had moreover evolved three new types of weapon which might well have affected the course of the war if they could have been brought into full use even at this date. These were a new type of submarine, jet-propelled aircraft, and rocket or self-propelled long-range missiles.

The new type of submarines embodied revolutionary features. They could travel at high speed under water and could operate submerged for long periods without rising to the surface. They were however only put into production late in 1943 and owing to Allied bombing none made their appearance till the spring of 1945. Various other improvements of the normal types of U-boat, to give better immunity from detection and better powers of defence against aircraft, had been effectively countered by the Royal Navy and the Royal Air Force, so that Admiral Dönitz, Hitler's Naval Commander-in-Chief, wrote bitterly in his diary for November the 12th, 1943, 'The enemy holds every trump card, covering all areas with long-range air patrols and using location methods against which we still have no warning. . . . The enemy knows all our secrets and we know none of his.' [2] It was true. The long battle of the Atlantic had been

---

[2] Chester Wilmot, *The Struggle for Europe* (London, 1952), p. 152.

won at least for the time being. Whether it could be reopened by the new U-boats in time to affect the course of the war remained to be seen.

A jet-propelled aircraft had been designed in Germany in 1937 and flown experimentally in 1941, shortly after a first British jet aircraft began flying trials. Two German armament firms continued experiments and in the winter of 1943 the great possibilities of a high-speed, jet-engined fighter were demonstrated to the Führer. Fortunately he was more concerned with the need of greater offensive air power and, against the advice of responsible air officers, he ordered the development of jet-engined aircraft as high-speed bombers—a change which delayed production for six months and denied the German air force a most valuable defensive weapon during the most critical months. Neither British nor American jet-engined aircraft were in use at the time and if the jet-propelled fighters which Messerschmitt and Heinkel had evolved had immediately been put into large-scale production the Allies' air superiority over Germany might have been seriously challenged.

The position in regard to the new long-distance missiles—the V-weapons—was different. In this case Hitler had an exaggerated belief that they could win the war and he therefore did his utmost to accelerate their production; it was the action of the Allied air forces which upset his plans. The story of how they did so belongs, however, to later chapters.

This glance at the German background to the forthcoming fighting in France discloses both the actual strength and relative weakness of the German position. She had vast armies—but they were committed on three fronts against yet stronger enemies and there was no central reserve. She had a huge and still increasing production—but it was also increasingly threatened by the Allied air offensive and, as was proved later, the destruction of key elements or the disruption of the means of distribution might quickly destroy its value. She had new weapons, all with great possibilities, preparing for use at sea, in the air and on land—but they could not be available in time to hinder the Allies' operations or affect the course of the war.

In planning Overlord the Allies had a good general appreciation of what they would have to face in France. They knew that they would have a hard task to break through Hitler's Atlantic Wall and thereafter to defeat von Rundstedt and Rommel and the divisions under their command. They counted on some aid—of what military value they could not foretell—from the French Resistance Movement. They realised that they would find a France who had endured agony under German occupation and Vichy misrule, where, often under enemy coercion, the civil administration of the country had however been carried on by officials who thought it their duty to obey legally constituted authority, in this case the shoddy tyranny of Marshal Pétain and his henchmen. They also realised that, while the Vichy régime was floundering to a shameful death in the quicksand of German appeasement, the framework of a new administration was developing in association with General de Gaulle, who, whatever his political future might be, would return to France the widely acknowledged leader of French resistance and rebirth. Finally they realised that while the German war-making capacity was still very great it was also very vulnerable.

CHAPTER IV

THE PLAN OF CAMPAIGN

> 'I have not a doubt, if proper measures are adopted, and if secrecy is observed, that at present a landing, in spite of the Batteries, may be effected to the westward of Boulogne.'
> Sir John Moore to War Office,
> October the 1st, 1805.

THE object of Overlord was to secure a lodgement area on the Continent from which further operations could be developed. The area must contain sufficient port facilities to maintain a force of some twenty-six to thirty divisions and make possible the augmentation of that force by follow-up shipments from the United States and elsewhere of additional divisions and supporting units at the rate of three to five divisions a month. Overlord was to be carried out in two phases. The first would include an assault landing on the Normandy beaches between Quineville on the east coast of the Cotentin peninsula and Cabourg les Bains to the east of the Orne, to be followed by the early capture and development of airfield sites and the port of Cherbourg. In the second the area won would be enlarged so as to include the Loire and Brittany group of ports.

The first or assault phase was named Operation 'Neptune'. Once General Eisenhower had approved the enlargement of the scale of attack it had not taken long to expand the plans which had already been prepared. On the assumption, but still with no certainty, that the necessary resources would be available the Neptune Initial Joint Plan of Admiral Ramsay, General Montgomery and Air Marshal Leigh-Mallory was issued on February the 1st. This settled the scope and method of the projected operation and enabled subordinate commanders of all three Services to elaborate their detailed plans. The Initial Joint Plan and the Service plans which were based on it were set out in many bulky and complicated documents and before attempting to epitomise them it will be well to point out that, apart from the obvious need for favourable weather, there are three essentials to success in any seaborne invasion of a defended coast. The first is such control of sea routes and mastery in the air as will prevent effective enemy interference with planned operations. Second is the largest obtainable measure of surprise, so that the enemy's defence may be handicapped. The third is ability to land and build up the invading armies with such speed and in such sequence that they can go swiftly into action and can maintain their attack with increasing weight and momentum. It will be seen how these fundamental requirements were met in the Neptune plans.

To ensure control of sea routes and mastery in the air, to surprise and confuse the enemy and increase the difficulties of his defence, various preparatory operations were to begin well before the launch of the main attack. At sea the Neptune operations were designed to seal off from U-boats and surface vessels the waters we intended to use, to keep them clear of mines and to restrict enemy movements in the Channel and its approaches; the Home Fleet would be ready at Scapa Flow in the Orkneys to deal with Hitler's surviving major warships if any put to sea. In the air, preparatory operations that had been continued with varying intensity since 1941 were to be greatly extended so as to damage and diminish the strength of the German air force and secure for the Allies mastery of the air, to hamper movement of the enemy's ground forces towards the battlefield by disrupting his communications and means of transportation, to weaken his coastal defences, and to confuse his commanders by disguising our intentions as to the time and place of our opening attack. These preparatory air operations were progressively intensified during the time which remained before the launch of the assault. They formed the essential prelude, the true beginning of Overlord, and as such will be described in a subsequent chapter.

The main purpose of the Neptune planning was to determine how, following the easement of their task by these preparatory operations, the Allies would land and build up their assaulting armies with such speed and strength that they could overbear the enemy's initial opposition and win a sure lodgement from which they could strike in force to compass his destruction. Two basic decisions have already been mentioned. The attack was to be launched against a stretch of the Normandy coast extending from the Cherbourg peninsula to the mouth of the river Orne; and troops of three airborne and five seaborne divisions were to make the first landings. All planning was governed by these decisions and by a further agreement that American armies should be on the right flank and British armies on the left. Since it was intended eventually to supply American forces directly from America, their use of Cherbourg and, later, of the Brittany ports would obviously simplify administrative control; for the British armies, advancing eastwards with the sea on their left flank, supply would be facilitated by the use of numerous small ports along the coast.

It followed naturally that the stretch of coast selected was divided into two sectors, American and British. These were subdivided into five areas, two of which, on the right, were allotted to divisions of the United States First Army and three, on the left, to divisions of the British Second Army, whose main forces, in each case, would follow their assaulting divisions as rapidly as possible. Thereafter, when an initial bridgehead had been secured, it would gradually be expanded to form a lodgement area capable of holding the two armies—British and Canadian—constituting General Montgomery's Twenty-First Army Group and the First American Army. The latter would subsequently be followed by their Third Army and would then be formed into the United States First Army Group under Lieut-General Omar N. Bradley.

But all this depended on the Navy's ability to effect the safe and timely arrival of our assaulting forces and the ability of the troops, supported by naval and air bombardment, to break the German defence and fight their way inland; and before examining the plans of the Services it may be useful to sketch in outline the underlying pattern of the opening assault.

While the Army is at sea it is under naval control and embarkation must be carried out under naval supervision. A marriage of the assaulting forces would therefore take place in England where the troops, supporting weapons and essential equipment would be loaded into the appropriate vessels for despatch in the order in which they would be needed. Guarded by naval forces and protected by air cover, the ships would sail in convoy at appointed times through mine-swept channels to the coast of France. The leading troop-carrying vessels would be specially adapted passenger ships, bearing the first wave of the assaulting troops and each carrying on deck a corresponding complement of small landing craft. In order to gain as much as possible of the priceless advantage of surprise and to reduce the danger from coastal batteries, each group of these 'landing-ships infantry' (L.S.I.) would be stopped several miles from the shore; there the troops on board would embark in the small 'landing-craft assault' (L.C.A.) which would be lowered and formed up for the final approach and run in with other larger craft loaded with tanks, armoured vehicles and artillery to assist in piercing the beach defences. The high proportion of these supporting arms with the leading waves was to be a special feature of the attack.

Concentrated heavy bombing by Allied air forces and intense naval bombardment of the enemy's more important coast defence batteries and other pre-selected targets would already have opened and this would later be swelled by the fire of destroyers and special support vessels as they shepherded the landing craft ashore, drenching beaches and enemy defence works with fire during the final approach. At the last moment the naval guns would lengthen range for the soldiers to fight their way across the beaches and advance inland, where certain key positions on either flank would already have been seized by airborne troops, landed some hours earlier. Succeeding waves bringing in reinforcements, including ammunition and priority vehicles, would follow swiftly till the beaches and hinterland were wrested from the enemy and a firm footing was secured; and as soon as the foreshore was in our hands, the beach organisation would take charge to marshal incoming traffic as it arrived and to direct its movement. At sea, the continuously mine-swept channels, guarded by warships and aircraft, would by then be busy fairways for shipping, with craft ferrying men and equipment ashore. That, stated in its simplest terms, was the pattern of opening assault which was provided for in the Neptune plans; with that outline in mind the detail that must be added is more easily understood.

As already mentioned, the front to be attacked was divided into two sectors and sub-divided into five areas. Each of the latter was distinguished by a code name as follows:

Area	Code Name	
1. The Cherbourg peninsula, northwards from the mouth of the river Vire.	UTAH	American sector
2. From the south-eastern limit of Utah to Port en Bessin (exclusive)	OMAHA	
3. From the eastern limit of Omaha to the river Provence.	GOLD	British sector
4. From the eastern limit of Gold to St. Aubin sur Mer.	JUNO	
5. From the eastern limit of Juno to the river Orne.	SWORD	

A further area extending eastward from Sword was named Band, but it was not used in the seaborne assault. See map facing page 168.

The naval plan, which was issued by Admiral Ramsay on February the 28th, conformed to the same pattern. Two 'Naval Task Forces' would be associated with the two armies—a Western Naval Task Force with the American First Army and an Eastern Naval Task Force with the British Second Army—and within these would be organised five 'Naval Assault Forces' to be associated with the five assaulting divisions. They would be known by the initials of the area code names. This five-pronged attack was the feature which all else in the naval assault plan was designed to further. An integral part of each task force would be bombarding warships, close escorts, minesweepers and numerous auxiliary vessels for special duties; these would be allotted to the five assault forces during the opening phase. The general structure of the seaborne assault is shown in the diagram opposite.

It will be noticed that two additional naval forces were associated with the troops who were to follow up the first landings—namely Forces B and L.

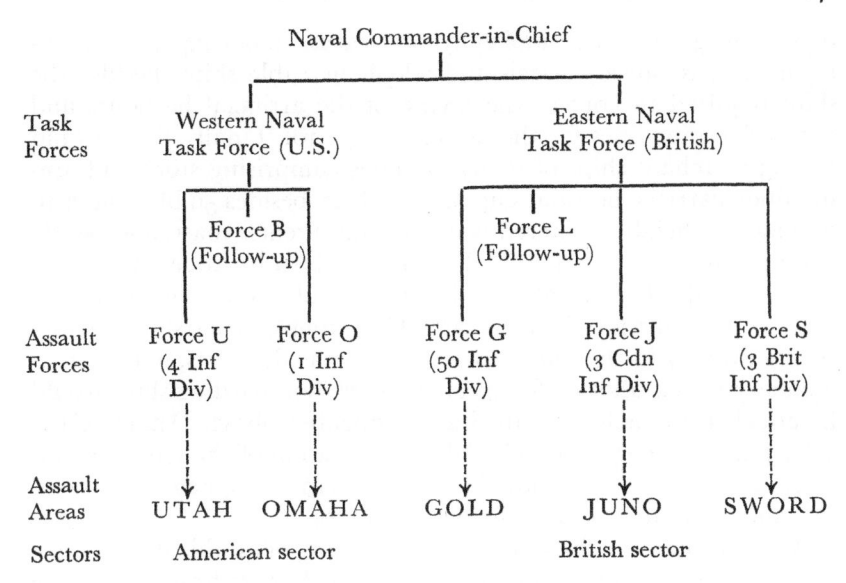

	Naval Commander-in-Chief				
Task Forces	Western Naval Task Force (U.S.)		Eastern Naval Task Force (British)		
	Force B (Follow-up)		Force L (Follow-up)		
Assault Forces	Force U (4 Inf Div)	Force O (1 Inf Div)	Force G (50 Inf Div)	Force J (3 Cdn Inf Div)	Force S (3 Brit Inf Div)
Assault Areas	UTAH	OMAHA	GOLD	JUNO	SWORD
Sectors	American sector		British sector		

Before proceeding with the naval plans it should be explained that both in peace and war British naval command in the waters of the Channel is normally divided between the Home Commanders-in-Chief at Plymouth, Portsmouth and the Nore, but the appointment of Admiral Ramsay necessitated a temporary variation of this arrangement. As Naval Commander-in-Chief of the Allied Expeditionary Force he was given full authority over all naval forces engaged in the invasion except those providing distant cover; he held direct command within the assault area off the French coast and he controlled all naval operations forming part of the general plan. Subject to this arrangement the Home Commanders-in-Chief continued to exercise their normal functions, carrying out the many planned covering operations and administering the many base services required by the expedition.

Altogether nearly 7,000 ships and craft would be operating. They would include 138 warships ranging from battleships to destroyers for bombardment duties; 221 destroyers, sloops, frigates, corvettes, trawlers and patrol craft as convoy escorts; 287 minesweepers and 495 light coastal craft for a variety of purposes. Included in the total would be 58 vessels forming anti-U-boat escort groups of the Western Approaches Command which were to control the western approaches to the Channel.

Landing ships, landing craft and barges of all types would number over 4,000; of these, nearly half were to cross the Channel under their own power, the remainder either in tow or on board the larger ships. In addition to the naval ships and craft there would be 441 ancillary vessels, exclusive of small craft, including amongst others depot ships, tugs, salvage vessels, smoke-laying vessels, mooring and buoy-laying vessels, survey vessels and telephone cable ships, besides the ships required to control the laying of the artificial harbours and submarine pipe-lines for the delivery of petrol. Finally there would be 805 merchant ships of many varieties comprising store and ammunition carriers, hospital ships and tankers, besides 59 blockships to provide 'artificially sheltered water' off the French coast, and nearly 300 miscellaneous small craft. Details are given in Appendix II.

Each of the five naval assault forces would consist of ships and craft to transport and land the attacking troops, of warships participating directly in the initial assault, close naval escorts, and various auxiliary vessels allotted for specific duties. Bombarding ships would be attached to each force during the opening phase. Details of the ships and craft engaged and of the organisation of the naval assault forces are given in Appendix II, and the map facing page 136 shows the convoy routes and naval covering forces.

Arrangements for the assembly and loading of all this shipping involved the use of almost every port and anchorage from Felixstowe on the east coast to Milford Haven in the west and about 750 additional berths were provided in the Solent to supplement the berthing facilities at Portsmouth and Southampton; for reasons of security and to avoid congestion the bombarding forces would assemble in the Clyde and at Belfast and the blockships at Oban.

Assault forces, protected by naval escorts and shore-based British and American fighters, were to move coastwise in convoy from their assembly ports to a rendezvous some fifteen miles south-east of the Isle of Wight, called 'Area Z'. In doing so they would follow routes which were in regular use for normal traffic (and were therefore continuously searched for mines) for as the enemy was aware of this considerable coastwise traffic the passage of the assault convoys would be less likely to arouse his suspicions. From Area Z the five forces would strike southward towards France and once they had turned towards the Normandy coast their destination would be apparent; thereafter, the preservation of secrecy would largely depend on success in preventing enemy observation from the air and in confusing his radar watch.

Each force would be preceded by minesweepers, for it was known that a German mine barrier extended across the line of advance in mid-Channel and other minefields were believed to exist further south; mine-free water might reasonably be expected in the German swept channel near the French coast and the 'lowering positions' for the landing-ships would therefore be in this area, about seven to ten miles off-shore. Minesweeping is an unspectacular but all-important task. In the phrase of the American Rear-Admiral D. P. Kirk, who commanded the Western Task Force, minesweepers were 'the keystone of the arch in this operation'. They were required to carry out the largest single minesweeping operation ever undertaken, falling into four phases. First they were to sweep and buoy ten channels, two for each assault force, one for fast and one for slow traffic, as far as the 'lowering positions'. This whole system of swept channels was known as the 'Spout'. Then they were to search and mark clear anchorages inshore for the bombarding ships and the great mass of assault shipping which would follow. Thereafter they were to widen the channels in the Spout, removing all mines swept, and finally they were to extend the swept waters inshore and open new channels along the French coast as required. Their task was unending, for all channels must afterwards be kept clear by continuous daily sweeping.

Twelve flotillas of fleet minesweepers would be employed, of which ten were British, one Canadian and one American. Besides these there would be ten flotillas of auxiliary minesweepers for special tasks and for inshore work, all but two being British. With attendant motor launches and dan-layers,[1] 255 of the minesweeping force were employed in the first phase. Its assembly was delayed and combined training suffered because several fleet flotillas had to be drawn from convoys to north Russia, from the Mediterranean, from Iceland, Canada and the United States; many of the crews thus lacked recent experience, particularly in the niceties of sweeping in cross tides by night, which involved unusual technical difficulties.

Fleet sweepers cannot operate effectively at a speed of less than $7\frac{1}{2}$ knots, but the speed of some of the convoys for which they were to clear a passage did not exceed 5 knots. Thus to avoid moving too far ahead the sweepers would have to 'waste' an hour and a half in the later stages of the approach by reversing course for about forty minutes. Sweeping would begin in a strong east-going stream and finish in one setting equally strongly to the west and, in the slack water between tides, the sweepers would have to change over their sweeps in the dark without loss of station. These exacting duties called for very skilful seamanship, courage and endurance and for unremitting toil. It will be seen later how splendidly the minesweeping crews rose to the occasion.

But mines were not the only danger to be overcome. The volume of Allied shipping that would be using comparatively limited waters would offer the nearby submarines and surface vessels of the enemy a unique temptation to attack. Apart from the protective measures of the Allied air forces to be described later, naval protection was to be afforded mainly by a strong defence in depth, for during passage the close escorts of the assault forces would be mainly engaged in

---

[1] A vessel employed to buoy the channels swept by the minesweepers.

controlling navigation and preserving the cohesion of convoys in the swept channels. Responsibility for deep defence was to rest chiefly on the Commander-in-Chief, Portsmouth, Admiral Sir Charles Little, supported and covered by forces under the Vice-Admiral, Dover, Vice-Admiral Sir H. Pridham-Wippell on the east and the Commander-in-Chief, Plymouth, Admiral Sir Ralph Leatham on the west. A seven-mile gun-zone would be established on each side of the Spout and along the southern side of the coastal channels; any ship discovered there during darkness must be treated as hostile. Destroyers were to patrol the outer fringes of this zone while more distant patrols of coastal craft would range at night over a wide adjoining area.

On the east, where movements were already restricted by minefields and shoal water, the Dover Command would provide four destroyers, two frigates and forty-six motor torpedo-boats and launches, to deal with any opposition. To extend radar cover and to act as rallying points for coastal craft, frigates were to be placed in advanced positions between Beachy Head and Cap d'Antifer, near le Havre. On the west, in the relatively open waters of the western Channel, a stronger defence was needed. To meet the threat of U-boats and surface craft working from Cherbourg and other westerly bases three patrols would be established, each consisting of four destroyers from the Plymouth Command. The first, composed of United States destroyers, was to protect the route followed by Assault Force U from the west country ports where it would assemble; the second, known as the Hurd Deep patrol, would cover the mid-Channel area on a line running north from St. Malo, in Brittany; the third, known as the Western Patrol, was to concentrate about fifty miles north-west of Ushant to intercept enemy destroyers should they appear. The last two patrols would be composed of British, Canadian and Polish destroyers and by night they would be reinforced by coastal craft.

Against the U-boats, further defence measures included both air and naval action. For many months past U-boats had had few successes in the Atlantic, but it was known that since their decisive defeat there in 1943 they were being re-equipped and reorganised and that a special group based on Brest and the Biscay ports was held there in readiness to intervene in the Channel. It was assumed that when the hour struck these would constitute the enemy's main form of counter-attack by sea. To prevent this succeeding, aircraft of the Royal Air Force would patrol continuously, by day and night, the area bounded by the coast of Ireland, Cornwall and the Brest peninsula in such density that evasion would be difficult if not impossible. The western part of the danger area—about a hundred and thirty miles west of Land's End—would be covered by aircraft of the

Fleet Air Arm from three escort carriers, supported by six antisubmarine escort groups, all drawn from the Western Approaches Command under Admiral Sir Max Horton, while four more antisubmarine groups of destroyers would operate from Plymouth and Milford Haven under the control of the Commander-in-Chief, Plymouth.

Defence of the anchorages off the French coast had also to be provided. An extensive programme of minelaying near the Brittany coast, which was designed to prevent an approach to the Spout by inshore routes, will be described with other operations which preceded the assault. In the days following the assault the invasion fleet might expect an increasing scale of attack as the enemy recovered his balance and drew reinforcements from elsewhere; his light surface vessels and aircraft, particularly minelaying aircraft operating by night, would be the greatest menace. To meet this danger permanent patrols to seaward and on the flanks of the assault area would supplement the day and night fighter cover, while organised striking forces composed of destroyers and coastal craft would be ready to counter any surface attack. In the anchorages smoke protection would be available and the many ships present would be ready to provide a great weight of anti-aircraft fire.

All these measures were planned to bear the armies safely to France. To support the landings and subsequent advance naval firesupport on an unprecedented scale would be provided by six battleships, two monitors, twenty-three cruisers and more than a hundred destroyers. The first targets for the heavy ships would be twenty coast defence batteries selected in consultation with the Army and because of the threat they constituted for assault shipping. Many of these batteries, as well as others, would already have been attacked by the heavy bombers, but experience elsewhere had shown that only the heaviest naval guns could neutralise them effectively over prolonged periods. As the hour of the landing approached, every available weapon would join in a crescendo of fire to plaster the beaches with bombs, shells and rockets so that the defenders could no longer serve their weapons and must seek shelter or be killed.

Leaving for the time being plans for the naval part in subsequent operations it will be well to turn to the army and air plans and convenient to take the air plans first, since, as will be seen, they were the first to come into force.

The Overall Air Plan which was issued by Sir Trafford Leigh-Mallory on April the 15th was designed to achieve and maintain an air situation in which the German air force would be incapable of effective interference with Allied operations, to provide continuous reconnaissance of the enemy's dispositions and movements, to disrupt enemy communications and channels of supply, to support the landing and subsequent advance of the Allied armies, to deliver offensive strikes against enemy naval forces and to provide the air lift for airborne forces. The foundations of this ambitious programme had been laid by the actions of both tactical and strategic air forces long before the Overall Air Plan was finally agreed, and it is well to bear in mind the distinctive position of the Allied air forces in that respect. For the past two years they had been actively engaged in what was, in a sense, an invasion of Europe. They were already involved in a continuous series of air battles, so that for them Overlord would be a culmination and intensification of their efforts rather than a new campaign. For months before the scale and scope of Overlord were decided they had, among other things, been fighting to win air superiority and to disrupt enemy communications as a general preliminary to an Allied invasion of the Continent; after the issue of the Overall Air Plan, and the approved plan for the strategic air forces which came into force at the same time (page 43), a new phase of the air war opened in that all Allied air operations were co-ordinated and specifically related to the Overlord campaign.

The massive scale and wide variety of air operations planned could only be met from huge resources and the Allies' combined air strength was indeed tremendous. As already mentioned (page 28) they expected to have over thirteen thousand aircraft concentrated in Britain, over eleven thousand of which would be available for Overlord. It was doubted whether the enemy could bring to battle on the day of the assault as much as one-tenth of that number!

In round figures, those available when it began may be classified broadly as follows:

		R.A.F. and associates	U.S.A.A.F.	Total
Heavy Bombers	(day)	—	1,970	1,970
,, ,,	(night)	1,470	—	1,470
Medium and Light Bombers	(day)	100	700	800
,, ,, ,, ,,	(night)	130	—	130
Fighters and Fighter Bombers	(day)	1,400	2,300	3,700
,, ,, ,, ,,	(night)	490	—	490
Troop Carriers and Transports		460	900	1,360
Coastal Command aircraft		1,030	40	1,070
Reconnaissance aircraft		350	170	520
Air/Sea Rescue aircraft		80	—	80
		5,510	6,080	11,590

In addition, the Allies would have over 3,500 gliders for the transport of airborne troops.

The varied nature of the Allies' planned air operations was well catered for by the variety of available resources. The highly concentrated experience of war had proved a great fertiliser of ideas and under its impulse rapid progress had been made in the application of scientific knowledge to the design, equipment and operation of the air arm.

The tactical air forces, the Allied Expeditionary Air Force of which Air Marshal Leigh-Mallory was Air Commander-in-Chief, are shown in outline in the diagram overleaf and in detail in Appendix VI. These also show the strategic air forces whose part in Overlord was under General Eisenhower's direction. The arrangements for the command of the strategic air forces have already been described (page 42); it will be well to explain here the command for the Allied Expeditionary Air Force.

The headquarters of Fighter Command, renamed Air Defence of Great Britain, had for years been situated at Stanmore in Middlesex and an elaborate network of communications had been installed there. This establishment was now developed by the Air Commander-in-Chief as his main headquarters during the assault, and he had with him at Stanmore his deputy, Major-General H. S. Vandenberg of the United States Army Air Force, and an integrated Anglo-American staff. From Stanmore he exercised overall air command except in relation to the strategic air forces which, when engaged on operations in support of Overlord, were to be directed and co-ordinated by Air Chief Marshal Sir Arthur Tedder as Deputy to the Supreme Commander.

At Stanmore the general co-ordination of air policy and plans was achieved in conferences attended by all the principal air commanders, their chief staff officers and senior representatives of other Services; and from Stanmore Sir Trafford Leigh-Mallory maintained close contact with the Supreme Commander, with the Commanders-in-Chief of the other Services and with Coastal Command, whose operations were under the operational control of the Admiralty. He retained command of the Air Defence of Great Britain and of the transport aircraft required for airborne troops, and he nominated targets of tactical importance which the *strategic* air forces were required to attack. But he delegated to the Commander of the British Second Tactical Air Force, Air Marshal Sir Arthur Coningham, operational control of the planning and operations of both the British and American *tactical* air forces. Air Marshal Coningham was known as Commander, Advanced Allied Expeditionary Air Force, with headquarters at Hillingdon House, Uxbridge.

ALLIED AIR FORCES—OUTLINE ORDER OF BATTLE
6th June 1944

SUPREME COMMANDER
General Dwight D. Eisenhower
DEPUTY SUPREME COMMANDER
Air Chief Marshal Sir Arthur W. Tedder

COASTAL COMMAND
Air Chief Marshal Sir W. Sholto Douglas

ALLIED EXPEDITIONARY AIR FORCE
Air Chief Marshal Sir Trafford L. Leigh-Mallory
DEPUTY Major-General Hoyt S. Vandenberg

ALLIED STRATEGIC AIR FORCES

BOMBER COMMAND	EIGHTH AIR FORCE
Air Marshal Sir Arthur T. Harris	Lieutenant-General James H. Doolittle

ADVANCED ALLIED EXPEDITIONARY AIR FORCE
Air Marshal Sir Arthur Coningham

AIR DEFENCE OF GREAT BRITAIN	SECOND TACTICAL AIR FORCE	NINTH AIR FORCE	AIRBORNE AND TRANSPORT OPERATIONS
Air Marshal Sir Roderic M. Hill	Air Marshal Sir Arthur Coningham	Major General Lewis H. Brereton	Air Vice-Marshal L. H. Hollinghurst
10 GROUP Day and Night Fighters, Fighter Bombers, Air/Sea Rescue Aircraft	**2 GROUP** Light and Medium Bombers—Day and Night, Reconnaissance Aircraft	**IX BOMBER COMMAND** Light and Medium Day Bombers	**38 GROUP** Troop Carrying, Glider-towing and Transport Aircraft
11 GROUP Day and Night Fighters, Air/Sea Rescue Aircraft	**83 GROUP** Day Fighters, Fighter Bombers, Reconnaissance Aircraft A.O.P. Aircraft	**IX TACTICAL AIR COMMAND** Day Fighters, Fighter Bombers, Reconnaissance Aircraft	**46 GROUP** Troop Carrying, Glider-towing and Transport Aircraft
12 GROUP Day and Night Fighters, Reconnaissance Aircraft	**84 GROUP** Day Fighters, Fighter Bombers, Reconnaissance Aircraft A.O.P. Aircraft	**XIX TACTICAL AIR COMMAND** Day and Night Fighters, Fighter Bombers	
13 GROUP Day Fighters	**85 GROUP** Day and Night Fighters	**IX TROOP CARRIER COMMAND** Troop Carrying, Glider-towing and Transport Aircraft	
	34 WING Reconnaissance Aircraft	**10 GROUP** Reconnaissance Aircraft	
	AIR SPOTTING POOL Fleet Air Arm and Royal Air Force Fighters		

When in support of Overlord – – – – – –
When in co-operation with Overlord • • • • • • •

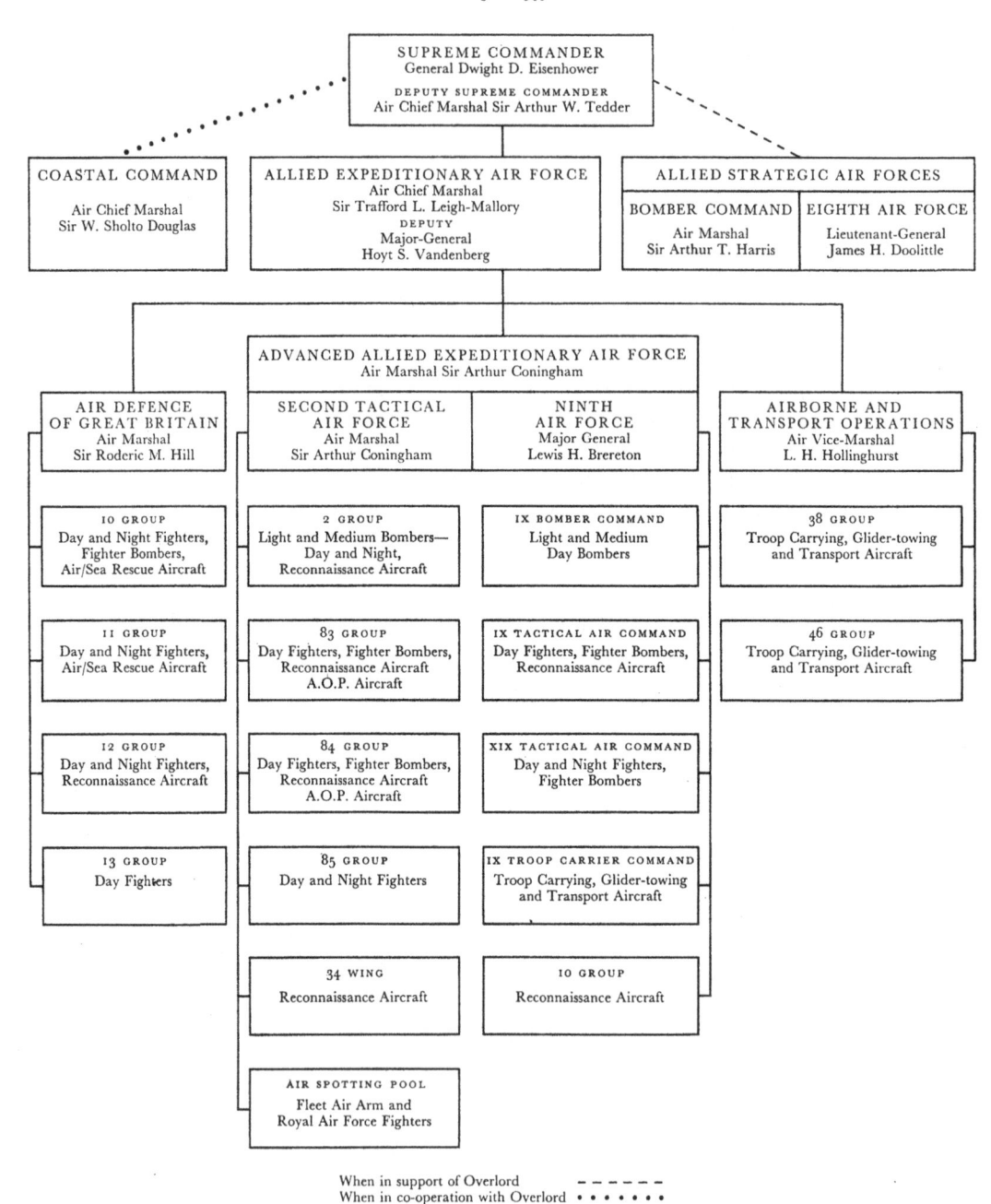

The reason for taking this step was that as long as General Montgomery had the command of all ground forces it was thought desirable that the command of all tactical air forces should similarly be unified. It was indeed understood and written into the plan that Air Marshal Coningham would be the only air commander with whom General Montgomery would normally have to deal. The opening tactical air battle would thus be directed by Air Marshal Coningham, to whom all requests for air action would be made. At his headquarters at Uxbridge there already existed an established network of communications and facilities for control, for it was the permanent headquarters of No. 11 Group, Air Defence of Great Britain, the group charged with the air defence of southern England and offensive fighter operations over northern France and Belgium. His Joint War Room, Combined Control Centre and Combined Reconnaissance Centre were all established at Uxbridge. From there he would direct executive air action in support of the armies; from there he would keep the Air Commander-in-Chief posted with the information reaching him about the tactical situation and with knowledge of General Montgomery's intentions and requirements. Only when the latter required strategic air forces to support operations would he notify the Air Commander-in-Chief direct, informing Air Marshal Coningham at the same time.

Both at Stanmore and at Uxbridge there would be senior Allied officers of the other Services for liaison duties, and at Uxbridge, alongside Air Marshal Coningham and sharing his responsibilities, would be the Commanding General of the United States Ninth Air Force, Major-General Lewis H. Brereton.

The Overall Air Plan was related first to naval plans which have been outlined and subsequently to the armies' operations on land. The enemy's opposition would take three forms. In the air was the continuing threat of aircraft which must be beaten off and destroyed; at sea there was the threat of U-boats, surface craft and mines; and on land there was the threat of the coastal defence system and of the rapid reinforcement of enemy ground forces. Against all these forms of opposition our air forces were to be heavily engaged. Protection of our forces while in passage and in the assault would depend mainly on fighters. Their task would begin in darkness with the escort of airborne troops and of heavy bombers for the opening of the bombardment. In daylight the assault forces would present such targets for enemy air attack that he could hardly ignore this challenge. A great air battle over the beaches was to be expected and it was likely to reach its crisis while the success of the actual assault still hung in the balance. The effectiveness of fighter cover at that time would profoundly affect the issue. Five squadrons would be maintained to cover the swept channels. Ten squadrons would be maintained over the beaches (five in the British and five in the American sector) and a pool of thirty-three squadrons would form a striking force for use as required. Approximately three thousand seven hundred of the Allies' fighters would be used in all, distributed as follows:

	British	American	Total
Shipping cover	—	15	15
Beach cover	36	18	54
Direct support of land forces	18	18	36
Offensive operations and bomber escort	—	33	33
Striking force	18	15	33
Total squadrons	72	99	171

While the co-ordination of all these fighter operations would be centralised at Uxbridge their tactical direction was to be exercised through a number of subordinate control centres at sea, completing a network of radio communications. In the assault area 'Fighter Direction Tenders',[2] under naval control, would operate as required by the air command. One was allotted to each of the British and American sectors; the third was stationed to seaward in the Spout. From these specially-equipped ships, personnel of the air forces would control day and night fighter cover over shipping and the beaches in those zones. After the beaches had been captured similarly-equipped stations would be established on shore and the direction tenders would then serve as satellites to the shore stations.

While fighters protected the assault forces from enemy air attack, heavy and medium bombers would join in the continued bombardment of the enemy's coastal defences. Heavy bombers of Bomber Command during darkness, and of the United States Eighth Air Force after daybreak, would concentrate first on the selected targets which would then be subjected to heavy naval bombardment. Squadrons of medium and light bombers and fighter bombers of the tactical air forces would attack strong points and defended positions which covered the beaches, joining with other arms in the final 'drenching fire' immediately before the first landings to keep the enemy's head down at this vital time. Their further actions would depend largely on the progress of the troops and on the armies' requests for air support. Intensive reconnaissance would be maintained to observe and report any enemy movements and the bombing of road and rail centres further inland would be sustained in order to make his movements difficult and dangerous. And always, then and thereafter, they would have to 'cleanse the sky' of hostile aircraft.

---

[2] For details, see Appendix II, page 515.

Milford Haven

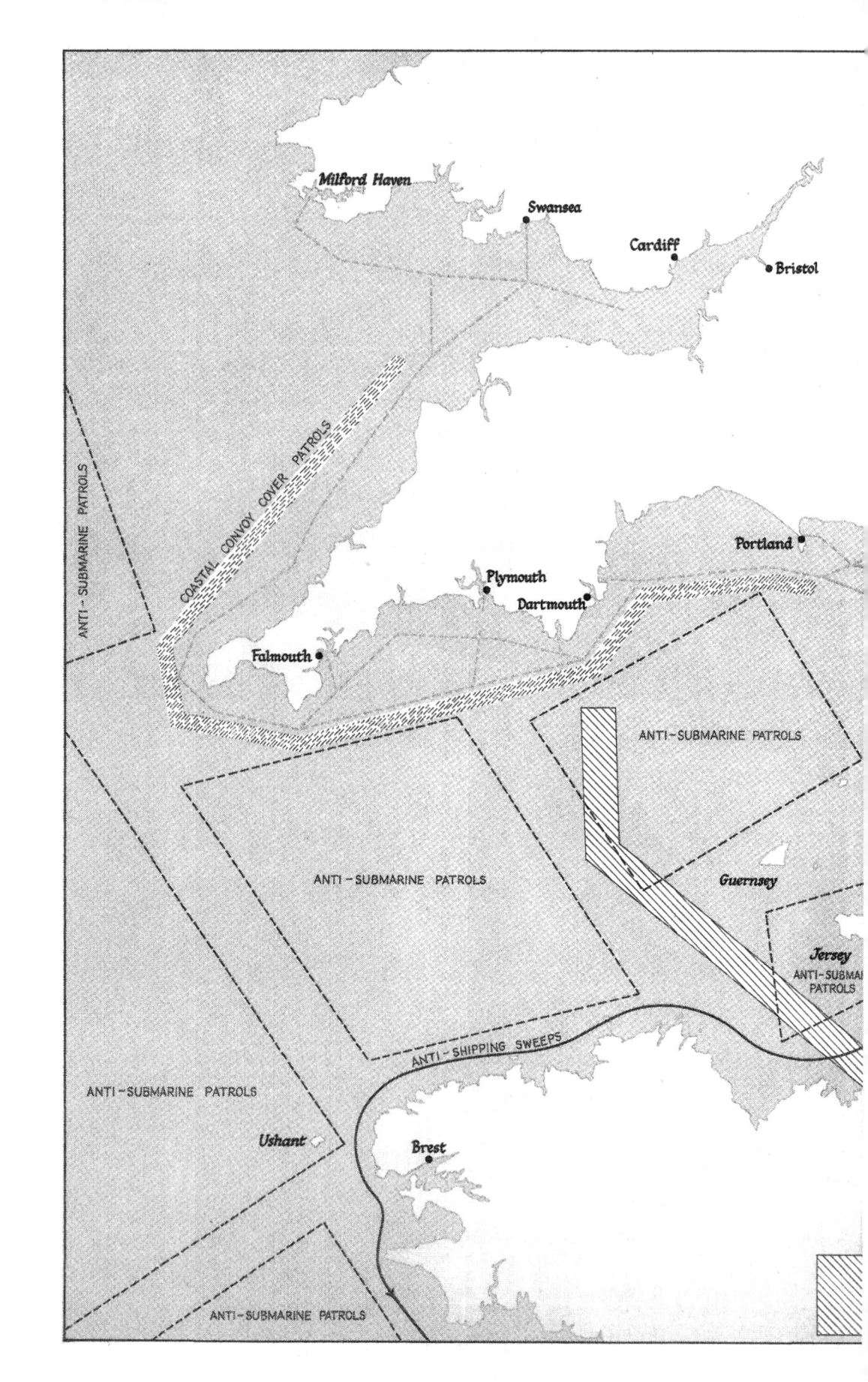

Swansea

Cardiff

Bristol

ANTI-SUBMARINE PATROLS

COASTAL CONVOY COVER PATROLS

Plymouth

Dartmouth

Portland

Falmouth

ANTI-SUBMARINE PATROLS

Guernsey

ANTI-SUBMARINE PATROLS

Jersey

ANTI-SUBMARINE PATROLS

ANTI-SHIPPING SWEEPS

ANTI-SUBMARINE PATROLS

Ushant

Brest

ANTI-SUBMARINE PATROLS

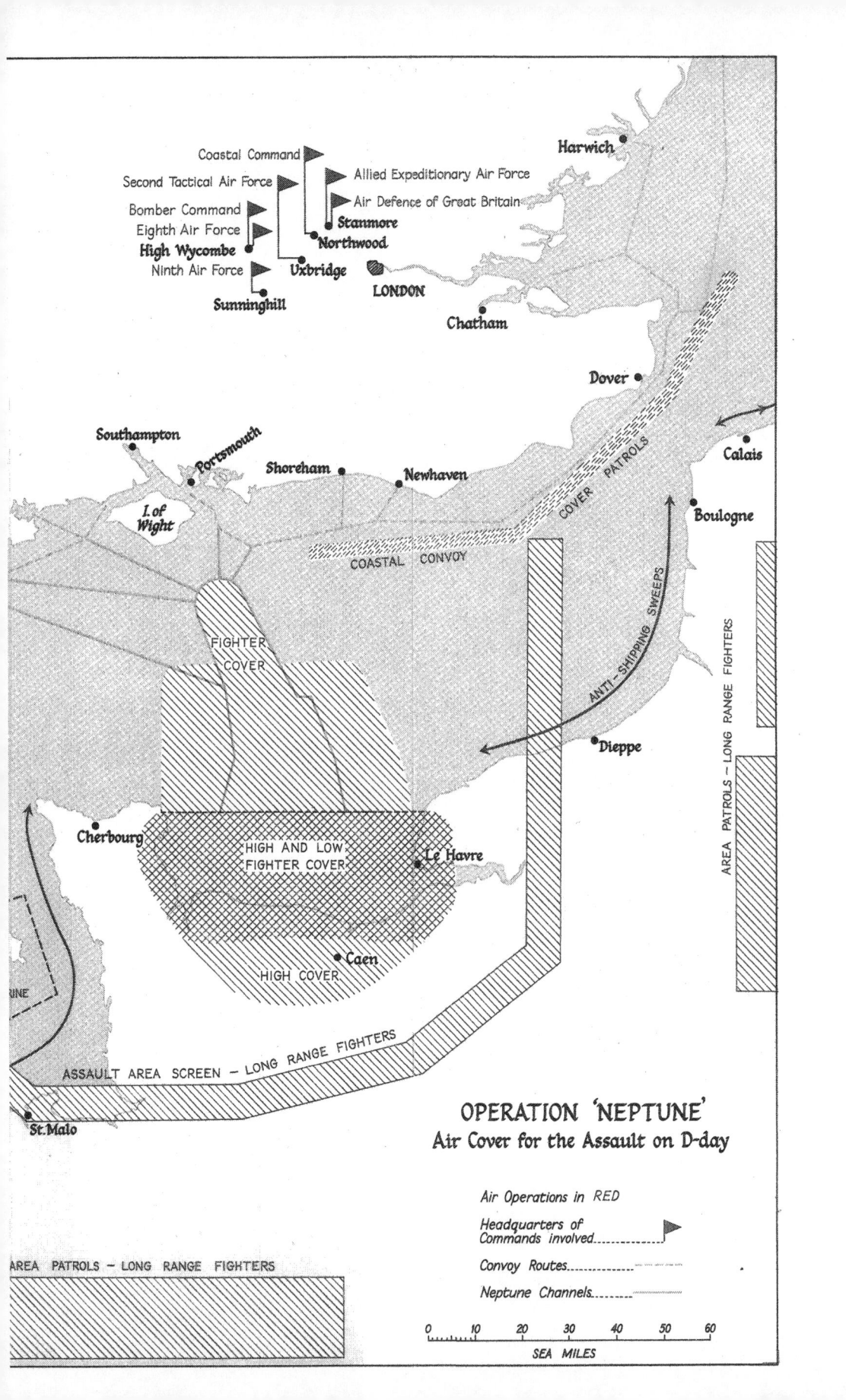

OPERATION 'NEPTUNE'
Air Cover for the Assault on D-day

As early as possible five airfield construction groups of the Royal Engineers and a field force basic construction wing of the Royal Air Force, and eighteen American aviation engineering battalions—two of them airborne—would begin work on a large programme of airfield construction so that the Expeditionary Air Forces could move to France in concert with the Allied armies. The programme aimed at the provision of three 'emergency landing strips' on the opening day, one British and two American; two British and two American 'refuelling and rearming strips' by the evening of the fourth day; ten British and eight American airfields by the end of a fortnight; and forty-five British and forty-eight American airfields available at the end of three months. The realisation of this aim would clearly depend on the speed with which the necessary ground was won and on the shape eventually taken by the opening battle. And it may be noted that, whereas the Cossac plan had specified that by the end of the first three months seventy-five per cent of airfields constructed would be 'within approximately sixty miles of the Seine', in the Overall Air Plan they would be constructed as far as was practicable 'within sixty miles of the limit of the Allied advance eastwards'.

There were of course many other matters covered by the Overall Air Plan including the air evacuation of casualties, the air-sea rescue service and the provision of air transport, a matter which assumed great importance and had considerable influence on operations as the armies advanced eastwards.

A system of control which could effectively direct the movements of so many and so varied aircraft in circumstances which changed from hour to hour depended not only on the structure of command which has been outlined but on an elaborate network of communications which could not be explained shortly in non-technical language—communications from land-to-land, land-to-ship, land-to-air, air-to-air, ship-to-air and ship-to-ship—all were involved. For the most part the means used was radio telephone but cable was made available later. During the assault, headquarters ships provided an essential radio link with air headquarters in England until stations on the French shore were established and, finally, the Expeditionary Air Force Headquarters itself moved to France in association with Shaef and the armies they were supporting. For all these naval and air operations were designed to help the armies' rapid capture of sufficient ground for the deployment of their full strength.

The armies to be employed were:

British Second Army
United States First Army } Assault armies

First Canadian Army
United States Third Army } Follow-up armies

The British Second Army, commanded by Lieut-General Sir Miles Dempsey, was to 'assault between Port en Bessin and the river Orne' and to secure and develop a bridgehead south of the line Caumont–Caen and south-east of Caen in order to 'secure airfield sites and to protect the flank of the First United States Army while the latter capture Cherbourg . . .' Lieut-General Omar Bradley's United States First Army was 'to advance as rapidly as the situation permits, capturing Cherbourg with the minimum delay' and developing the Omaha beachhead 'southwards towards St. Lô', in conformity with the advance of the British Second Army.

As soon as possible the First Canadian Army would follow the British Second Army and would take over the left or north-eastern sector of the front which by then should be expanding; the United States Third Army would follow their First to complete the First United States Army Group. After clearing the Brittany peninsula, capturing the Brittany ports and taking over the protection of the Loire flank, both American armies would face east. The Allied armies would then attack north-east towards the line of the Seine from above Paris to the sea.

But this is looking ahead, for it was never expected to reach the Seine in less than about three months. The armies must first breach Hitler's 'Atlantic Wall' and must hold off all opposition till they had gained 'elbow room' and gathered force to advance in strength.

The Baie de la Seine where the Allies were to land and to break through the enemy's defence is enclosed on the west by the Cotentin peninsula and on the east by the headland from which le Havre overlooks the mouth of the Seine. The coast—which will be described in detail later—varies, a rocky foreshore and steep cliffs in the west giving place eastwards to low undulating ground, sandy beaches and muddy flats. Dotted along the coast are nearly a dozen small watering places and three small harbours, Port en Bessin, Courseulles and Ouistreham. Inland it is gentle country. Except near the tip of the Cotentin, where the ground behind and overlooking Cherbourg rises in places to four or five hundred feet, the immediate hinterland is seldom more than two or three hundred feet above sea level and between the base of the Cotentin and the mouth of the river Orne it is often less; much of the area round the base of the Cotentin is easily flooded.

Inland, the country rises slowly to a belt of higher ground which sprawls across the base of the Cotentin peninsula and extends southwards for fifty to sixty miles and eastwards towards Chartres. It is broken country rising in a few places to a thousand feet or more, but intersected by steep valleys and cut by streams and rivers. It is served by a few main roads and a larger number of secondary roads and lanes, and one main railway runs through from east to west.

REVIEW OF PLANS

Much of this belt of country, known as the '*bocage*', is richly clothed with woods and orchards and starred by clusters of small farms gathered round their parish church. The chequered pattern of its little fields, its winding roads and dusty lanes, is bordered by steeply banked hedges. The pace of life there is slow and its most characteristic machinery is the unhurried ox-drawn plough. The progress of mechanised armies might well be slow too, for in this close country advantage would be with the defence.

Once clear of the *bocage* progress should be easier, for in the lowlands of the Loire valley to the south and in the plateau to the west of the Seine the country is more open and farming is done on a larger scale. Here and to the south-east of Caen are the areas most suitable for airfield sites. When the Seine had been reached the Allies would face the most fought-over French and Belgian country which had often been called 'the cockpit of Europe'. British soldiers had last fought there in 1940.

The initial organisation of the Allied armies is shown in the following diagram.

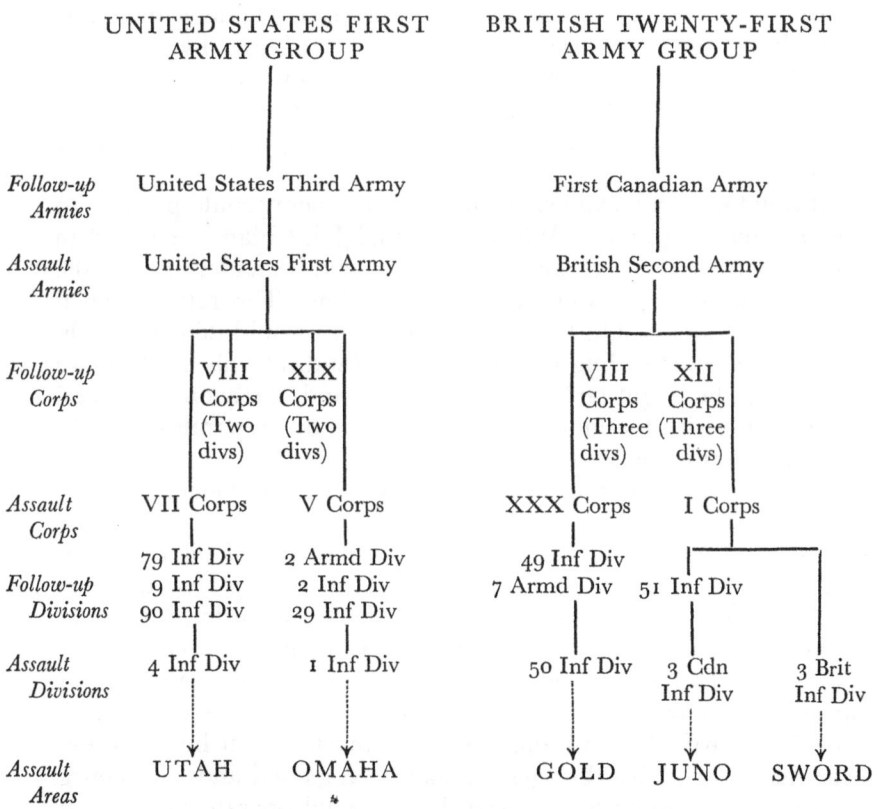

	UNITED STATES FIRST ARMY GROUP		BRITISH TWENTY-FIRST ARMY GROUP		
Follow-up Armies	United States Third Army		First Canadian Army		
Assault Armies	United States First Army		British Second Army		
Follow-up Corps	VIII Corps (Two divs)	XIX Corps (Two divs)	VIII Corps (Three divs)	XII Corps (Three divs)	
Assault Corps	VII Corps	V Corps	XXX Corps	I Corps	
Follow-up Divisions	79 Inf Div 9 Inf Div 90 Inf Div	2 Armd Div 2 Inf Div 29 Inf Div	49 Inf Div 7 Armd Div	51 Inf Div	
Assault Divisions	4 Inf Div	1 Inf Div	50 Inf Div	3 Cdn Inf Div	3 Brit Inf Div
Assault Areas	UTAH	OMAHA	GOLD	JUNO	SWORD

United States First Army under command of
British Twenty-First Army Group in opening phase

THE PLAN OF CAMPAIGN

The diagram shows the seaborne divisions which were to make the assault; it does not show the three airborne divisions which were to open the assault in darkness, landing behind the coastal defences on either flank. Of these the United States 82nd and 101st Airborne Divisions, to land behind the right flank, were to be under command of the United States VII Corps; the British 6th Airborne Division, to land on the left of the British sector, would come under command of the British I Corps after landing.

The diagram is enough to show in skeleton the Allied armies and the manner in which they were to be used in the opening attack. In the British Second Army, VIII and XII Corps would follow XXX and I Corps. Fuller detail of the five assault divisions of the leading corps is given later in the diagrams at pages 172 and 189 which indicate the order in which they would attack, the way in which they would be reinforced with additional troops and the named subdivisions of the beaches on which the landings were to be made.

It was planned to have landed the equivalent of over eleven British and American divisions on the opening day of the assault (D-day); thirteen by D plus 1, and seventeen by D plus 4, including in each case the three airborne divisions. The airborne divisions were then to be relieved and, excluding them, it was planned to have the equivalent of twenty-one divisions on the Continent by D plus 12, twenty-six by D plus 20, thirty-one by D plus 35 and thirty-nine by D plus 90.

It could not yet be known what forces the enemy could produce to oppose this programme. When the Initial Joint Plan was issued in February some fifty-five German divisions had been identified in the West, of which eight were armoured divisions. The rate at which further divisions would be brought against us would depend partly on the German reading of the situation (and, as will be seen, we hoped that he might be led to mis-read it) and partly on the Allies' interference with the movement of his troops by preparatory bombing and continuous air attack.

The combined plan of assault was explained by General Montgomery, Admiral Ramsay, Air Marshal Leigh-Mallory and other British and American commanders at a meeting of high ranking officers which was held at Twenty-First Army Group Headquarters on April the 7th. There General Montgomery also outlined in broad terms the course of operations which it was intended to pursue after the assault had succeeded and a firm footing had been won. It was obviously impossible to forecast with assurance the exact dates by which particular positions would be reached, but his intention was that after a firm bridgehead had been gained and Cherbourg captured the United States First Army would operate southwards towards the Loire, one corps of the Third Army, brought in through

5. Admiral Ramsay

6. Admiral Kirk

7. Admiral Vian

8. General Montgomery

9. General Bradley

10. General Dempsey

Cherbourg, moving westwards into the Brittany peninsula. The British Second Army would 'push its left out towards the general line of the river Touques' and at the same time would 'pivot on Falaise' and 'swing with its right towards Argentan–Alençon'. After this the armies would be directed on to the Seine. The First Canadian Army would by then have taken over the left or northern section of the front. It would face up to the Seine below Rouen, be prepared to force a crossing and operate northwards in order to cut off and capture le Havre. The British Second Army would move forward to the Seine between Rouen and Paris, while the United States First Army would be directed on Paris and the Seine above the city; it would be prepared to cross the river and operate to the north-east, while the United States Third Army protected its right or southern flank. General Montgomery thought that we might reach the Seine by D plus 90—i.e. about September the 1st.

Mainly for administrative planning purposes a map of the battle area had been drawn showing phase lines which might be reached by certain dates, so that the armies' needs would be met if they were realised. But in view of subsequent misunderstandings it is well to state here that neither at this meeting nor at any other time did General Montgomery commit himself to any detailed long-distance forecast of progress. He consistently emphasised the fact that military forecasts and projected phase lines are based on too many imponderables to be regarded as more than targets or shrewd conjectures. A paper dated the 7th of May was issued to the British and American army groups setting out his intentions 'so far as they can be formulated at this stage', with a note stating that 'Whether operations will develop on these lines must of course depend on our own and the enemy situation which cannot be predicted accurately at the present moment'.[3]

Some weeks before the April meeting General Montgomery had stated that 'his plan was to maintain a very firm left wing to bar the progress of enemy formations advancing from the eastwards, while his mobile armoured formations would press forward in a southerly direction. Before extending eastwards we should ensure that we had formed a firm base'; and his Chief of Staff, Major-General F. W. de Guingand, had reported that General Montgomery was not prepared to commit himself as to the time at which an eastern thrust would be launched 'as he has in mind the possibility that the enemy might concentrate their forces on this flank'.

---

[3] The following extracts are of particular interest:
'... The type of country immediately south of the initial bridgehead does not favour a rapid advance.... Once through the difficult *bocage* country, ... our aim ... should be to contain the maximum enemy forces facing the eastern flank of the bridgehead, and to thrust rapidly towards Rennes.'

The Supreme Commander was taking a still longer view of the strategy to be adopted in the conduct of subsequent operations. This is indicated in a paper dated May the 3rd which had been prepared for him by his planning staff at Shaef; with only one small modification suggested by his Air Commander-in-Chief, General Eisenhower approved it on the 27th of May. It will be found later that he adhered closely to the broad plan of campaign which was thus outlined well before the fighting began; it will be well therefore to note it here.

General Eisenhower's directive from the Combined Chiefs of Staff was to 'undertake operations aimed at the heart of Germany and the destruction of her armed forces'. The planners argued that although Berlin was the ultimate goal the Ruhr was the industrial and economic heart of western Germany and German resources would therefore be concentrated to defend it. 'Thus an attack aimed at the Ruhr is likely to give us every chance of bringing to battle and destroying the main German armed forces.' A study of the physical conformation of northern France and the Low Countries, the territory which lay between Normandy and the Ruhr, led to the conclusion that the two most promising lines of approach would lie 'north of the Ardennes, on the general line Maubeuge–Liège' and 'south of the Ardennes, on the general line Verdun–Metz–Saarbrücken'. Of these the northern route is the more direct; moreover, 'an advance along the Channel coast and north of the Ardennes is through the best airfield country available' and 'with the capture in turn of the Channel ports' as far east as Antwerp, the adoption of the northern route 'would facilitate the maintenance problem and enable a faster rate of advance to be sustained'. Yet the northern route alone 'should not be adopted as it leads only to a head-on collision of the opposing main forces on a narrow front with no opportunity of manœuvre'. It was contended that 'as operations progress and our superiority becomes more marked we must advance on a front sufficiently broad, to threaten an advance by more than one of the "gaps" into Germany. By so doing we should be able to keep the Germans guessing as to the direction of our main threat, cause them to extend their forces, and lay the German forces open to defeat in detail'. They concluded that 'the best method of undertaking operations aimed at the heart of Germany and the defeat of her armed forces would be to advance on two mutually supporting axes, in order to retain flexibility of manœuvre:—(a) with our main axis of advance on the line Amiens–Maubeuge–Liège–the Ruhr (b) with a subsidiary axis of advance on the line Verdun–Metz'. In view of the fact that General Eisenhower adopted substantially the strategy advocated in this paper and that the wisdom of this decision was later and is still challenged by some critics, it is worth noting that it was prepared and signed by Captain P. N. Walter, R.N., Brigadier K. G. McLean, and Group Captain H. P. Broad, R.A.F., three British members of the planning staff at Shaef.

Three days after approving the statement of future strategy, General Eisenhower issued a directive to the principal commanders, including Montgomery and Bradley, 'in order to permit advance planning of command and administrative control incident to eventual establishment of two distinct zones of advance on the Continent . . .' When ordered by the Supreme Commander the command of all U.S. and attached Allied ground forces in the American zone of operations would pass to the Commanding General, First U.S. Army Group, which would then become 'the Central Group of Armies' under its own Commander-in-Chief. At the same time Twenty-First Army Group (possibly strengthened by attaching a U.S. army or at least a reinforced U.S. corps) would become 'the Northern Group of Armies', with its separate Commander-in-Chief. Meanwhile General Montgomery would continue to command all ground forces on the Continent until reorganisation was ordered by the Supreme Commander.

The army plans covered a wide range of other matters on which success in the coming battles would largely depend. These included not only the detailed plans for operations but such general matters as arrangements for the concentration, marshalling and briefing of troops and their grouping in the assault formations and in 'residues' which would be sent out later; far-reaching provisions for security, and diversionary operations to mislead the enemy which would involve all three Services. It must indeed be realised that in order to epitomise the plans of the Commanders-in-Chief and of the three Services, so that their significance stands out clearly, all but their principal features have been omitted.

Among these was one of fundamental importance for which the planning required not only industry and technical skill, but also great imagination and foresight, namely the vitally important matter of administration and maintenance. It is easy to ignore these questions or to take them for granted when all goes well, but the maintenance overseas of large modern armies and air forces demands the very highest quality of administrative planning and executive ability. Only first-rate organisation will ensure that mighty forces, frequently on the move and liable to be extended over hundreds of miles, are continuously supplied with all their requirements. The material needs of modern armies and air forces are large and complex. Personal clothing and equipment, weapons and ammunition, and of course rations, are obvious necessities. But much more is required than these alone. A modern army moves on wheels or on tracks and so do the ground equipment and supplies of air forces. Without an adequate supply of vehicles and of the means to maintain and run them modern armies and air forces can neither live nor fight. So essential are they that it was deemed necessary to land some 12,000 vehicles on the opening day of the assault. It will be found later that questions of supply and maintenance had direct bearing on the conduct and conclusion of the campaign, but in this brief survey of plans it will be enough to indicate the principles and methods of maintenance laid down in the administrative planning for Neptune.

While the Supreme Commander's directive had made him responsible for the co-ordination of logistical arrangements on the Continent and of the requirements of British and United States forces under his command, responsibility in the United Kingdom rested with the Service Ministries, so far as British forces were concerned, and with the United States War and Navy Departments in the case of American forces. Throughout the gradual evolution and development of plans for a return to the Continent—the Combined Commanders studies in 1942, Cossac planning in 1943, and finally the Neptune plans of 1944—each time plans were modified a multiplicity of committees and staffs on both sides of the Atlantic worked out meticulous calculations afresh. Logistical planning probably involved a larger expenditure of thought, time and stationery than any other section of the campaign plans. It is unnecessary to describe fully the Joint Outline Maintenance Project/Administrative Plan which was issued on February the 8th in conjunction with the Neptune Initial Joint Plan. Some idea of both its complexity and importance can be appreciated from a mere recital of the main subjects dealt with. These included the policy for maintaining the forces engaged; the principles and methods of maintenance; control of base areas and reserves; assessment of stores required; movement and transportation; engineer works connected with roads, airfield construction, water supply, bulk petrol supply, hospital depots, electricity supply, accommodation, and the rehabilitation of civil installations; supplies; petrol, oil and lubricants; Expeditionary Force Institutes (N.A.A.F.I.); ordnance stores and vehicles; captured equipment; anti-gas clothing and equipment; ammunition reserves; repair and recording services; accommodation for hospital units, workshops, storage and personnel; salvage; waterproofing; postal service; fire service; printing and stationery; claims and hirings; local purchase; reinforcements; medical services; casualties; hygiene; discipline; prisoners of war; pay; burials; welfare; and civil affairs. Moreover, distinctive arrangements had to be made for administration and supply in United States areas.

While it is unnecessary to go into these matters in detail it is desirable to understand at least the general system of supply and maintenance by which the huge forces to be employed were to be sustained during the campaign that lay ahead.

The War Office was responsible for supply, movement to embarkation points, and despatch overseas of stores and equipment for the British armies, for certain items for the Royal Navy and Royal Air Force, and for 'common user' supplies (for example, fuel) for both British and American forces. American headquarters in the United Kingdom exercised similar duties regarding the movement of stores and equipment, subject to co-ordination with the War Office.

Before the campaign opened the British Army Main Base in the United Kingdom had built up reserves of all classes, and of equipment, amounting to seventy-five days' consumption at intense rates. Under the Bolero plan (page 9) American headquarters in the United Kingdom had built up 'a stockpile of two and a half million tons of equipment' in 'twenty million square feet of covered storage and shop space' and 'forty-four million square feet of open storage and hard standings'.

Logistical arrangements on the Continent, which would eventually come under the control of the Supreme Commander, would at the outset be a responsibility of General Montgomery and it may be well to explain the British Army system of maintenance in the field, as it had been modified by recent experience. Compared with the needs of the slow moving armies of previous wars those of modern mechanised armies vary far more greatly from day to day. Demands for petrol, ammunition, and engineering and ordnance stores, for instance, are liable to fluctuate rapidly and require a correspondingly flexible supply system; for ability to switch formations from one part of the front to another at short notice, which is one of the advantages of mechanisation, is largely dependent on flexibility in the system of supply. This means that supply and maintenance arrangements must be controlled and co-ordinated by the staff and that considerable stocks of all important commodities must be held well forward. To meet this need 'field maintenance centres' under corps control were introduced in the British system of supply.

From stocks held in the main base in the United Kingdom, supplies for current use and to be held as reserves would be accumulated overseas in a rear maintenance area—in effect the principal overseas base; from there they would pass along the lines of communication (by rail, road or air) to army rail or road heads; they would then be fed to the series of forward dumps in corps areas constituting the field maintenance centres; these would in turn supply divisional delivery points and so supplies would reach individual units. The system may be illustrated thus:

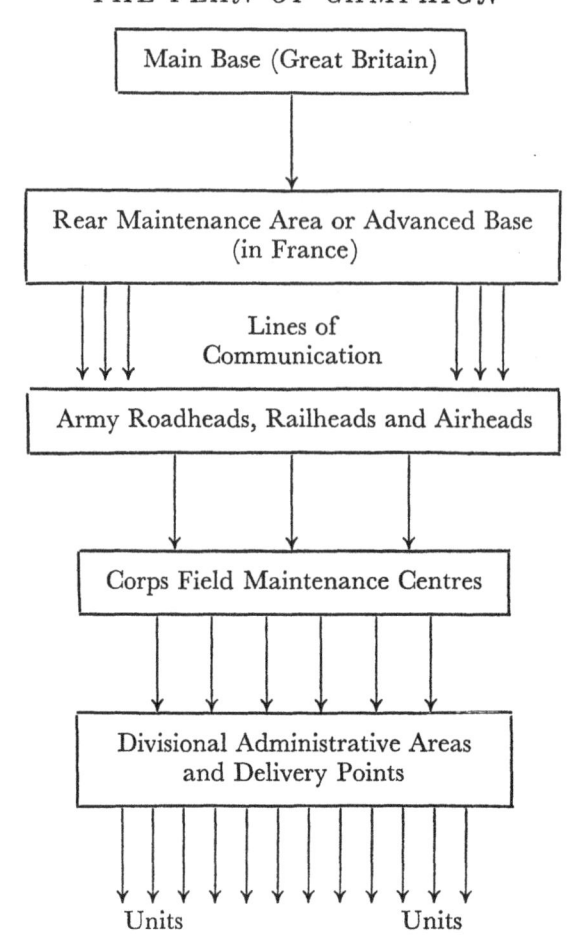

```
┌─────────────────────────┐
│  Main Base (Great Britain) │
└─────────────────────────┘
              │
              ▼
┌───────────────────────────────────┐
│ Rear Maintenance Area or Advanced Base │
│            (in France)            │
└───────────────────────────────────┘
    │ │ │      Lines of       │ │ │
    ▼ ▼ ▼   Communication     ▼ ▼ ▼
┌───────────────────────────────────┐
│ Army Roadheads, Railheads and Airheads │
└───────────────────────────────────┘
        │     │     │     │
        ▼     ▼     ▼     ▼
┌───────────────────────────────────┐
│    Corps Field Maintenance Centres    │
└───────────────────────────────────┘
     │   │   │   │   │   │   │
     ▼   ▼   ▼   ▼   ▼   ▼   ▼
┌───────────────────────────────────┐
│    Divisional Administrative Areas    │
│         and Delivery Points          │
└───────────────────────────────────┘
   │ │ │ │ │ │    │ │ │ │ │ │
   ▼ ▼ ▼ ▼ ▼ ▼    ▼ ▼ ▼ ▼ ▼ ▼
     Units              Units
```

The Rear Maintenance Area (comprising rear maintenance depots and advanced base depots) would eventually be distributed over a considerable district. The field maintenance centres would move forward with the corps they served.

It was of course important to get an overseas base—the Rear Maintenance Area—and a system of supply operating on the far shore as soon as possible, but this could only be achieved gradually. First a 'beach group' would be landed with each assault brigade; from initial dumps formed by these groups would be developed 'beach maintenance areas' under corps control, and by about D plus 5 Second Army would become responsible. During the next fortnight or so the lines of communication organisation would begin to take shape and two army roadheads would be established—one near Caen and the other near Bayeux. By D plus 17 the majority of Second Army's troops should have landed and the First Canadian

Army be on its way; this was to come in on the left of the British sector and in due course the army roadhead near Caen would be handed over to the Canadians. By then the Rear Maintenance Area should be able to replace the temporary beach maintenance areas; Lines of Communication should begin to play its full part, and field maintenance centres under corps control would be coming into operation. The final pattern would thus be taking shape.

It was intended to make use of the few little ports on the assault front, in particular Port en Bessin, and it might be possible to clear stores landed through them by rail to the Rear Maintenance Area, but apart from this it was not expected that railways could be of much use for about three months; meantime lines of communication would be road-operated. Eventually, road, rail and air transport would all play their parts. By the time that the railways were in use, about D plus 90, it was planned to have a reserve of twenty-one days' stocks in France.

Considerable provision for the assault formations was made by arranging, first, that unit transport and all ammunition vehicles of formations would land fully loaded and that an emergency ammunition reserve of three to four thousand tons would be landed in beached barges on D-day; second, that all vehicles would embark with full petrol tanks and would carry in addition three to five 'jerricans', each containing four and a half gallons; and, third, that each man would carry rations for two days. Armoured formations would land with three days' rations in their vehicles in addition to what the men carried.

It was hoped that Cherbourg and the Loire and Brittany ports would be captured by D plus 40; after they had been cleared and restored to working order they could be used for the United States build-up direct from America, and facilities in the Cotentin and at Omaha would then be available for use by the British until le Havre and Rouen were freed. Meanwhile, it was planned to construct two artificial harbours, one to serve the British sector and one the American. A full account of this remarkable and romantic enterprise, of the evolution of ideas finally embodied in their design and construction, of the novel problems which had to be solved and the difficulties which were encountered and overcome—though some of them only at the last minute—would be out of scale here. But they were an essential factor in the Neptune plans and as they will figure largely in the story of later operations it is necessary to explain what they were and what purpose they were planned to fulfil.

The idea of creating artificially sheltered water has a considerable history. Mr. Churchill had suggested the use of concrete breakwaters to form 'a weather-proof harbour' during the First World War and his mind had turned to the question of floating piers in 1942, when the Combined Commanders were studying conditions for a return to France.[4] His minute then (May the 30th) to the Chief of Combined Operations was headed 'Piers for use on open beaches'. It began, 'They *must* float up and down with the tide', and ended, 'Don't argue the matter. The difficulties will argue for themselves.'[5] Since then the War Office had been developing such piers but their combination with breakwaters to form a complete harbour was first raised as a matter of urgency by members of General Morgan's staff, who attended with him a conference convened by Admiral Mountbatten in June 1943 to study outstanding technical and administrative problems involved in Overlord. Those taking part included many of the principal commanders and staff officers of the Services and Service Ministries as well as American Service representatives. The conference agreed that the provision of such artificial harbours was an essential feature of the Cossac plan. Preparatory work could not begin till the plan was accepted in August; little more than eight months then remained for the technical development of the project and for the production of the great mass of equipment required, but the drive imparted through the Service Ministries and the aid of eminent engineers and contractors achieved remarkable success, as will be seen later. The designs finally adopted can be explained in simple terms though they were in fact highly complicated.

First, sheltered water was to be provided for the five assault areas by forming in each a breakwater composed of blockships known as 'Corncobs', brought in under their own power and sunk in line. These breakwaters were known as 'Gooseberries' and it was planned to complete all five by the fifth day of the invasion.

The Gooseberries lying off Gold and Omaha were then to be expanded into artificial harbours (each comparable in size with Dover harbour) by sinking large ferro-concrete 'caissons' (called 'Phoenix') to reinforce and extend the line of Corncobs and to continue them shoreward at both ends. Each harbour would have two entrances for shipping and berthing accommodation for a limited number of deep-draught ships and about twenty coasters, besides large numbers of landing craft, tugs and miscellaneous small vessels. Within the waters thus enclosed landing craft would be able to ply freely in all weathers. Piers would also be built of articulated steel roadway supported by pontoons and with pontoon pierheads all firmly anchored to the seabed but free to 'float up and down with the tide'. This equipment of piers was collectively known as 'Whale'. At the pierheads coasters and similar shallow-draught vessels would be able to discharge at all states of the tide. For deep-draught ships which could not be

---

[4] W. S. Churchill, *The Second World War*, vol. II (1949), p. 214 *et seq.*
[5] Op. cit., vol. V (1952), p. 66.

accommodated within the harbours additional breakwaters composed of heavy floating steel structures called 'Bombardons' would be provided to seaward of each harbour. The whole, including breakwaters, piers, moorings, buoys and other navigational aids and anti-aircraft guns for its protection, was known as a 'Mulberry' harbour. This outline with the attached diagram explains the general plan.

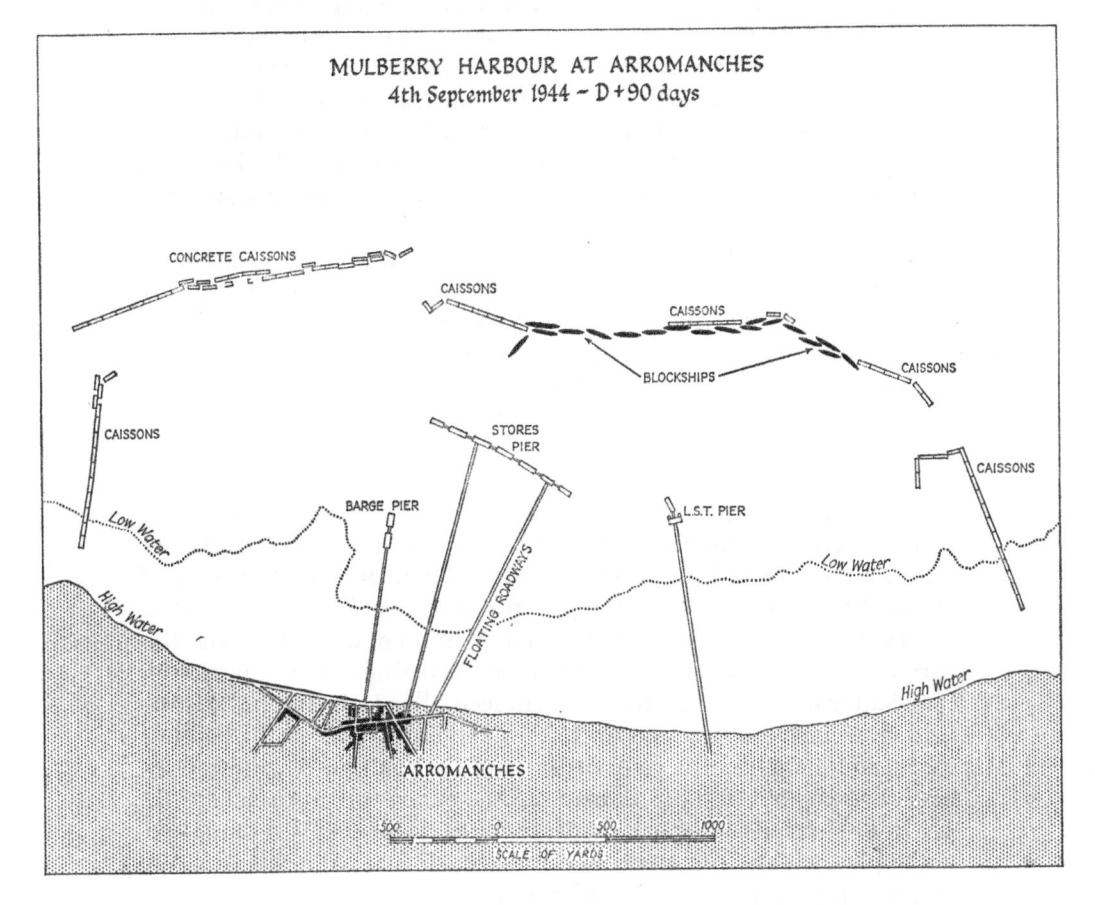

MULBERRY HARBOUR AT ARROMANCHES
4th September 1944 – D+90 days

Apart from the blockships, every main component had to be towed from its building-site to assembly areas and thence across the Channel to France, a task requiring the services of every available tug which could be mustered in Britain and from the United States. The magnitude of the project may be indicated by a few figures. Fifty-five merchant ships and four obsolete warships would be used as Corncobs.[6] There would be two hundred and thirteen caissons

---

[6] Fifteen more were added later.

varying in size according to the depth of water in which they were to be settled; the largest would be two hundred feet long, fifty-five feet wide and sixty feet high and would weigh over six thousand tons—'five-storey buildings' to be towed across the open sea. There would be twenty-three floating pierheads, ten miles of Whale roadway and ninety-three Bombardons of cruciform section, each two hundred feet long, twenty-five feet high and weighing about two thousand tons when partially flooded. In the aggregate the material to be moved by sea and installed quickly in exact position on the far shore, in a tideway and despite possible enemy interference, would amount to some two million tons of pre-fabricated steel and concrete, an enterprise to test the skill of many, including seamen, soldiers and civil engineers. When the time comes to describe how the harbours were brought into operation their construction will appear more fully.

Description of the means by which the Allied overseas forces were to be supplied has so far not mentioned the all-important naval link in lines of communication which connected those in England with those which would be developed in France. To appreciate this it is necessary to return to naval plans for after the opening assault the twin tasks of build-up and sustenance would depend on the navies' ability to maintain this link unbroken. On their success all else would turn.

To ensure a rapid start of the build-up fifteen personnel ships, seventy-four ocean-going merchant ships and over two hundred coasters were to be loaded before D-day. Thereafter eight convoys of ships, besides groups of landing craft, must reach the assault area every day in order to maintain the momentum of the battle. And the cargo of each convoy—and indeed of each ship—must match the particular needs of the force it was to feed. The right troops, ammunition, vehicles, armaments and stores had to be ready at the loading ports and loaded in the right order; and the route to be followed by each convoy, out and on return, and the escort to be provided, had all to be defined and timed as precisely as possible. Everything had to be planned and organised in duplicate, since separate British and American supply lines were to be maintained.

To match the day-to-day movements of shipping to the requirements of commanders and the planned build-up of overseas supplies, special inter-Service machinery was set up. A Build-up Control Organisation (known as BUCO) to co-ordinate and control build-up plans as a whole; a Movement Control Section (MOVCO) to direct the movement of men and vehicles from concentration areas to embarkation ports; a Turnround Control Organisation (TURCO) to ensure the smooth and rapid turn-round of shipping in the loading ports; a Combined Operations Repair Organisation (COREP) with tentacles in the chief ports to control the repair of damaged and defective ships and craft; and finally a body to control the fleet of tugs (COTUG) which would be needed for a great variety of duties.

The target date on which all planning was to be based was given in the Initial Joint Plan as May the 31st. But though necessary for planning purposes the target date was only approximate and the choice of an exact date for D-day was inseparably bound up with the choice of H-hour, that is the hour on D-day at which the first landing craft should strike the beach.

The British Army would have preferred to attack in darkness or at dawn in the hope of gaining a greater measure of tactical surprise, but for the Navy the advantages of an attack in daylight on this occasion far outweighed the risks entailed although, in previous Mediterranean operations, British practice had favoured landing in darkness. To subdue strong coastal defence works and so give the assaulting troops a chance to penetrate quickly without crippling losses, reasonable time must be allowed for preliminary naval bombardment which needs daylight for observation; the air forces, too, needed daylight for an accurate final attack on beach defences. A second consideration, on which only naval judgment was valid, was the impracticability of controlling with navigational precision the great number of craft involved in the assault if they had to approach the shore in darkness; errors in position and timing likely to result from such an attempt might well cause disastrous confusion, particularly if the weather were bad. A third factor eventually placed the matter beyond argument. In February the enemy was seen to be erecting on the Normandy beaches, and well below high water mark, obstacles, to be described later, which when hidden by the tide would gravely imperil approaching landing-craft. These could only be dealt with in daylight and when they were uncovered, so a landing in daylight and near low tide was necessary. All things considered, it was agreed that the best time to begin landing would be three to four hours before high water and some forty minutes after 'nautical twilight', which is said to begin when the rising sun is twelve degrees below the horizon. The exact time at which landings should start (H-hour) on each divisional front could not be determined till D-day was finally settled, for they would have to be related to the time of high water on that day at different points along the coast, and to the existence of shoal water off Juno. Except at Utah, where the ebb and flow take longer, the tide along the assault coast rises and falls rapidly and the high tide stands for about three hours. Good moonlight on the night before was also desirable both to ease the navigation of approaching shipping and, especially, to facilitate accurate airborne landings. These conditions could only be satisfied on about three days in each lunar month, or in every fortnight if the advantage of moonlight were ignored. Even so an overriding consideration must be suitable weather conditions, and weather could not be forecast far ahead. Until near the time therefore the exact date and hour could not be fixed but, while the target date remained as May the 31st, General Eisenhower and his principal commanders knew that D-day would have to be a day in the first week in June, unless bad weather necessitated postponement.

To complete this account of Allied plans it is necessary now to turn to those which were already being carried out in preparatory operations on which success largely depended.

CHAPTER V

PREPARATORY OPERATIONS

WHILE planning of the cross-Channel assault was being perfected and those who were to join in that great undertaking were being given their final training and rehearsal, while men and material were being assembled and the invasion fleets were gathering, the Allied air forces were already fighting relentlessly over the Continent; in support of the navies they were also harassing the enemy in the narrow seas by vigorous patrolling and the laying of mines. It would be difficult to exaggerate the importance of what was done by the air forces in the months immediately before D-day, for it contributed largely to the success of the opening assault and ultimately to the outcome of the whole campaign.

If the various air operations of this preparatory phase of Overlord are seen as a whole (though they originated at different dates and, in their execution, were interlaced with each other), their aim and principal features stand out clearly. Their aim, in the months immediately preceding D-day, can be summed up in three words—to assist Overlord. And in order to realise their aim they set out to do the four things mentioned on page 41, namely,

> to win and hold mastery of the air;
> to hamper the movement and supply of enemy forces;
> to weaken the enemy's coastal defences;
> and to confuse and mislead his commanders.

To win air mastery was the first condition of success, for only so could the offensive power of the Allies be fully exploited. To hamper the enemy's freedom of movement was particularly important in the opening phase of the campaign, because the Allies' own ability to build up large armies in France must inevitably be slowed by the initial handicap of a sea passage and by the necessity to land and maintain their forces over open beaches. To weaken the enemy's fortifications and to achieve surprise, desirable conditions in any military operation, were doubly so in this instance, for the Allies were compelled to make a frontal attack against a fortified position—a type of attack which any commander would avoid if possible.

Mastery of the air was not, of course, a new ambition; ever since the Battle of Britain was won the Royal Air Force had been fighting for it, at first with inadequate resources but as their strength increased with a growing measure of success, and in the past year they had been joined by the American air forces. Now, in the few months before D-day, a comprehensive series of operations combined to further this aim and strategic and tactical air forces of both nations played their parts in an all-round assault on German air power. In those months it was attacked at its source—in the enemy's aircraft factories and production centres; on the ground—at his airfields and control installations; and in the air—wherever his aircraft could be found. In this final preparation for Overlord a large proportion of the Allied air forces attacked the German air power, day after day and night after night, at one or other of the vulnerable points in its production and use. The attack went on with merciless persistence; the enemy air force was given no time for relaxation and insufficient time to recover from injury.

As indicated in the preceding chapters, the Allies' programme of preparatory operations, including this attack on German air power, was an integral part of the Neptune Overall Air Plan issued by the Commander-in-Chief of the Allied Expeditionary Air Force on April the 15th; but its full implementation was only made possible by another directive, issued by General Eisenhower on April the 17th, to the strategic air forces, when those to be employed on Overlord had just been put under his direction (page 43 above). Before that time the Combined Bomber Offensive, conducted under the Pointblank directive of the Combined Chiefs of Staff, had already included, as a priority in the general onslaught on the enemy's communications, industrial system and morale, a specific attack on the German fighter aircraft and ballbearing industries; and the Allied Expeditionary Air Force had been actively co-operating, both by supplying fighter protection for the strategic bombers and by searching out and engaging the enemy's fighters in aggressive sweeps over his territory. The night attacks of Bomber Command and the daylight attacks of the United States Eighth Air Force had kept in check the growth of German offensive air power and, by forcing the enemy to concentrate on the defence of his homeland, had progressively reduced his ability to defend France and other occupied countries in the West; simultaneously, the offensive sweeps of the Allied Expeditionary Air Force had also destroyed large numbers of the enemy's fighters. Over France and the Low Countries the Allies had, indeed, won a large measure of air superiority and the use of the American long-range fighters had gone far towards winning it by day over Germany too. Their concentrated attack had culminated in what became known to them as 'Big Week', in February, when a closely spaced series of daylight attacks were made against a dozen factories producing fighters and fighter components. In that week over 5,800 sorties by bombers and supporting fighters were dispatched by the Eighth and Ninth Air Forces based in England and over 900 by the

Fifteenth Air Force from Italy. Together this daylight attack cost the American air force 226 heavy bombers and 28 fighters—but it dealt German fighters and fighter production a very serious setback at a most critical time.[1] On six nights of this Big Week aircraft of Bomber Command also flew over 2,800 sorties to attack similar Pointblank targets. These included raids on Leipzig, Stuttgart, Schweinfurt and Augsburg in which heavy bombers flew over 2,700 sorties and lost 141 aircraft and over 1,000 men. But in darkness air superiority was not yet won, as is shown by the cost of Bomber Command's operations a month later. On four nights between March the 15th and March the 23rd Stuttgart, Frankfurt and Berlin were heavily attacked. On average, 834 aircraft were employed in each attack and on average forty-one aircraft were lost each time; and when 795 aircraft were sent to attack Nuremberg on the night of March the 30th/31st, 94 of our aircraft and some 650 men were lost and 71 aircraft were damaged, 12 irreparably—the heaviest casualties in any single attack by Bomber Command.

It has been claimed that the Allies had won such a measure of air superiority by day that they had ensured virtual mastery in the air. By this is meant that they had such a preponderant air power that they could dominate the position wherever they wished and could be confident of preventing serious enemy interference with their purpose. It does *not* mean that the German air force there or elsewhere had no longer any ability to hurt. They had a large and still expanding air force in spite of all the destruction they had suffered, and though they could not prevent the Allied attacks they could still, particularly at night, make them costly. Moreover, in addition to their air force they had considerably strengthened their ground defences against air attack. Allied air forces faced not only German fighters but *flugabwehrkanonen* (flak) in every raid. The percentage of aircraft lost is on record but it was not always possible to learn the cause in each case. For example, night operations of Bomber Command during May involved 11,822 individual flights. In these, two hundred and seventy-seven aircraft (2·4 per cent) were lost and two hundred and ninety-one (2·5 per cent) were damaged. But conditions varied greatly between different classes of target. Over German targets losses were 5·9 per cent and over strongly defended areas in northern France and Belgium they increased from 1·9 per cent in April to 4·3 per cent in May. This rise was accounted for partly by the increased number of German night fighters concentrated to intercept bombers and partly by improved organisation of their tactical control in areas which were the main scenes of bomber operations. The greater length of time which our aircraft had to

---

[1] W. F. Craven and J. L. Cate, *The Army Air Forces in World War II*, vol. III (Chicago, 1951), chap. II.

spend in target areas in order to make precision attacks at night was a further cause of heavier losses. It was estimated that enemy fighters were still the main cause of our losses in night attacks, only 21 per cent being attributed to flak.

The new directive (see below, page 100), issued by General Eisenhower a fortnight after the costly attack on Nuremberg in March, related operations of the strategic air forces more directly to Overlord, but targets in the Pointblank programme were still to be attacked in so far as the necessary forces were available, and in the seven weeks which remained before D-day Bomber Command attacked Brunswick (twice), Dortmund, Düsseldorf, Essen (in the Ruhr) and Schweinfurt, all Pointblank targets. They had still to face strong opposition, and of some 2,400 aircraft employed over 100 were lost in action. But these attacks against German towns represented less than a quarter of Bomber Command's total operations during this time, for, in concert with the Allied Expeditionary Air Force, the strategic forces also engaged in a variety of other preparatory operations, including further measures to weaken German air power.

Among the latter were attacks on German airfields and ground installations which had been increasing in strength since November 1943. With the co-operation of the heavy bombers these were to be greatly intensified in the last month of all-round attack on enemy air strength. During that time the Allied air forces set out to destroy the usefulness of the enemy's airfields and ground organisation including servicing, repair and maintenance facilities, especially those within a 150-mile radius of Caen. Beginning on May the 11th, this final onslaught was compressed into little more than three weeks. In that time ninety-one attacks were made, seventy-three by the American Eighth and Ninth Air Forces, who dropped over six thousand tons of bombs, and eighteen by the British Second Tactical Air Force and Bomber Command, who together dropped some nine hundred tons. By putting out of use many airfields adjacent to the assault area, the German air force was forced to fight from bases as far removed from the coming battle as were Allied aircraft while still operating from England.

Simultaneously a further and most damaging step was taken to weaken the German air force by disrupting the system of radar and wireless control, the eyes, ears and nerve system on which its effective employment largely depended. Early detection of approaching aircraft (or shipping) is the first means of defence against invasion. With eyes half-blinded, ears half-stopped and nerves torn and jangled, air forces can operate but fumblingly. So on May the 10th the Allied air forces also started to attack the German chain of radar and wireless communication stations which stretched from Norway to Spain

11. General Brereton   Air Marshal Coningham
General Eisenhower
General Vandenberg   Air Marshal Leigh-Mallory

12. BRITISH CHIEFS OF STAFF

Field-Marshal Dill Admiral Cunningham Field-Marshal Brooke Air Marshal Portal General Ismay

13. THE PRESIDENT WITH THE BRITISH AND CANADIAN PRIME MINISTERS

Mr. Mackenzie King Mr. Roosevelt Mr. Churchill

but was most thickly sited to face Britain from France and the Low Countries. Between Ostend and Cherbourg there were important installations every ten miles or so, those on the coast being backed by others inland.

The enemy's defence system comprised installations in depth of various types and sizes for detecting and reporting the approach of Allied aircraft from long and shorter ranges; for the control of his own fighters and anti-aircraft batteries; for shipping watch and the control of coastal guns; and for the interception of the Allies' wireless traffic from which their intentions might be learned. There were sixty-four installations covering in depth the coast between Ostend and Cap Fréhel near St. Malo. In view of other tasks it was not possible to destroy or damage all these; and some were by intention left virtually intact to mislead the enemy as to the Allies' intentions, in accordance with the cover plan; but enough was done in three weeks to spoil the proper functioning of the system. Most of this part of the air programme was carried out by the Spitfire and Typhoon dive-bombers and rocket-firing Typhoons of the British Second Tactical Air Force, but heavy bombers of Bomber Command were employed with great effect against some of the largest installations. In particular, on the night of the 3rd of June, ninety-five bombers guided by four Mosquitoes virtually destroyed the plant at Urville-Hague near Cherbourg, the most important headquarters of the German Signal Intelligence Service in North-West Europe. As these targets were heavily defended by anti-aircraft guns our own losses were severe; the saving of life on D-day through the comparative failure of the enemy's system of detection and control can be set against our air casualties in the preceding weeks.

The second thing which the Allies set out to accomplish in this preparatory air campaign was to hamper the movement and supply of enemy forces; this part of their programme was governed by what was known as 'the Transportation Plan'. The strategic bombers had already done much sporadic damage to German railways in the course of Pointblank attacks on the enemy's industrial system. The importance of a more intensive attack on the enemy's lines of communication had been adumbrated by Cossac; in the Transportation Plan it had been subsequently developed in detail by the planning staff of the Allied Expeditionary Air Force under Air Marshal Leigh-Mallory's direction, working in collaboration with the planners of Twenty-First Army Group, and with the help of expert advisers—notably Professor S. Zuckerman, who had been concerned in planning the Allied air attack on the enemy's railway system in the Italian campaign.

Because in the fight to establish their armies in France the Allies must be able to build up their forces more quickly than the enemy could bring forward his reserves, it was important to take all practical steps to delay the movement of his troops. The aim of the Transportation Plan was to achieve this by a concentrated and systematic attack on the railway and locomotive system on which he must largely depend and on major rail bridges leading to the battle area.

It would have been impossible to destroy or to put completely out of action the whole of the highly developed railway system of northern France, Belgium and western Germany, especially in the short time available, and nothing of the kind was planned. Moreover, it was realised that broken railway tracks could be repaired or circumvented comparatively quickly and it was known that forty to fifty thousand German railway workers had already been brought into France for this purpose. What was planned was first the destruction of nodal points in the railway system—the big centres with repair shops, servicing facilities, marshalling yards, and rail junctions where locomotives congregated—to break the system where its smooth working could most effectively be deranged; and in a final intensive phase to isolate the battle area.

Parts of the plan could be carried out by the Allied Expeditionary Air Force, and these indeed had been in progress since February the 9th when General Eisenhower had approved the general policy of the plan; during March medium bombers of the U.S. Ninth Air Force made fourteen attacks on rail targets in France. But the whole plan could not be realised without the full co-operation of the strategic air forces. It was here that acute differences of opinion were revealed. Air Marshal Harris questioned whether Bomber Command, trained for area bombing, could be used effectively at night for attacks needing such precision. To help in the reaching of a decision heavy bombers of Bomber Command staged nine trial attacks in March, the most notable being on the busy railway centre of Trappes, south-west of Paris, on the night of the 6th of March. Great damage was done to rolling stock, engine sheds and tracks, and none of the 263 aircraft employed was lost. As a demonstration of the fact that heavy night bombers *could* be economically employed on the precision targets of the Transportation Plan the attack was convincing, and, as on all these trial attacks, civilian casualties were far lighter than the opposers of the plan prophesied. Nevertheless, Lieut-General Carl Spaatz, who was in command of the United States Strategic Air Forces in Europe (the Eighth, stationed in England, and the Fifteenth in Italy), strongly opposed the use of heavy bombers envisaged by the plan, and Sir Arthur Harris of Bomber Command still held that nothing should be allowed to interfere with the area-bombing of Germany which (in his view), if fully developed, might of itself win the war. On the other hand, Sir Arthur

Tedder and Air Marshal Leigh-Mallory strongly supported the plan. Decision had to be reached, for it will be remembered that the strategic air forces were only to come under the direction of the Supreme Commander when a plan for the air support of Overlord had been approved jointly by the British Chief of Air Staff (Sir Charles Portal) acting on behalf of the Combined Chiefs of Staff, and General Eisenhower.

The arguments for and against the Transportation Plan are not difficult to distinguish. *For* the plan it was contended that while the combined attack on the German air potential must continue to have first priority, other Pointblank targets should no longer absorb all the strength of the strategic forces. The first consideration now was the success of Overlord and there was no alternative to the Transportation Plan which would give comparable assistance to Overlord in its first and most critical phase. The enemy's railway system was already strained severely, and if it were progressively attacked at its main assembly and repair centres enemy traffic would be disorganised, delayed and gradually canalised, so that by D-day it might well be virtually immobilised at key points. Although all railway traffic could not be stopped it could be greatly reduced if running to schedule were made impossible by the dislocation of the system and the reduction of locomotive power.

The argument *against* the plan was put most forcibly by General Spaatz. He contended that, while some reduction of rail traffic might be effected, the amount of damage that could be done to the enemy's huge rail system in the time remaining before D-day would be insufficient to interfere seriously with the movement of military traffic; it would not therefore help the Allies to win the opening battle. To use the strategic air forces against railway targets would be to misuse their power, for there was an alternative which would have greater effect on the subsequent campaign. His alternative proposal was that they should be employed in a sustained attack on the enemy's synthetic oil plants and refineries. He listed twenty-seven which, he said, accounted for 80 per cent of German synthetic production and 60 per cent of their refining capacity. The destruction of these would weaken, on all fronts, the enemy's power to fight and so should 'expedite the success of Overlord in the period subsequent to D-day'.

In that last sentence lay the crux of the whole matter. General Eisenhower was chiefly concerned at the moment to ensure the success of the Neptune assault and the opening fight. The oil plan would not help at that stage, for it was known that the enemy had accumulated large stocks in France, and only when these were used up would a stoppage of oil production affect military operations. On the other hand, even 'some reduction' of the enemy's railway traffic would be of immediate value to the Allied armies during their assault and build-up. Since it was admitted by all who were associated in this discussion that 'some reduction' *could* be effected, General Eisenhower decided with the full agreement of Sir Charles Portal that the Transportation Plan would be adopted, and with this joint approval of a plan for the air support of Overlord the direction of Allied strategic air forces passed, for the time being, from the Combined Chiefs of Staff to the Supreme Commander.

The strategic air forces were informed of the transfer on April the 15th and on April the 17th they were given their first directive by General Eisenhower. The Pointblank directive remained in force, but their 'particular mission', prior to Overlord, was 'to deplete the German air force and particularly the German fighter forces, and to destroy and disorganise the facilities supporting them', and 'to destroy and disrupt the enemy's rail communications, particularly those affecting the enemy's movement towards the Overlord lodgement area'.

But controversy on the Transportation Plan did not end there. The execution of the plan would involve heavy bombing attacks on key railway centres, some of which were in closely built-up areas of France and Belgium. Estimates of casualties varied widely, but there could hardly fail to be many among native civilians and the possible effect of these on the Allies' relations with France and Belgium was a political question. The War Cabinet, whose sanction was required, regarded it as a serious one and wanted to rule out all attacks which were likely to involve heavy civilian casualties. Moreover, they were not convinced about the efficacy of the plan itself especially in view of the divided opinion of many of the experts. The Supreme Commander, on the other hand, and most of the air staff held that restriction of the programme would vitiate the whole plan; and they regarded the bombardment of key railway centres as an immediate military necessity not to be surrendered for a future political advantage. The Defence Committee discussed the question at length during April while bombing continued on the less controversial targets. Re-examination of the list by Sir Arthur Tedder and a special committee led to changes which did something to reduce the estimated risk of heavy civilian casualties but did not wholly remove the Cabinet's opposition; nevertheless, the Defence Committee provisionally passed all but two of the targets on the 13th of April. Thus when on the 29th of April General Eisenhower suspended attacks on twenty-seven of the targets at the Prime Minister's request, a third of the plan had already been implemented. Although civilian casualties had continued to prove less than the lowest estimate, Mr. Churchill's disquiet was not abated. He tried vainly to persuade General Eisenhower to abandon the suspended targets and sent a telegram to the President setting out the reasons for his discomfort.

But President Roosevelt replied: 'However regrettable the attendant loss of civilian life is, I am not prepared to impose from this distance any restriction on military action by responsible Commanders that in their opinion might militate against the success of Overlord or cause additional loss of life to our Allied forces of invasion.' Seeing that not only the 'responsible Commanders' but also the Government's own military advisers, the British Chiefs of Staff, were by now convinced that the abandonment of the full plan might have both these effects, the War Cabinet's opposition was pressed no further. Bombing of the suspended list of centres was authorised by General Eisenhower on May the 5th with the proviso that the targets in the most densely-populated areas were not to be attacked until just before D-day.

Of eighty targets of first importance, thirty-nine were attacked by Bomber Command, twenty-three by the American Eighth Air Force, and eighteen by the Allied Expeditionary Air Force. By the end of April the damage done was already beginning to induce a creeping paralysis of the main railway systems of north-west France and Belgium. The attack was intensified in the month before D-day.

Meanwhile the slowing up and congestion which followed these attacks ministered to the success of the second measure by which the enemy's movement of men and material was to be hampered, namely the attack on locomotives and rolling stock on railways approaching the battle area. As damaged engines waited for repairs and trains moved slowly over newly-mended tracks or by improvised branch lines they became correspondingly more open to attack. On May the 21st, within a fortnight of D-day, the Allied Expeditionary Air Force began the final intensive assault. On that day large-scale fighter-sweeps were directed at such sitting targets—504 Thunderbolts, 233 Spitfires, 16 Typhoons and 10 Tempests operated throughout the day. On the same day over 500 of the long-range fighters of the American Eighth Air Force attacked similar targets in western Germany. Hundreds of locomotives and many trains carrying personnel, freight and oil were destroyed or damaged, often beyond all repair.

And while these operations continued, attacks began on rail and road bridges leading towards the Normandy battle area. Destruction of these would still further hamper the German ability to move up troops with which to oppose the Allies while they were building up their armies. Incidentally it would ultimately hamper the enemy's retreat if he were beaten in the opening battle.

By the nature of its construction and size a bridge is difficult to hit and even more difficult to destroy, and there were doubts as to whether the desired isolation of the battle area could be effected by air forces. These doubts were quickly dispelled. Among the first experimental attacks was one on the 725-foot steel girder railway bridge over the Seine at Vernon. Eight Thunderbolts of the American Ninth Air Force wrecked it by the use of only eight tons of bombs. More than one attack and a far heavier weight of bombs were needed in most cases, but by D-day the Ninth Air Force had cut or made unusable all the twenty-four bridges over the Seine between Paris and the sea. Twelve other much-used bridges over the rivers Oise, Meuse, Moselle and Loire and over the Demer, Escaut and Albert Canal in Belgium were also broken down or made unusable by fighters and medium bombers of the American Eighth and Ninth Air Forces, and of the British Second Tactical Air Force.

The success of an air attack which leaves a bridge broken by a huge gap, or with steel girders and piers collapsed in the river it had spanned, is easy to measure. But as the purpose of all these air operations was conceived as a whole it will be more profitable to judge their results as a whole. And before doing so there are still other items to be described—namely the attack on German coastal defences and measures to mislead and confuse the German commanders.

The enemy's coastal defences were already being progressively weakened by the attacks on his radar and wireless communications that have so far been treated as part of his air power, but these were also an integral part of his defences against attack from the sea. Having already lost command of the air he must rely first on radar to detect the approach of ships. And since he could not hope to fight the Allied navies at sea he must rely largely on his shore-based guns to ward them off. Coastal batteries therefore formed an important part of his 'Atlantic Wall'. Like the rest of his coastal defences they were strongest in the Pas de Calais area because it was there that he expected the main assault to be made, but it was estimated that there were about forty-nine battery positions in the Neptune area covering the coastal waters which the Allied navies must command and through which the Allied forces must be landed and supplied. Some of these positions appeared to be unoccupied but it was believed that in others there were about eighty-five guns of large calibre, 150-mm (approximately 6-inch) and upwards, and a considerable number of lighter weapons to dispute the landing: about three-fifths of these were in the British sector. Many of these guns were already heavily protected by steel and concrete which included overhead cover, but in other positions construction was incomplete. In the last chapter it has been explained how these were to be bombarded by Allied air forces and warships in the opening hours of D-day. In these preliminary operations the chief aim of the Allies was to delay building, and destroy or damage unfinished work.

Both tactical and strategic air forces were used in this programme, and about half the known batteries along the whole coast were attacked. On seventy-three sites nearly 24,000 tons of bombs were used. Much damage was done and work under construction was greatly set back. The condition of the German defences immediately before D-day will be realised when the results of all preliminary operations are examined.

At the request of Twenty-First Army Group a number of military targets—ammunition dumps, camps, depots and headquarters—were also attacked either by strategic or tactical air forces. Ammunition dumps at Chateaudun and Domfront in Normandy, for example, were largely destroyed, the former by aircraft of Bomber Command, the latter by Thunderbolts of the United States Ninth Air Force. The large military camp at Bourg-Leopold in Belgium was twice attacked by Bomber Command and heavily damaged. In some of these operations against well-guarded targets of military importance our losses, chiefly from enemy night fighters, were considerable (forty-two bombers were lost out of three hundred and sixty-two which attacked the tank depot at Mailly le Camp east of Paris on May 3rd/4th), but the destruction inflicted helped to weaken the enemy's military position and so prepare the way for our assaulting forces.

The carrying out of all these plans had been largely influenced by the Allies' determination to disguise their intentions and to mislead and confuse the enemy. It was impossible to hide from German commanders the fact that preparations for an assault were being completed. It might be possible, if good security were maintained, to hide from them knowledge of where and when it would be launched and to mislead them on both points, and in all the preparatory operations under review this was borne in mind. In the attacks on the airfields, radar installations, batteries, railway centres and bridges, great care was taken to avoid anything which might point to the Normandy coast as the probable point of assault. So for every installation attacked in the assault area two were simultaneously attacked outside it. This greatly increased the labours—and the losses—of Allied air forces during these hectic days, but it will be clear later that it achieved its purpose.

In the Allies' actions during these months the enemy saw nothing to indicate that Normandy would be the main point of their attack; on the contrary, the more heavy bombing of the Pas de Calais area strengthened his belief that the narrower waters of the Channel would tempt the Allies to launch their main assault on the nearest French coast. And as D-day approached other measures, combining to form a complete 'cover plan' ('Fortitude'), were to support this belief—measures in which all three Services played their deceptive parts. A comprehensive cover and deception plan—'Bodyguard'—had been made to misrepresent the Allies' strategy in Europe and thus to induce the German Command to make faulty dispositions. Fortitude was designed to give effect to this misleading strategic conception so far as Overlord was concerned.

The plan was based on a fiction—that the campaign would open with an attack on southern Norway launched from Scottish ports, but that the main attack would come in the Pas de Calais. This they were to launch about the third week of July, about forty-five days later than the real D-day. To achieve this deceit steps were taken, both before and after D-day, to mislead the enemy into the belief that the Normandy assault was but a diversionary attack. By artificial and indiscreet wireless traffic, and by means of dummy craft in south-eastern ports and harbours, it was made to seem that troops and air forces stationed in south-eastern England were assembled there for the Pas de Calais attack; various training schemes were arranged to add additional colour to this misreading of our real intentions. Other deceptive action taken before D-day and in the days following will be recounted later.

In describing these arduous air preparations for Overlord an activity on which all others largely depended has so far been omitted, namely the continuous air reconnaissance by which targets were identified and the result of the attacks observed. In 1942 the Photographic Reconnaissance Unit of the Royal Air Force had started a photographic survey of a thirty-mile wide strip of the coast from Holland to the Spanish frontier. Simultaneously a central interpretation unit had been built up, for the expert interpretation of photographs and the dissemination of results to the Intelligence departments of the three Services. The work of photographic reconnaissance had grown vastly since then, for during these months of preparation it not only provided invaluable information of many kinds but served as eyes which watched both the progress of enemy defences near at hand and the results of Allied bombing further afield. It was they who detected the enemy's batteries, emplacements, strong points, military depots and headquarters. It was they who saw whether a bridge had been broken or must be attacked again. It was they who built up such a picture of the assault area that the shape and make-up of the coasts and hinterland were known, and could be studied in detail before the attack had begun. When D-day came the coxswains of assault landing craft were given photographs of their allotted beach, taken from 1,500 yards off-shore at almost wave-top level so that they knew what it would look like as they approached land. Platoon commanders were provided with oblique photographs taken from low level so that they would recognise ground features; and further obliques from higher level were taken 1,500 yards inland to help those leading the attack inland to recognise the country and their own position. It was photographic reconnaissance aircraft that first disclosed that the enemy was placing beach obstacles below high-water level on the shores selected for landings. In all this air reconnaissance was quite invaluable. Flying often at low levels, the aircraft were vulnerable to attack from anti-aircraft guns and very open to sudden attack by enemy fighters from above. Losses were considerable, but there was no pause in their work.

Among much else, photographic reconnaissance revealed the building works from which the enemy planned to launch his much-vaunted long-distance weapons on England. The detailed account of the German attack with V-weapons belongs to the history of the defence of the United Kingdom, by Mr. Basil Collier,[2] rather than to the Overlord campaign, yet the steps taken to combat it in these months before D-day were for the most part taken by air forces preparing for Overlord and were thus a considerable addition to their many other tasks.

Evidence that the Germans were developing rocket-propelled and other long-range weapons for military use had been slowly accumulating since the autumn of 1939 but little was known as to their size and nature until 1943. By then it seemed certain that the rocket weapon was being developed, and possibly produced, at Peenemünde, an island in the Baltic. Photographs taken by a lone aircraft revealed a good deal about the size and shape of the works there, but it was not until June 1943 that two further photographic reconnaissance flights showed objects which appeared to be huge rockets. Photographic reconnaissance also confirmed reports of a new type of heavy construction work at Watten in northern France and, although there was as yet nothing definite to connect the two, close watch was kept on both. Regular flights to observe developments at Peenemünde were flown by Mosquitos and other flights to photograph further excavations and large structures then appearing in northern France were made by Spitfires.

In August 1943 a night attack was made on Peenemünde by nearly six hundred aircraft of Bomber Command. To ensure the best results the attack was made in full moonlight, although this gave every opportunity to the enemy night fighters. Forty bombers and one of our own night fighters were lost but great damage was done, and it was learnt through Intelligence sources that several of the most important designers and technical officers were killed and that all the production drawings of the V-2 rocket were destroyed. They had just been completed for issue to firms which were to manufacture the rockets, and their destruction delayed production for several months. In the same month the works under construction near Watten were twice attacked by Fortresses of the American Eighth

---

[2] Basil Collier, *The Defence of the United Kingdom* (H.M.S.O., 1957).

Air Force. As a result work on the site was suspended for over three months.

During the summer of 1943, however, Intelligence reports indicated that pilotless aircraft were also being built. The threat of this second long-range weapon took more definite shape during the autumn when the construction in France of works of a different type were photographed; they became known to the Allies as 'ski' sites. Sites of the same pattern were identified by further reconnaissance at Peenemünde and on one of these a small aircraft with a span of about twenty feet was recognised. From this and other evidence there was little doubt that the ski sites in northern France were then being built to launch 'flying bombs'. All were within 140 to 150 miles of London, most of them in a belt of country between Dieppe and Calais, with another group in the Cherbourg peninsula. Photographic reconnaissance disclosed eighty-eight sites by the end of the year and in December the code name 'Crossbow' was given to all operations, defensive and counter-offensive, against the threat of these two long-range weapons.

The counter-measures taken in France were a continuing drain on the strength of the air forces which could otherwise have been wholly devoted to preparatory operations for Overlord. Handicapped by recurrent bad weather, and with many Pointblank and Transportation Plan targets still to be attacked, the strategic air forces could only give limited strength to Crossbow targets and the attack on launching sites largely devolved on the Allied Expeditionary Air Force, though they too were needed for Overlord preparations. Their medium and low level attacks became progressively more hazardous as the enemy increased the anti-aircraft defences of the sites, and for all these reasons the endeavour to neutralise them all was not realised fully. By the end of May it was believed that eighty-six out of ninety-seven identified ski sites had been put out of action, and two out of seven rocket sites. In all, forty thousand tons of bombs had been used against Crossbow targets and the enemy's original plans had been largely nullified. But two months before D-day photographic reconnaissance revealed a new type of what became known as 'modified sites', easier to construct and less easy to distinguish. In the last three weeks many of these were recognised, but lack of time and other claims prevented their being attacked. Yet the Allies' counter-measures had at least had one most valuable result. The bombing of Peenemünde and other industrial works in Germany, the neutralisation of most of the original chain of launching sites in France and the dislocation of rail communications, by which both building materials and the weapons themselves must be borne to the sites, had between them prevented the enemy from launching the long-range attack on which Hitler built such exaggerated hopes while the Allied forces and shipping were massed for the Neptune assault. The first German flying bomb was not launched until June the 12th, by which time the Allied armies had already won a firm foothold in France.

While this aggressive programme of air operations over the Continent was in progress, measures were also taken to 'keep the ring' at sea for the coming Neptune assault—to prevent U-boats or surface craft from penetrating waters intended to be used as the Allies' 'highway' to France.

In keeping clear the waters round our coasts the Royal Navy and Coastal Command of the Royal Air Force worked in close partnership. The Admiralty specified the broad requirements; Coastal Command decided how and with what they should be met; control of day-to-day operations was effected through combined operations rooms at bases jointly staffed by the Royal Navy and the Royal Air Force. The critical south-west approaches to the Channel were patrolled by 19 Group with headquarters at Plymouth. 15 Group with headquarters at Liverpool, while mainly concerned with the defence of Atlantic convoys, was in position to deal with any U-boat which might evade patrols in the North Sea, where 16 Group guarded the eastern approaches to the Channel and the southern part of the North Sea. There the task was not only to protect our own invasion convoys but also to attack German supply shipping along the coast of the Low Countries and northern France. In the far north and east 18 Group[3] worked from bases in Scotland and Iceland against U-boats trying to reach the Channel or the Bay of Biscay through the Northern Transit Area between Norway and the Atlantic. There, from the 16th of May to the 3rd of June, 17 of the 32 U-boats in the area were sighted. Of these 15 were attacked, seven were sunk and four compelled to return to harbour. Subsequent research has however shown that only 13 U-boats out of the 32 were making for Biscay and the Channel. Of these four were sunk, and one was forced to return to Norway after it had been attacked; eight got through. But it is significant that, even in conditions of continuous daylight and fairly dense air patrol, only one of the seven *schnorkel*-fitted U-boats making for Biscay was located (and sunk), and then only because the captain rashly decided to defy air attack on the surface.

Thus the enemy's submarines, naval surface craft and coastwise shipping were liable to be met at every point by our naval and air patrols. Writing in his diary for May, Vice-Admiral Krancke, the Group Commander, West, lamented the fact that his forces 'were almost invariably attacked from the air as soon as they left harbour

---

[3] Composition of these groups is shown in Appendix VI.

and suffered numerous hits . . . darkness provided no relief. . . . The operations of motor torpedo-boats were handicapped by strong enemy patrols which prevented intended attacks and the laying of mines . . .' In the Admiral's opinion German minelaying could now make only a very small contribution to defence against invasion, for the number they could lay was too small and German minesweeping resources were insufficient to sweep the large number of mines being laid by the Allies.

For an intensive minelaying programme, carried out by the Royal Navy and Bomber Command, was another of the preparatory measures included in the Neptune plans. It was known as operation 'Maple' and was planned in five phases. Until the early days of April, routine offensive minelaying was continued by naval forces and Bomber Command using standard mines; in the next three weeks new and special types of mine were mixed with the standard mines. In the last three weeks of May this programme of mixed mining was intensified; and in the three or four days immediately before D-day only the special types were laid, the main concentrations being laid by minelayers off Calais, Boulogne, le Havre and Cherbourg, and by aircraft off the Dutch coasts and Brest. In the seven weeks before D-day nearly seven thousand mines were laid between the Baltic and the Bay of Biscay, most of them between Ijmuiden and Brest. Forty-two per cent were laid by naval forces and the rest by aircraft of Bomber Command. German records show that four steamships, fourteen auxiliary naval vessels (including minesweepers) and a tug were sunk, and five steamships, twenty-two auxiliary naval vessels, a torpedo-boat and a U-boat were damaged by our mines in April and May. Of the effect of Allied operations Admiral Krancke also wrote: 'The enemy's air mining . . . led to severe losses, and Cherbourg and le Havre had to be closed for considerable periods because of the initial difficulty of clearing the mines which were fitted with new types of acoustic firing mechanism.' So much was the German Admiral troubled by the damage incurred, one way or another, by his ships at sea that he wrote at the end of May that he 'would have to consider a further curtailment of their sea-going activities'. How different were the considerations affecting Admiral Ramsay's decisions! For while the Allies' naval and air forces continued to harass the enemy they were at the same time covering the concentration of their forces in the southern ports of Britain. Early in April the steady flow of ships and craft began along both the east and west coasts. Those forming the naval assault groups, the build-up shipping and numerous auxiliary vessels of many kinds were on the move to their loading and assembly ports, and as the weeks passed the flow swelled into a flood without any attempted interference by Admiral Krancke's forces.

ALLIED AIR SUMMARY

The vast and varied operations of the Allies in these months of preparation for Overlord merged without interval into the cross-Channel assault on D-day and the fighting which lasted till the heart of Germany was reached and the German armed forces were destroyed. Yet readers may well pause here and try to realise the magnitude of what the air forces had done in eight or ten weeks to prepare the way for the Allied invasion of Europe.

They had flown over two hundred thousand sorties and had dropped nearly as many tons of bombs at a cost of nearly two thousand aircraft and their crews. All the air commands of both nations played their part in operations against Germany as is shown by the following analysis of their records from April the 1st to June the 5th.

Command	Approximate number of sorties	Approximate tons of bombs dropped	Aircraft lost
Allied Expeditionary Air Force:			
Second Tactical Air Force	28,600	} 7,000	133
Air Defence of Great Britain	18,600		46
Ninth Air Force	53,800	30,700	197
Bomber Command	24,600	87,200	523
Eighth Air Force:			
VIII Bomber Command	37,800	69,900	763
VIII Fighter Command	31,800	600	291

In addition, aircraft of Coastal Command made over 5,000 sorties, attacking enemy coastal shipping, naval vessels and U-boats.

Their actions day by day were spread over the various objects included in the programme of preparatory operations. To illustrate this a single twenty-four hours' work may be quoted, namely that of May the 28th.

Command	Principal Targets	Sorties	Bombs dropped (tons)	Aircraft lost	Aircrew killed or missing
Second Tactical Air Force	Crossbow and transportation targets and radar stations	745		2	2
Air Defence of Great Britain	Offensive and defensive patrols	655		3	5
Ninth Air Force	Crossbow targets, bridges and radar stations	1,980	2,075	13	62
Bomber Command	Military installations, transportation targets and coastal batteries	1,110	3,900	27	189
Eighth Air Force	Aircraft factories and industrial plants	1,575	1,974	42	316

How far had the Allies' preliminary aims been achieved? Their first aim had been to obtain mastery of the air by hindering the enemy's aircraft production, by destroying his airfields, ground organisation and radar, and by destroying his aircraft in action and on the ground.

The Allies' Combined Bomber Offensive had not stopped German aircraft production, had not indeed prevented some expansion. But it had prevented anything like a full realisation of the largely increased effort which had been concentrated upon it. It also caused the enemy to tie up great resources of men and material on an air defence system over his home territories in efforts to combat that offensive. It inevitably had its effect on the local air situation in the Overlord area.

Of the havoc wrought by the Allies' attack on airfields the enemy's own verdict may be accepted. A study prepared by the German Air Historical Branch (8th *Abteilung*) two months later states that 'The systematic destruction of the ground organisation of the Luftwaffe, especially of the fighter airfields, was very effective just before and during the start of the invasion. Hardly a single airfield of those intended for fighter operations is still serviceable'. The same study records that 'Naval Radar Stations were attacked by bombers every day before the invasion and were largely put out of action'.

As to the number of enemy aircraft destroyed, the Germans' own record of those lost in the two months before D-day may also be quoted, for at least it is unlikely to be an overstatement. They show that in air operations against the Allied air forces which were based in Britain, the German Air Force lost 1,858 aircraft. Of this total 500 belonged to the Third Air Fleet based in France; the remainder were of the Reich Air Fleet responsible for the day and night defence of Germany.

Admiral Krancke considered that by the end of May the Allies had 'almost complete mastery of the air'. The historical staff of the German air force wrote that 'the outstanding factor both before and during the invasion was the overwhelming air superiority of the enemy'.

Subsequent events were to prove that all were true. Whatever operations were planned by the Allies, their commanders could now be confident that enemy air forces could not seriously interfere with them. The sting had been taken out of the German air force and over the battlefields of France it was left with little more than nuisance value.

The Allies' second aim had been to hamper the German movement of troops and supplies by disrupting his railway communications—the Transportation plan. The results of these efforts, as described in contemporary German records, show how it appeared to them at the time.

GERMAN RAILWAY REPORT

On May the 15th a 'Report on the German Transport Ministry's view of Recent Air Attacks on Railways' contains the following passages:

> 'In the occupied areas of the West, particularly in Belgium and northern France, the raids carried out in recent weeks have caused systematic breakdown of all main lines; the coastal defences have been cut off from the supply bases in the interior, thus producing a situation which threatens to have serious consequences . . . large-scale strategic movement of German troops by rail is practically impossible at the present time, and must remain so while attacks are maintained at the present intensity . . . In assessing the situation as a whole it must further be borne in mind that, owing to the widespread destruction and damage of important construction and repair shops, the maintenance and overhaul of locomotives has been considerably disorganised; this causes further critical dislocation of traffic.'

On June the 3rd, 1944, a 'top secret' report on 'Air Operations against the German Rail Transport System during March, April and May 1944' was prepared by the German Air Force Operations Staff. It included the following statement:

> 'In the area of northern France and Belgium—the zone of invasion in the narrower sense of the word—the systematic destruction that has been carried out since March of all important junctions of the entire network—not only of main lines—has most seriously crippled the whole transport system (railway installations, including rolling stock). Similarly Paris has been systematically cut off from long distance traffic, and the most important bridges over the lower Seine have been destroyed one after another . . . It is only by exerting the greatest efforts that purely military traffic and goods essential to war effort, e.g. coal, can be kept moving'. In the 'intermediate zone' between the German and French–Belgian railway system 'all the important through stations . . . have been put out of action for longer or shorter periods . . . In May the first bridge over the Rhine—at Duisburg—was destroyed "according to plan" in a large scale attack'. Of the Allies' intention the report deduced that in the western region the rail network was to be completely wrecked. 'This aim has been so successfully achieved—locally at any rate —that the Reichsbahn authorities are seriously considering whether it is not useless to attempt further repair work.'

In March 1945 a German report on the technical experiences of railway engineers in '*The Anglo-American invasion of France in the summer of 1944*' was sent to the Chief of Transport in the German Army High Command (OKH). Overleaf is a photographic reproduction of their map showing how the main railway system, leading from Germany through Belgium and north-east France to Paris and Rouen, was damaged during May by Allied bombing (shown in green) and by sabotage (in red). It will be seen that the bombing gave the enemy no indications that an Allied assault on *Normandy* was intended. Further maps showing how the pattern of Allied bombing developed in June and July are given at page 400.

The Allies' third aim had been to weaken the enemy's coastal defences. There is in German records abundant evidence of the damage done, but since this part of the Allies' preparatory programme was to culminate in the opening bombing and naval bombardment which would precede the first landings on D-day it will be time enough then to assess results.

While waiting for the further evidence of success which subsequent operations must provide before a final judgment can be formed it is permissible to record the opinion of the soldier in supreme command. Two years later, with unique knowledge of what had happened both before and after the Neptune assault was launched, General Eisenhower wrote: '... without the overwhelming mastery of the air which was attained by that time our assault against the Continent would have been a most hazardous, if not impossible, undertaking'.

The cost at which this achievement was purchased may be stated simply in the number of casualties. Between the 1st of April and the 5th of June the Allied air forces lost over twelve thousand officers and men in these operations and some two thousand aircraft. Of these, approximately four thousand men and over seven hundred aircraft belonged to the Royal Air Force. But these figures do not include men who were wounded or damaged aircraft. In any case the cost should not only be measured by figures; the whole cost was not paid by those who gave their lives or suffered obvious injury. The spiritual and physical strain borne by those who survived to fly their dangerous missions again and again has no measurement. Few fighting men are by nature fearless: in the minds of most fear is very present, and the courage which overcomes it, though upheld by confidence gained in training, by trust in equipment and comrades and by the tradition of his Service, is won by self-mastery and self-control which each action taxes anew. Something of what such operations involved has often been described. Nevertheless one illustration may be given as a reminder of their cost.

On the night of March the 15th, 863 bombers of Bomber Command were ordered to attack Stuttgart. They dropped 2,745 tons of bombs and lost 37 aircraft in doing so. This is how one which returned fulfilled its mission. Flying in darkness at a height of 22,000 feet a Lancaster (P2 of 626 Squadron) captained by Flight Sergeant C. R. Marriot was caught and held by enemy searchlights while still thirty miles away from the city. A German Ju.88 fighter approaching

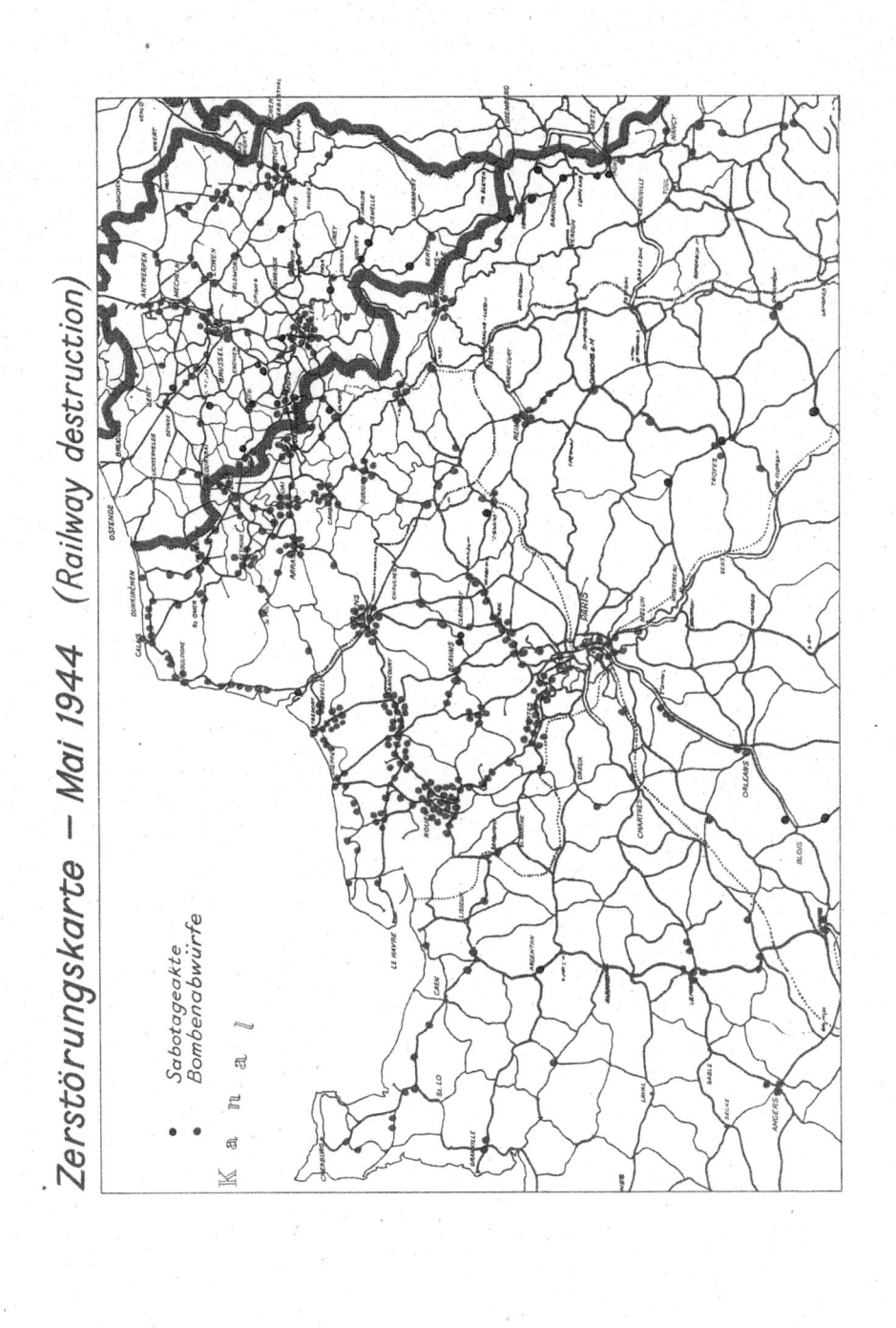

Zerstörungskarte – Mai 1944 (Railway destruction)

• Sabotageakte
• Bombenabwürfe
 Kanal

low on the starboard quarter opened fire at about 600 yards range. The Lancaster was extensively hit and, although the rear-gunner returned the enemy's fire, the German made a second attack from dead astern at only 250 yards range and more damage was suffered from cannon and machine-gun fire. The enemy was shaken off by evasive action and it was then found that the Lancaster's inter-communication and radio telephone system had been put out of action; the mid-upper and rear turrets had been made unserviceable and the oxygen supply to both cut; the tail plane and trimmers, fuselage and both turrets were badly damaged as well as the astro-dome and pilot's cockpit head; one petrol tank had been holed and two propellers damaged. A fire started below the mid-upper turret but was extinguished.

In spite of all this Flight Sergeant Marriot decided to carry on with the mission. The target was identified, the run in was made and the bombs were dropped without further damage from the local defence. Then P2 turned for home. The rear-gunner, Sergeant J. V. Brewer, had remained on duty in his broken turret, without oxygen, wounded in the foot and ankle and operating the turret with his hands. In the damaged mid-upper turret the other gunner, Sergeant R. Loughrey, also wounded, lay unconscious through lack of oxygen, and although Sergeant W. A. E. J. Willday, the flight engineer, and the wireless operator, Sergeant W. A. Palmer, succeeded in moving him on to the aircraft rest-bed he did not regain consciousness till some twelve hours after being landed in England. On the homeward run Sergeant C. R. Todd, the bomb aimer, kept observation by moving back and forth from his own station and the now empty turret. Through all this the navigator, Sergeant J. H. Barton, had held to a true course and P2 landed safely at its base. When the wounded rear-gunner, who had carried on without oxygen in his broken and exposed turret, was taken to hospital he was found to be suffering from severe facial frost-bite.

The captain of this crew of sergeants had already conducted night attacks on February the 22nd, 24th, 25th, 29th, March 1st, 4th, 5th and 10th, yet he did eight further attacks before D-day. His navigator and bomb aimer flew with him throughout.

CHAPTER VI

DEVELOPMENTS IN FRANCE

THE Allies' postponement of their assault gave the Germans a further month in which to continue the work on defences which Rommel was pressing forward. Much that was done was undone by Allied bombing. Much that was planned and ordered could not be carried out, for the dislocation of the railway system prevented the arrival in time of necessary material and air attacks constantly interrupted the use of what was available. The designed programme could be nothing like fully completed, yet progress was made and was daily noted and photographed by Allied aircraft.

The stretches of beach which were suitable for landings and for bearing the load of the subsequent build-up are shown on the map facing page 168: for example, on the British front they only amounted to less than a third of the total. By the end of May all were protected by several ranks of obstacles placed irregularly in the upper half of the tidal range; as seen from seaward there was one for every two or three yards. Some, known to the Allies as 'element C', were steel gate-like structures nearly nine feet high and nine wide, each weighing a ton and a half. Even more formidable were 'hedgehogs' made of seven-foot angled steel girders, riveted together so as to present sharp points in all directions; when struck they would pierce a craft or turn over, bringing other points up to impale it from beneath. There were 'tetrahedra' six feet high weighing nearly a ton, and ramps or heavy stakes, nearly all armed with mines or shells to explode on impact. An illustration is given opposite page 160.

On shore, coastal batteries covered the seaward approaches to the whole Neptune front, most of the heavier ones being situated in the vicinities of Cherbourg and the Seine estuary. Not all had been completed and the use of some had been abandoned before the Allies attacked. The situation of major batteries which were targets of the opening naval bombardment is also shown on the map at page 168.

Minor ports in the assault area, such as Port en Bessin, Courseulles, and Ouistreham were strongly guarded and along the whole front, sited to give mutual defence, were strong-points at every thousand yards or so incorporating pill-boxes, fortified buildings and trench systems covered by barbed wire and profusely sown minefields. These positions were usually manned by infantry at platoon or company strength; they all contained machine guns and most of them a mortar or two, and one or more field or anti-tank guns. The country in between them was frequently traversed by an anti-tank ditch. All the most likely exits from the shore were blocked by concrete walls or other obstacles—see sketch map at page 176.

With each increase of our knowledge of the German defences the way to overcome them was studied intensively. Ever since the construction of underwater obstacles was first discovered in February, small inter-Service parties had been visiting the French shore by night to examine the beaches and beach obstacles under the very noses of the defenders; many were photographed by low-flying aircraft. Minor landing craft might be stopped by any of these obstacles; heavier craft might drive through them but probably at the cost of severe damage and casualties. It would be necessary to demolish the obstacles *in situ* or to remove them bodily by tracked vehicles, and this could only be done when they stood above tide level or in less than two feet of water. Teams drawn from the Royal Navy and the Royal Engineers were jointly trained for this task. The naval teams equipped with special craft, explosives and shallow-water diving gear were to deal with underwater obstacles, the sappers with those still above water. Both would have to accompany the leading waves of the assault and at first work under fire. Only the clearance of narrow lanes ahead of the advancing tide could be attempted until the tide receded. It was fortunate that the Germans had not time or supplies to extend underwater obstacles into the lower half of the tidal range as they had intended to do.

Ingenuity and inventive skill had produced much new equipment to facilitate the attack on land defences: mat-laying tanks for crossing soft clay patches of beach, ramp tanks over which vehicles could scale sea walls, bridge-carrying tanks for crossing anti-tank ditches, assault engineer tanks with petards and other explosive charges for blasting concrete works, armoured bulldozers for moving earth and debris, flail tanks for mine clearance and Duplex Drive tanks which could swim ashore. These were all part of British equipment designed to out-match German ingenuity and ease the task of assaulting troops.[1]

Physically the forward defences of the assault coast, covered by the Channel, were very strong; their characteristic weakness was lack of depth. Once the outer crust was broken through there was no second organised line of defence to challenge a thrusting adversary's advance inland. Much therefore would depend on the garrison. In

---

[1] Since early 1943 all these special devices had been concentrated in the 79th Armoured Division so that one senior officer would be responsible for their development and for advising on their use. Throughout the campaign the division was to remain under direct command of Twenty-First Army Group, suitable portions being allotted to armies as operations required.
Further details will be found in Appendix IV on British equipment and weapons.

spite of the claims of the Russian and Italian fronts the forces of von Rundstedt's army of the West had been somewhat strengthened during the past two months; the changes of its composition are shown by the following figures.

	April 4	May 28
Static coast divisions	26	25
Infantry field-force and parachute divisions	14	16
Armoured and mechanised divisions	5	10
Reserve divisions	10	7
Total	55	58

But the mere number of divisions gives but an imperfect measurement of fighting value. Much of the increase was achieved by refitting, regrouping and training of reserves and some of the additional divisions shown above were still only in course of formation. Yet one significant change had taken place. The actual number of tanks in the West had increased from 752 at the beginning of January to 1,403 at the end of April; and though figures are not available there is reason to believe that they had been further increased by D-day.

The field force and so-called 'parachute' infantry and armoured divisions were to prove hard fighters. Although some of the static divisions were less good in quality and were not fully trained or equipped for mobile operations, they were to fight in well-prepared positions which they had occupied for some time and on ground with which they were by now familiar. Characteristics and strength of some individual formations will be given as far as they are known when they are encountered in battle. The disposition of the German armies in France and the Low Countries are shown on the map facing page 120. It will be seen that all the infantry divisions were in or directly behind the coastal defence zone and that the armoured divisions were widely distributed.

Fortunately it is not necessary here to describe fully the complicated German system of command prevailing under Hitler. After the war, Major-General von Buttlar, who in 1944 was Chief of Army Operations on the staff of Hitler's High Command of the Armed Forces (OKW), wrote that high-level organisation reflected 'the internal influence and inter-play of forces which affected the whole system of command'. The chain of command in the West was, he claims, no special handicap to the commander of the western theatre, for it was 'a burden to which Commanders-in-Chief in all theatres of war had to resign themselves'. But if that was how the matter appeared to General Buttlar at the centre, as seen at the circumference by Lieut-General H. Speidel, Rommel's Chief of Staff, 'the organisation and chain of command of the major commands in the

West was somewhere between confusion and chaos'. Even if it was not peculiar to the West, the fact that units such as the occupation troops, Waffen SS, and divisions stationed in France for rehabilitation and training were under von Rundstedt's control only for operational purposes, did not simplify his task; while officials such as the Chief Transportation Officer and inspectors general of armoured forces, infantry, artillery and engineers, and even some sections of the staff of von Rundstedt's own headquarters were, in different respects and to varying degrees, subject to control by OKW or other central *Reich* authorities. Nor was there close co-operation between the commanders of the three Services comparable to that of the Allies. But the 'confusion and chaos' which General Speidel lamented were also aggravated by the attitude and actions of his own chief, Field-Marshal Rommel.

It will be remembered (Chapter III) that the western theatre was not under control of the German Army Headquarters (OKH) but of what was virtually Hitler's personal staff, OKW; that the Commander-in-Chief of the western theatre, Field-Marshal von Rundstedt, was one of the most senior, most distinguished and respected soldiers Germany possessed; that early in 1944 the able but less experienced Field-Marshal Rommel had been appointed to command an army group of von Rundstedt's forces consisting of the Fifteenth and Seventh Armies, responsible for defence of the northern coasts of France and Flanders; and finally that these two field-marshals held different views on how the Allied assault, when it came, should be countered.

Von Rundstedt prepared a directive which made clear Rommel's position as subordinate to himself as Commander-in-Chief, but this definition of their relationship was unacceptable to both Rommel and Hitler. Instead, Rommel was given a *'Gummibefehl'* (an elastic directive) which was later to handicap von Rundstedt's power to influence operations.

The position of both men was ambiguous. As Commander-in-Chief von Rundstedt had, nominally, overriding command of all army forces in the West and was responsible for its defence. The two strongest and most threatened armies in his command were to fight under Rommel, but were still under his own headquarters for various matters such as training, equipment, and supply. Yet while Rommel's authority within the area of his own command was to that extent limited to the tactical conduct of two armies, as Inspector of Coastal Defences he had an influence outside the area of his operational command. In this dual rôle the importance attached to the Atlantic Wall and to the part which would be played by Army Group B in defending the Channel coast gave to Rommel a position of great intrinsic importance. He took full advantage of this position, for between mid-December and the end of February he not only personally inspected important stretches of coast from central Holland southwards to the Somme (particularly the Pas de Calais) but toured parts of the Atlantic and Mediterranean coasts. He drove forward work on the defences with great energy. It was said, for instance, that 'in several divisional sectors more land mines have been relaid (*verlegt*) in the last three weeks than in the previous three years'. But Allied bombing of communications seriously interfered with supplies and, although in the first six months of 1944 the number of mines in the coastal defence zone was tripled, the five or six million laid fell far short of Rommel's own minimum estimate of fifty million needed for continuous defence belts. This indefatigable industry, combined with his self-confidence, assertiveness and his favoured relationship with the *Führer*, enabled Rommel to win an influence on policy which over-shadowed the authority of the Commander-in-Chief.

Yet he was not content. In March he asked that the armoured divisions in his own sector (which von Rundstedt had intended to form into a reserve as 'Armoured Group West' under General Geyr von Schweppenburg) should be put under his, Rommel's, command; and also that he should be given control 'as far as work on coastal defences was concerned' over the armies allotted to the defence of the remaining coast of France (the First in the Atlantic and the Nineteenth in the Mediterranean sectors). His request was based on the policy of defence which he was pursuing in contrast with the policy which von Rundstedt advocated. Rommel held that the Allies must be defeated on the coast and must never be allowed to break through the defences of the Atlantic Wall; the coastal battle should be fought by a single commander and, as all depended on it, he should have all available forces under his immediate control. Though Hitler had himself laid down that the Allies must never be allowed to break through the Atlantic Wall and that the assaulting forces must be destroyed at sea or on the coast, he found that he could hardly retain von Rundstedt as Commander-in-Chief if he gave Rommel not only command of the two armies which were to defend the most threatened coast but also command of the reserves, and some control over von Rundstedt's other two armies. He got over the difficulty by an application of his favourite policy of 'divide and rule' which led to an unsatisfactory compromise. Neither von Rundstedt nor Rommel should have control of all the reserves. But by the middle of May Rommel was left in control of three armoured divisions (the 2nd, 21st and 116th) as an Army Group B reserve. The remaining armoured divisions to be stationed in the north (namely the 1st and 12th SS Panzer Divisions and the Panzer Lehr Division) were constituted as an OKW reserve under Hitler's direction from the 26th of April.

Thus, von Rundstedt had no reserve under his personal command and Hitler, by retaining personal control of the reserve, would inevitably have to intervene in the conduct of the battle. In an effort to balance his command and keep his hands free to exercise general control over the forthcoming battle von Rundstedt, at the end of April, formed his two armies in the south (the First and the Nineteenth) into a second army group, G, under Colonel-General Blaskowitz.

When the dispositions of the armoured divisions at the opening of the battle are examined on the map opposite, it will be seen that neither Rommel's views nor von Rundstedt's wholly prevailed.

According to Colonel-General Jodl's[2] diary notes for April the 13th, 'Rommel says mobile operations with armoured formations are a thing of the past'. This surprising opinion was apparently derived from Rommel's own experience in North Africa. There he had learned that massed armoured formations could not operate successfully where an enemy held mastery in the air. Now he argued that behind the Fifteenth and Seventh Armies of Army Group B the movement of armoured divisions from a reserve would be canalised on roads and railways, and in face of the Allies' air superiority it would be severely obstructed. Von Rundstedt on the other hand had little faith in the Atlantic Wall, which he subsequently described as 'an enormous bluff'. He felt that the Allies would be able to break through it but he could not be sure where the break would come, where therefore 'a centrally-located army' would be needed to counter-attack in force.

There is a further factor in this story of muddle, cross-purposes and mutual distrust which characterised the German system of command in the West. The German army, navy and air forces, charged with responsibilities for the defence against invasion, were under separate commands. The unification of command and the integration of staffs for planning and control which characterised the Allies' combined operations had no counter-part in the German system. The Commander-in-Chief in the West had no authority over the air forces stationed in France—the Third Air Fleet—or over Admiral Krancke, responsible for the naval defence of all the coasts of France. Many of the heavier shore batteries forming part of the Atlantic Wall defences were sited by naval authorities, often in disagreement with the army commander in the sector. In operations firing to seaward they were under naval control; firing on to the beaches or landward they were to come under army control. Similarly the disposal of anti-aircraft guns of the air force was decided by air force authority. Early in May, Rommel asked that the III Flak Corps which was 'scattered over the whole of central and northern France' should be

---

[2] Jodl was Chief of Operations Staff at OKW.

GERMAN ARMY DISPOSITIONS
Dawn 6th June 1944

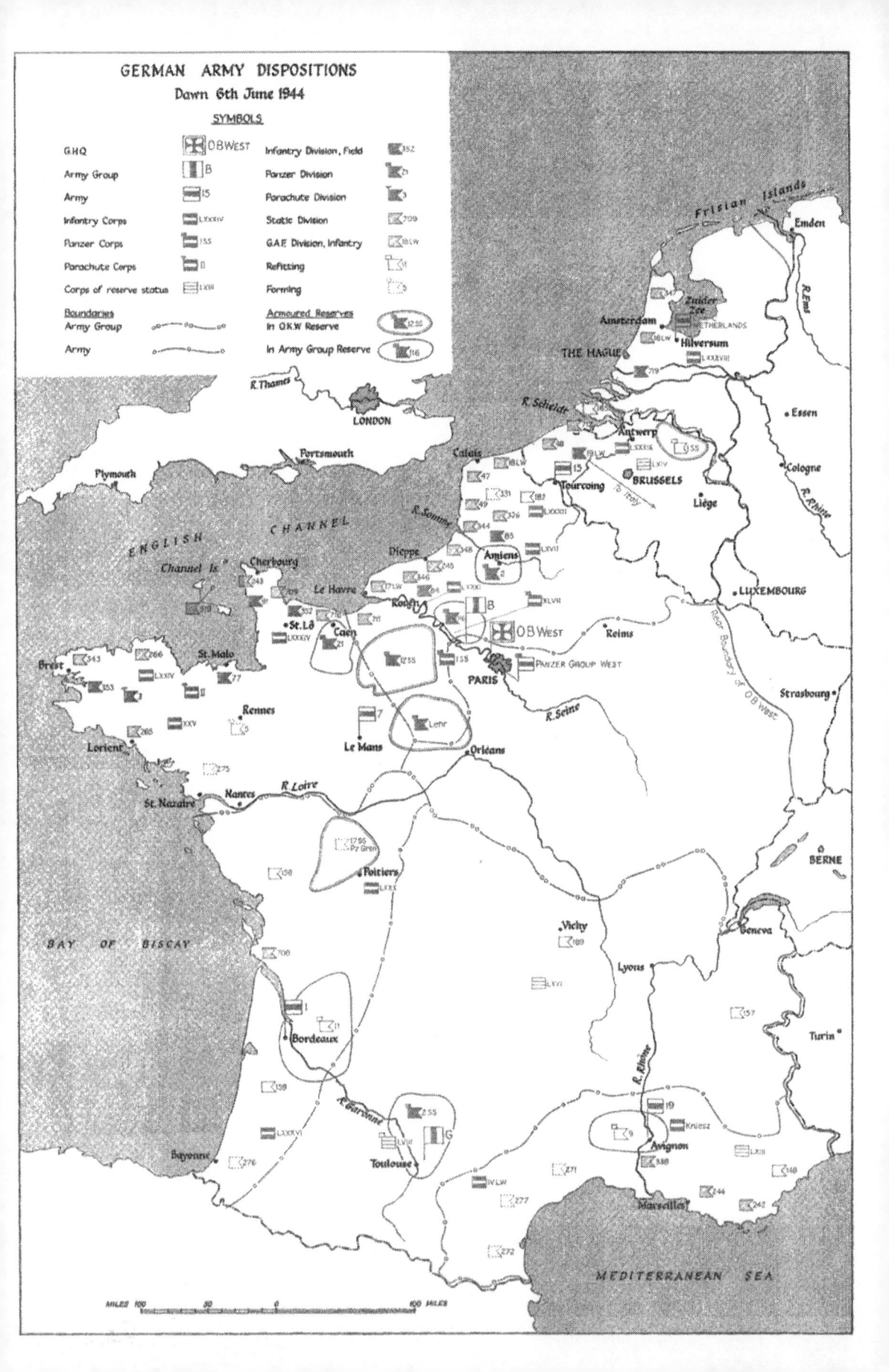

SYMBOLS

G.H.Q	OB West	Infantry Division, Field	352
Army Group	B	Panzer Division	21
Army	15	Parachute Division	3
Infantry Corps	LXXXIV	Static Division	709
Panzer Corps	I SS	G.A.F Division, Infantry	16LW
Parachute Corps	II	Refitting	9
Corps of reserve status	LXIII	Forming	9

Boundaries
Army Group
Army

Armoured Reserves
In O.K.W Reserve — 12 SS
In Army Group Reserve — 116

concentrated under his command. Its four regiments—twenty-four up-to-date batteries—would, he said, provide valuable fire-power for anti-aircraft and tank defence between the Orne and the Vire. Field-Marshal Göring refused his request.

It can be seen from the notes in Appendix VII how puny a force was the Third Air Fleet to oppose to the air might of the Allies, and how little it could do to support Rommel's armies. According to the German Air Ministry records the Third Air Fleet returned its strength on May the 31st as 402 bombers of various classes, 336 fighters, 89 reconnaissance and 64 transport aircraft. But not all would be operational on any given day, and other contemporary evidence states that of the fighters, for example, only about 200 were operationally available on D-day.

Also important from the Allied point of view were the fighter forces held by Germany for the defence of the Reich to which reference was made in the preceding chapter. Some of these were moved nearer to the scene of battle after the campaign opened, but their intervention could not make up for the weakness of the Third Air Fleet, or give the help that the Army would have needed to meet attack from air, land and sea.

The disposition of the enemy's naval forces in the West when the battle opened is shown in Appendix III. Admiral Krancke had at his disposal no major warships. Distributed round the coast, from Ijmuiden in Holland to Bayonne near the Spanish frontier in the Bay of Biscay, were five destroyers, six torpedo-boats, thirty-four motor torpedo-boats and nearly five hundred small patrol boats and mine-sweepers. Forty-nine U-boats were based on Brest and Biscay harbours for anti-invasion duty, and forty-three more for other uses. But not all these vessels were immediately available for service and they were clearly incapable of serious opposition to the great naval force to be employed in operation Neptune. Yet they might inflict considerable damage if they succeeded in getting among the thousands of ships and craft that would be crossing between England and France.

The damage and disorganisation wrought by the Allied air forces during the spring of 1944 was not the only handicap under which the enemy prepared for the coming battle. In the weekly reports of the German armies and army groups to the Commander-in-Chief (which were summarised in his own weekly situation estimates to OKW) a separate heading was included to record damage suffered through sabotage.

It is impossible to estimate with any exactitude the material damage wrought by the French sabotage activities. The best saboteurs do not keep the most careful records and such records as there are cannot produce a grand total which means anything. A list of 'successful' attacks on factories, for instance, tells little of value unless it also tells for how long and to what extent production suffered, and evidence available on such points is both incomplete and conflicting. Figures that have since been compiled must be treated with great reserve, but there is no doubt that the considerable damage done by saboteurs added much to the enemy's troubles.

One of their targets, perhaps the most effectively hit, was the railway system. Locomotives were sabotaged and derailments were caused by rail-cutting, which upset military transport of men and stores. To give one example, sabotage in a tunnel on the Besançon–Montbéliard line near Belfort blocked all traffic for nineteen days. The figures given in various calculations of damage done do not square, but such sustained pin-pricking had more than nuisance value; joined with the intensive Allied air attacks under the Transportation Plan, they were a continuing embarrassment to the enemy.

So, too, were sabotage activities in factories and other industrial works. A wide range of plants were damaged more or less seriously. Among these were electric and hydro-electric power plants, transformers, high tension cables and pylons; aero-engine and motor-vehicle works, others making air propellers and component parts, and ballbearing and aluminium factories. Over half a million litres of petrol and oil were destroyed, and a large minesweeper was sunk in Rouen harbour. Passive resistance, and in some cases bluff, added to the effectiveness of sabotage. An amusing story is recorded of a Canadian officer who went to the round-house of the Dieppe railway yards, immediately after the town's recapture on September the 1st, to re-establish the important supply line to Neufchâtel. 'Six engines were in the shed, all bearing placards stating their defects; the minimum repair period was stated to be three months. As the officer was expressing his disgust the foreman came into the shed and took down the placards, saying, "*Pour les Alliés demain soir*".'

So brief a survey cannot reveal the drama and dangers of these acts of sabotage. Many saboteurs were captured or killed, sometimes in their first venture, sometimes after one or more successes; most of the evidence of their work was lost with them. Not all were as competent as the famous 'Armada' team who worked in association with the British Special Operations Executive (S.O.E.). It was built round a fireman, Basset, and a garage mechanic, Jarrot, better known under the pseudonyms of 'Marie' and 'Goujon'. Their first mission in August 1943 was directed against the power supplies of the Creusot works. In October they carried out two missions against electric supplies for Paris and the canal system. With many able satellites (including one 'who specialised in the execution of Gestapo agents') they had a long run of well authenticated success. All their actions were carried out with *sang-froid* and discipline and without loss to the personnel of their teams or to the civilian population, and unlike many stories of the Resistance theirs had a happy ending. 'In July 1944 "Marie" and "Goujon" arrived a third time to organise the scattered Maquis round Lyon and Chalon sur Saône, and at the end "Marie" marched on Lyon at the head of some fifteen thousand Frenchmen.'

In the sabotage campaign French trade unions played a substantial part, notably the *Société Nationale des Chemins de Fer*, and, on rare occasions when it was practicable to co-ordinate plans, Allied bombing was not undertaken when sabotage could achieve the desired results. But although an astonishing amount of traffic was maintained between England and Resistance elements in France, the nature and composition of the Resistance movement inevitably limited co-operation and prevented its use as a positive factor in the Allied plans.

It has already been explained in Chapter III that the dispersed and variously constituted groups which formed the main corpus of the Resistance were, by the early months of 1944, associated with the organisation developing in France under the National Council of the Resistance, in turn represented on the National Committee of the Liberation over which de Gaulle presided in Algiers; it was represented in England at this time by General Koenig and his staff, constituted under de Gaulle's authority and acting as his Military Mission at Shaef. On June the 2nd his appointment as Commander-in-Chief of the Free French Forces of the Interior was recognised by the Supreme Commander, and he was accorded the status of an army commander with a right of appeal to de Gaulle. It has also been explained that while this widely, if loosely, organised movement was developing the British Special Operations Executive (S.O.E.) and the American Office of Strategic Services (O.S.S.) were also stimulating, guiding and supplying numerous small independent groups which remained untouched by the larger organisation. Soon after General Eisenhower's arrival S.O.E. and O.S.S. were brought under a Special Force Headquarters, as part of the Operations Division of Shaef, who subsequently appointed liaison officers to General Koenig's Staff. There was thus an attempt to co-ordinate the actions of both types of resistance operations, but the dichotomy which had been born of circumstances persisted till well after the campaign opened.

As that time approached the amount of assistance provided for groups of both categories was substantially increased. Ever since 1942 two squadrons of Bomber Command had been employed on this special duty, carrying emissaries of S.O.E. and supplies into enemy occupied territory and picking up our own men or French military or Resistance leaders to bring them to England. They were by now very skilful in finding 'reception committees' in obscure or ill-defined places and in landing and getting away quickly, on average in about three minutes. Since December 1943 their work had been supplemented by two squadrons of American Liberators, and after February by aircraft of 3 Group, Bomber Command and 38 Group, Airborne Forces. By May, supplies dropped in France included approximately 80,000 sten guns, 30,000 pistols and 17,000 rifles as well as several thousand bazookas, Piats, mortars, grenades and considerable demolition stores. A good deal of this material fell into enemy hands, but much reached its proper destination and strengthened the recipients morally as well as physically. It was calculated in May that some hundred thousand armed Frenchmen would take action on orders from London, apart from the thirty-five to forty thousand armed Maquis, of whom only about a quarter had ammunition for more than one day's serious fighting. Behind these a conservative estimate put the number of unarmed men ready to co-operate in passive resistance or a general strike at a million and a half.

Notwithstanding the growth of the movement and all that had been done to develop its organisation, its heterogeneous composition, paucity of equipment and lack of military experience, and the impossibility of calculating the size and efficiency of Resistance groups, prevented its playing an integral part in military operations which depended on exact and secret plans. From the Allies' point of view its achievements were to be regarded as a bonus. Yet as D-day drew near the need of closer contacts was felt by the Allies' planning staff and two further measures were taken. First, Special Force Headquarters organised and trained over ninety small inter-Allied teams of three men (known as 'Jedburghs'), at least one being an officer and another a wireless operator. On and after D-day these teams were to be dropped where needed to serve as foci of Intelligence and guidance to the neighbouring Resistance groups. Secondly, Special Air Service Troops, comprising some 2,000 officers and men, and eleven American 'Operational Groups', each of four officers and thirty men, were to be used as small 'striking forces' with specific objectives in association with Resistance groups.

In so far as Resistance activities directly affected the campaign with which this volume is concerned they will find their place in the story: but the full account of the movement and its achievements must be sought elsewhere, for much of it lies outside the scope of this British military history.[3]

No disinterested student of military affairs will be likely to question the Allies' wisdom in withholding their plans from leaders of the

---

[3] And see Appendix IX.

movement; the risk to security would have been too great. It does not require much imagination to picture what might have happened if the enemy had been able to obtain, through that or any other channel, accurate information as to the place and time of the invasion. All their major forces could with confidence have been concentrated behind the threatened coast and they could then have counter-attacked in overwhelming force. Even if they had failed to learn the exact date of the invasion they would have been in a strong position had they known that the main attack was to be made in Normandy and that the Allies would not attempt to land in the Pas de Calais or elsewhere. Mercifully the Allies achieved practically a hundred per cent security. Notwithstanding the fact that a considerable number of people had to be in the secret, it was not given away. Up to the end, even for some weeks after a footing had been gained in France, the German leaders were still left to guess the Allies' intentions, and by measures taken to deceive them they were encouraged to guess wrongly.

Throughout the long stages of planning and preparation infinite care had been taken to avoid any leakage of information, and as the day of assault approached and men, material and shipping had to be concentrated progressively in southern England, unheard-of measures were taken to prevent even accidental disclosure of the carefully guarded secret of the Allies' purpose. Normal civilian travel between the United Kingdom and Eire was stopped, for the Irish Government was not at war with Germany and still allowed German diplomatic representatives and agents in Eire to continue functioning unhindered. In Great Britain, in April, a coastal belt ten miles deep, on either side of the Firth of Forth and stretching from the Wash to Land's End, was closed to all visitors and only authorised travellers were allowed to enter or leave it. Finally a most drastic and unprecedented step was taken. Neither diplomats nor their couriers were allowed to enter or leave the country and all correspondence for transmission in the sacred 'diplomatic bag' was subject to censorship. This ban greatly annoyed Hitler when it was published; what was of more interest to the Allies was the fact that it greatly incensed General de Gaulle.

De Gaulle's political ambition has been referred to in an earlier chapter. In these last few months he had moved steadily towards the achievement of his desire to return to France at the side of the Allies as their partner and as the head of a liberation government. On May the 15th the Consultative Assembly which had been formed in Algiers ruled that the National Committee of the Liberation should henceforth be styled the 'Provisional Government of the French Republic'.

But while de Gaulle increased his authority with Frenchmen he made less progress with the Allies. The fact that no uncensored communications were allowed with his representatives in England; the fact that neither he nor his military commander in England, General Koenig, were allowed detailed knowledge of the Allies' plans; the fact that his 'Provisional Government' was not at once recognised as such by the Allies, stirred him to unconcealed anger. The political aspect of de Gaulle's leadership of the French liberation movement is only relevant here in so far as it impinged on the Allies' military preparations for the coming campaign and therefore little more need be said about it. On the Allies' request de Gaulle came to England on the day before the assault was launched and was then admitted to knowledge of their plans. He arrived in a difficult and unco-operative mood. He could not then affect plans, but he forbade the 120 French liaison officers with the Allied command to accompany the troops to France, on the ground that they could have no function to perform, seeing that they were agents of a French authority which had not reached agreement on civil affairs. He refused to sanction the Allies' arrangements for the issue of currency in France. He refused to join in a series of broadcasts to be made on D-day by the Allied and other national leaders and only consented to broadcast at a separate time a brief statement in which he omitted any direct mention of the Allies; 'immense means of attack, that is to say, of succour for us' was his only indirect reference. 'France', he said, 'will fight this battle with fury. . . . That is how, for 1,500 years, we have won each of our victories. . . . There is no problem for our Army, Navy and Air Force. They have never been more ardent, more skilled, more disciplined.' The toil and sweat which the Allied forces had already borne and the sacrifices of blood and treasure which they were preparing to make left him unmoved. From the Allies' point of view he seemed an ungracious and lonely figure. He did nothing to relieve and much to increase the anxieties which Allied leaders bore in those troublous days. In his somewhat grandiloquent reference to the French forces he no doubt had in mind the nucleus of a reconstituted French army which had been assembled in North Africa, after the German and Italian armies had been defeated there, and had been equipped by the Allies. A corps of four French divisions was already fighting under General Alexander's command in Italy, and was later to join in the Anvil attack in the south of France together with approximately three divisions training in North Africa. The 2nd French Armoured Division under General Leclerc arrived in England at the beginning of June to take part subsequently in Overlord. A number of French naval units, including two cruisers, were under Admiral Ramsay's command, and there were several French squadrons serving in the Royal Air Force.

The administration of Civil Affairs, which must be controlled by the Supreme Commander while the German forces were being driven out of France and other enemy-occupied countries, is being discussed in a separate volume[4] and will only be mentioned in this history of the campaign when it affects military operations. But it must be noted that it was one of the semi-military, semi-political matters with which General Eisenhower was charged and in which his commanders were involved. And it was a continuing source of conflict with de Gaulle and his colleagues as long as the Allies were conducting military operations in France.

The necessity to ensure absolute security has been shown to have increased the difficulty of Allied relations with de Gaulle. Other foreign governments stationed in England or elsewhere saw the reasonableness of the ban on free communications during this critical time and accepted it after some protest with a good grace. And while all information that might point to the date and place of the coming attack was closely guarded even from our own forces, the enemy was encouraged to deduce misleading inferences from evidence provided specially for him under the cover and deception plan, Fortitude, which has already been mentioned (page 103). Arrangements to simulate preparations for a preliminary attack on Norway were carried out under the Commander-in-Chief, Northern Command, Lieut-General Sir A. F. A. N. Thorne. The assembly in Scotland of a fictitious 'Fourth Army' was indicated by a volume of contrived wireless traffic from a skeleton headquarters consisting chiefly of signals staffs and equipment. This Fourth Army was supposed to comprise three corps, some of whose units were troops that were in fact stationed in Scotland while others existed only in imagination. Troop movements and exercises, indicated chiefly by wireless traffic (conducted with some purposeful indiscretions), offered evidence of preparation for landings on the Norwegian coast, and this threat was maintained until July in order to discourage any movement of German troops from Norway to France.

Meanwhile the Allies provided similarly false indications that their main attack on the German western front was to take place about the middle of July and to be directed against the Pas de Calais coast. The imaginary force was to comprise twelve divisions and these were to be built up in France to an army of fifty divisions. To give an appearance of reality to inspired suggestions that were skilfully imparted through diplomatic, press and underground channels, the formations which were in fact disposed in east and south-east England were made to appear more formidable by a large volume of wireless traffic with other 'formations' which only existed in imagination.

---

[4] F. S. V. Donnison, *Civil Affairs and Military Government in North-West Europe* (H.M.S.O., 1961). See also Appendix VIII.

The assembly of assault forces, real and imaginary, and the development of headquarters, camps, roads, airfields and launching facilities in the south-eastern counties was done openly and in some cases on an artificially exaggerated scale, while in the south-west similar activities, wholly necessary to meet real requirements, were hidden from the enemy as carefully as possible; the enemy's situation maps giving what they believed to be the disposition of Allied forces in Britain show how far the German command was muddled. False information reinforced the Germans' long-held belief that, although the Allies might well attempt a first landing in Normandy, the main assault would be made on the Pas de Calais coast; on D-day and for weeks afterwards further steps were to be taken to sustain that belief. The failure of German Intelligence to pierce the Allies' screen of deception and security was remarkable, though their various agencies at work vied with each other in supplying Hitler with reports.

Hitler's original conviction that the Allies' main assault would be directed against the Pas de Calais, and that therefore this sector should be most strongly guarded, was shared by all the German leaders. The nearness of England to France at that point, and the fact that it opened the shortest route to the Ruhr, made its selection obvious. But just as German plans for the invasion of England in 1940 had provided for landings in more than one place, so it seemed probable to Hitler and other German leaders that the Allies would launch one or more subsidiary assaults, designed to establish bridgeheads which would require a diversion of defending troops from the area of the main assault. Not only Norway, but the Atlantic coast, even Portugal and the Mediterranean coast of France, were at times considered to be likely places for such diversionary attacks; while as early as October 1943 von Rundstedt had pointed out that 'Normandy with Cherbourg, and Brittany with Brest are additional important areas on the Channel front'. In February, Hitler grew sensitive to the danger of Allied landings in Normandy and Brittany; on March the 4th he described them as 'particularly threatened'. On May the 6th Jodl informed von Rundstedt's headquarters that Hitler attached 'particular importance to Normandy', especially the Cherbourg area, and all possible measures should be taken to reinforce that area against attack short of committing the OKW reserves. As a result, the Cotentin peninsula was reinforced by the 91st Airlanding Division, then on its way to Brittany, and by the 6th Parachute Regiment and some smaller units from elsewhere. Together with transfers already in train at the end of April, namely, the 21st Panzer Division from Brittany to Caen and the Panzer Lehr Division from Hungary to Chartres, these moves amounted to an appreciable increase of the enemy strength in Normandy.

Von Rundstedt, too, continued to recognise Normandy as in the danger zone; the preparatory Allied air attacks reinforced his view on the 24th of April that the focal point 'is still the Channel coast from the Scheldt (inclusive) to Normandy, perhaps even to Brest (inclusive)'. On the 15th of May, in his situation report, he stressed the Allies' need to win large and capacious harbours. 'Le Havre and Cherbourg are primarily to be considered for this purpose, Boulogne and Brest secondarily. The attempt to form a bridgehead rapidly on the Cotentin peninsula in the first phase would therefore seem very natural. . . .' On May the 29th von Rundstedt concluded that the Allies' disruption and destruction of the traffic network, and the cutting off of the Channel front north of the Seine from direct contact with the Seine estuary and Normandy, by the attacks on the Seine bridges, 'may indicate enemy designs on Normandy (formation of a bridgehead)'. But the Allied air forces had gained such mastery over the Channel and sea approaches to the United Kingdom that German aircraft hardly attempted to observe what was going on in harbours along the English coasts. In a report dated June the 4th Admiral Krancke, while regretting that air reconnaissance during the month of May had been insufficient to give a clear picture of the state of enemy preparations for attack on the Atlantic and Mediterranean coasts of France, wrote that he was 'doubtful whether the enemy has yet assembled his invasion fleet in the required strength'.

On June the 5th, with no fresh information on which to base an opinion, Army Group B considered that the Allied concentration of air attacks on the Channel coast between Dunkirk and Dieppe pointed to 'the previously assumed focal point of the major landing' —that is, the Pas de Calais area. On the same day, in the portion of the weekly situation report reserved for his usual carefully worded synopsis, von Rundstedt expressed the opinion that the invasion was not yet imminent. 'The systematic continuation and noticeable intensification of enemy air attacks indicate a more advanced state of readiness for the descent. The main front between the Scheldt and Normandy is still the most probable place of attack. Its possible extension along the north coast of Brittany, including Brest, is not excluded. *Where* within this entire sector the enemy will attempt a landing is still obscure. Concentration of enemy air attacks on the coastal fortifications between Dunkirk and Dieppe, and on the Seine–Oise bridges, in conjunction with the paralysing of supply services and of the southern flank between Rouen and Paris (inclusive), might be indicative of the main front of a major landing intended by the enemy. However, the cessation of traffic across the Seine would equally affect troop movements required in the case of an enemy attack on the western part of the Baie de la Seine, Normandy and the north coast of Brittany. As yet there is no immediate prospect of the invasion.'

Nor was there any indication from the German Air Force of what was to come. While Allied reconnaissance aircraft flew far and wide over north-west France on the last two days before D-day but found nothing significant to report about the moves of German armoured divisions, the enemy failed to send any reconnaissance aircraft over Britain where there was much more to discover; on June the 5th —when the whole invasion armada was at sea—only five German aircraft flew over the Channel to carry out routine runs.

The German meteorological service, unable to maintain reporting stations far out in the Atlantic, had failed to catch the significance of changes taking place and had advised that invasion after June the 4th would be impracticable for several days. Naval patrols ordered for the night of June the 5th were cancelled because of the bad weather prevailing. An army war-game exercise that was to be held at Rennes on June the 6th was not cancelled and a number of divisional and other commanders of the Seventh Army were to attend it. Local leave for officers was open.

As for Rommel, he so little feared an immediate attack that he left his headquarters in France on June the 5th to spend a night with his family in Germany on the way to visit Hitler.

CHAPTER VII

THE END OF THE BEGINNING

It was a time of mounting tension for the Services. Only comparatively few knew exactly where they were to meet the enemy and no one yet knew exactly when, but everyone realised that the meeting was near at hand. Those who bore any measure of responsibility were conscious that the vast and complicated organisation of which they were a part would only function smoothly and punctually if no factor had been overlooked, no work scamped, no link badly forged. Very soon the validity of all the forethought, labour, and long and strenuous preparation would be tested. Millions of men, thousands of aircraft and ships, and vast quantities of machines, vehicles and stores were involved and all the contrivance to bring them to battle must work as planned; there must be no breakdown on the railways, no hold-up in congested harbours, no failure of communications which were to link all together under firm control. There was a lively sense of approaching crisis.

High morale and buoyant optimism characterised all the Services. General Eisenhower and his commanders had been indefatigable in visiting both formations in training and many of the industrial concerns engaged on the production of armaments and equipment. They had sought thus to establish personal touch with the forces and to inspire them and industrial workers with a true sense of partnership in the great enterprise that lay ahead, and to give them confidence in themselves and in their leaders.

> 'So service shall with steeled sinews toil
> And labour shall refresh itself with hope.' [1]

To reach a position in which each Service was well manned and prepared had not been plain sailing. The allocation of manpower between the fighting forces and industry, and between the separate Services, had involved continuous review and regulation by the War Cabinet. Each Service had increased its claims as planning proceeded and the nature and magnitude of its tasks were defined. Each Service had its own difficulties to overcome.

Most of the officers and men of the naval forces which formed the large combatant fleet under Admiral Ramsay's command had already gained experience in the long war at sea. But the Navy had also to train additional officers and crews for the thousands of landing craft

---
[1] Shakespeare—*Henry V.*

which were to play so large a part in forthcoming operations, for naval beach parties and many other special duties. These were met partly by an increased allocation from the joint intake of men and partly by the transfer of certain soldiers and airmen to the Royal Navy. The naval allocation to Combined Operations Command for initial training was greatly increased. The Royal Marine Division, formed in 1941 for amphibious operations, was disbanded and retrained to provide crews for minor landing craft (thus freeing seamen to man larger craft such as the 'landing-craft tank' or L.C.T.), for service in the Royal Marine Armoured Support Group or in Royal Marine Commandos. A large proportion of landing-craft crews and men in ancillary services had only a brief period of training in their special duties and relatively few had any previous battle experience. It will be seen later how remarkably successful was the Navy's assimilation of such large numbers for employment on an operation that had little precedent.

As finally constituted at this time, Twenty-First Army Group was largely composed of seasoned soldiers. There were many who had fought in France four years before and come home through Dunkirk; there were men of the divisions transferred from the Mediterranean theatre[2] who had fought in North Africa, or more recently in Sicily and Italy; and there were larger numbers who, though they had not had battle experience, had by now spent several years in the Army and were trained and practised soldiers. All were self-confident and eager to match their prowess against the enemy. By transfers and promotions, available fighting experience was spread as widely as possible. A high proportion of senior commanders had experience of recent fighting and all army and corps commanders and nearly all divisional commanders had seen some fighting during the war. Their average age was forty-eight, and that of lieutenant-colonels commanding infantry battalions or holding comparable commands of armoured troops, artillery, engineers or signals was thirty-five, compared respectively with fifty-four and forty-five in the British Expeditionary Force of 1940. Because there was some shortage of junior officers 673 were lent by the Canadian Army. Most of them served in their affiliated British infantry regiments; many were awarded distinction, and 465 became casualties.[3]

To foster regimental pride and the fellowship of larger formations, regimental and formation badges were to be worn in battle, contrary to the recent practice and despite the risk that the enemy might thereby obtain useful information. The regimental spirit has always

---

[2] The following had been transferred from the Mediterranean: 7th Armoured Division; 4th and 8th Armoured Brigades; 50th and 51st Infantry Divisions; 1st Airborne Division; XXX Corps Headquarters and Corps Troops.

[3] C. P. Stacey, *The Canadian Army, 1939–1945* (Ottawa, 1948), p. 295.

been a strong characteristic of the British Army; in this war, pride in the membership of a division or corps was also notably developed.

The Royal Air Force had to face its own manpower difficulties and at times to surrender numbers to the other Services. The Second Tactical Air Force had had to convert a static air force (provided with every need and with much help from civilian labour) to a highly mobile organisation entirely dependent on Service personnel and on its own equipment. But many of the airmen engaged in Overlord had already been fighting for months—many indeed for years—over France and North-West Europe and they were full of confidence.

After months of individual and combined training forces began to concentrate on the southern and western areas. In April, Force S[4] began to move from Scotland to the Portsmouth area; Force J was already based on the Solent while Force G, which was only formed on March the 1st when the expanded scale of Neptune had been confirmed, moved from the Weymouth–Poole area to the west Solent and Southampton. The American Force O was already in the Portland area; Force U, recently formed like Force G, began to concentrate in small west country ports in March, but many of its units did not reach England until April.

On the 26th of April began a final series of exercises in which each of the five naval assault forces combined with the troops who were to be associated with it in a rehearsal exercise at full scale, under conditions resembling as closely as possible those they would face on landing in France. Each involved the assembly and loading of convoys, a sea passage attended by minesweepers, the assault of a selected shore (in some cases accompanied by bombardment with live ammunition) and a build-up of troops and vehicles over the beach. On the first of these exercises, designed for the still incomplete Force U and its associated troops, there had occurred the only serious mishap during the whole series. The escorting destroyer, *Scimitar*, was damaged in collision with an American landing ship and had put into Plymouth for temporary repairs when, soon after midnight, enemy motor torpedo-boats attacked a convoy of landing ships engaged in the exercise. The corvette, *Azalea*, which had been left in charge of the convoy, was unable single-handed to beat off the attack before two landing ships were sunk and a third damaged; and although the enemy boats were sighted and chased by destroyers they made good their escape in the darkness. Over seven hundred American men were lost and a number injured, of whom two-thirds were soldiers. A subsequent German broadcast claimed that three ships had been sunk in convoy but did not apparently connect the event with preparations for invasion.

---

[4] For reference to this and other Forces mentioned here, see diagram on page 67.

There was no enemy interference with similar assault-landing exercises on the south coast during the first week of May—at Slapton (Force O), Hayling Island (Force G), Bracklesham Bay (Force J), and Littlehampton (Force S). Admiral Ramsay temporarily assumed operational control in the Channel for the purpose of these exercises. When they were concluded the assault ships and landing craft which had for months been employed in training schemes, often under extremely severe conditions, were in urgent need of repair. A heavy burden was laid on all concerned in repair facilities along the south coast, but so well did they rise to the occasion that, when the hour struck, 97·3 per cent of British and 99·3 per cent of American craft were fit for operations—a much higher proportion than was estimated in planning.

A final conference of high-ranking officers from all three Services of both nations was held at St. Paul's School on May the 15th under the aegis of Shaef. General Eisenhower afterwards described the meeting that morning as 'packed with dramatic significance'. His Majesty the King was present and the Prime Minister. Field-Marshal Smuts and members of the War Cabinet were there too and the British Chiefs of Staff. After General Eisenhower had spoken General Montgomery outlined the intended course of the Allied armies' assault, Admiral Ramsay and Air Marshal Leigh-Mallory described the operations of naval and air forces, and British and American naval, army and air commanders elaborated the story. The speakers' mastery of complex plans and their evident assurance deeply impressed those who heard them; a sense of sober confidence pervaded the room and, at the close, this was expressed by His Majesty and by Mr. Churchill.[5]

There had been no substantial change in the Army plan (outlined in Chapter IV) to attack with five assault divisions; the diagrams at pages 172 and 189 show in more detail how those divisions would land. Each division would attack with one or more infantry brigades, augmented by additional tanks, armoured cars, artillery, engineers and vehicles drawn from corps, army and G.H.Q. troops, the enlarged brigade being known as a 'brigade group', or in the American Army as a 'regimental combat team'. This reinforcement of basic formations for battle was a characteristic of Army organisation which four years of war experience had shown to be desirable. The main structure of the Army was unchanged with its groupings in divisions, corps, armies and army groups; but although the strength of an infantry division had been increased by nearly fifty per cent since 1940, its transport more than doubled, its fire power increased several times and the wireless sets (on which its communications

---

[5] Eisenhower, *Crusade in Europe*, p. 269; and see Churchill, *The Second World War*, vol. V, p. 542 *et seq.*

ASSAULT FORCES ASSEMBLING

largely depended) multiplied tenfold, it was commonly strengthened to fight as a 'divisional group' and its brigades never went into action without additional support for their three battalions of infantry. A battalion commander in one of the assault brigade groups would be able to call on supporting artillery and machine guns, tanks of an engineer assault regiment, amphibious ('D.D.') tanks and flame-throwing tanks, as well as naval support.

The average assault brigade group would comprise five to six thousand men, of whom approximately forty per cent were infantry and commandos and the remainder gunners, engineers, tank crews, signallers, beach and medical personnel. Eight of these brigade groups, or their American equivalents, would attack the named beaches, each having two battalions in the leading wave and one following in close support; but neither they nor any other unit or formation would land complete at first. It would only be possible to accommodate all the essential men and equipment needed in the initial stages of the attack by a drastic pruning of those not immediately required. For example, an assault division would only take with it for the initial attack about forty per cent of its vehicles, and an infantry battalion in an assault brigade group only about five hundred and fifty of its eight hundred men and a minimum of essential equipment. Once the landings began, units and formations would be completed gradually as ships and craft brought in men, ammunition, equipment and stores in planned sequence. It was because this was so that the composition of every ship-load and every boat-load of the thousands that were to be continuously employed had to be planned with reference to its destination and with its task known and provided for. As for its destination, the beaches selected for attack in each named area were divided and denoted alphabetically in signal parlance. It was thus possible to calculate exactly where every particular craft should land, the time at which it should touch down, and the anticipated situation that would confront it on shore; from these data the men and material to go in it could be assembled in due order. It will be realised how much thought and labour were involved in mounting the assault with such care for detail, seeing that troops, equipment and shipping had to be matched accurately in the scattered harbours of southern England from which they were to set out.

The magnitude and complexity of the naval arrangements for the loading and assembly of the vast amount of shipping and craft involved were indicated in the outline of Neptune plans in Chapter IV (pages 66–71), and the ports from which the various naval forces were to sail are shown on the map overleaf. The following table gives some further detail of the way in which the associated forces were assembled.

	Assembly Areas
Covering forces (destroyers)	Plymouth and Portsmouth
" " (coastal)	Dartmouth, Portland, Newhaven and Dover
Landing craft of Ferry Service	Chichester, Langston, and Poole harbours
Tugs, salvage vessels, depot and accommodation ships	Ports between Falmouth and Southend
Escorts and minesweepers	With their convoys
Bombarding ships—Eastern Task Force	Clyde
Bombarding ships—Western Task Force	Belfast
Blockships (Corncobs)	Oban
Mulberry harbour units:	
Phoenix	Selsey, Dungeness and Thames
Bombardon	Portland
Whale	Solent and Selsey
Pre-loaded merchant ships:	
Stores coasters	Thames, Solent and Bristol Channel
Mechanical transport ships	London, Southend and Bristol Channel
Personnel ships	Tilbury and Bristol Channel

In May, units taking part in the assault were assembled in concentration areas, mostly south of a line from the Wash to Milford Haven, where the 'residue' of men and baggage not required for the first stage would be separated and left behind. On May the 26th troops taking part in the assault moved to marshalling areas near their ports of embarkation. There they were 'sealed' in fenced-in camps and briefing began four days before they were split up into ship and craft loads. Until then only lieutenant-colonels commanding units and one other officer from each had been informed of the plan of attack; now company commanders and equivalent ranks were told, and in the final three days before formations were split up junior officers, N.C.O.s and men were briefed. Great trouble was taken to ensure that everyone understood what his task would be in the initial assault and immediate follow-up. A large number of models, photographs and maps were provided to explain this, exact in other detail but bearing artificial names and map references; information on these two important points was still withheld for security reasons. No one could be told the date on which the assault would be launched for that was not yet decided. And no one was yet told where they were to land in France, whether the beaches they

Map Labels

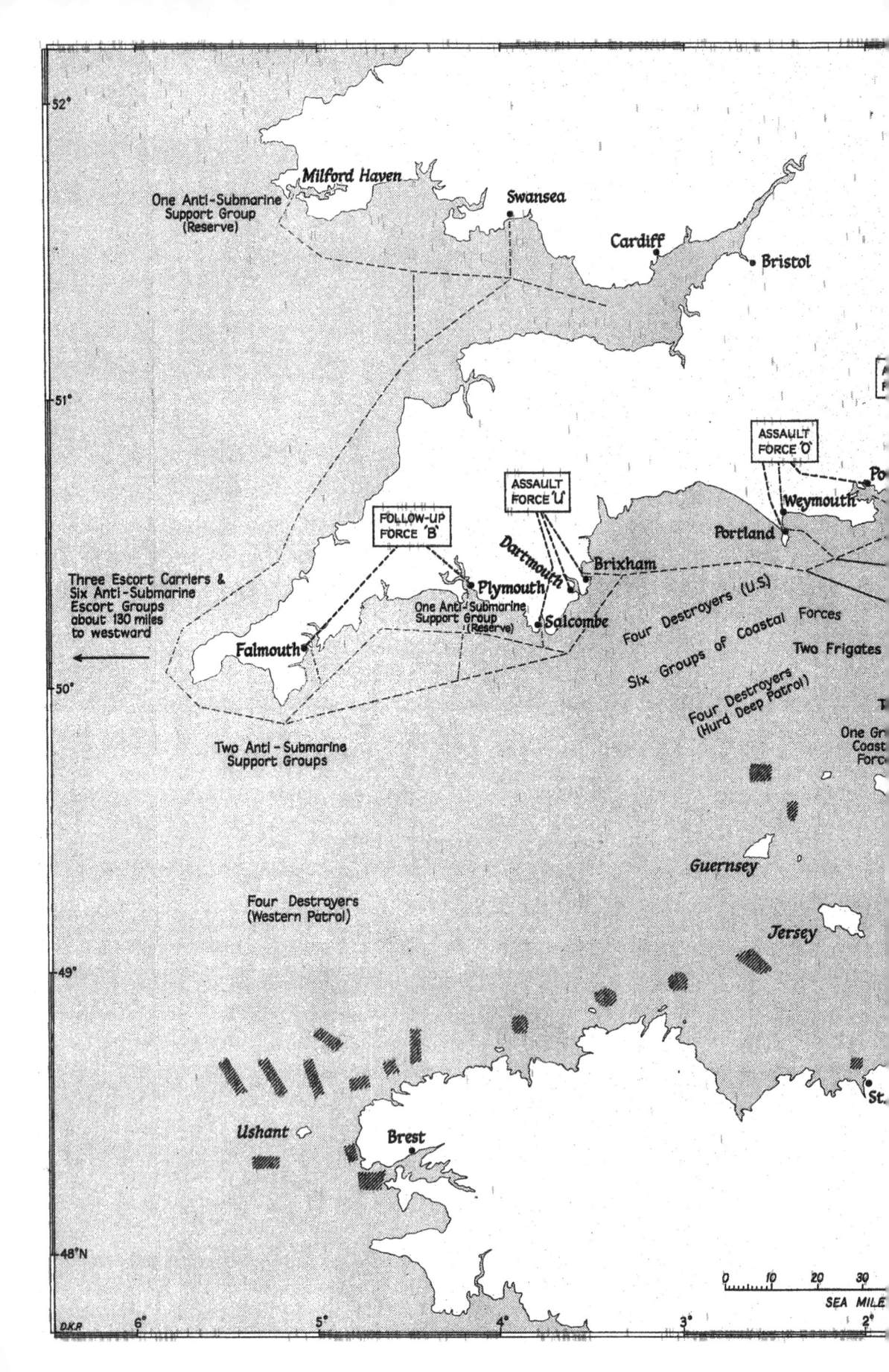

- 52°
- 51°
- 50°
- 49°
- 48°N

- Milford Haven
- Swansea
- Cardiff
- Bristol
- Falmouth
- Plymouth
- Dartmouth
- Brixham
- Salcombe
- Portland
- Weymouth
- Ushant
- Brest
- Guernsey
- Jersey

One Anti-Submarine Support Group (Reserve)

ASSAULT FORCE 'O'

ASSAULT FORCE 'U'

FOLLOW-UP FORCE 'B'

Three Escort Carriers & Six Anti-Submarine Escort Groups about 130 miles to westward →

One Anti-Submarine Support Group (Reserve)

Four Destroyers (U.S)

Six Groups of Coastal Forces

Two Frigates

Four Destroyers (Hurd Deep Patrol)

One Group Coastal Forces

Two Anti-Submarine Support Groups

Four Destroyers (Western Patrol)

0 10 20 30
SEA MILES

D.K.P.   6°   5°   4°   3°   2°

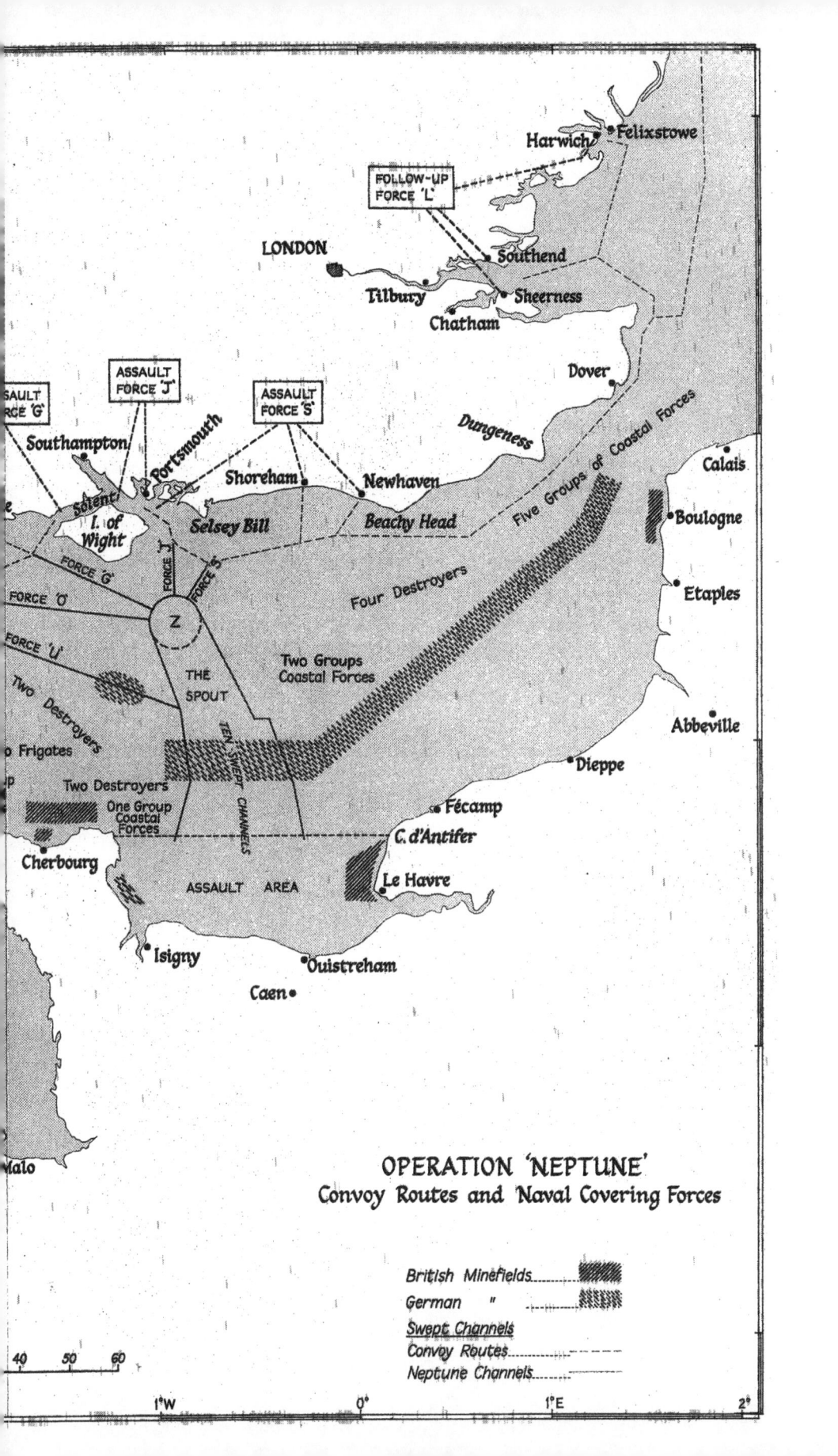

OPERATION 'NEPTUNE'
Convoy Routes and Naval Covering Forces

British Minefields
German   "
Swept Channels
Convoy Routes
Neptune Channels

were to capture were in Normandy or the Pas de Calais. They would only learn this when they were at sea, for only then would real maps be issued.

Ever since the planners had suggested the geographical limits within which an invasion of North-West Europe was considered feasible, and the probable trend of subsequent operations, the preparation of maps had begun. Before D-day about a hundred and seventy million were provided by the War Office for British and American forces, of various scales and for many distinctive uses. Some required much re-drawing of out-of-date maps, some were based on photographic survey; over two thousand were newly drawn. Special maps, diagrams and overprints were provided through collaboration of the Air Survey Liaison Section of the Royal Engineers, the Royal Air Force and the Hydrographic Branch of the Admiralty. 'Stop press' editions were published a few days before D-day for use in the final stages of briefing and assault. With all this precious and revealing information in print the fact that there was no leakage was a truly remarkable proof of good discipline and a high sense of responsibility in those who produced and handled this vast store of maps.

The final move of the assault troops was to their 'embarkation areas' at ports or 'hards'. It had long been realised that the ports available could not provide all the accommodation that would be needed for loading landing ships and craft carrying tanks and vehicles, and that sheltered beaches in their natural state would not stand up to the heavy traffic involved. So over a hundred and thirty hards had been specially constructed on selected beaches by the use of concrete and steel wire 'mattresses' which could be moved by four men; over half a million were made, for each of these hards needed on average four thousand.

Before embarkation every vehicle, tank, gun and wireless set in the assault was 'waterproofed' to prevent damage by sea water in wading ashore, often through four to six feet of water. Special solutions and other means were used to keep the sea from entering the engine or other vulnerable mechanism, and because a vehicle that had been fully waterproofed could only travel a limited distance, the considerable work involved had to be done in stages; it started in the concentration area, and was completed at the port of embarkation. Bearing in mind the huge numbers involved the magnitude of this single task may be indicated by the fact that it took about eighty-six man-hours to waterproof a single Bren carrier and two hundred and eighty-six for a tank—and after landing each vehicle had to be de-waterproofed.

While all else was now settled one important question was still in doubt, namely, how the two American airborne divisions should be used. There had never been any question that airborne troops could play a valuable and perhaps essential part in the assault; the original Cossac plan had assumed the use of two airborne divisions in the opening assault and the enlarged Neptune plan required the employment of three. There was no difficulty in finding these for there were now four airborne divisions available—two British and two American—in addition to the Special Air Service Troops comprising two British Special Air Service regiments, two French parachute battalions and independent companies of Belgian and Norwegian parachutists; there was also a brigade of Polish parachute units. The method of their employment was however conditioned in large measure by the number of transport aircraft and glider pilots that had by now been made available. Two troop carrier groups of the Royal Air Force (38 and 46) would have about 470 troop carrier aircraft and some 1,120 gliders available, and the Troop Carrier Command of the American Ninth Air Force would have 896 aircraft and 2,400 gliders. These could carry, respectively, two brigades of a British division in a first lift and the third brigade later, and the greater part of two American divisions by a first lift and the remainder later.

The rôle of the British 6th Airborne Division had been settled months before; they were to begin landing in the Caen area during the night preceding the first seaborne landings. But when it was proposed that the American 101st Airborne Division should, at the same time, begin landing behind beaches on the east of the Cotentin and the 82nd Airborne Division on the west of the peninsula, Air Marshal Leigh-Mallory expressed serious doubt as to the wisdom of the proposal. As planned it would require two long columns of towed gliders to take off in the dark, 260 to land at first light on D-day and 400 on the following morning. They would have to land in an area in which the enemy fighter and ground defence would have had time to be fully alerted and he prophesied that 'casualties will not only prove fatal to the success of the operation itself but will also jeopardise all future airborne operations'. An amended plan was subsequently agreed with General Montgomery and General Bradley, for which fewer glider-borne units would be used at the outset, parachutists of both divisions being taken in on the first night, but only 100 gliders at dawn and 200 at last light on D-day. But on May 25th it was learned that a fresh German division had arrived on the western side of the Cotentin peninsula in the area where the 82nd Airborne Division was planning to land. On learning this General Bradley proposed that the 82nd Division should be dropped some ten to twelve miles further east, alongside the 101st Division, for without the help of airborne divisions the attack on Utah would have to be abandoned. But to this Air Marshal Leigh-Mallory objected that 'if you do this operation you are throwing away two airborne divisions'. Nevertheless, General Montgomery supported General Bradley's view that airborne landings there were essential to the successful capture of the beaches on the east of the Cotentin and subsequently the decision to proceed was confirmed by Sir Arthur Tedder.

Still troubled, Air Marshal Leigh-Mallory wrote to General Eisenhower in a last attempt to get the plan changed. He pointed out that 915 aircraft (96 of them with gliders in tow) would have to fly from west to east across the Cotentin peninsula at less than 1,000 feet, at the time of the full moon and over known enemy concentrations. This would take three hours and at the end of it he doubted whether fifty per cent of the parachutists and thirty per cent of the glider loads would be effective for use against the enemy. But the Supreme Commander replied that 'a strong airborne attack in the region indicated is essential to the whole operation and must go on', though 'every single thing that may diminish these hazards' must be worked out to the last detail. It was already May the 30th when this was finally settled. After the war General Eisenhower said that he felt the burden of his responsibility even more keenly when he made this decision than he did when he decided to launch Overlord on June the 6th. In the latter case he followed the advice of experts—the meteorologists; they might be wrong, but they were the best authority available. In his decision to order the airborne operations in the Cotentin he acted *against* his Air Commander-in-Chief.

Early in May, Shaef established an advance command post for General Eisenhower conveniently near both to the battle headquarters which Admiral Ramsay had set up in the last week of April at Southwick House, Portsmouth, and to the Portsmouth Combined Headquarters. At the same time Twenty-First Army Group's main headquarters moved to the vicinity and shortly afterwards formed the tactical headquarters for General Montgomery which was to move to France as soon as a landing was effected on D-day.

That momentous date had now to be decided, and although in the course of this campaign General Eisenhower had other decisions to take of far-reaching consequence, he can hardly have had many that caused him so much anxiety as this one. For notwithstanding that he had the advice of his commanders, and of the best meteorological experts of both the British and American Services with their scientific paraphernalia for weather prediction, yet the Supreme Commander must make the final decision—the responsibility would be his and his alone. Not only the ultimate success or failure of the assault but the lives of many thousands of men would depend on his choice. He must have been very conscious of this as the time to choose drew near.

It will be remembered that certain of the conditions which must govern the choice had been decided in the earlier planning stage (page 91). The initial landings should be made soon after sunrise, on a day when at that early hour there would still be about three hours before high water; and it was desirable, if not essential, that there should be a good moon on the preceding night to facilitate accurate bombing and the landing of airborne divisions. In the first week of June, such conditions could only be fulfilled on three days—the 5th, 6th and 7th. All this was appreciated when the Neptune plans were agreed, but which of the three possible days to choose could not be decided so far ahead, for the final arbiter must be the weather. The wind must not be too strong nor the sea too rough and low cloud must not too heavily blanket the sky to allow for the planned operations of shipping and aircraft.

For convenience in long-term planning it had been decided that June the 1st would be referred to as Y-day. D-day must therefore be Y plus 4, 5 or 6 and it must be decided at latest by Y plus 2 as the machinery of assault must be set in motion two days before the event.

On May the 8th General Eisenhower decided provisionally that D-day would be Y plus 4—that is Monday, June the 5th. A signal to that effect was issued by Supreme Headquarters to the Commanders-in-Chief on May the 23rd.

No further action was called for as everything was already in train. On the receipt of this message the wheels of Neptune machinery began slowly to turn. First to move were the blockships to be sunk off the Normandy coast, which sailed south on May the 31st from the Scottish ports in which they had been made ready.

On June the 1st Admiral Ramsay assumed operational command of Neptune forces and general control of operations in the Channel.

It had been arranged that as D-day drew near General Eisenhower and his Commanders-in-Chief would meet daily, and twice daily if need be, to consider the weather forecasts. May had been consistently fine, but on Friday, June the 2nd, when they gathered at Admiral Ramsay's headquarters at Portsmouth, less favourable weather was predicted for D-day; there were indications that the relatively quiet weather which existed at that time might end about June the 6th. But the signs were not yet clear, and after discussion with his commanders General Eisenhower decided that existing orders should stand. Bombarding Force D sailed from the Clyde that evening and H.M.S. *Nelson* left Scapa for Milford Haven. Two midget submarines—X23 and X20—which were to act as markers off the French coast for Force S and Force J respectively, sailed from Portsmouth.

The mission of these tiny submarines, each manned by only two lieutenants and an engine-room artificer and each carrying a combined operations pilotage-party of two naval officers, was difficult, dangerous and responsible. They were to leave harbour before the assault forces, towed at first by trawlers; continuing the passage unescorted they were to reach the Normandy shore some twenty-four hours before anyone else. They were to identify the narrow Sword and Juno beaches—and then to submerge and lie hidden there till darkness came. On the morning of D-day, while it was still dark, they were to surface and show lights to seaward that would serve as leading marks for the assaulting craft destined to land on those beaches. These two beaches were not easy to identify. The few landmarks on the low shore would be hard to distinguish when approaching in darkness and even small inaccuracies in making a landfall might prove disastrous; for there were rocky outcrops off shore in some places and just east of Sword, where the Orne flows into the sea, mud flats stretch seaward for over a mile.

Cloud was lowering, wind increasing and the sea rising when dawn came on Saturday, June the 3rd. During the day the Western Task Force bombarding vessels sailed from Belfast and H.M.S. *Rodney* and Bombarding Forces E and K left the Clyde: late in the afternoon part of the first assault force convoys of Force U put to sea from Dartmouth, Salcombe and Brixham.

When General Eisenhower and his commanders met again at half-past nine that Saturday evening the experts' forecast for Monday was yet more pessimistic. Since Friday morning the whole meteorological situation had been growing less favourable; there had been doubt for a time as to how various factors should be weighed, but by now the unfavourable balance had swung too far to be righted by Monday; it looked as if D-day would have to be postponed. After full discussion General Eisenhower decided, however, to wait until one more report could be received.

Shortly after four o'clock on Sunday morning (the 4th) the commanders' conference met again. The forecast of worse weather on Monday was endorsed and was now too unfavourable to be ignored any longer, though outside the sky was practically clear and there was little wind. After discussion with his naval, army and air commanders General Eisenhower decided to postpone D-day for twenty-four hours. Accordingly D-day was moved forward to Tuesday, June the 6th, by the issue of a signal which meant that Overlord was postponed one day. In telegraphing his decision to the Combined Chiefs of Staff, General Eisenhower gave as his reason that approaching adverse weather conditions might make air and airborne operations impossible. He added that a second postponement of twenty-four hours might well be necessary. But any further postponement would have very serious effects. To put off the attack for one day was possible but on the following day ships already at sea would have to return to refuel and by the third day the required conditions in regard to time and tide would no longer obtain. They would not again obtain for a fortnight, even if the phase of the moon were ignored. The machinery of the assault, now wound up like a steel spring, would have to be released in that interval and rewound later. Apart from the trouble involved the risk to security would be greatly increased and acute disappointment would be likely to lower the forces' present high spirits.

On the postponement for twenty-four hours, convoys already at sea were ordered to reverse their courses and go to sheltered anchorages; those which had not yet sailed were to remain in harbour. The blockship convoys which were on passage from Scottish ports were diverted to Poole Bay and the bombarding forces already on the move reversed their courses, intending to remain at sea. Troops on craft still alongside the quays were taken on shore to stretch their legs, but those on ships which were loaded and lying at anchor remained aboard. Alternative air programmes for use in the event of postponement were put into operation. Before eleven that night the Commander-in-Chief, Portsmouth, reported that all Neptune convoys were anchored except one. This was one of the assault force convoys of Force U mentioned above as having put to sea on Saturday. It was a very large convoy, including 128 tank landing craft, nine escorts and a rescue tug; it had got some distance ahead of its planned positions and apparently missed the postponement signal issued early on Sunday morning. At nine o'clock that morning it was twenty-five miles south of the Isle of Wight and still steering for France, but within another hour it was turned back by a naval aircraft, hastily sent from Portsmouth, and was ordered to anchor and refuel in Weymouth Bay. The return progress was much delayed by the strong westerly wind and short steep sea and none of these craft were at anchor till after midnight; some did not anchor at all.

The submarines X23 and X20 had reached the French coast just before daybreak on this Sunday, the 4th of June; they have the honour of being the first of the Neptune forces to have done so. They lay at the bottom of the sea until daylight enabled them to fix their exact stations by rising to periscope depth to take bearings on the shore. There were no signs of movement on the sea around them or on land and having anchored they sank again. Throughout that day they remained on the bottom resting.

During the day the expected bad weather began to arrive. At eleven in the morning the Admiralty issued a gale warning to all shipping in the Irish Sea, and as the day wore on the weather grew worse. By half-past nine on Sunday evening, when General Eisenhower's conference met again, it was a rough and stormy night.

But while the gloom deepened outside, the spirits of those who assembled in the conference room had been dramatically raised already. During the afternoon the leaders had been told that the Chief Meteorological Officer, Shaef (Group Captain J. M. Stagg), and his colleagues now expected *better* weather on D-day. Their earlier forecast of unfavourable weather was being fulfilled near at hand (it was still raining heavily and blowing hard outside the conference room), but there had been rapid and unexpected changes over the Atlantic. A 'front' from one of the deep depressions in the north-west Atlantic had swept much further south than was expected; it was already almost over Portsmouth and would clear the Channel, at least on the English side, during the night. It would be followed by an interval of fair conditions which would last at least till dawn on Tuesday. Wind speeds and cloud should decrease. Cloud might increase after Tuesday night but there would be variable skies with considerable fair periods till Friday; it was too early to forecast conditions further ahead with any assurance, for they were likely to be unsettled by the vigorous shake-up which was taking place over the north Atlantic. Low pressure systems were forming, deepening and crossing at a rate that was more appropriate to mid-winter than to June.

Having heard the opinions of the three Service commanders, General Eisenhower decided to hold to his provisional decision that the postponed D-day would be Tuesday, June the 6th, but this would only be made firm if the new forecast still held good at four o'clock next morning. When the meeting dispersed it was blowing half a gale, low clouds swept overhead and it was still raining heavily.

If the assault were to be launched on June the 6th naval movements must begin without further delay. Admiral Ramsay therefore ordered them to proceed. The time of H-hour could now be decided. On the assault beaches in the Sword and Gold areas landings would begin at 7.25 a.m.; in Juno (where there was an off-shore shoal) at 7.35 and 7.45 a.m. The American landings were to start about an hour earlier, at 6.30 a.m., for reasons which will be noted when their landings are described. It should be remembered that British Double Summer Time was being used, and that these times for H-hour would have been two hours earlier if Greenwich Mean Time were used.[6]

The midget submarines, still believing Monday to be D-day, kept wireless watch till at one o'clock in the morning they received a wireless message that D-day had been postponed for twenty-four hours. They must lie hidden at their stations for another day.

When the conference met again at four o'clock on Monday morning Group Captain Stagg reported that he and his colleagues held

---

[6] British Double Summer Time corresponded with German Summer Time (i.e. Central European Time plus one hour).

to their more favourable forecast of the evening before. 'The fair interval, which had set in then at Portsmouth and would clear all South England during the night, would probably last till into the later forenoon or afternoon of Tuesday; conditions in this interval would be less than 5/10ths [cloud], based 2,000–3,000 feet with good visibility and wind on the coast of the assault area not more than force 3. Later in the day a period of 10/10ths with cloud base 1,000 feet would come over the area, associated with a warm front. Over Wednesday to Friday, when the front had passed, there would be an average of 7/10ths cloud based mainly at 2,000 to 3,000 feet. In this period there would be periods of 10/10ths at 1,000 feet but there would also be considerable fair to fine periods. Visibility would be good throughout and wind not above force 4 on the English side and force 2 to 3 on the French side.' It was too early to predict the weather after Friday.

The provisional decision which General Eisenhower had taken on Sunday evening had now to be confirmed or countermanded (with the serious consequences that have been described), for soon it would be too late to recall shipping already at sea and heading for the French coast. At this most critical moment the Supreme Commander did not hesitate. After hearing the views of his commanders he quickly gave the fateful order to go ahead. It was half-past four on the morning of the 5th when the date of the assault was at last 'finally and definitely settled'.

D-day would be Tuesday, June the 6th.

Once the decision was taken, the long-prepared organisation went at once into action. All along the coast of Britain a torrent of ships and craft began pouring out into the Channel. Enthusiasm was in the air; the twenty-four hours' postponement had not damped the spirits of the troops, for the signs of the last few days were unmistakable; this was clearly the real thing and not just another exercise. The sorely-tried slow groups of Force U which had already been at sea for two days were the first to move; after turning back the previous day some had had scarcely four hours' respite in the comparative calm of Weymouth Bay, others had not entered harbour at all. From east and west the great armada gathered, and once at sea the soldiers began their final briefing with the newly-opened maps which no longer bore bogus names, each man studying in detail his individual task. Grenades were primed, weapons stripped and cleaned once more and a final check made of all fighting equipment. Messages from the Supreme Commander and the respective Commanders-in-Chief, making clear the great issues at stake, were read out and were supplemented by personal messages from the several Force Commanders.

As the first British units, the leading groups of Force S, sailed from

14. Field-Marshal von Rundstedt

15. Field-Marshal Rommel

16. Field-Marshal von Kluge

17. Field-Marshal Model

18. Aircraft for the British airborne assault

PREPARATION FOR D-DAY

19. Landing craft for the naval assault

Spithead at 9 a.m. that Monday morning, June the 5th, Rear-Admiral A. G. Talbot ran up the signal 'Good luck: drive on'—and kept it flying till his flagship sailed in the evening. All day the craft streamed out from the Solent, Southampton Water and harbour and from Portsmouth (in the twenty-two square miles of the Solent there was not one vacant berth) and from Poole, Portland and Weymouth: American 'follow-up' groups started from ports further west and similar British groups from the east coast. The reserve group of Force S coming from Newhaven battled its way to the westward against a head wind and sea to join its consorts off the Isle of Wight and had a hard fight to make this westing on time.

The sailing of the British forces from the Portsmouth area proceeded smoothly. Force J and the main part of Force S from Spithead and Cowes used the Nab entrance while Force G came through the Needles channel, some craft finding difficulty in rounding the Needles in the stiff westerly weather. Force O was somewhat delayed in clearing Portland harbour by the congestion in Weymouth Bay owing to the presence of many weather-bound craft of Force U. Yet by the evening all was in order and off St. Alban's Head Rear-Admirals J. L. Hall and D. P. Moon in their respective flagships U.S.S. *Ancon* and U.S.S. *Bayfield* were joined by their bombarding squadrons which had sailed from Belfast two days earlier.

The wind, slightly south of west, was force 5 (sixteen to twenty miles an hour) with a moderate sea and a slight swell, severe conditions for the heavily laden landing craft and their complement of soldiers and sailors, but in the words of Rear-Admiral Sir Philip Vian, who commanded the Eastern Task Force, 'their spirit and seamanship alike rose to meet the greatness of the hour and they pressed forward in high heart and resolution; there was no faltering and many of the smaller craft were driven on until they foundered'. As the meteorologists had predicted, the early bleak conditions improved as the day wore on. The wind veered to N.N.W., both wind and sea decreased slightly and the clouds lifted before evening.

The protective measures which had been and were being taken by naval and air forces have already been indicated in Chapter V; the anti-submarine patrols between south Ireland and Brittany, over coastal waters used by the assault forces, and in the Channel on either flank of the ships in passage, are shown on the maps at pages 76 and 136. The anti-submarine patrols in the main area of U-boat threat, the south-west approaches, were carried out by squadrons of Coastal Command, while their twin-engined aircraft helped in protecting the assault convoys against attacks by E-boats[7] and other enemy light surface craft. Cover for squadrons engaged in operations

---

[7] The term E-boat, as used in contemporary British reports, covered not only the German motor torpedo-boats but various other types of small surface craft.

near the French coast was provided by fighters of Air Defence of Great Britain, and for convoys, sailing along the south coast of England to the assembly points for the assault, by squadrons of the Fleet Air Arm under the operational control of Coastal Command. At four o'clock that afternoon, as the ships were about to turn towards France, four groups of Lightnings from the U.S. Eighth Air Force flew out to cover their passage. They maintained patrols till half-past eight, when their place was to be taken by three groups of the U.S. Ninth Air Force. From ten o'clock until the sun rose on D-day night-fighters patrolled over the shipping lanes and assault area.

For the passage each British assault force was organised into sixteen or eighteen groups according to the speed of the various units and their intended times of arrival in the assault area; the Americans favoured a larger grouping, planning that only craft required in the opening phase should arrive on the first tide. Rear-Admiral Moon with Force U had perhaps the most exacting task. It had by far the greatest distance to cover from its embarkation ports. It was the last to be formed, the craft assigned to it had only recently arrived in England and in many cases had had practically no special training; owing to the limited resources of the west country, its 865 ships and craft had to be loaded and sailed from nine different ports in twelve convoys, assembling and meeting their escorts in most cases at sea.

Forces J, G and O made for the rendezvous in Area Z south-east of the Isle of Wight. From there they continued in a south-easterly direction to the northern end of the group of approach channels, through the enemy minefields in mid-Channel, to the assault area. The minesweeping flotillas were already busy cutting ten lanes for the safe passage of the convoys, a fast and a slow lane for each of the five assault forces—the group of channels known as the Spout. Force S, having to pick up its group from Newhaven, kept slightly to the east of Area Z, while for Force U on the west a special channel was swept to the northern end of the Spout to shorten the distance its convoys had to travel. On June the 4th just after the postponement signal had led to the turning back of the Force U convoys, the minesweepers had discovered newly laid mines south of the Isle of Wight. On his own initiative their commanding officer had remained to sweep and buoy a channel through this dangerous area, destroying seven mines. Force U now passed through safely, but the minefield claimed the first casualty of the operation—the U.S. minesweeper *Osprey*.

The leading groups pressed steadily on and were entering the Spout before darkness fell to cloak their further advance, by this time pointing directly to the Normandy coast. During the afternoon Admiral Vian in his flagship H.M.S. *Scylla* closed the various groups and judged that the larger landing craft should have no great difficulty in keeping up, but for the minor landing craft and the Rhino ferries in tow it was a question which time alone would answer.

Meanwhile, minesweeping operations were going almost precisely as planned in spite of unexpectedly strong tidal streams. The leading fleet minesweepers were protected by minesweeping motor launches of shallow draft ahead of them and two mines were cut by them in Channel 7 ahead of the flotilla leaders. The intricate business of changing over sweeps at the turn of the tide was safely accomplished by all flotillas, even though two of them were forced to do so while actually in a minefield. A total of twenty-nine mines were cut in Channels 2, 6 and 7, while in Channel 5 sweep-cutters were encountered but no mines. Equally important was the buoying of the safe channels with lighted dan-buoys and this too was admirably done by the danlayers. All these activities were completely disregarded by the enemy, even though one flotilla was in sight of the French coast near Cap Barfleur by 8 p.m. and two hours later, despite the gathering dusk, could distinguish individual houses ashore. Only then could the sweepers turn back to carry out the process of 'wasting time' while the leading slow convoys overtook them.

The convoys in general found little difficulty in locating the swept channels, the entrance to each of which was pointed by a motor launch, but a few mistakes were made. Four groups of Force J and one of Force S entered the wrong channels, all to the westward of the correct ones, but without immediate inconvenience to the proper users. Later the importance of the error was shown, for when approaching the assault area in the early morning they had to cross over to the eastward to regain position and in consequence some of them were too late to take their planned place in the assault. The American forces had a similar experience, but such divergencies were no more than was to be expected with slow-moving craft, navigating in heavy weather and in a strong cross tide. Some groups were forced to steer as much as forty degrees off their true course to allow for the tidal set, and station keeping in the dark was very difficult. The tail of the long columns trailed down tide, but although some of those in the rear were carried out of swept water no harm resulted. Apart from the U.S.S. *Osprey*, already mentioned, the only casualties due to mines at this stage were the British destroyer *Wrestler* and one tank landing craft belonging to a later convoy in Force L. The *Wrestler* had been rounding up stragglers in unswept water in order to further their punctual arrival. At 6.45 a.m. on the 6th she was mined while a short distance outside channel, but managed to limp back to Spithead.

At battle headquarters Admiral Ramsay and his staff were closely watching progress. Before midnight he felt able to report that although conditions in the Channel were unfavourable only a few major craft were falling astern and a number of small craft in tow had been cast adrift; the assault forces in general were conforming to the plan.

Three miles from the French shore the two midget submarines surfaced just before midnight, having lain all day on the sea bottom in eleven fathoms. Soon after surfacing they received a wireless signal confirming the earlier message that the assault would take place next day. Then they bottomed again to wait till they should show lights to guide in-coming craft.

CHAPTER VIII

D-DAY: AIRBORNE ASSAULT AND OPENING BOMBARDMENT

> 'Twas on a Summer's day—the sixth of June—
> I like to be particular in dates,
> Not only of the age, and year, but moon;
> They are a sort of posthouse where the Fates
> Change horses, making History change its tune,
> Then spur away o'er Empires and o'er States.'
> Byron—*Don Juan*.

IN the middle of the night, when the leading ships were steadily nearing the coast of France, British and American airborne divisions began their flight to the scene of battle. The British 6th Airborne Division's task was to seize and hold the Orne bridges between Caen and the sea, to deny the enemy use of the country between the Orne and the Dives and to silence a battery which threatened the left flank of the seaborne landings. To soldiers of the division this meant that they were to be flown through the windy night until, on an order, they must jump into darkness which shrouded both the ground below and the enemy who held it, or must land in a glider to meet they knew not what unseen obstructions or German troops. From their training they knew full well the hazards involved; their courage is the more noteworthy.

Two brigades of the division were to carry out the first operations in darkness before the seaborne landings began—an advanced guard of the British armies which were to fight their way to victory. The 5th Parachute Brigade were to capture and hold the Orne crossings while, to the east and south of them, the 3rd Brigade Group were to cut the bridges carrying roads over the Dives, by which the enemy might bring up troops to attack the British left flank, and occupy high ground from which they would command these approaches; they were also to capture the battery near Merville referred to below (page 154). In each case advance parties would land by parachute or glider at a selected 'dropping zone'; with them would go 'pathfinders' to mark the zone by lights for the guidance of following aircraft when they flew in the main bodies in two successive waves.

When darkness fell on this evening before D-day, 38 and 46 Groups of the Royal Air Force had formed up on airfields south of Oxford to carry the soldiers to Normandy. The map at page 212 shows the dropping zones for which they were destined—'N' near Ranville, 'K' near Touffreville and 'V' near Varaville. The first was to be used by the 5th Brigade, the other two by the 3rd Brigade, and both brigades' pathfinders and advance parties were timed to drop at twenty minutes after midnight; the second wave would take about twenty minutes to land the main bodies and was timed to begin dropping them at a quarter to one; the third wave, with divisional headquarters, heavy engineering equipment, anti-tank guns, bulldozers, jeeps and other stores would land about two hours later at twenty past three. It would be dark till about five o'clock, for it must be remembered that the Allies were using double summer-time: the sun would not rise until about five minutes to six. Since the two brigades had objectives which were not directly connected they must be separately described, but it should be borne in mind that their actions were taking place at the same time.

From Caen—past Ouistreham to the sea—runs the river Orne: beside it, five hundred to a thousand yards away, the Caen Canal follows a parallel course. The only road which crosses these waterways is carried by twin bridges at Bénouville on the west and Ranville on the east; from there, at Hérouvillette, it joins the road from le Havre to Caen via Houlgate and Cabourg. The task of the 5th Brigade was to capture these Bénouville and Ranville bridges, to establish bridgeheads on both and to clear and protect the nearby dropping zone N, so that further airborne troops could be landed there later in the night and next evening.

A *coup de main* party consisting of five platoons of the 2nd Oxfordshire and Buckinghamshire Light Infantry and thirty officers and men of the 249th Field Company, Royal Engineers, crossed the French coast in six Horsa gliders a few minutes after midnight; there the gliders were released. 'Everything was so quiet that it seemed we were merely carrying out an exercise over England.' The first three gliders landed on time and, although it was dark, in exactly the right place. The nose of the first was in the barbed wire round the German post guarding Bénouville bridge and the second and third within a hundred yards. The bridge was rushed and captured intact though the leading platoon commander was killed. Two of the other gliders landed a hundred and fifty yards from the Ranville bridge and also quickly captured it. Within fifteen minutes both were in our hands. They were checked by the engineers and found free from explosives, but it remained to prove whether they could be held till troops of the main body arrived, for the enemy occupied the villages of Bénouville and Ranville on either flank. There was a good deal of sniping and shortly afterwards a patrol of three tanks approached but withdrew after the leader had been hit and set on fire by a Piat. The German officer in charge of the bridge defences drove up in a car and was taken prisoner: other prisoners taken came from the 736th Grenadier Regiment of the 716th Infantry Division.

While this well executed *coup de main* was in progress the sixth glider of the party had been released too far east and had landed some eight miles away and the drops of the pathfinders and the advance parties on the nearby zone N were less successful. The men were heavily laden with equipment, weapons and ammunition and so encumbered the rate of their release from moving aircraft was in some cases slower than had been calculated. As a result they were widely dispersed across the south-east corner of the area. The position was complicated by the fact that a pathfinder party of the 3rd Brigade destined for K was dropped by mistake on N, set up guiding lights and began sending the code-letter K thinking that they were there; more troops of the 3rd Brigade followed them before the mistake was rectified.

The 5th Brigade consisted of the 7th, 12th and 13th Parachute Battalions and within half an hour all but five of their hundred and twenty-nine aircraft had dropped their troops, though not all in the right places. For again they were dispersed and had to search the darkness both for equipment-containers and for the rendezvous. By half-past one about half of the 7th Battalion, and a detachment of the 591st Parachute Squadron, Royal Engineers, had reached the rendezvous, and although without most of their machine guns, mortars and wireless sets they went to reinforce the troops that had seized the Bénouville bridges. There was confused and continuous fighting round the nearby village and le Port. The regimental aid post was at one point overrun by the enemy; the medical officer was missing and the chaplain killed. Fighting was still going on when day broke, but the bridgehead was held.

The 12th Battalion had set out in thirty-two aircraft. Fifteen loads were dropped accurately, seven were within a mile of the area, the rest were widely dispersed. The battalion was to hold the approaches to the Ranville bridge from the east and by four o'clock had occupied le Bas de Ranville, having taken prisoners from the 736th Grenadier Regiment. The 13th Battalion was to protect, clear and improve landing strips on zone N in conjunction with a detachment of the 286th Field Park Company and the 591st Parachute Squadron of the Royal Engineers who had come with them, and to complete the bridgehead by clearing and capturing Ranville itself. By four o'clock they had done so, prisoners having come from the 125th Panzer Grenadier Regiment of the 21st Panzer Division stationed south-east of Caen. Landing strips were ready by three-thirty when the third wave began to arrive. Of sixty-eight Horsa gliders which had brought them from England, fifty were released over the landing area with few casualties, though twenty-five aircraft had been damaged by flak as they came in. Either the tow ropes of those missing had parted or they had been cast off in the low cloud which now obscured the coast of France.

Major-General R. N. Gale commanding the division, with some of his headquarters, had arrived with the third wave, bringing heavy engineer stores and equipment and guns of the 4th Airlanding Anti-tank Battery, Royal Artillery. Nine 6-pounders and two 17-pounders were soon in position. The commander of the 5th Brigade had flown in with the main body two hours before, and when he met General Gale he was able to report that the Orne bridges had been captured and bridgeheads were being held.

The main body of the division's 3rd Brigade was by this time disposed in or making for positions on the ridge of high ground which runs from Sallenelles to Troarn along the west side of Bavent woods; but a great deal had happened before this. For the brigade's three battalions—the 8th and 9th Parachute Battalions and the 1st Canadian Parachute Battalion—and the 3rd Parachute Squadron, Royal Engineers, had carried out five widely separated tasks while the 5th Brigade was capturing and consolidating their hold on the Orne bridges. Taking first the actions of the 8th Battalion; it was to land further south near Touffreville in zone K and from there to cover the engineers while they destroyed the bridges over the river Dives at Troarn and Bures. Unfortunately the battalion was split in the early drops. As mentioned above, half the pathfinders and advance party and some of the following second wave troops landed in error on zone N three miles away to the north. In both cases too there was a good deal of dispersion and loss of equipment. Those landed correctly on zone K included the battalion commander, who had only been able to assemble about a hundred and sixty men and had ascertained by reconnaissance and the questioning of local residents that Escoville, Sannerville and Troarn were all occupied by German troops. There was a good deal of sporadic enemy fire and his battalion was clearly not yet strong enough to attack Troarn, so he concentrated his small force on high ground to the south-west of Bavent woods to cover the party who were blowing the Bures bridge.

The troops which had been landed by mistake in N zone had meanwhile congregated in two parties—the mortar officer and about sixty men of the battalion in one, and in the other Major J. C. A. Roseveare with about sixty of his sappers of the 3rd Parachute Squadron, four or five hundred pounds of explosive and demolition equipment in six trolleys, and a jeep and trailer with medical stores. Twenty or thirty infantry of the battalion also joined his party and marching south-east by different ways the two parties met on the high ground on the west of Bavent woods. Here the infantry were left to form a firm base, the main body of sappers and most of their

THE DIVES AND MERVILLE

material were sent to blow the Bures bridge, while Major Roseveare with an officer and seven sappers remained. They reloaded the jeep and trailer with the rest of the demolition equipment and, crowding into them, the audacious party of nine set out to blow the Troarn bridge.

The road into the village had been blocked by the garrison and the jeep ran into a barbed wire knife-rest from which in the darkness it took them twenty minutes to cut their way clear. While they did so a scout who had been sent forward shot a German cyclist and this roused the garrison. When the jeep entered the village 'the fun started as there seemed to be a Boche in every doorway shooting like mad'. The sappers fired back as well as they could from the swaying overloaded jeep and trailer as, gathering speed, they careered through the village down the road which falls steeply to the river. One man with a Bren gun who had been covering their rear from the trailer was missing when they reached the bridge but no one else had been hit and a wide gap was quickly blown in the centre span. Then, abandoning the jeep and swimming a number of small streams, they went northwards across country to rejoin the men who meanwhile had blown the bridge at Bures. When day broke the 8th Battalion's first tasks were accomplished and they were disposed on the ridge down the western side of the Bavent wood.

Further north the drop intended for the Varaville zone V fared badly. The advance party was larger than the others, for it included a company of the 1st Canadian Parachute Battalion to capture an enemy headquarters and signal station before the main body arrived. Most of the company were landed west of the Dives, but again they had exit troubles and other misfortunes. One of the pathfinder parties made a good landing and had a beacon light in position for the main body; the other was about a thousand yards away, and though some of the men reached the area later, nearly all their equipment was lost among flooded dykes near the river. The main body when it began coming in at about a quarter to one was no more successful. Just before they arrived Bomber Command had made a heavy attack on the battery near Merville and dust and smoke added to the clouds which obscured the approach to the landing area. Only one of eleven gliders landed in the right place and less than half of their parachute aircraft dropped their loads on the zone or within a mile of it; several loads were dropped in flooded ground on either side of the Dives, more than two miles away.

The advance company of Canadians with some sappers of the 3rd Parachute Squadron blew the Varaville bridge and attacked the nearby headquarters in a château defended by a 75-mm gun in a pill-box and surrounded by weapon pits, mines and wire. The château was cleared, the gatehouse taken and the pill-box closely invested, and three sections of enemy infantry who had tried to reinforce it were killed or captured; but the Canadians had considerable casualties and the pill-box was not taken before daylight came. The nearby woods were full of snipers; three were shot by a Frenchman who had collected a red beret and rifle in the fight. Other French civilians helped by tending the wounded. The brigade commander and his headquarters then moved on towards le Mesnil. Meanwhile other men of the Canadians were making their way to Robehomme on the Dives and by six-thirty about sixty had collected. The demolition material had not arrived but with the help of an engineer sergeant and explosives carried by the infantry, enough was made up to put the bridge out of action. Then a position was taken up on the hill which overlooks the river and road with a good observation post in the church tower.

The fifth of the 3rd Brigade tasks, and a very stiff one, fell to the 9th Parachute Battalion; it was to destroy the enemy battery just clear of the woods to the south of Merville–Franceville Plage. This was thought to contain four guns that could dominate the most easterly beach on which the British 3rd Infantry Division was to land. They must therefore be destroyed before daylight, when the seaborne landings would begin. The guns were in steel-doored concrete emplacements six feet thick, two of which were also covered by twelve feet of earth. They were in a fenced area of seven hundred by five hundred yards within which was a belt of barbed wire, double in places, fifteen feet thick and five feet high. An anti-tank ditch was incomplete but mines had been sown profusely and there were a dual-purpose gun position and about fifteen weapon pits. Outside the main position was a wired-in strong-point with five machine-gun emplacements and several other anti-aircraft gun positions. Not only would brave and resolute men be needed to destroy the battery but also equipment to deal with obstacles and minefields and to blow up the guns. And the drop, assembly, march from Varaville and capture of the battery must all be done in the four and a half hours of darkness which remained before the seaborne landings began. It was intended to use a small reconnaissance party and three companies. One company was to hold a firm base on which to rally and make a diversion against the main entrance, one to breach the defences, one to assault, and a party in three gliders was to crash-land on the battery as the assault went in.

The reconnaissance party dropped accurately twenty minutes after midnight with the pathfinders and the former set off for the Merville battery at once. But only half of the three companies dropped within a mile of the rendezvous. Moreover, the mine-detectors and marking tape and much other equipment were lost in marshy land. At five minutes to three the commanding officer marched with a hundred and fifty men. No engineers had reached them and they had no engineer stores, mortars or anti-tank guns; one Vickers machine gun and twenty Bangalore torpedoes[1] were all they had besides their personal weapons.

On reaching the position it was found that the reconnaissance party had done their work well. Having cut the outer wire they had marked with their feet paths through the minefield to the inner fence and had neutralised a number of trip-wire booby-traps. On hearing this seven parties were formed: two to breach the main wire, four to make for the four guns and one to make the diversionary attack on the main entrance. At this moment two of the Albemarles towing gliders which were intended to make a crash-landing on the battery arrived and circuited low over the position. It was hard to locate in darkness for the troops had not been able to put out lights; both pilots of the Albemarles took great risks while flying around to look for it. Eventually the gliders were released; they landed about two hundred yards away and their troops were at once involved in fighting in the outer defences. But gaps in the wire had been blown and the assault parties made for the guns; the breaching parties joined them and the diversionary party forced the main gate. After a short sharp fight the garrison were overcome and the guns (found to be 75-mm) were put out of action. The success signal was sent up at quarter to five and the battalion signal officer took a somewhat ruffled pigeon from his pocket and released it to carry the news to England.

Eighty survivors of this stout-hearted band rallied at the firm base. Of the five officers and sixty-five other ranks who were casualties, the wounded were left in a nearby building under the care of two medical orderlies and a captured German doctor. A party of the 1st Canadian Parachute Battalion came up and acted as rearguard to the little column which marched away to the 9th Battalion's next objective—high ground near le Plein.

Before continuing the story a provisional assessment may be made of the 6th Airborne Division's achievement by the time that daylight relieved something of the strain they had been bearing. All their primary tasks had been accomplished. The bridges over the Orne had been captured and bridgeheads on both sides were being held and strengthened. To the east three bridges over the Dives had been cut, at Troarn, Bures and Robehomme, and a fourth over the tributary stream near Varaville. The battery at Merville had been put out of action and troops of the 3rd Brigade were disposed at a number of places on the high ground which runs from le Plein to

---

[1] A Bangalore torpedo is a prepared charge for making a gap through a wire obstacle. It consists of 5-foot lengths of 2-inch pipe, filled with explosive, which are joined together and pushed through the obstacle. When exploded it blows a gap about 12 feet wide.

Troarn, in positions to delay, even if not strong enough to prevent, an enemy attack on the left flank of the British assault. Out of 264 parachute aircraft despatched from England only seven were missing: and out of 98 gliders twenty-two. On the other hand, many were landed in the wrong places. Exact figures are not obtainable but it is thought that not more than sixty per cent (and possibly less) of the four thousand eight hundred who were landed in France were able to join in the early operations described. Similarly a large proportion of equipment was released—17 anti-tank guns, 44 jeeps, 55 motor cycles and 1,214 containers—but not all was recovered at the time; some was retrieved when men who had failed to join up in darkness were able to do so later. The risks taken and the losses incurred may well be considered to have been justified by the measure of safety assured to the left flank of the seaborne troops. It was due to the courage of those who took part in the airborne operations and fought in darkness on this memorable morning. And among those it may not be thought invidious to notice especially the men of the Glider Pilot Regiment. They had to land their precious charges in the dark, in some places where the enemy had planted high stakes ('Rommel's asparagus') on purpose to destroy them. Of 196 employed 71 were casualties. Many of those who landed safely joined in the fighting which followed.

While the 6th Airborne Division was thus engaged on the left flank of the British assault the American 82nd and 101st Airborne Divisions were in action in the Cotentin peninsula behind the right of the American sector. They had a more ambitious and in some respects a more difficult programme, for double the number of troops were to be dropped, not in such open, hedgeless country as is found eastward of the river Orne but among the close hedgerows which characterise the Normandy *bocage* and in an area constricted by extensive floods. Moreover, German troops were in the vicinity in greater numbers and 'all units in the Cotentin had been briefed to expect airborne operations'.[2]

Put shortly, the rôle of the American airborne divisions was to aid the assault of the United States First Army and facilitate the capture of the Cotentin peninsula. The 101st Airborne Division was to secure the western exits of the flooded area behind Utah beach and the line of the river Douve on the north side of Carentan, to capture Carentan and join up with the troops landing on Omaha beach. The 82nd Airborne Division, dropping further inland astride the river Merderet, was to seize Ste. Mère Eglise and bridgeheads over the river to facilitate a subsequent thrust across the Cotentin by forces landed at Utah.

---

[2] G. A. Harrison, *Cross-Channel Attack* (Dept. of the Army, Washington, D.C., 1951), p. 278.

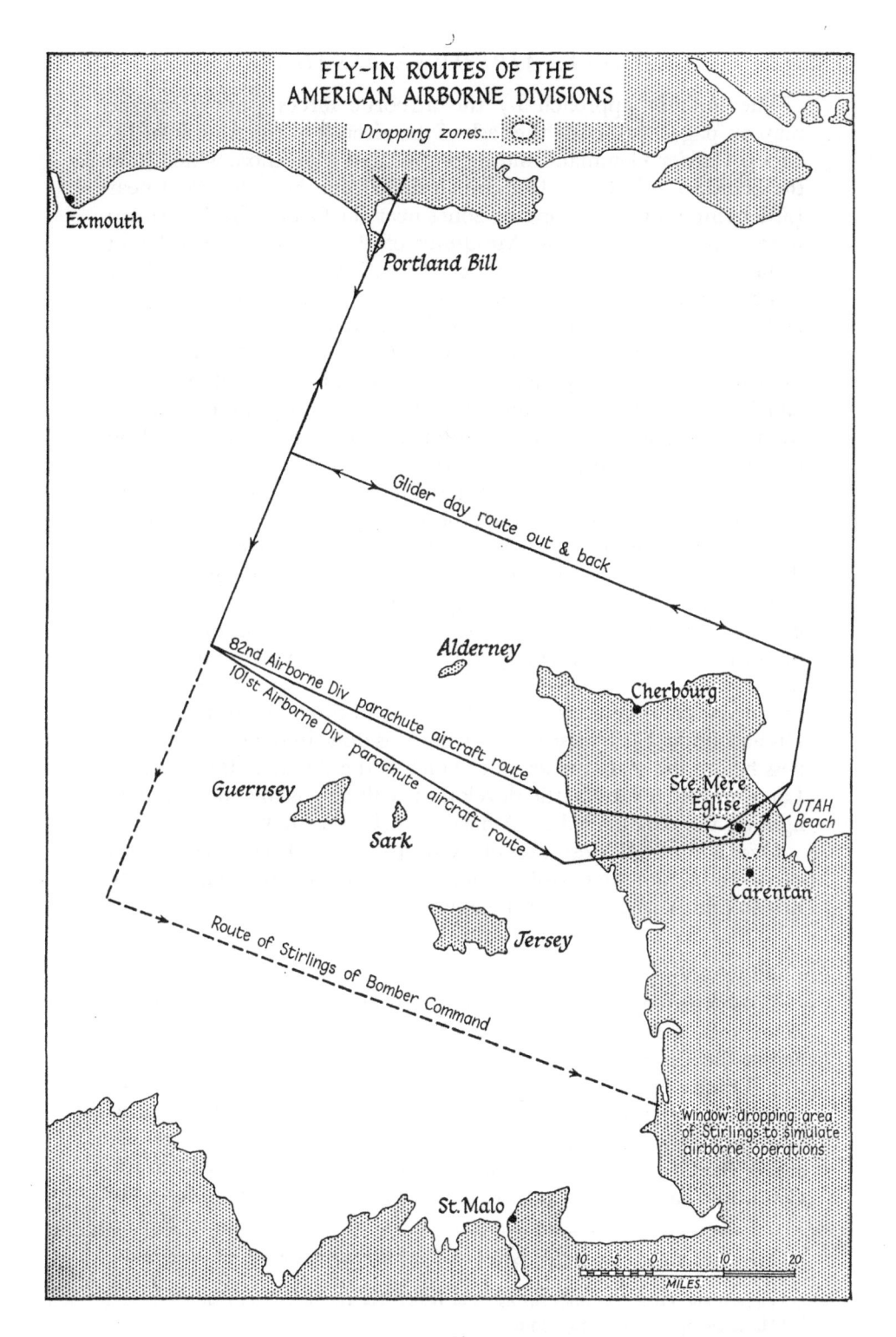

FLY-IN ROUTES OF THE AMERICAN AIRBORNE DIVISIONS

158 D-DAY: AIRBORNE ASSAULT

The indirect approach by the airborne forces (shown on the map on page 157) made the task of the aircraft of the American IX Troop Carrier Command more complicated than those which bore the British 6th Airborne Division straight from the south coast near Littlehampton to the dropping zones near the Orne. The Americans were protected *en route* by Mosquitos of the Air Defence of Great Britain and their passage was masked from enemy radar by Stirlings of Bomber Command, dropping 'window',[3] which preceded them and went further south to simulate diversionary landings. But when the airborne forces turned east near the Channel Islands and crossed the Cotentin coast they met heavy anti-aircraft and small-arms fire and thick cloud; 'formations tended to break up, and even the trained pathfinders experienced difficulty in identifying their drop targets ... The main drops ... were generally scattered.'[4]

The American historian states that 'Records of airborne operations in the Cotentin are very sketchy: those of the 101st Airborne Division in particular are all but useless'. The account he gives is, he says, 'based on a set of comprehensive interviews ... with officers and men of the airborne units', subsequently developed in a number of battalion and regimental studies. 'The first actions of all airborne units in the Cotentin on D-day were attempts by small groups of men to carry out in the fog of the battlefield their own portion of the assigned plan. There could be little over-all direction from above.'[5] His account does not distinguish what was done in the hours of darkness before the seaborne assault, which is the theme of this chapter. Later on, when their battle develops, it will be possible to gain more light on the part played by American airborne troops.

Over a hundred Mosquitos of 2 Group, Second Tactical Air Force, carried out offensive patrols throughout the night, covering both the British and American airborne operations.

To complete the story of this night it is necessary to go back to the hours around midnight when the assault fleet was ploughing its way across the Channel and the airborne divisions were being carried into France and the heavy bombers of Bomber Command were setting out to attack ten of the enemy's most formidable coastal batteries—map at page 168. The first three of these—near Merville east of the Orne and at Fontenay and St. Martin de Varreville in the Cotentin—had to be attacked early, for soon after midnight the

---

[3] Metallised strips of paper dropped from aircraft in order to confuse the enemy radar defences.
[4] Craven and Cate, *The Army Air Forces in World War II*, vol. III, p. 188.
[5] Harrison, op. cit., pp. 278, 279 n. 26.

airborne troops would be landing in their vicinity; the remaining seven—at la Pernelle, Maisy, Pointe du Hoe, Longues, Mont Fleury, Ouistreham and Houlgate—were to be bombed between quarter past three and five o'clock so that their defenders would have little time to recover before the naval bombardment opened with the coming of daylight. Altogether over five thousand tons of bombs were dropped by 1,056 Lancaster, Halifax and Mosquito aircraft, an average of about a hundred aircraft and five hundred tons for each battery; eleven aircraft and seventy men were lost. Flares and the glow of explosions from these attacks were increasingly visible to the oncoming ships. All night the latter pursued their arduous way. Conditions at sea had somewhat worsened and to the troops on board, waiting in the acute discomfort of throbbing, labouring ships and lashed by the cold spray driving across their decks, the night seemed interminable. The hours passed slowly in growing tension and the chill of suspense; to many who suffered the sheer misery of sea-sickness, their present ordeal seemed to them less bearable than what lay ahead. Seldom have modern armies gone straight into battle from such uncomfortable conditions, yet seldom have troops set out with more ardent spirit or higher morale. Physically and mentally they were in fine training, and if the night seemed long while they could only wait for it to end, their discomfort would soon be forgotten when day called them to action.

One thing was puzzling commanders. It has already been mentioned that before darkness had fallen on this historic night some of the Allies' minesweepers could have been seen off the coast of Normandy and already the assault fleet was at sea. During the few dark hours of the early morning thousands of ships and craft of many sorts were streaming across the Channel, thousands of airborne soldiers were landing in France, and a thousand or more heavy bombers were plastering key points in the Atlantic Wall. Yet the enemy made no sign at all. His complete inactivity at sea and in the air was disconcerting, even sinister. Had he something unforeseen up his sleeve? Apparently the Allies had again won tactical surprise as they had done in the landings in Sicily and at Anzio. They had indeed been at great pains to do so in the preparatory operations already described. Now, while two squadrons from 100 Group of Bomber Command fitted with radar jamming equipment masked the enemy's coastal radar warning system, further deceptive measures were being taken. To confuse the enemy's reading of the British and American airborne landings, dummy landings were being made at Maltot south-west of Caen and at Marigny west of St. Lô; and a third was being made at Yvetot, twenty miles inland of the coast between Dieppe and le Havre, to supplement naval and air operations and suggest that an Allied attack was impending north of the Seine. Four squadrons of Bomber Command carried out these diversions, dropping large quantities of 'window', dummy parachutists and fireworks which sounded like rifle and gun-fire. About midnight two other misleading operations began up-Channel. Off the Pas de Calais feint attacks were made against suitable beaches near Boulogne by six harbour-defence motor launches of the Dover Command and a squadron of Bomber Command. The radio counter-measures of the motor launches, towing balloons with reflectors and using special equipment and smoke, and of the aircraft dropping 'window', were intended to emulate the echoes that would be received by radar from large ships and give the impression of an approaching convoy; other aircraft patrolling in the Somme area and also using window would suggest the presence of a large air force to give top cover for the shipping. The ruse had some measure of success for the enemy's shore guns and searchlights were turned on the imaginary convoy and for three hours before daylight his night fighters hunted for the ghost air force.

A similar combined feint was made off the coast further south between Dieppe and le Havre by eight motor launches of the Portsmouth Command and a squadron of Lancasters. The aircraft, forming a 'box' twelve miles wide by eight miles deep which approached the coast at convoy speed, dropped window as they circuited. The aim was to disguise the true left flank of the Allies' actual assault and in this case there was no visible reaction. Nor can the effectiveness be measured separately of a third deceptive action down-Channel in which four motor launches under the naval commander of Force U, and aircraft of Bomber Command, operated about six miles off Cap Barfleur to distract the attention of the enemy's radar installation at the north-east of the Cotentin. Apart from these deceptive operations and the air forces' direct attacks on the enemy's chain of radar stations, two hundred and sixty-two ships and craft employed in the assault were fitted with specially-designed radar jammers to avoid early detection by any remaining enemy radar stations and to distract their attention from the approaching ships. This jamming barrage was also planned to prevent the enemy from using radar to control his coastal batteries, a measure of protection which was vitally important to the successful operation of battleships, cruisers and monitors in the bombardment of enemy defences. It was too early to know how all these measures affected the enemy's conduct, but his inactivity certainly appeared to show that he did not yet appreciate what was happening.

At eight minutes past five a green light showed to seaward off Sword beach and shortly afterwards a second appeared off Juno

20. Enemy beach obstacles

21. Engineer tanks of the 79th Armoured Division

22. Mine-clearing (flail) tank

23. Gliders near Ranville

AIRBORNE ASSAULT

24. Benouville bridge and gliders of *coup de main* party

beach. The first came from the midget submarine X23 and the other from X20. Seventy-six hours had elapsed since they left Portsmouth on the evening of June the 2nd; sixty-four hours had been spent under water. For the five men confined in each of these tiny craft it had been a severe test of nerve, skill and endurance. Their sense of relief must have been very great when at last their long and exhausting vigil was over and the log entry could be made: '0500. Surfaced and checked position by shore fix in dawn light. Rigged mast with lamp and radar beacon' and, shortly after, 'Commenced flashing green light . . .'

Four miles further out to sea the British bombarding squadrons which had reached ahead of the landing ships were now following the minesweepers down the approach channels to their allotted anchorages almost as if taking station for a review. To the distant sound of explosions a glow spread in the east as 114 Lancasters dropped 580 tons of bombs on battery positions near Ouistreham. It was growing light when the last of the night bombers left the target area at quarter past five and quiet reigned on the coast for a few minutes. On the American front the bombing had stopped earlier. Now at about half past five the guns of the fleets roared out along the whole front.

Never has any coast suffered what a tortured strip of French coast suffered that morning; both naval and air bombardments were unparalleled. Along the whole fifty-mile front the land was rocked by successive explosions as the shells of the ships' guns tore holes in fortifications and tons of bombs rained on them from the skies. Through billowing smoke and falling debris defenders crouching in this scene of devastation would soon discern faintly hundreds of ships and assault craft ominously closing the shore. If the sight dismayed them, the soldiers borne forward to attack were thrilled by the spectacle of Allied power that was displayed around them on every hand.

At the approach of dawn a great shield of day fighters had been spread overhead—over the ships in passage and the seas on either flank, over the assault coast and its hinterland, over the country from which enemy aircraft or army reinforcements might approach the battle area. While aircraft of the Air Defence of Great Britain guarded shipping within forty miles of the English coast, the protection during darkness which had been given outside that limit by night fighters of the Royal Air Force was now taken over and extended by day fighters of the American Eighth and Ninth Air Forces. From now on four squadrons of Lightnings maintained ceaseless patrol over the mineswept lanes across the Channel and the adjacent seas, their operation controlled from a fighter direction tender (F.D.T. 13) stationed in the swept channels leading to the assault area; and a further six squadrons were held in readiness to reinforce them immediately if required. Over the assault coast itself six squadrons of Spitfires from the Second Tactical Air Force gave low cover, flying beneath the cloud base at three to four thousand feet, or less if need be; while above the clouds, at eight thousand feet or more, flew three squadrons of Thunderbolts from the United States Ninth Air Force. To maintain constant patrols at such strength, thirty-six British and sixteen American squadrons were needed, while in order to ensure flexibility and readiness to reinforce swiftly in case of need, thirty additional squadrons were reserved of which, throughout the day, six were always ready to act as an immediate striking force. Two fighter direction tenders controlled this double fighter cover over the coastal areas, one (F.D.T. 217) over the British sector and the other (F.D.T. 216) over the American sector. The sight of Allied fighters in such strength, serenely demonstrating their unchallenged supremacy over the battle areas, inspired confidence in the seamen and soldiers below them, but their eager pilots saw no German aircraft during the whole of those fateful hours.

Beneath the protection of this great force of fighters the bombarding warships had taken up their stations, moving to the positions shown on the map facing page 168. On the most vulnerable and therefore most strongly-defended eastern flank the powerful bombarding force (Force D) included three ships mounting 15-inch guns —H.M.S. *Warspite*, *Ramillies* and *Roberts*. Shortly before 5.30 a.m. these opened fire on the coastal defences east of the river Orne, *Warspite* engaging the most distant battery at Villerville from a range of about 30,000 yards, *Ramillies* and *Roberts* attacking the batteries at Bénerville and Houlgate respectively. All along the British front the battleships and cruisers opened fire on the targets shown on the map. Later the destroyers and support landing craft would join in the attack. Admiral Krancke entered in his war diary, 'it was only to be expected that no effective blow could be struck at such a superior enemy force'.

In fact one attempt to intervene was made by German surface craft. *Warspite*, *Ramillies*, *Roberts* and *Arethusa* were already anchored; *Scylla*, *Mauritius*, *Danae*, *Frobisher* and the Polish cruiser *Dragon* were anchoring along the swept loop channel; the bombarding squadron had opened fire but the destroyers were waiting to be swept into their inshore positions; a convoy, bringing up amphibious tanks, was just coming up to the lowering position.

> 'Our own aircraft streaked low across the eastern flank at about this time and laid a most effective smoke screen to shield the Force from the heavy batteries at Havre. Unfortunately, three

German torpedo-boats took advantage of this to carry out a torpedo attack and, although engaged by the bombarding squadron, were able to make good their escape in the smoke. Two torpedoes passed between H.M.S. *Warspite* and H.M.S. *Ramillies* and at 0530 one hit H.Nor.M.S. *Svenner* close on the port beam of H.M.S. *Largs*. Another torpedo was seen approaching H.M.S. *Largs*; her engines were put emergency full astern and the torpedo passed a few feet ahead of her. It then came to rest and sank just short of H.M.S. *Virago* (one of the destroyers of Force S).'

The *Svenner* had been hit under the boiler room; her back was broken and she sank rapidly but most of her men were picked up, and after this brief excursion the German navy made no further effort to interfere that morning.

For the most part the reply from batteries ashore was desultory and ineffective and soon faded away almost completely; but a few garrisons showed more spirit and determination. The four-gun battery at Longues was engaged by *Ajax* at 5.30 a.m., but just before six o'clock it opened fire on the headquarters ship *Bulolo* anchored in the lowering position in Gold area. By 6.20 a.m. it had been silenced but soon afterwards resumed the attack on *Bulolo*, causing the ship to move seaward. After further engagements by *Ajax* and *Argonaut* it was at last silenced at about 8.45 a.m.; its reduction had needed a hundred and seventy-nine shells from the cruisers; two of its four guns had been put out of action by direct hits through the embrasures. The battery at Bénerville, silenced initially by the *Ramillies*, afterwards opened on the *Warspite* (who had to shift berth), and during the day prompt counter-battery action was called for when some other batteries showed renewed activity.

Control of all naval bombardment was exercised from joint command posts in the headquarters ships in which the naval commanders and the divisional generals with their staffs were carried, with air force representatives. These headquarters ships were the nerve centres from which the battle was fought until the military command was established on shore.[6]

Before landings were effected the bombarding ships relied solely on aircraft to observe and report the fall of their shells. They were provided by four squadrons of Seafires of the Fleet Air Arm, five squadrons of Spitfires and Mustangs from the Royal Air Force and fifteen Spitfires manned by United States naval pilots. Single-seater, high-performance aircraft had never attempted this on such a scale before, and with about a hundred and sixty employed, each maintaining radio communication with the particular ship to which it was

---

[6] Details of these specially equipped headquarters ships are given in Appendix II.

allotted, it is not surprising that contact was occasionally broken; but the airmen served the naval gunners faithfully though seven aircraft were lost that day. Air spotting continued for many weeks but with the initial landings specialist Army observers on the ground were also used. These, known as 'Forward Observer Bombardment' (F.O.B.), with naval signallers and radio sets, moved forward with the troops to transmit calls for fire, point out targets and observe and report the results.

The convoy of ships and craft bearing the troops who were to capture the chosen beaches in Sword, Juno and Gold areas—convoys named correspondingly S, J and G—had begun reaching their lowering positions at about half past five. Their headquarters ships *Largs*, *Hilary* and *Bulolo*, flag ships respectively of Rear-Admiral A. G. Talbot, commanding Force S, Commodore G. N. Oliver, commanding Force J, and Commodore C. E. Douglas-Pennant, commanding Force G, anchored in position (map at page 168). From the shelter of their bridges commanders could see how well their charges had come through the ordeals of that troubled night. In general they were arriving fairly punctually. There were some stragglers but these were now making up lost time; and there had been some losses among the landing craft which had set out to make their way across Channel under their own power or in tow. Some of these, notably assault craft carrying tanks of the Royal Marine Armoured Support Regiment, were over-weighted with top hamper and proved to be unseaworthy in prevailing weather conditions, and others being towed across armed with mortars and sixty-pound spigot bombs to blast lanes through beach minefields also fared badly. In all the loss of fifty-four small craft in passage was attributed to weather, twenty of them being Rhino ferries or their tug units. This was a very small proportion of the thousands engaged in an operation which required, in Admiral Ramsay's phrase, 'a degree of efficiency and seamanship never attempted hitherto with landing craft'. Considering the number and various characteristics of the ships and craft engaged, the widely dispersed harbours from which they had gathered, the distances they had covered and the conditions they had weathered, it seems little short of a miracle that all this energy and effort was so skilfully focused on the French shore that troops would soon begin landing there almost to the minute.

The scene at the lowering positions was beginning to look like some fantastic regatta. The manning and lowering of the assault craft carrying troops from the decks of the large landing ships, and their formation in groups for the run-in to the beaches, were proceeding smoothly. Soldiers and sailors had been well practised in the drill for getting the small craft away from their parent ships, but when loaded each weighed over thirteen tons and great skill was needed to release them smartly and safely into the short steep seas. These shallow craft are lively and wet and the fact that all were got away without a single mishap was proof not only of skilled seamanship but of good training, good organisation, and good discipline.

The leading groups already heading for the shore could be seen deploying into their assault formations. In the van were landing craft carrying D.D. tanks which would be launched at sea to swim in ahead of the assault, covered by guns in support craft lying off shore. Behind these other craft were forming up or already moving forward in succession, carrying assault companies of infantry, engineers and their armoured vehicles, self-propelled artillery, more engineers, more infantry, more tanks, more artillery and equipment. On either flank destroyers waited to close the beaches while auxiliary minesweepers swept ahead of them. All round the headquarters ships craft were waiting to take their places in succeeding groups and, from the north, ships and craft could be seen approaching in endless sequence.

On the map facing page 168 the blue boundary line defining the swept channels looks clear enough, and the lowering positions do not look far from the coast. The sailors saw no such guide lines on the sea but only a wilderness of tumbling grey waters, and the coast was still seven miles away and not yet visible from water-level. The final seven miles severely tested the seamanship of sailors responsible for clumsy, unweatherly assault craft and not all could reach the shore in exactly the right spot or at precisely the planned time; wind and sea, enemy fire, accidents or personal error intervened in some cases but that was only to be expected in the seas that were running. A stiff wind blew and the waves of a rising tide were already breaking on the seaward line of exposed beach obstacles as the craft drew in to the shore.

While they drove uneasily forward towards their destination, a new note was added to the roar of the heavy naval guns. For now the destroyers closed the shore in groups of ten or more 'Fleet'-class destroyers, mounting four or eight 4·7-inch guns, reinforced by 'Hunt'-class destroyers with 4-inch guns and shallower draft. Some approached to within a few thousand yards of the beaches and, all firing by direct observation, attacked strong-points and other targets on their immediate front until the landings began; then they would support the troops, first attacking other targets on their flanks and behind the beaches, and afterwards giving fire when called for. Destroyers played a notable part in the reduction of the enemy's defence throughout the assault and gave invaluable assistance to the troops.

In the American sector similar scenes were being enacted. At Omaha eight United States destroyers and three British were filling the same rôle. 'Lacking complete knowledge of their own troops' position and hard pressed to pick out enemy positions, they closed in some cases to within eight hundred yards of the beaches. It is certain that they destroyed many enemy positions and it is probable that without their assistance the casualties on the beach would have been considerably higher.' At Utah, too, the naval bombardment was very effective.

But the guns of destroyers could produce only part of the close support planned. All targets were not suitable for attack by high velocity, flat trajectory naval guns; some could be attacked more effectively from the air or by close-support weapons mounted in special craft. In the last phase of the combined bombardment the intensity of fire was stepped up to a new level as the fire-power of all three Services was focused on the beaches and their defences. To the merciless fire of the naval guns there was added, first a great outburst of covering fire from specially adapted support landing craft carrying 4·7-inch guns, 6-pounders or 2-pounders and self-propelled guns of the army's field artillery which would land later to join the fight of their divisions ashore. Details of these close-support craft are in Appendix II, page 506. On each brigade front they went into action about forty-five minutes before the first landings, when their fire was lifted or diverted to the flanks to avoid endangering the assault troops. From the destroyers and close-support craft over thirty thousand shells of 4-inch and upwards had been directed on the beaches and beach defences in the British sector before the first troops began to land.

On top of this great combination of fire power there was next imposed a concentrated attack from the air by some sixteen hundred aircraft of the United States Eighth and Ninth Air Forces. The configuration of the coast and its effect on the tide had led to the adoption of plans which differed in two main respects as between the British and American sectors. The areas in which American troops were to land—Utah and Omaha—lay at right angles to each other in the west of the bay. Ships at anchor off the coast there would thus be exposed to the fire of heavy guns from their front and in particular from those on the embracing arm of the Cotentin peninsula; moreover high tide occurred earlier on the Cotentin shore. Taking these facts into account, it had been decided by the American commanders that in their sector the lowering positions (in American terms the 'transport areas') should be eleven miles from the shore as against seven miles in the British sector; and that H-hour would be approximately half past six, whereas in the British sector it was to be about an hour later, the exact time varying somewhat to suit conditions on each beach. The final bombing of the beach defences, which was timed to end only ten minutes before landings began, had therefore started earlier in the American sector when 269 medium bombers (Marauders) of the Ninth Air Force had bombed the defences of Utah beach. Flying low, under the cloud base, they were able to take visual aim and they largely succeeded in silencing the defence. But because of bad visibility over Omaha and the British front the heavy bombers of the Eighth Air Force were unable to make a visual pin-point attack on batteries and strong points covering the beaches but had to adopt an alternative method; successive waves of aircraft were to fly in line abreast over the shore, releasing their bombs on orders of pathfinders aiming by instruments.

Because of the earlier H-hour for Omaha, there next came 329 Liberators. Flying high over cloud, and delaying the release of their bombs so as to avoid endangering assault craft and troops nearing the shore, many of the bombs they dropped 'did not hit the enemy beach and coast defences at all but were scattered as far as three miles inland', according to the American historian.[7] The successful bombing of Utah defences and the comparable failure to hit those at Omaha were to be reflected in the sharply contrasted experience of troops who had to capture these American beaches. Over the British beaches the heavy bombers were also only partially successful. By the masterly performance of a 'Pre-dawn Assembly Plan' over a thousand Flying Fortresses and Liberators, drawn from airfields distributed through England, had carried out a series of complicated movements which began while it was still dark. Now at about twenty minutes to seven they flew over in successive waves, each of thirty-six bombers flying in line abreast, and together they dropped nearly three thousand tons of bombs. But as at Omaha they bombed from above the cloud-overcast on the instance of pathfinders relying on instruments to distinguish their targets; they observed similar precautions to safeguard oncoming assault troops; and, broadly speaking, their attack had similar results. Some bombs fell on the close defences of the shore but many of them fell well inland. Besides inflicting widespread damage the severity of their attack certainly helped to shake the nerves of garrison forces, and if it did less destruction to the beach defences than was intended it induced the enemy to keep under cover while it lasted, as planned, till within ten minutes of H-hour. And with that short interval came the culminating feature of the Joint Fire Plan, the final addition to the attack which had been opened by the heavy bombers of Bomber Command while it was still dark, and had been followed in daylight by the continuing fire of the naval guns, by guns of the Royal Marines and the Royal Artillery firing from support craft during the run-in and by the successive attacks of American medium and heavy bombers.

---

[7] Harrison, op. cit., p. 301.

Now, about five minutes before the first troops landed, clouds of five-inch explosive rockets rose in succession to fall on the beaches in a deluging rain of destruction.[8] They had been electrically fired in quickly following salvos from assault craft (L.C.T.(R)) each of which could discharge about a thousand in the space of a minute and a half.

As the noise of exploding rockets died away troops of the British Second Army began landing in France.

---

[8] Over twenty thousand were fired on the British front and some eighteen thousand in the American sector.

OPERATION 'NEPTUNE' — T

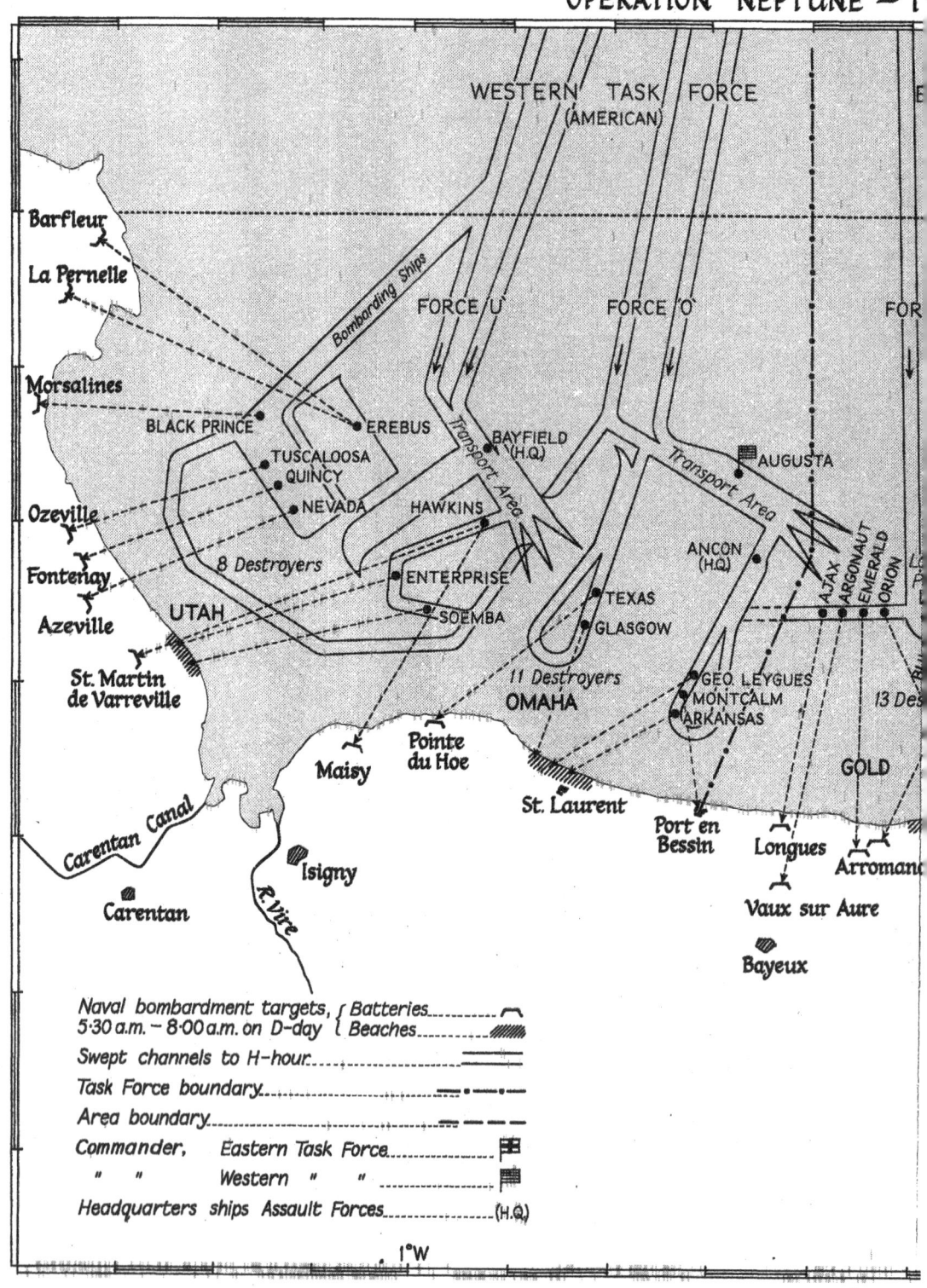

WESTERN TASK FORCE
(AMERICAN)

Barfleur
La Pernelle
Morsalines
  BLACK PRINCE
  • EREBUS
  TUSCALOOSA
  QUINCY
  • NEVADA
Ozeville
  HAWKINS
  Bombarding Ships
  FORCE 'U'   FORCE 'O'   FOR
  BAYFIELD (H.Q.)
  Transport Area   Transport Area
  ■ AUGUSTA
  ANCON (H.Q.)
  AJAX ARGONAUT EMERALD ORION
Fontenay
  8 Destroyers
  • ENTERPRISE
  • SOEMBA
Azeville
  UTAH
St. Martin de Varreville
  • TEXAS
  GLASGOW
  11 Destroyers
  OMAHA
  • GEO. LEYGUES
  MONTCALM
  ARKANSAS
  13 Des
  Maisy Pointe du Hoe
  St. Laurent
  Port en Bessin   Longues   GOLD
  Arroman
Carentan Canal
  R. Vire
  Isigny
  Vaux sur Aure
Carentan
  Bayeux

Naval bombardment targets, { Batteries.........
5·30 a.m. – 8·00 a.m. on D-day { Beaches..........
Swept channels to H-hour................
Task Force boundary.....................
Area boundary...........................
Commander, Eastern Task Force.............
    "   "   Western   "   " ....
Headquarters ships Assault Forces........(H.Q.)

1°W

THE NAVAL BOMBARDMENT

EASTERN TASK FORCE
(BRITISH)

Northern Limit of Assault Area

49°40′

FORCE 'G'   FORCE 'J'   FORCE 'S'

Bombarding Ships

● WARSPITE

● RAMILLIES

Le Grand Clos

● ROBERTS

Le Havre

Lowering Position

● MAURITIUS

R. Seine

Lowering Position   FLORES BELFAST DIADEM   Lowering Position   LARGS (H.Q.)   SCYLLA   DRAGON FROBISHER

(H.Q.)   HILARY (H.Q.)   DANAE   ARETHUSA

Villerville

11 Destroyers   13 Destroyers

JUNO

Bénerville

Mont Fleury ches

SWORD

Ver sur Mer   Moulineaux   Riva Bella   Houlgate

Colleville sur Orne   Outstreham   Merville   Le Mont

49°15′N

Caen Canal   R. Orne   R. Dives

Caen

0 1 2 3 4 5   10
Nautical Miles (approx)

0°30′   0°

CHAPTER IX

D-DAY: SEABORNE LANDINGS

THE enemy's long-range fire had been effectively subdued by naval bombardment and air attacks, and under cover of the support-fire of all arms the assault craft approached the shore with little to trouble them except the difficulty of navigation in the turbulent sea and sea-sickness, which was not confined to soldiers. In spite of this some of the men sang as their craft moved shorewards and a bugler of the East Yorkshire Regiment sounded the General Salute as his craft passed their command ship. But as they neared the beaches in the last lap of the run-in, when supporting fire had to be switched to the rear and flanks of the beaches, the enemy's artillery, mortars and machine guns that had escaped destruction opened on them. Not much damage was done while they were still afloat, but along the fringe of waves breaking on the shore craft grounding and unloading in the surf provided the enemy with easy targets and casualties increased.

Amphibious tanks, obstacle clearance groups, flail tanks, assault engineers and infantry were all timed to land within a few minutes of H-hour. Such exact timing could not everywhere be maintained; all were soon landing practically at the same time. On some beaches D.D. tanks landed first, on others naval and engineer obstacle clearance groups, flail tanks, engineers' armoured vehicles (AVREs) or infantry were the first to reach the shore. At the water's edge naval parties, often submerged by the waves, began their dangerous work of clearing mined underwater obstructions which were being rapidly covered by the incoming tide, while sappers worked on those which were still exposed. Across the beaches flail tanks began beating lanes through possible mined areas while armoured vehicles of the sappers bridged or battered their way forward to make exits from the shore for incoming vehicles. All worked at high pressure often under enfilading fire, and there were many casualties to men and vehicles. The infantry, not waiting for the completion of these tasks, broke across the beaches to gain cover and to capture the positions from which fire was sweeping the foreshore. The enemy's fire increased along the coast, still punctuated by the roar of bursting shells from the continuing naval bombardment, now countered by the fire of tanks which had swum ashore or been landed already, by bursting petards of the assault engineers' tanks, and by the crackling of machine-gun and rifle fire. Overhead flew clouds of fighters and at frequent intervals the din was increased by the roar of fighter-bombers and rocket-firing Typhoons of the Second Tactical Air Force, attacking strong-points or other targets inland.

Eighteen squadrons of Typhoons from 83 and 84 Groups and twelve squadrons of Mitchell and Mosquito bombers from 2 Group attacked in the British sector, and Thunderbolts of the Ninth United States Air Force in the American sector. Most of the Typhoon fighter-bombers were armed with eight rockets, each with a 60-pound warhead, the remainder carried 2,000-pound bombloads. A few minutes before the touch-down the leading squadrons dive-bombed strong-points near the beaches, particularly le Hamel and la Rivière in Gold, Courseulles in Juno, and Hermanville in Sword. Other formations of Typhoons then attacked batteries, defended localities and military headquarters further inland. They continued their attacks throughout the morning, either working to previously made plans or on requests received from the army in the course of the fighting. In response to an early morning request from Twenty-First Army Group a vicious attack was made soon after 8.30 a.m. on the headquarters of the German LXXXIV Corps near St. Lô which bad visibility had prevented our pilots from finding the evening before.

While trying to picture the scenes that were developing all along the coast the reader will do well to consult the diagram at page 172 and the map facing page 212. He will see there the line of the French coast where the Second Army was to land; the Gold, Juno and Sword areas into which it was divided and the named beaches to be captured in the first instance. The diagram shows the details of the five brigade groups who were now beginning to land and the rest of the assault divisions—that is of the 50th, 3rd Canadian and 3rd Divisions—in the order in which they would follow; the further formations of XXX Corps and I Corps are also indicated. It thus shows at a glance who they were who had the honour of opening the ground attack on Hitler's Atlantic Wall. Yet in one respect it may be misleading, for the diagram is apt to give an impression that the troops were much thicker on the ground than was really the case. The coast-line of the British sector stretched for twenty-four miles, but less than five miles were to be attacked at the outset. Each of the five beaches to be captured was only about a mile wide, some a little more and some a little less. There was a gap of over ten miles between the most westerly British beach in the Gold area and the American beach in Omaha; there was approximately a mile-wide gap between each of the beaches to be captured by the four brigade groups of the 50th and 3rd Canadian Divisions, and of about five miles between the Canadians and the assaulting brigade group of the 3rd Division. Until landings were effected and these gaps

50TH DIVISION IN GOLD AREA

closed it is necessary to follow the happenings on each assault beach in turn, although in reality all were under simultaneous attack. It must also be borne in mind that the D-day task of the assaulting divisions was not only to capture and then link up the beaches along the coast between Port en Bessin and the Orne, but to strike rapidly inland and, by the evening of D-day, to occupy a bridgehead which would include Bayeux and Caen and be joined to the ground east of the Orne which the 6th Airborne Division had already seized. It was known that the enemy's nearest armoured division available for prompt counter-attack was stationed immediately east and south of Caen; the quick capture of that key city and the neighbourhood of Carpiquet was the most ambitious, the most difficult and the most important task of Lieut-General J. T. Crocker's I Corps. The capture of Bayeux, eight miles inland, and the high ground on which it stands, and the protection of the American army's east flank were the tasks of XXX Corps under Lieut-General G. C. Bucknall.

It will be seen from the diagram that the 50th Division (the leading division of XXX Corps, associated with Assault Force G) was to attack in the Gold area with two brigade groups. The 231st Brigade was to capture 'Jig' beach, the 69th was to take the beach named 'King'. The coast in both is low-lying and sandy, offering no such natural obstacles as the bluffs of the rock-bound shore which stretches from Arromanches to Port en Bessin in the western half of Gold. Only low sand dunes fringe the shore of Jig and King but there are soft patches of clay in the tide-washed foreshore on which heavy vehicles would be liable to sink; and behind the lateral road which runs near the sea front much of the ground is soggy grassland, criss-crossed with dykes which must hinder movement. Jig beach could be covered by fire from strongly defended positions at le Hamel and Asnelles sur Mer and from a smaller strong-point near les Roquettes; King beach was protected by defences at la Rivière and by strong-points at Hable de Heurtot on the coast, and on higher ground near Mont Fleury and Ver sur Mer. The whole front between le Hamel and la Rivière was defended by beach obstacles and by a continuous belt of mines and barbed wire.

For the 231st Brigade, attacking on a two-battalion front with the 1st Hampshire on the right and the 1st Dorset on the left, it was obviously important to capture quickly the position at le Hamel. This was known to include on the west a number of fortified houses and entrenchments, well protected by barbed wire and mines and by an anti-tank ditch; on the east, commanding Jig beach, the defences consisted not only of more fortified buildings, including a large and conspicuous sanatorium, but also a number of concrete and steel pill-boxes and infantry positions, again protected by barbed wire and minefields. The position was held by about a company of infantry

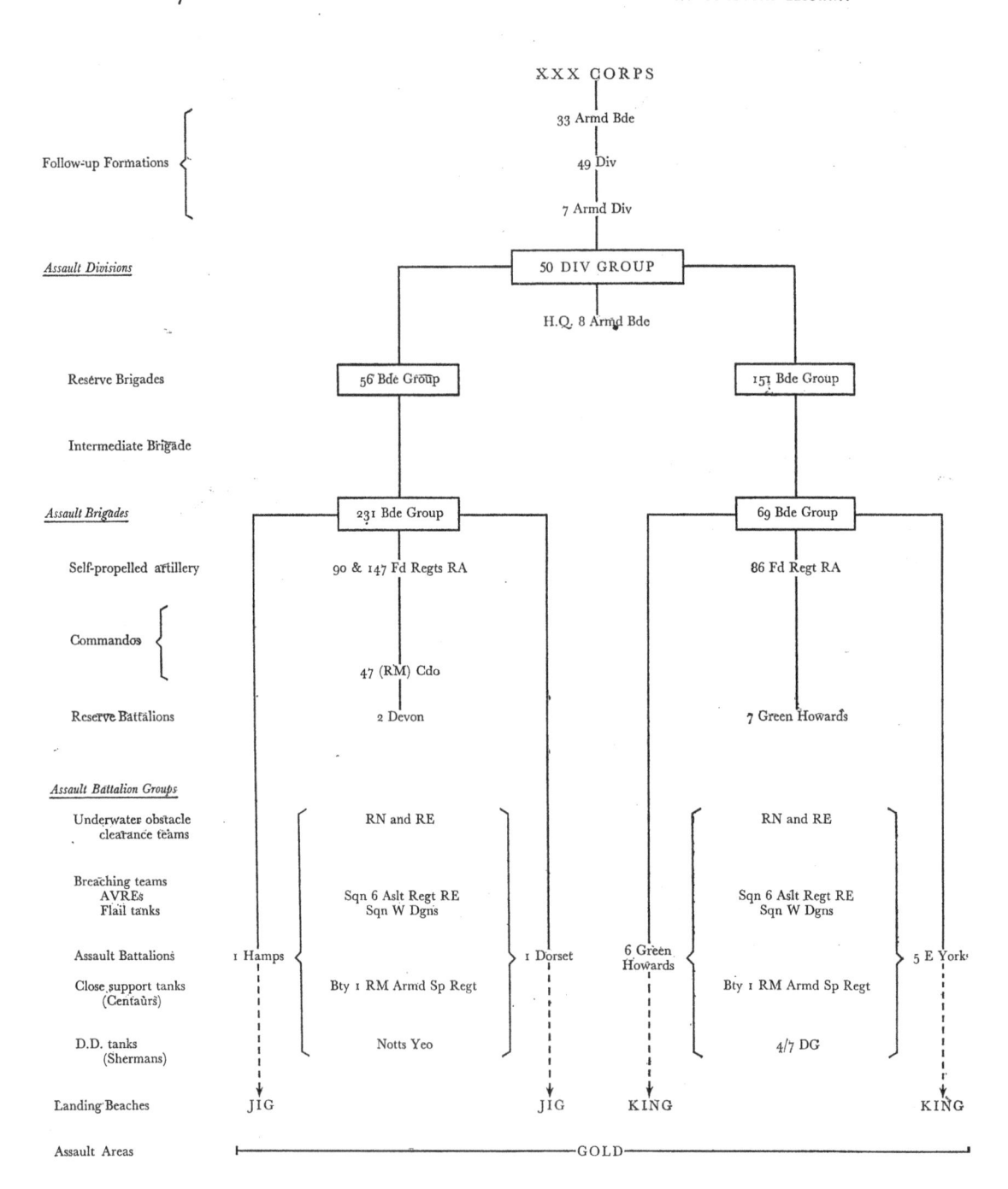

	XXX CORPS	
Follow-up Formations	33 Armd Bde 49 Div 7 Armd Div	
Assault Divisions	**50 DIV GROUP**	
	H.Q. 8 Armd Bde	
Reserve Brigades	56 Bde Group	151 Bde Group
Intermediate Brigade		
Assault Brigades	231 Bde Group	69 Bde Group
Self-propelled artillery	90 & 147 Fd Regts RA	86 Fd Regt RA
Commandos	47 (RM) Cdo	
Reserve Battalions	2 Devon	7 Green Howards
Assault Battalion Groups		
Underwater obstacle clearance teams	RN and RE	RN and RE
Breaching teams AVREs Flail tanks	Sqn 6 Aslt Regt RE Sqn W Dgns	Sqn 6 Aslt Regt RE Sqn W Dgns
Assault Battalions	1 Hamps 1 Dorset	6 Green Howards 5 E Yorks
Close support tanks (Centaurs)	Bty 1 RM Armd Sp Regt	Bty 1 RM Armd Sp Regt
D.D. tanks (Shermans)	Notts Yeo	4/7 DG
Landing Beaches	JIG JIG	KING KING
Assault Areas	GOLD	

British Second Army

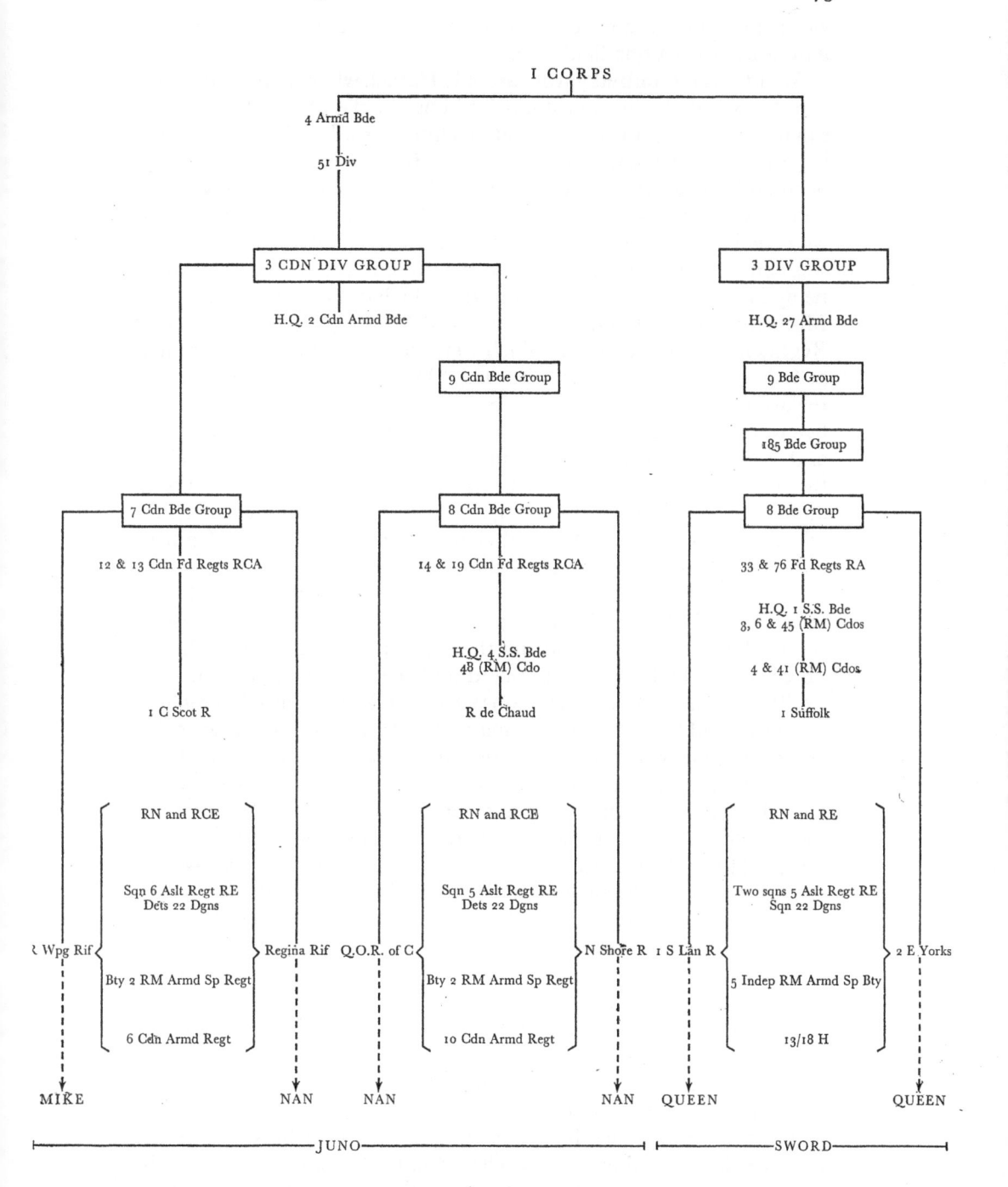

```
                                    I CORPS
                                 4 Armd Bde
                                   51 Div
               ┌───────────────────────┴───────────────────────┐
         3 CDN DIV GROUP                                  3 DIV GROUP
         H.Q. 2 Cdn Armd Bde                            H.Q. 27 Armd Bde
                                   9 Cdn Bde Group        9 Bde Group
                                                         185 Bde Group
      7 Cdn Bde Group              8 Cdn Bde Group        8 Bde Group

   12 & 13 Cdn Fd Regts RCA    14 & 19 Cdn Fd Regts RCA   33 & 76 Fd Regts RA

                                                          H.Q. 1 S.S. Bde
                                                        3, 6 & 45 (RM) Cdos
                                H.Q. 4 S.S. Bde
                                 48 (RM) Cdo              4 & 41 (RM) Cdos

      1 C Scot R                   R de Chaud              1 Suffolk

       RN and RCE                   RN and RCE              RN and RE

   Sqn 6 Aslt Regt RE          Sqn 5 Aslt Regt RE     Two sqns 5 Aslt Regt RE
      Dets 22 Dgns                Dets 22 Dgns             Sqn 22 Dgns

 Wpg Rif        Regina Rif  Q.O.R. of C      N Shore R   1 S Lan R         2 E Yorks

 Bty 2 RM Armd Sp Regt       Bty 2 RM Armd Sp Regt      5 Indep RM Armd Sp Bty

   6 Cdn Armd Regt              10 Cdn Armd Regt              13/18 H

     ↓              ↓          ↓            ↓            ↓                ↓
    MIKE          NAN         NAN          NAN         QUEEN            QUEEN
   ├─────────────────── JUNO ────────────────────┤   ├────── SWORD ──────┤
```

well supplied with mortars and machine guns and with two anti-tank guns and at least one field gun.

About seven hundred yards east of le Hamel, where a by-road leads past les Roquettes to a customs building on the coast, there was a small well-wired post with several machine guns. Landing craft bearing the leading companies of the 1st Hampshire were carried by wind and tide some distance eastward of their intended landing place and touched down nearly opposite les Roquettes. D.D. tanks which were to have preceded them were still at sea, for on this front it was considered to be too rough to swim them ashore and they were being brought in by their landing craft which did not arrive till later. Misfortunes had overtaken the 1st Royal Marine Armoured Support Regiment. Of the ten tanks which were to have landed on Jig beach at H-hour, in order to join with the D.D. tanks in giving support to the attacking troops until the field artillery could be brought in, only five were landed and about a quarter of an hour late, and all but one of these were hit by shell-fire from le Hamel soon after landing. Thus the first troops to land on Jig beach had no tanks to support them and had little answer to the gun, mortar and machine-gun fire which swept the shore. It was obvious that the defence of le Hamel, although it had been attacked shortly before by twelve Typhoons using 1,000-lb bombs, was unsubdued. Owing to the loss of two control vessels during the passage, le Hamel had to be omitted from the field artillery's shoot during the run-in; most of the Eighth Air Force bombs had fallen well inland and the destroyers were unable to silence guns and other weapons sited to take the shore in enfilade and protected from seaward by massive earth-banked concrete walls. Interpretation of photographic reconnaissance here and elsewhere along the front had failed to reveal the fact that many of the guns near the shore were thus sited solely for enfilade fire on the beaches; they could not fire to seaward but neither could they be effectively attacked from the sea, except by cross-fire. Had this been known the naval fire plan might have been differently framed. On the flat sands craft grounded some distance from dry land. The engineers' armoured bulldozers, track-laying, bridging and ramp tanks had therefore to negotiate a considerable stretch of surf, while men of many units often bearing heavy loads of explosives or other equipment, had to struggle ashore through the waves, raked all the way by the enemy's fire.

Yet the leading men of the 1st Hampshire had comparatively light casualties in getting ashore and they quickly rushed the post at the customs house near les Roquettes and turned to attack le Hamel. At once they met intense fire. Their commanding officer and with him the forward observation officer for the supporting ships and a battery commander from the field artillery all became casualties. The battalion headquarters wireless sets were put out of action and they were thus unable to call for support from the destroyers or the self-propelled artillery ready to fire whilst still at sea. When the remaining companies of the Hampshires came in, twenty minutes after the first landings, an out-flanking attack through Asnelles was organised; without artillery support direct attack by way of the beaches was proving costly and making little progress. To handicap the battalion still further the second-in-command was killed soon after taking charge.

Meanwhile the naval and military obstacle clearance teams, working under fire and suffering heavy casualties, partially cleared one narrow gap on Jig before the rising tide put a stop to this work. The breaching teams of sappers with the assault vehicles were at the same time busy clearing exits from the beaches to the coast road behind and the build-up of the brigade continued steadily, though the beach was still under fire from le Hamel.

While this was happening on Jig beach the brigade's second battalion, the 1st Dorset, landing east of les Roquettes, had fared better. Flail tanks of the Westminster Dragoons and armoured vehicles of the engineers had landed punctually and were quickly at work clearing mines and beach obstructions. The infantry crossed the beach and leaving a company to form a firm base at les Roquettes they pushed inland. After capturing a machine-gun post at Meuvaines they by-passed le Hamel and advanced westwards towards Buhot and an enemy position, at Puits d'Herode, which covered Arromanches and the nearby shores from the south. Though troops on the beach east of les Roquettes were less exposed to fire from le Hamel the breaching teams were still having casualties in clearing two exits to the coast road.

At about a quarter past eight the brigade's third battalion, the 2nd Devon, began landing as planned close to le Hamel. Beach obstacles were still intact and le Hamel still unconquered, so they had a hazardous time in landing and getting clear of the beach. One company joined the Hampshire in the fight for le Hamel and the rest of the battalion moved round Asnelles on the south and pressed westwards towards Ryes, about two miles south of Arromanches.

Close on the heels of the Devon the 47th (Royal Marine) Commando landed. Since H-hour the tide had risen considerably, submerging obstacles before it was possible to clear them. On these, three of the five landing craft bringing in the Commandos were damaged and sunk by attached explosives. Many of the Marines swam ashore, but forty-three men and much precious wireless equipment were lost; yet in spite of the fire from le Hamel about three hundred concentrated at the back of the beach. After acquiring another wireless set from 231st Brigade Headquarters (which by then had landed) the Commando started off across country. They were to move inland and, avoiding contact with the enemy, to make westwards for Port en Bessin on the inter-Allied boundary.

About a thousand yards further east, the 50th Division's 69th Brigade had begun landing punctually on King beach—the leading companies of the 6th Green Howards on the right and on their left the 5th East Yorkshire. Obstacle clearance groups and AVREs had begun landing just before them. The main enemy defences here were the fortified positions at la Rivière on the left flank and on higher ground near Mont Fleury and round the lighthouse; there was also a strong-point at Hable de Heurtot where a by-road from Ver sur Mer reaches the coast. On the map opposite, German defences as recorded by Allied Intelligence are marked. Similarly overprinted maps were issued for all sectors of the assault front.

The Green Howards, landing to the west of la Rivière, quickly cleared the strong-point at Hable de Heurtot where they were closely supported by engineer tanks. When four pill-boxes had been reduced[1] with the help of petards, two of the tanks charged over the sea wall and routed the rest of the garrison who had been firing and throwing grenades from behind it. The advance was quickly resumed and the Green Howards next took the battery position near Mont Fleury. It had been struck by the bombers and H.M.S. *Orion* had registered twelve hits. There was no sign that its four guns had ever fired a shot and the gun crews, cowed by the bombardment, offered no resistance.

The East Yorkshire landed near the outskirts of la Rivière and for a short time were pinned down by fire under the sea wall. They called for naval support, and destroyers and support craft closed the shore and shelled the position heavily. A flail of the Westminster Dragoons silenced an 88-mm gun in a concrete emplacement and the East Yorkshire captured the position, taking forty-five prisoners. Even so it needed several hours' fighting to clear the whole village and its capture cost, in killed and wounded, six officers and eighty-four other ranks. The rest of the battalion had gone on to capture the strong-point at the lighthouse near Mont Fleury. From there they took two guns and thirty prisoners and then moved on towards Ver sur Mer.

The 69th Brigade's third battalion, the 7th Green Howards, landed at about twenty past eight, and made at once for Ver sur Mer. There were no enemy in the village and the battalion continued to the battery beyond it. Bombing and a two-hour bombardment by H.M.S. *Belfast* had left the garrison with little further will to fight and fifty were taken prisoner; their four 10-cm gun-howitzers in

---

[1] Sergeant-Major S. E. Hollis of the Green Howards was awarded the Victoria Cross for his 'utmost gallantry' in this action.

Symbol description	
Light machine gun ; A A machine gun	↑ ; ⌀
Mobile gun – light ; medium ; A/tk	╫ ; ╪ ; ╫
Open emplacement ; gun casemate	⌒ ; ⊞
75mm ; 155mm guns – in open emplacement ; in concrete	⁷⁵╤ ; ¹⁵⁵⊞
Concrete artillery O.P. ; wireless station	⍓ ; Ψ
Communication trench ; dug-out shelter	∿ ; ⊐
Concrete shelter ; hutted camp	□ ; H
Steel 'Hedgehogs' ; A/tk ditch	⋈⋈ ; ▲▲▲▲
Barbed wire obstacle ; single fence	xxxx ; —*—*—
Mines ; dump	∩∩∩∩ ; ⌒
Under construction ; constructional activity	U/C ; WK
Unconfirmed ; unspecified infantry weapon	? ; ↑

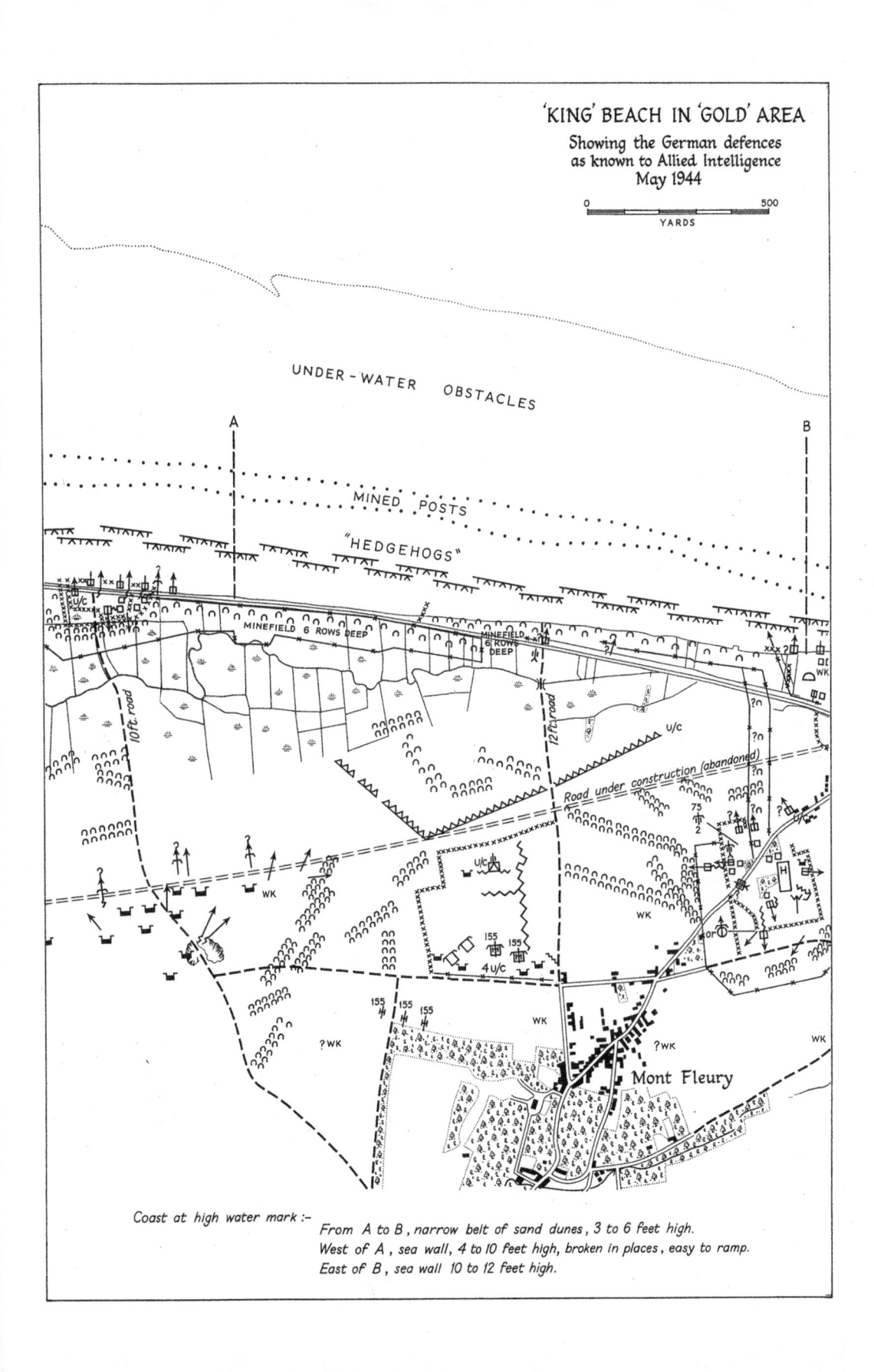

'KING' BEACH IN 'GOLD' AREA

Showing the German defences as known to Allied Intelligence
May 1944

Coast at high water mark:—
From A to B, narrow belt of sand dunes, 3 to 6 feet high.
West of A, sea wall, 4 to 10 feet high, broken in places, easy to ramp.
East of B, sea wall 10 to 12 feet high.

concrete emplacements had apparently fired eighty-seven rounds before they gave in.

The two assault brigade groups of the 50th Division were now ashore and fighting their way inland. On the coast the engineers had cleared two paths through beach obstacles and two exits for vehicles; and the two brigades were being steadily built up. D.D. tanks of the 4th/7th Royal Dragoon Guards and the Nottinghamshire Yeomanry had been brought in by landing craft soon after the leading infantry, with more tanks of the 6th Assault Regiment, Royal Engineers, and flails of the Westminster Dragoons. Self-propelled guns, of the 86th, 90th and 147th Field Regiments, Royal Artillery, Bren carriers, machine guns, mortars, anti-tank guns, jeeps and small trucks were being landed.

Shortly before nine o'clock two tanks of the 1st Royal Marine Armoured Support Regiment had landed on King beach and in the next hour or so six more came ashore. The circumstances of these Marine regiments need explanation. They had been formed only a few months before D-day to meet the army's desire for guns to support early-landing troops until the field artillery could be brought in. They were armed with 95-mm howitzers mounted in out-moded Centaur tanks with troop leaders in Shermans carrying 75-mm guns. After firing on the run-in they were to land a few minutes before the infantry, to fire from the beaches or within a mile of the sea. Unfortunately they were not given much chance to fulfil this important rôle, since they were despatched in landing craft, hurriedly adapted and fitted with side armour, which made them unseaworthy in the prevailing weather. Some foundered on passage, some broke down at sea and had to put back; others were damaged by under-water obstacles or enemy fire as they grounded on the French coast. On all five beaches only twenty out of eighty Centaurs landed within the first quarter of an hour *after* H-hour and only twenty-eight more within the first four hours. Those that were not quickly put out of action after landing did good service, the Marines showing their characteristic enterprise.

Among others who had begun landing on each assault beach with the first troops and had started work while the shore was still under enemy fire were men whose task it was to resolve the confusion which was inevitable at first, when craft of every sort were arriving minute by minute to discharge men and vehicles hurriedly on beaches which the rising tide was narrowing rapidly, and from which an adequate number of exits were not yet cleared. They were the naval assistant beachmasters with small advance parties, forerunners of the naval organisation on the far shore that would eventually be needed for the reception and direction of ships and craft, the control of unloading operations, and the turn-round and despatch of return convoys;

and the beach groups which were an essential part of each assault brigade group, to be gathered later into the divisional sub-area and the vast supply organisation that would subsequently be needed.

The first task of these reconnaissance elements of naval and military beach organisation was to make a rapid survey of local hazards, both off-shore and on land, and to decide the precise location of beach exits to be cleared; to begin marking positions for ammunition and supply dumps for the guidance of incoming craft and of vehicle drivers; and at the earliest possible moment to set up signal stations. The Main Beach Signal Station on each brigade front, manned on an inter-Service basis, was to enable local commanders to control both the tactical situation and the flow of traffic to the beaches and to be the clearing-house for all local information. This work of beach organisation began while beaches were still under enemy fire and in some cases men engaged in it joined in fighting to overcome near-by enemy posts which were hindering progress. Like others employed on the beaches in this early stage they had a full share of casualties. It will be seen later that as ships and craft continued to arrive and men, vehicles and supplies were landed in ever-increasing numbers, naval and military organisation of the beaches was a determining factor in the progress of operations. Unless the incoming flood of craft and troops was well directed and efficiently distributed and controlled, congestion on the shore would delay movement and the momentum of the assault must suffer.

Apart from the hold-up at le Hamel, the leading brigades of the 50th Division were making good progress and about eleven o'clock the first of its reserve brigades—the 151st—began to land on the beaches that had been captured by the 69th Brigade. About an hour later the 56th Brigade started landing near Hable de Heurtot so as to avoid fire from le Hamel which was still sweeping across Jig beach where it was to have landed. By early afternoon all four brigades of the 50th Division were ashore. But this is anticipating events and before following the division's movements inland it will be well to see how the simultaneous assaults of the 3rd Canadian and British 3rd Divisions had fared in these early hours.

Nearly two miles away to the east of la Rivière leading troops of the 3rd Canadian Divisional Group had been landing on 'Mike' and 'Nan' beaches in the Juno area. The same low-lying coast is protected there by a reef of off-shore rocks, exposed at low water; only in a mile-wide gap, opposite the mouth of the river Seulles and the little seaport of Courseulles, is the approach free from navigational danger, and there the beach obstructions had been thickened and the water-front fortified. Behind mined areas and barbed wire, houses had been strengthened for defence and concrete protection built for numerous machine guns and mortars; guns, sited to fire east and west along the shore, were emplaced on either side of the harbour entrance and were well protected by concrete from bombing and naval bombardment. The town itself lies mainly to the east of the river, stretching nearly a mile inland along the road which runs southwards to Caen. Behind the harbour, on the west bank of the river, lies the village of Graye sur Mer. The capture of Courseulles and Graye was the first task of the division's 7th Canadian Brigade Group. A mile or more further east the 8th Canadian Brigade Group was to land at Bernières sur Mer and at St. Aubin sur Mer. There, again, houses on the front and behind the sea wall were fortified and barbed wire and minefields covered machine-gun and mortar positions protected by concrete. The only road which leads directly from the shore had been blocked by a concrete wall.

It had been planned to begin landing the 7th Brigade at 7.35 a.m. and the 8th ten minutes later, but in view of the fact that rough weather seemed likely to delay some of the landing craft, the local joint commanders postponed both landings for ten minutes. Even so some groups were late in arriving and the planned sequence could not be adhered to. Most D.D. tanks were swum ashore (though some from a shorter distance than had been planned). On only one sector of the divisional front did the D.D. tanks beach ahead of the infantry and at once engage the defences; on all other Canadian sectors the tanks arrived after the infantry. Most of the craft which carried the engineers' tanks were delayed through having got into the wrong swept channel during passage, and the leading infantry were a little late too. The covering fire of destroyers and support craft, including the field guns firing while still at sea, was accurately timed and so effective that there was little enemy shooting before craft touched down. But although by delaying the time of landings they gained the advantage of higher water over off-shore rocks, they now had to land *among* beach obstructions instead of *ahead* of them. The obstacle clearance groups could do little before the rising tide put a stop to their efforts, for the sea was too rough for under-water work. The larger landing craft had therefore to drive on-shore in spite of obstructions and the smaller craft to worm their way through if they could. The courage and resolution of their crews matched the occasion and they showed much skill and daring in bringing them in; there was no pause in the landings but the loss and damage to landing craft was severe. Out of three hundred and six landing craft of all sorts employed by Force J on that morning ninety were lost or damaged in breaking their way ashore or in withdrawing after discharging their loads.

One illustration must typify what was happening all along the British front. The extract is from the report of a lieutenant of the Royal Canadian Naval Volunteer Reserve on the performance of five landing craft from the flotilla under his command, carrying infantry in the initial assault.

> 'The lowering of craft began at 0617 . . . The forming up with other assault flotillas . . . carrying troops was satisfactory . . . and the passage to the release position . . . uneventful . . . Upon leaving the release position . . . the beach was clearly visible . . . the tide was considerably higher than had been anticipated and the beach obstructions were partly covered with water. There were six rows of obstructions but we were able to weave our way through them. At 0840 all craft . . . were beached. There was quite a heavy swell and a strong current on our starboard quarter . . . On the beaches there was considerable enemy fire, mostly from mortars.
>
> About three quarters of the troops had been disembarked from L.C.A. 1150 when an explosion caused either by a mine or by a mortar bomb blew in the port side. One soldier was wounded. The port side of L.C.A. 1059 was blown in by the explosion of one of the mined obstructions after about one third of the troops had been disembarked. Casualties in this craft were two soldiers killed. Another explosion holed L.C.A. 1137 and stove in the starboard bow. All troops were cleared from the craft without casualties. All troops had been disembarked from L.C.A. 1138 and the craft was about to leave the beach when a wave lifted it on to an obstruction. The explosion which followed ripped the bottom out of the craft . . . the boat officer in the craft suffered several shrapnel wounds in his legs, a fracture of the right fibula and slight head injuries. All troops were discharged from L.C.A. 1151 without loss . . . I ordered the crews of the sunken craft to embark for return passage to the ship. By this time there was a cleared channel through the obstructions . . . but as we were leaving an approaching L.C.T. forced us to alter course. An obstruction ripped the bottom out of L.C.A. 1151. The crews then transferred to an L.C.T. and were eventually brought back to the ship.'

The flotilla had done its job but at a cost of four out of the five landing craft involved. It was indeed a common experience that, despite all difficulties, landing craft bearing infantry made their way to the shore and landed the soldiers with very few casualties. It was while lying in the breakers among the obstacles or when withdrawing from this perilous position that they suffered most heavily. Mercifully most of their crews were saved.

The Centaurs of the 2nd Royal Marine Armoured Support Regiment again fared badly owing to trouble with their unseaworthy landing craft, three of which were capsized and two had to return to port: out of forty tanks with which the regiment was to support the Canadian landings only about six were ashore on D-day.

Of two groups of small landing craft 'Hedgerow' allotted to Juno to clear lanes through beach minefields, one arrived intact and delivered its bombs across the beach near Bernières ahead of the infantry. Of the other group only one craft survived the sea passage.

The 7th Canadian Brigade was attacking the beaches on both sides of Courseulles harbour, The Royal Winnipeg Rifles on the right and The Regina Rifle Regiment on the left, with D.D. tanks of the 6th Canadian Armoured Regiment supporting them. One company of the Winnipegs attacked the defences on the west of the entrance while the rest of the battalion moved round behind the harbour to capture Graye sur Mer. But the main defences of the port lay in Courseulles, east of the river, and these were attacked by The Regina Rifles. Like le Hamel, Courseulles was stubbornly held and eventually a troop of the Royal Marine Centaurs and tanks of the 26th Assault Squadron, R.E., also became involved in the bitter street fighting. It was not finally captured until well into the afternoon. One of the reserve companies of The Regina Rifles coming ashore twenty minutes later suffered heavily when two of its landing craft were mined on obstacles, yet although reduced in strength it straightway set out with the battalion to capture Reviers, two miles inland at the junction of the rivers Seulles and Mue.

The brigade's reserve battalion, The Canadian Scottish Regiment, had sent forward with the first wave of the assault one company under command of The Winnipeg Rifles. Landing on the west flank they had met little opposition and finding that the naval bombardment had demolished a nearby coastal post, which included a 75-mm gun in a concrete emplacement, they went on to Vaux. There also they found the gun abandoned and they pressed southwards towards Ste. Croix. The rest of their battalion landed behind the Winnipegs and, avoiding Courseulles, they also struck southwards for Ste. Croix.

The hold-up at Courseulles, which meant that the nearby beaches were still under enemy fire, and the fact that landing craft carrying the assault engineers' breaching crews were coming in late and irregularly, was delaying the clearance of exits from the shore; already there were signs that congestion might delay the movement of troops and vehicles as these continued to come in.

The development of beach exits may not seem a difficult task; here is an illustration of what it might involve. Half of the 26th Assault Squadron, Royal Engineers, landed just west of Courseulles, after infantry and D.D. tanks had already begun to gain ascendency, and set out to make an exit from the shore. Facing them was a line of sand dunes twelve to fifteen feet high, then two to four hundred yards of low-lying land which had been flooded by the damming and heavy cratering of a stream, and beyond that the lateral road from

Courseulles to la Rivière to which the exit was to lead. Mines had been thickly scattered among the barbed wire, which was in large quantities in the dunes and the ground to be crossed.

A bridging tank of the sappers laid its bridge against the dunes and three flail tanks of the 22nd Dragoons went up it. The first had flogged its way for about forty yards through the minefield when a mine exploded under its track; the second was stopped by mechanical trouble and the third so entangled in wire that it could not get further. Progress was now impeded by a German tank trap, fifteen feet wide and nine deep. A fascine was laid in it and a bulldozer set to work to fill it in. Beyond the trap the flooded stream had passed through a culvert; this had been blown up and a huge crater full of water took its place. Another fascine-carrying tank tried to fill it but the 'tank slid into the crater and gradually disappeared from view except for its fascine.' The crew baled out but were all killed or wounded by mortar fire before they could reach cover. Other sappers freed the fascine by explosives and a bridge 'was dropped from the seaward side on the sunken tank which acted as a pier' but left a gap on the far side; this was filled with logs carried from the shore where the Germans had collected them for the construction of obstacles. 'A causeway was built out and about 0915 hours the first D.D. tank got across behind the assaulting companies' and more followed. Then field guns arrived but the first 'totally misjudged the bridge and bellied itself on it . . . Three bulldozers were linked together but failed to pull him off; two AVREs were therefore brought up and, after a lot of trouble, succeeded in getting him off.' The horse and cart of 'a disinterested farmer' was impressed to complete the track with rubble from damaged houses, and from then on the way was open for traffic.

The 8th Canadian Brigade's leading battalions—The Queen's Own Rifles of Canada and The North Shore (New Brunswick) Regiment—landed meanwhile on Nan beaches opposite and a little east of Bernières. The D.D. tanks of the 10th Canadian Armoured Regiment had been launched close to the shore from their landing craft, one of which with four tanks on board was sunk by shell-fire. The rest of the tanks waded in. Two were lost at the water's edge but thirty-four arrived in time to support the infantry already ashore.

The front at Bernières was bounded by a sea wall, in places twelve feet high, and houses behind it had been fortified. Although many had been demolished by naval bombardment the place remained a formidable strong-point whose defences had largely survived. These included two 50-mm anti-tank guns, two heavy mortars and eight machine guns, in addition to infantry in prepared positions. Landing on the right of the sea front The Queen's Own Rifles suffered severely from enfilading fire as they rushed the beach and stormed the sea wall, but once they had done so they attacked from the flank and the enemy soon surrendered.

East of Bernières leading companies of The North Shore Regiment had a similar experience in landing near St. Aubin sur Mer. It is a somewhat larger watering place and it too was firmly defended. Its reduction with the help of the assault engineers' tanks took about three hours and, even after the main position had been taken, sporadic fire from hidden snipers continued intermittently till nightfall. The battalion's reserve company, which landed twenty minutes after the initial landing, immediately moved southwards towards Tailleville.

The division's third brigade—the 9th Canadian Brigade—began landing at about half past eleven. By then many damaged landing craft encumbered the water's edge; only a narrow strip of beach was still uncovered by the rising tide and this was crowded by men and vehicles. Some beach exits had been cleared but these were being jammed from time to time by vehicles hit by enemy shells or temporarily broken down. Until Bernières was cleared and additional exits facilitated movement, not only the beach but Bernières itself became choked with troops and vehicles struggling to assemble and get forward. Nevertheless by two o'clock the whole of the 3rd Canadian Division was ashore with its four regiments of field artillery (12th, 13th, 14th and 19th) and its third regiment of armour (the 27th).

On the left of the Canadian brigade No. 48 (Royal Marine) Commando had landed at about nine o'clock in the morning. By that time most of the beach obstacles were submerged, and in rough water many of their landing craft (L.C.I.(S)) suffered widespread damage; being built of wood this type was particularly vulnerable. Three, carrying headquarters of the 4th Special Service Brigade, and two with troops of the Commando on board, struck mined obstacles and another was hit by shell-fire. The men who reached the shore came under close-range machine-gun fire from St. Aubin as they rushed the sea wall and little more than two hundred (about half their strength) started eastwards to attack Langrune sur Mer, hitherto kept under fire from the sea by guns of the support craft.

Only three miles away along the coast to the east of St. Aubin lies a little watering place called Lion sur Mer and two and a half miles still further east is the larger seaside town of Ouistreham, at the mouth of the river Orne. The coast between Lion and Ouistreham is flat and the coastal road which joins them is fringed with houses along its whole length. Lion and Ouistreham were both fortified as strong-points and about halfway between them was another strong-point at la Brèche, with the familiar casemated guns, mortars, machine guns and wired trench positions for infantry. This stretch of coast was the Sword area and the beach to the west of la Brèche was known as 'Queen'; the British 3rd Division was to attack there on a single brigade front. Its 8th Brigade Group was to land first and be followed in turn by the 185th and the 9th Brigades. This concentration of attack on a narrow front was planned to put as much weight as possible into the blow which the division was to strike for the rapid capture of Caen and the link-up with the airborne division. Details of the supporting troops are shown on the diagram at page 172.

The experience of the 8th Brigade was similar to that of the other assault brigades. It landed at the time fixed and in the chosen place. The protection given by the fire of destroyers and support craft during the run-in was so effective that there was little enemy fire till the shore was neared. Thirty-four out of forty of the D.D. tanks of the 13th/18th Hussars were launched at sea and only two failed to reach the coast; six more were taken in in landing craft and all were landed. Six tanks were knocked out in the surf and four shortly after; twenty-eight were available to support the infantry though they were not there before the first infantry landed. Two troops of the 5th Independent Battery, Royal Marine Armoured Support Regiment, reached the land within the first quarter of an hour and a third came in later; craft carrying the breaching teams and armoured vehicles of the assault engineers and Dragoons were landed with the leading infantry and were the only supporting troops ashore at the outset. The wind was driving the sea inshore so rapidly that obstacle clearance groups could only mark one clear passage until the tide receded. In trying to neutralise mines and shells attached to the obstacles some sappers were soon exhausted and several were swept away; for the time being they could only work above the water's edge. The majority of craft arriving with the first assault troops had to risk obstacles and drive ashore as best they could and there were inevitably many casualties.

The landings here, as on the other assault beaches down the coast, were on the whole so successful that it is easy to miss the significance of how much was due to the faithfulness of those in charge of the landing craft. The majority were organised for the run-in as small flotillas under the immediate command of young officers of the Royal Marines or the Royal Naval Volunteer Reserve. The records of what happened to craft under their command, in spite of their bald statements of fact, must fill the reader with pride.

A flotilla of ten landing craft carrying assault engineers and their armoured vehicles, under command of a lieutenant of the Royal Naval Volunteer Reserve, touched down at 7.26 a.m., one minute late. All craft succeeded in unloading with the exception of one which only managed to unload one flail; as a second was about to move down the ramp it was hit by a mortar shell which exploded the

Bangalore torpedoes being carried. The explosion killed Lieut-Colonel Cocks, the Royal Engineers' commander, and two other ranks; seven other ranks were wounded; three vehicles were disabled on board which prevented further unloading. None of the other craft was seriously damaged though two were hit by shells and mortar fire.

Of seven craft carrying tanks of the Royal Marine Armoured Support Regiment two were lost after unloading. One of them received several direct hits from mortar bombs and was soon on fire. It was commanded by a temporary sub-lieutenant of the Royal Naval Volunteer Reserve with two other officers of the same rank; all three and some of the crew were killed. The second craft was mined and hit by shell-fire; one of the crew was killed and a junior officer and four ratings were wounded; the craft became a total wreck.

And here is the story of one craft commanded by another temporary lieutenant of the Volunteer Reserve; it carried self-propelled guns of the field artillery and 'received a hit from a mortar shell when about a hundred yards from the beach. The shell hit the after end of the tank deck and ignited the petrol supply of the three field guns. A few minutes later the craft beached and disembarked all but the three burning guns and the fire was soon brought under control.' No soldiers were available to move the damaged guns, for two of their detachments had landed with those not damaged and the rest were casualties from burns. In spite of the 'unpleasant experience' of fire on board and shell damage the craft unbeached and went to the assistance of another damaged craft which was in danger of sinking. Its crew and some wounded soldiers were taken off and it was taken in tow stern first. The tow rope parted three times but both craft reached the southern exit of the swept channel where the towed craft was handed over to a tug and the wounded transferred to a vessel with a surgeon on board. On continuing its own return journey to England the engines failed as water had entered the fuel tank through a shell hole. The official report concludes: 'This gallant craft was then taken in tow . . . and eventually reached the collecting area at Portsmouth at 1600 on 7th June.' In spite of all they had gone through the crew had suffered no casualties since it had sailed from England two days before. It was one of eighteen that carried the self-propelled guns of the 7th, 33rd and 76th Field Regiments, Royal Artillery, which were landed after firing while at sea during the opening phase of the assault. Of these eighteen craft six were damaged by enemy fire, five by obstacles and three by mines; two of these fourteen became total wrecks.

But although these are typical examples of what many experienced, there were many others which came through unscathed. Twenty landing craft, for instance, bore the first wave of assaulting infantry of the 8th Brigade to the shore and, successfully avoiding all obstacles, landed them without a casualty. They were the leading companies of the 1st South Lancashire Regiment on the right and the 2nd East Yorkshire Regiment on the left. They started landing at half past seven on the beach between la Brèche and Lion sur Mer and were to be joined about twenty minutes later by the rest of their battalions.

The tide was rising fast and the foreshore was already narrowed to about fifteen yards. A belt of barbed wire separated it from the road along the sea front and, irregularly spaced behind it, were a number of machine-gun posts. Fire from the la Brèche strong-point swept the water's edge and the beach but the troops crossed this without many casualties to break their way through to the narrow built-up area which faced them. One company from each battalion joined in an attack on the strong-point, the others started to clear the enemy from the housing belt along the coast. A company of the South Lancashire moved out to guard the right flank and was soon joined by No. 41 (Royal Marine) Commando, much weakened by casualties on the beach, whose task was to pass through and capture the enemy position at Lion sur Mer; the East Yorkshire turned left towards Ouistreham and were followed, shortly afterwards, by No. 4 Commando and two French troops from No. 10 (Inter-Allied) Commando whose primary rôle was to capture Ouistreham and destroy the battery there. While the fight for the la Brèche position continued, the rest of the South Lancashire battalion landed and struck inland for Hermanville sur Mer which they occupied by nine o'clock. The rest of the East Yorkshire battalion set out to capture two enemy positions near the south-west corner of Ouistreham.

Soon after ten o'clock, after nearly three hours' fighting, the la Brèche position was captured. Its three guns and three heavy mortars, machine guns and rifle posts had done much damage to incoming and unloading craft during that time and had caused the attacking troops many casualties. Among those killed was the commanding officer of the South Lancashire, who lost, in all, five officers killed and six wounded with ninety-six other ranks killed or wounded. The East Yorkshire losses were equally heavy. And here as elsewhere along the British front the fact that with few exceptions the near defences of the coast had been silenced did not yet mean that the beaches were free from danger. A high wind had driven the full tide up the beaches to within ten yards or so of the sand dunes. Vehicles, now being landed in large numbers, were so tightly packed along the water front that it was almost impossible to move along the shore to a prepared exit; the delay was already upsetting the time-tables. The narrow beaches were still under fire from gun positions inland and from beyond the Orne—the exposed left flank of the British assault. Barrage balloons were put up as protection from air attack but were soon cut adrift when it was found that they were being used as ranging marks by enemy gunners. The 8th Brigade's third battalion—the 1st Suffolk—also had a troublous experience in landing.

The rest of the 3rd Division, the 185th and the 9th Brigades, and the 1st Special Service (Commando) Brigade came ashore during the morning and early afternoon.

The initial American landings were made by troops of VII Corps in association with the Naval Force U on the Utah beaches of the Cotentin coast; and by V Corps with Force O on Omaha beaches between the mouth of the Vire and Port en Bessin (map, page 222). The first landings at Utah had been made under more favourable conditions and against less opposition than any others on the whole Allied front; at Omaha, on the other hand, conditions were in some respects more difficult and the local opposition was certainly more effective than anywhere else. It is therefore not surprising that widely different results had been achieved during these early hours.

As already mentioned, the American leaders had decided to begin landings at half past six,[2] that is about an hour earlier than the British; the tide would be lower then, thus giving more time for the clearance of obstacles. They had also decided not to open the naval bombardment till ten minutes to six as against the British opening at half past five. The prearranged fire support had thus lasted for only forty minutes when the American landings began, whereas the British front had been bombarded for two hours before H-hour. Admiral Kirk, commanding the Western Task Force, subsequently reported that 'the period of bombardment was extremely heavy but was of too short duration to silence or neutralise all the defences, particularly in the Omaha area'. Rear-Admiral Hall who commanded Force O held the same view: 'the time available for the pre-landing bombardment was not sufficient for the destruction of beach defence targets'.

The lowering positions ('transport areas') were about eleven miles from the coast (as against the British seven) so troops had to endure at least three hours in small craft while closing the shore. During much of this long run-in craft making for Utah moved in comparatively sheltered water under the lee of the Cotentin peninsula; those making for Omaha were exposed to a stronger wind and rougher seas. Behind the sand dunes at Utah the land is only a few feet above sea level for the first few hundred yards inland; the chief protection of the coast consisted of a further wide extent of meadow land below sea level, normally drained by dykes but now flooded. At four widely-separated points there were banked-up roads serving as narrow

---

[2] Two hours earlier the undefended St. Marcouf Islands flanking Utah beach had been occupied.

causeways through the inundations, and American airborne troops were already fighting to gain possession of their western exits. By contrast, the foreshore at Omaha is everywhere overlooked by formidable bluffs which, rising in places to about a hundred and fifty feet, command the water's edge and the beaches to be captured. The close defences on the narrow strip of unflooded land behind Utah had been effectively bombarded and bombed; the bombers had missed the defences covering Omaha which were so protected from seaward attack that the naval forty-minute bombardment had not silenced them. Finally, to complete this comparison of conditions which affected the American assaults, the troops defending the Omaha beaches were of better quality and in greater strength than those at Utah.

One disadvantage encountered by Force U was an undetected minefield offshore. This caused the loss of the navigational leader (control vessel) of the left-hand assault group, a landing craft carrying four D.D. tanks and, later, the destroyer *Corry*. The other control vessel of this left group had been disabled in the transport area. Of the right hand group only one control vessel remained in the van to lead the assault, the second having turned back to guide the group of craft carrying the D.D. tanks, delayed by the mining of one of their number. Owing to these misfortunes, the obscuring of landmarks by smoke and the effects of a strong current, craft were beached about a mile further south than had been planned, but this turned out to be an advantage for both beach obstacles and forward defences were less formidable there than they were further north.

The organisation of the American assault is shown in the diagram opposite;[3] from this it will be seen that the opening attack on Utah was to be made by the United States 4th Infantry Division. The division consisted of three 'regimental combat teams' (the 8th, 12th and 22nd), each of which was composed of an infantry regiment of three battalions and of artillery, tanks, engineers and other supporting troops, and thus corresponded approximately to a British brigade group. The initial attack was made by the 8th Regimental Combat Team, with two of its battalions landing first and the third following in close support. The infantry started landing punctually at half past six and meeting very little opposition they quickly overcame the adjacent enemy posts defending the shore. The twenty-eight D.D. tanks which were available, after the landing craft mentioned above had been sunk, were all launched at sea about three thousand yards from the shore and all swam in safely but were a few minutes after the infantry. The tide had not yet reached the beach obstacles and little enemy fire was directed at them; within an

---

[3] For a detailed account of the American assault, see Harrison, *Cross-Channel Attack*, chap. VIII.

The Seaborne Assault—United States First Army

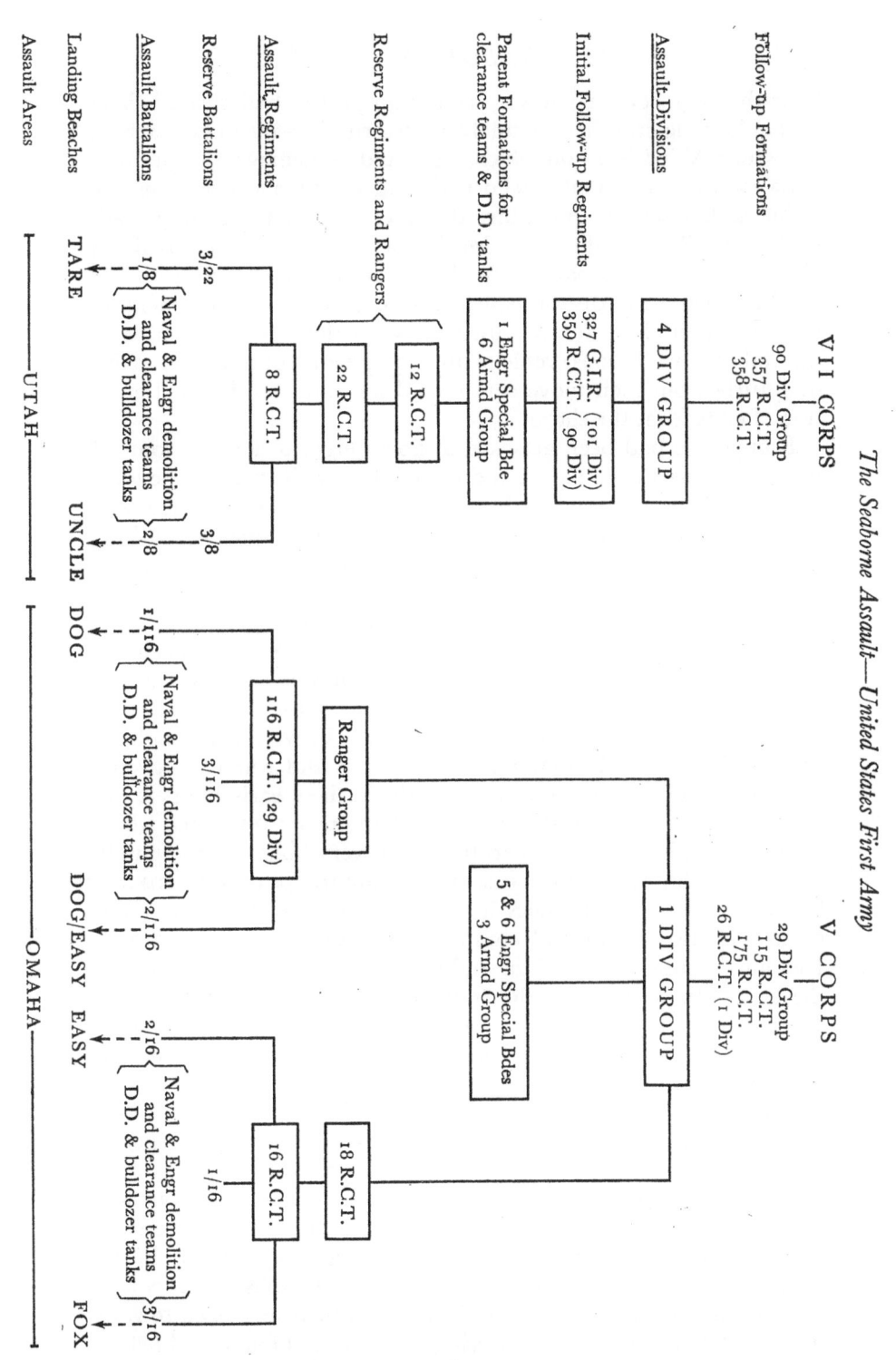

	VII CORPS	V CORPS	
Follow-up Formations	90 Div Group 357 R.C.T. 358 R.C.T.	29 Div Group 115 R.C.T. 175 R.C.T. 26 R.C.T. (1 Div)	
Assault Divisions	4 DIV GROUP	1 DIV GROUP	
Initial Follow-up Regiments	327 G.I.R. (101 Div) 359 R.C.T. (90 Div)		
Parent Formations for clearance teams & D.D. tanks	1 Engr Special Bde 6 Armd Group	5 & 6 Engr Special Bdes 3 Armd Group	
Reserve Regiments and Rangers	12 R.C.T. 22 R.C.T.	Ranger Group 18 R.C.T.	
Assault Regiments	8 R.C.T.	116 R.C.T. (29 Div)	16 R.C.T.
Assault Battalions	1/8 → 3/22 2/8 → 3/8	1/116 → 3/116 2/116	2/16 → 1/16 3/16
Naval & Engr demolition and clearance teams D.D. & bulldozer tanks			
Reserve Battalions			
Landing Beaches	TARE — UNCLE	DOG — DOG/EASY	EASY — FOX
Assault Areas	—— UTAH ——	—— OMAHA ——	

hour the engineers and naval demolition parties had cleared them so that landing craft had an unobstructed run-in—the only beach on the whole Allied front on which this could be achieved so quickly.

As soon as the infantry who had landed first had overcome the defences they set out to capture the three southern causeway roads leading to Pouppeville, Ste. Marie du Mont and Audouville la Hubert. A sea wall separated the land from the shore and until this was breached and exits for vehicles had been cleared, movement off the shore and along the narrow causeways through the floods was inevitably slow. Troops, vehicles and equipment continued to arrive undisturbed but their movement inland was hindered by the limitation of exits from the shore.

Pouppeville had been attacked at about eight o'clock by some of the parachutists who had been dropped during the night. The force was a small one and some of the garrison held on till noon; a few who tried to escape to the coast were taken prisoner by infantry pushing inland from the beach; it was there that contact was first made between seaborne and airborne troops.

By ten o'clock in the morning six battalions of infantry with a considerable quantity of supporting arms were ashore, the beach was not under accurate fire and beach organisation was taking shape, but movement along the narrow causeways available was still slow. Some of the infantry tried to quicken the pace by wading through the flooded fields, but the water was waist deep and where it covered dykes men were often out of their depth. In these early hours it was delay imposed by the flooding rather than enemy resistance which prevented rapid progress. Apart from this everything was going well.

Fifteen miles away to the east the leading troops of V Corps had begun the attack on beaches in the Omaha area. The attack was opened by two regimental combat teams, the 116th (of the 29th Division) landing on the right and the 16th (of the 1st Division) on the left. Both were under the commander of the 1st Division who was given the 115th Combat Team of the 29th Division to support the landings on the right and had his own division's 18th Combat Team to support the attack on the left beach: in addition, two battalions of Rangers (corresponding approximately to British Commandos) were employed in the assault, their task including a special mission to capture the enemy position on Pointe du Hoe.

As the transport area was so far from the shore, and as H-hour was only about half an hour after sunrise, the assault craft had to start for the shore in darkness. 'Due to the darkness and confusion in the Transport Area' the landing craft carrying D.D. tanks, artillery and demolition parties 'straggled considerably in their approach toward the line of departure'. Two, carrying artillery, had foundered before reaching the transport areas: one strayed to the Force U area and did not return until several hours later: two more 'had gone so far to the eastward that they could not get back in time for their part in the initial assault wave'. Of thirty-two D.D. tanks which were launched six thousand yards from the shore twenty-seven foundered; fifty-one were taken to the shore in landing craft but eight of them were knocked out in the surf by enemy gun-fire. 'At least ten' of the craft carrying infantry were swamped on the way in and much of the artillery was sunk.[4] The Americans had planned to ferry the leading artillery ashore in DUKWs.[5] In the prevailing weather the heavy loads proved too much for these craft. Twenty-two out of thirty of the howitzers of two field artillery battalions and an infantry cannon company were lost. 'In short, the artillery that was planned to support the infantry attack particularly in the advance inland did not reach the shore.'[6]

Off Omaha no enemy gun was fired while the assault craft moved in towards the coast. But once assault craft reached the shore and landings began, a withering fire from guns, mortars and machine guns opened on beached craft and soldiers wading to land. Faulty navigation and ineffective control of the landing craft made the task of the troops more difficult since they were scattered and many were landed too far to the east, not always with the formation to which they belonged.

While making their arduous course from the transport areas landing craft moved under the direction of 'primary' and 'secondary' control vessels. Of these, Admiral Hall states in his official report on Force O that 'neither were adequately trained': the former had received only 'a few days instruction', had taken part in one large-scale exercise and had been taken out 'several times' for special drill as control vessels; the latter 'had had no instruction and no training'. He adds, 'they did not arrive in the theater soon enough'. Wind, waves, the set of the tidal current and the masking of landmarks by mist and smoke from the naval bombardment proved too much for them. The American historian gives a grim account of what happened.

> '. . . units became scattered on the final approach. Since the men had been briefed only for their particular areas, they were confused by the changed picture . . . Debarking in water sometimes up to their necks, the troops on some sectors of the beach were met with a hail of bullets that drove some to seek shelter under the surf, others to scramble over the sides of the craft . . . The troops, overladen with heavy clothing and equipment, waded slowly through the surf and through fire that increased as

---

[4] Harrison, op. cit., p. 309.
[5] Amphibious lorries—a most valuable American equipment.
[6] Loc. cit., p. 313.

they approached the beach. Some stopped to rest or seek shelter behind obstacles. Some lay at the water's edge and were able eventually to crawl in with the tide ... The first wave should have landed nine companies evenly spaced along the beach. Because of withering enemy fire and mislandings, however, the right wing all but disintegrated; two companies bunched in front of les Moulins, and the remainder of the landings (elements of four companies) clustered in the Colleville sector. One company was carried so far to the east that it landed an hour and a half late.'[7]

Immediately after the leading infantry were to come the engineers to clear obstacles and exits from the shore. 'Half the demolition teams were delayed in landing and only a third of them touched down on their appointed sectors' and much of their equipment was lost. They had very heavy casualties and after half an hour the rising tide had made further clearance of the beach impossible. The American authorities had decided not to use the variety of armoured vehicles which proved so valuable to the Royal Engineers in the British landings, relying mainly on bull-dozers for clearance work. Of sixteen bull-dozers allotted to the 116th Infantry 'only three could be put into operation on the beach, and one of these was prevented from maneuvering freely by riflemen who sheltered behind it'.[8]

When the succeeding waves began coming in the surviving men who had landed in the first wave were still at the water's edge, or sheltering either under the bank of shingle at the top of the sands or the wall at the foot of the bluff. Obstacles had not been cleared and were now largely under water; no exits from the beaches had been opened; the enemy's gun-fire was still unsilenced and machine-gun fire from the overlooking bluffs swept the water's edge and the beach. Admiral Hall wrote, of this time:

> '... the landing craft were allowed to fall into confusion, and wave after wave was dispatched from the line of departure close in on the preceding wave, where the combined effect of the wind and tide soon converted the waves into a milling mass in which little semblance of order remained. Had it not been for the appearance on the scene of the Deputy Assault Group Commanders and their prompt action in withdrawing and reforming these craft, the success of the entire landing would have been jeopardized.'

The American historian, with a German report before him, adds:

> 'To the German officer in command of the fortifications at Pointe et Raz de la Percée it looked in these first hours as though

---

[7] Harrison, op. cit., p. 313.
[8] Loc. cit., p. 317.

25. British warships open fire
Detail from painting by Norman Wilkinson

SEABORNE APPROACH

26. Assault craft head for the beaches

27. Infantry and amphibious (DD) tank

LANDINGS ON D-DAY

28. Royal Marine Commandos

the invasion had been stopped on the beaches. He noted that the Americans were lying on the shore seeking cover behind the obstacles, that ten tanks and a "great many other vehicles" were burning. The fire of his own positions and the artillery, he thought, had been excellent, causing heavy losses. He could see the wounded and dead lying on the sand.' [9]

Yet the German officer was mistaken in thinking the invasion had been stopped. From about seven-thirty onwards small parties of soldiers had broken through the barbed wire which bounded the shore and had been working their way up through the mine-sown slopes. At this juncture eight United States and three British destroyers closed the shore and opened fire on many of the enemy positions. Almost imperceptibly at first the general situation began to improve. Individual movements forward began to take effect and by about nine o'clock parties of soldiers had reached the crest between defence posts and were turning to attack them and to feel their way forward towards St. Laurent and Vierville. Opposite Colleville a small gap had been opened with the help of fire from a destroyer and a strong-point guarding the defile through the hills was being stormed.

Three companies of the Rangers landing near Pointe du Hoe had scaled the cliffs with ropes and ladders and under cover of fire from the destroyers *Satterlee* (U.S.) and *Talybont* (British) had stormed the battery positions and 'eliminated' the garrison remaining. The guns had been removed but were found later well concealed inland.

By ten o'clock there were indications that the assault was making some progress as more American troops climbed the heights above Omaha, and the British 50th Division pressing inland began to threaten the German position by turning its eastern flank. The invasion was far from being 'stopped', but the American troops were to have much hard fighting before the Omaha sector was securely won.

By now the world knew that the Allies had begun their long-deferred attack from the West, for at five minutes past nine a press communiqué had been issued from Supreme Headquarters which read:

'Under the command of General Eisenhower, Allied naval forces supported by strong air forces began landing Allied armies this morning on the northern coast of France.'

It was too early to disclose the most astonishing news of all, namely that no German aircraft had yet appeared. How different from the days, four years before, when British troops were withdrawn from France! Then ships and small craft lying off the beaches at Dunkirk

---

[9] Loc. cit., pp. 319–320.

O

or alongside the mole of its outer harbour, and three hundred thousand soldiers holding the bridgehead or on the sand hills and in the surf waiting their turn to leave, had endured the all-out attempt of the German air force to stop evacuation. Now a far larger target of Allied shipping was offered and far larger armies had begun landing on the coast of Normandy. On the British beaches alone over thirty-one thousand men, over three hundred guns and another seven hundred armoured vehicles had already been landed within two and a half hours of the opening of the assault. In all that time the German air force was conspicuous by its absence; it appeared to be completely daunted by the Allied air forces covering and furthering the assault. Absolute immunity from air attack was perhaps the most surprising phenomenon of these early hours of D-day.

Another disclosure was the failure, amounting to fiasco, of the Atlantic Wall. Nowhere were the defence works on which so much labour and material had been expended providing any decisive hindrance to the Allied landings. It is true that some strong-points had still to be taken, it is true that the captured beaches had still to be joined up and it is of course obvious that, until the Allied armies were ashore in greater strength and occupied firmly a larger bridgehead, the Allies' foothold in France would be precarious. Yet it was already true that the coastal defences of the assault beaches which had taken years to construct were being swept away in almost as many hours.

In spite of what has been said it would be wrong to pretend that everything was going exactly as planned. Though leading troops had broken through the beach defences and were pushing inland, most of the beaches were still under enemy fire from gun-positions able to reach the shore. Under-water obstacles were still reaping a harvest of damaged landing craft and the clearance and construction of tracks to enable tanks and vehicles to move inland was still very incomplete; as a result there was serious congestion on most of the beaches and progress everywhere was behind schedule. It has been explained that the beaches being attacked by the British were, in total, less than five miles wide. On that small space there had been landed, by about half past ten, fifteen infantry battalions, seven commandos, seven tank regiments; two engineer assault regiments; nine field artillery regiments; portions of two Royal Marine armoured support regiments and elements of five beach groups with detachments of the Royal Navy and the Royal Air Force.

It is hardly surprising that while all these men with large quantities of vehicles and equipment were being landed without pause there were times when they appeared to be so jammed together that movement was impossible. Tanks and self-propelled guns were on the beaches in some cases for an hour or more before they were able to move off the shore. Some field guns were deployed so near the sea that, as they opened fire in support of the troops moving inland, the tide lapped against them. At one place the beach was only fifteen yards wide where a hundred and fifty yards was expected, for the wind had raised an unusually high tide.

It is impossible to say exactly when the first beach exits were open. People were too busy to keep looking at their watches and some exits, opened fairly quickly, were later blocked by knocked-out vehicles or traffic jams. It had been foreseen that the rate of landing would be governed by the availability of exits and it had been planned to open twenty-eight in the first hour. The 3rd Division and the 50th appear to have had their first exits opened not much later but not nearly all that were needed; two hours or more had elapsed before the first was opened on the Canadian beaches. The delay in each case had slowed the landings of the reserve brigades and this inevitably had far-reaching effects on the day's progress. But before following their movements inland it will be well to get a clearer understanding of what they were up against and to learn what the German commanders were doing in these early hours of the assault.

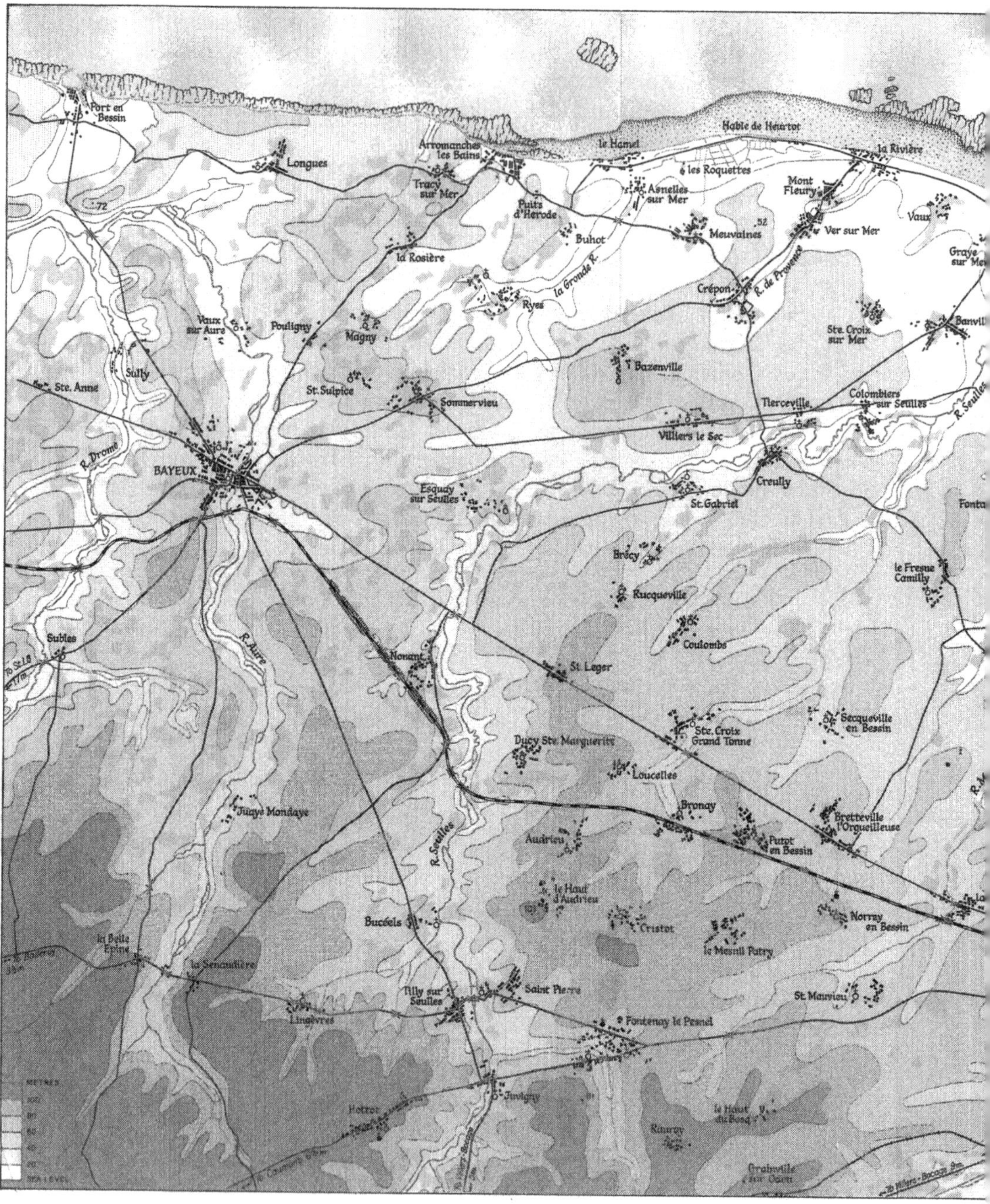
Port en Bessin
Longues
Arromanches les Bains
Tracy sur Mer
Puits d'Herode
le Hamel
Hable de Heurtot
les Roquettes
Asnelles sur Mer
Meuvaines
Mont Fleury
la Rivière
Ver sur Mer
Vaux
Graye sur Mer
Buhot
la Rosière
la Grande R.
Ryes
Crépon
R. de Provence
Banville
Ste. Croix sur Mer
Vaux sur Aure
Pouligny
Magny
Sully
Ste. Anne
St. Sulpice
Sommervieu
Bazenville
Tierceville
Colombiers sur Seulles
R. Seulles
Villiers le Sec
R. Drome
BAYEUX
Esquay sur Seulles
St. Gabriel
Creully
Brécy
Rucqueville
le Fresne Camilly
Subles
R. Aure
Nonant
St. Leger
Coulombs
Secqueville en Bessin
Ducy Ste. Marguerite
Ste. Croix Grand Tonne
Loucelles
Juaye Mondaye
Bronay
Putot en Bessin
Bretteville l'Orgueilleuse
Audrieu
R. Seulles
le Haut d'Audrieu
Cristot
Norrey en Bessin
Bucéels
le Mesnil Patry
la Belle Epine
la Senaudière
Tilly sur Seulles
Saint Pierre
St. Mauvieu
Lingèvres
Fontenay le Pesnel
Juvigny
Hottot
le Haut du Bosq
Rauray
Grainville sur Odon
METRES
SEA LEVEL

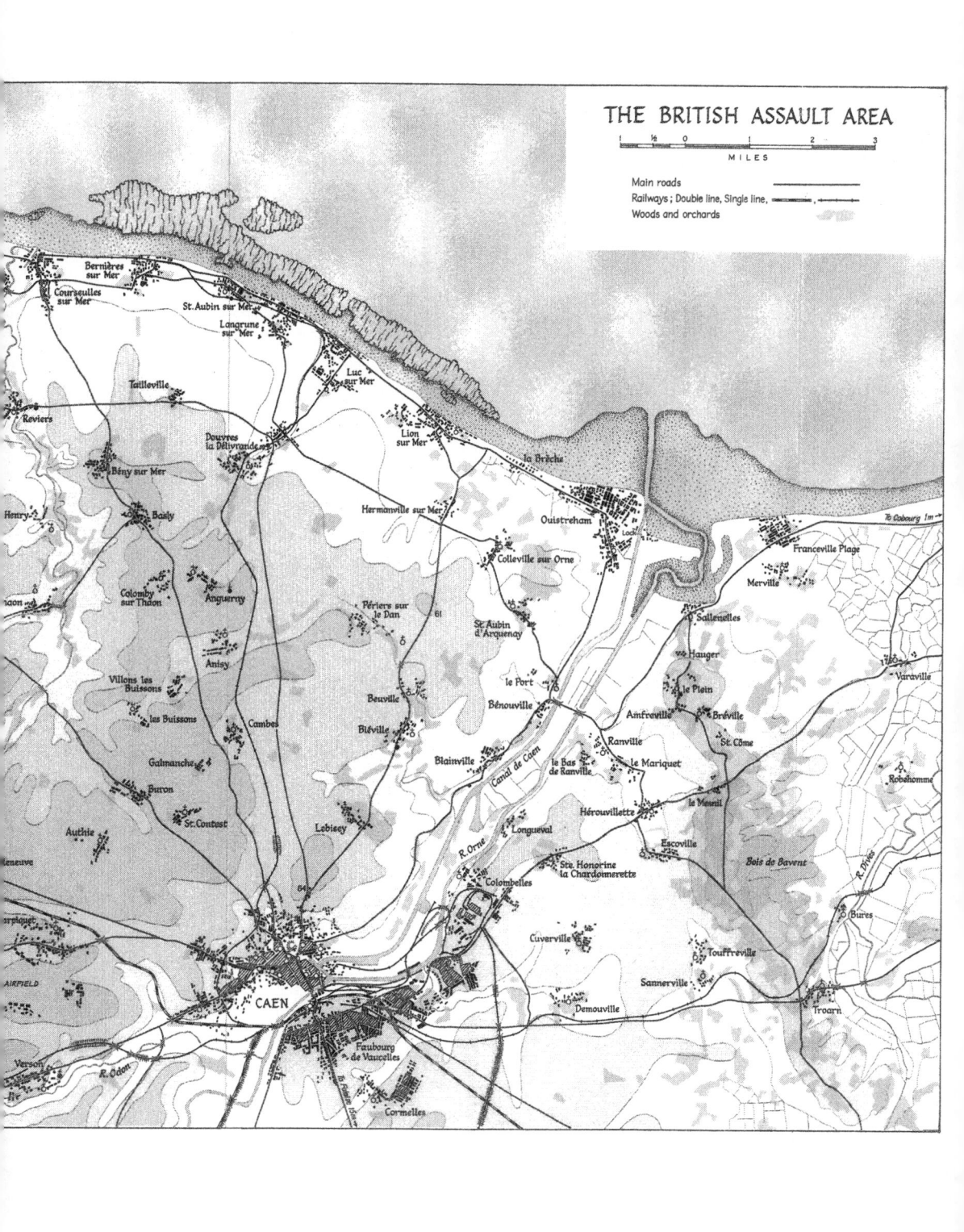

THE BRITISH ASSAULT AREA

CHAPTER X

D-DAY: ADVANCE INLAND

THE German opposition did not only consist of the beach defences within three or four hundred yards of high water mark that have already been described and the so-called coastal batteries; behind these was a defended coastal belt of country from four to six miles deep, whose southern edge is marked on contemporary German maps as 'land front'; in the rear area beyond that there were a very few unfinished defence works.

The twenty-four mile length of coast which the British Second Army had set out to capture on D-day was defended by eight battalions of infantry, ten of whose companies occupied the forward beach defences while the remainder held defensive positions in the coastal belt. With the infantry in these *beach defences* were some ninety single guns of 88-mm calibre or less, nearly fifty mortars and between four and five hundred machine guns. In addition to the infantry in the *coastal belt*, and largely within range of the beaches, were twenty-two batteries of field, medium and heavy artillery containing a further ninety guns, and two companies with twenty-one heavy anti-tank guns. In the *rear area* were five more battalions of infantry or panzer grenadiers, five more batteries with twenty-two medium and heavy guns, and two more battalions of anti-tank artillery mustering thirty-four self-propelled '88's. Thus the assault divisions of the Second Army faced in all some thirteen battalions of infantry, about two hundred and sixty guns of all kinds and about five hundred mortars and machine guns. Moreover, some artillery stationed outside the British sector, east of the Orne on their left and in the American sector on their right, could also fire on the flanks of the British assault.

The German army principally concerned was the Seventh, but the Fifteenth on their east flank was also involved to a less extent. In the Seventh Army area the corps responsible for the defence of the British sector was LXXXIV Corps, its forward defences from the neighbourhood of le Hamel to just east of Franceville Plage being held by the 716th Infantry Division and those from le Hamel to Port en Bessin by part of the 352nd Infantry Division which was also responsible for Omaha. The former was a 'static' division which had been occupying the coast for many months; the latter was a 'field' division, trained for mobile operations, which had recently been brought forward to strengthen the defence in Gold and Omaha areas. In the Fifteenth Army area its LXXXI Corps was responsible, forward defences being held by the 711th Infantry Division. Stationed south-east of Caen (but with some of its troops pushed forward on either side of the Orne between Caen and the sea) was the 21st Panzer Division of Army Group B; in the Fifteenth Army area, but held in OKW reserve under Hitler's control, were the 12th SS Panzer Division, south of Rouen, and the Panzer Lehr Division, near Chartres. These and the German forces defending the American sector are shown in the map facing page 120.

On June the 5th the German naval, army and air forces were all completely ignorant of the fact that the huge invasion fleet had already put to sea. The weather deterred naval surface craft from venturing out on patrol and the presence of Allied aircraft discouraged any serious attempt at reconnaissance by the Third Air Fleet. So neither knew anything of the forces driving relentlessly towards them. The British Broadcasting Corporation's 'Voice of Shaef' broadcast that evening coded messages to the French Resistance, which led the German Fifteenth Army to warn its corps and headquarters at about half past ten that night that intercepted code messages were pointing to invasion within forty-eight hours. German post-war statements are contradictory but no contemporary evidence has been found that Seventh Army knew of the issue of that warning message; as already mentioned, orders requiring certain divisional commanders to attend an exercise at Rennes on June the 6th were not cancelled.

But Admiral Krancke's headquarters knew of the Fifteenth Army's warning and his diary comments that Naval Group West did 'not attach any special significance to this news', believing the B.B.C. messages to refer to acts of sabotage as former messages had done. At half past one on the morning of D-day he learned of the American airborne landings from the Admiral Commanding Channel Coast. The news must also have reached the headquarters of von Rundstedt and of the Third Air Fleet, for the naval diary says that all three took the view that 'no major enemy landing is imminent'. Nevertheless, Krancke himself ordered a state of 'immediate preparedness' for his own command and both the Seventh and Fifteenth Armies issued the 'highest alert'. At about the same time both the 711th and 716th Divisions reported British airborne landings east of the Orne to the headquarters of LXXXI Corps at Rouen and LXXXIV Corps at St. Lô.

At a quarter past two the Seventh Army Chief of Staff (Major-General Pemsel) told General Speidel, Rommel's Chief of Staff at Army Group B, that 'the sound of engines can be heard coming from the sea on the eastern Cotentin coast . . .' and that 'Admiral Kanalküste [Channel coast] reports presence of ships detected in the sea area Cherbourg'. In Pemsel's view this activity pointed to a major operation. Speidel did not agree and von Rundstedt did not agree either: 'OB. West does not consider this to be a major operation'. Pemsel, however, stuck to his opinion. From then on reports of Allied action multiplied. At ten minutes to three came a naval report of 'sea targets' north of the Cotentin peninsula and off the 716th Division's sector; at half past three landing craft were noted for the first time off the mouth of the Vire and 'sailing quickly to the Orne estuary'. A few minutes before this Admiral Krancke had ordered his mobile forces to patrol coastal waters in the Baie de la Seine. This brought the 5th Torpedo-boat Flotilla and a flotilla of patrol craft from le Havre and led to the attack on the bombarding ships off the mouth of the Orne described in Chapter VIII; they had fired fifteen torpedoes but their only victim was the destroyer *Svenner*. Further west two flotillas of motor torpedo-boats left Cherbourg but they were back in harbour by six-thirty 'having found nothing'. In the Bay of Biscay the three available ships of the 8th Destroyer Flotilla were ordered north to Brest and the *Landwirt* group of U-boats, held especially for anti-invasion duties, were brought to instant readiness.

Further reports of airborne landings came in from many quarters and at a quarter past five Seventh Army told Army Group B that a 'large-scale enemy assault' was indicated by the depth of Allied airborne landings on both flanks, in conjunction with radar-located targets at sea off the Orne, Port en Bessin, the mouth of the Vire and the Cotentin. Soon after this the Allied heavy bombing of coastal defences was reported and at six o'clock, 'naval forces in some strength have opened fire on the coast near the Orne estuary, near Bernières s.M., Arromanches, Colleville, Grandcamp. Landing craft approaching Bernières s.M.' The Seventh Army, though convinced that a large-scale attack was indicated by the depth of the parachute landings, yet added '. . . purpose of coastal bombardment not yet apparent. It could be a diversionary attack in conjunction with attacks to come later at other points. Air and sea reconnaissance have brought no further news since daybreak.'

Uncertainty and disagreement as to whether this was the beginning of the Allies' main attack or a diversion to cover a major assault elsewhere was already hindering firm decision. The two armies directly concerned took the threat of airborne landings seriously from the outset. As early as 2.35 a.m. Seventh Army had given the 91st Airlanding Division, which was in reserve in the Cotentin, to LXXXIV Corps which, with the 709th Division in the Utah area, was to clear up the situation created by the American airborne landings on the western flank. At seven o'clock the 21st Panzer Division was also put under LXXXIV Corps to help in dealing with the British descents on the eastern flank beyond the Orne.

Some of the British airborne troops had been landed in the area of the 711th Division whose boundary with the Seventh Army ran south from a point on the coast about two miles west of Cabourg and passed along the Dives valley just east of Troarn. News of these descents alarmed the Fifteenth Army. Before two o'clock in the morning they asked that the 12th SS Panzer Division should be alerted and moved up. After a first refusal by Army Group B, further argument so far prevailed that before five o'clock (that is before the Allied naval bombardment opened) von Rundstedt gave orders to Army Group B for the division to be moved up in rear of the 711th Division to be ready for 'immediate intervention', and the Panzer Lehr Division to make ready to do so. Before seaborne landings began he put 12th SS Panzer Division under Army Group command. But it was in OKW reserve under Hitler and von Rundstedt's action was soon countermanded. At ten o'clock he was informed that the 12th could move but Panzer Lehr was not to move, and neither would be committed *without orders from OKW*. And there for the time being the matter rested.

During these early hours of D-day it was the Allied airborne landings which occupied the attention of the German Command. In the east, detachments of the 736th Grenadier Regiment of the 716th Division and of the 125th and 192nd Panzer Grenadier Regiments of the 21st Panzer Division attacked (and continued to attack repeatedly during the morning) the various positions on both sides of the Orne held by the British 6th Airborne Division, but failed everywhere to dislodge them. The 7th Parachute Battalion and the 2nd Oxfordshire and Buckinghamshire Light Infantry detachment holding the Bénouville–Ranville bridges across the Caen Canal and the river Orne, the 13th Parachute Battalion near le Mariquet, and the 12th Parachute Battalion on rising ground south of le Bas de Ranville repulsed all attacks, though at times they were all hard-pressed and a party in the village of Bénouville, a mile or so to the south of the bridge, were cut off and surrounded but held out.

In the west, in the area of the Cotentin, the unintentionally wide dispersion of the American airborne troops made it difficult for the Germans to appreciate clearly the size or seriousness of what was happening. The appearance of airborne troops in so many places magnified the apparent scale of the threat, and soon after half past two German troop movements began. Well before any seaborne landings, the 91st and 709th Divisions in the Cotentin and the 915th Regiment near Bayeux had been ordered in turn to move against the airborne threat that was developing to westward of the Vire.

But after the seaborne landings began it was the British area which occupied the Seventh Army's chief attention. At 8.45 it first heard of British tanks landing east of Asnelles and fifteen minutes later

LXXXIV Corps reported that 'from 7.15 a.m. onwards landings in some strength were being made from the sea on both sides of the Orne Estuary, especially to the west of Bernières, Asnelles, Meuvaines, Grandcamp, with infantry and armoured forces. . . .' Apparently news of the landings at Utah had not come through, and though it was known at 9.25 a.m. that there had been some penetration of the 352nd Division's front at Omaha, that division took an optimistic view of the situation—and continued to do so all morning. Rather naturally therefore the area of the 716th Division was regarded as the more dangerous. British tanks had reached the German artillery positions and seeing that the defence in this sector was beginning to disintegrate the LXXXIV Corps Commander decided to modify his plans and to pull out the 21st Panzer Division from the east of the Orne and send it into action against the British landings west of the river. The 21st Panzer was a well-found division of about sixteen thousand men, some of whom had fought in Rommel's Africa Corps against the British Eighth Army. It included a hundred and twenty-seven Mark IV tanks, forty assault guns and twenty-four 88-mm anti-tank guns. But on this morning its troops were widely distributed. Its two grenadier regiments had one battalion forward on either side of the Orne, facing the British 6th Airborne and 3rd Divisions; its anti-tank guns had been put on the Périers ridge with a battalion of field guns to the south of it; its anti-aircraft guns were around Caen and the rest of its artillery on high ground about fifteen miles south-east of Caen; its tanks were disposed a few miles north-east of Falaise. The forward infantry which were already involved in fighting the 6th Airborne Division were left to contain their bridgehead beyond the Orne and to keep open the road from Troarn, but the two battle groups containing the tanks, which the divisional commander himself had launched against the airborne troops, were now ordered to change direction and to cross the Orne at Colombelles and Caen.

The 3rd Division's assault brigade group (the 8th) had indeed made good early progress. By the middle of the morning the South Lancashire had taken Hermanville, the East Yorkshire were clearing the defences south of Ouistreham and the Suffolk, having taken Colleville, were attacking two strong-points a mile or so to the south, known to the Allies as 'Morris' and 'Hillman'. The former, containing four field guns, was taken easily since the area had suffered heavily from naval and air bombardment and its garrison of sixty-seven came out with their hands up as soon as the attack opened. But Hillman, half a mile further south, was a stronger position covering about four hundred by six hundred yards, well protected by wire, mines and weapons and containing a concrete redoubt and underground accommodation. It proved to be the headquarters of the 736th Regiment. The Suffolk's first attack, with artillery and mortar support and assisted by a squadron of the 13th/18th Hussars, took the outer defences but failed to capture the inner redoubt and a further full-scale attack was organised. It was launched late in the afternoon but the position was not captured till after eight o'clock in the evening. During the whole day's fighting the Suffolk casualties were light (seven killed and twenty-five wounded), but the failure to take Hillman earlier was to cost another battalion dearly.

The company of the South Lancashire and the 41st Commando who had started early to capture the strong-point Lion sur Mer (page 186) had been unsuccessful. After severe casualties in a series of hand-to-hand fights among the houses a fresh attack was made with the help of three armoured vehicles of the 5th Assault Regiment, Royal Engineers, but all these were quickly knocked out by the strong-point's gun and the position remained untaken.

On the opposite, Ouistreham flank the clearance of the coast was more successful. There four Centaur tanks of the Royal Marine Armoured Support Regiment had assisted the commandos to capture the strongly fortified but heavily bombarded Riva Bella battery position (from which the guns had been removed), and ten armoured vehicles of the 79th Assault Squadron, Royal Engineers, had pushed on to the mouth of the canal, taking sixty prisoners and three anti-tank guns. The lock gates and bridge were checked for demolition charges but the enemy had blown the bridge's eastern span.

The 185th Brigade Group had landed nearly up to time and the infantry were assembled in woods half a mile inland by about eleven o'clock. The brigade was to be the spearhead of the division's attack inland; it was to advance with all speed and if possible to capture Caen and the ground immediately south of it that day. The advance was to be led by a mobile column of the 2nd King's Shropshire Light Infantry, riding on tanks of the Staffordshire Yeomanry and supported by the 7th Field Regiment, R.A.; but at noon the infantry's heavy weapons and vehicles were still not clear of the congestion on the shore and the tanks that had succeeded in getting through were being held up by a minefield. Leaving these to overtake them as quickly as possible, the infantry started marching south *en route* to Caen at about half past twelve and by two o'clock they had climbed the Périers rise. The leading Yeomanry had overtaken them but enemy guns in woods to their right knocked out five tanks of the Staffordshire and four flails of the Westminster Dragoons and a company of the infantry were sent off to join the Yeomanry in taking the position. The rest of the column moved on towards Beuville and Biéville while a squadron of the Staffordshire occupied a commanding position at Point 61.

The main body of the 185th Brigade (the 2nd Royal Warwickshire and the 1st Royal Norfolk) did not advance till some hours had elapsed. At three o'clock the Norfolk were ordered to secure high ground on the left of the Shropshire Light Infantry and, believing that St. Aubin d'Arquenay was occupied by the enemy (though in fact the 1st Special Service Brigade had passed through it at noon), they struck across country between it and the still uncaptured Hillman. Moving through a large field which the strong-point could command, about half the battalion lost direction in the high standing corn covered by the Hillman machine guns; in a very short time they had had some 150 casualties. The rest of the battalion pressed on and overcoming the few enemy in front of them they were established on high ground between Beuville and Bénouville by seven o'clock in the evening. There they were halted for the night. The 2nd Warwickshire were not ordered forward till later in the afternoon and did not reach St. Aubin till about six o'clock. By then events were beginning to vary the planned programme.

At intervals throughout the morning air reconnaissance indicated that the 21st Panzer Division was moving up on Caen and as early as eleven o'clock General Dempsey had asked the air forces to attack troop movements into Caen from the south and south-east. From then on German movement towards Caen was attacked from the air almost continuously. Early in the afternoon it was learnt that the 21st Panzer Division's reconnaissance unit was probing far afield and other reports pointed to the fact that the division would be committed north and north-west of Caen that evening. The divisional commander, Major-General Feuchtinger, has since stated that once over the Orne (where it flows through the southern outskirts of Caen) his armoured regiment with ninety effective tanks and two battalions of infantry attacked northwards.

The situation of the 3rd Division at about that time—four o'clock in the afternoon—was as follows. The 8th Brigade was well established in Hermanville, Colleville sur Orne and Ouistreham, with one of its battalions, the 2nd East Yorkshire, closing with the battery position known as 'Daimler' south of Ouistreham, and the 1st Suffolk about to renew its attack on Hillman strong-point. Just clear of the beach the 9th Brigade was assembling but was not yet ready to debouch into the four-mile gap of country between Hermanville and the Canadian sector. The 185th Brigade's main body (the Norfolk and Warwickshire battalions) were moving in the direction of Caen by the west bank of the canal. Ahead of them the Shropshire Light Infantry and accompanying troops had reached Beuville and Biéville on the direct road to Caen; the infantry's 6-pounder anti-tank guns had caught up and were disposed to cover the advance and they had near them some 17-pounder self-propelled guns of the 20th Anti-tank Regiment. One squadron of the Staffordshire

Yeomanry was with them, another was supporting the Suffolk attack on Hillman, and a third was disposed on the Périers ridge commanding the brigade's right flank.

Soon after four o'clock a troop of the Staffordshire Yeomanry scouting ahead reported enemy tanks advancing from Caen. The squadron with the Suffolk at Hillman strong-point was hastily moved to Biéville and had just taken up position to the west when about forty enemy tanks, moving very fast, attacked. Two were knocked out by the Yeomanry and two by the Shropshire anti-tank guns and the enemy turned away into the woods. They were pursued by the Yeomanry and by field-gun fire, and when they showed again some more were destroyed. They swung off again and were joined by others, and making a wide détour they came in towards the Périers ridge. There they met the squadron of the Staffordshire posted at Point 61 for just such an occasion. Three more were knocked out and again they drew off. Thirteen had then been knocked out to our knowledge (our only loss was one self-propelled gun), but they had already been persistently harassed by aircraft while they were south of Caen. On the western outskirts of the town eight Typhoons of the Second Tactical Air Force had dive-bombed tanks moving up to join the fight and had left two in flames and four others smoking. Feuchtinger has since said that his division started the day with 124 tanks and by nightfall had only 70 left. In view of his figures British records were over-modest.

Once the enemy's attack near Biéville was driven off a company of the Shropshire led off again down the road to Caen, but their way was blocked by enemy holding strongly the Lebisey woods athwart the road. It was growing dusk and with the necessity to guard their right flank against renewed attack by the German armour it was decided to halt for the night, holding Biéville and Beuville. Caen was about three miles away.

Of the 185th Brigade the Warwickshire had found that le Port just north of the Bénouville bridge still contained a few of the enemy. Shortly before nine o'clock as they prepared to attack, two columns of transport aircraft of 38 and 46 Groups, towing gliders, came in low from the Channel, strongly escorted by fighters. One column of about 100 released their gliders over Colleville to land near the canal north of Bénouville; the other column of about 140 went on to Ranville for the gliders to land on the nearby zone N. This mass fly-in, which was seen by both sides, greatly cheered British troops but had an opposite effect on the German commanders. Their Seventh Army telephone log records a statement that 'Attack by 21st Panzer Division rendered useless by heavily concentrated airborne troops', and their report to Rommel said that it had 'been halted by renewed air landings'. According to other German statements, a few forward tanks had reached the coast near Lion by seven o'clock and others were trying to slip past the British guns on Périers ridge when the sight of large airborne reinforcements to their rear led the panzer division to call off its counter-attack, and to withdraw to a line running eastwards from Cambes to the canal, that is between the Shropshire positions and Caen.

The Warwickshire cleared le Port and, after making contact with the airborne troops holding the bridge, went on to attack Bénouville and the château to the south of it. It was nearly midnight when at last the stalwart party of the 7th Parachute Battalion who had held out in Bénouville since early morning, surrounded by the enemy but unconquered, were at last relieved. Then, with the troops who had held the bridge, they joined the rest of their battalion on the east of the Orne. The Warwickshire continued southwards till halted for the night at Blainville.

The effective strength of the 6th Airborne Division had been doubled by the reinforcements flown in, namely two strong battalions of infantry, the armoured reconnaissance regiment with light tanks and jeeps, some light field artillery, anti-tank guns and medical and supply units; and six hundred containers of stores and ammunition, dropped by parachute.

The original position of the airborne troops had already been improved when the 1st Special Service Brigade, marching to the skirl of the Brigadier's piper, had crossed the Orne bridges to join them during the afternoon. The main danger appeared to lie to the south, for the enemy still held Longueval (from which the bridgehead can be overlooked) and Hérouvillette. The parachutists' positions at le Bas de Ranville and le Mariquet had warded off several attacks with difficulty; No. 3 Commando was diverted to reinforce them, and No. 6 Commando and the 45th (RM) Commando were turned north to take the Bréville feature and to secure Merville. Meanwhile parties of engineers from the 17th and 71st Field Companies, and part of the 106th Bridging Company of the Royal Army Service Corps, began the construction of Bailey bridges over the canal and river that would carry any existing British or American tank. The sites had to be cleared of mines and booby traps and the sappers suffered heavily from snipers and mortar fire as the work continued.

Enemy attacks continued at intervals till the late evening, and at one time the forward bombardment officer directed fire from the destroyer *Serapis* on German infantry near Longueval. The reinforcements to this sector (the 1st Royal Ulster Rifles and the 2nd Oxfordshire and Buckinghamshire Light Infantry who had just arrived in the gliders) prepared to attack Hérouvillette and Escoville at first light next day.

At the southern end of the high ground to the west of the Bavent woods, German troops attacking the 8th Parachute Battalion from near Troarn had been thrown back in confusion, leaving behind them a large lorry full of stores. In the centre round the cross roads at le Mesnil the Canadian Parachute Battalion had not been molested. Further north the position was not so satisfactory, for the enemy still held Bréville and the gap in the wooded ridge near the village. Beyond the gap airborne troops held the hill at le Plein and Hauger, but the Bréville area, where a battery of artillery lay hidden in an orchard, was to cause trouble for a week.

During the afternoon the 3rd Division's plans had been modified by events. With the 21st Panzer Division loose in the country between the 185th Brigade and the Canadians, Major-General T. G. Rennie decided to make sure of the British left flank and ordered the 9th Brigade to establish itself so as to cover the Orne bridges against attack from the west. The brigade had been late in coming in and while moving to the assembly area a German mortar bomb had landed on the headquarters, severely wounding the brigade commander and several of his staff. The commanding officer of the 2nd Ulster Rifles had assumed command and the brigade took up positions on the high ground between Périers sur le Dan and St. Aubin d'Arquenay for the night. In front of them was the 185th Brigade and behind them the 8th who, after the Suffolk had finally captured Hillman and the East Yorkshire Daimler, were ordered to concentrate for the night in the Hermanville area.

The final positions held that night by the 6th Airborne Division and the 3rd British Division are shown on the map facing page 212. Forward positions held by the enemy are also indicated. From the latter it will be seen that the 12th SS Panzer Division was coming up. Hitler's ban had in fact been removed at about two-thirty in the afternoon, when von Rundstedt was at last authorised to move both the 12th SS and the Panzer Lehr Divisions up to the front. Movements of the SS Division had been observed and reported by our reconnaissance aircraft and it was realised that it could not now reach the battle that day but must be expected on the day following.

In the 3rd Canadian Division's sector, as elsewhere, congestion on the beaches delayed the start of movement inland. Not only was it difficult to clear the shore while troops, vehicles and equipment continued to land more quickly than exits could be made and kept open; as long as the Courseulles defences held out on one side, and part of St. Aubin on the other was still unconquered, those who got off the beach were almost inevitably led to congregate where there was freedom from enemy fire. Owing to wrecked craft and congestion, disembarkation could not be spread as widely as planned and most of the reserve brigade (9th Canadian) was landed opposite Bernières.

Bernières was no sooner clear of Germans than it was filled with Canadians, for at first any attempt to debouch into open country drew heavy fire from '88's and machine guns. Soon it was so choked that reorganisation of troops crowded in the town was a slow process and it took longer still to get up heavy weapons and vehicles and to marry them and the units with which they were to move inland.

The country to be seized by the Canadian division is, for the first few miles inland, undulating, slowly-rising agricultural land whose wide fields stood deep in corn. South of the Seulles, contours are steeper and the valleys of the river and of its tributaries are in many places narrow and wooded; especially is this true of the Mue valley which separated, broadly speaking, the areas to be captured in the first instance by the Canadian 7th and 8th Brigades. The advance of the former was led by The Royal Winnipeg Rifles and the assault company of the 1st Canadian Scottish, with tanks of the 6th Canadian Armoured Regiment (1st Hussars). They were followed by the rest of the Canadian Scottish and later by The Regina Rifle Regiment. Their task was to secure the high ground south of the Seulles between Creully and Fontaine-Henry and then to push on and get astride the Bayeux–Caen road. There were no major strongpoints in their path, but infantry with machine guns and artillery were widely distributed to cover the principal villages, roads and river crossings. A contemporary German map of coastal dispositions shows eleven anti-tank guns of the 716th Division spaced across the Canadian front between la Rivière and Bernières, within a mile or so of the coast; and widely disposed in the country south of the Seulles another eighteen '88's.

The Winnipegs leading, and the Canadian Scottish closing soon afterwards, made good progress in capturing Banville and Ste. Croix sur Mer, taking 'hordes of prisoners' in the field positions which they overran. Then the Winnipegs made for the Seulles crossing at Tierceville, and the Scottish for Colombiers sur Seulles. The Regina Rifles meanwhile occupied Reviers and the crossing there. By four o'clock most of the 7th Brigade Group were across the Seulles and, half a mile away on their right, troops of the British 50th Division held Creully. There was evidence that three companies of the 726th Infantry Regiment had withdrawn in some disorder in face of the Canadian advance.

The Regina Rifles with tanks of the Hussars moved south again at about four o'clock. In the neighbourhood of Fontaine-Henry they were heavily shelled by '88's but the advance was continued. Leaving the Mue valley, they struck south-westwards and took le Fresne-Camilly on the Arromanches–Creully–Caen road.

During this time the second assault brigade—the 8th—had

advanced on the left. The reserve battalion, Le Régiment de la Chaudière, had assembled at the southern edge of Bernières by ten o'clock, but it was noon when with artillery and a squadron of the 10th Canadian Armoured Regiment (The Fort Garry Horse) their advance began. Then they worked forward capturing a battery about a thousand yards west of Tailleville and skirting another of eighty fused rockets, which had not been fired as their cables had been cut by the bombing. Bény sur Mer was taken by half past two with some fifty prisoners and another battery of four 10-cm guns of the 1716th Artillery Regiment on which the cruiser *Diadem* had rained over two hundred 5·25-inch shells.

Further left, The North Shore Regiment had advanced on Tailleville, leaving one company to clear the strong-point at St. Aubin on the coast. A battalion headquarters and a company of the 736th Grenadier Regiment were holding Tailleville with cover in shelters connected by tunnels. Much of the housing had been destroyed by the bombers but the ruins were not cleared till late in the afternoon. Shortly after four o'clock the Chaudière Regiment began to advance southward from Bény with tanks of The Fort Garry Horse. Soon after five they were in Basly and shortly afterwards they seized Colomby sur Thaon. On their left The Queen's Own Rifles, moving south, captured Anguerny and neared Anisy, but skirmishes with enemy detachments continued till nearly midnight.

Back on the coast St. Aubin had been captured (though sporadic shooting continued during the night) but further east Langrune sur Mer still defied capture. Tanks of the Royal Marine Armoured Support Regiment and the fire of naval close support craft offshore had reinforced the repeated attacks of the 48th Commando, but the enemy in fortified houses protected by minefields and road blocks were not subdued. About two and a half miles still separated the Canadians and the British 3rd Division.

While the assault brigades thus advanced some four to five miles inland the 9th Brigade had struggled through Bernières and assembled south of the town by about half past two. Its objective, Carpiquet just west of Caen, was ten miles away and its route lay through Bény sur Mer. But the 8th Brigade was not clear of Bény till late afternoon and the 9th was not all there till after seven o'clock. Half an hour before, The North Nova Scotia Highlanders had set off with companies carried on the tanks of the 27th Canadian Armoured Regiment (The Sherbrooke Fusiliers). Mortars and anti-tank guns firing from their right were surrounded and captured, and by dusk the head of the column reached the outskirts of Villons les Buissons. It was too late to go further. Tanks of the 21st Panzer Division were between them and the nearest troops of the British 3rd Division about three miles away and they were ordered to form a 'fortress'

29. Canadian troops

LANDINGS ON D-DAY

30. Follow-up units

31. Beach organisation taking shape

32. Mulberry harbour under construction. *Note sheltered water*

round the point where the road between Anisy and Villons les Buissons crosses the Courseulles–Caen road. The rest of the 9th Brigade had been held in the neighbourhood of Bény sur Mer.

During the evening the 7th Brigade had been ordered to halt for the night in the positions they had reached at Fontaine–Henry, le Fresne-Camilly and the high ground south of Creully. Earlier in the evening two troops of the 1st Hussars had lost touch with their infantry and had reached the day's final objective—the main road and railway between Bayeux and Caen. Meeting no opposition worth mentioning, they went through Bretteville l'Orgueilleuse and almost to Carpiquet. Then finding that they were not followed they rejoined their squadron about an hour and a half later. The Canadian armoured regiments had indeed done well throughout the day; between them they had knocked out more than a dozen of the enemy's '88's.

The country in which the Canadians fought on D-day and the positions occupied that night are shown on the map facing page 212.

In the last chapter it was told how the assault brigades of the 50th Division (the 231st and the 69th) had landed in Gold area to the west of the Canadian beaches.

Starting at about eleven o'clock the reserve brigades, the 151st and the 56th, had landed in succession; the whole of the 50th Division was ashore by soon after midday and its task can be seen as a whole. On the right the 231st Brigade was to push westwards in the coastal area, taking Arromanches and the battery at Longues, while the 47th (Royal Marine) Commando went ahead to capture Port en Bessin and join up with Americans from Omaha. On the left, the 69th Brigade was to strike southwards and crossing the Seulles in the St. Gabriel–Creully area to secure the Bayeux–Caen road near Ste. Croix Grand Tonne. The reserve brigades were to advance between these two—the 56th on the right to Bayeux and beyond it to the river Drome; the 151st on the left to seize the Caen road and railway between Bayeux and the Seulles.

By the time le Hamel was finally conquered the 231st Brigade had just taken Ryes and had already occupied the radar station at Arromanches. The battery south of the village had been heavily shelled by the cruiser *Emerald* and its four 105-mm guns had been abandoned without being fired. The western half of Arromanches was then attacked after bombardment by a destroyer and the 147th Field Regiment, R.A.; the place was taken but was not finally cleared until about nine o'clock that night. The light was fading, Tracy sur Mer was full of enemy snipers, and after la Rosière had been occupied it was decided to postpone further advance until first light next day. The 47th Commando making for Port en Bessin had had a sharp fight at la Rosière earlier that evening and it was dark when they

P

reached Point 72, the prominent hill a mile and a half south of Port en Bessin; they dug in there for the night ready to attack in the morning.

Leading troops of the 56th Brigade had also passed through la Rosière and turned southwards astride the road to Bayeux. As they approached Pouligny radar station the enemy set fire to it and decamped. The South Wales Borderers, in the van, pushed on to Vaux sur Aure and secured the Aure bridge shortly before midnight. The nearby battery had been shelled by the cruiser *Argonaut* and the vicinity had been bombed; it was now found deserted. The 2nd Essex on the left of the brigade advance had meanwhile reached St. Sulpice after meeting 'light enemy forces' and the 2nd Gloucestershire had followed into Magny. In those positions they were halted for the night. The brigade had been concentrated in the woods between Buhot and Ryes before six; it had taken four to five hours to advance about three miles, though virtually unopposed, and Bayeux was untaken.

On the left of the 56th Brigade, the 151st had moved forward in two groups supported by the 90th Field Regiment, R.A. Starting from near Meuvaines the right-hand group, led by the 9th Durham Light Infantry, took roughly the line of the Crépon–Bayeux road. On their left, the 6th Durham Light Infantry and a squadron of the 4th/7th Dragoon Guards went south from Crépon to Villiers le Sec and there turned westwards towards Bayeux. Between Crépon and the Seulles the 69th Brigade met considerable opposition from a battle group of the 352nd Division. Its 915th Grenadier Regiment stationed near Bayeux had been ordered, early that morning, to move westward to deal with a reported airborne landing between the Vire and Carentan. When it was proved that no such landing had taken place but that a battalion round Mont Fleury had been overwhelmed, the grenadier regiment was ordered to retrace its steps, to move eastwards and to counter-attack towards Crépon. On the way back one of its battalions and some assault guns were diverted to oppose the threatened American penetration at Omaha. The rest of the battle group consisting of the 1st Battalion, 915th Regiment, the 352nd Fusilier Battalion and ten guns of the 352nd Anti-tank Battalion reached the country between Villiers le Sec and Bazenville at about 4 p.m. In the ensuing fight with the 50th Division, the German commander was killed and his infantry forced to withdraw across the Seulles, where some were taken prisoner near St. Gabriel by troops of the 69th Brigade who were already south of the river.

An entry in the German Seventh Army log records a 'strong penetration in the area of the 915th Grenadier Regiment east of Bayeux . . .' and another German account states that only ninety men survived of the battle group engaged. The remnants were attached to the 726th Regiment which was now ordered to establish a line from Coulombs to Asnelles—that is through the country already occupied by the 50th Division! But although this task was obviously beyond their power there was still much mopping-up to be done before the area was wholly free of the enemy. Near Crépon, for instance, an '88', four '75's and fifty prisoners were captured from a hidden position in the nearby woods early on the following day.

By about half past eight, advance troops of the 151st Brigade had reached the Bayeux–Caen road and were ordered to halt for the night in the Sommervieu–Esquay sur Seulles area. Tanks of the 4th/7th Dragoon Guards were by then reporting that there was little resistance for three thousand yards to the south in the direction of St. Leger, but earlier in the evening the situation had looked very different. Advanced troops of the 69th Brigade, brushing opposition aside, had crossed the Seulles at Creully after fighting in which the Dragoon Guards lost four tanks. At about half past six aircraft reported forty German armoured fighting vehicles between Rucqueville and Brécy. On the request of a forward observer bombardment officer these were engaged by H.M.S. *Orion* about an hour later, and though some shells fell among our own troops, three enemy armoured vehicles were hit and the remainder scattered. Again at half past eight the spotting aircraft reported three large guns which moved south 'when engaged', presumably by *Orion*'s guns. Typhoons of the Royal Air Force on armed reconnaissance also reported attacking a few 'tanks', half-tracked vehicles and lorries north-east of St. Leger just before nine o'clock.

In addition to the early morning bombing, to the maintenance of continuous air cover over ships crossing and recrossing the Channel, the successive carriage and landings of airborne troops, the anti-submarine and anti-shipping patrols further afield and the protection of the assault area and beaches, the Allied air forces were engaged all day in giving tactical support to the armies advancing inland. The daily log of the Second Tactical Air Force records more than a hundred operations over the British area in which alone over two thousand Mitchells, Mosquitos and Bostons, Typhoons, Spitfires and Mustangs were employed. They attacked army headquarters, strong-points, batteries and gun sites, road junctions, troop movements and airfields with bombs, rockets, cannon and machine guns; and both by visual and photographic reconnaissance they watched and recorded the situation in order to keep Allied Intelligence up to date. Thunderbolts and Mustangs of the Eighth Air Force attacked similar targets south and east of the battle area. In the American sector these operations were carried out by nearly three thousand aircraft of the Ninth Air Force whilst, in order to increase further the difficulties of enemy reinforcements moving up to the battle area, over six hundred heavy bombers of the Eighth Air Force bombed 'choke points' in such towns as St. Lô and Caen, or transportation targets near the assault area from Coutances in the west to Lisieux in the east.

Hardly any of these thousands of Allied aircraft saw any sign that the German air force still existed. In the British sector thirty-six German aircraft were seen at wide intervals during the whole twenty-four hours; only twelve of these showed fight, of which seven were brought down and three damaged. The Ninth Air Force claimed another five destroyed and one damaged, but it seems that these Allied claims were over-modest. For the Third Air Fleet's own return of air losses on June the 6th gives thirty-one destroyed and seven damaged 'by enemy action'; and (surely an illustration of the lack of experienced pilots) five destroyed and eleven damaged on operations 'but not by enemy action'.

The tasks which the Third Air Fleet had been given were: reconnaissance of Allied preparations, attack on convoys and shipping, destruction of all enemy forces which had landed, attacks on airborne and parachute forces, fighter protection of bombers, and cover and close support to prevent air attack on ground forces. What a contrast there was between programme and performance! Never has the meaning of 'air mastery' been more clearly exhibited than it was that day by the Allied air forces. The German Third Air Fleet had been prevented from trying to carry out even one of its many tasks; for all the damage they did that day they might almost as well not have existed and certainly they had no effect on the progress of Allied land forces.

The positions reached by the 50th Division on the night of D-day are shown on the map opposite. This also shows the location of each divisional commander's battle headquarters. Generals Bucknall and Crocker went ashore during the day and visited their divisions but, in order to maintain good signal communications, their headquarters remained afloat for the night, XXX Corps in *Bulolo* and I Corps in *Hilary*. General Dempsey, with a small staff, had crossed the Channel during the afternoon. After seeing Admiral Vian he joined *Hilary*, where he remained until the next morning.

The operations of all three divisions had made a good start but had subsequently developed too slowly for the main (and perhaps over-ambitious) object to be *fully* realised—namely, the capture of Bayeux and the road to Caen, the seizure of Caen itself and the safeguarding of the Allies' left flank with a bridgehead east of the Orne. Partly this was due to a physical cause—the unexpectedly high tide and the resulting congestion on the shore which delayed the start of the advance inland. Partly it was due to the strength of the

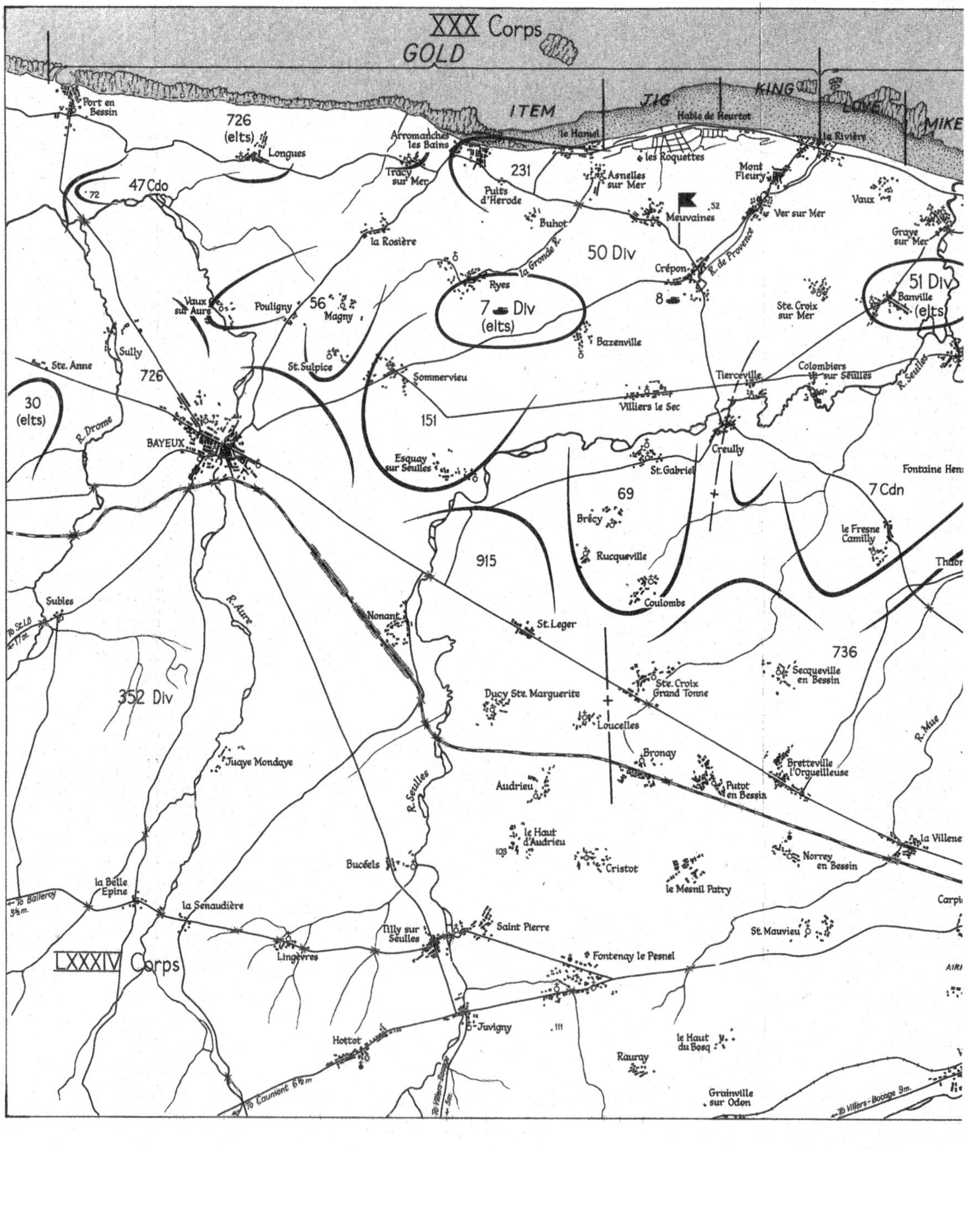

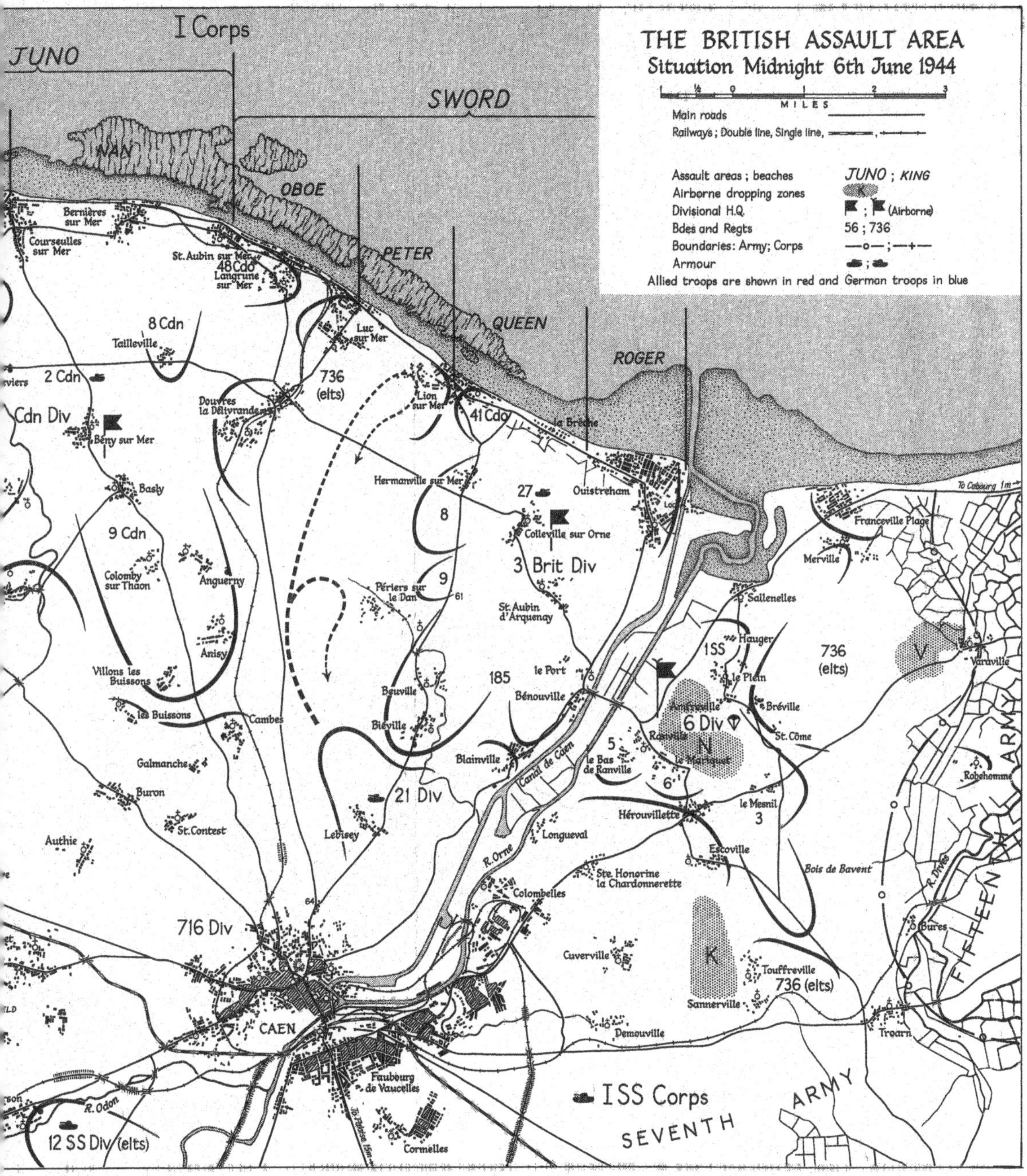
THE BRITISH ASSAULT AREA
Situation Midnight 6th June 1944
MILES
Main roads
Railways ; Double line, Single line,
Assault areas ; beaches
JUNO ; KING
Airborne dropping zones
Divisional H.Q.
(Airborne)
Bdes and Regts
56 ; 736
Boundaries: Army; Corps
Armour
Allied troops are shown in red and German troops in blue
I Corps
JUNO
SWORD
NAN
OBOE
PETER
QUEEN
ROGER
Bernières sur Mer
Courseulles sur Mer
St. Aubin sur Mer
48 Cdo
Langrune sur Mer
Luc sur Mer
8 Cdn
Tailleville
2 Cdn
736 (elts)
Lion sur Mer
41 Cdo
la Brèche
Douvres la Délivrande
Cdn Div
Bény sur Mer
Basly
Hermanville sur Mer
27
Ouistreham
9 Cdn
8
Colleville sur Orne
3 Brit Div
Franceville Plage
To Cabourg 1m
Merville
Colomby sur Thaon
Anguerny
Périers sur le Dan
9
61
St. Aubin d'Arquenay
Sallenelles
Anisy
Villons les Buissons
185
le Port
1SS
Hauger
736 (elts)
le Plein
V
Varaville
Bénouville
Amfreville
Bréville
les Buissons
Cambes
Beuville
Biéville
6 Div
Ranville
N
St. Côme
5
Blainville
Canal de Caen
le Bas de Ranville
le Mariquet
6
Robehomme
Galmanche
Buron
21 Div
Hérouvillette
le Mesnil
3
St. Contest
Lebisey
Longueval
Authie
Escoville
R. Orne
Bois de Bavent
Ste. Honorine la Chardonnerette
Colombelles
R. Dives
64
716 Div
Bures
Cuverville
K
Touffreville
736 (elts)
Sannerville
CAEN
Demouville
Troarn
FIFTEENTH ARMY
Faubourg de Vaucelles
R. Odon
I SS Corps
SEVENTH ARMY
12 SS Div (elts)
Cormelles

opposition at certain points and to the fact that the 21st Panzer Division had had time to intervene. But partly it was also due to the pace at which the assault divisions' operations were carried out. Caen is eight miles from the coast from which the attack was launched and Bayeux six or seven. There was no possibility of taking them that day unless the advance was made as rapidly as possible, and at times there was little evidence of the urgency which would have to characterise operations if they were to succeed fully. Yet it must be remembered that the troops had had little time for rest and no relaxation of strain since they left England on the previous day. Their attack had been launched not from a firm base but from unstable waters breaking on an enemy-held coast. Starting under such conditions, to have swept away all but a few isolated fragments of Hitler's Atlantic Wall and to have fought their way inland for an average depth of four to six miles on most of a twenty-four miles front, was surely a notable feat of arms.

The grim struggle to win a foothold at Omaha continued all day and casualties and confusion made it difficult for both the opposed commanders to measure progress with any certainty. The American corps commander was able to report at one o'clock that his troops were beginning to reach high ground beyond the beaches; half an hour later the German 352nd Division reported 'the division has thrown back invaders into the sea'. In fact, American troops had begun climbing on to the high ground three hours before and the two further regimental combat teams under the command of the 1st Division had begun landing soon afterwards; by four o'clock in the afternoon both were ashore and moving inland and the German commander was then reporting developments as 'unfavourable'.

During the morning the position on the beaches had not greatly improved. The mined beach obstacles could not be cleared while the tide was in, and the naval group which brought in the 18th Regimental Combat Team that morning lost, in doing so, twenty-two small assault craft, two larger infantry landing craft and four tank landing craft. The impression of the troops who were landed was that 'the beach shingle was full of tractors, tanks, vehicles, bull-dozers, and troops—the high ground was still held by Germans who had all troops on the beach pinned down—the beach was still under heavy fire from enemy small arms, mortars, and artillery'.[1] But the position soon changed. A destroyer close in to the shore turned quick and accurate fire on the pill-boxes guarding the nearby re-entrant and when the infantry attack opened the garrisons surrendered. Soon

---

[1] *Omaha Beachhead* (War Dept. Historical Division, Washington, D.C., 1945), p. 83.

engineers were clearing mines from the track which led from the shore to higher ground, bull-dozers were busy and a way inland was open and in working order. There were five places on the assault front at which a track from the shore led up to a re-entrant in the bluffs. Each was covered by a strong-point which commanded the entrance and the shore, and the initial penetration had been made by soldiers who climbed up the mined hillside on to high ground between them. Three of these natural exits had now been captured but two were still in enemy hands.

Even when the coastal plateau was reached the country favoured the defender. Small parties of German infantry were sited among the hedgerows, well placed to delay advancing formations which inevitably needed reorganisation after all they had gone through to reach the high ground. And the troops they met here came from two regiments of the German 352nd Division, holding ground on which they had exercised and knew well. Units of the American 116th, 115th, 18th and 16th Regimental Combat Teams, in Vierville, Château de Vaumicel and le Grand Hameau, were in contact with German forces. Some in the centre had advanced south of the road between St. Laurent and Colleville, and the 26th, arriving later, moved south in support. Colleville was still held by the enemy but was almost surrounded. The Rangers and infantry in Vierville and Château de Vaumicel had had a hard fight and, no further reinforcements reaching them, held on to their positions two miles away to the west of the main penetrations near St. Laurent. Further west still the Rangers who had taken Pointe du Hoe were virtually besieged but maintained their lonely position with support from destroyers which stood by throughout the day. Similarly the troops holding le Grand Hameau in the east had not been reinforced.

It had been a very hard day for the infantry. A high proportion of the tanks had been lost in the approach to the land and only a few reached them by midnight. They were short of field artillery and of ammunition. In fact, there was a shortage of everything. Engineers got to work energetically on beach obstacles as soon as the tide fell but only about a third were cleared that day. Some exits were not yet open and vehicle parks on shore had not been established. Pockets of enemy still held on at places along the coast and the beaches were under observed artillery fire most of the day. Casualties had been heavy; the official history puts them at about two thousand though frankly admitting that this is a guess.[2] Of the larger craft that had brought them ashore, six large infantry landing craft and thirty-one tank landing craft had been lost or damaged.

The position of the American troops at Omaha that night is

---

[2] Harrison, *Cross-Channel Attack*, p. 330.

shown on the map facing page 222. In spite of all misfortune and in face of strong opposition they had secured, in the words of the American historian, 'a toehold on the enemy shore nowhere more than a mile and a half deep'.[3] Over thirty-four thousand men had been landed.

The bridgehead positions in the Utah area of the Cotentin peninsula, which had been seized early in the day by troops of the 82nd and 101st Airborne Divisions and by the 8th Regimental Combat Team landed from the sea, had not been significantly increased but had been considerably strengthened. The quick clearance of beach obstacles and possession of causeways through the flooded area behind Utah had facilitated the landing of the rest of the 4th Division unhampered. At about half past seven in the morning the United States destroyer *Corry* had been sunk by a mine and during the day a control vessel, three tank landing craft and a flak craft had also been lost, apparently from a similar cause. But apart from these, Force U had landed the division without loss and that day about 23,250 men, 1,742 vehicles and 1,695 tons of stores had been put ashore.

The right flank of the American position had been pushed north by the 4th Division's 22nd and 12th Regimental Combat Teams which had been landed intact during the morning; it now extended from a point on the coast just short of Hamel de Cruttes to Beuzeville au Plain about four miles inland. Further west a small detachment of the 82nd Airborne Division fought all day to hold Neuville au Plain on the Cherbourg–Carentan road, down which a battle group of the German 91st Division were trying to advance on Ste. Mère Eglise, where the airborne division's strongest concentration was. To the west of Ste. Mère detachments of airborne troops were on the east bank of the Merderet covering the crossings near la Fière and Chef du Pont, and smaller scattered parties of two parachute regiments that had been landed on the west of the river were gradually collecting, the strongest on Hill 30; these were not yet able to co-operate with other detachments on the eastern bank but their presence helped to delay a counter-attack from the west by the German 1057th Regiment.

Troops of the 8th Regimental Combat team working westwards towards Ste. Mère Eglise were still opposed by Germans in strength. Some reinforcements for the 82nd Airborne Division were landed from the sea to prepare ground north of les Forges for additional airborne reinforcements, but all their efforts to advance were unsuccessful and when the airborne troops arrived in gliders they were greeted by intense enemy machine-gun fire and had heavy casualties, some landing in the enemy lines.

---

[3] Op. cit., p. 329.

Another thirty-two gliders of IX Troop Carrier Command brought reinforcements for the 101st Airborne Division near Hiesville; eleven landed in or near the correct position but many crashed or fell into enemy hands. Detachments of the 101st Division held scattered positions on the south flank of the beachhead, covering bridges near la Barquette and near Brévands; but the German 6th Parachute Regiment, ordered to counter-attack from Carentan, had infiltrated two battalions between these detachments and other American troops further north.

While therefore troops of the American VII Corps had not yet extended the beachhead at Utah, either westwards across the Merderet or southwards to Omaha, and although there was a large enemy pocket between Turqueville and Fauville and some penetration from the south, yet the area held was large enough for manœuvre and safe enough for the build-up to proceed with confidence.

Shortly before 5 p.m. the German Seventh Army's Chief of Staff was told that it was 'the desire of OKW that the enemy in the bridgehead be destroyed by the evening of June 6 as there is a danger of fresh landings by sea and air. According to General Jodl's orders all available forces must be diverted to the point of penetration in Calvados.[4] The bridgehead must be cleared today.' General Pemsel declared this to be impossible; the 12th SS Panzer Division could not attack until the next day and Panzer Lehr would be another twenty-four hours behind it. Nevertheless, on Rommel's instructions he was told that the 21st Panzer Division must attack immediately (it was already doing so) with or without reinforcements, for OKW had given orders that the bad weather conditions must be utilised to the full for bringing up reserves during the night of June 6th–7th.

By this time in the afternoon orders had been issued for the two new panzer divisions, with 21st Panzer and the 716th Division, to come under I SS Panzer Corps and the corps commander had received his instructions from von Rundstedt. He was to '. . . attack from the vicinity of Caen and drive the British into the sea'.

With the main effort thus set in train, further complementary measures were concerted during the course of the evening. A battle group from the 346th Division near le Havre was to be ferried across the Seine after dark and join the 711th Division in attack against the 6th Airborne Division the following day. On the opposite flank the 275th Division was ordered from St. Nazaire by rail towards Bayeux and a battle group of the 265th Division from Lorient by road to St. Lô. But a request by the Seventh Army commander for the 77th and 266th Divisions, on the north coast of Brittany, to be moved

---

[4] The Department of France in which the landings had taken place.

up was rejected by Rommel. They were to be alerted but the field-marshal would not agree to their being moved for the time being.

In the British sector, as the morning tide fell, naval 'frogmen' and engineers renewed their efforts to clear the beach obstacles which were causing so much trouble. Some idea of the strenuous nature of their task may be gathered from the fact that in a three and a quarter mile stretch of the assault beaches in Gold (i.e. Jig and King sectors) there were found to be nearly two thousand five hundred obstacles, embodying nearly nine hundred tons of steel, concrete or wood, most of which had fused mines or shells attached to them. All these obstacles—the larger ones having to be first systematically crushed or broken by explosives—had to be dragged to one side. Similar conditions were met on all other assault beaches. Yet by midnight all sectors of the beaches in use had been cleared and craft were able to land on the next tide with comparatively little damage or delay.

The risks and dangers braved by assault shipping before obstacles had been removed have already been illustrated. By the end of the day in the British sector 258 landing craft of various kinds had been lost or disabled but over seventy-five thousand men, over six thousand vehicles and over four thousand tons of stores had been landed. Exact figures are not available, for inevitably some records are incomplete and it is often not clear whether a particular landing was made before or after midnight. A careful study of all available evidence suggests that while the number of men landed approximated closely to the number planned, the number of vehicles represented about fifty to sixty per cent and the weight of stores about sixty to seventy-five per cent of the planned totals. The vehicles landed included about nine hundred tanks and armoured vehicles against a planned total of a thousand and fifty, for one armoured regiment (the 24th Lancers) was not disembarked till the following day. Some 240 field guns, about 80 light anti-aircraft guns and approximately 280 anti-tank guns came ashore for the Second Army during the day, and three machine-gun battalions with Vickers guns and heavy (4·2-inch) mortars. The main deficiencies were in medium artillery and heavy anti-aircraft guns.

Considerable anxiety was caused by the knowledge that on both British and American fronts operations were somewhat behind schedule, particularly as it was thought that the boisterous weather might get even worse during the next few days. The ultimate success of Allied operations would clearly depend on the ability to build up forces and supplies more quickly than the enemy could bring up reinforcements to oppose them. For this the Navy bore the first responsibility. With every increase in the number of troops landed, the volume of stores, supplies and ammunition must match their needs and good organisation must ensure that they were readily available. Beach organisation was a most urgent task in which all three Services were concerned. The landing of their advance parties early in the morning has been noted (page 177). The naval task, to direct all movements of shipping and craft in the assault area with regard for the army's operational requirements, involved the establishment of naval control centres on shore and afloat.

While naval organisation for the control of incoming and outgoing shipping and craft (under the naval officers in charge with their beachmasters and naval personnel) was being developed, army organisation of the congested beaches gradually took shape. On each

INITIAL BEACH ORGANISATION — BRITISH SECTOR

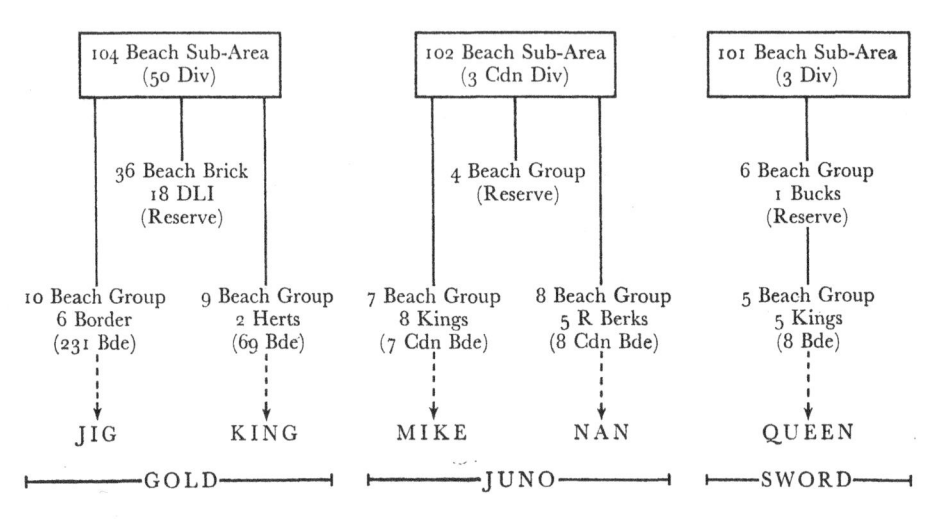

104 Beach Sub-Area (50 Div)		102 Beach Sub-Area (3 Cdn Div)		101 Beach Sub-Area (3 Div)
36 Beach Brick 18 DLI (Reserve)		4 Beach Group (Reserve)		6 Beach Group 1 Bucks (Reserve)
10 Beach Group 6 Border (231 Bde)	9 Beach Group 2 Herts (69 Bde)	7 Beach Group 8 Kings (7 Cdn Bde)	8 Beach Group 5 R Berks (8 Cdn Bde)	5 Beach Group 5 Kings (8 Bde)
JIG	KING	MIKE	NAN	QUEEN
——GOLD——		——JUNO——		——SWORD——

of the assault beaches the basis of the army organisation at first was the 'beach group', a loosely knit formation, eventually four to five thousand strong, with which naval and air force units were associated. Later on these groups were joined to form 'beach sub areas' for each of the divisional areas in Gold, Juno and Sword. Each beach group contained units of the Royal Engineers, Royal Army Service Corps, the Royal Army Medical Corps and other specialist formations, and a specially trained battalion of infantry whose commanding officer was the beach group commander. The main task of the infantry was to provide working parties for the specialist units concerned with the unloading of stores and vehicles and clearance of beach defences and wreckage, the salvage and recovery of 'drowned' or damaged vehicles, the formation of dumps and depots, the development of beach exits and lateral roads, the establishment of field dressing stations, and the control and direction of traffic; but at first most of the beach battalions (shown on the diagram opposite) were involved in fighting to subdue enemy posts which had not been cleared when the assault troops moved inland. In this fighting they had considerable casualties, including the commanding officer of one battalion, and much of the day passed before they were free for other tasks.

But as time wore on the position steadily improved. By midday shore exits were generally available, if not so many as had been intended; lateral roads were being developed and traffic control was working, though at times long blocks formed and held up movement; field dressing stations were dealing with the wounded and the confusion of the early morning was largely resolved.

The Royal Air Force not only played its part in organising the reception and distribution of its own stores and material for the construction of the first airfields, but also provided for the control of the balloon barrage to protect the shore and anchorage from enemy aircraft. They too suffered casualties and loss of equipment while the beaches were still under enemy fire.

The Air Force beach organisation consisted of a 'beach squadron' each for Gold, Juno and Sword, with a 'beach flight' for each subsector, comprising sections dealing with landings, ammunition, equipment, motor transport, fuel and provost duties. All their advance units were under 83 Group, which was to be the first group established in the bridgehead. Part of 83 Group Headquarters and staff came ashore during the afternoon and an advance party began setting up a group control centre; its ground control interception unit for the control of night fighters was able to begin operating that night though less progress was made than had been planned.

During the day the shipping awaiting discharge had moved further inshore to prearranged anchorages to save time in unloading but the rough weather was interfering everywhere with the ferrying of stores ashore from tank landing ships and coasters, and the unloading of landing craft and beached barges was also behind schedule. Admiral Talbot who landed at Sword beach during the afternoon arranged for naval working parties to go ashore next morning to help in clearing the beaches.

The convoys of Force L bringing the first follow-up formations—the fighting echelons of the 7th Armoured Division and the 153rd Brigade of the 51st (Highland) Division—were due to arrive from the Thames in time to land on the second tide. They included a convoy of large personnel ships, the first big British ships to pass through the Straits of Dover for four years. Enemy gun-fire from the French coast had sunk a motor transport ship in the preceding convoy, but, using radio counter-measures and smoke, the passenger ships passed through without interference.

SEAWARD DEFENCE SYSTEM
ASSAULT AREA

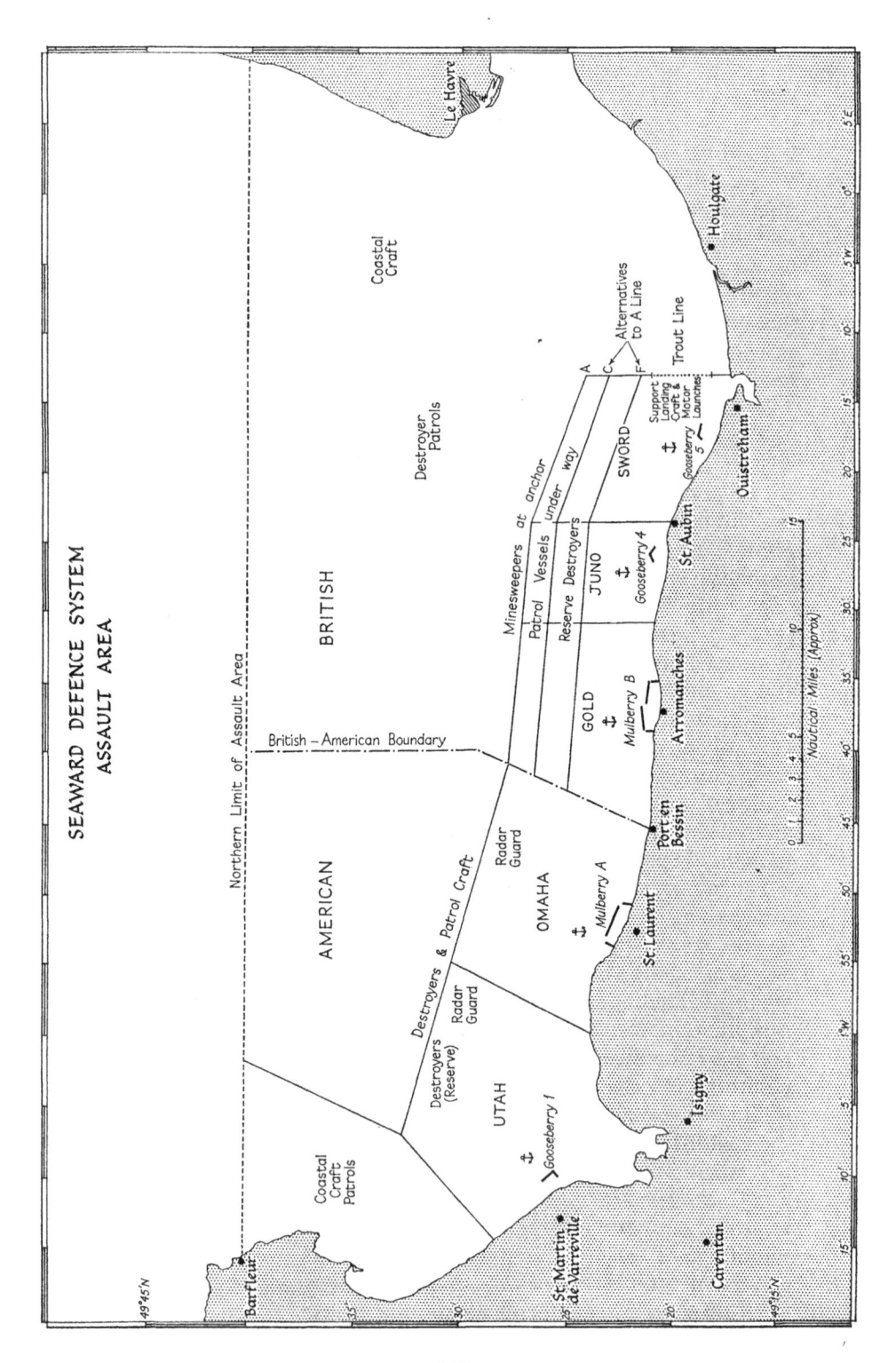

During the day Admiral Vian had visited each assault area and his flagship *Scylla* had joined in the bombardment of targets in Sword and Gold. At six o'clock in the evening he met his assault force commanders off Juno to concert with them naval dispositions for the coming night. The safety of the mass of shipping now lying off the coast was the first consideration. It was improbable that U-boats or warships could penetrate the area in view of the Allied naval strength; the laying of mines by ships or aircraft seemed the enemy's more likely form of attack. To meet the threat of surface attack in the British sector a cordon of minesweepers was anchored at half-mile intervals about six miles from the shore, covering all shipping near the beaches. Admiral Vian in *Scylla* anchored off Sword near the eastern end of the line. Along the eastern flank the line was extended shorewards into shallow water east of the Orne by support landing craft, anchored two hundred yards apart, forming what was known as the 'Trout line'. To seaward of the minesweepers roving patrols of destroyers and motor torpedo-boats covered the approach channel from the Spout, while inside the assault area lay the Captain (Patrols) in a frigate under way, ready to reinforce any threatened point. Assault force commanders were responsible for the inner defence of the anchorages where auxiliary minesweepers were anchored to observe the fall of any mines laid by aircraft. Smoke was also used to screen shipping but this was discontinued as it obscured observation.

In the American sector destroyers and patrol craft under way continued the British defence line to westward and motor torpedo-boats patrolled the shallow water of the northern approaches to Utah; a group of four destroyers under way inside the western end of the line provided further protection.

The defence system, covered during the night by six squadrons of Mosquitos and at dusk and dawn by British and American squadrons of day fighters, was successfully maintained throughout the Neptune operation, though modified in detail as a result of experience.

Admiral Vian had returned to Sword area soon after ten o'clock that evening and saw the fly-in of airborne reinforcements described on page 204, as many of the gliders passed over the anchorage. It was an impressive spectacle, but at 10.50 p.m. orders were given to cover the anchorage with smoke in anticipation of an enemy air attack. About half an hour later the attack began, just before the arrival of the last re-supply mission by transport aircraft of 46 Group. This was precisely the contingency Admiral Ramsay had foreseen when, discussing the airborne plan, he had emphasised the danger of routeing aircraft in proximity to naval forces at dusk or in darkness; should a simultaneous enemy air attack develop their safety could not be guaranteed though all anti-aircraft fire was forbidden.

Admiral Vian saw a German bomber pass down the side of *Scylla* at masthead height and a few minutes later two of our Dakotas flew overhead at about a thousand feet. Anti-aircraft fire opened up on the British aircraft from certain merchant and landing ships and later from anti-aircraft batteries on shore—some of them British. In all, five aircraft were lost and fourteen damaged and there was considerable dispersion; only twenty tons of supplies out of a hundred and sixteen they had brought were collected. With the original airborne attack some equipment had been brought in by gliders, and twelve hundred containers had been dropped from parachute aircraft; earlier in the evening of D-day further equipment had been landed in gliders, and six hundred containers dropped by tug aircraft. Much material had been lost, but the following supplies and equipment had been received during the course of the day: over a hundred thousand rounds of ·303 ammunition; eleven hundred 3-inch mortar bombs; five hundred anti-tank mines; fifty-eight light machine guns; ninety-seven wireless sets; eight 75-mm pack howitzers; thirty-five 6-pounder guns and two 17-pounders; eight light tanks and a hundred and fifty jeeps.

The British and Canadian casualties among troops landed from the sea are believed to have been in the region of three thousand, of whom about a third were Canadians. So far as can be ascertained casualties to airborne troops by the end of the day were about six hundred killed and wounded and about the same number missing; in addition nearly a hundred glider pilots were killed, wounded or missing. The total American casualties on this day in both airborne and seaborne assaults amounted to approximately six thousand.

Before leaving this account of a day which was 'making History change its tune' some of the figures that have been quoted and a few others may well be brought together.

Personnel employed in	British	American	Other Allies
Warships	78,244	20,380	4,988
Landing ships, craft and barges	32,880	30,009	—
Naval shore and miscellaneous parties	1,700	2,500	—
	112,824	52,889	4,988
Total, Allied navies		170,701	
Allied merchant navies (estimate)		25,000	
Grand Total		195,701	

A full measure of success was due to the hundreds of thousands of men and women in all three Services whose work in Great Britain lay behind the day's operations, and to the still greater number of

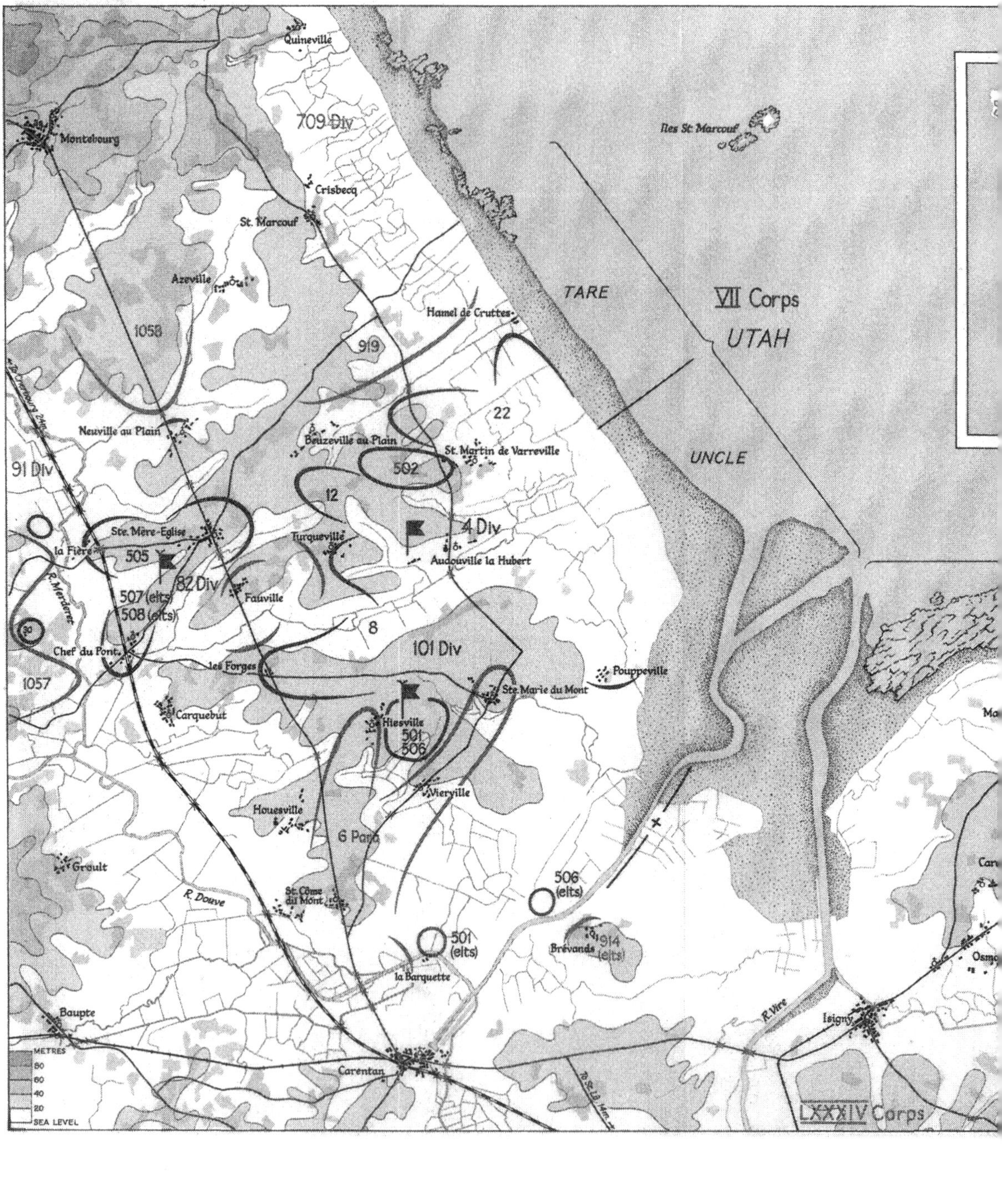

Quineville
709 Div
Montebourg
Crisbecq
St. Marcouf
Iles St Marcouf
Azeville
1058
Hamel de Cruttes
TARE
VII Corps
UTAH
919
22
Neuville au Plain
Beuzeville au Plain
St. Martin de Varreville
502
UNCLE
91 Div
12
Ste. Mère-Eglise
la Fière
505
Turqueville
4 Div
Audouville la Hubert
82 Div
R. Merderet
507 (elts)
508 (elts)
Fauville
8
101 Div
Chef du Pont
1057
les Forges
Pouppeville
Ste. Marie du Mont
Carquebut
Hiesville
501
506
Vierville
Houesville
6 Para
Groult
506 (elts)
R. Douve
St. Côme du Mont
501 (elts)
Brévands
914 (elts)
la Barquette
R. Vire
Baupte
Isigny
METRES
80
60
40
20
SEA LEVEL
Carentan
LXXXIV Corps

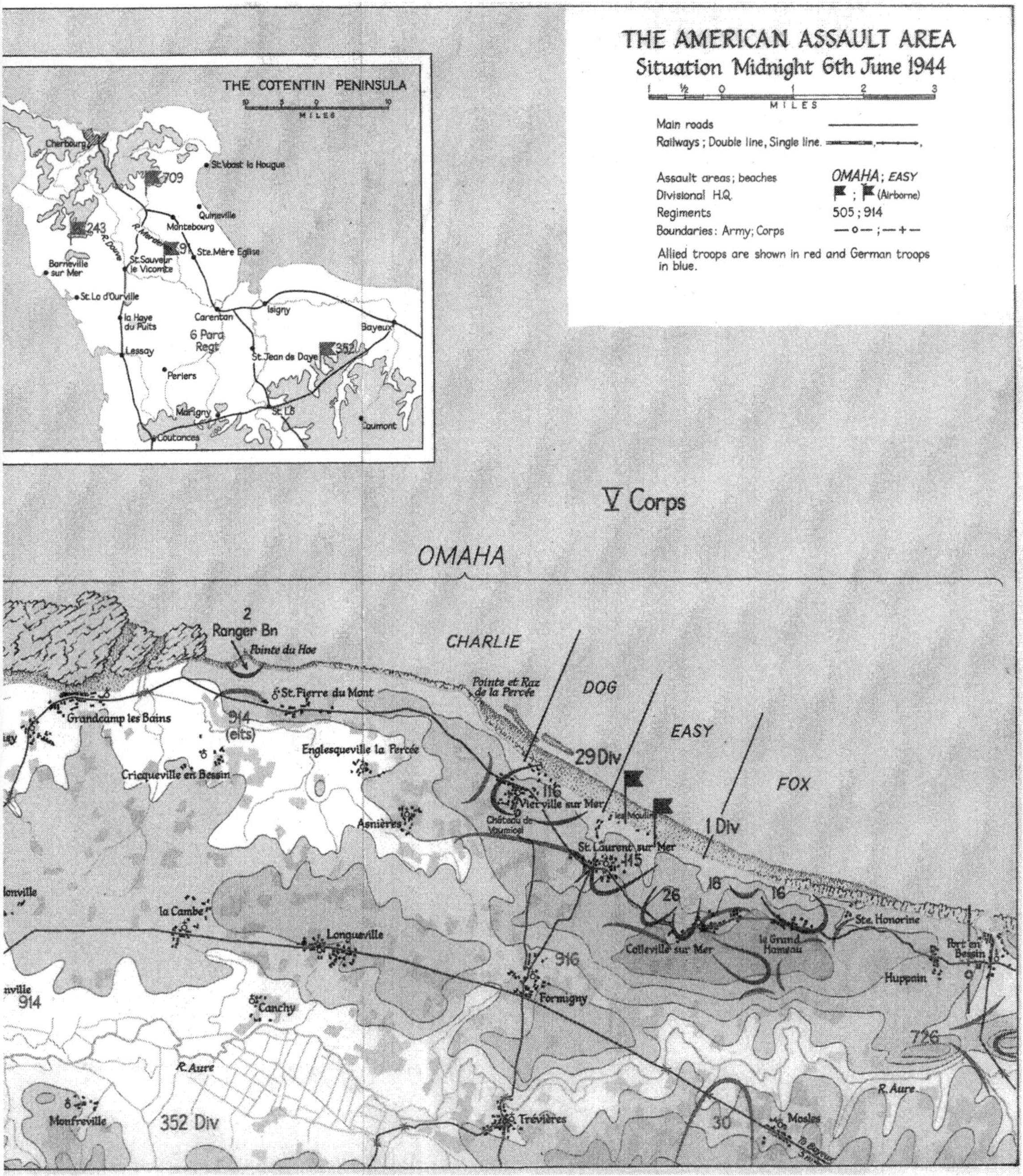
THE AMERICAN ASSAULT AREA
Situation Midnight 6th June 1944
MILES
Main roads
Railways; Double line, Single line.
Assault areas; beaches
OMAHA; EASY
Divisional H.Q.
(Airborne)
Regiments
505; 914
Boundaries: Army; Corps
Allied troops are shown in red and German troops in blue.
THE COTENTIN PENINSULA
MILES
Cherbourg
St. Vaast la Hougue
709
Quineville
243
Montebourg
R. Douve
91
Ste. Mère Eglise
Barneville sur Mer
St. Sauveur le Vicomte
St. Lo d'Ourville
Isigny
la Haye du Puits
Carentan
6 Para Regt
Bayeux
Lessay
St. Jean de Daye
352
Periers
Marigny
St. Lô
Caumont
Coutances
V Corps
OMAHA
2 Ranger Bn
Pointe du Hoe
CHARLIE
Pointe et Raz de la Percée
DOG
St. Pierre du Mont
Grandcamp les Bains
914 (elts)
EASY
Englesqueville la Percée
29 Div
Cricqueville en Bessin
FOX
116
Vierville sur Mer
les Moulins
Château de Vaumicel
Asnières
1 Div
St. Laurent sur Mer
115
26
18
16
la Cambe
Ste. Honorine
Longueville
Colleville sur Mer
le Grand Hameau
Port en Bessin
916
Huppain
Formigny
914
Canchy
726
R. Aure
R. Aure
Monfreville
352 Div
Trévières
30
Mosles

those in civil employment who had laboured unceasingly in ship-yards and factories, in workshops and offices to prepare and equip these forces. This cannot be shown by statistics.

In naval operations over a hundred and ninety thousand men were engaged afloat on this first day. The above approximate figures are based on Admiralty records and the reports of Force Commanders which are not, however, always complete.

In air operations during the night of June the 5th and on D-day, Allied aircraft of all types had flown over fourteen thousand sorties. For that huge total a hundred and twenty-seven aircraft had been lost and sixty-three damaged.

Of the Allied armies, over a hundred and thirty thousand men were landed from the sea on D-day as nearly as can be calculated. Their distribution along the Normandy shore was approximately as follows:

British Sector	Gold	24,970	*American Sector*	Utah	23,250
	Juno	21,400		Omaha	34,250
	Sword	28,845			

Total British and Canadian 75,215   Total American 57,500

In addition, over twenty-three thousand airborne troops were landed by the Allied air forces. The records are not complete but, including glider pilots, their approximate numbers appear to have been 7,900 British and 15,500 American. Thus in spite of the Atlantic Wall over a hundred and fifty-six thousand men had been landed in France during the first day of the campaign.

CHAPTER XI

CONSOLIDATING GAINS

THE night of D-day passed without serious interference by the enemy but the short hours of darkness gave little rest to the commanders and their troops. Some, after a night of active patrolling, would have to resume the advance at an early hour; others, having laboured to straighten out affairs on the beaches, must be ready to accept a flood of supplies and reinforcements as soon as day broke. Those fortunate enough to snatch a few hours' sleep were roused more than once by a few German aircraft which dropped bombs or mines on the beaches or in the crowded anchorages, and by the answering noise of anti-aircraft fire from ships and shore. So far the German air forces had shown little desire to give battle and had made only feeble attempts to hit the wonderful targets offered to them. Allied air forces, on the other hand, had had a busy night. Air reconnaissance on D-day had reported that the 12th SS Panzer Division was already on the march from near Rouen and had noted that military trains were being loaded near Chartres and Amiens, where two armoured divisions—Panzer Lehr and the 2nd Panzer—were known to be, and south of the Loire where the 17th SS Panzer Grenadier Division was. To delay the movement of troops from these areas and from Brittany, Bomber Command attacked in darkness rail and road junctions along an arc which stretched from Paris to the base of the Cherbourg peninsula; they flew over a thousand sorties that night, from which twelve aircraft failed to return. Mosquitos and Mitchells of the Second Tactical Air Force also dealt with roads which converged on the bridgehead, creating choke points at key places such as Falaise and Villers-Bocage, and attacking columns on the move.

At dawn on the first day after the landings the Allied armies were quickly on the move. Behind their forward troops were many enemy pockets to be cleared and their D-day tasks had still to be completed. The Americans had to take Isigny and Carentan, join up their two bridgeheads, and in the Cotentin thrust westwards across the peninsula and isolate Cherbourg in preparation for its capture. The British had to take Caen and Bayeux and establish their left flank on the Dives, while on their right they would link up with the American army at Port en Bessin. When General Montgomery saw General Bradley and General Dempsey between six and eight o'clock that morning he had no need to issue any fresh orders but only to emphasise the urgency of these tasks. He added that the newly arriving 51st Division might cut in behind Caen, moving east of the river Orne. (Map at page 197.)

Except near Caen, where there is an area of hedgeless, big-field cultivation, Normandy is close and broken country, thickly hedged and heavily wooded, a land of hill and valley intersected by winding roads and waterways—lovely to look at but difficult to fight in. Each thrust forward was likely to leave ground on either hand still held by a by-passed enemy. Progress in such country, if stoutly opposed, must inevitably be slow, and with each advance clearance of the enemy left behind must occupy many troops and many hours. There was as yet nothing like a firm German front, nothing to show where the enemy would make a firm stand; a small gain, here recorded in a sentence, was often the result of a strenuous day's fighting and many casualties to those engaged. Our forces were as yet comparatively thin on the ground and between the forward positions there were still wide gaps. General Montgomery had impressed on his army commanders the need to link up the initial bridgeheads as quickly as possible, but while this was being done the Allies must retain the initiative and must guard against any setbacks or reverses. It would take time to 'get the whole organisation sorted out and working smoothly; while this was happening there was a danger of the enemy catching us off-balance'.[1]

The next few days were indeed largely occupied in consolidating and strengthening the hold gained on D-day, but the initiative was retained by pressure all across the front. Least progress was made on the vulnerable left flank, for it was there that such armoured formations as the enemy had already available were concentrated to restrict, if not to eliminate, our bridgehead and to prevent nearer approach to Caen. Sustained efforts were made to enlarge the small bridgehead east of the Orne which had been won by airborne troops, but casualties on D-day had reduced the strength of the six parachute battalions to some two hundred men each, and though two of the airlanding battalions had had very few casualties the third did not arrive (by sea) till the afternoon of the 7th; the commandos of the 1st Special Service Brigade had about four hundred men each. With these small forces not much immediate progress could be looked for in face of strong opposition.

While the 3rd and 5th Parachute Brigades engaged in active patrolling, in warding off enemy attacks and in strengthening the defences of the main position covering the Ranville bridges, Royal Engineers were already putting up the first of the 1,500 Bailey bridges which they were to build for Twenty-First Army Group in this campaign. To the north, commandos tried to extend the bridgehead

---

[1] B. L. Montgomery, *Normandy to the Baltic* (1947), p. 50.

to Franceville Plage and along the coast, and to recapture the Merville battery position which the enemy had again occupied. At both places there was hard fighting but, though supported by the cruisers *Arethusa* and *Mauritius*, the commandos were too weak to achieve success and were eventually withdrawn to the positions already held along the le Plein ridge. It was essential to deny the enemy the advantage of observation which its high ground would afford and there were not yet enough troops to do that and also to extend the bridgehead to the coast. Meanwhile the 6th Airlanding Brigade sought to enlarge the bridgehead southwards towards Caen. The 1st Royal Ulster Rifles and the 2nd Oxfordshire and Buckinghamshire Light Infantry took and held Longueval and Hérouvillette on the 7th, but after strenuous fighting they failed to wrest from the enemy Ste. Honorine and Escoville on that day or in renewed attacks two days later.

By then the German Fifteenth Army had been made responsible for all troops east of the Orne and the destruction of the British airborne bridgehead there had been made the task of LXXXI Corps. Its troops comprised not only the 346th and 711th Divisions and elements of the 716th Division but also a battle group from the 21st Panzer Division made up of infantry, tanks and assault guns.

Each day the Germans attacked at one point or another, but all these attacks were beaten off with loss. The most serious was on the 9th when, after we had made a second unsuccessful attack on Ste. Honorine, our positions around Ranville were heavily shelled and mortared and, shortly afterwards, a two-pronged attack was made by the battle group of the 21st Panzer Division. But when the left prong, having by-passed Longueval, came out into the open, devastatingly accurate, pre-arranged defensive fire of the 3rd Division's guns from across the Orne broke the back of the attack and local sorties brought it to an end. The other prong had meanwhile attacked Hérouvillette but there too it failed; the enemy got a foothold in one company area but a counter-attack drove them out, leaving forty dead and four tanks and armoured cars behind.

In view of the strength of the opposition it was clear that the bridgehead east of the Orne could not be enlarged without further troops. The 51st (Highland) Division was being sent there and meantime the airborne division did well indeed to hold the ground already won; nowhere had the enemy been able to dislodge them. Behind their defence the engineers, often working under shell-fire and frequently attacked by enemy aircraft,[2] were steadily strengthening

---

[2] A troop of the 3rd Division's light anti-aircraft regiment brought down a number of enemy planes which attacked the bridge site. In addition to the divisional and corps light anti-aircraft regiments, eight anti-aircraft brigades with searchlights and both heavy and light guns were included in G.H.Q. Troops. One brigade landed with

the life-line, by bridges over the river and canal, which joined their bridgehead to the ground to the west of the Orne that had been won by the rest of I Corps. They too were not yet strong enough to make much headway against the enemy's determination to hold Caen.

The immediate task of the 3rd Division was to seize the high ground north of Caen, to close the gap on their right where the 21st Panzer Division had penetrated on D-day, and to link up there with the 3rd Canadian Division. On the morning after D-day the 185th Brigade renewed the attack on Lebisey. Though assisted by the fire of three regiments of field guns and a cruiser, the attack was not successful. North of Lebisey is open country through which the road to Caen passes over a ridge crowned by Lebisey woods. The attack, started by the 2nd Warwickshire early in the morning and reinforced later by the 1st Norfolk, continued all day. The Warwickshire penetrated for some distance into the thickly grown woods and a few reached the outskirts of the village on the far side; but the enemy held the main attack in the woods with machine guns, well disposed in thick undergrowth, that were hard to reach, and when darkness fell the troops still fighting there were withdrawn. They had had heavy casualties, and while they reorganised in the next two days the attack was not renewed. (I Corps orders issued before D-day had recognised that if the enemy prevented our seizing Caen on the first day it would be necessary to mask the city for three or four days till the 51st Division and the 4th Armoured Brigade were available to join in a general attack.)

The 9th Brigade on the right had meanwhile occupied Périers sur le Dan on the 7th and had unsuccessfully attacked Cambes, one of the enemy's strongest positions in this part of the front, but a junction with the Canadians was made and two days later the 2nd Royal Ulster Rifles and the East Riding Yeomanry again attacked. They had to cross over a thousand yards of flat open land, shelled, mortared and machine-gunned heavily, and they had nearly two hundred casualties and lost four tanks, but after hard fighting they gained their objective. Later in the evening the 1st King's Own Scottish Borderers joined them in making the new front secure at this important point.

On the 7th the 3rd Canadian Division bore the brunt of a strong counter-attack by the 12th SS Panzer Division which had begun moving up on D-day (page 206) and was the second armoured division to be opposed to the British advance.

---

each assault corps and two more followed during June. Closely linked to the naval and air force commands in Normandy, these brigades were responsible for protecting the base area, the Mulberry harbour and, until relieved by the Royal Air Force Regiment in July, the British airfields. As June passed, with the enemy's air attacks on a small scale, a number of heavy anti-aircraft regiments joined in the support of ground operations—a practice which became general as the campaign progressed.

The Canadian 9th Brigade led by the 27th Canadian Armoured Regiment and The North Nova Scotia Highlanders, struck southwards down a by-road that leads through Villons les Buissons, Buron and Authie to Carpiquet. Les Buissons was soon cleared and an '88' and a six-barrelled mortar (the first seen) were accounted for; Buron was taken, with another '88', but as the Canadians pushed on and entered Authie they were heavily shelled from St. Contest on their left. Cambes at that time had not yet been taken by the British 3rd Division and the left flank of the Canadian attack was therefore exposed to the enemy holding Cambes, Galmanche and St. Contest; supporting field artillery was out of range or on the move and calls for naval fire were not getting through. In view of this it was decided to halt the advance and make good a position to the north of Authie, but as this move was in progress tanks of the 12th SS Panzer Division broke in among them, overrunning some of their positions. The 27th Canadian Armoured Regiment became fully engaged and there was a stern fight and many casualties on both sides as the Canadians fell back on Buron. The German tanks pressed their attack till they reached the outskirts of the village, but there a counter-attack beat them off. Both sides had lost heavily, and when darkness fell the Canadians were withdrawn to the higher ground at les Buissons; Buron was left as a 'no man's land' between the contestants. On the west of the Mue stream the 7th Canadian Brigade had meanwhile pushed southwards for about four miles and had occupied Putot en Bessin and Bretteville l'Orgueilleuse and established outposts at la Villeneuve and Norrey en Bessin, on either side of the railway and south of the Caen–Bayeux road.

Before daylight on the 8th German patrols were active and there were soon indications that an armoured counter-attack was imminent. The outpost at Villeneuve was withdrawn and a first attempt by enemy tanks to cross the railway was driven off, but thereafter attacks on Putot and Bretteville developed and went on far into the night. Tanks from a second battle-group of the 12th SS Panzer Division got into Bretteville in the growing darkness. 'Altogether twenty-two Panthers circled about battalion headquarters [of The Regina Rifle Regiment] and A Company's position during the night and it is hard to picture the confusion which existed. Contact with all but D Company was lost. Fires and flares lit up the area, and the enemy several times appeared to be convinced that the opposition had ceased . . .!' But the opposition had *not* ceased. The Regina Rifles were still there and there they stayed despite several more attacks, holding all their positions until relieved some days later.

About half past six on the morning of the 8th The Royal Winnipeg Rifles drove off infantry and tanks from a battle group of the 26th SS Panzer Grenadier Regiment, a battalion of 'Panther' tanks and some self-propelled guns which tried to cross the railway. With increasing support of their guns and mortars, the enemy's infiltration between the Canadian positions became general; by early afternoon all three of the Winnipeg's forward companies were encircled and short of ammunition and some of their positions were overrun. A withdrawal was made on to the reserve company between Putot and the Caen road and the village was shelled heavily. Then the Canadians counter-attacked with the 1st Battalion, The Canadian Scottish Regiment and a squadron of tanks, supported by two field regiments and some 4·2-inch mortars. Though costly, the attack was successful. The railway crossing and the village were once more in our hands.

A strong counter-attack by I SS Panzer Corps (21st and 12th SS Panzer Divisions) had been ordered for this day, to 'drive the British into the sea', but the British and Canadian operations had forced the enemy to commit his available forces in order to hold them; no large scale counter-attack was now possible.

On XXX Corps front the 50th Division was the only division landed on D-day and the following days were spent in consolidating and expanding the ground they had won. Their 69th Brigade, adjoining the Canadians, had made the deepest thrust on D-day by reaching Coulombs and Brécy; on the 7th they advanced a further three or four miles southwards and, crossing the high ground and the Bayeux–Caen road at St. Leger, joined the Canadians near Bronay and captured Ducy-Ste. Marguerite. A German radar station protected by concrete installations, minefields and wire was taken with few casualties and about fifty prisoners. But enemy infantry and tanks were still in the wooded country on the east bank of the Seulles river when, on the 8th, the 8th Armoured Brigade moved down through the front of the 69th Brigade to exploit southwards through Audrieu and to capture the high ground above Villers-Bocage, fifteen miles south of Bayeux.

The advanced guard of the 8th Armoured Brigade Group, mainly composed of the 50th Division's 61st Reconnaissance Regiment on the right and the 24th Lancers on the left, was hotly engaged as soon as it neared the railway line near Loucelles and Bronay, and the Lancers were involved with troops of the 12th SS Panzer Division who at that time had temporarily driven the Canadians out of Putot en Bessin. While this fight was in progress the Nottinghamshire Yeomanry from the main body of the brigade made a detour on the right and, outflanking the resistance at Loucelles, forced its way across the railway and made a speedy run up to Point 103, two miles beyond it. Anti-tank guns and machine guns were brought up after dark and during the evening infantry of the Dorset Regiment (detached from the 231st Brigade) and tanks of the

4th/7th Dragoon Guards cleared the opposition at Loucelles and reached the Audrieu area but had to share the straggling village with the enemy for the night.

Early next morning (the 9th) Audrieu was cleared and the 8th Durham Light Infantry were brought up from the 151st Brigade. They reached Point 103 in the afternoon and about six o'clock, following a preliminary bombardment, they advanced and took Saint Pierre, a village on the right bank of the river Seulles, opposite Tilly. It had been a costly attack but, with the assistance of tanks, the infantry eventually cleared the place except for a bridge over the river which remained in the enemy's hands. There was thus a small salient at this position with enemy forces building up on each side of it. Tanks, frequently reported to be in the neighbouring woods in the Seulles valley, were from the first elements of the Panzer Lehr Division which was now coming into action—the third armoured division opposing the British advance.

While the 8th Armoured Brigade was thus fighting its way southwards towards Tilly sur Seulles the 151st Brigade had reached the high ground astride the direct road from Bayeux to Tilly between the Seulles and the Aure. The 56th Brigade on its right had taken Bayeux (on the 7th) and, having occupied defensive positions blocking approaches to the city from Caumont and St. Lô, captured Sully on the Drome after a tough fight but were unable to take the enemy's main defences west of the river. In the coastal area the 231st Brigade had pushed westward taking the Longues battery position with 120 prisoners. Empty shell cases showed that the German guns had fired 115 rounds before they were finally silenced by H.M.S. *Ajax* on D-day; two had been put out of action by naval shells which passed through the embrasures and the whole area was heavily cratered.

Two miles further westward the 47th (Royal Marine) Commando had begun a stiff fight for Port en Bessin early on the 7th. It lies in a hollow between high cliffs on which commanding strong-points had been constructed in positions which were difficult to reach. While a damaged wireless set was being mended and supporting fire arranged, fighting began in the narrow streets and packed houses of the town. In the afternoon H.M.S. *Emerald* and three squadrons of rocket-firing Typhoons attacked the overlooking strong-points and first a post on the edge of the town and the positions on the west cliff were taken. Then in the gathering dusk the Marines began to scale the eastern heights and attack the stronger position on the cliff-top. Fighting went on throughout the night and not until four o'clock on the morning of the 8th was the position taken; the commander with three hundred of his men surrendered. The capture of Port en Bessin had cost the Marines heavy casualties but the harbour was to prove of great value, and almost before it was safely in our hands naval parties had been landed to survey its facilities. The 231st Brigade had gone on to capture a strong position on the river Drome near Port en Bessin on the 8th and had made first contact with American troops fighting eastwards, but between there and Sully the enemy still held the west bank of the river Drome in an effort to prevent the link-up of the British and American bridgeheads.

The American V Corps had meanwhile steadily enlarged the foothold gained in the assault on Omaha beach. There had indeed been a complete metamorphosis of the position there in the first forty-eight hours. At the end of D-day it had been still the most tender spot in the Allied line; two days later the defence of the German 352nd Infantry Division, which had opposed the landings at Omaha so strongly, had been broken and the Omaha bridgehead firmly established. The American 1st Division had pushed eastwards, and as mentioned above by the evening of the 8th had made contact with the British near Port en Bessin. Later that day they attacked down the main road to Bayeux from Formigny. Reaching Ste. Anne after dark, they had a violent and confused fight with German units striving to keep open a way between Ste. Anne and the British on the east bank of the Drome. During the night surviving elements of the German 352nd Division and the formations attached to it escaped southwards; its right flank had given way after losing heavily. The Americans followed hard on their heels and during the 9th reached Agy four miles south-west of Bayeux on the road to St. Lô. A serious gap was thus opening in the German defence. Although the 352nd Division had avoided capture its left flank had now gone too and the American 29th Division captured Isigny and pushed southwards almost to the Carentan–Bayeux railway. Patrols from Isigny had also made contact with troops of the 101st Airborne Division, the first junction of the American V Corps from Omaha and their VII Corps from Utah. (Map facing page 248.)

After clearing-up operations on the 7th, VII Corps in the Cotentin had organised a strong attack northwards in order to eliminate batteries still firing on the Utah beaches and to widen the base for a drive westwards. On the morning of the 8th the 82nd Airborne and the 4th Infantry Divisions attacked abreast with the Quineville–Montebourg ridge as their first objective. Aided by naval guns and air support they made steady progress, and by the evening of the 9th had advanced four or five miles beyond Ste. Mère Eglise. A bridgehead across the Merderet had also been formed by the evening and was being exploited westwards, and contact had been made with the isolated detachments of the 82nd Airborne Division, while an attack on Carentan had been launched from two directions. Its capture was most important, for it was there that the two American bridgeheads were to be joined together. Thus everywhere the Allied gains on D-day had been solidified and extended in spite of all that the Germans could do. In these achievements guns of the Allied navies had continued to support the armies' operations with powerful long-range fire and the Allied air forces to play their essential part; for the moment only operations on land are being noted, but both the other Services were also deeply involved in maritime operations in the Channel, where the great volume of Allied shipping had to be protected from surface, submarine and air attacks. These maritime operations will be described later.

The immediate tasks of the air forces during these first few days may be bracketed under three heads. First they had to maintain their protection of the home base in England and the shipping areas, assault beaches and bridgehead; secondly they had to prevent or delay the enemy's reinforcements and supplies from reaching the battle ground and to deny their air forces the use of convenient airfields; thirdly they had to join in supporting the fighting troops in prearranged attacks or, where called to help, in the course of the battle. In fulfilling all these tasks they sought to destroy the German aircraft wherever and whenever they were met. The importance of fighter cover increased after the first few days as the German Third Air Fleet's aircraft were gradually reinforced and showed rather more enterprise. Yet so effective was the Allies' air activity that nowhere did the *Luftwaffe's* attacks have any effect on the movements of Allied troops, nowhere were Allied plans interfered with by enemy air forces. How different was the effect of Allied air attack on the enemy's operations! But then how different was their strength and their attitude, the scale of their operations and the objectives to which they were matched. It has been shown (page 121) that the German Third Air Fleet in France had 891 aircraft of all types when the campaign opened. Only 497 of these were serviceable on D-day, but no doubt they brought some more into operation in the days that followed. Be that as it may, their return of daily losses shows that in the first four days they lost 208 aircraft and had 105 damaged. After a few days they began to receive some reinforcements and their records show that in the first thirty days they flew on average between four and five hundred sorties a day; but a large proportion of these were defensive patrols, well outside the battle area, attempting to ward off the Allied attacks on communications which were so seriously hampering the movement of reinforcements and supplies. A contemporary German report says: 'The policy of never operating in strength in good weather against enemy bomber formations' was adopted; 'there was no point in attacking four-engined formations since the destruction of a single aircraft would make little difference to the effect [of bombing] on targets'. They realised that Allied air forces avoided combat on the way to their targets and sought to engage German aircraft on their return flight. 'The losses on these occasions', the report said, 'were two to three aircraft out of every ten sent up' and 'fighter losses on average worked out at three to one in the enemy's favour'.

In these first few days the bombing of transportation targets was concentrated on routes leading to the battle area. By day, bombers and fighters of the American Eighth Air Force attacked such junctions as Lisieux, Falaise, Flers, Argentan and Laigle astride the two main rail and road routes from Paris, and in the Nantes–Rennes–Laval area routes running north from the Loire. The heavies were supplemented by mediums of the Ninth Air Force attacking subsidiary junctions between the two main areas. On top of all this came the British and American fighters and fighter-bombers ranging over the roads and railways between the choke-points. The combined effort was on an immense scale but the area was large, the country was close and the routes many. It was not expected that all day-movement could be stopped but the delaying effect was immediate and considerable. The Panzer Lehr division was forced to move after daylight on a very wide front, using five roads. Its commander, Lieut-General F. Bayerlein, described the air attacks as 'terrible' and 'incessant'; the road out of Vire, he said, was a '*Jabo Rennstrecke*' or 'fighter-bomber race-course'. He estimated that over eighty of his half-track vehicles, self-propelled guns and prime-movers were destroyed. A battle group of the 275th Division, ordered by train from St. Nazaire to Bayeux, took all D-day and most of the night to assemble and load under the Allies' air attacks, and not till the morning of the 7th were its trains at last on the way. A few miles from Avranches the first was attacked by medium bombers and then by Thunderbolts and was destroyed with all its vehicles and equipment, while the troops suffered heavy casualties. The second train had meanwhile been halted by an attack which cut the line short of Avranches. It, too, was then attacked and had to be abandoned and the rest of the journey to the front had to be made on foot.

While attacks such as these went on at some distance from the bridgehead there were many others closer in—for example on traffic centres and batteries in the Cotentin, junctions between Carentan and Bayeux, on Tilly sur Seulles and Villers-Bocage opposite XXX Corps and on Mézidon in front of I Corps.

Supplementing the flow of information from the reports of returning aircraft, the tactical and photographic reconnaissance squadrons flew far and wide and fighters and fighter-bombers of the tactical air forces were out daily on armed reconnaissance. They also answered an increased number of support calls, and air spotting for naval

ALLIED AIRCRAFT DELAY ENEMY MOVES

gunfire was continuous. American squadrons dealt with targets such as the Cotentin batteries, Montebourg, Carentan and St. Lô, while the British Typhoons and Mustangs operated between Lisieux, Falaise and Caen, or further south about Alençon and Vire. On the 8th the hard-pressed Canadian brigade at Putot en Bessin and the airborne troops east of the Orne were among the several British formations which called for Typhoon attacks on the enemy opposing them. There was a notable example of Anglo-American co-operation at Omaha where Typhoons combined with fighter-bombers of the Ninth Air Force to attack enemy positions at and east of Isigny in response to calls from the 29th Division. On that day over one thousand of the Eighth's fighters had, as the Americans described it, '... a general beat up of railways outside the battle area ...' and '... roamed a great area stretching from the south of Nantes to the north-east of Paris, shooting up everything they saw moving'.

Each night Bomber Command continued the air attack. On the night of the 7th 330 heavies attacked key points on the Paris Ceinture railway. It was moonlight and the bombing was made from a low level. Twenty-eight aircraft were lost from the enemy's flak defences and night fighters but the results were rated '... a considerable success'. At Juvisy, for example, every track was cut and the Seine bridge was wrecked—a further blow to the passage of formations from the north. Also that night another two hundred heavy bombers bombed the Forêt de Cerisy south-west of Bayeux where the American First Army believed there was a build-up of German armour. Next night they sent over five hundred bombers to attack railways at Alençon, Mayenne, Fougères, Rennes, Pontaubault and the railway tunnel at Saumur on the Loire. A special force from Bomber Command's 5 Group attacked this with 12,000-lb bombs—'Tallboys' used in action for the first time. Eighteen Tallboys were aimed at the tunnel's southern end (previously marked by a salvo of flares from Mosquitos), a direct hit was scored and the tunnel made unusable; it had not been repaired when captured by the Americans two months later. On the 8th the weather deteriorated and many places were eventually obscured by cloud. Out of nearly 1,200 bombers despatched in the morning by the Eighth Air Force only 735 were able to attack, and of 250 Ninth Air Force mediums all but thirty had to be recalled.

On the evening of the 9th conditions improved slightly and Bomber Command flew five hundred aircraft to Eampes, targets in the Orléans gap, and airfields which the weather had prevented the day bombers from attacking. Despite the thick cloud the bombing was well concentrated, especially at the le Mans airfield. On each night, too, light and medium bombers of the Second Tactical Air Force patrolled the approaches to the battle area, attacking all movements seen; but the enemy made good use of cover and camouflage and were quick to halt on the approach of an aircraft.

Though not so affected by weather as the bombers, the fighters were forced to work at much lower heights and their losses from ground weapons were increased appreciably. Covering the western sector the Ninth's protective patrols saw very few Germans, but the Spitfire formations of the Second Tactical Air Force were more fortunate, particularly near Caen and over the Sword beaches. On the 8th Australian, New Zealand and Belgian squadrons made contact with over thirty aircraft and shot down seven of them without loss.

Rommel's opinion that massed armoured formations could not operate successfully where an enemy had mastery of the air (page 120) was being abundantly justified and the effectiveness of the Allies' air policy is witnessed in all contemporary German records of this period—especially in the official war diaries of the Commander-in-Chief, West (von Rundstedt), Army Group B (Rommel), the Seventh Army (General Dollmann), and those of subordinate commands. Hitler was a long way off and at first could only reiterate orders that the bridgeheads must at once be eliminated and the Allies driven back into the sea. Von Rundstedt and Rommel, nearer to the scene of action, were quick to realise the failure of this prearranged strategy and how large a share Allied air forces were taking in the frustration of German designs; for these presupposed the ability to strike back in armoured strength while the enemy's foothold was still insecure, but in fact the Allied air attack on communications was preventing any quick concentration of the necessary troops.

The German commanders claimed that the delay in getting permission from OKW (page 200) to counter-attack at once with three armoured divisions—the 21st, 12th SS and Panzer Lehr Divisions—had meant that only the 21st Panzer Division was able to attack on D-day, and that its failure single-handed to secure any material result had allowed the Allies to renew their advance on the 7th. Certainly the delay was of advantage to the Allies. Yet it seems very unlikely that either the 12th SS or the Panzer Lehr Division could, in any case, have intervened in the battle on D-day seeing that the former had to come from the south of Rouen (over seventy miles away) and the latter from the south-west of Chartres (over one hundred miles) and that both went by road under constant Allied air attack and could not move quickly. It was the fact that the German command were taken by surprise and that movement was delayed by Allied air attack, as much as Hitler's delay, which prevented any concerted counter-attack by I SS Panzer Corps on D-day. And when, on the 7th, the first elements of the 12th SS Panzer Division reached the front, they had to be committed at once on the left of the 21st Panzer Division in order to stem the advance of the Canadians at Authie. It was two days later before the first units of Panzer Lehr Division, much delayed and damaged by air attacks *en route*, began to arrive and were put straight into battle on the left of the 12th SS Panzer Division in order to hold the attack of the British XXX Corps near Tilly sur Seulles. Thus the British divisions were given time to improve their position and maintain their offensive. By the 10th of June the already damaged armoured divisions of the enemy were strung out across the British front, trying precariously to hold their ground under pressure which gave them no time to concentrate for a major counter-attack or make good their losses.

While these steps were being taken to check the British advance others were ordered against the Americans. It is not always possible to discover from the records who initiated orders, for both von Rundstedt and Rommel record them in the war diaries as if they were their own; the point is not very important, however, for there is little to suggest that now there was any difference of opinion between them. Everything had to be done to ensure that the Allies did not get a firm foothold.

Apart from the danger of the British landings in the east, the American bridgehead at Utah and airborne landings in the Cotentin together implied an attempt to cut off the peninsula and capture Cherbourg. Early on the 7th, in agreement with von Rundstedt, Rommel ordered two divisions to move at once to the west of the Cotentin—the 77th Infantry Division from near St. Malo and (with Hitler's consent) the 17th SS Panzer Grenadier Division in OKW reserve from south of the Loire. On the same day it was agreed that the 3rd Parachute Division should also be moved up from Brittany; all three divisions were to be under II Parachute Corps which in turn would be subordinated to LXXXIV Corps.

The German capture of some American orders on the 7th confirmed von Rundstedt's expectation that the American forces landed at Omaha and Utah were to join up and the latter to thrust north and take Cherbourg; the danger of 'a new enemy land front' was apparent, and 'our attempts to build a new defensive front between Bayeux and the Vire . . . are being severely impeded . . .' The Allies were striving to delay arrival of II Parachute Corps and 'our troops without new reinforcements must be forced on to the defensive'.

Von Rundstedt now ordered three more armoured divisions to the battle area, namely the 2nd Panzer and the 1st and 2nd SS Panzer Divisions,[3] the 8th Werfer Brigade, and artillery units mobilised

---

[3] 2nd Panzer Division was in Army Group B reserve near Amiens, but the 1st SS, in OKW reserve and only movable with Hitler's permission, was in Belgium, and the 2nd SS, in Army Group G reserve, was near Toulouse.

from three named artillery schools. He also ordered the preparation of two infantry divisions to relieve the armoured divisions already committed and sent OKW a personally signed request for further reinforcements. By the 9th 'the point of main effort' was said to be in the region of the Vire estuary and Carentan, where the flank of 352nd Division had been torn open by American attacks and orders had been given for its withdrawal to a line covering St. Lô. II Parachute Corps was now directed towards Carentan, though its 77th Infantry Division was to move up through the western side of the Cotentin to Valognes for defence and counter-attack and placed under command of LXXXIV Corps.

There had been a further change of German commands. All Seventh Army formations between the Orne and the Vire (I SS Panzer Corps, 716th and 352nd Divisions) were put under General Geyr von Schweppenburg of Panzer Group West whose headquarters, given an operational rôle on D-day, had been transferred to Army Group B and allotted to the Seventh Army. As it moved up to the battle from Paris three-quarters of its wireless equipment was destroyed by fighter-bomber attacks and it was not fully operational till the 9th. The task of holding the Cotentin had been laid on General Marcks commanding LXXXIV Corps, which had II Parachute Corps coming up on its right.

But the Allied air forces had almost as much say in such movements as the German commanders. Where were the divisions of the II Parachute Corps on the evening of the 9th when the Seventh Army was urging movement 'with the greatest speed'? Although the 17th SS Panzer Grenadier Division had some reconnaissance elements within ten miles of Bayeux, one of its two grenadier regiments was near Avranches and the other east of Laval. According to Seventh Army the whereabouts of its tracked vehicles and other units moving by train were '. . . not exactly established at this time . . .' The bulk of the 77th Division was about Avranches with, it was hoped, one battalion on ahead. The 3rd Parachute Division had most of a battle group about ten miles east of Avranches, but two of its parachute regiments were still well back in Brittany.

It was claimed in the C-in-C West war diary that the transfer of Allied reinforcements from the British Isles 'which are near and abundantly equipped is more rapid [by sea] than the movement of our reserves by rail and road', and the build-up of strength was described as 'a race in which conditions inevitably favour the enemy'. To consider that travel by road and rail was now more difficult in France than the crossing of a hundred miles of tempestuous sea, subject to the danger of attack by aircraft, surface vessels and submarines, was a pleasant compliment to the Allied air forces but a landsman's under-valuation of maritime power and naval skill.

Moreover, the worsening weather was a greater handicap to the Allies' build-up than any German opposition, and the maintenance of cross-Channel communication was only achieved by perpetual vigilance and not without cost.

In the first week the effect of weather, shortage of craft and consequent delay in turn-round, combined to hinder the progress of the Allied build-up, which was falling considerably behind schedule; but if we were not realising all that had been planned, either in that regard or in the operations on land, the battle was going well for the Allies and badly for the enemy. General Montgomery had been quick to see that while, tactically, operations were not making the progress aimed at, strategically the piecemeal absorption of German armour on the left flank was to our advantage. On the other hand, von Rundstedt and Rommel had already come to the hopeless conclusion that for successful counter-attack it was 'important for the *Luftwaffe* so to eliminate, at least temporarily, the activity of enemy warships on the coast that the attack can be pressed through *and* the main defensive line finally re-occupied' and 'to prevent enemy bombers intervening at the central point of attack'.

The German war diaries for this period are indeed full of references to the effect not only of air force attacks but also of naval gunfire in land operations. Of the opening assault the Seventh Army recorded that:

> 'Weapons sited in defensive field works had to be dug out before use owing to the preliminary bombardment by enemy warships. Coastal defence guns were in most cases put out of action by direct hits on emplacements.[4] Counter-attacks, successful everywhere at first, later suffered unusually high casualties in the neighbourhood of the coast through enemy naval gunfire.'

Five days later von Rundstedt was reporting to Hitler that 'the guns of most enemy warships have so powerful an effect on areas within their range that any advance into the zone dominated by fire from the sea is impossible . . . The ships keep constant watch on the coast inland, up to the limit of the range of their guns.'

During the first few days all types, from battleships to gun landing-craft, helped to give fire support along the whole front; later, as the fighting moved inland calls from the armies for naval support were less frequent but an average of two battleships or monitors, from four to ten cruisers and a few destroyers were held in readiness in the British sector with corresponding provision on the American front.

---

[4] This was an overstatement, but the main object of the Allies' naval bombardment was to silence the German batteries and undermine morale—and in that they certainly succeeded.

The main concern of the Allied maritime forces was, however, to ensure the safe conduct of reinforcements and supplies for the build-up of the battle ashore. The German Naval Commander-in-Chief, Admiral Krancke, with the meagre resources of his command, was doing his best to interfere; but their few successes had no noticeable effect on Allied operations in the Channel and, leaving for the moment the story of the fighting in Normandy, it will be well to trace the course of maritime operations during the first ten days of the campaign.

From the table in Appendix III it can be seen that apart from five destroyers in the Gironde and la Pallice (of which only three were serviceable) the only offensive surface vessels at Krancke's disposal on D-day consisted of six torpedo-boats (five at le Havre and one at Brest) and thirty-four motor torpedo or E-boats of which fifteen were at Cherbourg and the rest at Boulogne, Ostend and Ijmuiden. The other surface craft shown in the table—minesweepers, patrol boats, artillery barges and tugs—were of little offensive value, though some could be used for minelaying. There were also the thirty-five U-boats of Group *Landwirt* that were ready for sea on D-day, and five of Group *Mitte* in south Norway which had just cleared past Iceland into the Atlantic and were ordered to the Channel area.

Early that morning (June the 6th) the three available destroyers sailed northwards from the Gironde and all thirty-five U-boats of the *Landwirt* that were ready were ordered out; the nine fitted with schnorkel apparatus were to make for an area twenty-five miles south of the Isle of Wight; seven without schnorkel were to operate off the south coast of England between Start Point and the Scilly Isles; the remaining nineteen were to form an off-shore screen across the Bay of Biscay to guard against any further Allied landing there. The five of Group *Mitte* that had cleared Iceland were told to make for western France. The motor torpedo-boats waited for the cover of darkness, for they could not risk movement in daylight in face of the Allied sea and air strength. To get a clear picture of the German naval effort, and of the Allies' reply during these first weeks, it will be well if the actions of destroyers, U-boats and motor torpedo-boats are followed separately.

Two of the destroyers belonged to the German Z class of 2,600 tons with a speed of thirty-six to thirty-eight knots; each had eight torpedo tubes and five 15-cm guns. The third was an ex-Dutch destroyer of 1,600 tons with similar speed. All three were spotted by reconnaissance aircraft as they left the Gironde, and at once the 10th Destroyer Flotilla of the Plymouth Command was ordered from the Hurd Deep patrol to a new position off Ushant in order to intercept them. Beaufighters and Mosquitos of Coastal Command attacked them twice on their passage northwards and damaged one before they put into Brest. They left Brest on the 8th with the torpedo-boat there (one of the T class, with six torpedo tubes and a speed of thirty-three knots).

The Allied flotilla of eight destroyers waiting for them, led by H.M.S. *Tartar*, established contact by radar at 1.15 a.m. on the 9th and ten minutes later opened fire at a range of five thousand yards. The Germans turned to fire torpedoes but the British pressed on, throwing the enemy into confusion. The torpedo-boat and one destroyer turned away southwards: they were pursued and damaged by the Canadian destroyers *Haida* and *Huron* but escaped in the darkness to Brest. Of the other two, one (the ex-Dutch destroyer) was hit by the *Tartar* and stopped. The other, commanded by the German leader, turned away northwards firing at the *Tartar*. Four of her shells burst in rapid succession about the *Tartar's* bridge, bringing down her trellis foremast and radar gear and causing damage and casualties. *Tartar* returned the fire and, though reduced in speed, pursued the German with *Ashanti* in company; but sighting her original opponent—the ex-Dutch destroyer—she sank her, the ship blowing up with a 'spectacular explosion'. Meanwhile the *Haida* and *Huron* returning from their pursuit of the Germans to Brest met the German leader now also trying to reach harbour. Turning and twisting she sought in vain to escape, but was hotly engaged and finally driven ashore a burning wreck. What was left was destroyed later by Allied bombers. The only German destroyer force in the West was thus eliminated in the first three days, for the torpedo-boat and destroyer that had got back to Brest never fought again; when, later, American armies advanced into Brittany both were withdrawn to la Pallice and eventually scuttled there. So much for the destroyers. In such night-fighting between fast ships the need for quick decision in a rapidly changing scene is vividly illustrated by this affair.

The sixteen U-boats ordered to the Channel made but slow progress, for naval forces and aircraft of 19 Group Coastal Command[5] hunted them relentlessly as they worked their way northwards and day by day their numbers were reduced. On the night of the 6th one was sunk, on the 7th three, and on the 9th and 10th one was sunk each day. Already by the evening of the 10th, of the seven non-schnorkel boats on these missions five had been sunk and two damaged by air attack. An entry in the German war diary records that 'on account of the large number of air attacks and the extensive damage suffered, above all on U-boats without schnorkel, all further sailing of these boats has been stopped for the present'.

Of the nine schnorkel boats striving to reach the 'Spout' one had been sunk and two others damaged and forced to return to Brest. The

---

[5] Which included four Fleet Air Arm and three U.S. Navy squadrons. Four Fleet Air Arm squadrons were also with 16 Group.

six remaining worked slowly northwards almost continuously submerged—tactics which limited their movement and proved exhausting to their crews. When a week had elapsed one turned back with defects, another entered St. Peterport, Guernsey, with empty batteries, a third followed there next day and subsequently went back to Brest. The fourth succeeded in sinking the frigate, H.M.S. *Blackwood*, between Cherbourg and Portland but was herself so damaged by counter-attack that she too made back to Brest; the fifth was sunk by a Wellington bomber on the 18th. Only the sixth ever reached her intended position south of the Isle of Wight where she arrived on the 15th and only remained for three days, harried continuously by Allied patrols. Her only success was the destruction of one tank landing craft and, after having attacked but missed two battleships, she withdrew and returned to Brest.

On the 15th the first of the five U-boats from Group *Mitte* had reached the western entrance to the Channel. There she had an early success by torpedoing the frigate H.M.S. *Mourne* of the 5th Escort Group which blew up with heavy loss of life. The U-boat succeeded in evading subsequent counter-attacks only to be sunk on the 18th by the 14th Escort Group of destroyers (*Fame, Inconstant* and *Havelock*). Little had come of Admiral Dönitz's U-boat offensive in the first fortnight, but the U-boats had shown their fortitude and devotion and were still far from being defeated.

Finally, the third form of naval attack, by fast motor torpedo-boats, had also only very limited success. Responsibility for defence of the main convoy routes from the Isle of Wight lay with the Commander-in-Chief, Plymouth, on the west and the Commander-in-Chief, Portsmouth, on the east while additional groups operated, up Channel, under the command of the Vice-Admiral, Dover; their forces deployed on the flank consisted of groups of motor torpedo craft supported by destroyers and frigates. Each night the E-boats tried to penetrate these covering forces and to reach the cross-Channel convoy routes and the assault area. In most cases they were detected, but these small 90-ton boats with two torpedo tubes and a 3·7-inch gun had a speed of thirty-five to forty knots and, working in darkness, it was almost inevitable that such fast-moving little craft could sometimes elude the protecting forces, to make tip-and-run attacks on shipping streaming across the Channel.

Each night the German 5th and 9th E-boat flotillas from Cherbourg and later others, which were transferred to le Havre from ports further east, attempted to penetrate the defence. On the first night they met with no success; some were intercepted by British M.T.B.s, one group reached the Spout but was driven off by the destroyer *Hambledon*, another group was forced into a German minefield off Cherbourg where two were sunk. On subsequent nights an occasional minor success could be set against their own increasing losses.

On the night of the 8th, a group of E-boats from le Havre reached the Spout unobserved and attacked a convoy of seventeen landing craft with only one motor launch in close escort. In the ensuing mêlée three landing craft were torpedoed. Two sank with some loss of life; others and the motor launch were damaged by gun-fire before the E-boats were driven off. In the darkness and confusion the convoy had scattered and at daybreak the motor launch still guarding a group of the craft found herself close to the French coast near Cap d'Antifer. Fortunately they were hidden from enemy shore batteries by morning mist and made their way safely to their destination in Juno area. But in most cases E-boat attacks were beaten off by destroyers or coastal forces before they reached the convoy routes.

The damage inflicted by E-boats in their nightly sorties was insignificant when compared with the volume of Allied shipping that was crossing the Channel daily and was certainly not enough to have any effect on the Allies' build-up in France. Losses from E-boats were one motor torpedo-boat, two tank landing ships (American), three small merchant ships, two landing craft and two tugs towing Mulberry components; in the same period six E-boats were sunk and ten others damaged but in the next week their challenge was virtually eliminated.

Air reconnaissance had revealed a quantity of ships and craft in le Havre and at Admiral Ramsay's request 346 aircraft of Bomber Command made daylight attacks on the port twice in the late evening of June the 14th. By a fortunate coincidence the Germans had banned the use of anti-aircraft fire at that time to safeguard their own operations and the bombers struck with devastating effect. Eleven E-boats were destroyed outright in their shelters and three others seriously damaged; only one remained operational. And in the harbour three of the five T class torpedo-boats, twenty minesweepers and patrol boats and nineteen tugs were sunk and eight other craft, including another T class torpedo-boat, were damaged. Admiral Krancke described it as a 'catastrophe' and his war diary recorded: 'it will hardly be possible to carry out the operations planned with the remaining forces ... the naval situation in the Seine Bay has completely altered since yesterday's attack on le Havre'. That was written on the 15th, but almost as it was written Bomber Command did it again. On that evening 274 bombers struck at the shipping in Boulogne harbour. They destroyed a depot ship and twenty-six light craft, and damaged eight others as well as the floating dock and harbour installations.

In addition to the losses in U-boats which have already been told, the German naval casualties in surface vessels inflicted by Allied naval and air forces from the 6th to the 16th of June, inclusive, according to the war diary of the German Group Command West, were:

	Sunk	Damaged
Destroyers	2	1
Torpedo-boats	3	2
E-boats	17	13
Minesweepers, patrol vessels and other small craft	82[6]	29

This destruction was not achieved without cost to ourselves. During the same eleven days 26 aircraft of Coastal Command were lost in attacking U-boats or coastwise shipping, mostly from anti-aircraft fire; in the attacks on le Havre and Boulogne Bomber Command lost two bombers. Allied shipping losses at sea during this period, from these and other causes, are summarised later, for a more serious menace to shipping was the enemy's nightly air attack in the assault area, partly by bombs but mainly with mines. On every night save one in the first half of June up to fifty or more low-flying aircraft, often operating singly, attacked shipping in the anchorages of the assault area. The bombing attacks achieved comparatively little. The headquarters ship *Bulolo* was damaged by bombs on June the 7th, the frigate *Lawford* was sunk on the 8th, and the destroyer *Boadicea* was sunk by a torpedo bomber on the 12th/13th while escorting a convoy off Portland; in addition one landing craft and two merchant ships were sunk by air attack in this period. Thus out of the hundreds of ships at sea up to June 16th only five were destroyed by direct air attack. Air-mining, coupled with some mines laid by surface craft, took a heavier toll of shipping.

Although a number were brought down by our own air forces, defence in darkness against single, low-flying aircraft laying mines was difficult, for a low cloud-base on most nights forced Allied night fighters also to fly low, and the fact that radar efficiency was much reduced in low altitudes increased the difficulty of identification. The greatest danger was from the enemy's two newly-introduced types of mine. Both were actuated through the momentary reduction of pressure on the sea bed when a ship passed over them in shallow water. One defied all known methods of minesweeping and the other could only be swept in favourable weather; in any case the sweeping of a congested anchorage was very difficult. Fortunately a mine fell on shore in Sword area and was recovered and the vital parts were at once flown to England. Counter-measures were

---

[6] Included one depot ship and nineteen tugs.

quickly evolved, and although no complete answer was found the risk was reduced by drastically reducing the speed of all vessels mooring in shallow water and by towing large ships when moving in the anchorage. Up to June the 16th in the British sector losses from mines were remarkably small, namely a motor gunboat, three landing craft and the Trinity House vessel *Alert*, used as a buoy-laying ship. In the American sector losses from mines in the same period were much heavier for they included five destroyers and other vessels, some of which were lost in the moored minefield off the east coast of the Cotentin peninsula (as shown in the map facing page 136) which was only located on D-day.

Apart from ships and craft lost on D-day in the original assault, the Allied losses at sea owing to enemy action from the 7th to the 16th of June are shown in the following table.

Allied Losses at Sea
7th June to 16th June inclusive
Cause

	E-Boats	U-Boats	Mines	Aircraft	Other Causes	Total
Warships	1 M.T.B.	2 Frigates	4 Destroyers (3 U.S., 1 French) 3 Minesweepers 1 M.G.B. 1 Netlayer	1 Destroyer 1 Frigate		14
Landing ships and craft	3 L.S.T. 1 L.C.T. 1 L.C.I. (L)		3 L.S.T. 6 L.C.T.	1 L.C.I. (L)	21 L.C.	36
Merchant ships	3 Ammunition coasters 2 Tugs		1 M.T. ship 1 Buoy-laying vessel 1 (unspecified)	1 M.T. ship 1 Coasting tanker	3 Coasting tankers 1 (unspecified)	14
TOTAL	11	2	21	5	25	64

In the same period seven warships, seven merchant ships (including two hospital carriers), the headquarters ship *Bulolo* and three landing craft were damaged by enemy action, but in four cases the damage was slight and the ships remained operational. In addition, seven warships were damaged by grounding or collision.

Against these losses should be set the fact that, *not counting shipping which arrived on D-day*, up to midnight on June the 16th, 93 passenger ships, 636 other merchant ships and 1,300 landing ships and craft had crossed the Channel safely.

CHAPTER XII

EXPANSION OF THE BRIDGEHEAD

To describe the maritime operations of the first ten days, the account of fighting ashore was interrupted on the evening of June the 9th. By then the Allied front was already a continuous one from the east of the Orne to the Vire at Isigny and the junction of the two American corps across the Vire estuary was imminent. The American V Corps was now ordered to capture Caumont and to secure a firm junction with Carentan, while on their right VII Corps was to take Carentan and drive westwards in order to cut the Cotentin peninsula and to isolate Cherbourg.

In the British sector the German armoured divisions' strong opposition to a direct advance on Caen decided General Montgomery to outflank and encircle the position. On the east wing I Corps would pass the 51st Division into the bridgehead east of the Orne, from there to attack southwards towards Cagny, six miles south-east of Caen; to the west XXX Corps would launch the 7th Armoured Division southwards to Villers-Bocage and Noyers, and then strike across the Odon to high ground above Evrecy. When these positions had been reached the 1st Airborne Division, waiting in England, would be flown in to close the gap between Cagny and Evrecy, but though operations would start on the 10th this final stage would not be reached for some days.

When General Montgomery made this plan known Air Marshal Leigh-Mallory opposed the intended use of the 1st Airborne Division, arguing that for various reasons it would not be landed in sufficiently concentrated strength to fulfil General Montgomery's intention. As however neither British corps attained its objective, and neither Cagny nor the high ground above Evrecy was reached when these operations were broken off, no opportunity to use the 1st Airborne Division in fact arose.

Of the twin attacks that were designed to outflank Caen, the start of the operation from the airborne division's bridgehead east of the Orne was delayed, for neither the 51st Division nor the 4th Armoured Brigade, each of which was to attack southwards, had completed its assembly there by the morning of the 10th; the 51st Division's 153rd Brigade was to cross the Orne that evening and the new operation should be developing by the 12th. Meanwhile fighting round the airborne bridgehead continued.

The position of the opposed forces on the morning of the 10th is shown on the situation map overleaf. That morning the enemy renewed the attack on both sides of the Bréville gap. Commando positions on the ridge north of Bréville were attacked early and a few of the enemy succeeded in reaching Hauger and Amfreville villages, but local counter-attacks ejected them and by early afternoon the situation had been stabilised again. During the morning other enemy attacks were made further south against the 3rd Parachute Brigade's positions near St. Côme and its château. In the late afternoon these reached their climax with an assault by about a battalion of infantry and some self-propelled guns. But the bombardment officer (F.O.B.) was in wireless touch with H.M.S. *Arethusa* and within fifteen minutes the cruiser's 6-inch salvos were falling among the enemy. The parachutists then went in with the bayonet and finally disposed of the Germans. A badly wounded unit commander of their 346th Division, taken prisoner in the action, remarked that his battalion had been virtually wiped out in the last twelve hours.

Meantime the enemy's main attack was against Ranville. After an hour's heavy shelling and mortaring, about 9 a.m. the Germans began to work across the old landing ground, making good use of the cover afforded by the wrecked gliders after their supporting fire had stopped. But the defenders held their fire till the enemy were only fifty yards away and opening up with every rifle, machine gun and mortar, broke up the attack. Some German troops took cover in the adjacent woods but a counter-attack helped by tanks summoned from across the river drove the Germans back towards Bréville, leaving behind them a hundred prisoners and still more dead. The German corps war diary admitted that the 2nd Battalion of their 858th Regiment had been reduced to a hundred men; another battalion had been badly shaken and disorganised.

Late in the evening the 51st Division's 153rd Brigade crossed the Orne but owing to the troublesome situation was held near Ranville and only the 5th Black Watch was put under the 3rd Parachute Brigade to capture Bréville on the 11th. A detachment of the parachutists meanwhile occupied the château of St. Côme so that it would serve as the jumping-off place for the attack.

At 4.30 a.m. on the morning of the 11th, after a bombardment by mortars and five field regiments, the Black Watch advanced from the château but when the guns stopped the enemy quickly came to life and inflicted severe casualties on the leading companies and others preparing to follow; with the Germans bringing mortars, assault and anti-aircraft guns into action, the Black Watch eventually withdrew to the château having had about two hundred casualties in this their first action in Normandy.

Elsewhere east of the Orne the day had been quieter but there was much probing and patrolling by both sides during the night and the sound of tracked vehicles moving up to Bréville could be heard

Cap de la Hague

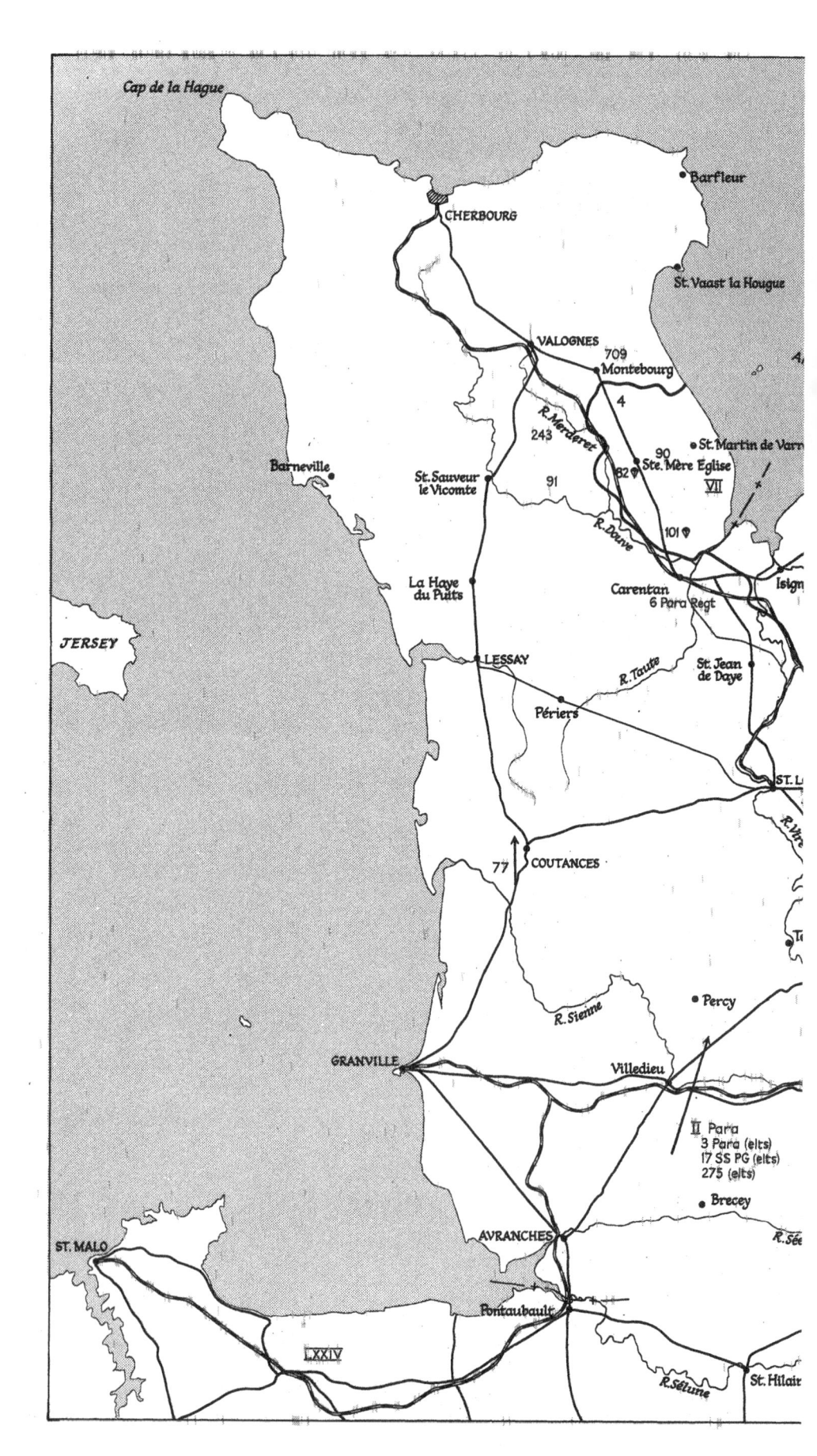

Barfleur

CHERBOURG

St. Vaast la Hougue

VALOGNES
709
Montebourg
4
R. Merderet
243
90
St. Martin de Varr
St. Sauveur le Vicomte
82
Ste. Mère Eglise
91
VII
Barneville
R. Douve
101
La Haye du Puits
Carentan
6 Para Regt
Isign

JERSEY

LESSAY
R. Taute
St. Jean de Daye
Périers

ST. L

77
COUTANCES

R. Sienne
Percy

GRANVILLE
Villedieu

II Para
3 Para (elts)
17 SS PG (elts)
275 (elts)

Brecey

ST. MALO
AVRANCHES
R. Sée
Pontaubault

LXXIV
R. Sélune
St. Hilair

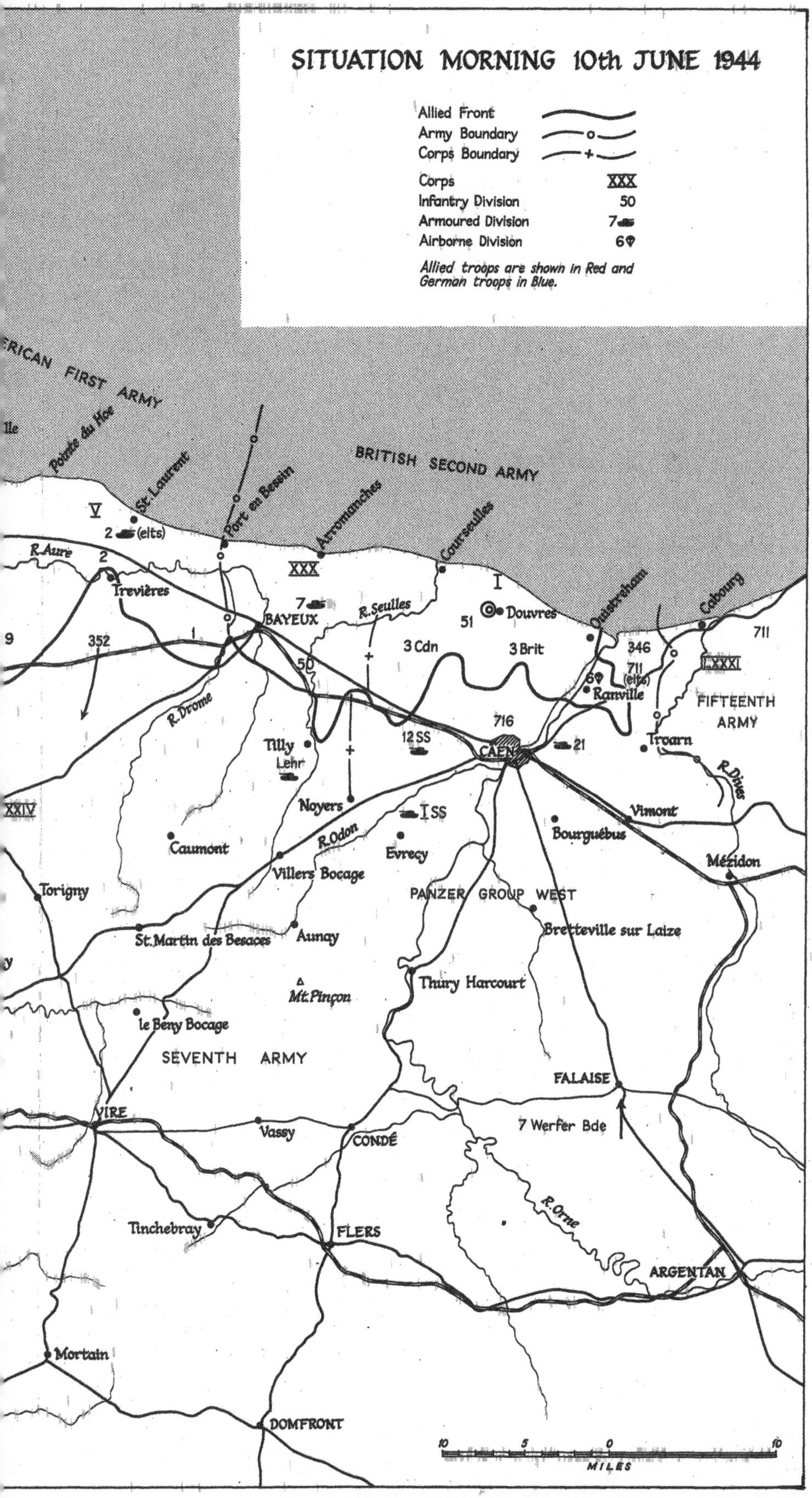

SITUATION MORNING 10th JUNE 1944
Allied Front
Army Boundary
Corps Boundary
Corps XXX
Infantry Division 50
Armoured Division 7
Airborne Division 6
Allied troops are shown in Red and German troops in Blue.
AMERICAN FIRST ARMY
BRITISH SECOND ARMY
Pointe du Hoe
St. Laurent
Port en Bessin
Arromanches
Courseulles
Ouistreham
Cabourg
V
2 (elts)
R. Aure
2
Trevières
XXX
7
BAYEUX
R. Seulles
I
Douvres
51
3 Cdn
3 Brit
346
711
711 (elts)
LXXXI
6
Ranville
FIFTEENTH ARMY
9
352
1
50
R. Drome
716
12 SS
21
CAEN
Troarn
R. Dives
Tilly
Lehr
Noyers
I SS
Vimont
Bourguébus
XXIV
Caumont
R. Odon
Evrecy
Villers Bocage
Mézidon
Torigny
PANZER GROUP WEST
Bretteville sur Laize
St. Martin des Besaces
Aunay
Thury Harcourt
Mt. Pinçon
le Beny Bocage
SEVENTH ARMY
FALAISE
VIRE
Vassy
CONDÉ
7 Werfer Bde
R. Orne
Tinchebray
FLERS
ARGENTAN
Mortain
DOMFRONT
10 5 0 10
MILES

plainly. From midday on the 12th shelling and mortaring of the British positions continued and about three o'clock an enemy attack was launched by the 3rd Battalion of the 858th Regiment supported by a company of assault guns. A desperate fight ensued with the Black Watch in and around the château and with the 9th Parachute Battalion in the woods behind. Casualties were severe on both sides but all our positions were held. As the Germans were reinforced by odd companies and platoons from other regiments, the British battalions were joined by tanks of the 13th/18th Hussars and a company of the Canadian Parachute Battalion of the 3rd Parachute Brigade. Attack and counter-attack went on until after nine o'clock, at which time the German commander returned to his command post at Bréville to collect what further troops he could. As he got there the British began a heavy bombardment of the place.

For the fighting had convinced General Gale that the Bréville gap, the one hole in his otherwise intact perimeter, must be filled once and for all, and reasoning that 'after the extreme severity of the day's fighting [the enemy] would scarcely credit us with the ability to stage a counter-attack, anyhow until the following day . . .' he decided to attack that night.

He had on hand only the 12th Parachute Battalion 'sadly under strength', about sixty men of the Independent Parachute Company and a squadron of the 13th/18th Hussars. Preliminary bombardment of the enemy's Bréville position by the supporting artillery opened at a quarter to ten (just when the German commander was trying to collect his troops) and at ten o'clock the attack was launched through the commando positions at Amfreville. From the first, the parachutists had heavy casualties from the enemy's defensive fire, the commanding officer of their battalion being killed and the commanders of both the commando and airlanding brigades badly wounded. Le Plein, Amfreville and Bréville were burning fiercely when the attack went in with great dash, the tanks being well up in support. Two enemy companies were overrun, Bréville church was quickly reached and the whole village was in our hands before midnight.

The cost was grievously high. The parachute battalion, who had started with only about 160 officers and men, had 141 casualties, but the 3rd Battalion of the German 858th Regiment which had borne the brunt of the day's fighting could now only muster 146 of the 564 men who had entered battle three days before.

General Gale afterwards summed up the action in these words:

> 'There is a turning point in all battles. In the fight for the Orne bridgehead the Battle of Bréville was that turning point. Neither in the north nor in the south were we ever seriously attacked again.'[1]

---

[1] R. Gale, *With the 6th Airborne Division in Normandy* (1948), pp. 99–101.

The day before, that is on June the 11th, the rest of the 51st Division's 153rd Brigade had secured Touffreville without difficulty as flank protection for the projected attack southwards. The 152nd Brigade, by then assembled near Ranville, was to advance on the 13th against Ste. Honorine, Cuverville and Démouville. That morning an advance from Longueval got a footing in the northern half of Ste. Honorine but troops moving on Cuverville met a strong counter-attack by the 'Luck' battlegroup of 21st Panzer Division. Both the leading battalions became embroiled and after several hours of severe fighting the brigade was withdrawn to Longueval and the high ground south of Ranville. For the time being the attempt to expand the bridgehead was discontinued.

Meanwhile the complementary attack on the west of the British front had begun on June the 10th. General Montgomery's intention has already been indicated—to attack through Villers-Bocage and Noyers and from there cross the Odon to seize the high ground above Evrecy. Orders by XXX Corps for the opening phase of this operation gave as the immediate aim 'to seize the ground in the area of Hottot . . . and the high ground east of Juvigny'—objectives which were south and south-east of Tilly sur Seulles (map, page 256). The 7th Armoured Division was to attack through the 50th Division's front between the Seulles and the Aure and to capture Hottot: the 8th Armoured Brigade, at present in the salient east of the Seulles, would then pass from the command of the 50th to the 7th Armoured Division to join it in the further attack southwards.[2] The junction with the Canadians would still be held by the 69th Brigade, but the main task of the 50th Division was to guard the right flank of the 7th Armoured Division as far south as the Tilly-Balleroy road. Before the operation began on June the 10th the cruiser H.M.S. *Orion* fired 186 rounds on Lingèvres. In all she fired over a thousand rounds of 6-inch shell that day on key points ahead of the advance with a relay of seven aircraft observing her fire. The naval long-range support then and on the following day included the shelling of Hottot at a range of 33,100 yards by H.M.S. *Nelson*'s 16-inch guns and of other positions by the Netherlands gunboat *Flores*, who increased range by 'listing' ship to elevate her guns.

---

[2] The 7th Armoured Division's main tank was the Cromwell of 28 tons, which mounted a 75-mm gun firing both H.E. and armour-piercing shot.
  The main tank of the independent 8th Armoured Brigade was the Sherman of 32 tons with the 75-mm gun.
  In both cases the armoured regiments included Sherman 'Firefly' tanks, roughly in the ratio of 1 to 4. These mounted a 17-pdr. gun but it was only provided with armour-piercing shot at this time.
  For reconnaissance work every armoured regiment had in addition ten Stuart ('Honey') tanks of 14 tons with a 37-mm gun.

The Second Tactical Air Force (which included four naval fighter squadrons) played a conspicuous part in co-operation with the naval and army artillery. Close armed reconnaissance was maintained over the battle front and for some fifteen miles or so further south, searching places which the Army named where the enemy was expected and flashing information and urgent calls to England where sorties were held ready for prompt action.

But on June the 10th it was the enemy who attacked first. Early that morning after a sharp artillery and mortar bombardment of the 8th Armoured Brigade's position at Saint Pierre, German troops, making good use of the narrow lanes and deeply hedged orchards, worked their way into several parts of the village and also attacked the nearby positions round Point 103. By the stubborn resistance of the infantry and the fire of tanks, artillery and warships, our main positions were held and after the fighting died down Point 103 and the northern half of Saint Pierre remained in our hands at the end of the day. While our advance from this flank had been checked, the main effort west of the Seulles had meanwhile made little progress.

Taking the road from Bayeux to Tilly sur Seulles as its main axis the 7th Armoured Division began its advance at half past six with the 22nd Armoured Brigade in the lead. First contact was made by the reconnaissance screen as it approached Bucéels, about two miles north of Tilly. Then, by using an additional route a mile further to the west, two armoured regiments were deployed across the front. This hedge-bound *bocage* country was new to the 'Desert Rats' and the enemy's small infantry detachments, each with a tank or anti-tank gun or two and a couple of 'eighty-eights' lurking in the background, were able to cause considerable delays by skilfully exploiting the close country. Some, hidden in the hedgerows, tried to lob grenades into the tanks' turrets or to fix 'sticky' bombs on them as they moved through the deep lanes. Fortunately the enemy bowled a good proportion of 'wides' and their bombs were not lethal enough to cause major damage, but it was clear that our tanks must have infantry to work with them. The infantry brigade had however been ordered to follow in rear of the armour and it was early evening before they caught up and joined the battle. Then they cleared Juaye Mondaye on the right and occupied the high ground beyond it at Hill 112. On the left they dealt with snipers along the original centre line and joined the tanks in mopping up Bucéels. During the day there had been few casualties and only four tanks had been lost, but no further progress was made. Major-General G. W. E. J. Erskine, commanding the 7th Armoured Division, recognised that progress had been slow; yet he reported that he 'never felt serious difficulty in beating down enemy resistance . . .' He proposed to continue the advance towards Villers-Bocage at first light on the 11th.

But no better progress was made on the 11th. The attack was re-organised; two groups were formed with tanks and infantry in each —the first, under command of 56th Infantry Brigade to renew the attack on Tilly sur Seulles: the second, under the 22nd Armoured Brigade to capture Lingèvres on the Tilly to Balleroy road. At Tilly the 56th fought their way into the middle of the town by the evening but the tanks failed to make progress round the flank; the enemy still held the main part of the town when it grew dark and the group was withdrawn for the night to a nearby position on the north. The other group had taken the wooded Verrières country north of Lingèvres by the evening and its armour drew off to harbour for the night. Shortly afterwards enemy tanks broke into the infantry positions among the woods. They were eventually driven away but about midnight, after a bombardment by guns and mortars, the enemy launched a stronger attack with tanks, infantry and a self-propelled flame-thrower. The 2nd Essex had about a hundred and fifty casualties in the grim night-fighting that ensued but they lost no ground and, by calling down artillery fire 'almost on top of themselves', they beat the Germans off.

While the 7th Armoured Division had thus spent the day fighting between the Seulles and the Aure the 50th Division was engaged in the country on either flank. East of the Seulles the 69th Brigade had sought to enlarge the salient which ran through Audrieu to Saint Pierre. From le Haut d'Audrieu the 6th Green Howards and the 4th/7th Dragoon Guards had moved to attack Cristot, advancing in waves of tanks followed by others of infantry, but the two got separated. Lying low in the hedgerows and ditches the enemy infantry left the first wave of tanks to be dealt with by anti-tank guns in the rear, and then came to life and held up the infantry. There was severe and confused fighting and the attack made no more progress. Nine Dragoon tanks pushed forward alone through the Cristot orchards but one by one they were hit by guns which, for the most part, they never saw. Only two got back when the attacking troops were withdrawn to join the reserve holding high ground round Point 103. Following up, the Germans then tried to recapture that position, tanks and infantry having worked round both flanks; but it was firmly held and as night fell the enemy withdrew.

While all this was happening the 3rd Canadian Division had been involved on the 69th Brigade's left. More than once the enemy had infiltrated parties through the open flank along the Mue and the position in front of Putot en Bessin and Bronay needed strengthening. It had therefore been decided to carry out a limited offensive with the 2nd Canadian Armoured Brigade to clear up the Mue valley thoroughly on the 11th and then, on the 12th, to push the front southwards to higher ground at le Haut du Bosq and Grainville sur Odon. Before the Mue clearance began, General Dempsey decided to bring forward the armoured brigade's whole operation to the 11th in order to relate it to that of the 69th Brigade which has already been described above. Unfortunately orders did not reach the 2nd Canadian Armoured Brigade and their associates The Queen's Own Rifles till the morning of the 11th. There was little time for reconnaissance and not enough either to brief the troops adequately or to plan artillery co-operation before the advance started. In the result it was a costly failure.

The 6th Canadian Armoured Regiment started with infantry riding on their tanks and, passing through Norrey en Bessin in spite of considerable shelling, they deployed in the open cornfields north of le Mesnil Patry under machine-gun and mortar fire. The leading squadron drove forward into le Mesnil Patry, getting well among the enemy and doing considerable execution; but when they emerged they found enemy tanks and anti-tank guns waiting for them in position across their front and others opened fire on the Canadians both from St. Mauvieu on their left front and Cristot on their right. Touch with the leading squadron was lost and, seeing that his small force was in danger of being surrounded, the regimental commander ordered a withdrawal to the Caen road. The regiment had lost thirty-seven tanks and the infantry ninety-six killed, wounded and missing from the vanguard company alone. That night the 2nd Canadian Armoured Brigade concentrated about three miles behind the front. It was believed that thirteen enemy tanks (mostly Panthers) had been destroyed.

On the other flank of the 7th Armoured Division, west of the Aure, the 50th Division had pushed southwards to the cross-roads at la Belle Epine while American troops on their right, meeting little opposition, advanced towards Caumont.

On the morning of the 12th XXX Corps (General Bucknall) realised that Panzer Lehr's obvious determination to hold firmly the ground between the Seulles and the Aure made it unlikely that the 7th Armoured Division could achieve a rapid advance there. But west of the Aure there seemed to be a 'soft spot' in the German defence which should be exploited, for the Americans were nearing Caumont without serious opposition. In fact, as is now known, the enforced withdrawal of their 352nd Division on the night of the 9th had left a gap which the German commanders were finding it hard to fill (page 238). XXX Corps accordingly decided (after consultation with General Dempsey) that while the 50th Division continued the battle for the existing front, the 7th Armoured Division would side-step across the Aure and, outflanking the German front on the

Tilly–Balleroy road, would push southwards to the Caumont neighbourhood; turning then to their left they would seize the Villers-Bocage ridge from the west. Their capture of this high ground behind Panzer Lehr Division might compel its withdrawal or surrender.

Most of the 7th Armoured Division started that afternoon (the 12th) and since its own brigade of lorried infantry, the 131st, was now available to move with it the 56th Brigade reverted to the 50th Division. The move went well. Crossing the Aure the 7th Armoured turned south and by ten o'clock that night the leading troops of its 22nd Armoured Brigade reached Livry, two miles from Caumont and five from Villers-Bocage. In order to hide their intentions they halted near Livry for the night while the leading units of the infantry brigade closed up behind them.

Early next morning—June the 13th—the 22nd Armoured Brigade group wheeled to the left to seize the Villers-Bocage ridge. The Sharpshooters (4th County of London Yeomanry) led with a company of the motor battalion, the Rifle Brigade. Behind this advanced guard were the second armoured regiment (5th Royal Tanks) and two infantry battalions of the 131st Brigade (1/5th and 1/7th Battalions, The Queen's Regiment). Squadrons of the divisional reconnaissance regiment (8th Hussars) and the armoured car regiment (11th Hussars), covering their flanks, met a number of enemy tanks, but Villers-Bocage was reached without difficulty. A squadron of the Sharpshooters with its regimental headquarters and a company of the Rifle Brigade drove through the town and out along the wood-flanked road rising to Point 213 on the way to Caen. While tanks went forward, the Rifle Brigade company and the rest were halted behind the crest of the hill, when Tiger tanks swept the column with fire from roadside woods and destroyed all its vehicles. Meanwhile other enemy tanks and infantry covered the eastern exit from the town and all attempts by the rest of the Sharpshooters to free the road and join their advanced guard failed. The latter had found Point 213 held by a mixed force of tanks and infantry. After a fight lasting for some hours the squadron was surrounded and eventually overwhelmed. In all 25 tanks, 14 armoured trucks and 14 Bren carriers had been lost in the engagement.

Though the first troops had got through Villers-Bocage without opposition German tanks and infantry had been in other parts of the town. The 1/7th Queen's were called up but only succeeded in clearing the western half and meanwhile the road behind them through Tracy-Bocage was under attack at several points. Moreover, German prisoners taken were found to come from infantry of the 2nd Panzer Division, evidence that troops of another armoured division were coming into action on their southern flank. When this was realised General Erskine decided, with the corps commander's approval, to break off the fight for Villers-Bocage and to strengthen his position on the high ground by Tracy-Bocage which was 'to be held at all cost'.

Next day (the 14th) the 50th Division continued the battle for Tilly sur Seulles and the road westwards through Lingèvres and la Senaudière—on which the German hold had in fact been strengthened. First the Royal Air Force attacked all three places with bombs, rockets and cannon from eleven squadrons of 83 and 84 Groups. Then two brigades attacked on a four thousand yard front, supported by the divisional and corps artillery and by guns of the Royal Navy and of the American V Corps on their right. Fighting continued all day. The 151st Brigade captured about half of Lingèvres village and on their right the 231st Brigade captured la Senaudière. But nowhere could they break the German front; the fact that seven miles away to the south the 7th Armoured Division had thrust an arm into the enemy's side had not weakened his determination to hold his forward positions. It was the British armoured division which was ordered to draw back its outstretched arm that night, in order to prepare for a stronger thrust in a few days' time. By then a second armoured brigade (the 33rd) which had been delayed in landing would be able to join it.

In reaching these decisions the divisional and corps commanders were influenced by the knowledge that while the 7th Armoured Division was outstretched deep in country held by the Panzer Lehr Division, the 2nd Panzer Division was in turn coming into action against it from the south. Until the 50th Division made headway and the armoured division was strengthened by the addition of the 33rd Armoured Brigade, its precarious positions at Tracy-Bocage and the near-by Amaye sur Seulles were only a liability.

All day enemy detachments of tanks and infantry had been testing the armoured brigade's defences, coming in from both sides of the route to Tracy-Bocage, and strong joint infantry and tank picquets had had to be put out to keep the road open. There were signs that the enemy was assembling troops south of the British positions and about eight o'clock in the evening attacks developed against both Tracy-Bocage and Amaye sur Seulles. They were engaged with every available weapon and great execution was done; what probably settled the issue was the fire brought down by something like 160 British and American guns of various calibres. Here are some extracts from an account written by one commanding officer:

> 'The enemy had quite appreciable artillery and mortar support and his infantry were supported by some of his heaviest tanks . . . but this time it was we who were sitting still and the

German tanks who were moving and ... quite a number of them were brewed up ... and after that the infantry rather lost heart ... the Horse Gunners firing air bursts at 400 or 500 yards ... really rather enjoyed their party. Then the Americans took a hand ... their S.P. 155s had been supporting us throughout ... We had an OP officer ... who certainly knew all the answers. As the firing died down ... there were quite a number of German infantry in a certain wood to our right front. The American OP then called for a special concentration on it. I think its code name was "Pandemonium": at all events ... it meant that every gun within range had to engage and it could only be ordered by an American General. However, it came down within about a minute and a half and it certainly was a real "pandemonium". Afterwards, two Germans who surrendered said ... in the wood they must have had some 800 or 900 casualties. Although this is no doubt a gross exaggeration it will give you some idea of the sort of shoot it was. It may have caused telegrams from Washington due to the colossal amount of ammunition expended but it certainly put "finis" to any further German attack ...'

The withdrawal of the 7th Armoured Division began half an hour after midnight on the 14th/15th, covered by the noise of over three hundred heavies of Bomber Command who dropped over 1,700 tons on German concentration areas south and east of Villers-Bocage at Aunay sur Odon and Evrecy, on the request of Second Army. While this was in progress the enemy made no attempt to interfere and at five in the morning of June the 15th the 7th Armoured Division reported that it had disengaged. Pending the arrival of the 33rd Armoured Brigade it was stationed between the 50th Division and the Americans at Caumont.

If the results of the 7th Armoured Division's first action in Normandy appear to be unimpressive it should be recognised that circumstances were much against it. It had gained its reputation in open desert warfare; fighting in the close *bocage* country needed a very different technique. This called for a trustworthy marriage of tanks and infantry, but the tanks and infantry associated in the first two days' fighting were complete strangers to one another. With Panzer Lehr still holding up the advance of 50th Division and with a second armoured division coming up unexpectedly against them the 7th Armoured Division could hardly have achieved full success. As it was, the immediate result of these operations was disappointing.

Meanwhile, in the American sector progress had been made on both sides of the Vire estuary. By nightfall on the 10th the 1st Division of Lieut-General L. T. Gerow's V Corps (the one nearest to the British XXX Corps), had its right at Balleroy on the edge of the Forêt de Cerisy; the forest itself had been cleared by the 2nd

VILLERS BOCAGE

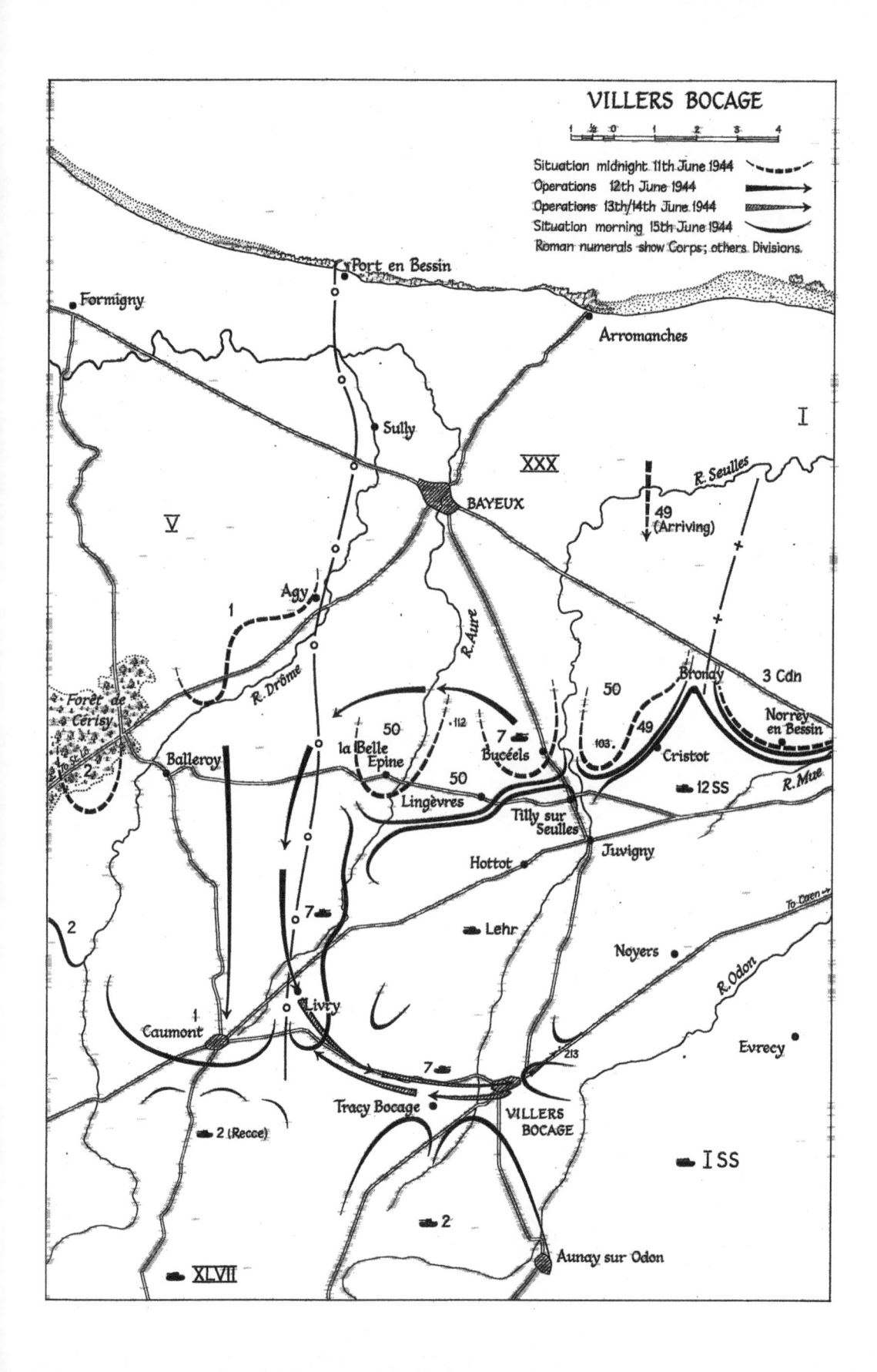

Situation midnight 11th June 1944
Operations 12th June 1944
Operations 13th/14th June 1944
Situation morning 15th June 1944
Roman numerals show Corps; others, Divisions.

Division and, on its right again, the 29th Division's front ran northwestwards to the neighbourhood of Isigny.

After the United States V Corps had passed through the Forêt de Cerisy on the 10th it had proceeded to widen the salient so formed, particularly in the direction of the British sector, and by the 12th, when the 7th Armoured Division was on its way to its new axis, General Gerow's left was at the outskirts of Caumont. To the northwest, the two American corps had been finally joined together early on that day, when VII Corps completed the capture of Carentan. There the German garrison had '. . . used up every scrap of ammunition . . .' and a supply dropped by air was too little and too late to save the situation. To deepen the front at this point, and generally to face towards St. Lô, the Americans now brought in XIX Corps between the other two.

In accordance with Montgomery's directions Bradley intended to hold Caumont firmly, in order to support Dempsey's thrust to Villers-Bocage, and to take St. Lô later. He did not wish to push V Corps too hard for the time being; the introduction of a new corps must involve a pause for regrouping and he was conscious that the urgent and main task of his army at this stage was to cut the Cotentin peninsula and capture Cherbourg.

In pursuit of those objectives VII Corps at Utah had been having much hard fighting, but by the evening of the 12th it was evident that German opposition to the Merderet bridgehead was cracking and a speedy advance westwards could be expected. Further north Montebourg was still holding out but VII Corps was closing around it and, with strong support from the naval guns, had secured a footing on the Quineville ridge north-east of the town.

The Germans were indeed steadily losing the battle.

The bridgehead of their Anglo-American enemies had been consolidated and was progressively being extended; at Caen in the east, between Bayeux and the Vire in the centre, and in the Cherbourg peninsula on the west the Allies were seriously threatening to break their defence. All their available reserves were being committed as they arrived at the front but the dominance of Allied air power made their movements slow and dangerous. The German air force was of little help. 'Out of the first twelve fighter-bomber attacks carried out by serviceable aircraft . . . only in two attacks did our aircraft penetrate over the front line. During the other sorties the bombs had to be released over our own territory so that our aircraft could take up fighter combat.' Their own air headquarters judged the 'success' of their fighter forces as 'only negligible'. It was obvious to von Rundstedt and Rommel that neither the German naval nor air forces could effectively interfere with the Allies' transfer of strength to Normandy or in the battle that was being fought there. They could neither stop nor match the Allied build-up and could not bring to the battle in Normandy the full German strength in the West; for both commanders believed that a second landing in northern France or Belgium was soon to come and that therefore the substantial forces of the Fifteenth Army must be held in readiness to meet it.

On the 8th von Rundstedt had appealed urgently for reinforcements, having already ordered the bringing up of three additional armoured divisions and the preparation of two infantry divisions to relieve the armoured formations that were being employed in emergency to hold the British advance. On the 9th Rommel had ordered 'the absolute prevention' of the loss of Cherbourg and of the junction of the Allied bridgeheads 'west of the Orne and west of the Vire'. But on the following day von Rundstedt ordered the destruction of all Cherbourg harbour installations that were not indispensable for German naval operations, showing that in his view its loss was only a matter of time. On the 10th the Seventh Army war diary recorded that 'the German command's calculations are largely ruled out by the enemy's control of the air'. On that morning the Second Tactical Air Force had been asked to destroy the headquarters of Panzer Group West, newly established near Thury-Harcourt. That evening rocket-Typhoons of 83 Group and Mitchell squadrons of 2 Group attacked heavily. The building was not badly damaged but the orchard where vehicles were parked was saturated and everything in it destroyed; seventeen officers, including the Chief of Staff, were killed. What remained of the headquarters went back to Paris to be reconstituted and I SS Panzer Corps took over its duties. On the 10th C-in-C West's war diary records that 'the Seventh Army is everywhere forced on the defensive', and next day von Rundstedt and Rommel met to discuss the very serious position that was developing. They were in complete agreement and decided that they would report independently to the Führer.[3] It is unnecessary to quote both for there is no material difference between them. They give similar appreciations of the Allies' intentions and of the German situation. 'The formations of Army Group B fighting in Normandy are forced on to the defensive between the Orne and the Vire. Offensive operations cannot as yet be conducted in this broad sector for lack of forces and because the armoured divisions, with their striking power, had to be used for defence. Any attacks launched would not succeed and would only consume men and material.' The further forces which were arriving were to be used 'for defence, so that a cohesive front is built up'. In the Cotentin it was proposed to attack the Allies from the west and from the north 'in order to prevent a breakthrough to Cherbourg,

---

[3] Von Rundstedt's report was sent to OKW on the 11th, Rommel's a day later.

and to press these enemy forces back to the east and south' but 'it is not yet possible to tell whether, if this succeeds, the enemy east of the Vire can then be attacked . . . with the forces thereby released'. This is from von Rundstedt's report; Rommel puts it more bluntly. The proposed attack in the Cotentin is 'to annihilate the enemy there' and 'only when this has been accomplished can the enemy between the Orne and the Vire be attacked'. Both emphasise the necessity for infantry to relieve the armoured divisions now holding the defensive front in order that the armour may be freed for offensive action. And both describe four considerations which may delay the realisation of their plans.

> '(a) The numerical superiority of the enemy air force is so great that no major movement by day is possible. The rapid supply of reinforcements, ammunition, and fuel is made almost impossible by constant, heavy air attacks on nodal points of the road system, inhabited places, bridges and railway stations . . . Movements on the battlefield, and behind it when assembling for an attack, necessary tactical transfers, etc., are immediately and severely bombed from the air . . . From the long term point of view this superiority of the enemy air forces will paralyse all movement and control of the battle, and make it impossible to conduct operations.
>
> (b) The guns of most enemy warships have so powerful an effect on areas within their range that any advance into this zone dominated by fire from the sea is impossible . . .
>
> (c) The material equipment of the Anglo-Americans . . . is far superior to that of our infantry divisions operating here.
>
> (d) The enemy can use his very strong parachute and airborne troops in such numbers and with such weight and flexibility that our troops suffer heavy losses, especially if the airborne troops are dropped amongst or behind them. . . .'

'I must point out that with this disparity in material a situation might arise compelling us to take basic decisions. This would be the case if the enemy perchance succeeded in achieving a real break through southwards with strong armoured forces supported by his far superior air force.'

Von Rundstedt added that the troops were fighting excellently, 'spirit and morale are good, but the material superiority of the Anglo-Americans must in the long run have its effect on any troops'. Finally, both requested that their reports should be submitted to the Führer, von Rundstedt adding 'verbatim'.

Hitler's reaction on the 11th of June was to order II SS Panzer Corps (consisting of the 9th and 10th SS Panzer Divisions) to be transferred to Normandy from the eastern front and to direct that 'the enemy bridgehead between the Orne and the Vire must be attacked and destroyed piece by piece. As a first operation the enemy will be annihilated east of the Orne in order to free 346 Infantry Division'. The promise of the armoured reinforcements was welcome news but it would be some time before they could arrive on the western front. For the rest, the 346th Division had already suffered so severely in *failing* to 'annihilate' any part of the British bridgehead east of the Orne (pages 248 *et seq.* above) that Rommel now proposed to withdraw the German defence in the north-east behind the flooded river Dives and then to attack the bridgehead again from the south with the 346th Division, the 'Luck' Group of the 21st Panzer Division and the 7th Werfer (Mortar) Brigade. But Hitler would have none of this. There was to be no withdrawal to the Dives and no moving of the 346th Division to the south; his general orders governed the battle in the Cotentin, and in Normandy there could be no question of retiring to a new line of resistance. 'Every man shall fight and die where he stands.'

On June the 15th another Hitler directive was received but, while rehearsing the troop movements ordered or in progress, it contained little that was new beyond the fact that replacements for infantry divisions which were to relieve the armour in Normandy would come from Norway, Denmark and the Reich. They could not therefore arrive quickly. The directive showed no realisation of the urgent need for immediate action. The strong armoured counter-attack which alone would offer any hope of reducing the Allied lodgement must apparently wait till I SS Panzer Corps was relieved by the infantry divisions not yet available and until II SS Panzer Corps had arrived from Russia. But meanwhile the situation grew more dangerous hourly. The two field-marshals had tried to make this clear in their recent reports to Hitler and from the first there had been much daily telephoning by the leading staff officers of the two commands in the West, reporting the growing seriousness of the position to OKW. After receiving the unhelpful directive of the 15th von Rundstedt now asked that Jodl or his deputy might be sent to his headquarters for personal conference and subsequent report to the Führer. When Hitler was told of this, on the 16th, he decided that he would himself fly to the West next day to discuss with von Rundstedt and Rommel the future conduct of operations.

While the German commanders were greatly troubled by their realisation of the way the battle was going, General Montgomery was quite content. *His* general policy remained unchanged, namely: 'to increase and improve our own build-up through the beaches, to do everything possible to hamper and delay the enemy build-up by air action and other means', and 'to pull the Germans on to the British Second Army and fight them there so that First U.S. Army can carry out its task easier'. It is obvious that the greater the success of this strategy the swifter must be the corresponding adjustments of British tactics to the growth of enemy opposition. As already told above, the unexpected appearance of the 2nd Panzer Division had led to a pause in the 7th Armoured Division's thrust through Villers-Bocage towards Evrecy. Air reconnaissance had previously reported heavy rail traffic towards Paris from the north which was believed to be carrying the 1st SS Panzer Division from Belgium; it was not thought that the 2nd Panzer Division in reserve for the Pas de Calais sector would be released at this time because the German commanders still believed that a second Allied landing was imminent. The division's appearance in Normandy on June the 13th had therefore come as a surprise and General Montgomery had written to the C.I.G.S. on June the 14th, 'when 2nd Panzer Division suddenly appeared in the Villers-Bocage–Caumont area it plugged the hole through which I had broken' and 'I had to think again' and be careful 'not to get off balance. . . . So long as Rommel uses his strategic reserves to plug holes that is good', but he (Montgomery) 'had not got sufficient strength to be offensive on both flanks of Second Army'. He had therefore decided 'to be defensive in the Caen sector on the front of I Corps, but aggressively so', and to use all the offensive power of XXX Corps on the right of the Second Army. 'I shall hold strongly and fight offensively in the general area Caumont–Villers-Bocage, i.e. at the junction of the two Armies.'

In the next few days I Corps did in fact beat off a further attack on the Ranville bridgehead and keep the rest of 21st and 12th SS Panzer Divisions pinned to their positions north and west of Caen by vigorous patrolling and active artillery fire. They also captured the fortified radar station at Douvres that had originally been by-passed, taking some two hundred prisoners. In XXX Corps sector, meanwhile, the 49th Division in further stiff fighting re-took Saint Pierre and captured Cristot from the 12th SS Panzer Division and, by the 19th, 50th Division finally drove the enemy out of Tilly sur Seulles and pushed south to the outskirts of Hottot. On their right they joined up with the 7th Armoured Division who held the general line of the Aure as far south as Livry while gathering strength for a renewal of the drive eastwards towards Evrecy; they were in touch with the Americans now holding Caumont firmly.

The United States First Army had meanwhile been concentrating on the cutting of the Cotentin peninsula. While V and XIX Corps strengthened their positions, VII Corps attacked westwards from the Merderet bridgehead on the 14th. By the evening of the 16th they had crossed the upper Douve and taken St. Sauveur le Vicomte and late on the 17th their leading division reached the west coast and was astride the western road to Cherbourg. VII Corps was now to turn north as the newly arrived VIII Corps moved in to guard its rear, facing south between Carentan and the west coast.

Rommel had foreseen the American attempt to break across the Cotentin and to cut off Cherbourg. In his view two divisions were sufficient for the defence of Cherbourg; all others were to concentrate on preventing the break-through. If however the Americans succeeded, the troops cut off to the north should withdraw into the fortress 'in one movement'; other troops which had the necessary transport should move southwards to avoid being locked up in Cherbourg. On the morning of the 16th, however, Hitler intervened to forbid any withdrawal towards Cherbourg; the existing front was to be held at all costs.

The situation map opposite shows the positions of the opposed forces on the 17th of June (D + 11) and it is possible to make a comparative estimate of their strength.

But the enemy formations shown must not be taken at their nominal value, for while Allied losses in action had continuously been made good the German losses had not. By the 18th of June they had lost some 26,000 killed, wounded and missing, including a corps commander, five divisional commanders and nearly fifty other 'commanding officers'. Moreover, the reinforcing formations ordered forward since the Allies had gained a foothold in France had, as explained already, been reaching the front slowly and many of those shown on the map were still very incomplete. During most of the first week after D-day II Parachute Corps was struggling forward: one of its divisions had a battle group near the Forêt de Cerisy but the rest of the division was still south of St. Lô. The 17th SS Panzer Grenadier Division (motorised infantry) had not arrived in time to counter-attack on the 11th when the Americans captured Carentan, because Allied bombers had prevented the prompt arrival of its assault guns and it was short of petrol; when it did counter-attack on the 13th the town was firmly held and the attack was decisively thrown back. By the 17th of June the three infantry divisions ordered forward, the 265th, 275th and 353rd, had each only one battle group at the front. XLVII Panzer Corps headquarters had been brought up to take command of the 2nd Panzer and 2nd SS Panzer Divisions; but the former was still short of its armoured regiment and the latter had not yet arrived.

The German Third Air Fleet had also received a small reinforcement of about three hundred or so fighters and about a hundred assorted bombers. Its work by night over the anchorages was described in the last chapter and it also had a few lucky hits on army ammunition dumps ashore; by day it could do little over the battle area in face of the Allied air supremacy and the destruction of its nearest airfields; but the fighter and anti-aircraft defences

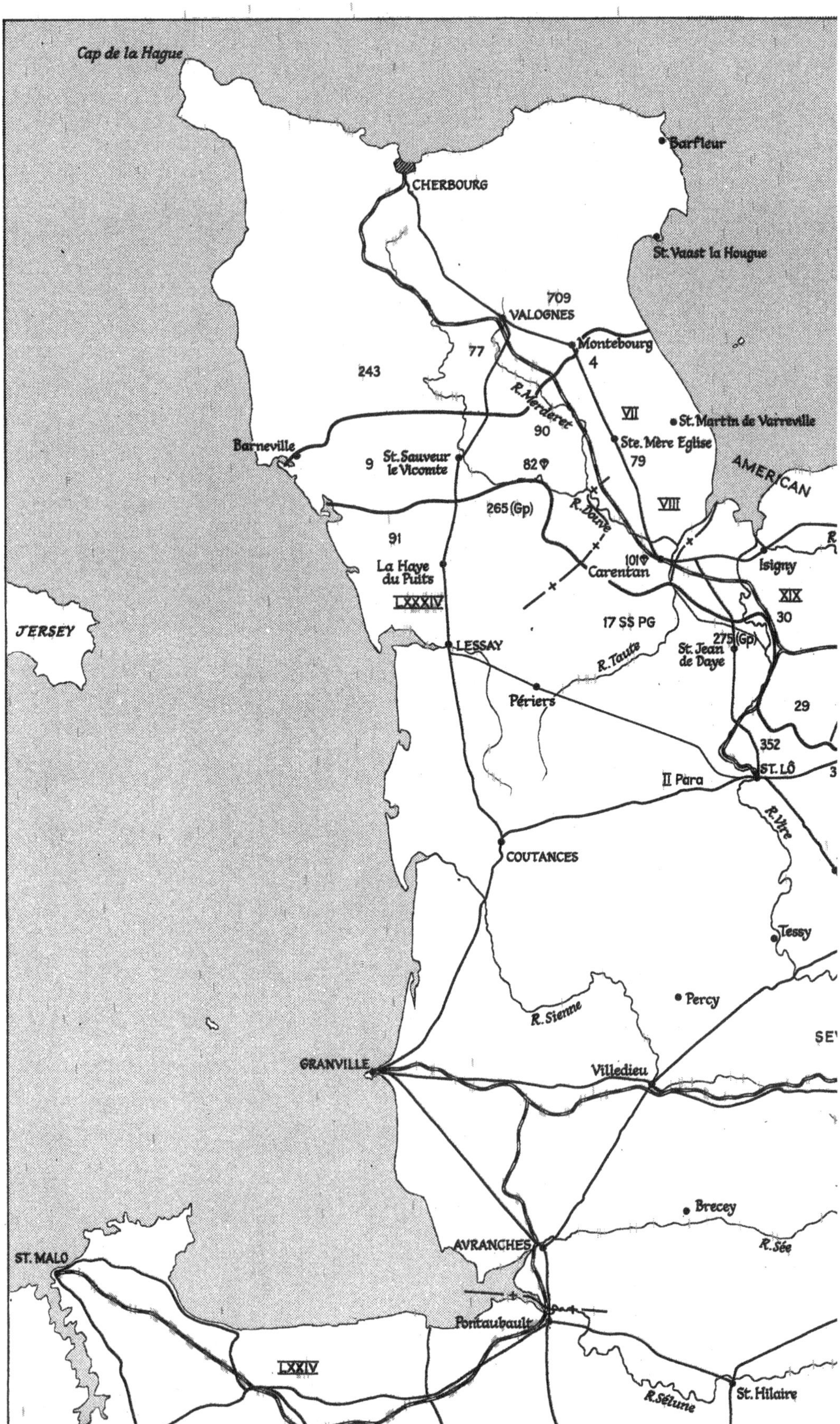
Cap de la Hague
Barfleur
CHERBOURG
St. Vaast la Hougue
709
VALOGNES
Montebourg
4
77
243
R. Merderet
VII
St. Martin de Varreville
90
Barneville
St. Sauveur le Vicomte
9
82
Ste. Mère Eglise
79
AMERICAN
R. Douve
VIII
265 (Gp)
91
101
Isigny
La Haye du Puits
Carentan
XIX
LXXXIV
30
JERSEY
17 SS PG
LESSAY
275 (Gp)
St. Jean de Daye
R. Taute
Périers
29
352
ST. LÔ
II Para
R. Vire
COUTANCES
Tessy
Percy
R. Sienne
GRANVILLE
Villedieu
Brecey
AVRANCHES
R. Sée
ST. MALO
Pontaubault
LXXIV
R. Sélune
St. Hilaire

SITUATION MIDNIGHT 17th JUNE 1944

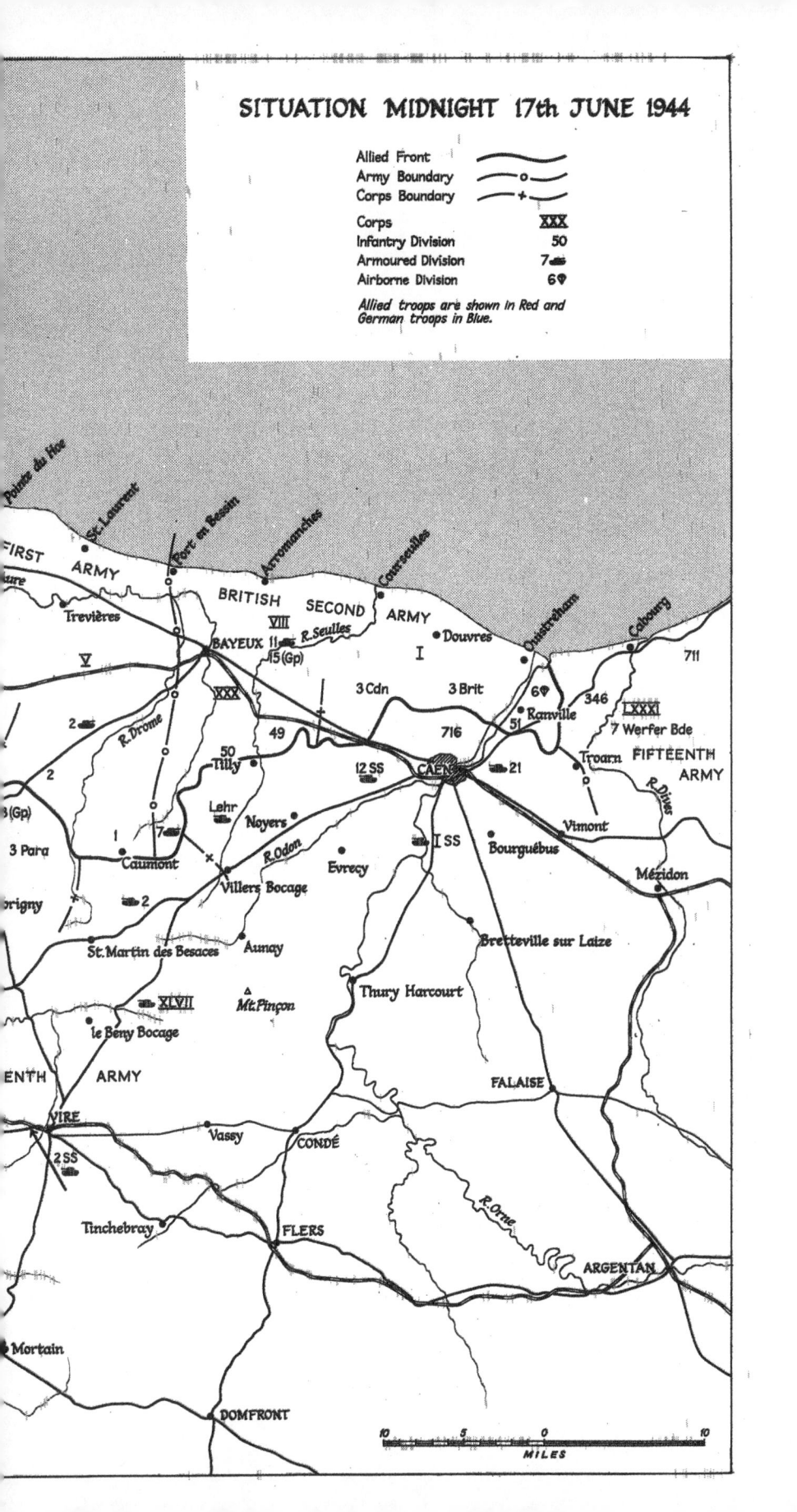

Allied Front
Army Boundary
Corps Boundary

Corps — XXX
Infantry Division — 50
Armoured Division — 7
Airborne Division — 6

Allied troops are shown in Red and German troops in Blue.

near Paris caused considerable losses to Bomber Command and the Eighth Air Force in their heavy bomber attacks in the Seine area. Nothing that the enemy could do was able to interfere with the Allied build-up. In those first ten days many of the early difficulties had been surmounted and reinforcement in men and material was now proceeding more smoothly. A fuller account of the build-up and of the difficulties which had to be overcome will be given later.

The provision of artificially sheltered water off the assault beaches had begun on D-day, when the movement of blockships and Mulberry harbour components had started. On the following day the planting of the first blockships to form Gooseberry breakwaters began, explosive charges being used to sink them on an even keel. The three Gooseberries in the British sector were completed by the 10th and the two in the American sector a day later. The first Phoenix concrete caissons had also sailed on D-day and had begun arriving on the 8th. Much skill was needed to sink each unit correctly, for the tidal stream ran at speeds of up to $2\frac{1}{2}$ knots and the rise and fall of the tide was more than twenty feet. Caissons were equipped with flooding valves but took up to half an hour to settle after flooding began, and during that time tugs had to hold these huge contraptions in position in spite of wind and tide. The naval officer controlling this operation, the 'planter', with working parties of seamen and soldiers, had a difficult task and the results on the whole were most satisfactory. Within the harbour thus being created at Arromanches the building of the Whale piers by Port Construction Companies of the Royal Engineers had begun promptly and by the 14th the east pier had been completed; to seaward of the harbour the Bombardons had also been laid.

At most of the assault beaches one or two piers had been built of American naval pontoons. These consisted of rectangular steel tanks bolted together; in lengths of about 180 feet they could be carried at sea slung to the sides of tank landing ships. In Juno there were two piers each 700 feet long: at Omaha two of much greater length. On these, troops and vehicles could be landed dry-shod. For the rest, the sheltered water provided by Gooseberries greatly facilitated boat work and the transfer of loads from ship to shore. On June the 7th Admiral Ramsay ordered the drying-out on beaches of tank landing ships (L.S.T.s) and suitable coasters. Though this greatly increased the pace of landing vehicles, the delay by waiting for the tide to refloat the ships contributed to the difficulties of maintaining a punctual flow of sailings.

The two small harbours at Courseulles and Port en Bessin were opened on the 12th and between them handled 15,000 tons in the next week. Considerable strides had been made in organisation ashore. Signal networks, signposting and reception arrangements were working effectively and Lines of Communication headquarters were relieving the assault corps of responsibility for the beaches and ports, while two army roadheads had been established by the Second Army through which forces ashore were being maintained.

Yet of course all was not perfect. In such huge and complicated operations, involving three Services and having to face such difficult conditions, it was inevitable that out of many thousands engaged some should prove unequal to their job and that however carefully things were planned some things should go wrong. Liaison between responsible authorities at sea and on shore was not always effective to prevent muddles and some serious delays, and there were times when a volume of shipping lay at anchor off the coast though their cargoes were urgently required on shore. In one instance, troops of one division remained on board their anchored transports for two days after arrival though the division was anxiously awaited at the front. And there were inevitable mistakes and mishaps which must be allowed for. Yet in spite of all, in spite of bad weather, accidents and personal failings, what had been accomplished by this date was a magnificent achievement.

There is some doubt about the actual numbers of men, vehicles and stores landed in the first three hectic days, for the records of the Navy and the Army do not tally, but thereafter they agree substantially and the following figures are believed to be reasonably accurate:[4]

Allied Landings 6th to 16th June, both inclusive

	Men	Vehicles	Stores (in long tons)
American	278,000	35,000	88,000
British	279,000	46,000	95,000
TOTAL	557,000	81,000	183,000

These figures are impressive yet they alone do not tell the whole story. Formations were coming in as planned, *but on average at least two days late.* To that extent the Allies were forfeiting some of the advantage gained from delays inflicted on the enemy's build-up of reinforcements. It is easy to see the effect of this in the recently described operations designed to outflank Caen. If the infantry brigade of the 7th Armoured Division, the 33rd Armoured Brigade with its 150 tanks, and some at least of the 49th Infantry Division had arrived two days earlier on their due dates, they could have

---

[4] For the American figures, see Ruppenthal, *Logistical Support of the Armies*, vol. I, pp. 416–421.

taken part in the later phases of XXX Corps' operations in the west; Villers-Bocage and the high ground beyond it might well have been captured and firmly held before the 2nd Panzer Division reached the battle. With more satisfactory progress in the west, the intended thrust east of the Caen canal need not have been scaled down so that I Corps could hold part of the 51st Division and the 4th Armoured Brigade in reserve; with both available, the attack in the east could have been driven home before the 7th Werfer Brigade with its heavy mortars had arrived to strengthen the enemy defence, and before the '88's of the III Flak Corps[5] had come up south and east of Caen to baulk our progress. It seems possible indeed that Caen might have been taken by now if our build-up of formations had kept to the planned time-table.

With about seven days' rations in hand there was no shortage of food. The two British corps had petrol for 150 miles with them and there was a fair reserve on shore behind them. Ammunition had been rationed throughout Second Army but there is no evidence that, as yet, it had been lacking in an emergency or insufficient for the operations undertaken.

With the capture of Caen still delayed and the unexpected arrival of the 2nd Panzer Division, some of the British air commanders were beginning to feel anxious about the future, and if territorial gains were the only criteria of success the Second Army's operations must seem disappointing. But the critics were premature in expressing their fear that the military situation 'had the makings of a dangerous crisis' as Sir Arthur Tedder described it at the daily meeting of Allied air commanders on June the 14th.

It will be well to set beside this gloomy view a truer estimate of the situation. The day after the triumphant success of the opening assault General Montgomery had reported that General Dempsey, commanding the British Second Army, was to proceed relentlessly with the original plan. He would hold a flank on the river Dives and capture Caen and Bayeux; he would then pivot on Caen and swing his right forward. Bayeux had indeed been captured on June the 7th and thereafter the advance of XXX Corps had made progress southwards in face of increasingly strong opposition. But after ten days' fighting we did not yet 'hold a flank on the river Dives' and Caen was still firmly held by the enemy; and although the ground won on D-day by I Corps and the 6th Airborne Division had been consolidated and was now firmly held it had not yet been substantially expanded. To that extent the enemy had indeed been able to prevent the immediate realisation of the original plan and General Montgomery had been compelled to modify the method of its achievement.

---

[5] See Appendix V, page 554, for detail.

For the time being, as has been told, direct attack on Caen had been discontinued and while, as he wrote, remaining 'aggressively defensive' in the Caen sector he had decided to use his main offensive strength on the west of the British front.

The enemy's success in holding Caen was indeed handicapping the planned expansion of the British lodgement area. Nevertheless the Second Army's achievement and the general military situation ought not to be measured chiefly by that fact. Only those who fail to recognise that 'whether operations will develop' on the lines predicted before the campaign opened 'must of course depend on our own and the enemy situation' (page 81) are likely to miss the most significant result of this fortnight's fighting—as some did at the time. For General Montgomery had always foreseen that the enemy's strongest opposition might well be encountered on the eastern flank of the Second Army and had planned to hold it there so as to facilitate advance in the American sector. Taking a long view, he was justified in feeling that Rommel was now playing his game. We *had* established 'a firm left wing', even though it did not yet include Caen or extend to the Dives; Rommel was putting his armoured divisions into battle piecemeal and all that had arrived *were* being held on the British front; and the American armies, with no armoured divisions opposing them, were enlarging their lodgement area and proceeding to isolate Cherbourg.

It is difficult to discern in this 'the makings of a dangerous crisis'.

In the early hours of June the 13th four 'flying bombs' dropped in England—one at Gravesend, one in Sussex, one in Bethnal Green and one near Sevenoaks; four people were killed and nine injured. The threatened attack with long-range weapons had begun, though it had made a poor start. It was renewed on the 15th and by noon on the 16th 244 flying bombs had been aimed at London. Up to midnight on the 16th 155 had been observed by the defence, 144 crossed the coast and 73 reached London.[6]

It is not part of this history of operations on the Continent to describe the attack on England by long-range weapons but it is necessary to note that the Air Defence of Great Britain, under the command of Air Marshal R. M. Hill, was part of Leigh-Mallory's responsibility; and that the counter-offensive ('Crossbow') against flying-bomb and rocket sites and on the centres of their manufacture, would absorb at times parts not only of the Second Tactical Air Force but also of the Strategic Air Forces. At present the latter were largely engaged in tactical collaboration with the Allied armies

---

[6] See Basil Collier, *The Defence of the United Kingdom*, chap. XXIV (ii).

VIEWS OF OPPOSING COMMANDERS

but still liable for the strategic bombing of transportation targets, German industrial towns, aircraft factories and oil installations. On June the 18th, after a flying bomb had struck the Royal Military Chapel at Wellington Barracks during morning service, killing 131 and seriously wounding 68 members of the congregation, General Eisenhower ruled that for the time being Crossbow targets must take precedence over 'everything except the urgent requirements of the battle'.

Ten days had passed since the Allies began landing in France and it is worth pausing at this point to see what the opposed commanders had been thinking as they watched the battle developing, and what they were now foreseeing as its probable future course. There is no need to speculate or to rely on post-war recollections for on both sides there are contemporary records which reveal their minds. General Montgomery wrote or telegraphed frequently either to General Eisenhower, to his own Chief of Staff (de Guingand), or to the C.I.G.S. (Field-Marshal Sir Alan Brooke) setting out his current appreciation and his intentions for future action. He issued few written orders to his army commanders but saw them almost daily to keep touch with their operations, to make known his intentions and to give them directions. And after these meetings he frequently issued an *aide mémoire* of what had been decided. From his first association with Overlord he had expressed confidence in its outcome and before it was launched he had shown that he had a clear picture in his mind of the general strategy he would employ and his tactical plans for the opening phases. In these first ten days the enemy had been strong enough to delay the full realization of his tactical aims yet he was quite unperturbed about that and was indeed 'well satisfied' with the way the battle was developing. He had said from the first that the early capture of Caen was essential. His mind on that point had not changed though ten days had passed and Caen was not yet captured: he still regarded it as a necessary step towards the end he had in view which was the *defeat of the German armies in Normandy*. But he was content for its capture to be delayed if meanwhile the German armoured divisions were being so fully required for its defence that they were unable to gather strength for effective counter-attack. Though few of the British operations he had ordered had so far attained their named objectives yet he was none the less contented, for most had made some progress and each had led to a further frittering away of German armoured strength in the east while the Allies enlarged their bridgehead in the west. The capture of Caen was needed as a means of further expansion: the destruction of the German Army was an end in itself. Watching the course of the battle General Montgomery's attitude was consistently, almost aggressively confident.

The attitude of the German commanders in Normandy was very different. Before the landings began neither von Rundstedt nor Rommel had been confident that an Allied invasion could be defeated; after ten days they knew that they were fighting a losing battle. For different reasons both had been dissatisfied with the original disposition of reserves: both now knew that the prearranged plan of defence could not be realised. On their side everything had gone amiss. Their Intelligence had failed to give effective warning of the attack and they were taken by surprise. The concrete and steel of the Atlantic Wall had crumbled away in a few hours. The counter-attack that was to drive invaders back into the sea had not been possible. The *Luftwaffe* had been able neither to silence the Allies' naval guns nor to ward off their air forces' devastating attacks. And though the German armies were fighting stoutly they had not been able to prevent the consolidation and expansion of the Allies' lodgement: at best they had slowed the pace of advance only by using their precious armour in a defensive rôle. As von Rundstedt and Rommel went to meet Hitler on June the 17th they knew that they were out-matched at sea, on land and in the air.

They met him at Margival near Soissons, in a concrete bunker built in 1940 to serve as his headquarters for the invasion of Britain. With Hitler was Jodl, Chief of the Operations Staff of OKW; with von Rundstedt and Rommel were their chiefs of staff, General Blumentritt and General Speidel, and there were some subordinate officers. Nothing new came of the meeting—no recognition of the fact that the growing Allied forces could not for long be contained in the existing bridgehead; no relaxation of the orders to hold everything everywhere; no thought of strategic withdrawal; no permission for even tactical withdrawals; no greater discretion for commanders-in-chief (even the proposed movement of an infantry division from one point to another was countermanded); and no new strategy. When the necessary reinforcements arrived and the armoured divisions holding the front had been relieved by infantry there would be a strong armoured counter-attack which was to make a break between the Allies and drive them back to the sea. Till then all existing positions were to be held. Hitler's preoccupation with the effects of the V-weapon attack on England and of new mines to be dropped at sea occupied much time. The naval representative left the meeting hurriedly at about twelve o'clock and sent a teleprinter message to Admiral Dönitz, the German Naval Commander-in-Chief, reporting that the Führer considered the only possible way to ease the situation on land was to eliminate or neutralise the enemy's naval forces, particularly his battleships. What Dönitz thought of this is not on record and there is no contemporary record of what von Rundstedt and Rommel thought. What Rommel's chief of staff thought in retrospect is told in statements he made to the Allies while in captivity and subsequently reproduced in his book. In contemporary records of the meeting there is no hint of the strong words and tense atmosphere which Speidel described, nor of the field-marshals' request for freedom to conduct future operations without being tied to a static defence of all France and with no liberty of movement. Whether or not Speidel's post-war recollections are accurate, the negative outcome of the meeting is as clear in his version as in contemporary accounts. Talk of V-weapons and new mines could not have done much to make von Rundstedt and Rommel more confident of victory in the battles they were fighting. 'The discussion', as von Rundstedt wrote after the war, 'had had no success.' Confidence is a great battlewinner. In this battle all the confidence was on our side.

CHAPTER XIII

THE STORM, 'EPSOM' AND CHERBOURG

His Majesty King George VI visited the British and Canadian forces in Normandy on June the 16th. He had crossed in the *Arethusa* and was accompanied by Admiral Ramsay, Admiral Sir Andrew Cunningham (First Sea Lord), Air Chief Marshal Sir Charles Portal (Chief of the Air Staff) and Major-General R. E. Laycock (Chief of Combined Operations Headquarters). The King landed on Juno beach where he was met by General Montgomery. His visit was greatly appreciated.

On June the 18th General Montgomery issued a new directive. In it he first summarised the results of the past twelve days' fighting. The Allies had gained a good lodgement area and, by keeping the initiative, had got the enemy into an awkward predicament. Rommel's mobile reserves were being exhausted, for he had been forced to use them to plug holes and all their local counter-attacks had been beaten off; he still lacked good infantry to relieve his armoured divisions so that they could be grouped for a full-blooded counter-offensive. 'We must now capture Caen and Cherbourg as the first step in the full development of our plans.'

Accordingly the British Second Army was ordered to launch a new version of the pincer attack on either side of Caen, in order to establish a strong force on the high ground north-east of the Bretteville sur Laize area and so dominate the exits from Caen to the south; the First United States Army was meanwhile to press on with the capture of Cherbourg and also, without waiting for it to fall, to push southwards.

It was originally intended to launch the main British attack on the extreme left but subsequently decided that in the small bridgehead on the east of the Orne there was not enough room to mount a strong attack; the left arm of the British pincer would again therefore only undertake a minor operation in the first instance to extend the bridgehead southwards; the main attack would be made by the right arm, its final objective being the named country south of Caen. This main attack was to be made by the now-landing VIII Corps with a supporting operation by XXX Corps, and was to begin on June the 22nd.

But while it was being prepared bad weather intervened. Ever since D-day the weather had caused anxiety. Fresh to strong winds, bad visibility and troubled seas had continuously affected the rate of unloading and had limited air activity. The erection of Mulberry harbours was making good progress. By the 16th the breakwaters were about half completed; two pierheads were available for traffic in the British Mulberry and one in the American. But the despatch of piers and roadways had been delayed by the weather and five tows of Whale roadway and two Phoenix caissons had been lost at sea. On June the 17th there were renewed signs of deterioration in the weather, but on the 18th the day was more promising and the twenty-four tows of Whale roadway which had been held back (each 480 feet long) set out to cross the Channel. They were well on their way when, in the early hours of the 19th, an unexpected strong wind sprang up from the north, increasing the difficulties of these ungainly tows and making it almost impossible to work small craft in the assault area. Rapidly increasing as it veered to the north-east the wind was blowing at over thirty knots by the afternoon, raising waves of six to eight feet. The storm continued to rage for three days, with winds increasing at times to gale force; no such June storm had been known in the Channel for over forty years.

A raging gale on a lee shore is a seaman's nightmare. Ships and craft crowded into the shelter of the Gooseberry breakwaters and the Mulberry harbours but there was not enough room for them all. As huge waves broke in the shallow water off the land, ground tackle of heavier landing craft did not always hold and numbers were driven ashore; there, pounded by the surf, many broke their backs or were badly damaged. Rhino ferries were swept high up the beaches, reducing to matchwood small craft in their path. The shuttle service from England was suspended but craft which had already left for France when the storm arose arrived in the assault area to add to the congestion and increase the number that met with disaster. The tows of Whale equipment—in all some two and a half miles of articulated steel roadway—which were crossing the Channel when the storm broke, were almost all lost at sea or, reaching the coast when the storm was at its height, were sunk or cast ashore and wrecked. When at last, on June the 22nd, the storm abated the whole invasion coast was strewn with wreckage. About eight hundred craft of all types were stranded, most of them heavily damaged and many entirely destroyed; on some beaches wrecked craft were piled on one another in dreadful confusion.

Yet absolute disaster had been averted by the 'improvised sheltered water' which the Cossac 'Outline Plan' had regarded as essential for the invasion's success. Within the protection of the Gooseberry break-waters and the uncompleted Mulberry harbours many hundreds of ships and craft rode out the storm in safety, and unloading never wholly ceased. Off the Juno beaches the Gooseberry breakwaters survived the ordeal virtually intact and eighteen L.S.T.s were cleared during the storm; but off Sword the Gooseberry had been sited to meet winds from the north-west and so gave only limited protection. At Arromanches, where the Gooseberry breakwater was strengthened and extended by Phoenix caissons to form the embracing arms of the Mulberry harbour, and where the Calvados shoal to windward of the anchorage gave some additional protection from the heaviest seas, the breakwaters withstood the storm well. The main breakwater held, with its blockships and caissons more or less intact though the safety margin was extremely fine; in the western arm, though less exposed, six caissons disintegrated, leaving gaps. Damage to existing piers and pierheads was considerable but not disastrous, and was mostly caused when landing craft out of control were driven against them. But the floating breakwater of Bombardons, further to seaward, was virtually destroyed. Many of its component units broke from their moorings and were driven ashore to the west of the harbour and those that remained at their moorings swung head on to the wind. Whether or not the loose Bombardons driving shorewards damaged the western arm of the harbour is a matter of dispute. Despite misfortunes the harbour at Arromanches successfully gave shelter to some 500 landing craft and other vessels and some unloading continued without intermission. Without its protection the losses of small craft might well have been crippling to future operations.

The American sector suffered much more severely. In the Gooseberry breakwater off Utah, squarely opposed to the full force of the gale, a number of blockships broke up, opening gaps to the raging seas; by the evening of the 21st the breakwater had lost nearly all its protective value. But it was in the Mulberry harbour at St. Laurent (off the Omaha beaches) that the devastation was greatest. Partly because of the pattern in which the blockships and Phoenix caissons had been laid and partly on account of physical conditions which differed from those off Arromanches a great weight of driven water overwhelmed the breakwaters. Many of the blockships settled in the sands owing to the tidal scour and two broke their backs as the heavy seas pounded them: out of thirty-five Phoenix caissons in position when the storm broke only about ten were intact when it subsided. Inside the harbour the two piers which had been completed were wrecked as landing craft were driven down on them. Many of the seaward Bombardons came adrift and, again, expert opinion differed as to whether Bombardons driving ashore increased the disintegration of the harbour.

In both British and American sectors the scenes of destruction were truly appalling and although the work of clearance and recovery was begun at once with great energy, some days would be needed to learn the full extent of the damage and longer still to overcome it. For the time being therefore it may be well to leave the coast and to see what effect the storm had had on the conduct of the Allied campaign ashore.

In the first place it had seriously interfered with the planned build-up of the Allied strength in Normandy. This can be seen easily in the following figures which show the daily average of men, vehicles and stores that had been landed in the four days which had preceded the storm, and the daily average landed while the storm lasted.

Daily average landed	Men		Vehicles		Stores (tons)	
	British	American	British	American	British	American
June 15th to 18th	15,774	18,938	2,965	2,929	10,666	14,308
June 19th to 22nd	3,982	5,865	1,375	1,051	4,286	3,064

In the four days affected by the storm the Americans had planned to bring one additional regiment and other troops needed to complete formations already ashore; but in the British Second Army, already two brigades behind schedule when the storm broke on June the 19th, the deficiency had increased to three *divisions* when it abated on the 22nd.[1]

Secondly, the British attack had had to be postponed. The limited attack east of the Orne was now to start on June the 23rd and the major, right-hand thrust on the 25th. In the third place, the storm had given the enemy four days' grace in which to strengthen his defences and move up additional troops in so far as they could escape the delaying effect of Allied air operations. The armour of the 2nd Panzer Division joined the infantry of the division who had come into the line west of Villers-Bocage over a week before; the 353rd Division arrived on the Cotentin front to oppose the American advance on the west; a battle group of 266th Division and a heavy anti-tank battalion reached the area of operations west of the Vire and also the remaining units of the 3rd Parachute Division (which had begun moving up from Brittany on the 13th); a mortar brigade and a battery of artillery reached II Parachute Corps area; the arrival of LXXXVI Corps' headquarters to the east of the Orne was completed and one medium battery and three troops of heavies had arrived in the corps area.

The purpose of the limited British attack on the extreme left was to capture Ste. Honorine la Chardonnerette on the east bank of the Orne. It was to be made by the 152nd Brigade of the 51st Division

---

[1] For the American figures, see Ruppenthal, *Logistical Support of the Armies*, vol. I, pp. 416–421, tables 7, 8 and 9.

and was opened before daybreak on June the 23rd by the 5th Cameron Highlanders, supported by the 13th/18th Hussars, artillery and engineers.

Unheralded by artillery preparation the infantry advanced in silence and, taking the German garrison by surprise, captured the village while it was still dark. Later in the morning German infantry and tanks of 21st Panzer Division's 'Luck' Group counter-attacked strongly and the Camerons' leading company was at first compelled to give some ground; but the enemy's successive attempts to recapture the village were stopped by artillery fire or beaten off with the help of the Hussars, the Camerons being reinforced by a company of the 5th Seaforth Highlanders. Fighting continued all morning but by midday Ste. Honorine was clear of the enemy and firmly held. Thirteen enemy tanks had been destroyed.

The major operation on the British west flank, operation 'Epsom', was a much more serious affair, involving both XXX Corps and VIII Corps. The former had borne the strain of continuous fighting since it began landing on D-day; VIII Corps, fresh from England and eager for battle, had only just landed and had not yet been engaged. Some of its divisions (11th Armoured, 15th (Scottish) and 43rd (Wessex) Infantry Divisions[2]) were not yet quite complete but the corps was to be strengthened for the coming fight by the addition of the 31st Tank and the 4th Armoured Brigades, bringing its tank strength up to over six hundred of all types. The total strength of VIII Corps when the battle opened was some sixty thousand (including three thousand officers). Its own artillery numbered nearly three hundred guns, and the artillery of XXX Corps on its right and of I Corps on its left were to bring the total number of guns available for support up to over seven hundred; three cruisers and the monitor *Roberts* were also to co-operate. A large air support was to include not only strong fighter cover but bombing attacks against enemy positions on the flank and in the enemy's rear.

The general map opposite shows the nature of the country in which the Odon battle was fought, and the map at page 286 its start-line on June the 25th and the ground won by the 30th. On the 25th XXX Corps was to launch an operation ('Dauntless') whose object was to secure the Noyers area and protect the right

---

[2] The reconnaissance regiment of the 43rd Division had suffered heavy misfortune. Their ship (T72/M.T.S.) arrived off Sword beach on the evening of the 20th and anchored for the night. In the morning a high sea and enemy shelling prevented unloading and with these conditions continuing they were kept there at anchor for three days. Each night enemy aircraft dropped mines in the area and when the ship was moved to Juno beach early on the morning of the 24th a mine was exploded under the after cabins where the troops were sleeping, an ammunition lorry was set on fire and oil on the sea burst aflame. Landing craft and other warships were quickly alongside and great gallantry was shown by all troops, but though 105 wounded were rescued 180 men were lost. Regimental headquarters and one squadron formed ashore but the remaining squadrons were not built up from England till late in July.

THE ODON BATTLEFIELD

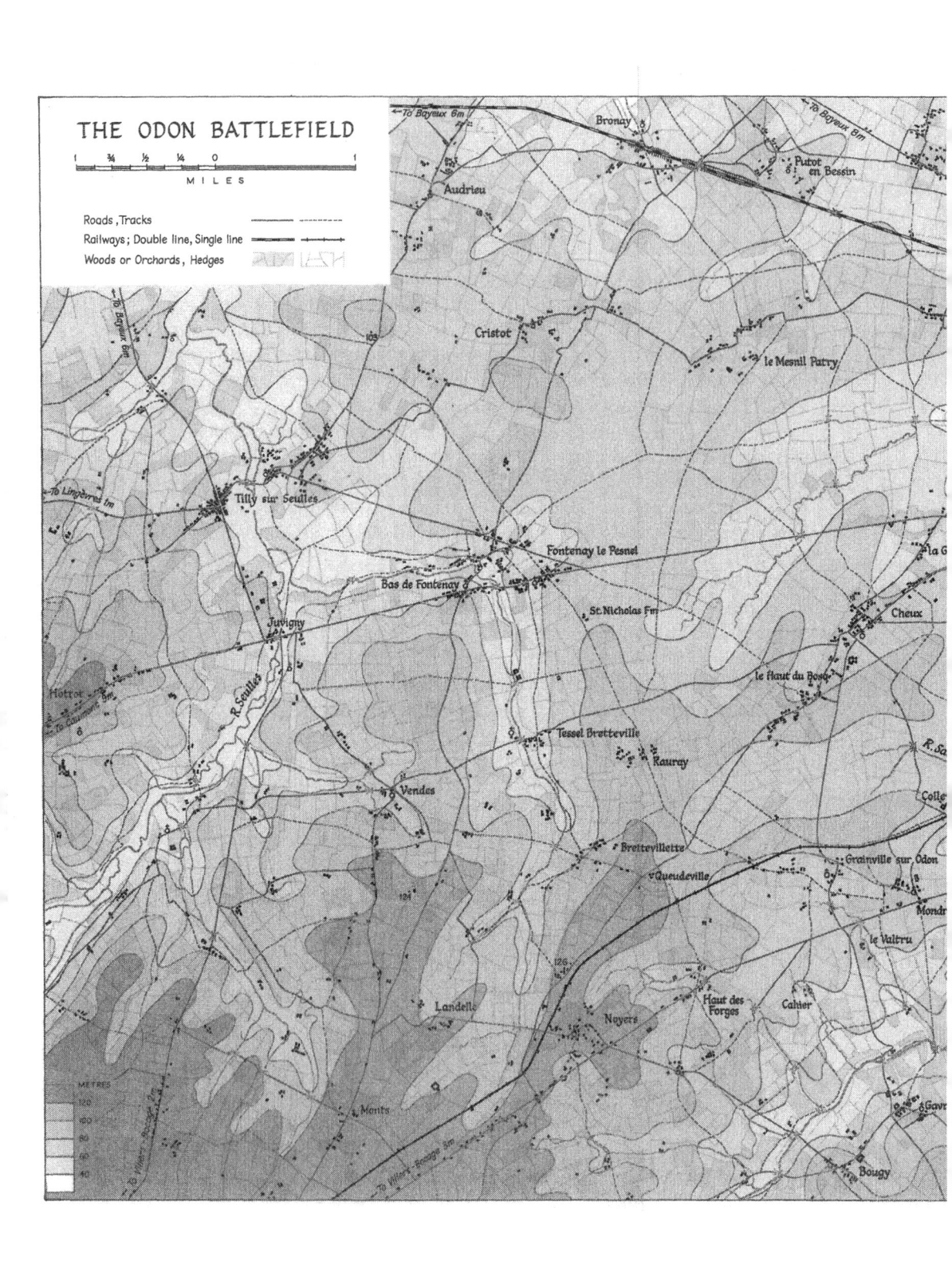

Bretteville l'Orgueilleuse
Rots
Buron
St. Contest
Epron
To Luc sur Mer 8m
Authie
Cussy
Norrey en Bessin
R. Mue
St. Mauvieu
Marcelet
Carpiquet
St. Germain la Blanche Herbe
AIRFIELD
CAEN
To Caen Sta
Bretteville sur Odon
Verson
Mouen
Bas de Mouen
R. Odon
Louvigny
Tourville
Gournay
Eterville
Fleury sur Orne
R. Orne
Tourmauville
Baron
Maltot
Hill 112
112
59
To Evrecy 1m
Esquay
Feuguerolles sur Orne
To Thury-Harcourt 11m
St. André sur Orne

flank of VIII Corps. Its first task was to capture Rauray on the spur of high ground overlooking the country through which VIII Corps was to begin the main attack southwards on the following morning and secure the line Rauray–Vendes–Juvigny; when that was achieved it would exploit well to the south. Starting from the front held by the 3rd Canadian Division between Bronay and Bretteville l'Orgueilleuse, and protected at first by XXX Corps on its right, VIII Corps was to force in turn the crossings of the Odon and the Orne and subsequently to establish itself on high ground north-east of Bretteville sur Laize, where it would command the roads converging on Caen from the south. As its advance progressed I Corps would support its eastern flank by capturing Carpiquet.

The course of the battle that was beginning was largely influenced by the nature of the ground—the rich cultivated ground of Normandy. At the start was an area of wide hedgeless fields of standing corn, falling slowly to the Mue, an insignificant stream. From there southwards the landscape is more typical of the *bocage*, its small farms and orchards enclosed by thick and often steeply banked hedges, its villages half hidden in hills and its outlines broken by woods and coppices. From the south-west a ridge of higher ground extends across the battlefield with spurs running northwards towards Fontenay le Pesnel and Rauray on XXX Corps front and on VIII Corps front towards le Haut du Bosq with a final hump south-east of Cheux. This ridge conceals the ground beyond, which falls to the thickly wooded valley of the Odon and rises again to commanding hills on the south of the river. The main roads and railway and the river Odon all run in the same direction between Villers-Bocage and Caen. It is difficult country through which to attack and its broken contours and abundance of cover make it almost ideal for defence. The 12th SS Panzer and parts of 21st Panzer and Panzer Lehr Divisions had been holding it for nearly three weeks and when the British attack opened they were familiar with its intricacies and knew every point of vantage. Infantry and machine-gun positions had been chosen with skill and strengthened by wire and minefields; each was supported by two or three tanks and '88's sited in hidden positions but able to move to others if detected.

If VIII Corps were obviously set a hard task for their first operation so also were XXX Corps, as experience showed when they made their preliminary attack on June the 25th. The capture of Juvigny, Vendes and Rauray was allotted by XXX Corps to the 49th Division; this also would be engaging in its first operation as a division. An additional field regiment and a battery of self-propelled anti-tank guns were added to its artillery and for this first day it could also call on the additional support from VIII Corps, on its left, of five field regiments and part of two anti-aircraft brigades acting in a ground rôle. The front to be attacked was held by the right of Panzer Lehr Division and the left of the 12th SS Panzer Division, with sixty to eighty 88-mm guns of III Flak Corps in support.

Soon after four o'clock on the morning of the 25th, in a thick ground-mist that persisted for some hours, the 49th Division advanced on a two-brigade front, with 146th Brigade on the right and 147th on the left; its third infantry brigade (70th) and the 8th Armoured Brigade were held in support. By 9.15 a.m. the 146th Brigade, attacking with two battalions, captured Bas de Fontenay against stiff opposition and by early afternoon went on and reached the edge of the woods that crown the spur north of Vendes. Meanwhile the 147th Brigade on their left, attacking with only one battalion, found the larger village of Fontenay firmly held, and though they fought hard and suffered heavy casualties they could not get beyond the northern outskirts. For some reason that is not explained a second battalion did not go forward to pursue the attack until nine o'clock in the evening. Most of the straggling village was then occupied but it was not cleared of the enemy and fighting continued throughout the night. Of the 49th Division's fight that day the situation report of the German Army Group B recorded: 'After heavy fighting on the severely weakened left of the 12th SS Panzer Division and right of Panzer Lehr Division, attacks by successive waves of enemy troops, supported in the air by continuous enemy sorties, succeeded in tearing open a gap 5 km wide and 2 km deep'. But the Rauray spur on the flank of VIII Corps was still in enemy possession when that corps attacked next morning.

On June the 26th flying weather was so bad in England that the large programme of air support for the opening of Epsom had to be cancelled and, for the first time since D-day, practically no aircraft based in England left the ground. Only 83 Group, stationed in Normandy, would be able to help VIII Corps, and though they flew over five hundred sorties their support was handicapped by low cloud and heavy ground-mist. For it was a lowering, misty day when at 7.30 in the morning the 15th Division set out to capture the Odon bridges, five miles away to the south, so that 11th Armoured Division could then pass through them to seize further bridges over the Orne and open the way to high ground south of Caen.

It had rained heavily in the night and the dripping crops and sodden ground made the going heavy. The 44th (Lowland) Brigade were on the left and the 46th (Highland) Brigade on the right and they set off behind a strong moving barrage and were supported by the 31st Tank Brigade. Steady progress was made at the outset but, as the barrage moved on, enemy posts that had been well dug-in came to life again and in overcoming them the Scotsmen soon lost the close protection of the bombardment. German prisoners taken that morning described what happened. 'We had gone to ground and had emerged only to find ourselves surrounded by tanks or furious Scotsmen throwing grenades.' The 'furious Scotsmen' themselves lost heavily in this close fighting, especially as they neared the villages where the enemy had done all they could to strengthen their positions. La Gaule was taken after a sharp fight, but St. Mauvieu, Cheux and le Haut du Bosq were entered only with hand-to-hand fighting and it took a long time to overcome all the parties which held out to the last in ruined buildings, farmyards and orchards. St. Mauvieu, after its first capture, was twice counter-attacked by tanks and infantry of the 12th SS Panzer Division and a tank company of the 21st Panzer Division; but both counter-attacks were beaten off, largely by intensive artillery fire. The Glasgow Highlanders (of the 46th Brigade) who were occupying Cheux were persistently shelled and mortared from higher ground to the south, till the village was half blocked by debris and reduced to a shambles. They lost twelve officers and had nearly two hundred casualties in this their first day's warfare. Only the northern outskirts of the long straggling village of le Haut du Bosq were taken; the rest of the village, the wooded country on either side, and the rising ground to the south were still held firmly by the enemy, with tanks dug in and infantry covered by machine guns, mortars and minefields.

Soon after midday the 11th Armoured Division (which had been following up the Scotsmen) was ordered to push through to Tourmauville and Gavrus where the Odon is bridged. Its 29th Armoured Brigade found however that all attempts to deploy south of Cheux were met by determined opposition, and after some hours of costly and abortive fighting it was clear that the Odon bridges could not be rushed by tanks that night. At six o'clock therefore the 15th Division was ordered to resume the advance and its third infantry brigade (227th) moved up. Progress was slow. Much time and many men were lost on this day by the frequent hold-up of troops and vehicles of all sorts, bottle-necked in the congested ruins of Cheux. Numerous tracks and roads converge there; it is an obvious target for enemy guns and mortars posted in the hills to the south. But the only two roads to the Tourmauville and Gavrus bridges lead from Cheux. One, on the east, crosses a dip in the ridge to Colleville and goes on to the bridge near Tourmauville; the other, to the west, goes over the ridge to Grainville sur Odon and on past le Valtru to the twin bridges near Gavrus. The brigade's leading battalions started from Cheux by both roads at about six o'clock in the evening and in torrential rain. On the eastern road the advanced guard reached the outskirts of Colleville but the main body was held up near the Salbey stream, about a mile south of Cheux, and got no further that night;

on the western road only the ground skirting Cheux was reached, when the infantry and supporting tanks were embroiled in confused fighting, there and round le Haut du Bosq. In the fading light and blinding downpour there was not enough time left to oust the enemy from their strong hold of the ridge over which the road to Grainville climbs. Further west, XXX Corps had been fighting all day to gain possession of the Rauray spur, but the main artillery support was being given to the Epsom attack on their left and though they fought hard and had heavy casualties they had captured only the northern part of it.

So ended the first day of Epsom. The Odon had not been reached but the leading troops were within shorter striking distance of the coveted bridges, and though the enemy showed no signs of weakening and still held most of the high ground in the path of the British advance, they had suffered considerable losses of men and tanks and had not been able to make any effective counter-attack. Army Group B recorded this as 'a complete defensive success' achieved only by I SS Panzer Corps 'employing its last reserves' and 'with all the forces of 12 SS Panzer Division and Panzer Lehr Division taxed to their utmost . . . All available elements of 1 SS Panzer Division and of II SS Panzer Corps are being brought up to the point of penetration.' It was intended 'to send into action the II SS Panzer Corps which, with all its available elements and the tank battalion of 2 Panzer Division and the 8 Werfer Brigade under command, will attack northwards with its right resting on the Orne on 27.6' but 'the formations of II SS Panzer Corps and the 1 SS Panzer Division have been considerably delayed in their move up by intervention from the air'. Twenty-First Army Group Headquarters had learnt on the 20th that 1st SS Panzer Division had begun moving from Belgium three days before, and in the days that followed both Allied air forces attacked the railway system almost continuously. Key targets in Belgium and France were struck by heavy bombers, and medium and fighter-bombers attacked railway targets in the Mantes–Orléans gap and the Paris–Chartres–Dreux area and marching troops who had been forced to detrain south of Paris and continue by road. Some infantry of 1st SS Panzer Division was committed to action on the 28th, but the division as a whole did not reach the battle area till July the 9th.

During the night the 43rd Division began taking over the ground already won so that the 15th Division could continue the attack, and at five o'clock on the morning of the 27th the advance was resumed.

Bad flying weather still prevented air support from England and perhaps realising this German aircraft appeared, soon 'seen off' by 83 Group fighters. But the 43rd Division had hardly taken over the

St. Mauvieu–Cheux area when the enemy began making probing attacks. All these were beaten off, though in the most serious (at about 9.30 a.m.) enemy tanks penetrated Cheux from the west, causing temporary confusion and knocking out several guns which were being moved in at the time. But the attack was repulsed with the loss of six enemy tanks. A German report stated that I SS Panzer Corps was attacking that morning with sixty tanks.

Meanwhile the 15th Division started early. On the western road to Grainville no progress was made and fighting went on all day in the Haut du Bosq area; but on the eastern road Colleville, Tourville and Mondrainville were taken. Then after a pause for reorganisation the 2nd Argyll and Sutherland Highlanders (of the 227th Brigade) advanced again and overcoming light opposition captured intact the bridge over the Odon near Tourmauville and formed a small bridgehead on the south bank. Soon afterwards leading tanks of the 11th Armoured Division (the 23rd Hussars) crossed the bridge and moved out to the lower slopes of a hill to the south-east, which was to be the scene of much fighting. The ground rises steeply from the Odon before levelling off to a wide, flat-topped summit known to the British as Hill 112. Close behind the Hussars, the 11th Armoured Division's infantry brigade (159th) and the rest of the 29th Armoured Brigade began passing through them to cross the Odon.

The 15th Division, now holding the eastern road to the river, set out from Colleville to cut the enemy's possession of the western road by attacking Grainville from the east. The outskirts of the town were reached but too late to attack that night, for it was found to be strongly held. So the Scotsmen drew off and prepared to attack next morning.

Tanks of the 31st Tank Brigade and of the 4th Armoured Brigade had been supporting the VIII Corps infantry and feeling for the enemy on the eastern flank. They were therefore now stationed for the night in positions to resist any attack from either flank. Late that afternoon XXX Corps had finally captured Rauray but the high ground south of it was still strongly held.

The 12th SS Panzer Division had lost more tanks in the numerous small and disjointed actions which had marked the day but had been reinforced by a battalion of tanks from the 2nd Panzer Division and by others from the Tiger battalion of I SS Panzer Corps.

Aircraft of 83 Group had flown a number of defensive sorties to restrict the *Luftwaffe's* increased activity and in answer to the Army's requests had made dive-bombing or rocket attacks on gun positions, villages and other targets, destroying an enemy headquarters and badly damaging Carpiquet airfield buildings where tanks were reported assembling. Flying weather improved in the afternoon and when night fell Mosquitos and Mitchells using flares attacked enemy

33. Rocket-firing Typhoon

34. General de Gaulle returns to France
Bayeux, 14th June 1944

35. Air Marshal Harris

36. General Doolittle

37. General Spaatz

38. Lancasters of Bomber Command attack armoured divisions near Villers-Bocage

39. Near Paris

AIR ATTACKS ON RAILWAYS

40. At Vire in Normandy

troops on the roads or assembled in woods behind the battle area with bombs, cannon and machine guns. Bomber Command sent out over a thousand aircraft; most of their targets were flying-bomb sites further up the coast but some two hundred attacked a rail centre between Strasbourg and Paris and the junction at Vaires in the Paris suburbs, through which reinforcements were coming from Germany.

By daybreak on the 28th the bridgehead south of the Odon was being strengthened and enlarged as the 11th Armoured Division passed over the river. The 159th Infantry Brigade formed a firm perimeter and the 29th Armoured Brigade moved out through the wooded ground near Baron to continue their attack on Hill 112. But the Germans had tanks, anti-tank guns and mortars well hidden in the surrounding country and the British attack was met by fire from the neighbouring hills to their right, from the slopes of the hill itself and from the woods north-east of Baron in their rear. Inconclusive fighting went on all morning and soon after midday the 11th Armoured Division was ordered to maintain and improve its bridgehead position but not to advance to the Orne until the 15th and 43rd Divisions had cleared the area between Cheux and the Odon.

For north of the Odon enemy pressure was increasing on both sides of VIII Corps and frequent air reports showed that additional troops were coming into action against it. Their air force was providing both weak fighter cover and strong flak defence in the Villers-Bocage area to the south-west, and for the first time the movement of German troops from that direction was being risked in daylight. Bad flying weather again prevented the Allied air forces in England from taking much part in the day's fighting but 83 Group did well. They brought down twenty-six of the enemy's aircraft and destroyed or damaged a greater number of troop-carrying and other army vehicles and tanks on the roads or halted in woods.

The left shoulder of the salient, where it joined the front of the 3rd Canadian Division, was now strengthened by the addition of the 32nd Guards Brigade (recently arrived in France as the forerunners of the Guards Armoured Division) who were put under command of the 43rd Division and stationed south of Bretteville l'Orgueilleuse and on either side of the Caen–Bayeux road. Further south Mouen was taken, but by a strong counter-attack tanks of the 21st Panzer Division recovered it; the close country from there to the river remained in German hands. There was evidence that troops and vehicles were assembling in Verson and on Second Army's request the place was heavily attacked by Typhoons.

On the western flank two battalions of the 15th Division with tank support started a drive southwards to clear the ground between the road to Grainville and the Rauray spur. Strong opposition was met as they approached the railway west of Grainville and after a stiff fight the infantry were forced to give ground and got no further that night. The enemy had attacked Grainville during the afternoon and had penetrated the town but were eventually driven out again and a number of tanks in the vicinity were beaten off. Meanwhile infantry and tanks had cleared the country between Colleville and Grainville. Overcoming strong enemy pockets near the railway and west of Mondrainville they crossed the Caen road and captured le Valtru. The close country to the south, through which the road leads over the Odon to Gavrus, was still held by the enemy but Gavrus and the nearby bridge were by then occupied by the Argyll and Sutherland Highlanders. For after being relieved by the 11th Armoured Division of responsibility for the first bridge which they had captured near Tourmauville, they had moved westward through the wooded country on the south bank of the river and had seized Gavrus and its bridges. There they remained in isolation, with the road between them and le Valtru held by the enemy.

The 29th Armoured Brigade had had to fight hard to retain their hold on the northern part of Hill 112 and the Baron area. Enemy tanks covered by a heavy mortar barrage had counter-attacked in the afternoon in an effort to drive them off the hill, but the 3rd Royal Tank Regiment and part of the 8th Battalion, The Rifle Brigade had beaten back the attack and had improved their positions.

At the end of that day (the 28th), though no further advance had been made, the ground won by VIII Corps was more firmly held and the corps was in a better position to withstand the counter-attack which appeared to be imminent. In the course of the day's fighting prisoners had been taken not only from the 2nd Panzer Division but also from the 1st and 2nd SS Panzer Divisions. The 1st SS had just begun to arrive from near Bruges. The 2nd SS had come from near Toulouse and had been greatly delayed *en route* by fights with the Resistance and by the attentions of the Allied air forces; moreover, about half had been unable to move because it had no motor transport. On arrival at the front it had been stationed south of St. Lô in army group reserve, but a battle group had been moved hurriedly eastwards after Epsom began and the first of its units to arrive had been put straight into battle against 49th Division on the 28th. There was evidence too that the formidable II SS Panzer Corps, with the 9th and 10th SS Panzer Divisions, had now arrived in the neighbourhood from Russia. It was this cumulative evidence of preparation for a major counter-attack which had decided Lieut-General Sir Richard O'Connor, commanding VIII Corps, not to push the attack further till the position north of the Odon was more secure. The British salient was over five miles deep into the enemy front but still less than two miles wide. Round it were apparently gathering all the Germans' armoured divisions in Normandy. Till the salient was broadened and its flanks made safe a further advance would invite disaster. XXX Corps on its right, though now established on the Rauray spur after hard and prolonged fighting, had been forced out of Brettevillette (which had been taken earlier in the day) and the enemy still held the ground carrying approaches to the salient from the south-west; on the left flank I Corps had postponed for the time being its projected attack on Carpiquet, the western gateway of Caen. General Montgomery's desire to fight the German armour on the British front had so far succeeded but it would only be justified if the armour were held and there was no setback. For the time being that was the most important consideration.

The morning of the 29th broke bright and clear and air reports of large-scale enemy movements towards the battle flowed in continuously. The Second Tactical Air Force was out in strength and great damage was being inflicted both by aircraft and by the artillery who also were in action early. Key positions on approaches to the battlefield, troop concentrations and headquarters, and movement on roads were all attacked with good effect as was soon to be proved.

The Germans were apparently not yet ready to attack, for the morning passed quietly, small counter-attacks on XXX Corps front being driven off. On the eastern flank the 43rd Division attacked Mouen and by eleven o'clock had taken it and the neighbouring village of Bas de Mouen. The day before they had occupied Marcelet to the north of Mouen; they now succeeded in clearing the close country southwards to the Odon and had one battalion beyond the river.

On the west flank the 15th Division resumed their drive southwards. When the railway near Grainville was reached they met strong opposition and were forced back, but they firmly held a track from the woods west of Grainville which leads over the hill to Rauray, crossing the road from Noyers to Cheux. In the course of the afternoon a German officer was taken prisoner carrying plans of the counter-attack for which he was reconnoitring, and about six o'clock the counter-attack began, coming in from the south-west. Tanks and infantry in about three-battalion strength attacked astride the Noyers–Cheux road. There was hard fighting and a few tanks broke through one of the Scottish battalions and got as far as Cheux before they were knocked out; the rest of the attacking troops were driven back, the situation was restored and the holding troops reorganised. The artillery had played a large part in defeating the attack and later in the evening a regiment of the 4th Armoured Brigade swept the country between Grainville and the Noyers road where pockets of enemy were still found.

About the time of this counter-attack another was in progress further south against le Valtru. At first it made progress but by six o'clock in the evening the enemy had been driven back and the situation restored. A third attack had been made by the enemy south of the Odon. The tanks and infantry of 11th Armoured Division had extended their hold on the Baron area, pushed southwards to the Esquay road and at last established a company of the Rifle Brigade in the wood on the southern slopes of Hill 112. Then a sharp counter-attack coming in from the wooded ground near Bougy compelled withdrawal from advanced positions facing Esquay and Gavrus. But the Argyll and Sutherland Highlanders still held their position covering the nearby bridge, often under heavy shell and mortar fire. A final attack, this time from the east, never materialised. Forty or so tanks which had been moving from Caen into Carpiquet were so heavily attacked by Typhoons that no more was seen of them that day.

The 29th had been an anxious day. There had been sharp fighting all round the salient but every attack had been defeated and several attempts to concentrate for others had been broken up by artillery fire. Much of the day's success was indeed due to the guns, not only of VIII Corps but also of XXX and I Corps on the flanks. The tactical air forces had flown a thousand sorties. More German fighters had been met and 'seen off', and the German troops had suffered much from Mustang, Typhoon and Spitfire attacks. The German Seventh Army telephone log noted that the counter-attack planned by II SS Panzer Corps could not start till the afternoon because of continuous artillery and air bombardment, and its commander, SS General Hausser, when subsequently questioned in England, confirmed this: the counter-attack by both I SS and II SS Panzer Corps 'was scheduled to begin at seven o'clock in the morning but hardly had the tanks assembled when they were attacked by fighter-bombers. This disrupted the troops so much that the attack did not start again till two-thirty in the afternoon. But even then it could not get going. The murderous fire from naval guns in the Channel and the terrible British artillery destroyed the bulk of our attacking force in its assembly area. The few tanks that did manage to go forward were easily stopped by the British anti-tank guns.'[3] Neither General Dempsey nor General O'Connor could of course know this and both felt that the attacks made by the Germans that day were probably only preliminary to the major attack for which the enemy's armoured divisions had been assembled round the British salient. The last of these had now been identified in action—infantry and tanks of the 9th SS Panzer Division in the attacks on the west flank, and troops of the 10th SS Panzer Division in the attack which had recaptured ground near the Esquay road and Gavrus.

---

[3] Quoted in G. S. Jackson, *Operations Eighth Corps* (1948), pp. 51–52.

Assuming that a stronger counter-attack was yet to come, VIII Corps was disposed in strength. General Dempsey ordered the bridgehead south of the Odon to be reinforced by a brigade of 43rd Division and the 159th Brigade to come under command of 15th Division; 11th Armoured Division should withdraw its armour from advanced positions in the Baron area and on Hill 112, and be stationed in the salient ready to meet the expected attack. After dark the 29th Armoured Brigade withdrew from the hill they had fought so hard to win, disappointed by an order for which they could not know the reason. During the night more than two hundred heavy bombers of Bomber Command dropped over 1,000 tons of bombs where enemy armour was concentrating in the Villers-Bocage area.

On June the 30th the Germans made no move: presumably they were getting ready their counter-attack—as the British commanders were preparing to meet it with their forces well disposed and the guns of VIII and XXX Corps closely co-ordinated. During the night much activity behind the German front and the sounds of tracked vehicles on the move were reported by patrols and at 3.30 a.m. on July the 1st, after a heavy mortar bombardment, a strong infantry attack began on the Gavrus sector of the Odon bridgehead. It was met by the defensive fire of the infantry and of twelve regiments of artillery and was dispersed before it reached the British positions. Later it was twice renewed, spreading to the Baron sector, but each time was stopped by heavy defensive fire.

A second attack had meanwhile been launched north of the Odon, this time on a front of about a mile and a half, stretching from VIII Corps flank near Grainville, across the Noyers–Cheux road and the high ground where the 49th Division of XXX Corps held Rauray and Tessel-Bretteville. The attack was covered by a smoke screen and was pressed hard by infantry and tanks, some of whom got through forward positions in both corps sectors. But eventually the enemy was driven off with heavy loss. Infantry and their anti-tank 6-pounders claimed many of the tanks which had reached our front and many more were destroyed as they tried to close in by the fire of our own tanks and artillery. By 9.45 a.m. General Speidel, Rommel's chief of staff, had already telephoned to von Rundstedt's headquarters that '. . . the resumption of the attack by II SS Panzer Corps had been stopped by very strong artillery concentrations'. Two hours later enemy tanks appeared again, moving towards the flank of VIII Corps, and were again stopped by the fire of our tanks and artillery. After this second failure a local German commander, reporting his midday situation to 9th SS Panzer Division, finished his message with a quotation: '. . . abandon hope all ye who enter here (Dante) Signed M . . .' However, a further attack was attempted (and was broken up) in the early afternoon and yet again, and finally, at about half-past four. This time the infantry came up the road from Noyers in troop-carrying vehicles, and proceeded to dismount and form up with their tanks near Queudeville in full view and at no great distance away. Every available machine gun, mortar and gun was brought to bear on them and they were driven off before ever getting into action.

The hunting down of small parties of enemy left isolated within our forward position after the previous attacks had meantime continued with the help of flame-throwing tanks and at the end of the day all original positions had been re-established and strengthened. Identifications showed that infantry, anti-tank guns and tanks of the 9th SS Panzer Division and a battle group of the 2nd SS Panzer Division had been engaged in the actions north of the Odon, and troops of 10th SS Panzer Division in those against the bridgehead south of the river. It was there that the last flicker of life was noted that evening. About 6 p.m., when the Rauray action had begun to wane, the 159th Brigade saw the Germans 'assembling' between Gavrus and Esquay, but the movement was brought to nothing by our defensive fire. On the eastern side of the VIII Corps salient there had been less activity, though the 32nd Guards Brigade had knocked out a few tanks of the 12th SS Panzer Division and there had been some skirmishing in the Carpiquet area.

The day's claims came to over forty tanks and, though some may have been duplicated, air photographs taken four days later show clearly twenty-two burnt out German tanks lying abandoned in the open in less than a mile square of the battlefield. Our own casualties had been considerable but our position was unshaken. The enemy had suffered a sharp defeat, yet comparing the scale of his actions with the number of his armoured divisions in the area it was still reasonable to suppose that they covered preparations for the stronger armoured counter-offensive. Of the whole Allied position this was where the enemy's potential for offensive was strongest, the only place where he was in a position to make a serious attack on the Allied front. Yet Epsom had in fact forestalled and spoiled the last German effort to break the Allied front that could be made while there were still some fresh armoured divisions with which to attempt it; from then on much armoured strength was gradually frittered away as it had to be used to plug holes in their own defences.

The operations that have been described were the principal events on the British front during the last weeks of June. Apart from these, I Corps positions on the east had been slightly advanced by an attack by the British 3rd Division, which captured the Château de la Londe, north of Epron, after two days' fighting. To the west of the battle for the Rauray spur, XXX Corps had had continuous hard

THE EPSOM BATTLE

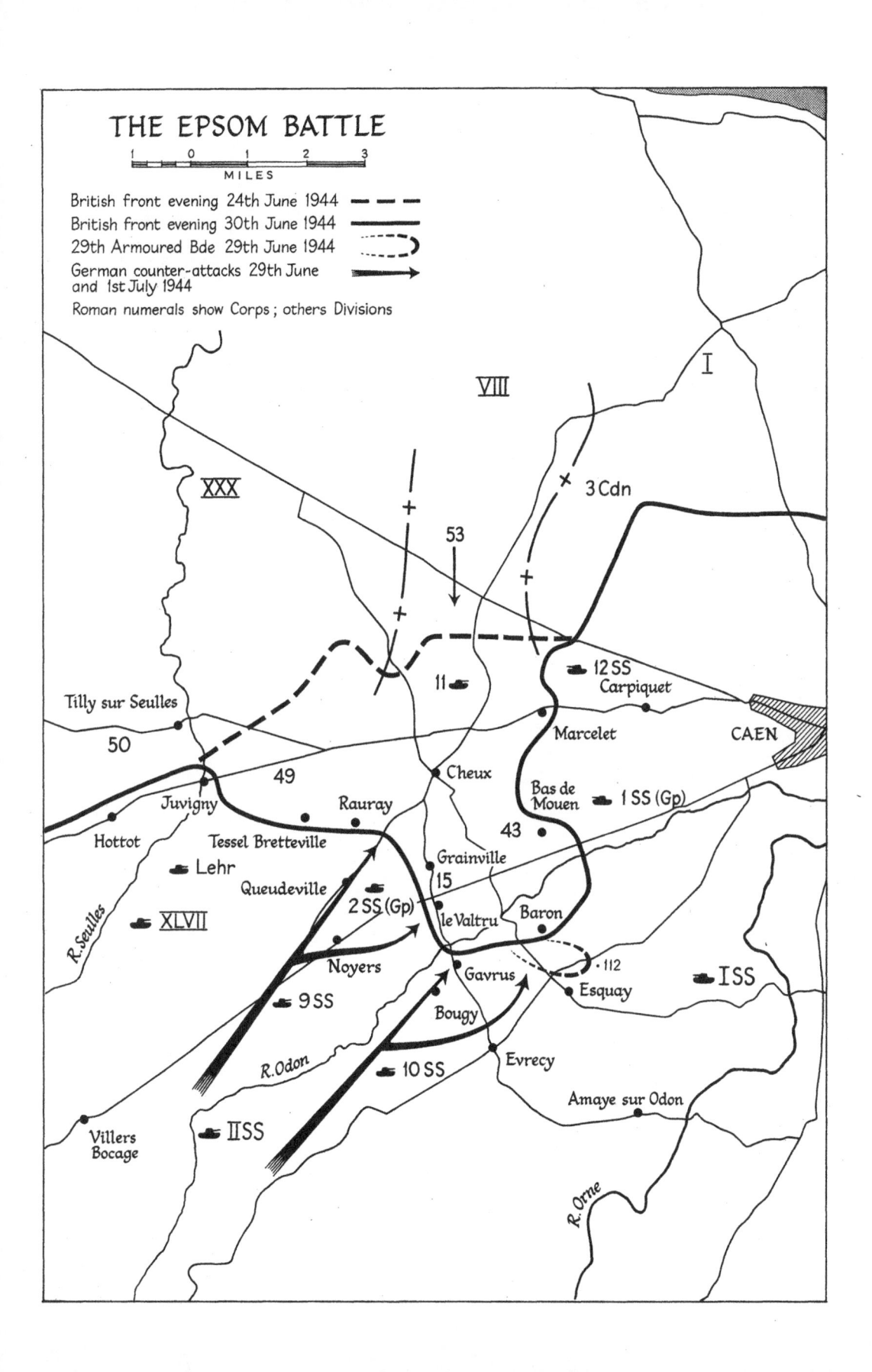

Scale: MILES (1 0 1 2 3)

- British front evening 24th June 1944 — – – –
- British front evening 30th June 1944 — ———
- 29th Armoured Bde 29th June 1944
- German counter-attacks 29th June and 1st July 1944 →
- Roman numerals show Corps; others Divisions

XXX · VIII · I
3 Cdn
53
12 SS Carpiquet
Tilly sur Seulles
11
CAEN
50
Marcelet
49
Juvigny
Rauray
Cheux
Bas de Mouen · 1 SS (Gp)
Hottot
Tessel Bretteville
43
Lehr
Grainville
Queudeville
15
2 SS (Gp)
le Valtru
Baron
XLVII
R. Seulles
Noyers
Gavrus
·112
Esquay
I SS
9 SS
Bougy
Evrecy
R. Odon
10 SS
Amaye sur Odon
Villers Bocage
II SS
R. Orne

fighting south-west of Tilly and especially about Hottot which was twice entered but each time retaken by the enemy. Four miles away westwards Longraye was captured, and from there XXX Corps joined up with the American left flank just east of Caumont.

But before turning to affairs in the American sector it is desirable to add something to what has already been written in previous chapters of the part that was being played by the Royal Air Force in the furtherance of Overlord. The Second Tactical Air Force and Air Defence of Great Britain were so closely associated and such essential partners in army operations that to describe them every time would involve much needless repetition. The reader should remember that day by day, and every day, while the army fought on the ground the air forces fought from the sky. In describing army operations it is not always necessary to particularise the part played by, say, infantry or artillery; similarly, it should not be necessary to record on every occasion the part played by aircraft in warding off any German planes that ventured near the scene of operations, by photography or observing, reporting and attacking the enemy's movements, by helping to stop attempted counter-attacks and, on the army's requests, by attacking strong-points, gun sites or enemy troops that were holding up progress. It must also be remembered that the air forces the battlefield reached out over a far larger area than the ground being fought over by the armies and that their work included the constant attack on railways, roads and bridges which was doing so much to prevent or hamper the enemy's operations.

It remains to be told shortly what else Bomber Command had been doing since D-day to further the progress of Overlord through the less closely associated strategic air offensive and in other ways. To the air offensive against the German air force, oil, railway communications and industry General Eisenhower had added, on June the 18th (page 267), that attacks on the German flying-bomb sites were to be given precedence over everything except the urgent requirements of the battle. Since then much of Bomber Command's resources had been devoted to the attacks on flying-bomb targets but there were very few days and nights on which other targets were not also attacked. Between D-day and the end of June forty-four separate attacks were made on railway communications converging on Paris from the east and the south, and nine on German oil plants and fuel depots; and mines were dropped almost daily for the Navy. In a fairly typical twenty-four hours, the 27th/28th, over seven hundred heavy bombers and Mosquitos dropped more than three thousand tons on flying-bomb sites; about two hundred attacked two key railway centres with some seven hundred tons, while sixty engaged in radio counter-measures to divert German night fighters; fourteen Bomber Command aircraft laid marine mines and thirty-six carried arms and ammunition to French Resistance groups. A comparable programme was carried out daily; there was no pause in Bomber Command's offensive.

Similarly, the American air force maintained both strategic and tactical air operations. In their case, however, less attention was paid to the attack on flying-bomb targets and more to those designed to limit aircraft production and oil. In the attack on communications they paid special attention to the destruction of bridges over the Seine and the Loire and the prevention of their repair.

The American front at the end of June ran generally from Caumont to the west coast of the Cotentin above la Haye du Puits. In winning the sector between Caumont and the Vire–Taute canal, V and XIX Corps had found, as had the British corps, that an advance against stubborn opposition in the close *bocage* country was a slow and costly business. The line was temporarily stabilised within about five miles of St. Lô, while the fight to clear the Cotentin and capture Cherbourg was completed and preparations were made to advance to the south.

In the Cotentin, VII Corps had had conspicuous success. The new VIII Corps had assumed responsibility for the front which faced south, and VII Corps had turned northwards after fighting which had carried them from the original Utah beach to the west coast and so had cut off the German forces to the north which were to defend Cherbourg.

That was on June the 18th. The VII Corps left was that night on the west coast near Barneville sur Mer; by the night of the 19th it was twelve miles further north and by the 20th was within five miles of Cherbourg, facing the line of landward defences planned by the Germans earlier in the year. By then the storm was raging in the Channel. It interrupted the landing of build-up requirements at Utah and Omaha and although this did not directly prejudice VII Corps operations it coincided with an inevitable pause; for its advance had been so rapid that it must close up and collect its strength before launching the final attack on Cherbourg. With the storm abating on the 22nd, the attack was resumed. The hopelessness of the German position had been broadcast by the Americans to the Cherbourg garrison and the general in command of some twenty-one thousand troops had been given till 9 a.m. in which to capitulate. When no response was made, the assault began soon after noon. For eighty minutes first ten squadrons of the Royal Air Force and then twenty-three groups of the United States Ninth Air Force attacked enemy positions, strong-points and forts. Following this the advance began and for three days there followed hard fighting, as one by one the outlying defences and forts were captured, each with its complement of defending troops. Pressure was everywhere sustained with

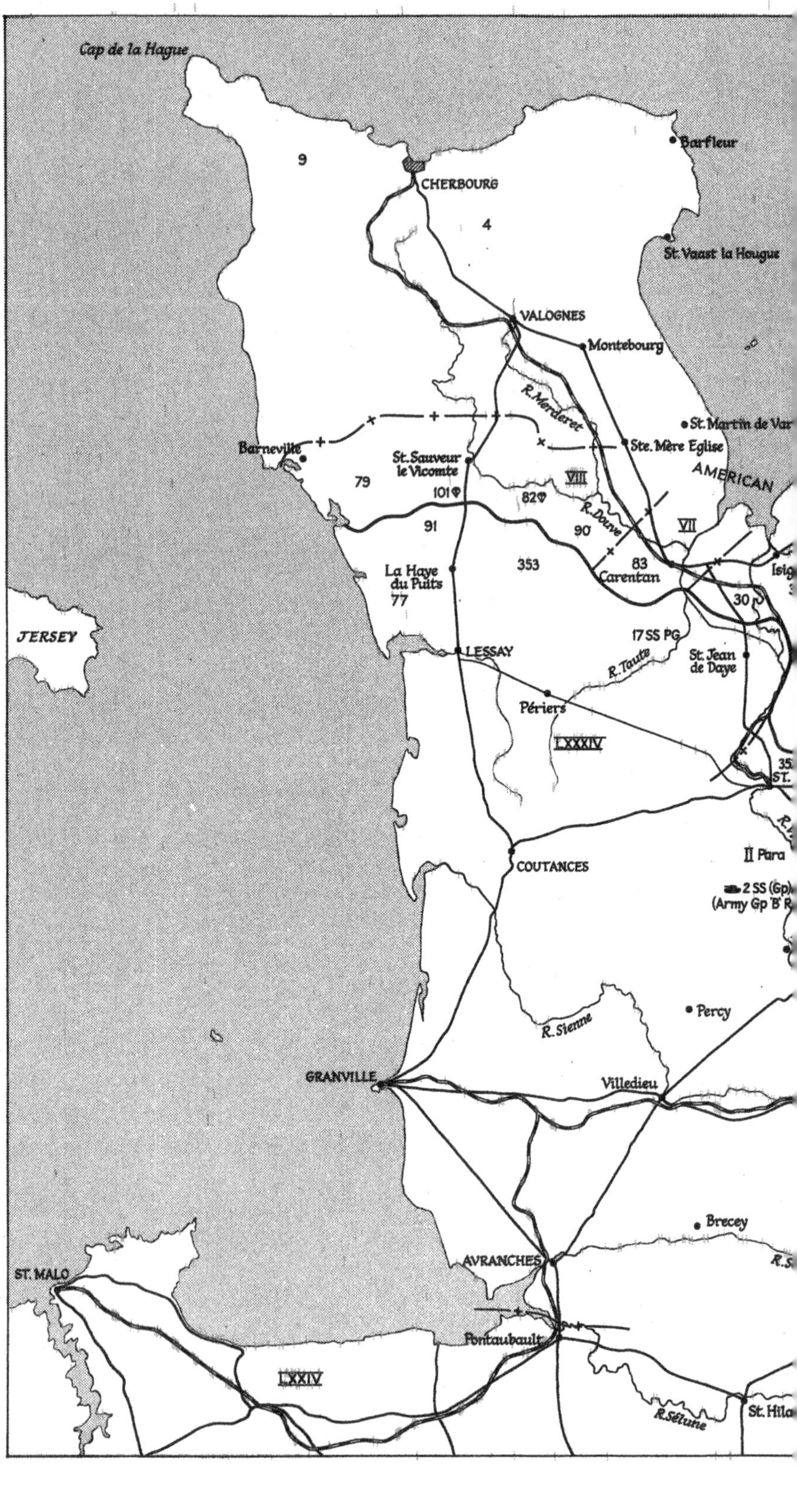
Cap de la Hague
Barfleur
9
CHERBOURG
4
St. Vaast la Hougue
VALOGNES
Montebourg
R. Merderet
St. Martin de Var
Ste. Mère Eglise
Barneville
St. Sauveur le Vicomte
VIII
AMERICAN
79
101
82
R. Douve
VII
91
90
La Haye du Puits
353
83
Carentan
77
30
JERSEY
17 SS PG
LESSAY
R. Taute
St. Jean de Daye
Périers
LXXXIV
II Para
COUTANCES
2 SS (Gp)
R. Sienne
Percy
GRANVILLE
Villedieu
Brecey
AVRANCHES
ST. MALO
Pontaubault
LXXIV
R. Sélune

SITUATION MIDNIGHT 30th JUNE 1944

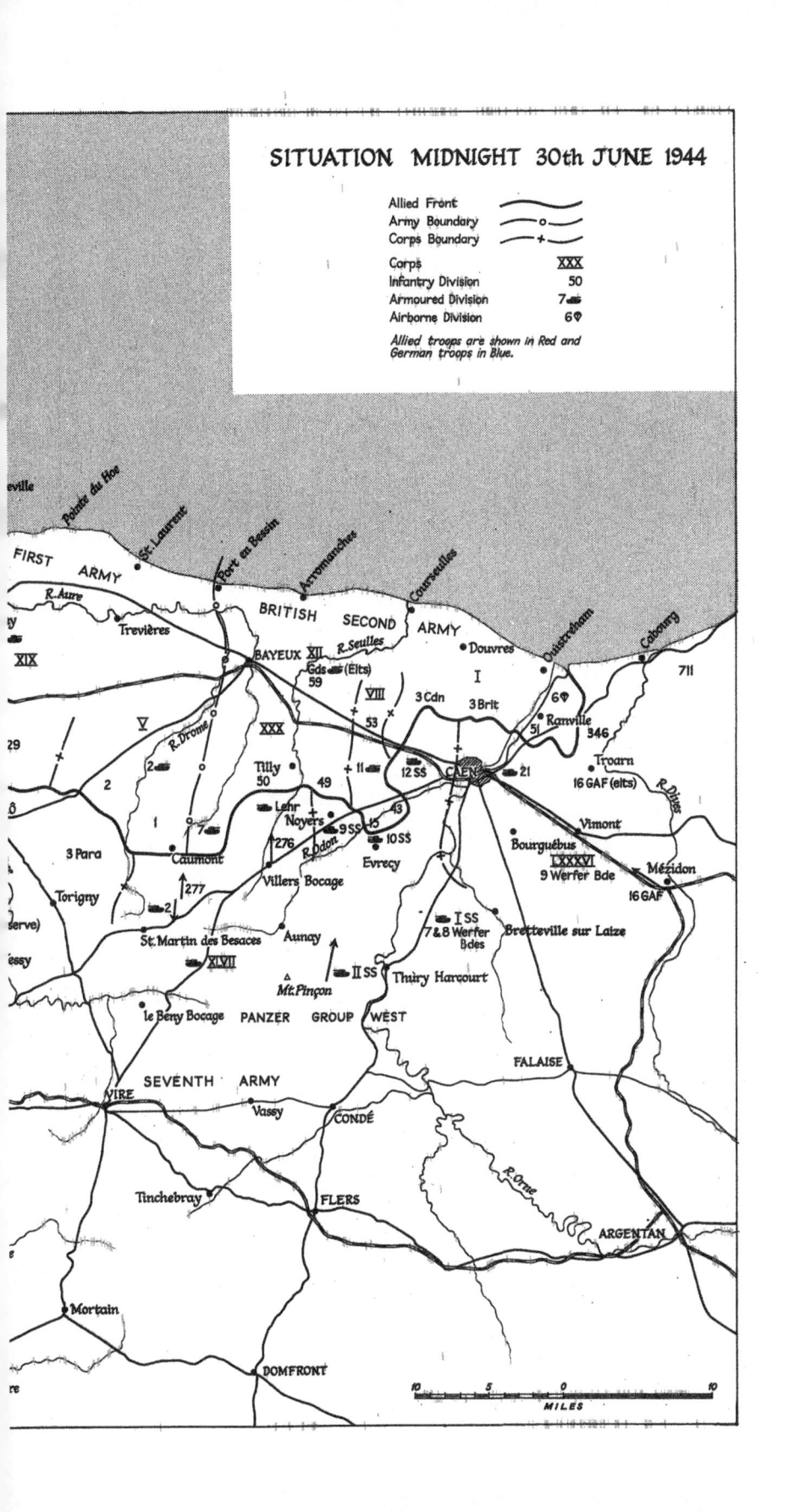

Allied Front
Army Boundary
Corps Boundary
Corps — XXX
Infantry Division — 50
Armoured Division — 7
Airborne Division — 6

Allied troops are shown in Red and German troops in Blue.

MARITIME SUCCESSES

great vigour and Cherbourg reached on the 24th. On the 25th the town was entered while for three hours a naval force bombarded the protecting defences at the Army's request (page 291 below). There was much close fighting and no general surrender that day but on the 26th the commander of the garrison and the local naval commander surrendered with some eight hundred men. More prisoners were captured as the defences were overcome. The extremities of the outlying positions, resting on the coast, were the last to be taken but all opposition had ceased by July the 1st and the whole of northern Cotentin was then in American hands. All Cherbourg's port equipment and facilities had been destroyed by the Germans and its waters were blocked by sunken ships and heavily mined. Many weeks and much hard work would be needed before it could be cleared and re-equipped for use, but the Allies were at least sure of a harbour before long.[4]

The adjoining map shows the Allied front in Normandy at the end of June, but before going further with the story of the land battle what had meanwhile been happening at sea must be recorded.

On June the 17th it had been reported to Admiral Dönitz (page 268) that 'the Führer sees the only possible relief for the land forces in the elimination or harassing of enemy naval forces, particularly battleships'. Since then, however, German naval operations had been on an even smaller scale because of the destruction of their remaining surface vessels and the toll taken of submarines. With what they had they did little damage during the rest of June. The unrelaxing vigilance of the Allied sea and air forces and their instant reaction to any enemy threat ensured that the stream of shipping between England and Normandy was virtually immune from naval attacks, and casualties from that source during these weeks were minute.

The U-boat menace was stifled by the air cover of Coastal Command and ceaseless patrolling by the Allied navies, fulfilling their complementary rôles. The first U-boat had succeeded in reaching the 'Spout' on June the 15th (page 242); the second did not do so till the 25th. By the 30th two more had arrived but only one, U.984, was successful. Coming up to the Channel she had torpedoed and badly damaged the frigate *Goodson* on the 25th; arrived in mid-Channel she attacked a convoy of south-bound American ships in the Spout on the 29th and torpedoed four. Three were successfully towed in and beached but became a total loss; the fourth continued her voyage to France. After this the U-boat made her way back to Brest. This isolated incident shows what damage might have been done by the twenty-five U-boats that had been ordered by the end of June to attack

---

[4] See Harrison, *Cross-Channel Attack*, chap. X.

shipping in the Spout if the Allied defence had been less vigilant. In fact, of the twenty-five, seven had been sunk and three damaged and forced to return, five had given up or turned back with defects, and six were still making their way up Channel at the end of June. Only four had succeeded in reaching the Spout and of these two were already returning to base. Meanwhile Allied aircraft had sunk five others patrolling in the western Channel or Bay of Biscay, making a total of twelve sunk during June. Three more submarines were ordered to mine Cornish waters. One was damaged and turned back soon after leaving Brest. The others laid their mines off Plymouth and Land's End.

Away from the scene of these actions Coastal Command kept watch on U-boats trying to pass north of Scotland in order to attack shipping in the Channel or the Atlantic. Their work over those lonely waters may be illustrated by the story of how one U-boat was sunk 120 miles north of Shetland on June the 24th. U.1225, bound for the Atlantic, was sighted and attacked by a Catalina flying-boat of the Royal Canadian Air Force and elected to fight it out on the surface. The aircraft was badly damaged by enemy fire during the run in but staggered on to straddle and sink the U-boat with depth charges. By then the Catalina was unmanageable; the starboard engine fell out and, burning furiously, the flying boat was put down into the sea. The crew got clear and were in or clinging to the dinghy for twenty-one hours before being rescued by a launch of the Air/Sea Rescue Service. Two had died of exposure; the captain, Flight Lieutenant D. E. Hornell, died soon after he was pulled from the water. He was posthumously awarded the Victoria Cross.

After the bombing of le Havre and Boulogne the E-boats did no further damage in June. On the 18th those remaining at Cherbourg managed to escape to St. Malo and a few days later they broke back to the eastward and successfully reached le Havre. In this risky passage across the Allied front they were pursued, but in the darkness and poor visibility their high speed enabled them to escape. At this time the enemy attempted to evacuate shipping from Cherbourg and British coastal forces fought a number of actions near the Channel Islands in which they sank a German minesweeper, one escort vessel and four coasters without loss to themselves.

E-boats had some minor success later against convoys between Dungeness and Beachy Head, but they had virtually ceased to be a factor in the Normandy fighting and at the beginning of August all but six at le Havre and Boulogne were out of action.

During these last days of June the enemy increased night activity in the air, adding to the minelaying by low-flying aircraft attacks, torpedo attacks, and, occasionally, flying bombs. An early victim was the cruiser *Scylla*, flagship of Admiral Vian, which was mined on the evening of the 23rd. She was towed to England for repair and Admiral Vian transferred his flag to H.M.S. *Hilary*.

Naval co-operation with the armies ashore (and the enemy's fear of the naval guns) has already been noted in describing the progress of the fighting. There is no need to elaborate in detail the day to day part which the warships played, for its significance has been recognised. The biggest call for naval assistance on shore was General Bradley's request for help in the final reduction of Cherbourg which was mentioned on page 289. Cherbourg's heavy guns, well concealed in almost indestructible concrete emplacements, were distributed not only in the port itself but in a ring of outlying forts and a number of strong-points; the three largest batteries mounted 280-mm (11-inch) guns. The bombarding force was to subdue the chief of these guns while the final assault went in. Commanded by Admiral M. L. Deyo, U.S.N., it comprised three United States battleships and four cruisers (two of them British) with a screen of eleven American destroyers. Ahead of these moved a large number of British and American minesweepers. Fire opened at 14,000 yards (about 8 miles) from Cherbourg and the defending guns there replied vigorously. For three hours the duel was continued. The battleship *Texas*, the cruiser *Glasgow* and three destroyers received hits and others were damaged by splinters; there were fifty-two casualties, killed and wounded. Nineteen of the twenty-one missions which the ships had been given were completed when the ships were withdrawn. As already told, the Cherbourg garrison commander surrendered next day.[5]

It was to be expected that the harbour and port facilities would have been reduced to a shambles and as soon as the surrender had been completed Commodore W. A. Sullivan, U.S.N., and Commodore T. McKenzie, R.N.V.R., heads of the American and British Salvage Sections, flew to Cherbourg to survey the damage. The harbour was thickly strewn with mines of every description, many of them fitted with anti-sweeping devices, delayed-action firing mechanism, or trip lines to entangle sweepers or divers. Access to the docks and basins was blocked by sunken ships great and small, and large numbers of tugs, barges and small craft. Almost all the deep, water quays had been demolished; cranes, elevators and railway

---

[5] There is an amusing story, in Froissart's 'Cronycle', of Edward the Third's landing at St. Vaast La Hougue, south of Barfleur, in the 14th century. 'Whane the kynge of Englande arryved in the Hogue saynt Wast, the kyng yssued out of his shyppe, and the firste fote that he sette on the grounde, he fell so rudely, that the blode brast out of his nose. The knyghtes that were aboute hym toke hym up and sayde, Sir, for Goddessake entre agayne into your shyppe, and come nat a lande this day, for this is but an yvell signe for us. Than the kyng answered quickely and sayd, Wherfore, this is a good token for me, for the land desyreth to have me. . . . So that day and nyght the kyng lodged on the sandes, and in the meane tyme dyscharged the shyppes of their horses and other bagages.' The nearby 'Cherbourgue' is described as 'stronge and well furnysshed with men of warre'. (From Pynson's edition of 1523 and 1525. Translated by Sir John Bouchier. Vol. I, cap. CXXII.)

wagons had been blown into the water, and the quay walls blasted in on top of them. On shore, the *Gare Maritime* and naval arsenal and base were wrecked, and along the whole water-front buildings and workshops had been reduced to ruins.

The work of recovery began as soon as the fortress fell and the last outlying batteries had been captured on June the 30th. On that day the first Allied vessel, a British minesweeping motor-launch, passed the outer breakwater but for some time only small craft feeling their way with the utmost caution were permitted to enter the harbour. The most urgent task was mine clearance, for no ship could enter port with the essential engineers' equipment for reconstruction work until at least part of the anchorage had been made reasonably safe. At Admiral Ramsay's suggestion, Admiral Kirk accepted the loan of Commander J. B. G. Temple, R.N., to direct the mine-clearance operations and the work was entrusted mainly to the British 9th and 159th Minesweeping Flotillas, with other British and American units assisting. Normal sweeping methods within the wreck-strewn harbour were not enough. Some of the mines were inaccessible to sweepers and these were tackled by 'P' Parties, British teams of young men, all volunteers, trained in under-water bomb disposal and the use of shallow-water diving equipment. In the muddy waters of the lower Thames they had practised the grisly art of tackling all manner of German mines, guided only by a sense of touch. In the course of six weeks from the beginning of July, these 'P' Parties explored nearly the whole floor of the harbour and they were also continually on call to deal with explosives and booby traps found among the wreckage obstructing the quays.

Apart from mine clearance, the reconditioning of the port went ahead as a joint Anglo-American enterprise under American control, Commodore Sullivan being in general charge of salvage assisted by Commodore McKenzie and the British salvage team. In other respects reconstruction was controlled by U.S. naval and military authorities. With the loss of three minesweepers and seven other small vessels over a hundred mines were accounted for by July the 16th. On that day the first deep-draught ships were safely brought into the outer harbour and anchored; they had been waiting outside for days, loaded mainly with essential equipment for port development. From then on a trickle of supplies for the army began, carried in Dukws over the beaches within the harbour to dumps inland. The trickle eventually swelled slowly into a flood. Cherbourg, which in peace-time was mainly a passenger port and intended to develop to a capacity of 9,000 tons a day, eventually reached more than double that daily average; until Antwerp was available it was the mainstay of the port system serving the American forces.[6]

---

[6] See Ruppenthal, op. cit., vol. II, chap. III.

Away on the extreme eastern flank the abandonment of General Montgomery's original intention to extend the British left flank to the Dives had left the coastal country beyond the Orne in enemy hands. Numerous mobile batteries were concealed in wooded country and beyond the Dives were two heavy casemated batteries at Bénerville and Houlgate. These continued to shell Sword beaches and anchorage and seriously interfered with their use. Counter-battery fire by battleships and cruisers had destroyed some of the heavier guns and silenced the batteries temporarily from time to time, but in spite of persistent effort and the firing of over a thousand heavy and medium shells neither battery was put out of action permanently; and neither the bombarding ships nor the artillery could silence the enemy's mobile guns firing from hidden positions in the woods. A number of landing ships were damaged and, though all were unbeached successfully, drying-out here was stopped and all personnel ships were transferred to Juno for unloading. The small headquarters ship *Locust*, a corvette and some ferry craft were also damaged, and an ammunition coaster was hit and set on fire. From June the 25th all landing ships and coasters were also transferred to more westerly areas and the use of the Sword beaches was finally discontinued, in agreement with the Army, at the end of June.

By that time the fall of Cherbourg, the firm establishment of a growing lodgement area, and the attrition of the enemy's submarines and surface vessels made it possible for Admiral Ramsay progressively to reduce the assault forces as originally constituted and to release bombarding ships and craft which were now needed for the projected assault on the Mediterranean coast. An account of the long and sometimes heated discussion on whether, when and where this second landing should take place is given in Mr. Ehrman's history of grand strategy during this period.[7] It is enough to note here that on the last day of June the British Chiefs of Staff advised Mr. Churchill to give way to American opinion 'for the sake of Allied solidarity' and agree that Anvil should be launched as soon as possible, August the 15th being set as the target date. Only later, when the forces who landed there came eventually under General Eisenhower's command, do their operations play a direct part in this history.

On June the 24th Rear-Admiral J. W. Rivett-Carnac set up his headquarters ashore at Courseulles as Flag Officer British Assault Area and, in turn, Commodore Oliver withdrew from Juno (on the same day), Commodore Douglas-Pennant from Gold (on the 27th) and Rear-Admiral Talbot (on the 29th) from the then nearly deserted Sword anchorage. Similarly Force Commanders in the American sector withdrew after Rear-Admiral J. Wilkes, U.S.N.,

---

[7] John Ehrman, *Grand Strategy*, vol. V, chap. IX.

had established his headquarters ashore as Flag Officer West. On June the 30th Admiral Vian, the British Task Force Commander, withdrew to England (he was followed by Admiral Kirk, U.S.N., three days later) and on that day Operation Neptune was officially concluded. Its planning, organisation and execution had been wholly successful and although, as the assault phase of Overlord, Neptune was now completed this did not affect the navies' continuing responsibilities, as will be seen in subsequent chapters. They were still responsible for naval protection of the daily convoys carrying their precious cargoes of men and supplies to France and bearing to England thousands of casualties and German prisoners of war; they were still responsible for the naval protection of the anchorages and harbours, and as long as the armies were fighting within the range of their guns they would continue to assist them with the gunfire which the enemy so dreaded. The navies' contribution would not be completed till victory was won.

The following figures indicate some of the results of the Neptune operation.

By June the 30th there had been landed in France 850,279 men, 148,803 vehicles and 570,505 tons of stores.

During that time every effort by the enemy to interfere with the Allies' naval movements had been defeated and thousands of our ships and craft had crossed and recrossed the Channel safely. As the table opposite shows, 51 had been lost and 76 damaged by enemy action, while 8 more had been lost and 44 damaged by other causes. It is worth noting that of the total casualties attributable to enemy action (127), nearly half (59) were caused by mines; the united efforts of enemy U-boats, surface vessels and aircraft, which resulted in 68 casualties, were little more dangerous than hazards of the sea, from which the 52 casualties are shown under 'other causes'.

It will be well to see, now, how these events were affecting the German command. A study of contemporary documents shows clearly that while fighting was being conducted with skill by local commanders and stubborn bravery by their troops, the battle as a whole was being directed by Hitler. His control was not limited to the issue of broad directives; not even a division could be moved without his concurrence and several divisional moves that had been ordered by von Rundstedt or Rommel were promptly countermanded by Hitler. The field-marshals were being treated as little more than subordinate commanders; hundreds of miles away at his headquarters the Führer knew, better than they who faced realities in Normandy, how their fight should be conducted! He discounted their statements and distrusted their judgment, and he ignored their repeated requests that someone from OKW should visit the front to report independently on the true state of affairs. All power of

Allied Shipping Losses in Operation Neptune—6th to 30th June 1944
(*Excluding landing craft and other miscellaneous small craft*)

Cause of Loss	Warships		Merchant vessels and auxiliaries	Remarks
	Larger vessels	Smaller vessels		
SUNK				
By Mines	9 (a)	7	10	(a) 7 Destroyers and 2 Fleet Minesweepers
U-boats	2 (b)	–	4	(b) 2 Frigates
Aircraft	2 (c)	–	3	(c) 1 Destroyer and 1 Frigate
Gunfire	–	2	3	
Surface craft torpedoes	1 (d)	–	8	(d) 1 Destroyer
Other causes	–	1	7	
Total sunk	14	10	35	
DAMAGED				
By Mines	12 (e)	7	14	(e) In one case damage was superficial
U-boats	2	–	2	
Aircraft	2	1	4	(f) In two cases damage was superficial
Gunfire	13 (f)	5	10	
Surface craft torpedoes	2	–	2	
Other causes	9	6	29	
Total damaged	40	19	61	

initiative was hamstrung by his close control and his overriding and reiterated order that there must be no withdrawal anywhere.

So far as offensive action was concerned, von Rundstedt had proposed on June the 15th that the available armoured divisions and those that were on the way should be massed for a major counter-attack as soon as infantry divisions arrived to relieve the armour at present holding the British front. 'The direction of this thrust', he wrote, 'has still to be determined.' Later his intention was to split the Allies' bridgehead 'east of St. Lô'. Hitler agreed to this at the conference on the 17th (page 268) and three days later sent a directive in that sense, naming the divisions to be used. Meanwhile planning for it had started. On the 19th Rommel had sent two sketch maps of alternative developments to Geyr von Schweppenburg (who as commander of Panzer Group West would be responsible for the counter-attack) and on the 26th the latter replied with proposals for his basic plan. Meanwhile, on the 24th, von Rundstedt's war diary had noted that the counter-attack could not start until July the 5th–7th. Yet, on the same day, Hitler ordered him to examine the possibility of an attack 'during the next few days' against 'the rear of the 1st U.S. Army which is attacking towards Cherbourg. After destroying these forces the aim of further operations is to relieve Cherbourg.' This was to be 'in addition to the plans for an offensive which have been reported'—

that is the major counter-attack already being planned. Von Rundstedt replied almost at once that neither sufficient force nor supplies could be assembled for an attack towards Cherbourg within the next few days, and until the launch of the major counter-attack 'the area round and east of Caen' must continue to have most importance. Next day the war diary noted von Rundstedt's belief that the Allies planned to attack there and that these plans 'require our own reserves to be assembled correspondingly'. He conferred with Rommel on the 26th and sent a memorandum to OKW explaining in detail why both regarded Hitler's proposed counter-attack towards Cherbourg as not possible, adding, 'it may become necessary, undesirable as it is, to use all the new forces now coming up to intercept, attack and destroy the English offensive which is expected within a short time from the area round and west of Caen. . ..' (This was the day on which Epsom began and the commander of Cherbourg surrendered.)

Hitler however was unimpressed by the considered views of his field-marshals. On the 27th he gave von Rundstedt another order to examine the possibility of an attack against enemy forces west of the Vire. 'The Führer holds firmly to the idea of attacking not the strength, but the weakness of the enemy west of the Vire where weaker American forces are located on a broad front.' (So 'weak' that they had just swept most of the enemy from the Cotentin and had captured Cherbourg!) His 'basic idea' was to attack the Americans with four or five named armoured divisions; to 'support' the bridgehead between the Orne and the Vire by 'infantry divisions and battle groups'; and also to attack east of the Orne as soon as possible 'not merely after the main attack'. This order was received on the day that saw VIII Corps across the Odon. It was too much for von Rundstedt. Ignoring this further order to consider a counter-attack west of the Vire, he said that if the German troops there were not soon to be encircled commanders should '*now*' be given freedom to withdraw to a more favourable line. 'In conjunction with Field-Marshal Rommel, I [von Rundstedt] therefore ask for a free hand to order even extensive adjustments of the front . . . and for a corresponding directive.'

On the following day both field-marshals, travelling separately by road as they were not allowed to go by air or train, set out on a six hundred mile journey to Hitler's headquarters at Berchtesgaden for conference with the Führer. On the same day (28th) Dollmann, commander of the Seventh Army, died suddenly of heart attack.

The conference did not begin till six o'clock in the evening of the 29th. There were present besides Hitler and the two field-marshals only Field-Marshal Keitel, head of OKW, and General Jodl, chief of the OKW Operations Staff, for von Rundstedt had asked for a

A VISIT TO HITLER

private meeting. Subsequently Göring, Dönitz, Sperrle and a number of staff officers were brought in and a personal meeting was changed into a general conference at which Hitler did most of the talking. He gave no indication however of any new policy. The only notes on policy which Jodl made in his diary for that day doubtless express what seemed to him a summary of what was significant. 'We are now compelled to ward off the English attack, instead of counter-attacking. . . . Then if all goes well, we could still advance against the Americans.' Official records of the conferences and such personal reports as have survived do not differ materially. Hitler was to issue a new directive that night and what followed the meeting will be told in the next chapter. Von Rundstedt's request for greater freedom of control remained for that day unanswered.

CHAPTER XIV

THE CAPTURE OF CAEN

AT the end of June, with Cherbourg captured and the Second Army on the Odon, General Montgomery reviewed the situation with his army commanders and outlined his plans for the next phase. Before examining these it will be well that the reader should have some further knowledge of the general state of affairs.

On the conclusion of Neptune and the gradual withdrawal of the Assault Forces, naval protection of the all-important lines of communication between the main Allied base in England and the assault area off Normandy was reorganised. The supply convoys sailing regularly under the Home Commands continued to be protected by their own escorting warships. Arriving in the assault area they now came under Admiral Rivett-Carnac's orders for he was responsible (under Admiral Ramsay's direction) for naval command of the British assault area including local operations, defence from seaward, sailing of homeward bound convoys and administration of naval personnel in the area; he was at the same time to maintain close liaison with the local military and air force commanders. Under him general responsibility for the defence of the vulnerable eastern flank was given to Captain A. F. Pugsley, R.N., who as Captain (Patrols) had operational control of all vessels allocated for patrols and striking forces (destroyers, control frigates, corvettes, anti-submarine trawlers, coastal craft and minesweepers), including minesweepers employed on the night defences described in an earlier chapter. A new 'Support Squadron Eastern Flank' was formed of some seventy-six small craft drawn from the original assault forces; its commander was Commander K. A. Sellar, R.N., and its purpose to man the eastern defence or 'Trout' line by night (page 221) and to support the army when required by day. Its main task by day was to bombard enemy forces along the coast, operating often in enemy-mined waters beyond the Orne and threatened by shore batteries. In these conditions the Support Squadron had a difficult and dangerous duty and a very responsible one, for the enemy's possession of this stretch of coast, which had enabled him to make the Sword area practically unusable (page 293), also helped hostile craft based on le Havre to creep round the coast in darkness under cover of shore batteries and to shelter in its small harbours, Cabourg and Trouville.

At sea a number of clashes occurred between enemy E-boats (which had been reinforced by some brought from the Baltic) and the

Navy's motor torpedo-boats and supporting frigates. Most of these actions in darkness between small, fast-moving boats were inconclusive. There were some casualties on both sides but the enemy did no damage to the steady stream of ships passing to and from the assault area and had only two successes against convoys moving slowly through the Channel. On the night of the 26th/27th two ships in convoy were damaged off Dungeness and four days later, off Beachy Head, four were damaged of which one sank.

At the beginning of July there were two U-boats at large in the 'Spout' area and others either approaching it or returning to Brest. After their initial losses in June only U-boats fitted with *schnorkel* were used in Channel operations and against these aircraft were less effective as they seldom exposed themselves. Even so the result of the month's anti-submarine operations is sufficiently striking.

Eighteen sorties were made during the month against the Channel convoy routes and the effect on the seventeen U-boats concerned (for one made two separate sorties) was as follows:

Destroyed by the Navy in the Channel	.	6 (U.390, 678, 212, 672, 214, 333)
Damaged by the Navy in the Channel	.	3 (U.671, 741, 275)
Completed their patrol undamaged	.	5 (U.218, 953, 673, 309, 621)
At large in the Channel on 31st July	.	3 (U.984, 667, 671 second trip)

Between them these seventeen U-boats had sunk one infantry landing ship, a merchant ship and an anti-submarine trawler; two other merchant ships had been damaged.

During the same period two U-boats were sunk by aircraft[1] in the Bay of Biscay and a third foundered close off Brest on an air-laid mine.

In the early hours of July the 6th a new menace suddenly appeared. A 'strange object' was seen moving slowly through the Trout line and was at once engaged by gunfire from the Support Squadron. Thereupon it released a torpedo and disappeared. There followed a hectic interval in which similar objects, widely dispersed, were discerned in the darkness and similarly dealt with by the vigilant defence. They were in fact 'human torpedoes'.[2] These had been

---

[1] Flying Officer J. A. Cruikshank, R.A.F. Coastal Command, was awarded the Victoria Cross for his gallantry in fighting one of these till it was sunk, after his navigator was killed and he and his crew were badly wounded.

[2] Known to the Germans as a *marder* (marten) it was an improvised weapon composed of two torpedoes fastened together one above the other. The speed of this contraption was only about $2\frac{1}{2}$ knots and it was not submersible. Astride the upper torpedo (from which the explosive had been removed) sat the pilot, sheltered by a Perspex hood only part of which showed above the water. The under-slung torpedo when released by the pilot travelled at 20 knots towards its target, leaving the pilot to elude the defences and escape back to base—if he could.

EFFECTS OF STORM

met in action three months before off Anzio in Italy but this was their first appearance in the Channel. The German records show that on this night twenty-six had set out from le Havre. Two broke down before reaching the assault area, nine were sunk by the defenders, fifteen escaped back to their base. Two small minesweepers had been torpedoed.

Two days later another attempt was made to pierce the defence by twenty-one of these human torpedoes launched from Houlgate. Their attack began at three o'clock in the morning and continued during the forenoon. All twenty-one were brought to action and the German records show that all were sunk; a few pilots were picked up from the sea. In this crushing defeat one minesweeper was lost and the Polish-manned cruiser *Dragon* severely damaged. She was an old ship and had played her part in the naval bombardments; but still she would continue to serve, for on abandonment she was sunk where she would form a needed extension of the Gooseberry breakwater off Sword beach. After the Support Squadron had dealt so faithfully with this new form of attack several weeks passed before it was renewed.

After the storm the most energetic measures were taken to repair the trail of damage and destruction in the assault area. Salvage was a herculean task, made more difficult by the fact that many wrecked craft had been driven high up the beaches and those which were repairable could not be refloated till the July spring tides. The full salvage organisation was brought into action at once and additional resources were made available including a repair ship and skilled ratings, many of them drawn from the Home Fleet. Many craft were temporarily repaired where they lay and by the 8th of July some 600 stranded craft, besides coasters and other small vessels, had been refloated. Another 100 were safely brought off on the high tides a fortnight later, and in order to cope with the sudden influx of damaged craft from the assault area, the repair organisation in home ports was also expanded.

On reviewing the situation with expert assistance the Supreme Commander decided that no attempt should be made to restore the piers and equipment of the American Mulberry harbour off Omaha; only its Gooseberry breakwaters would be repaired and strengthened to give shelter to small craft; such equipment as remained there after the storm was to be used to complete the British Mulberry at Arromanches, where the harbour was to be strengthened to withstand as far as possible the onset of winter gales. This would involve the production of forty new Phoenix caissons of stronger construction and the work of 'winterisation' would not be completed till late in the autumn. Meanwhile one stores pier was already finished and two more were in hand. By the 20th of July the harbour would be in full operation on a maximum scale, with moorings for seven deep-draft cargo ships and for a larger number of coasters within the shelter of the breakwater; and all three piers were by then in use.

The set-back in the rate of landing vehicles and stores occasioned by the storm could not be wholly overtaken but in the week that followed—June the 23rd to the 30th—there was a remarkable recovery in view of the destruction and disablement of so many landing craft. In that first week after the storm, the daily averages landed were as shown:[3]

Daily average landed	Vehicles		Stores (tons)	
	British	American	British	American
June 19–22 (storm) . .	1,375	1,051	4,286	3,064
,, 23–30	3,337	3,271	17,410	20,188

The overall supply situation was generally satisfactory, but a shortage of some essential types of ammunition had at times caused anxiety to both British and American commanders. On June the 22nd there had been only one day's reserve of 25-pounder and 4·2-inch mortar ammunition in the British army roadheads; by then their total ammunition stocks had fallen from 29,800 tons to 9,562 and some rationing had been imposed. But by special shipments and, in the American sector, some delivery by air the situation was quickly improved. By the 1st of July British roadheads held nine days' stocks of 25-pounder and fifteen days' of 4·2-inch mortar ammunition and contained 64,942 tons of ammunition of all kinds. There is no evidence that lack of ammunition seriously handicapped or delayed British operations at this time, but the American history states that their offensive southwards would have been started earlier had it not been for shortage of ammunition.

By the beginning of July the planned arrangements for ensuring the supply of petrol to the growing Allied forces in France were making good progress. These were to take two forms. The first, essential in the early stages of the campaign, consisted of the establishment of petrol and oil storage depots fed through buoyed pipelines from tankers moored off-shore; this plan was known as 'Tombola'. The second was a more novel and ambitious plan to supply petrol from England through Pipe Lines Under the Ocean ('Pluto'). The history of Pluto, of its origin, the technical difficulties that were overcome and its eventual outcome are told later. At the beginning

---

[3] For the American figures, see Ruppenthal, *Logistical Support of the Armies*, vol. I, pp. 416–419.

THE NORMANDY BASE

of July the laying of cross-Channel pipes had not yet started but the Tombola scheme was already coming into use. The British depot was built at Port en Bessin and the American two miles further west near Ste. Honorine. The first 6-inch pipeline for the former was completed on June the 25th and the first for the American depot a week later; by July the 14th there were two in use for each depot and three shorter lines were hauled ashore for American use at the eastern end of Omaha. The supply of petrol for the Allied armies and air forces in Normandy was for the time being assured.

The armies' administrative organisation ashore was by now well developed. In the British sector Second Army had relieved the original assault corps of responsibility for back areas and Headquarters, No. 11 Lines of Communication Area had taken control of beach- and port-working. The organisation, shown in outline, was as follows:

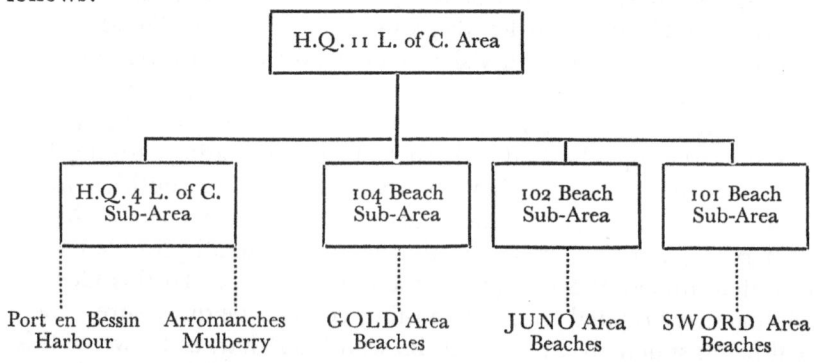

```
                        H.Q. 11 L. of C. Area
         ┌──────────────────┬──────────────┬──────────────┐
   H.Q. 4 L. of C.      104 Beach      102 Beach      101 Beach
     Sub-Area            Sub-Area       Sub-Area       Sub-Area
       ┊   ┊                ┊              ┊              ┊
Port en Bessin  Arromanches   GOLD Area    JUNO Area    SWORD Area
   Harbour      Mulberry      Beaches      Beaches      Beaches
```

Two roadheads through which the British forces were being maintained were under command of Headquarters, Second Army Troops; No. 1 Army Roadhead was near Douvres la Délivrande and No. 2 round Bayeux. Signal networks, signposting and traffic control were fully adequate and newly landed personnel could find their destination quickly. Since the storm an average of approximately 14,400 men a day had landed in both British and American sectors, but the British leeway had not yet been made good and Second Army was still short of three divisions at the end of June.

By this time the number of men landed was British 397,819, American 452,460, a total of 850,279. If the approximate number brought in by air in the airborne assaults and the subsequent airlifts be added, the grand total of the Allied landings was about 875,000 men.

While delay of the early build-up was due mainly to bad weather, limitation of tactical progress had also handicapped the development of administrative plans. The pre-D-day forecasts had contemplated that a lodgement might extend as far as Lisieux, Alençon, Rennes and St. Malo by the 1st of July (D plus 25); actually it enclosed rather less than one-fifth of that area. The space between the beaches and the front line was inadequate for the base installations which had been planned, and with anything up to 10,000 vehicles a day passing through some of Second Army's traffic posts congestion was acute; it would have been unmanageable if the Allies had not held command of the air.

Headquarters of Twenty-First Army Group was still in England, General Montgomery having with him in Normandy only his small Tactical Headquarters. Until June the 22nd this was at Creully, with General Dempsey's Second Army Headquarters and the Headquarters of Air Vice-Marshal H. Broadhurst, commanding 83 Group, within a mile or two. On June the 22nd General Montgomery had moved to Blay in the American sector six miles west of Bayeux, where he was within easier reach of General Bradley's First Army Headquarters at Grandcamp les Bains on the coast near Omaha. The Supreme Commander had visited Normandy several times and had stayed there with General Bradley from the 1st to the 5th of July. He was showing some anxiety about the pace of the Allied advance. On June the 25th he had written to General Bradley, urging him '. . . to rush the preparations for the attack to the south'; and on July the 7th had said in the course of a letter to General Montgomery: '. . . It appears to me that we must use all possible energy in a determined effort to prevent a stalemate . . .' To this General Montgomery replied '. . . of one thing you can be quite sure—there will be no stalemate . . .' It will be seen later that, as he wrote this, further operations had begun for the capture of Caen and were making good progress.

The First Canadian Army commander (Lieut-General H. D. G. Crerar) had arrived in Normandy on the 18th of June with a small staff but General Montgomery had come to the conclusion that, until Second Army had completed its landings and the front was further advanced, there would not be room for another army headquarters and its large complement of army troops. First Canadian Army headquarters was therefore retained in England and did not become operational until the 23rd of July. In the circumstances the need for a headquarters, Lines of Communication (under the direct control of Twenty-First Army Group) was not urgent and the organisation represented by the diagram on page 303 generally held good until the middle of July. In the meantime the incoming Canadian formations were under the command of Second Army (which temporarily would contain five corps) till the First Canadian Army was constituted in France.

Much the same thing happened to the American follow-up army (the Third, under Lieut-General G. S. Patton) which had been expected to operate from about the 25th of June. He landed early in July but for three weeks was hidden in the Cotentin *bocage*—that the Germans might continue to believe he was in England commanding the Allied army which they still expected to attempt a second landing in the Pas de Calais area. Meanwhile his divisions went under the First Army as they arrived on the Continent.

Lack of space had also limited the provision of airfields. By the beginning of July the British had constructed twelve[4] airfields, but three or four were still denied them by shellfire; the Americans had another eleven in use. Altogether, these represented about three quarters of the programme for this date. By the 5th of July the whole of 83 Group and nine groups of the Ninth Air Force would be operating from the Normandy fields.

Yet even though bad weather had hampered air operations there had been no inadequacy of air support for the armies, no loss of air mastery, no failure to prevent air interference by the enemy. In the foregoing chapters a broad outline of air operations in June has been included; a separate book would be needed to describe them in detail. Here it is only possible to indicate their scale and scope by figures; readers must be left to picture for themselves the effort that lay behind them.

A usual measurement of the scale of air operations is the number of sorties involved, a sortie being one mission—a single there-and-back flight—of one aircraft, so that, for example, a bombing attack by ten bombers is described as involving ten sorties. Obviously a sortie may be comparatively short, easy and safe, or long, difficult and very dangerous; in one the pilot may see nothing of the enemy, in another he may have to fight off enemy aircraft and brave a hurricane of anti-aircraft fire; a fighter patrol may take less than an hour but a Catalina flying boat may spend ten hours on anti-U-boat patrol. Nevertheless there is no other single standard by which to measure the great variety of air operations. Measured, then, in this way the combined effort of the Allied air forces involved 163,403 sorties as shown in the table overleaf.

In these multifarious actions the Royal Air Force lost 3,083 air crew,[5] killed or missing, and the American Eighth and Ninth Air Forces 3,170. Of the total 6,253 airmen lost, 5,006 were in Bomber Command and the Eighth Air Force, for while the total aircraft lost (1,508) were fairly evenly distributed between the tactical (740) and

---

[4] Chief Engineer 21 Army Group's Report of Situation at 0900 hrs 1 July gives British sector ten completed airfields, plus one emergency landing strip and one glider landing strip. Nine of the airfields appeared to be in R.A.F. use. Report of 4 July gives one more rearming and refuelling strip (Amblie) completed.

[5] In one of these bomber operations, Pilot Officer A. C. Mynarski of the Royal Canadian Air Force was awarded the Victoria Cross for sacrificing his life in order to save a badly wounded member of his crew.

the strategic (768) air forces, the loss of each heavy bomber involved a much larger crew.

Allied Air Operations, June 6th to June 30th, 1944

Nature of operation	Sorties flown				
	2nd T.A.F. and A.D.G.B.	Bomber Command	Coastal Command	U.S. 9th Air Force	U.S. 8th Air Force
1. *Direct and Indirect Support of Operations*					
(a) Offensive operations by fighters and fighter bombers	9,871			14,650	5,436
(b) Attacks by heavy, medium and light bombers	2,923	7,088		8,820	18,435
(c) Fighter escorts, support for bombers, intruders, spotting for naval gunfire	4,074	680		590	8,548
(d) Visual, photographic and weather reconnaissance	5,010	70	1,150	2,800	648
(e) Troop carrying and glider towing in airborne operations. Support for Resistance Forces by Special Duty Squadrons	907	270		1,662	350
(f) Day and night fighter cover for home bases, shipping and lodgement area	23,167			12,348	1,766
2. *Maritime Operations*					
(g) Anti-U-boat patrols			3,983		
(h) Anti-shipping patrols	1,335		1,987		
(i) Minelaying		325			
(j) Air/Sea Rescue	1,140		200		
3. *Operations against V-weapons*					
(k) Attacks on launching sites, supply depots and flying bombs in flight	2,800	4,660		1,500	2,210
4. *Long-term Operations*					
(l) Attacks on synthetic oil plants		975			2,360
(m) Attacks on industries and cities		200			3,590
(n) Fighter escorts and light bomber support for heavy bombers		780			4,095
Total sorties	51,227	15,048	7,320	42,370	47,438

Total Allied Air Force Sorties — 163,403

While the Allied air forces thus flew over 130,000 sorties in support of the armies, the fighters, fighter bombers, bombers and reconnaissance aircraft of the German Third Air Fleet together flew a grand total of 13,829 sorties. In that comparatively small effort they lost 808 aircraft while the Reich Air Fleet lost a further 185 in fighting the Allied attacks on targets in Germany. An officer detached by the German Historical Branch to report on the air position in the West visited the Third Air Fleet area in July. From a long and detailed report one paragraph may be quoted:

> 'The effect of Anglo-American air supremacy on the Normandy front and as far as Paris is so great that all convoy traffic is restricted to night time and even single vehicles are only used by day in the most extreme emergencies. The main highway, Paris–Versailles–Dreux, is ploughed up by direct hits from the western end of Versailles to the goods yard at St. Cyr. The villages of Laigle, Argentan and Falaise are reduced to ruins. The losses in motor vehicles amounted in some units to as much as 40% of the original strength and at the same time large quantities of reserves of munitions and fuel were destroyed.'

He noted that 'owing to the enemy's air superiority no photo reconnaissance could be made to ascertain the effect of V.1 attacks on London'; the figures for June are given here. As the table opposite shows Crossbow operations against launching installations and flying bombs since D-day had involved 11,170 sorties. Since June the 13th, 2,049 flying bombs had been launched; 22 had been shot down by our fighters before they reached the English coast; of 1,557 which had crossed the coast fighters had shot down 504 in flight, 224 had been brought down by anti-aircraft fire, 41 by barrage balloons and 5 by the Royal Air Force Regiment's guns; 783 had reached London.

In the last fortnight of June a few flying bombs which had apparently gone astray dropped in the assault area without causing any damage to shipping.

One further matter must certainly have been present in General Montgomery's mind when he outlined his plans for future operations at the end of June, namely the resources both in France and elsewhere on which he could count. Casualties up to then had been considerably less than had been allowed for in Overlord planning and so far they had been made good by replacements. The Army figures are as follows:

Allied Battle Casualties—June 6th to June 30th

	Killed	Wounded	Missing	Total	Remarks
British and Canonical .	3,356	15,815	5,527*	24,698	* Men at first reported missing who later rejoined have been deducted.
American . .	5,113	26,538	5,383	37,034	
TOTALS	8,469	42,353	10,910	61,732	

Replacements dispatched to make good these losses were: British and Canadian 38,000; American 41,000; total Allied replacements 79,000. So far then, losses were being more than made good.[6]

At the beginning of July the British and American armies in France were approximately equal in strength; each had the equivalent of some fifteen or sixteen divisions. The Americans had nine further divisions waiting to cross from England and a steadily increasing force preparing in the United States which would eventually make up their Overlord armies to sixty-one divisions. But only the equivalent of some six British and Canadian divisions waited in England to join Twenty-First Army Group and its full strength would never exceed twenty divisions. It was not even certain that the British manpower situation would make it possible to maintain all these if the war continued for long. Knowledge of these circumstances had therefore to be taken into account in planning future operations.

At the end of June elements of eight panzer divisions had been identified between Caen and Caumont; none had yet been met on the rest of the front and the United States First Army was able to reorganise and regroup without hindrance. This was what General Montgomery had been aiming at, for his intention was to hold the maximum number of German divisions on the eastern flank between Caen and Villers-Bocage and '. . . to swing the western or right flank of the Army Group southwards and eastwards in a wide sweep, so as to threaten the withdrawal of such enemy divisions to the south of Paris'. The Seine bridges between Paris and the sea would be kept permanently out of action by the Allied air forces. A strong force established in the area of le Mans and Alençon would therefore be a serious threat to the enemy concentrated near Caen and to their line of withdrawal through the Paris–Orléans gap.

His plans depended for success on two factors, on whose importance he was most emphatic. The (British) left flank was the pivot on which the main stroke would hinge; it must therefore always remain secure, otherwise the whole movement might lose its balance. As a corollary the (American) right flank must forge ahead with the utmost speed before the enemy had time to switch his more mobile troops from the positions into which we had just succeeded in drawing them.

As events will show, General Montgomery here set the general pattern of the campaign for the next six or seven weeks.

---

[6] Army Group B's casualty return up to June 30th was admittedly incomplete, for at that date the losses in the defence of Cherbourg and its surrounds were not known. They are said to be included in the returns for June 6th to July 7th. For that time the German casualties were given as: 1,830 officers (including 9 generals, 109 commanders and 7 General Staff officers), 75,166 NCOs and men, 3,787 'Russians', Total 80,783.

The immediate task of the British Second Army was to hold the main enemy forces between Caen and Villers-Bocage and '... to develop operations for the capture of Caen as opportunity offers— and the sooner the better'. First United States Army was required to begin on the right flank an offensive southwards on the 3rd of July and then, pivoting on its left at Caumont, to swing eastwards to the general line Caumont–Vire–Mortain–Fougères. When the base of the Cotentin peninsula was reached, near Avranches, the right-hand corps (VIII) should be turned westwards into Brittany and directed on Rennes and St. Malo. Plans must now be prepared for the rest of General Bradley's command to '... direct a strong right wing in a wide sweep south of the *bocage* country to successive objectives as follows: (*a*) Laval–Mayenne, (*b*) le Mans–Alençon'.

On the 1st of July the capture of Carpiquet, which had been postponed during Epsom, was now ordered for the 4th; the major attack, on Caen, was to follow about the 8th, by which time the 59th Division would have landed and be ready to take part alongside the 3rd British and 3rd Canadian Divisions. Carpiquet airfield had been used for some years by the occupying Germans; it contained a lot of concrete and wire, many pill-boxes and anti-aircraft posts. Since D-day the whole area had been converted into a strong-point to guard the western approaches to Caen. Its garrison now consisted of the 26th SS Panzer Grenadier Regiment and some tanks of the 12th SS Panzer Division, all well entrenched. (Map, page 275.)

The attack was to be made from west to east by the 8th Canadian Infantry Brigade, who would start from a firm base at Marcelet, held by the 32nd Guards Infantry Brigade still under the command of the 43rd Division. To prevent interference from the south the latter's 214th Brigade temporarily occupied Verson and the adjoining village on the Odon without incident during the night before the attack.

For its task the 8th Canadian Brigade was given an additional infantry battalion and also had under command, or at call, a regiment of gun tanks, three squadrons of special tanks from the 79th Armoured Division, a battalion of machine guns, twenty-one regiments of artillery, H.M.S. *Rodney* and two squadrons of rocket Typhoons.

On the evening of the 3rd the *Rodney* with a spotting aircraft fired fifteen rounds from her 16-inch guns from 26,200 yards on the buildings round Carpiquet as a preliminary to next morning's attack, and at 5 a.m. on the 4th the artillery opened. Fifteen minutes later three infantry battalions began to move forward with tanks close behind them. The enemy replied promptly with a counter-barrage which took a steady toll of casualties, but the two battalions on the left kept up their advance and by half past six had reached their objectives—the village of Carpiquet and the nearby hangar area. On their right flank smoke and mist caused the third battalion to lose touch with its supporting tanks and it was nine o'clock before it had fought its way to the first of the hangars on the west of the airfield. It was there met by a hail of fire from strongly held positions at the other end of the airfield and eventually, after hard fighting, had to withdraw.

While mopping-up around Carpiquet village was still not complete, and before it was realised that the attack on the hangars at the west end of the airfield had failed, the fourth battalion went forward towards the village intending to pass through and capture the control buildings at the east end of the field. By 11 a.m. the battalion was in Carpiquet but there became involved with the other two battalions in mopping-up the village. All of them with tanks and other supporting units were heavily shelled and mortared, while coveys of German tanks drove around in the distance. In the afternoon the right battalion returned to the attack and again reached the hangars on the west, but was then counter-attacked by tanks and driven out once more; it was then ordered back to the base at Marcelet.

During most of the day the weather was so bad that the air force could do little to bring immediate help to the Canadians. But it improved in the late afternoon and Typhoons of 83 Group went into action against the enemy at the east end of the airfield where about seventeen tanks appeared to be dug in among the buildings. A counter-attack launched by I SS Panzer Corps, begun during darkness, went on into early morning and reached its height about eight o'clock on July the 5th when a thrust from the south succeeded in penetrating some of the Canadian positions. With help from the guns and from the Typhoons the situation was eventually restored; several Panthers were knocked out and many Germans killed and before midday Panzer Group West made a report to Army Group B that 'the attempt to recapture Carpiquet has failed'. They had had enough and fell back on shelling and mortaring, while the Canadians postponed any further attempt to complete the capture of the airfield till Caen itself was attacked on the 8th.

On that day I Corps, strongly reinforced and now comprising about 115,000 officers and men, was to clear Caen as far as the river Orne and establish bridgeheads across the river south of the city. Meanwhile VIII Corps on its right was to be ready at twenty-four hours' notice to launch a new attack towards the upper reaches of the Orne.

In the previous four weeks the German defences north of Caen had been greatly strengthened. The anti-tank ditches and weapon pits begun before D-day had been extended and supplemented by a wealth of minefields and other obstacles. Every incident of the ground had been skilfully used in forming a defensive belt two or three miles deep. This included mutually supporting positions based on what were by now virtually tank-proof villages (Lebisey, la Bijude, Galmanche, Gruchy, Franqueville, Cussy and Couvre-Chef) and was studded with dug-in tanks, assault guns and multi-barrelled mortars to support the infantry. Behind this belt, round the fringe of the city, were other artillery and mortar positions; on the west were the unsubdued positions at Carpiquet airfield. The front from Hérouville on the Caen canal, through Lebisey to the railway near Cambes was held by infantry of the 16th Luftwaffe Field Division of LXXXVI Corps, with some tanks of the 21st Panzer Division in support (though its main body had gone out to rest). From there, through Gruchy to Carpiquet airfield and the Odon near Verson, the front was held by I SS Panzer Corps with the 12th SS Panzer Division, the 7th Werfer Brigade and detachments of the 1st SS Panzer Division. In reserve near the Orne about five or six miles south of Caen lay the rest of the 1st SS Panzer Division which was only now completing its move, and distributed in the corps area were the dual-purpose 88-mm guns of at least one regiment of III Flak Corps. West of Verson stood II SS Panzer Corps facing the British VIII Corps salient. (Map overleaf.)

It was a strong position and I Corps planned to attack with three infantry divisions (3rd British on the left, 59th in the centre and 3rd Canadian on the right) supported by the 27th and 2nd Canadian Armoured Brigades and a number of flail, engineer and flame-thrower tanks of the 79th Armoured Division. In addition to the artillery of the three attacking divisions the guns of the Guards Armoured and 51st Divisions and of the 3rd and 4th AGRAs would be available with those of the battleship *Rodney*, the monitor *Roberts* and the cruisers *Belfast* and *Emerald*. In the late afternoon of July the 7th H.M.S. *Rodney's* 16-inch guns fired twenty-nine rounds from a range of 25,000 yards on to the hill (Point 64) just north of Caen on which the roads from Epron and Lebisey join before running down to Caen. The Germans regarded this position as a key point of the Caen defences.

Later that evening heavy bombers were to be used for the first time for tactical support of the Army's forthcoming operation. In order to safeguard the attacking troops it had previously been decided that pending further experience the bombline should be 6,000 yards ahead of the nearest troops. This meant that the bombs would fall on the enemy's rearward defences on the northern outskirts of Caen, some three miles behind the strongly defended forward area which the infantry and tanks would have to capture. As the attackers

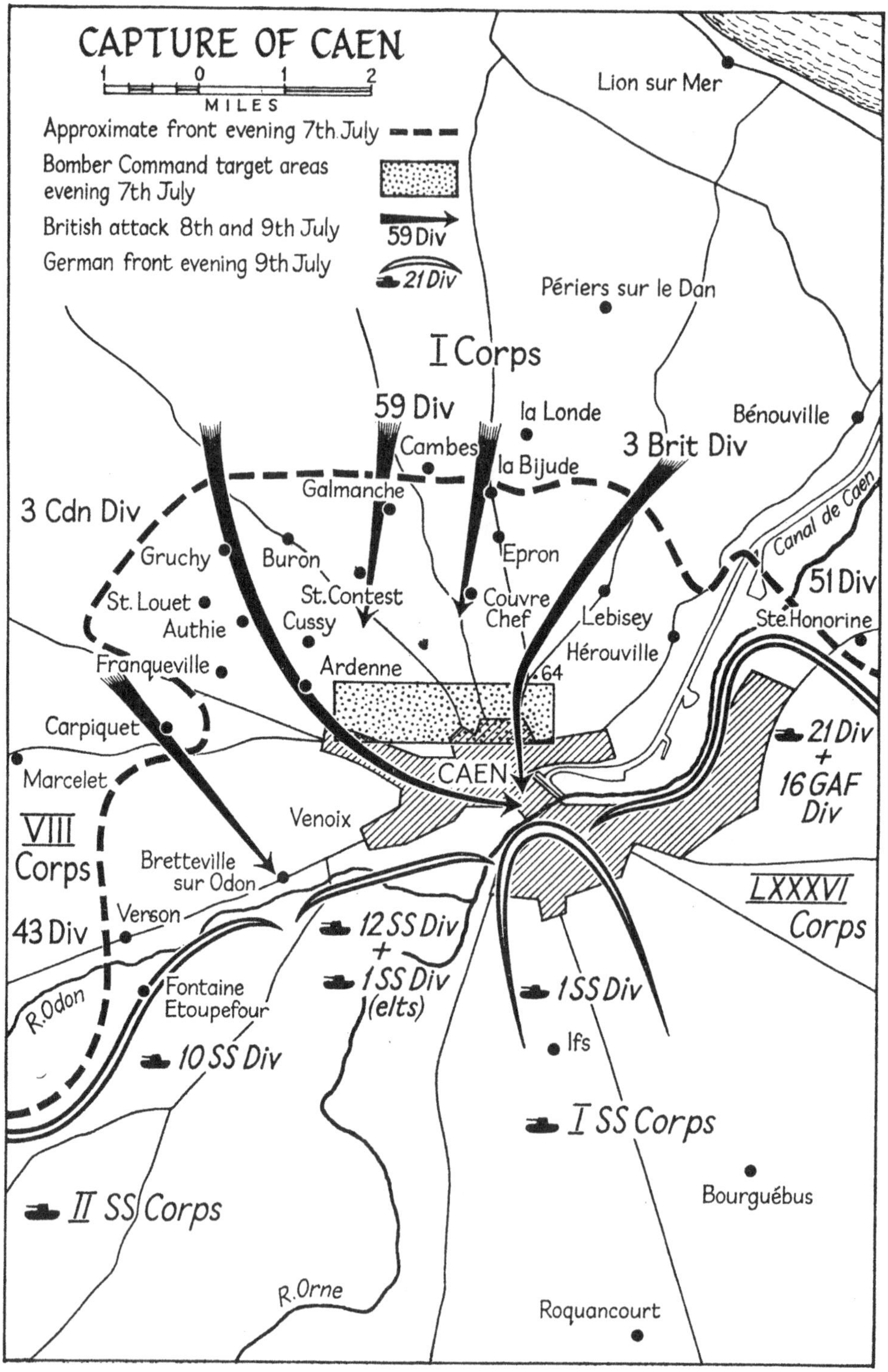

CAPTURE OF CAEN
1 0 1 2
MILES
Approximate front evening 7th July
Bomber Command target areas evening 7th July
British attack 8th and 9th July
59 Div
German front evening 9th July
21 Div
Lion sur Mer
Périers sur le Dan
I Corps
59 Div
la Londe
Bénouville
3 Brit Div
Cambes
la Bijude
Galmanche
3 Cdn Div
Canal de Caen
Gruchy
Buron
Epron
51 Div
St. Contest
Couvre Chef
St. Louet
Authie
Cussy
Lebisey
Ste. Honorine
Hérouville
Franqueville
Ardenne
64
Carpiquet
21 Div + 16 GAF Div
Marcelet
CAEN
VIII Corps
Venoix
Bretteville sur Odon
LXXXVI Corps
Verson
43 Div
12 SS Div + 1 SS Div (elts)
Fontaine Etoupefour
R. Odon
1 SS Div
10 SS Div
Ifs
I SS Corps
Bourguébus
II SS Corps
R. Orne
Roquancourt

could thus not follow closely behind the bombers it was decided that the bombing of rearward defences should be done on the evening of the 7th so that this would not only facilitate the advance of the troops when they reached that area but would meanwhile prevent the enemy from bringing forward reinforcements during the night and block the movement of his tanks through Caen.[7]

Shortly before dark, as the men of I Corps completed their arrangements for the morrow, a long stream of Lancasters and Halifaxes of Bomber Command, with a strong escort of Spitfires, began to pass overhead in the direction of Caen. From 9.50 p.m., while guns of VIII Corps fired on the enemy's anti-aircraft positions, over 450 bombers struck at the selected points on the northern outskirts of Caen. The leading aircraft met some fire from the target area and from guns to the south of Caen, but as the attack went on the response wavered and eventually ceased; all was over in an hour, a demonstration of power and accuracy which gave great confidence to the soldiers who would soon be advancing to attack, and provided valuable lessons for future supporting operations by heavy bombers.

As the heavy bombers turned for home the light bombers and intruders of 2 Group came in to harass movement behind the enemy lines. A good deal of activity was seen during the night and among other targets twenty-six trains were attacked. At 11 p.m. the artillery of I and VIII Corps opened and, reinforced by the naval guns, began softening up the village strong-points and the enemy batteries.

At 4.20 a.m. on July the 8th the full force of the artillery came down in front of the 3rd British and 59th Divisions, who then moved forward in the first phase of the attack. Progress was comparatively rapid and, within an hour, the leading brigade of the 3rd Division (moving 'one up') had reached Hérouville and Lebisey, and the two brigades leading the attack of the 59th were in the outskirts of both la Bijude and Galmanche—their first objectives.

The weather was fair, though cloudy, and Second Tactical Air Force fighters were already at work just ahead of the assault. Soon after 7 a.m. 250 medium bombers of the Ninth Air Force joined in the battle and for the next two hours attacked strong-points, likely forming-up places, gun areas, bridges and headquarters; their fighters went further afield against the enemy's roads and railways.

---

[7] It has since been stated that the reason for bombing several hours before the army attack opened was an adverse weather report, but this was not so. The records show that the air forces in France were warned on the 6th that an appreciable air effort would be needed on the evening of the 7th, and at the Air Commanders' morning meeting on the 7th it was agreed that the evening attack should be made by Bomber Command with the double purpose quoted above. In neither case was any reference made to weather, and in fact the forecast supplied to the air staff that day was favourable both for the bomber attack and for their return to base.

H.M.S. *Rodney* again shelled Point 64 and later in the day she fired on enemy transport near Ifs and at a group of thirty-five German tanks waiting in country south-east of Caen, and hit them with 16-inch shells at a range of 32,000 yards. The report on the shoot reads: 'Enemy paid dearly with a "flamer" and several "smokers" and a disorderly retreat'. Typical targets for the cruisers were bridges over the Odon and railways on which H.M.S. *Belfast* fired. Accurate shooting on targets far out of sight without the help of 'spotting' aircraft would not have been possible. The spotters had to fly in view of the target slowly enough to observe the fall of shell and to wireless back corrections. Only a few days before this one had been brought down by enemy fire and a second damaged. In 10th SS Panzer Division's 'Lessons from the Normandy Front' it was said, 'the greatest nuisance of all are the slow-flying artillery spotters, which work with utter calmness over our positions'.[8]

The corps commander ordered the next phase to start at 7.30 a.m. The two 59th Division brigades were to pass fresh troops through to capture their second objective (the villages of Epron and St. Contest) and the 3rd Canadian Division on their right were to join the attack with one brigade aiming firstly at Buron and Gruchy and then at Authie. The main weight of the corps artillery was now switched to the front of these divisions, and under cover of a new series of concentrations the second phase duly started.

Affairs on the extreme left, about Lebisey, went well but in the centre the 12th SS Panzer Division fought back hard and parties held out against the 59th in la Bijude and Galmanche. Similar struggles were soon developing in Epron and St. Contest, while no progress was being made between them where the way was barred by a trench system just west of la Bijude. Seeing this, General Crocker told the 3rd British Division to push some armour forward on to the high ground (Point 64) just north of Caen and later in the morning he put his reserve (the 33rd Armoured Brigade) under the division's command.

The Canadians were in Buron by half past eight but the 12th SS Panzer Division were prepared to fight to the end amongst the rubble and it took most of the day to master them. The Germans made repeated attempts to eject the Canadians with tanks but they were eventually defeated by the Canadian armour and by a 17-pounder anti-tank battery which itself was credited with thirteen 'kills'. The casualties around Buron were heavy on both sides; by the end of the day the assaulting infantry battalion had lost 262 officers and men, killed and wounded, and its supporting squadron was left with only four of its original fifteen tanks. At Gruchy, on the right, things had

---

[8] H. J. Parham and E. M. G. Belfield, *Unarmed into Battle* (1956), p. 78.

gone better, though not without a sharp fight. What probably settled the issue here was the somewhat unorthodox action of about sixteen Bren carriers of the divisional reconnaissance regiment which suddenly charged, in cavalry fashion and with all guns firing, right into the middle of the German position.

The heavy fighting at Buron had delayed progress but at 2.30 p.m. a fresh attack was begun and, in an hour or so, the Canadians had secured both Authie and St. Louet; and when parties of enemy were seen from Carpiquet withdrawing to the south a battalion was speedily despatched to Franqueville. The way was now clear for the next phase and a second brigade began an attack on Cussy and Ardenne at 6.30 p.m. By 8.30 p.m. the Canadians had captured Cussy and knocked out six tanks from a number which attempted a counter-attack; Ardenne was secured next morning, the enemy having withdrawn during the night.

The 59th Division and their supporting troops had kept up the pressure all day and succeeded in taking St. Contest and what was left of la Bijude, but their other objectives still defied them. The 3rd British Division had completely cleared the Lebisey area and, apart from some heavy shelling and mortaring from east of the Orne and a short-lived tank sortie against Hérouville, were not seriously impeded. In the early evening, supported by the 33rd Armoured Brigade, they captured the high ground round Point 64 and were then overlooking Caen from the position they had hoped to gain on D-day. Patrols reached the outskirts of the city but it was getting dark and further penetration was hampered by debris.

By nightfall on the 8th the wings of the attack were little more than two miles apart, and the corps commander decided to leave the clearance of Caen to the flank divisions and told the 59th to clear up the hard core of resistance on its immediate front but not to go on into the city.

Meanwhile, Second Army ordered that the VIII Corps operation (to be called 'Jupiter') would begin on July the 10th, and shortly before midnight a brigade of the 43rd Division set out to secure a suitable start line just across the Odon from Verson.

During the night intruders of the Second Tactical Air Force attacked a good deal of movement on the other side of the Orne and the pilots thought that most, if not all of it, was heading away from Caen, but patrols were busy probing enemy positions along the front and the fighting which flared up here and there seemed to show that no general withdrawal had begun. In fact, Rommel had agreed that the heavy weapons of all three corps (LXXXVI, I and II SS Panzer) should be withdrawn from Caen during the night. Strong infantry and engineer forces were to remain behind to hold a close perimeter round Caen, and only if attacked by superior forces were they to withdraw to a new line along the east bank of the Orne and thence across to Venoix and Bretteville north of the Odon.

Early in the morning (July the 9th) the divisions were on the move again. The 3rd British pushed tank patrols against the flank of the opposition in the centre sector and then began to move into Caen. There were snipers and mortars but these gave little trouble compared with the bomb craters, the rubble and the large blocks of locally quarried stone which choked the narrow streets. While the division struggled to get through, the 59th had been working forward steadily and were on all their objectives by midday. The Canadians had cleared Carpiquet and finding little opposition had made sure of Bretteville sur Odon as well. At about half past two their armour had met with the 3rd British Division, and by 6 p.m. I Corps had reached the Orne at Caen and was also up to the Odon above the junction of the two rivers. Some of the bridges were still intact but they were either blocked by rubble or denied by German troops on the opposite bank. To oppose our further progress, the 1st SS Panzer Division had been moved nearer to Caen during the day.

Apart from a little mopping-up the operation was over. The hard character of the fighting is shown by the high losses on both sides.

In I Corps the casualties were about 3,500 with the 59th and the 3rd Canadian Divisions each having more than a thousand. About 80 of our tanks were destroyed or out of action. According to the German war diaries all the battalion commanders of the 16th G.A.F. Division's regiment west of the Orne had either been killed or wounded and it had lost 75 per cent of its strength; the total infantry strength of the 12th SS Panzer Division had been reduced to the equivalent of one battalion. On the 8th twenty of its tanks had become a total loss and most of its anti-tank guns had been destroyed. Nearly 600 prisoners were received in the I Corps cages.

About a third of Caen's 60,000 inhabitants had remained in the city during the siege which had lasted since D-day. Despite their privations they greeted our soldiers with a generous, if pathetic, welcome. For some they could provide flowers, for all they had cheers and good wishes.

With the capture of Caen and with the Americans nearing St. Lô, the time was riper for the decisive action towards which General Montgomery had been working—namely a double attack designed at once to enlarge and strengthen the eastern open flank of the Allied position and compel the enemy to fight there with his strongest armoured forces; and simultaneously to break out of the American sector to the open country south of the *bocage* and turn eastwards towards the Seine. Some days must elapse while troops were being regrouped for these twin attacks, and meanwhile the pot was kept

FIGHT FOR HILL 112

boiling by a limited action to hold the enemy armour in the east and to round off the ground won in the Epsom battle and by the capture of Carpiquet airfield and Caen city. The bridgehead south of the Odon was to be expanded by the capture of Eterville and Maltot and by the recapture of Hill 112. The troops to be employed were the 43rd Division reinforced by the 4th Armoured, 31st Tank and 46th (Highland) Infantry Brigades. They were to be supported by additional artillery of the 11th Armoured and 15th Divisions and by 3rd and 8th AGRAs. They would start from the shallow Odon bridgehead which now stretched from Verson to Baron, for the 214th Brigade had crossed the river to come in on the left of the 129th Brigade on the night of the 8th. The attack was to open at 5 a.m. on the 10th.

As shown in the map of the Odon battlefield, facing page 275, high ground which separates the valleys of the Odon and the Orne rises to its highest point on Hill 112. The hill is crossed by the road from Caen to Evrecy passing through the straggling village of Eterville as it climbs to the hill-top; about a mile away on the far side Maltot nestles in the Orne valley. Though Hill 112 dominates the surrounding country, much of the battlefield is in full view from beyond the Orne and from hills around Evrecy to the south.

Following the opening bombardment early on the 10th, leading troops of the 43rd Division reached Eterville and were well up on the slopes of Hill 112 by eight o'clock; the advance towards Maltot started soon afterwards. Eterville was taken and held. Maltot was entered in spite of sharp opposition but by mid afternoon armoured counter-attack and heavy mortaring made it clear that the low lying village could not be held until Hill 112 was in our hands. Meanwhile there was hard fighting for possession of the hill. Defending infantry were hidden by the corn and tanks lay waiting in copses. One battalion reached the road over the hill top but could get no further and the rest of the brigade was pinned down below the crest. A fresh attack by the 5th Duke of Cornwall's Light Infantry supported by the 7th Royal Tank Regiment was launched in the evening and by nightfall Hill 112 and the small nearby woods were occupied. From there to Eterville the 43rd Division had all four infantry brigades and much of its armour on the ridge and on the slopes behind it at the end of the day. North of Eterville a brigade of the 3rd Canadian Division had crossed the Odon to strengthen the left of the bridgehead where the 1st SS Panzer Division had been identified.

Those who hoped for a quiet night were disappointed. Counter-attacks began soon after midnight and were repeated at several places along the front till late on the 11th. More than once German troops penetrated Eterville but all were thrown out and 100 dead were left behind. On Hill 112 the Duke of Cornwall's Light Infantry were heavily attacked and after all their anti-tank guns had been put out of action and they had lost 240 casualties they had to fall back to the hill-top road.

In all there were two thousand casualties in this two-day action and little ground had been gained; yet 10th SS Panzer Division, 102nd SS Heavy Tank Battalion and part of 1st SS Panzer Division had been held in the fight. Panzer Group West's war diary records that General Eberbach told the commander of II SS Panzer Corps on the 11th that Hill 112 'is the pivotal point of the whole position ... in no circumstances may it be surrendered ... The loss of Eterville might be borne, but not that of Hill 112'. Yet they had lost half of it, for the 43rd Division had captured the northern slopes and were halfway across the almost level hill-top. Before them were the wide hedgeless cornfields in which much blood had already been spilt. Standing out on the skyline in the centre of this front is a lonely crucifix and near-by a memorial has been raised to record the courage and sacrifice of the 43rd Division.

Meanwhile in the American sector the task of the First Army was very difficult, largely owing to the lie of the country there. Its 40-mile front ran roughly in a quarter-circle from Caumont, through Carentan, to the west coast beyond St. Sauveur le Vicomte. Behind this line communications were, for the most part, unfavourable. In front of it on the left, between Caumont and the river Vire, the country was hilly and broken and rose steadily as it approached St. Lô; west of the Vire there was a belt of low ground six to ten miles deep, covered with marshland and intersected by numerous sluggish streams; only near the west coast was there a narrow corridor of dry land. (Map, page 288.)

General Bradley's first object was to secure the general line St. Lô–Marigny–Coutances. This would bring the First Army clear of the restricting defiles and provide it with a good lateral in the St. Lô–Lessay road. He decided to begin on the extreme right with an attack by VIII Corps down the corridor near the west coast. The other three corps were to join the battle later on his orders.

In heavy rain and thick cloud, which cancelled the air support programme, the offensive opened on the 3rd of July with three divisions of VIII Corps attacking due south for la Haye du Puits. The enemy's resistance was stubborn and only some 6,000 yards were gained in the next three days. On the 4th VII Corps entered the battle in the Carentan sector, aiming at Périers, about ten miles to the south-west. Confined to an isthmus of dry land only about two miles in width, the corps made little more than a mile's progress in two days' hard fighting. XIX Corps then joined the offensive and on the 7th made assault crossings of the river Vire and the Vire–Taute canal, the intention being to secure the rising ground just to the west of St. Lô. By nightfall a two-pronged attack was going well and had reached the neighbourhood of St. Jean de Daye. It appeared to General Bradley that this sector offered a good prospect of success and he therefore ordered an armoured division (the 3rd) to reinforce the bridgehead that night. It was then directed to drive for the objective south-west of St. Lô.

Meanwhile First Army intended that another three divisions should take up the attack east of the Vire on the 9th, and thrust through the hills which immediately protected St. Lô.

American troops were being opposed for the first time in this campaign to elements of the enemy's armoured divisions. One of the German infantry divisions (the 276th) that had been coming up to release armoured divisions holding the front in the British sector took over the front of Panzer Lehr Division on July the 5th, though a battalion of Panzer Lehr's tanks and most of its anti-tank battalion were left behind in support of the newly arrived infantry. The remainder of the armoured division, which it had been intended to rest and refit, was instead ordered to move westwards to strengthen the defence threatened by the American attack north of St. Lô. At the same time 2nd SS Panzer Division, including its two battalions of tanks, its guns and three battalions of infantry, was also ordered to move still further westwards to the area round Périers.

While progress on the Allied side was steadily advancing General Montgomery's plan, on the enemy side, by comparison, plans and counter-plans were being debated. The whole Hitler-controlled conduct of the battle had been questioned and memorable decisions had been taken—but the German position had steadily worsened. To understand what had occurred it is necessary to recall the meeting at Berchtesgaden on June the 29th at which much had been discussed but little decided. At its conclusion a new directive was promised and this was issued by OKW late that night. By then von Rundstedt and Rommel had already started on the long journey back to their respective headquarters. There they found the new directive waiting for them when they arrived late on the evening of the 30th. Its only significant references to policy were the admission that a further attack against the British forces east of the Orne was dependent on the arrival of another field division and on 'the withdrawal of enemy naval forces'; and that an attack in the west against the Americans was 'not possible at present'; that 'the most important tasks for the immediate future' were: '(a) A flank attack to destroy the enemy forces thrusting through Baron [that is the Epsom attack of the British VIII Corps] towards the Orne. (b) 7th Army must not allow themselves to be driven into open country. 2nd SS Pz. Division "Das Reich" will have to remain where it is in reserve [that is south of St. Lô] until the main body of 17th SS Pz. Grenadier Division has been successfully relieved by infantry . . .' Other subjects dealt with were matters of detail.

But on von Rundstedt's return he also learnt that Rommel had meantime received situation reports from Hausser, acting commander of the Seventh Army, and Geyr von Schweppenburg, commander of Panzer Group West, both of whom advocated an immediate evacuation of Caen and withdrawal to a new line, further south, that would be out of range of naval guns. Von Rundstedt at once informed OKW of this by telephone and without waiting for sanction he authorised Rommel to order immediate preparation for a planned withdrawal from Caen. He then followed up his telephone message by sending forward to OKW the text of the reports from Hausser and Geyr von Schweppenburg and the covering letter from Rommel strongly endorsing their recommendations. His own personal approval of the proposed measures and request for freedom to act on them at once read as follows:

> '1. I agree with the estimates of Field-Marshal Rommel, and of the Cs.-in-C of 7th Army and Pz. Group West. I request that I may *immediately* be allowed a free hand to carry out a planned evacuation of the Caen bridgehead and, after this, to adjust the front, at my discretion, to the approximate line Orne–Bully–Avenay–Villers-Bocage–Caumont area. It is just when II SS Panzer Corps' thrust is making itself felt that I consider that a suitable opportunity for the adjustment of the front has presented itself: covered by II SS Panzer Corps, the infantry divisions can, as they arrive, form a new front line withdrawn from the reach of the enemy's naval guns. Through this planned evacuation, particularly of the Caen bridgehead, irreplaceable units of I SS Panzer Corps, that is, 1st SS "Adolf Hitler" Panzer Division, 12th SS "Hitler Youth" Panzer Division, and units of 21st Panzer Division, will be released in good time from an ever-narrowing encirclement and will thus be set free for any further operations. These troops, which are our best, must be preserved east of the Orne at fighting strength; this decision is urgently necessary, lest valuable forces should once again be destroyed by the enemy.
>
> '2. In spite of the proposed withdrawal of the front from the whole Caen bridgehead to a line from east of the Orne to the Caumont area, there will be for the time being no alteration in the present planned attack which all available forces are making astride the River Odon towards Caen. Because of the situation an immediate decision is essential.
>
> [signed] von Rundstedt
Field-Marshal'

Although von Rundstedt and Rommel had asked for greater freedom before they went to Berchtesgaden it had not been conceded and when Hitler received this budget of letters and reports, all

41. Spitfires in flight

42. Air Marshal Sholto Douglas

43. Air Marshal Hill

44 and 45. In the Normandy *bocage*

embodying a counter-proposal to the course he had prescribed only a few hours after his meeting with them, he must have received a shock. Here were his commander-in-chief in the West, the commander of the army group responsible for fighting the battle, the commander of the principal army involved, and the commander of most of his armoured divisions all combining to advocate a radically different policy and a free hand to carry it out. Evidently they thought they knew better than their Führer! They distrusted his judgment and thought they could do better without his direction! Moreover his displeasure is likely to have been heightened by the fact that von Rundstedt had forwarded (and both he and Rommel had approved) the report of a subordinate condemning in scornful terms the Führer's policy of defence. For in advocating immediate withdrawal from Caen to the new line described in von Rundstedt's covering letter, Geyr von Schweppenburg had written:

> 'It is no longer possible (a) to achieve a break-through to the coast . . . (b) to hold lines with panzer divisions, without their dwindling or already depleted units . . . being consumed in a very short time; (c) to expect a change in the situation by badly equipped or mediocre infantry divisions, which have indeed been allocated but cannot get here within the predictable future . . . A clear cut choice must be made between the inevitable patchwork of a rigid defence, which leaves the initiative to the enemy, and flexible tactics which give us the initiative sometimes at least . . . An elastic conduct of operations is the better course.'

As von Rundstedt had approved this it was clear that the freedom he asked for was in fact freedom to alter the whole conduct of the German defence; he must think that even Geyr von Schweppenburg was wiser than the Führer! Then von Rundstedt (and von Schweppenburg) must go.

That afternoon von Rundstedt received the immediate answer to his request in a message from OKW.

> 'The present positions are to be held. Any further breakthrough by the enemy will be prevented by tenacious defence or by local counter-attacks. Assembly will continue and further mobile formations will be released by infantry divisions as they arrive. Detailed orders will follow.'

This was received by von Rundstedt at 5.40 p.m. on the 1st July. At once he cancelled preparations for the evacuation of Caen and gave orders for Hitler's directive to be carried out.

Events then moved quickly. On the 2nd Hitler's adjutant Lieut-Colonel Borgmann arrived at von Rundstedt's headquarters. He gave the field-marshal a letter from the Führer saying that he was superseded and, at the same time, handed him the Oakleaves to his Knight's Cross. At eleven o'clock on the 3rd Field-Marshal Günther von Kluge arrived and assumed command. It was given out by OKW that von Rundstedt had been allowed to retire at his own request for reasons of age and health, but after the war von Rundstedt strongly denied this false explanation and his dismissal after what had happened was, surely, almost inevitable. On the 4th Geyr von Schweppenburg was also superseded by Hitler's order, and General Eberbach was given command of Panzer Group West. Four days later, on July the 8th, Hitler issued a new and fuller directive. The first two paragraphs are given below.

'Directive for the conduct of operations in the West.

(1) The enemy has succeeded in landing in Normandy and in seizing with astonishing speed the Cotentin Peninsula together with the fortress of Cherbourg.

He expected but has failed to achieve the rapid widening of the bridgehead from Elbeuf to S. of Granville.

In the next stage of operations it will very probably be the enemy's intention to make a thrust along both sides of the Seine towards Paris and then to employ the bulk of his highly mobile forces in a war of movement.

Consequently, in spite of all the attendant risks, the enemy will probably attempt a second landing in the 15th Army's sector, all the more so, as public opinion will press for the elimination of the sites of the long-range weapons firing on London. The dispositions of the forces still available in England suggest attacks primarily against the sector between the Somme and the Seine by divisions assembled north of the Thames, but also against Belgium and Southern Holland. At the same time, however, surprise attacks designed to effect the capture of one of the large ports in Brittany cannot be ruled out.

Similarly, an attack against the French Mediterranean coast may also be expected. The time chosen for it will depend upon the enemy's intentions and progress in his operations in general. It is unlikely that he will conduct two large-scale operations in the Mediterranean theatre simultaneously.

(2) The present relative strengths of the opposing forces and the fact that the majority of all our mobile formations are already committed preclude for the time being any major offensive aimed at the destruction of the enemy in the bridgehead. Nevertheless, in no circumstances may the bridgehead be allowed to increase in size to any appreciable extent, otherwise our forces will prove inadequate to contain it and the enemy will break out into the interior of France, where we do not possess any comparable tactical mobility with which to oppose him.'

The success of the Allies' elaborate precautions to ensure tactical surprise in their initial assault had been matched by an equal success of the steps taken to deceive the enemy as to their intentions. It will be remembered that as part of these they set out to provide false indications that although they might attempt a first landing in Normandy their main attack was to take place about the middle of July and be directed against the Pas de Calais coast. Hitler's directive shows how well this deception had been sustained; although at times von Rundstedt and Rommel had seemed to question the imminence of a second assault they had agreed that the defence of the threatened coast must not be weakened. Indeed they underlined the danger of a second landing there at the end of June, when they urged a change of policy. In an estimate of the situation on the 27th von Rundstedt had written that if strong forces assembled in the south-east of England were used for landings anywhere from the Somme down to the Seine, in conjunction with 'Army Group Montgomery's' probable thrust towards Paris, the German forces behind Fifteenth Army were 'too weak to face this'. The reader will not fail to realise how valuable it was that the Fifteenth Army was thus being held in idleness all this time while a few miles away the rest of Rommel's army group was being defeated in Normandy.

The Allies were now so strongly established in Normandy that they need fear nothing that the enemy might do to prevent their continuing the attack, but the German forces were stretched to the limit in their attempt to prevent a break-out from the lodgement area. By July the 16th their losses amounted to over 100,000 men. Such reinforcements as could be scraped together were coming forward slowly and painfully, under constant attack by the Allied air forces and further delayed by the sabotage of Resistance groups; moreover, many of the reinforcing formations were poor in quality, with insufficient training for battle and indifferent equipment. Thus while the Allied strength increased daily the German strength daily diminished. And neither at sea nor in the air were their efforts to hamper Allied operations having any significant effect.

It was a grim situation that von Kluge inherited and its difficulties were aggravated by Hitler's reorganisation of the command to which he was appointed at this critical juncture. The forces opposing the Allies were grouped in the Seventh Army facing the Americans on the west, and in Panzer Group West confronting the British on the east; both had been given new commanders. Command of the Seventh Army had been given to the SS General Hausser, in spite of Rommel's recommendation that General Kurt von der Chevallerie, commanding the First Army, should be transferred to the Seventh. The new commander of Panzer Group West, General Eberbach, an able soldier with much experience of armoured warfare, had latterly been serving in Germany as Inspector of Armoured Troops; he was a very different type from the volatile Geyr von Schweppenburg whom he replaced. Thus, of the previous commanders in the West only Rommel remained and he too was now to serve under a new commander-in-chief. In view of his somewhat restive acceptance of von Rundstedt's authority and his confidence in himself, he can hardly have been easily reconciled to his subordination to a new chief who had neither von Rundstedt's experience of French affairs and proved wisdom nor his own knowledge of the Normandy situation. He had submitted to Hitler's orders for the future control of operations but he had shown that he had no confidence in Hitler's judgment; he had no reason to feel any greater confidence in the leadership of his new commander-in-chief.

The briefing which von Kluge had had from Hitler and the staff of OKW before taking up his new appointment 'had convinced him that the events in the West were the result of mistakes and omissions on the part of commanders and troops'.[9] He had also been warned about Rommel's intransigence. Immediately after taking over from von Rundstedt on July the 3rd he had a meeting with Rommel. The only official record found is a paragraph in C-in-C West's war diary which reads:

> 'The most important points stressed by the new C-in-C West were as follows: Defence. The present line to be held at all costs (situation on the left wing still not clear). Our own position to be improved by advancing our line wherever this is really advantageous, that is to say, by attacking after the most careful preparation. Defence in depth to be built up with all available means.'

But according to Speidel (writing after the war) von Kluge 'spoke in the Berchtesgaden style without any first-hand knowledge of conditions at the front' and 'Rommel, raising his voice, protested against the unjustified criticisms by Hitler and the High Command'. The conversation became so heated that Speidel and the other staff officers were ordered to leave the room.[10] Two days later, on the 5th, Rommel sent von Kluge the following letter:

> 'I send you enclosed my comments on military events in Normandy to date. The rebuke which you levelled at me at the beginning of your visit, in the presence of my Chief of Staff and Ia, to the effect that I, too, "will now have to get accustomed to carrying out orders", has deeply wounded me. I request you to notify me what grounds you have for making such an accusation.'[11]

---

[9] Speidel, *Invasion 1944* (Stuttgart, 1949), p. 131. An English edition, entitled *We Defended Normandy*, appeared in 1951.
[10] Loc. cit., p. 132.
[11] *The Rommel Papers*, ed. B. H. Liddell Hart (1953), p. 481.

The memorandum enclosed was concerned with past events. Its final paragraph referred to Rommel's conviction that the German channels of command were unsatisfactory and that 'only the unified close-knit command of all three Services, on Montgomery's lines, will ensure final success'. Four days previously (on the 1st) he had already proposed that the naval and air forces in the West be put under his command.

After their first stormy meeting von Kluge made a two days' tour of inspection. According to Speidel, he had not been able to escape 'the overwhelming evidence of the facts, the unanimous views of all the military commanders, and the logic of the situation; he had temporarily been bemused by Hitler's phrases. He took back all his accusations.' [12] After his return he did not interfere with Rommel's control of the battle and they seem to have worked in harmony.

Two measures were put in train in order to implement Hitler's directives. The first was related to the order that *the present positions were to be held* (page 321 above).

On taking over the command of Panzer Group West General Eberbach discussed the situation with Rommel and two days later issued a directive. The Group's immediate task was to hold the existing front. At present this was only a line; what was needed was a system of defence in depth. He set out the principles on which this should be conducted and ordered that all troops and weapons should be dug in and all otherwise unemployed men of services behind the front should be used for the preparation of rearward defence positions. A week later he toured the front to stimulate a more active preparation of defences in depth.

The second order on which action was taken was Hitler's directive that: 'The most important tasks for the immediate future are (*a*) a flank attack to destroy the enemy forces thrusting through Baron towards the Orne . . .' (page 319). Planning for this followed but in its final shape the plan was not reported to OKW till July the 17th. There is no need to examine the plan in detail for it was overtaken by events and was never used, but certain features are worth noting because they show how completely unrealistic it was. It proposed to use all three armoured corps (comprising seven armoured divisions) and it named August the 1st as the target date by which infantry divisions must have completed their relief at the front; the attack was then to be made on a three-mile front between Grainville sur Odon and Juvigny, striking behind the British forces in the Caen area towards Luc sur Mer. In other words, it discounted the threat of the Americans to break out in the west and proposed to use almost all its armoured divisions to break into the British position in the east.

---

[12] Speidel, op. cit., pp. 132–133.

Von Kluge noted 'the execution of this attack is entirely dependent on the development of the situation in the Normandy battle area in the next few days and weeks'. That Rommel himself did not take this plan seriously is shown by the fact that when forwarding it to von Kluge on July the 15th Rommel sent forward next day a statement of his personal observations for the Führer. After rehearsing the losses incurred, the paucity and poor quality of the equipment of reinforcements, supply difficulties and the steady growth of Allied strength, he concluded that 'in these circumstances we must soon expect the enemy to succeed in breaking through our thinly held front, especially that of 7th Army, and to thrust deep into France . . . The [German] troops are fighting heroically everywhere, but the unequal struggle is nearing its end. It is in my opinion necessary to draw the proper conclusion from the situation. I feel it my duty as Commander-in-Chief of the Army Group to express this clearly.'

Two days later, on July the 17th, the motor car in which he was being driven was attacked by Allied aircraft. The driver was killed and Rommel was seriously injured and removed to hospital.

CHAPTER XV

OPERATION 'GOODWOOD'

'To engage the German armour in battle and "write it down" to such an extent that it is of no further value to the Germans as the basis of the battle. To gain a good bridgehead over the Orne through Caen and thus to improve our positions on the eastern flank . . .'
General Montgomery's instruction to General Dempsey before 'Goodwood'.

'To deliver a concentric attack with all available forces against the enemy that has thrust down towards the south between the Dives and Caen and at all costs to push him back northwards to his starting position.'
Field-Marshal von Kluge's order to Army Group B on the afternoon of 'Goodwood'.

GENERAL BRADLEY's First U.S. Army was continuing its hard and costly fight to reach St. Lô and ground to the west of that place, from which to break out of the lodgement area. In an effort 'to pick a soft point in the enemy's line' he had directed Major-General T. H. Middleton's VIII Corps to push down the coastal sector to Coutances, but the enemy had put up a strong defence and little progress had been made there or further inland when General Montgomery conferred with his army commanders on July the 10th. What they decided was embodied in a directive which General Montgomery issued that day. The broad policy was unchanged—to draw the main enemy forces into battle on the eastern flank and to fight them there, so that affairs on the western flank would proceed more easily. The fact that the enemy had been able to bring up some infantry reinforcements and to transfer Panzer Lehr Division to the American front, emphasised the need to stage British operations in the east so that they would prevent further transfers and thus have direct influence on events in the west. 'Having captured Caen . . . we must now gain depth and space in our lodgement area. We require space for manœuvre, for administrative purposes, and for airfields . . .' To the south of Caen, Second Army was to 'operate strongly in a southerly direction with its left flank on the Orne', and during its progress southwards was 'to retain the ability to be able to operate with a strong armoured force east of the Orne in the general area between Caen and Falaise'. The First U.S. Army was meanwhile to push on southwards speedily and in strength; on reaching Avranches one corps with one armoured division would be turned westwards into Brittany and 'as regards the remainder of the Army', plans should be made to 'direct a strong right wing in a wide sweep south of the *bocage* country towards successive objectives as follows:

(*a*) Laval–Mayenne
(*b*) Le Mans–Alençon'.[1]

The development of this programme in the next few days can be traced in contemporary records and although the intention was always clear to Dempsey and Bradley some of the phrases used were given a different interpretation at Shaef and so led to misunderstandings which were unfortunate.

On *July the 12th* Montgomery told the C.I.G.S. that Dempsey's operation would begin west of the Orne on the 15th and east of the river on the 17th, and he wrote to General Eisenhower asking for the fullest air support on the 17th.

On *the 13th* he sent a telegram to Eisenhower explaining his intentions more fully.

> 'Am going to launch a very big attack next week. Second Army begin at dawn on 16 Jul and work up to the big operation on . . . 18 Jul when VIII Corps with three armoured divisions will be launched to the country east of the Orne. Note change of date from 17 to 18 Jul. First Army launch a heavy attack with six divisions about five miles west of St. Lô on . . . 19 Jul. The whole weight of air power will be required for Second Army on 18 Jul and First Army on 19 Jul. Have seen Coningham and explained what is wanted.'

To this Eisenhower replied expressing his enthusiastic support but, reading his message with the knowledge of after events in mind, it seems doubtful if he fully appreciated the essential relationship of the British and American attacks as Montgomery saw it. In Montgomery's conception the main break-out attack was to be launched by Bradley on the 19th and, in order to make Bradley's task easier *by holding the enemy armour away from the American front*, Dempsey would attack the day before. But Eisenhower concluded his reply with the statement that Bradley could be counted on 'to keep his troops fighting like the very devil, twenty-four hours a day, *to provide the opportunity your armoured corps will need* . . .' [2]—which seems to view Montgomery's plan upside down.

On *the 14th* Montgomery signalled to Tedder emphasising the importance of the part which the air forces could play on the 18th and

---

[1] Repeating his directive of June 30th, quoted on page 309. See map, page 27.
[2] Author's italics. Quoted in F. C. Pogue, *The Supreme Command* (Dept. of the Army, Washington, D.C., 1954), p. 188.

EVOLUTION OF PLANS

19th of July, adding, 'if successful the plan promises to be decisive and it is therefore necessary that the air forces should bring their full weight to bear'—'the plan' being the plan for complementary attacks on both flanks.

On the same day Montgomery sent a long letter to the C.I.G.S. For the most part this was to explain more fully plans he had indicated in his directive of the 10th, but it was also to expose certain considerations which he had in mind in deciding that the British attack on the 18th should start with three armoured divisions in the van.

> '... The Second Army is now very strong; it has in fact reached its peak and can get no stronger. It will in fact get weaker as the manpower situation begins to hit us. Also, the casualties have affected the fighting efficiency of divisions; the original men were very well trained; reinforcements are not so well trained, and this fact is beginning to become apparent and will have repercussions on what we can do. The country in which we are fighting is ideal defensive country; *we* do the attacking and the Boche is pretty thick on the ground. I would say we lose three men to his one in our infantry divisions...
>
> But the Second Army has three armoured divisions, 7, 11, and Gds. These are quite fresh and have been practically untouched. A fourth armoured division will be complete in here by 27 July, i.e. the Canadian Armd. Div.
>
> Having got Caen, my left flank is now firm; my whole lodgement area is very secure and is held by infantry divisions. And available to work with the infantry I have eight independent armoured Bdes ... with a tank strength of over 1000 tanks.
>
> And so I have decided that the time has come to have a real "show down" on the Eastern flank, and to loose a corps of three armoured divisions in to the open country *about the Caen–Falaise road*.' [3]

As though anxious to make sure that his purpose was not misunderstood, his Military Assistant (Lieut-Colonel C. Dawnay) was sent over on the same day to explain Montgomery's intentions verbally to the Director of Military Operations at the War Office. He was instructed to make clear that:

> 'The real object is to muck up and write off enemy troops. On the eastern flank he [Montgomery] is aiming at doing the greatest damage to enemy armour. Caen–Falaise is the only place this can be done. If the proposed plan can be completed, next British move would be westwards in order to ring round Evrecy ... General Montgomery has to be very careful of what he does on his eastern flank because on that flank is the only British army

---

[3] Author's italics.

there is left in this part of the world. On the security and firmness of the eastern flank depends the security of the whole lodgement area. Therefore, having broken out in the country south-east of Caen, he has no intention of rushing madly eastwards and getting Second Army on the eastern flank so extended that that flank might cease to be secure. *All the activities on the eastern flank are designed to help the* [American] *forces in the west while ensuring that a firm bastion is kept in the east.*[4] At the same time all is ready to take advantage of any situation which gives reason to think that the enemy is disintegrating.'

This emphasis on Second Army's task did not involve any change of the directive to 'operate strongly in a southerly direction in the general area Caen–Falaise', but circumstances on the American front made it necessary to stress the importance of the first part of the plan which promised 'to be decisive'—namely the dual attack in the east on one day and in the west on the day following. For the American First Army was still making only slow progress. Because of this General Bradley had ordered the discontinuance of the push towards Coutances and had decided to launch the breakout attack (to be named 'Cobra') from ground just west of St. Lô; but St. Lô and the ground to the west of it was still held by the enemy. Since July the 3rd, when General Bradley's army had started to fight its way through the hedgerows and swamps north-west of St. Lô, it suffered approximately 40,000 casualties before St. Lô was taken. When captured at least two days would be needed to regroup forces before the Cobra attack could begin. It was now hardly possible for Cobra to follow immediately the attack on the 18th, so the German armour brought to battle south of Caen might well have to be held there for some days till the American attack could be launched. The first and most important task therefore was to win a stronger position from which to fight the German armour on the Caen flank.

On July 15th General Montgomery, realising this, gave Dempsey a written instruction that the immediate objectives of the armoured divisions' attack on the 18th (to be known as 'Goodwood' [5]) should be limited at the outset to the high ground south of Caen and should not seek to establish a division over twenty miles south of Caen in the Falaise area. The instruction is as follows:

'1. *Object of this operation*

To engage the German armour in battle and "write it down" to such an extent that it is of no further value to the Germans as a basis of the battle.

---

[4] Author's italics.
[5] A name identified in England with a famous race meeting.

To gain a good bridgehead over the Orne through Caen and thus to improve our positions on the eastern flank.

Generally to destroy German equipment and personnel, as a preliminary to a possible wide exploitation of success.

'2. *Effect of this operation on the Allied policy*

We require the whole of the Cherbourg and Brittany peninsulas.

A victory on the eastern flank will help us to gain what we want on the western flank.

But the eastern flank is a bastion on which the whole future of the campaign in N.W. Europe depends; it must remain a firm bastion; if it became unstable the operations on the western flank would cease.

Therefore, while taking advantage of every opportunity to destroy the enemy, we must be very careful to maintain our own balance and ensure a firm base.

'3. [Enemy divisions in area]

'4. *Operations of XII Corps and Canadian Corps—16th and 17th July*

Advantage must be taken of these to make the Germans think we are going to break out across the Orne between Caen and Amaye [sur Orne].

'5. *Initial operations of VIII Corps* [on 18th]

The three armoured divisions will be required to dominate the area Bourguébus–Vimont–Bretteville [sur Laize], and to fight and destroy the enemy, but armoured cars should push far to the south towards Falaise, spread alarm and despondency, and discover "the form".

'6. *II Canadian Corps*

While paragraph 5 is going on, the Canadians must capture [Faubourg de] Vaucelles, get through communications, and establish themselves in a very firm bridgehead on the general line Fleury [sur Orne]–Cormelles–Mondeville.

'7. *Later operations VIII Corps*

When 6 is done, then VIII Corps can "crack about" as the situation demands.

But not before 6 is done.

'8. *To sum up for VIII Corps*

Para 5
Para 7

Finally

Para 6 is vital.'

Shaef did not, apparently, learn of this definition of Goodwood's first objectives and, since Goodwood was to begin on the 18th though there was now little likelihood that Cobra could be launched on the 19th, Shaef began to think of Goodwood as a separate operation. Montgomery's request for such massive air support seems to have caused General Eisenhower and his airmen to expect more from Goodwood than Montgomery ever had in mind, and to look for a separate break-out from the British attack on the 18th. To Montgomery, however, the air support was needed for his immediate aim. In order to keep the German armour away from what Bradley had selected as 'a soft point' for the American break-out, Montgomery was going to attack the strongest point in the whole front, the place where the Germans' greatest strength had been assembled and their defence organised in depth, the place where they were most determined to stand firm. To make *any* progress at that point the Army would need the largest measure of help that the Air Force could give, and whether Goodwood gained much ground or little it would serve Montgomery's purpose if it engaged and severely damaged the German armour while Cobra was being launched away in the west. But, although he had made it clear to the C.I.G.S. and the War Office that Goodwood was not an attempt to break out eastwards, he hoped that it might appear so to the German command. It will be seen later that not only the German leaders mis-read his intentions.

Since the capture of Caen Second Army had been regrouped and the opposing Panzer Group West had been engaged in the long-deferred replacement of armour by infantry in their front line defences. The forces which now faced each other in the British sector were approximately as shown opposite.

At first glance it may seem that only in infantry had the British any considerable advantage, for in armour their three armoured divisions and seven armoured brigades were matched by the German six armoured divisions and three heavy tank battalions; but in fact British formations were fully up to strength, while all but the latest German arrivals (1st SS Panzer Division and four new infantry divisions) were reduced by losses that had not been made good.

Yet although the Germans had far fewer tanks they were disposed in depth, with well-prepared and advantageous positions, fortified by minefields and covered by numerous long-range anti-tank guns of III Flak Corps and multi-barrelled mortars of three werfer brigades, and it is not surprising that Montgomery sought the full weight of the air force in attacking so formidable a defence. Moreover, as was

OPPOSING FORCES

Opposing forces in the British Sector—mid July

(British and German corps held sectors approximately opposite each other)

BRITISH SECOND ARMY

(Reserve, VIII Corps—Guards, 7 and 11 Armd Divs)

Caumont–Rauray Sector	Odon Salient	Caen Sector	Lower Orne Sector
XXX Corps	XII Corps	II Cdn Corps	I Corps
49 Inf Div	15 Inf Div	2 Cdn Inf Div	3 Brit Inf Div
50 ,, ,,	43 ,, ,,	3 ,, ,, ,,	6 Airborne ,,
59 ,, ,,	53 ,, ,,		51 Inf ,,
8 Armd Bde	4 Armd Bde	2 Cdn Armd Bde	27 Armd Bde
33 ,, ,,	31 Tk ,,		1 S.S. ,,
	34 ,, ,,		4 ,, ,,
↓	↓	↓	↓
↑	↑	↑	↑
276 Inf Div	271 Inf Div	272 Inf Div	711 Inf Div (part)
2 Pz ,,	relieving	relieving	346 Inf Div
	10 SS Pz Div	1 SS Pz Div	16 GAF ,,
	277 Inf Div		21 Pz ,,
	102 SS Hy Tk Bn	101 SS Hy Tk Bn	
326 Inf Div	9 SS Pz Div	12 SS Pz Div	503 Hy Tk Bn
(*en route* from	(corps reserve)	(corps reserve)	(corps reserve)
Boulogne to			
relieve 2 Pz Div)			
XLVII Pz Corps	II SS Pz Corps	I SS Pz Corps	LXXXVI Corps

Distributed among sectors
{ III Flak Corps (three regts)
7, 8 and (most of) 9 Werfer Bdes
654 Hy A-Tk Bn (Jagdpanther) }

GERMAN PANZER GROUP WEST

learnt afterwards, the German Intelligence report of July 15th from 'Foreign Armies West' contained the following sentence:

> 'According to information derived from photographic reconnaissance of the lodgement area, the enemy command is planning to start a major operation across the Orne towards the south-east from about 17 July onwards. It is worthy of note that this date coincides with the period most favourable for new landing operations.'

And on the 17th, Army Group B's weekly report stated that the British Second Army's intention 'is to push forward across the

Orne in the direction of Paris'. The enemy was therefore prepared for the coming attack though mistaken as to its direction and final object.

Preliminary British operations began on the night of the 15th with attacks which extended across the whole front between the west of Caen and Tilly sur Seulles. XII Corps starting from the Odon bridgehead was first to secure a firm base on the road running south-east from Bougy through Evrecy, with a view to a subsequent advance towards Aunay sur Odon or Thury-Harcourt 'as the situation may indicate'; XXX Corps was meanwhile to secure the Noyers area and be prepared to exploit to the high ground north-east of Villers-Bocage 'if a favourable opportunity presents itself'. (Map page 275.)

From the night of the 15th till the launching of Goodwood on the 18th both corps fought hard and continuously against stout opposition and repeated counter-attacks by tanks and infantry. In XII Corps area on the left, Bougy and Gavrus were taken by the 15th Division; Esquay was entered but could not be held and after repeated attacks and counter-attacks remained in German hands. On their right 53rd Division captured Cahier but were heavily counter-attacked and only with difficulty maintained their gain. Westwards XXX Corps extended the battle front with 59th Division attacking Haut des Forges, Noyers and Landelle and 49th Division fighting for Vendes and its neighbourhood. Though the positions were everywhere improved territorial gains were inconsiderable. Haut des Forges was captured and held; Noyers was attacked again and again, but the enemy garrison from the 277th Division was reinforced and only the railway station and nearby Point 126 were finally held. The 49th Division, in spite of taking heavy casualties, captured Vendes in two days' fighting with the Germans' recently-arrived 276th Infantry Division, backed by tanks of the 2nd Panzer Division. While these were strongly engaged by the 49th, the 50th Division captured Hottot which through bitter fights had defied them for more than a month.

The most satisfactory result of these two days' hard fighting, which had gained but little ground at a cost of over 3,500 casualties, was the fact that the 1st SS, 10th SS and 2nd Panzer Divisions had been kept in the battle, and 9th SS Panzer Division from corps reserve had been called in to help with counter-attacks. The fighting had served 'to make the Germans think we are going to break out across the Orne between Caen and Amaye' and so to disguise the intention to attack on the east of the river.

For a number of reasons the Goodwood battle has especial interest. In the first place, the decision to gain as much advantage as possible from surprise by a hidden movement of armoured divisions eastwards and to attack in an unexpected quarter from the shallow and congested bridgehead east of the Orne, meant that the conduct of the battle would be largely conditioned by geography. (See map of battle plan facing page 350.)

No considerable body of armoured troops could be assembled without the enemy's knowledge, for the British position and approaches across the river and canal were closely watched and shelled by the Germans from vantage points outside the perimeter, and they had sufficient air reconnaissance to detect any unusual activity. Till the battle opened the three armoured divisions of VIII Corps which were to lead the advance had to wait in the country well to the west of the Orne; then they must follow each other across the river and canal by three double bridges between Ranville and the sea. They could not therefore enter the battle together but must follow into action one after the other. Moreover, though the artillery of I Corps, VIII Corps and II Canadian Corps could employ more than twice as many guns as the enemy opposing them in the early stages of the battle, in the later stage they, too, would be handicapped by geography. For the bulk of the artillery, particularly that supporting the main attack, had to be kept to the west of the river and canal till all the armoured divisions had crossed into the bridgehead and, as the battle progressed southwards, their effectiveness would be limited till they too could follow across the river.

A second distinctive feature of Goodwood was the unique volume of air support that was given by the largest force of both tactical aircraft and strategic bombers that was ever employed in direct support of ground forces in a single action.

Thirdly, the attack was to be made not where the enemy was weak but where he had prepared his strongest defence, in country which gave him almost everywhere the advantage of ground observation and fields of fire.

Finally, Goodwood is of particular interest because the conduct of the battle and its achievements were afterwards subjects of criticism and controversy and in due course it will be desirable to examine the reasons for both.

From Ranville, in the 'airborne' bridgehead, open cornfields stretch southwards between a chain of villages, backed by the Bréville ridge and the Bavent woods on the left, and the closely built up industrial suburbs of Caen on the right. Through the intervening farmlands run two embankments carrying railways from Caen to Troarn and to Vimont; south of the Vimont line the fields rise gradually towards high ground which forms the southern sky-line behind Bourguébus (five miles from Caen) and is crowned by woods near Garcelles-Secqueville. Falaise lies a further sixteen miles south of Bourguébus. Villages in the country hereabouts vary greatly in size but they are mostly stone built and bedded in strongly hedged orchards.

Holding the country to be attacked were three German infantry divisions (346th, 16th G.A.F. and 272nd) and two armoured divisions (21st and 1st SS Panzer); as a result of Hitler's orders the 12th SS Panzer Division was being moved to Lisieux to be in LXXXVI Corps reserve, for he now believed that the Allies' expected effort to break out eastwards from the Orne would coincide with a second landing between the Orne and the Seine. Under Eberbach's direction the front had been organised in considerable depth, strengthened by numerous defended villages and by commanding gun positions in the woods and hills on the east and to the south which framed the open country to be attacked. Second Army's estimate of about three hundred enemy guns seems to have been reasonably correct, but it did not mention the fact that there was in addition almost a similar number of heavy mortars, many of which were multi-barrelled. The German armoured divisions might employ, it was estimated, some 230 tanks.

Confronting these German forces would be the British I Corps and the Canadian II Corps, fighting to strengthen and extend the flanks, while VIII Corps struck southwards between them. The infantry of the flank corps would be supported by some 350 tanks; VIII Corps would have another 750 tanks. Put shortly General Dempsey's orders to his corps commanders for July the 18th were as follows:

I Corps was to establish the 3rd British Infantry Division in the east flank area of Bures–Troarn–St. Pair–Emiéville–Touffreville and to hold it against attack from the east and south-east.

VIII Corps, in the centre, was first to get the main bodies of its armoured divisions so firmly established in the areas of (*a*) Vimont, (*b*) Garcelles-Secqueville and (*c*) Hubert-Folie and Verrières that there could be no enemy penetration between them, and enemy armour brought against them would be defeated. Vigorous patrolling and exploitation would be carried out to the south-east, south and south-west, but their main bodies would not be moved further without reference to the army commander—for he must be satisfied that the Canadians had established behind the armour a very firm bridgehead south of Caen before any further advance by VIII Corps.[6]

II Canadian Corps on the right was to capture and hold Giberville and Faubourg de Vaucelles, to build bridges over the Orne at Caen and be prepared to advance its front to the line Cormelles–Fleury sur Orne and across the river to Eterville. The provision of bridges at Caen was 'a vital part of the whole operation'. To the

---

[6] See Montgomery's instructions, page 331 above, paras. 6 and 7.

46. General Hodges

47. General Patton

48. General Crerar

49. Lancaster bomber and Spitfire fighter

50. Cromwell and Sherman tanks advance south of Caen

51. Infantry with Churchill tanks attack in the cornfields

west of Caen, XII Corps would develop a thrust towards Amaye sur Orne, maintaining the illusion that Second Army intended to cross the Orne from that direction; while the actions of XXX Corps on the extreme right of the British sector were designed to improve its positions and to draw enemy reserves into the close country on its front and hold them there.

The measure by which it was hoped to counter-balance the strength of the enemy's position in the opening attack was the overwhelming support to be given by the Allied air forces, all of whom were to co-operate in a carefully worked out plan. Bomber Command was to lead off by attacking defended areas on both flanks of the corridor of open farmlands through which the armoured divisions of VIII Corps were to advance. On the left flank they were to bomb an area of nearly 1,000 acres (marked H on the battle plan) containing fortified villages which were to be captured by the British 3rd Division—Touffreville, Sannerville, Banneville, Guillerville and Manneville; for this task heavy cratering was allowable and 1,000- and 500-pound bombs were to be used. On the right flank another area of about 1,000 acres (marked A) containing the extensive steel-works at Colombelles, strongly defended and likely to be hard to capture, was also to be attacked by heavy bombs. Bomber Command would attack a third area of about 340 acres (marked M), which contained the strongly-defended village of Cagny, lying in the path of the armoured advance; for this area instantaneous fuses were to be used to minimise cratering.

Heavy bombers of the American Eighth Air Force were to attack three areas with 100-pound high-explosive bombs, 20-pound fragmentation bombs and incendiaries. One area of about 500 acres (marked I) lay on the extreme left, covering Troarn; the other two were to the south of the armoured attack where much of the enemy's artillery was sited on rising and wooded country—namely, about 2,000 acres (marked P) which included Soliers, Hubert-Folie and Bourguébus and some 500 acres (marked Q) between Bourguébus and Frénouville. So much for the tasks of the heavy bombers. It may be noted that the wooded area near Garcelles-Secqueville was not included though it was known to contain a large number of enemy guns.

The medium bombers of the American Ninth Air Force were to attack the enemy's forward positions (marked C, D, E, F and G) facing VIII Corps in the corridor through which the armoured divisions were to drive southwards. They would use 500-pound bombs against the villages of Cuverville, Giberville and Démouville, but on defences in the intervening country only 260-pound fragmentation bombs would be used so as to avoid cratering.

During and after the concentrated bombing of defined areas the fighter-bombers of 83 Group, with six wings of 84 Group under command, would attack a large number of pre-selected gun positions, strong-points and defence works throughout the country involved, bridges over the Dives and the Orne, and areas in which 21st, 1st SS and 12th SS Panzer Divisions were believed to be situated. During the battle they would give continuing support to the Army as requests for help were received. They would be kept in touch with the Army's needs through tentacles of the Air Support Signal Unit attached to each armoured brigade, division and corps. In addition, a Visual Control Post housed in a tank was attached to the armoured brigade of 11th Armoured Division. It carried an experienced Air Force Controller with a very-high-frequency wireless set which enabled him to communicate directly with fighters operating above. The two groups would also maintain armed reconnaissance over a wide area to observe and attack any movements of enemy troops to and from the battlefield. Fighter cover to prevent any interference by German aircraft, and escorts for the Bomber Command heavies were being provided by Air Defence of Great Britain, while more fighters from the Eighth and Ninth Air Forces escorted the American bombers and made attacks on the enemy's airfields. In all, over 4,500 Allied aircraft were to take part in this first day of Goodwood.

By nightfall on July the 17th the armoured divisions had reached positions from which they could cross to the east of the Orne at the times ordered; they had been travelling by night (two of them from the Bayeux–Tilly area) so that movement from west to east would not be revealed to the enemy. Headquarters of 11th Armoured Division and its infantry brigade (159th) had already crossed to the east of the river but its armoured brigade (29th) waited for darkness on the western side. About one o'clock on the morning of the 18th one infantry brigade of the 3rd Canadian Division, which was to attack the village of Giberville and the industrial areas of Colombelles and Mondeville, crossed the 'London' bridges near Bénouville. Then the armoured brigade of 11th Armoured Division followed and headed for its forming-up position east of Ranville. From then on troops of VIII Corps moved steadily eastwards by sign-posted roads and tape-marked tracks leading to and through the bridgehead. It was a fine morning, bright and clear, with practically no wind. An infantryman, waiting to cross one of the bridges, wrote down his impression:

> 'High in the sky and away to our left a faint and steady hum caught our attention and, as we watched, it grew into an insistent throbbing roar and the first aeroplanes appeared high up in the pale sky. Then the whole northern sky was filled with them as far as one could see—wave upon wave, stepped up one

above another and spreading out east and west till it seemed there was no room for any more. As the first passed overhead guns began to open up on our right and the wonderful hush of the morning was finally shattered. The bombers flew in majestically and with a dreadful, unalterable dignity, unloaded and made for home; the sun, just coming over the horizon, caught their wings as they wheeled. Now hundreds of little black clouds were puffing round the bombers as they droned inexorably to their targets and occasionally one of them would heel over and plunge smoothly into the huge pall of smoke and dust that was steadily growing in the south. Everyone was out of their vehicles now, staring in awed wonder till the last wave dropped its bombs and turned away. Then the guns took up in a steadily increasing crescendo the work which the bombers had begun.' [7]

The artillery had opened fire on the German anti-aircraft defences shortly before half past five and for the next forty-five minutes Lancasters and Halifaxes had bombed their targets. On each of areas A and H over 2,500 tons of bombs rained down and in the final ten minutes 650 tons fell on Cagny (area M). Guided by pathfinders, over 1,000 aircraft took part in these attacks; six were brought down by enemy flak before it was silenced by the bombardment.

As the heavy bombers finished, guns of H.M.S. *Roberts*, *Mauritius* and *Enterprise* and artillery of the three corps began to bombard all known German batteries within range and under their cannonade, which continued till 7.35 a.m., the leading divisions began to move forward through the minefields which stretched across the whole front, using passages which had previously been cleared. Over the country through which the armoured divisions were to advance hung a great cloud of dust and smoke, caused by the heavy bombing. When the medium bombers of the Ninth Air Force had arrived at seven o'clock about a quarter of them found their targets (areas C, D, E, F and G) so obscured by dust that they had to turn back without bombing; so too did some of the Eighth Air Force Liberators who went to attack area I on the eastern flank. Before the bombers turned for home fighters and fighter-bombers of 83 and 84 Groups began their pre-arranged attacks on batteries in the Dives area, on guns and mortars near Garcelles-Secqueville and le Mesnil-Frémentel, and on troop positions and bridges in the Orne valley. Then they took up their day-long obligation to give close support for the advance. At half past eight Liberators of the Eighth Air Force began attacking areas P and Q with 100-pound and 20-pound fragmentation bombs and continued in relays until 9.30 a.m. With their action the heavy bomber effort for the day was concluded.

At 7.45 the artillery had opened again all across the front and the

---

[7] Quoted in L. F. Ellis, *Welsh Guards at War* (1946), p. 175.

attacking troops went forward behind their barrages and timed concentrations. Though troops of all three corps were engaged simultaneously it will be easier to appreciate the course of the battle if the central operations of VIII Corps are first described and afterwards what happened in the fighting on the flanks, by I Corps on the left and by II Canadian Corps on the right.

Behind a barrage fired by some 200 guns (while some 200 more fired concentrations on selected sites) the 11th Armoured Division started from just south of the minefield belt between Escoville and Ste. Honorine; the armoured brigade (29th) was on the left and the infantry brigade (159th) on the right. The former's first task was to take the le Mesnil-Frémentel area about three miles ahead and beyond the first railway line; and then to capture the higher ground about Verrières and Rocquancourt some five miles further on. The infantry brigade, with the armoured reconnaissance regiment, was meanwhile to clear Cuverville and Demouville and then join the armoured brigade on its final objective. The advance went well. The enemy seemed to be completely demoralised by the bombardments and many gave themselves up to the oncoming tanks. But the barrage moved rather too quickly for the leading tanks (3rd Battalion, Royal Tank Regiment) and those following (2nd Fife and Forfar Yeomanry) were soon pressing on their heels. When the first railway was reached at about half past eight and the barrage paused, the gunners were asked to delay its resumption for twenty minutes but even so the tanks had not all crossed the railway when it started to move forward again. Yet the advance continued and more of the enemy were overrun and rounded up by the motor companies. Just after nine o'clock the barrage ended; by then most of the field guns had reached the limit of their range till they could cross the river and move forward. Leaving the motor battalion (8th Battalion, The Rifle Brigade) to clear up le Mesnil-Frémentel with the help of flails and AVREs, and the 23rd Hussars covering Cagny on the flank, the first two armoured regiments pushed on to the second railway embankment and their leading tanks were over it by about 9.30 a.m. The infantry brigade had already reached Cuverville and they cleared it by ten o'clock; their next task was to capture Démouville.

So far all had gone very well but now the situation was changing. The flow of traffic over the bridges and southwards towards the battle front was getting behind schedule and the enemy was recovering from the bombardment and offering stiffer resistance. Much of the more heavily bombed area had been passed and, although Cagny was reduced to ruins, the '88' guns which defended it and Tiger tanks in the Cagny woods had escaped destruction, as had the defences of Emiéville and other gun areas to the south.

Leading units of the Guards Armoured Division were halted

about half a mile behind the tail of 29th Armoured Brigade at about 9.45 a.m. and, in turn, the first tanks of 7th Armoured Division, using another bridge, were baulked by the rear Canadian brigade held up by tenacious resistance at Colombelles, and when they got forward became mixed up with the Guards.

The resulting congestion was already apparent to VIII Corps headquarters and the Guards were ordered to '. . . get the armoured brigade down to Vimont as fast as you can . . .'; but the opposition was also stiffening. Ahead of the 2nd Armoured Grenadier Guards, who were leading their brigade, could be seen the rear squadron of the Fife and Forfar Yeomanry and the whole of the 23rd Hussars having a costly fight with German '88's and tanks; about twelve Shermans were already in flames. The Hussars were urgently needed to join the rest of their brigade now debouching beyond the Vimont railway line, but it was impossible for them to do so till the Guards arrived in sufficient strength to take responsibility for the dangerous left flank.

As soon as the Grenadiers crossed the first railway, with the 1st Armoured Coldstream Guards following on their left, they were heavily engaged from the flank by detachments of tanks and anti-tank guns disposed between Emiéville and Cagny, and the armoured brigade was soon forced to modify its plan. While the Grenadiers attacked Cagny, and the Coldstream moved to the right in order to pass behind the village and advance on Vimont along the line of the railway, the 2nd Armoured Reconnaissance Welsh Guards were to seek a way through the German defence screen somewhere near Emiéville. These manœuvres inevitably added to the congestion and delay, for the Coldstream found they had to make a long detour round le Mesnil-Frémentel which took them across the intended path of the 7th Armoured Division. Thus it was nearly half past twelve before the 23rd Hussars could leave to join the two regiments of the 29th Armoured Brigade who had been fighting for some time on the slopes of the Bourguébus ridge.

At half past nine a counter-attack by the 21st Panzer Division had been set in motion from the south-east and, soon afterwards, the 1st SS Panzer Division was ordered to launch a converging attack from the south, for the enemy was determined to hold the Cagny area, fearing that its loss would enable the British to drive a wedge between LXXXVI Corps on the east flank and I SS Panzer Corps in the country south of Caen. Both attacks were some time in getting under way. The 21st Panzer, with the 503rd Heavy Tank Battalion under its command, had started the day with about a hundred tanks, thirty-nine of them Tigers, but the Bomber Command attack on the left flank (area H) had destroyed or damaged so many that it was nearly midday before the survivors could be made fit to fight.

Most of the 1st SS Panzer Division had been in positions to the south of the bombed areas, and two battle groups, with forty-six tanks and some assault guns, were available to attack. They advanced against the Guards and the 11th Armoured Division at many points, but complete lack of air cover prevented their making the concentrated effort necessary to regain the Caen–Troarn road, as had been ordered.

Meanwhile comparatively few of the 11th Armoured Division's tanks were across the second railway. There they were in full view of the enemy's guns and mortars on the rising ground before them; the Eighth Air Force bombs (intended for areas P and Q) had been too widely dispersed to be really effective. The two armoured regiments of 29th Armoured Brigade, alone south of the railway, suffered heavily as they tried to fight their way up the slopes and by midday were virtually pinned down. As they strove to get forward a violent battle continued all afternoon, with German battle groups attacking from the la Hogue–Tilly la Campagne area, and the garrisons of Four, Soliers, Hubert-Folie, Bras and Bourguébus adding to the weight of fire. Our artillery engaged many targets, the medium guns, with the aid of air observation planes and Forward Observation Officers, shooting to the limit of their range. Numerous formations of Second Tactical Air Force fighters scoured the countryside, bombing and rocketing any enemy tanks they could see, sometimes within half a mile of our own. They answered many calls from the army and nine separate Typhoon attacks were made between two and five o'clock. To some extent they were handicapped when the air force officer in the Sherman tank of the 29th Armoured Brigade's Visual Control Post was wounded, but the young tank commander took over and, when he was unable to control a strike, the aircraft were directed to an alternative target by the Group Control Centre. Much damage was done to the enemy but, though some armoured cars eluded the opposition and penetrated the German defences on the high ground for several miles southwards, the main attack was unable to get forward to capture the villages which served as strongpoints in the enemy's line. Further back, the 11th Armoured Division's infantry brigade, supported by the tanks of the reconnaissance regiment (2nd Northamptonshire Yeomanry), had taken Démouville (and 250 prisoners) in the early afternoon; the infantry then moved on to occupy positions round le Mesnil-Frémentel for the night.

While the Welsh Guards had been trying unsuccessfully to force their way through the opposition in the Emiéville woods, the rest of the Guards Division had concentrated on Cagny and neighbouring enemy positions. The 2nd Armoured Grenadiers, with infantry of the 32nd Guards Brigade, were well into the village by six o'clock and had cleared it completely about an hour and a half later. Squadrons of the 2nd Armoured Irish Guards, by-passing Cagny on the north, had secured a footing on the ridge to the east after hard fighting at close quarters with the 21st Panzer Division; but the Coldstream, abreast of the railway line, were eventually brought to a halt by well-positioned anti-tank guns in le Poirier and Frénouville.

The 7th Armoured Division had had a frustrating time. Owing to the persistent congestion on the east bank of the Orne, its leading unit (5th Battalion, Royal Tank Regiment) was not wholly clear of the bridges until midday, and was then slowed by other troops moving in the corridor. Despite all its own efforts, pressure from the corps commander and the exertions of his staff, the division had only succeeded in getting one armoured regiment into action south of the Caen–Vimont railway before nightfall; this had arrived too late and was not strong enough to affect the issue of the day.

On the left flank the British 3rd Infantry Division of I Corps, with a brigade (152nd) of the 51st Division under command and supported by the 27th Armoured Brigade, moved forward at 7.45 a.m. behind a barrage and concentrations. They met a varied reception. At some places the bombing had been most effective—Sannerville and Banneville la Campagne had been well hit and their dazed defenders could offer little resistance; both were in British hands soon after midday. Touffreville on the other hand was on the fringe of Bomber Command's area H, and though some of the over-spill had fallen there it held out till the evening. There was heavy fighting too in the mined and broken country to the south of the Bavent Wood, through which the road runs down to Troarn. Attacking by that route and from Sannerville, the division found Troarn to be still strongly defended and when night fell our troops were halted for reorganisation about a mile short of the town. South of the Troarn–Caen road there was also a stiff fight in the area between Manneville and Guillerville against German infantry of 711th Division, hurried down from the coast on bicycles to counter-attack with the support of some Tiger tanks. It was midnight when both villages were cleared and only Emiéville and Troarn remained to the enemy. Most of the fighting on this eastern flank had been with the German 346th Infantry Division and the 16th G.A.F. Division, a large number of whom had been taken prisoner; it had cost the British 500 casualties and 18 tanks.

On the western flank, meanwhile, II Canadian Corps had been having a hard and not uneventful fight. Starting from near Ranville at 7.45 a.m., the leading brigade (8th) of the 3rd Canadian Infantry Division with support from the 2nd Canadian Armoured Brigade had moved against the factory area of Colombelles. The greatest density of bombs had fallen on the eastern half of the area and the ground towards Giberville, and good progress was made on the left till Giberville was reached; but by the time that the Canadians fought their way to the town and to the industrial Colombelles area nearer the river the infantry of 21st Panzer Division who were holding it had had three hours in which to recover from the early bombing. A second brigade of 3rd Canadian Division (9th) joined in the fight and like beaters at a shoot had to work methodically through the wrecked buildings and large bomb craters, where parties of the enemy held out well into the night. The tenacity with which they were fighting is illustrated by the following reported messages from a German battalion fighting grimly in the ruins of Colombelles:

> 8.00 p.m. 'Shall I withdraw?'
> 8.09 p.m. 'Enemy already broken through in encircling movement.'
> 8.19 p.m. 'Enemy has cut off this battalion.'
> 8.20 p.m. 'Battalion HQ surrounded. Long live the Führer.'

Enemy counter-attacks near Giberville at dusk were fought off and the town was cleared by nine-thirty, 200 prisoners being taken. Meanwhile a patrol of the division's third brigade (7th), guided by a member of the French Resistance, had made its way across one of the damaged bridges in Caen and seized a foothold on the other side; the rest of the battalion soon followed and began driving the recently arrived troops of 272nd Division out of the factories and railway yards on the south bank of the Orne. By midnight they were joined by troops of the 9th Canadian Brigade and meanwhile the Canadian engineers got quickly to work building bridges.

On the right of the corps sector the 2nd Canadian Division began crossing the Odon that evening. One brigade (4th) attacked Louvigny and had cleared half of the place by nightfall; a second brigade (5th) then got a battalion across the Orne into the western part of Vaucelles by a kapok footbridge, while the rest waited to cross as soon as there were bridges to take them.

The final outcome of the battle was yet to be decided and information as to the exact positions was still uncertain. Inevitably, some of the reports received at headquarters were inaccurate and on this day General Montgomery must have been misinformed about the true state of affairs, for at 4.20 that afternoon he sent the following message to the C.I.G.S.:

> 'Operations this morning a complete success. The effect of the air bombing was decisive and the spectacle terrific. VIII Corps advanced at 0730 hours. Present situation as follows.
> 11th Armd Div reached Tilly 0760 [Tilly la Campagne]—Bras 0663. 7th Armd Div passed area Démouville 1067 and moving on La Hogue 0960. Guards Armd Div passed Cagny

and now in Vimont. 3rd Div moving on Troarn. Have ordered the armd car regts of each div, supported by armed recce regts, to reconnoitre towards and secure the crossings over Dives between Mézidon and Falaise. Canadians fighting hard in Vaucelles.

Have issued a very brief statement for tonight's 9 p.m. B.B.C. news and am stopping all further reports today.

Situation very promising and it is difficult to see what the enemy can do just at present. Few enemy tanks met so far and no (repeat no) mines.'

This report was unfortunately inaccurate and misleading. The 11th Armoured Division had not reached either Tilly la Campagne or Bras; the few troops of the 7th Armoured who had passed by Démouville still had four miles to go before they could reach la Hogue, and the Guards were never within three miles of Vimont. Whoever this information came from must have failed to realise that, since about eleven o'clock in the morning, no new ground had been won in the south.

Casualties of I, VIII and II Canadian Corps were approximately 1,500 of all ranks and some 200 tanks. At that cost the small bridgehead east of the Orne from which Goodwood had been launched had been enlarged and strengthened on the east and extended for six miles to the south. The whole of Caen and its industrial suburbs were now comfortably within the British front and, when bridges were completed, would give new freedom of access to more open country in the south.

The opening air bombardment had made possible the quick conquest of the enemy's forward defences, but the handicap of cramped conditions at the Orne crossings and congestion in the initial bridgehead had not been overcome; only the 11th Armoured Division and the infantry divisions on the extreme flanks had been able to follow up the bombers before the enemy had recovered their power to fight back strongly. The 11th Armoured on its own could not be expected to get as far south as General Dempsey had hoped.

But if in that respect it had been a disappointing day for the British it had been a bad day for the German command. Von Kluge had left at nine o'clock to visit his First Army headquarters at Poitiers, two hundred miles away. At that time Eberbach had reported the opinion that 'it is not yet the anticipated British offensive that we are dealing with, but an attempt by the enemy to provide himself with a suitable jumping-off position for the offensive that may be expected in two or three days . . . The British are clearly anxious to avoid heavy losses which would result from a major attack launched from the present bridgehead.' But as subsequent reports were received, Panzer Group West's war diary noted that the situation was 'getting more serious every hour'. Later in the day von

Kluge, kept in touch by telephone, had ordered that in no circumstances would the enemy's salient be merely sealed off; Panzer Group West, by 'concentric' counter-attacks, was to 'push the enemy back across the line from Caen to Troarn', for he would not tolerate any gain by the enemy of new ground east of the Orne. Yet none of the ground which had been lost after the morning bombardment and the following attack had been regained; 21st Panzer and 1st SS Panzer Divisions had lost 109 tanks 'under ceaseless air attacks', and when the day ended Eberbach was trying to establish a new front running roughly from Troarn through Frénouville and Soliers to about Maltot. Moreover, so serious was the British threat that von Kluge had sought permission from OKW not only to recall 12th SS Panzer Division from Lisieux but also to bring 116th Panzer Division from the Seine to reinforce the troops opposing the British advance. During the night infantry, driven out of other places that had been lost, were sent to buttress the defenders of Troarn, Emiéville and other 'hedge-hogs' (such as Four, Bras, Soliers, Hubert-Folie and Bourguébus) and spent the night feverishly digging themselves in.

Our air forces were out that night to hinder movement and harass the enemy, but much of the country was blanketed by mist and they saw little. For once enemy aircraft made a night raid near Ranville. It caused many casualties among the personnel of the headquarters and administrative echelons of 11th Armoured Division, and among relief tank crews both for them and for the Guards Armoured Division. But they failed to hit the bridges and during the night the remaining units of VIII Corps crossed the Orne. Among these was the belated infantry brigade of 7th Armoured Division.

When dawn broke on the 19th, infantry of the 3rd British Division were already working their way through the orchards about Troarn. The place was well defended, with outlying, well-sited infantry positions surrounding it. Four successive attacks, supported by tanks, were launched against it during the day but none succeeded and late in the evening the action was broken off and defensive positions were taken up overlooking the town. Meanwhile all attempts to take Emiéville also failed, but with Banneville la Campagne and the Manneville–Guillerville area in 3rd Division's hands the country between Troarn and Emiéville was strongly guarded.

Apart from active reconnaissance the depleted armoured divisions of VIII Corps spent the morning reorganising for further action. At midday General O'Connor met his divisional commanders and the attacks were resumed that afternoon.

On the left the infantry brigade (32nd) of the Guards Armoured Division advanced and captured le Poirier, but Frénouville proved to be very strongly held. Air support was arranged and it was decided to attack early next morning. The armour improved its position east of Cagny but could make no real progress against the strong anti-tank line that faced it.

At five o'clock in the afternoon, when its infantry brigade was at last beginning to reach the Démouville–Grentheville area, the 7th Armoured Division set out to take Four and Bourguébus. Four was eventually captured but Bourguébus, though at one time almost encircled, was still in enemy hands at nightfall.

The 11th Armoured Division began attacks on Bras at about four o'clock, and after a first effort had failed a second succeeded; the garrison, an infantry battalion of 1st SS Panzer Division, was practically wiped out and many were taken prisoner. Subsequently, after suffering heavy losses from Tiger tanks and '88's, the 11th Armoured Division captured Hubert-Folie. The infantry brigade then took over the defence of both places.

Divisions of II Canadian Corps had been early on the move. The 3rd Canadian Division were engaged all day in clearing up small rearguard parties that were found in the ruins of Vaucelles. Snipers, mines, booby traps and mortars made mopping up a slow business but Cormelles was also taken and cleared. Meanwhile the 2nd Canadian Division advanced through the country between the Falaise road and the Orne and, when the completion of bridges made it possible to bring enough troops forward, Fleury sur Orne was captured and the high ground about Point 67. As the infantry dug in for the night the enemy counter-attacked but was thrown back. Just before dark Ifs was attacked and by the early hours of the 20th was securely occupied.

Poor visibility had handicapped air operations throughout the day though some 300 sorties had been flown; occasionally a few German fighters emerged from the clouds for a few minutes and once eighteen Messerschmitts succeeded in machine-gunning a brigade headquarters—without hitting anyone. Indeed the very few German air sorties were entirely ineffective.

Little further advance had been made for it had been necessary to consolidate the ground won. Every step had been contested by the enemy and our hold on ground won had been tested by local counter-attacks as a matter of course; but Eberbach had decided by midday that it was now impossible to carry on the general attempt to rescue lost territory; all he could do was strengthen the hold on his present position. The 16th G.A.F. Division had been practically destroyed and the 21st Panzer Division reduced to the equivalent of about one battalion; the units of the returning 12th SS Panzer Division had begun arriving early in the morning and had taken over the defences opposite Cagny; and Eberbach had ordered both XLVII Panzer and II SS Panzer Corps to send reinforcements to I SS Panzer Corps. Two battalions of tanks and a battalion of panzer grenadiers, a reconnaissance battalion and a battalion of artillery were being moved to the threatened front. The 116th Panzer Division was already on the way to the Falaise area.

On the 18th, when Goodwood began, the first American troops were entering St. Lô and on the 19th the ruined town was fully occupied. As planned at that time Cobra, the attempt to break through in the west, should now be launched on the 21st. By the 19th it was clear that the main, underlying purpose of Goodwood was being realised—to hit the enemy hard in his most susceptible place in order to attract his armour there and so weaken his capacity to resist the American effort to break out in the west. For the German command's attention was still being largely focused on what they mistakenly regarded as the Allies' main intention—to break out on the east. Because of that threat they were hurriedly moving armoured troops eastwards on the Caumont to Caen front; because of that, they were moving the 116th Panzer Division westwards from the Fifteenth Army, notwithstanding their fear that a second Allied landing impended. It is indeed clear from German war diaries of the time that although the American concentration was seen to threaten a large-scale attack in the west the higher commanders were mainly preoccupied with what they regarded as the more dangerous British attack on the Caen front. But Goodwood's immediate purpose—'to gain a good bridgehead over the Orne through Caen and thus to improve our position on the eastern flank . . . to engage the German armour in battle and "write it down" to such an extent that it is of no further value to the Germans as a basis of the battle'—this was only partially achieved. We had indeed enlarged our bridgehead across the Orne and greatly improved our tactical position on the eastern flank, and we had inflicted serious damage on the enemy's armour. But we had not gained as much ground as we hoped and the German armour, though considerably 'written down', still remained a strong force which enclosed the eastern flank ready to contest any further advance. Realising this, General Dempsey saw that the immediate task was to secure the position won and meantime to give his armour time to refit. That afternoon (the 19th) he ordered that I Corps would remain responsible for the left flank and should be joined as soon as possible by the 49th Infantry Division and the 33rd Armoured Brigade from XXX Corps. VIII Corps must complete the capture of Bourguébus and having done so would hold its front with infantry till relieved by II Canadian Corps. While the armour of VIII Corps was refitting (they had lost 271 tanks though many would be recovered and repaired) the corps would be reinforced by an armoured brigade (the 4th) and its front would be narrowed. Then II Canadian Corps would take over Bras and Hubert-Folie and be responsible for all the country westwards to the

Orne, establishing a forward division to the west of Bourguébus on the Verrières ridge. West of the Orne XII Corps would conform with II Canadian Corps' operations, working forward from Hill 112 to Maltot and the nearby Point 59, while further west still XXX Corps was also to work forward.

The 20th of July broke with low threatening cloud that prevented flying operations all morning. On the left front the infantry brigade (32nd) of the Guards Armoured Division took Frénouville with little opposition, 12th SS Panzer Division having thinned out its garrison during the night. The neighbouring country was now firmly held but all the division's attempts to advance towards Vimont were stopped by anti-tank guns and no further progress was made in that direction.

On the right of the Guards the 7th Armoured Division occupied Bourguébus at first light, finding it had been abandoned by all but a solitary Tiger tank. They pushed forward westwards of Bourguébus to the road to St. André sur Orne and from Beauvoir Farm at Point 72 tried to seize Verrières but found it too strongly held to rush with a small force. By now II Canadian Corps had taken over Bras and Hubert-Folie and were waiting to attack the Verrières ridge, so 7th Armoured Division were withdrawn to positions of observation and support east of the Falaise road.

The real focus of the battle on that day (July the 20th) was on the front of the II Canadian Corps. The 2nd Canadian Division, and particularly the 6th Brigade, waited some hours for 7th Armoured Division to get clear in order to attack the Verrières ridge. The delay was unfortunate for the Germans were now prepared for a renewal of the attack at that point. Verrières itself was being hele by troops of the German 272nd Division; in support were the 1st SS Panzer Division with some 70 tanks and, under command, a battle group of 2nd Panzer Division hurriedly transferred from the Noyers–Caumont front. In all, probably some 100 tanks were deployed against the Canadians. Moreover artillery of II SS Panzer Corps was able to be used against the Canadians from the country west of the Orne. The men of a division which had not been in action since the Dieppe raid in 1942 were to be severely tested.

Four battalions from the 2nd Canadian Division's 6th Brigade with two squadrons of tanks, supported by the corps artillery and Typhoons of 83 Group, went forward to attack in the early afternoon; they were Les Fusiliers Mont-Royal, The South Saskatchewan Regiment, and The Queen's Own Cameron Highlanders of Canada, with The Essex Scottish Regiment from the 4th Brigade under command. The road from Hubert-Folie to St. André was reached and two farms on it were occupied. On the left the advance on Verrières was continuing when a counter-attack by tanks and infantry came in from the left flank. The advanced troops were cut off and the remainder driven back to the road, which was held with difficulty. Meanwhile, on their right the attacking troops had reached their objective further along the ridge, which runs away to the south-west, and their anti-tank guns were moving up when they in turn were counter-attacked before the gunners could put the trails down. A confused fight followed and gradually the Canadians were again driven back to the road. Further to the right St. André sur Orne and St. Martin de Fontenay were captured and held under heavy shell-fire from across the Orne, but only after bitter fighting and a succession of counter-attacks had been beaten off. Panzer Group West's war diary recorded that day that all the artillery of II SS Panzer Corps was being directed on St. André. German opposition was not the only thing with which the Canadians had to contend. A violent thunder-storm broke over the battlefield in the late afternoon and soon turned the powdery soil into mud. Wireless communication became difficult, movement was slowed and air support greatly hampered. The early morning cloud had only cleared for a few hours before the storm cut short air attacks which British and Canadian squadrons were making on guns, infantry and tanks to the south.

Next morning—the 21st—the enemy began early to attack the Canadian position on the east bank of the Orne from Point 67 to St. André, and on the by-road across the front which had been the scene of such hard fighting the day before. Four separate attacks were beaten off by half past ten that morning with the help of the artillery, and of the 2nd Canadian Armoured Brigade which had now been put under the command of the 2nd Division and made the German tanks pay heavy toll. In the afternoon a further enemy attack broke through the road defence near Point 72, and tanks and infantry fought their way forward almost to the outskirts of Ifs. A fresh Canadian battalion, supported by tanks on either flank and preceded by a creeping barrage, drove them back up the hill; the lateral road was reached once more and the gap again filled.

As darkness fell the enemy attacked yet again and some tanks got into parts of the two roadside farms. But there was no break-through and elsewhere the attack was beaten off and the Canadians' hold on the road was maintained.

A point had been reached at which neither side was anxious to launch a major attack until they had reorganised, and though fighting flared up again at intervals during the next few days Operation Goodwood was ended. That evening (the 21st) General Montgomery issued a new directive. This reaffirmed the policy already laid down and stressed the fact that '... we must improve and retain firmly our present good position on the eastern flank and be ready to take quick action on that flank ... the enemy must be led to believe that we

THE GOODWOOD BATTLE PLAN

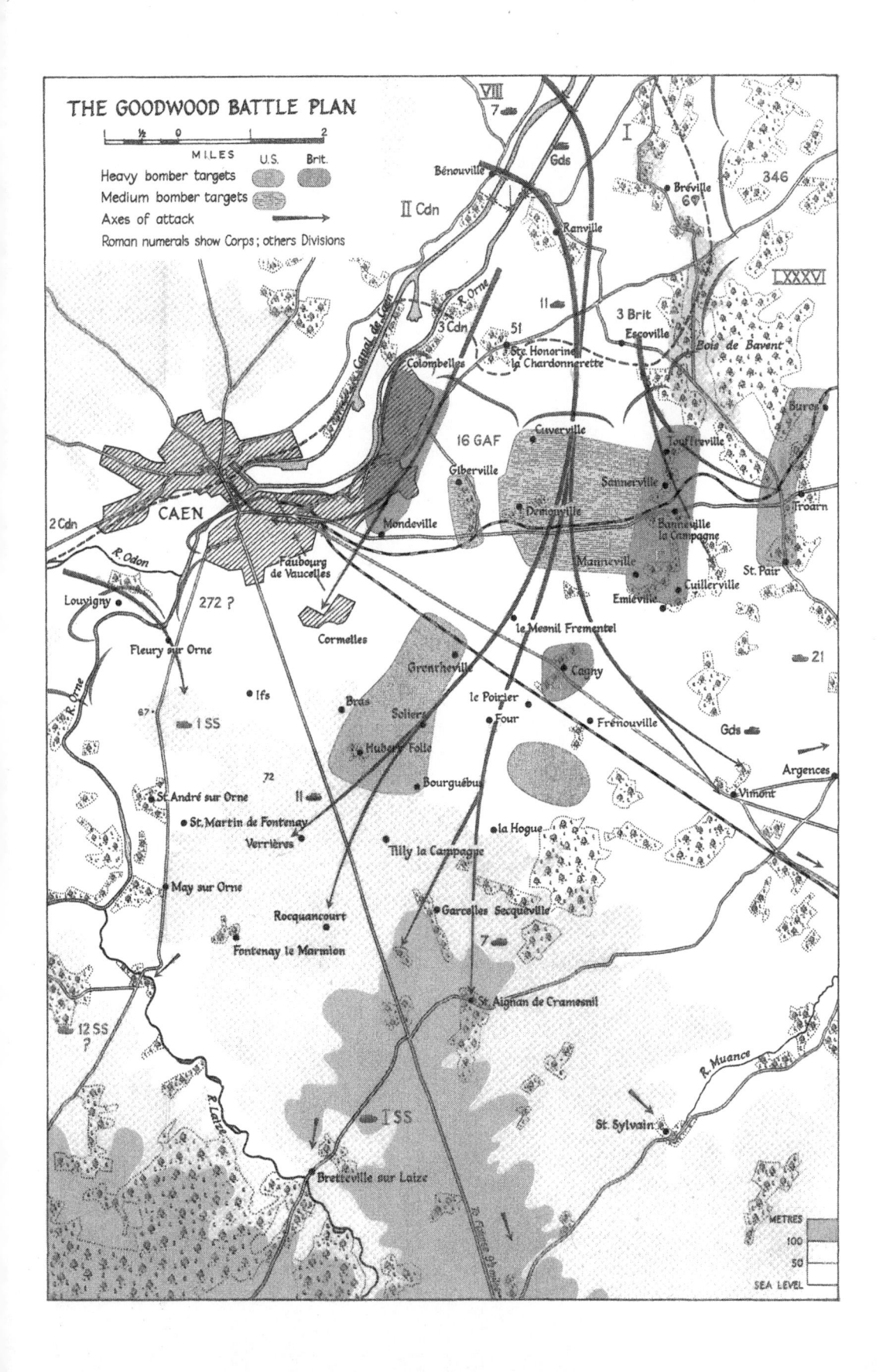

MILES
½ 0 1 2

          U.S. Brit.
Heavy bomber targets
Medium bomber targets
Axes of attack
Roman numerals show Corps; others Divisions

contemplate a major advance towards Falaise and Argentan, and he must be induced to build up his main strength to the east of the river Orne, so that our affairs on the western flank can proceed with greater speed'. For though the Americans were now ready to launch Cobra the break in the weather made its essential air support impossible. Neither the enemy nor the public at home and in America knew that General Bradley waited only for good weather to launch the decisive attack near St. Lô, but General Montgomery knew, and he knew how important it was to hold the German armour in the east.

Though Goodwood had achieved its main purpose in that it had greatly improved our position on the eastern flank and had kept the enemy's armoured divisions fighting there, it had not attained all that was intended. As pointed out already the task set was a very difficult one. It is indeed open to question whether the plan to make the main attack from the bridgehead, with three armoured divisions in the van, was a sound one, but this can be considered later when the conduct of the Overlord campaign as a whole is reviewed. Meanwhile it must be recognised that in some respects execution fell short of intention. (Final situation shown overleaf.)

First, in regard to air support and fire plans. The preliminary air bombardment, though faithfully carried out, did not prove equally valuable everywhere. The Royal Air Force heavy bomber attack on the two flanks fulfilled its purpose but the bombing of the Cagny area did not prevent its defence from holding out till evening. The American Eighth Air Force bombing was less effective. A large proportion of the 13,000 100-lb bombs and 75,000 20-lb fragmentation bombs which were used failed to reach their target areas, some falling in various places as far south as Bretteville sur Laize. It is true that in this region were some of the enemy's main gun positions and immediate armoured reserves, but lightly-spread attacks by such small bombs did little more than warn the defenders that a ground attack was about to follow.

The Army counter-battery work could not be expected to silence all the enemy's guns in well-prepared and largely hidden positions, particularly those in his strongest gun areas among the woods around Garcelles-Secqueville almost out of range of our heaviest guns. Since it had been foreseen in the early planning that 'in this area the armour will meet with considerable gun opposition which it will be difficult to neutralise' it seems to have been a mistaken policy which used 500- to 1,000-lb bombs to facilitate the first stage of the advance but nothing heavier than the 100-lb bombs dropped by the Eighth Air Force against the enemy's guns.

But the most immediate reason for the slowing down of the armoured advance was the congestion which was allowed to develop in the Cagny area. The original plan had been to 'mask' Cagny while the armoured advance continued but, once armour of both the 11th and Guards Divisions became deeply involved there, the momentum of the advance was soon lost and the enemy was allowed to focus forces for defence and counter-attack. While tanks of several regiments were milling about round the Cagny area, thousands of vehicles of the armoured divisions were crossing the river and canal and moving forward in the bridgehead. Descriptions of the resulting confusion provide unedifying reading and show that the carefully prepared traffic control plan was unable to ensure that approaches to the corridor were kept open. It is also questionable whether it would not have been better to use the infantry brigade and armoured reconnaissance regiment of 11th Armoured Division to back up the armour, instead of committing them at the outset to the clearing of Cuverville and Démouville. But if mistakes are recognised frankly they should not be allowed to obscure the fact that the armour had been asked to break a strong defence, organised in considerable depth, when its more normal rôle would have been to exploit a gap that had first been made by infantry.

In England and America during July some dissatisfaction had been expressed at the slow progress made by the Allies in Normandy. It was natural that this should be so. High hopes that had been justified by the successful landings and the early days of the campaign were inevitably deflated when the smallness of the ground subsequently recovered in France was thoughtlessly contrasted with the Russians' far larger gains during the same period. The British Press had shown commendable restraint and confidence in General Montgomery's leadership and there had been little open criticism but, as the weeks passed with the Allied armies still enclosed by the German defence, the static warfare of the First World War began to be recalled and the threat of stalemate to be mentioned, especially in America. A wave of enthusiasm consequently greeted the first news of Goodwood with its seeming promise of a break through the enemy front; and there was a corresponding reaction when again the attack was stopped with the German defence still intact. The official communiqué issued from General Montgomery's headquarters on the evening of the 18th contained the statements that: 'Early this morning British and Canadian troops of Second Army attacked and broke through into the area east of the Orne and south-east of Caen . . .'. Vaucelles was being cleared and 'strong armoured and mobile forces are operating in the open country farther to the

THE GOODWOOD BATTLE

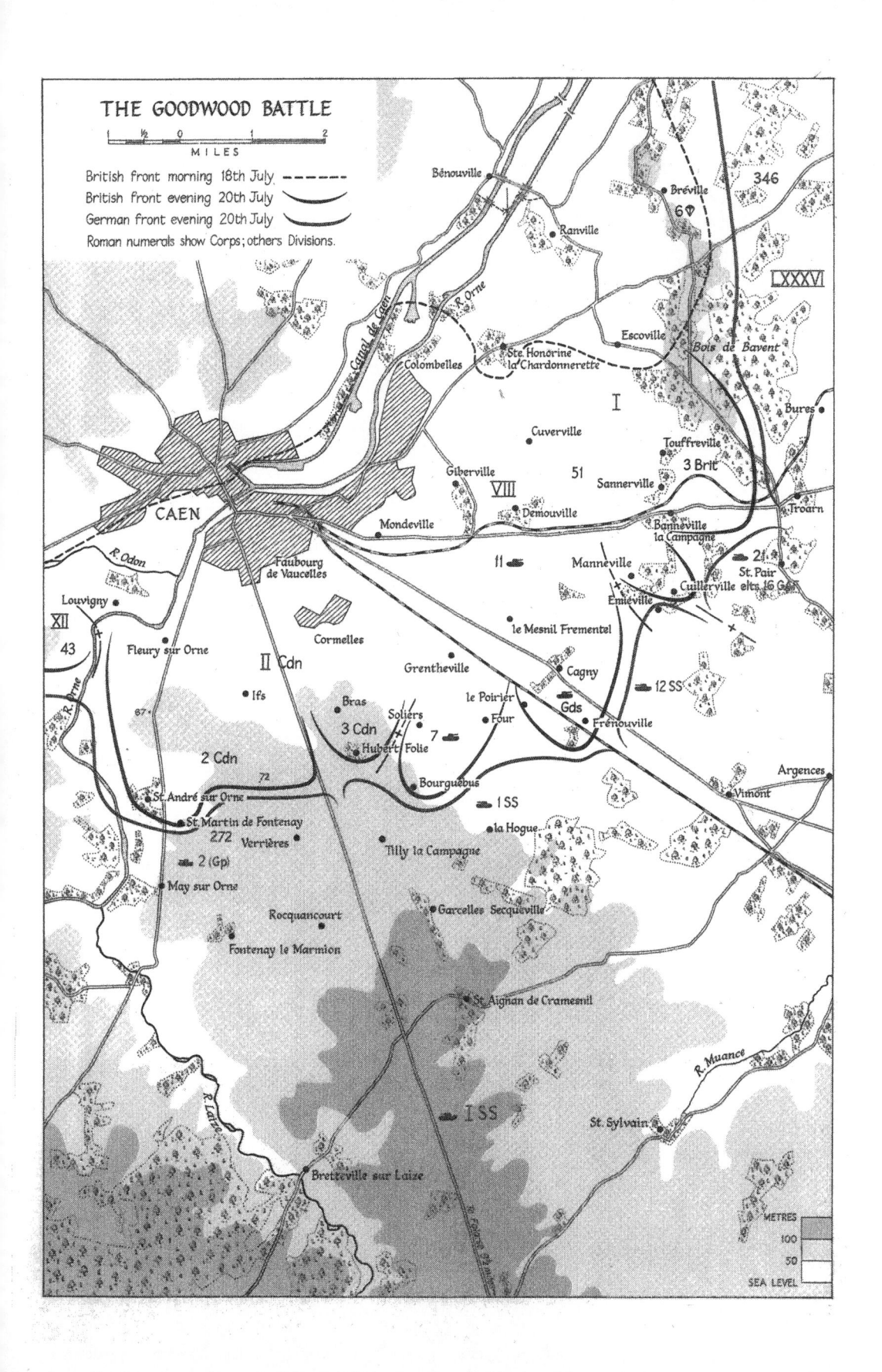

south-east and south . . .' While this was literally accurate the headlines under which *The Times* published it shows how easily it could be misinterpreted: 'Second Army Breaks Through—Armoured Forces reach open country—General Montgomery well satisfied'. The phrases 'break through' and 'open country' were thus understood to imply something like 'break through the enemy defences into open undefended country'. Not only the general public but Supreme Headquarters misread Montgomery's announcement, and both were proportionately disappointed when the actual positions reached were realised. Three days afterwards *The Times* headline was 'Lost Momentum of Break In', and later in the week it explained: 'The word "break-through" used in early reports can only be said to have a limited meaning. The German defensive perimeter round Caen has been broken but the German armour has not . . . Possibly the offensive was too much boomed when in its initial stages. It is always better to do the booming after complete success has been secured.'[8] 'Allies in France Bogged Down on Entire Front' and 'Critics assert Americans and British are making a Vice of Overcaution' are typical headlines of the *New York Herald Tribune*, and an article written by a correspondent at Shaef said: 'It is not for war correspondents sitting hundreds of miles behind at General Eisenhower's headquarters to master-mind the battle of Normandy, but it should be reported that the progress in Normandy has fallen far short of what headquarters had led correspondents to expect'.[9]

What was more important was criticism at Shaef itself. This had been started by air planners, had been developed by Sir Arthur Tedder, and had finally infected the Supreme Commander. Air Marshal Leigh-Mallory's planners at Shaef had been dissatisfied before ever Overlord was launched. When the Cossac plan was enlarged to meet the policy of General Eisenhower and General Montgomery they had argued that 'success in the Caen area is . . . essential to the success of the whole operation, and plan II [the enlarged plan] prejudices such success'. With their eyes fixed on suitable airfield country south-east of Caen they subsequently saw the failure to take Caen quickly as a fulfilment of their prophecy. Sir Arthur Tedder's fear, after only a fortnight's fighting, that the situation in Normandy 'had the makings of a dangerous crisis' (page 265 above) developed into a positive distrust of General Montgomery's leadership and outspoken criticism of his conduct of operations.

It would have been odd if the expression of such opinions by his British Deputy had had no influence on the mind of the Supreme Commander, and there is evidence in Eisenhower's correspondence

---

[8] *The Times*, 19th, 22nd and 25th July, 1944.
[9] *New York Herald Tribune*, 25th July, 1944.

with Montgomery that he too was becoming troubled about the slow rate of progress in both sectors. As early as June the 25th he had written to General Bradley urging him 'to rush the preparations for the attack to the south'. He also wrote to Montgomery on July the 7th of the need to expand the Allies' bridgehead in order to get more space for manœuvre, and though he was aware of Montgomery's plan to hold the main weight of German opposition on the left while gaining room on the right, in his view it had not yet proved its value, for the American advance there was slow and some of the German armoured divisions were beginning to regroup. He urged the need to use 'all possible energy' and stated that 'we have not yet attempted a major full-dress attack on the left flank supported by everything we could bring to bear'.

Caen was taken two days later and, after further hard fighting in both sectors, St. Lô was entered as Goodwood was launched on July the 18th. The Supreme Commander's optimism revived but, when Goodwood was concluded without realising the results he had looked for and Cobra was still held up, he was greatly disappointed and Montgomery's 'satisfaction' seemed to him unjustifiable. He visited Montgomery's headquarters on the 20th. There is no record of what took place but next day he recapitulated in a letter something of what was said 'to assure myself that we see eye to eye on the big problems'. He repeated objects named by Montgomery in his letter of July the 8th—'to get the Brittany peninsula', not to get 'hemmed into a relatively small area, generally to kill Germans'. He agreed with Montgomery's statement that 'we are now so strong and so well situated that we can attack the Germans hard and continuously in the relentless pursuit of our objectives', but he obviously considered that there was a discrepancy between this statement of Montgomery's intentions and the execution of his policy. '. . . you should insist that Dempsey keep up the strength of his attack . . . In First Army the whole front comes quickly into action to pin down local reserves and to support the main attack. Dempsey should do the same'—a somewhat curious remark since Dempsey's sustained pressure was successfully pinning down almost all the German armour and most of the infantry reinforcements. While the Americans had been fighting for Coutances and St. Lô since July 3rd only one new infantry division (5th Parachute), part of another (275) and one weak armoured division (Lehr) had reached the American front; *but four new infantry divisions (271, 272, 276 and 277) had appeared on the British front in the same period.* Another (326) and an armoured division (116) were to arrive within the next four days on the British front, without any corresponding increase opposite the Americans.

A copy of General Eisenhower's letter went to his Deputy, but

Sir Arthur Tedder was not satisfied. On July the 23rd he expressed his dissatisfaction in writing to the Supreme Commander. His letter is too long to quote here in full but its purpose can be gathered from a few extracts. 'I can see no indication of the bold offensive action which the time factor demands and the relative strengths of the combined sea, land and air forces justify.' He was 'shocked by the satisfaction with the situation' expressed in General Montgomery's directives. 'I can see no grounds for satisfaction with the operations in the Eastern Sector . . . On the Eastern flank, despite our overwhelming superiority, we were apparently unable to exploit our advantage . . . the airfield programme, which should have been completed by D + 40 is still only half complete . . .' Quoting from Montgomery's directive that the enemy 'must be induced to build up his main strength to the East of the river Orne, so that our affairs on the Western flank can proceed with greater speed', he wrote, 'I have no faith in such a plan. . . I have every faith in General Bradley and his Commanders, and in their impending attacks, but I do not feel that we can expect rapid moves in that area owing to the nature of the terrain.' He added that he would again urge Eisenhower to set up his tactical headquarters in France and take over direct control, and put an end to the arrangement by which General Montgomery had operational control of both British and American forces in Normandy. He assured General Eisenhower that he would support 'any action you may consider the situation demands'. Sir Arthur sent a copy of his letter to the Chief of the Air Staff at the Air Ministry.

But the Supreme Commander did not think the situation demanded any such action and in the next few days General Montgomery's policy was justified and Sir Arthur Tedder's views disproved. While the British fought the strongest German forces in the east General Bradley's troops *were* able 'to proceed with greater speed' in the west and 'rapid moves in that area' were *not* prevented 'owing to the nature of the terrain'.

General Montgomery was himself partly responsible for the dissatisfaction at Shaef. Those who have followed the accounts of British operations so far will have realised that General Montgomery's named intentions were stated clearly and with great accuracy; that in no case were their geographical objectives reached; yet when each operation concluded with its stated object unrealised he asserted that he was satisfied with the result. To observers who saw each end with a fresh failure to realise his intentions, the satisfaction he professed was incomprehensible. It is indeed not easy to understand why he failed to realise the need to explain that, while others judged each operation by its territorial gains, he judged it by its contribution to the realisation of his long-term plan. And part of the dissatisfaction at Shaef was apparently due to the fact that his long-term plan was not understood. After the war had been won General Eisenhower wrote:

> 'A sound battle plan provides flexibility in both space and time to meet the constantly changing factors of the battle problem in such a way as to achieve the final goal of the commander. Rigidity inevitably defeats itself, and the analysts who point to a changed detail as evidence of a plan's weakness are completely unaware of the characteristics of the battlefield.' [10]

The critics at Shaef should have realised the truth of General Eisenhower's dictum that 'a sound battle plan provides flexibility in both space and time', and in regarding the fact that the Allied armies had not reached certain positions by certain dates (e.g. D + 40 quoted by Sir Arthur Tedder) 'as evidence of a plan's weakness' the critics were 'completely unaware of the characteristics of the battlefield'.

General Montgomery's battle plan was indeed concerned 'to meet the constantly changing factors of the battle problem' in such a way as to achieve his goal. He was not thinking of phase lines drawn by planners months before the battle opened but of how to defeat the enemy in Normandy and be ready to cross the Seine and advance into Germany. Foreseeing that the enemy was likely to concentrate on the open eastern flank he determined from the first to hold him there, maintaining a strong position, while the Americans won ground from which the Allies could wheel towards the Seine. The diagram opposite is taken from a map drawn by his staff *in April* before Overlord was launched to show how he was planning to develop the battle—Diagram I. There were no dates to indicate when he hoped to reach particular positions but it shows that he did not expect to start wheeling eastwards towards the Seine till the Americans had reached Avranches and the country further south— certainly not while they were still held at the St. Lô–Caumont line where they were on the 24th of July—Diagram II. Until adequate room had been won in the west his principle was to hold the bulk of the enemy armour on the east. The action which he had said might well be 'decisive' was a dual attack launched in the Caen area and St. Lô on consecutive days. And it will be found later that, although at the western attack was delayed for six days after Goodwood, the bulk of the enemy armour was still held by continued British attacks on the Caen front and, this being so, advance on the west when it was launched was rapid and deep. By August the 1st the Allied position was as shown on Diagram III below, approximating closely

---

[10] Eisenhower, *Crusade in Europe*, p. 281.

to that shown in the pre-D-day Diagram I as the position from which the wheel eastwards would begin.

After the war General Eisenhower said of the operations that preceded the break-out in Normandy, 'Field-Marshal Montgomery's tactical handling of this situation was masterly'.[11] General Bradley too wrote afterwards, 'Monty's primary task was to attract German troops to the British front that we might more easily secure Cherbourg and get into position for the break-out. In this diversionary mission Monty was more than successful.'[12]

Yet despite these post-war appreciations it is doubtful whether General Eisenhower ever fully understood Montgomery's intentions. In the Supreme Commander's Report to the Combined Chiefs of Staff, dated July 1945, he acknowledged that the British forces by

Diagram I

Development of battle forecast in April

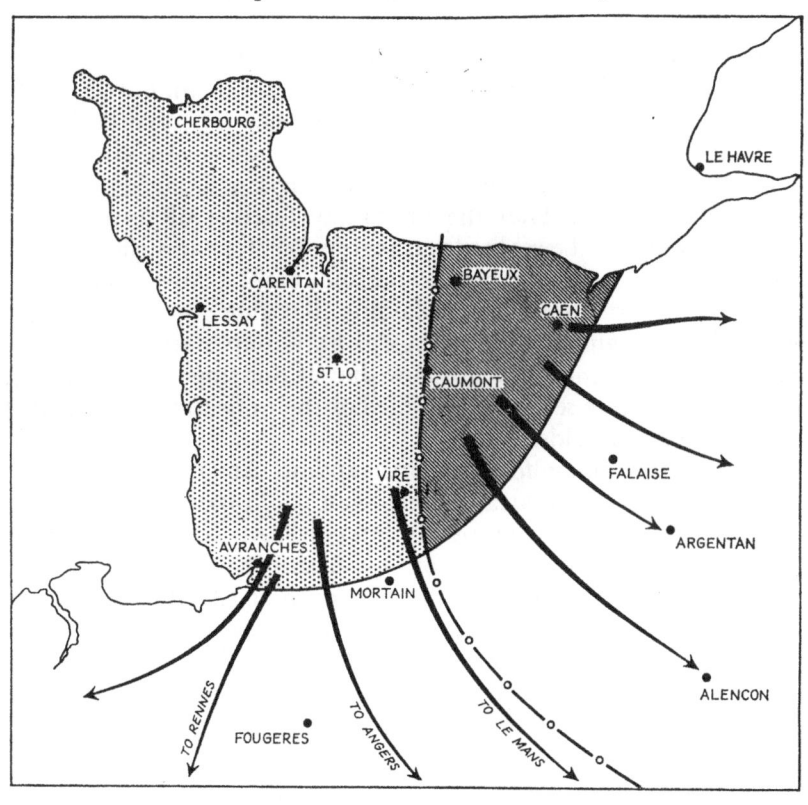

---

[11] *Report by the Supreme Commander to the Combined Chiefs of Staff* . . . (H.M.S.O., 1946), p. 41.

[12] Omar N. Bradley, *A Soldier's Story* (London, 1951), p. 325.

their increasing pressure had never given the enemy 'the respite necessary to withdraw and mass his armoured resources' but he added, 'nevertheless, in the east *we had been unable to break out toward the Seine*'; and he described the aim of Goodwood as 'a drive across the Orne from Caen toward the south and south-east, *exploiting in the direction of the Seine basin and Paris*'.[13] Yet as Diagram I on page 357 shows, General Montgomery had from the first realised that the time to 'break out towards the Seine' would not come till the Americans had gained room southwards from which to wheel towards the east and he would indeed have been foolish if, having fought so persistently to attract the enemy's strongest forces away from the American front and to hold them on the eastern flank, he had tried to break out there, where the bulk of the German armour had been purposely concentrated.

Despite pressure from the Supreme Commander, even indirectly from the Prime Minister (who visited him after Goodwood), Montgomery steadfastly refused to attempt to break out south-eastwards until he was satisfied that the time was ripe. It was to be made at his discretion, not to satisfy a set plan. He would exploit opportunities as they arose, and he would do his best to create them, but he would not sacrifice men needlessly when by patience he could make the Germans fight the battle his way. In this he was consistent even if at times, both before D-day and after it, he envisaged quicker progress than was achieved. That the pre-D-day forecast of airfield construction could not be realised was regrettable, for the airfields in the British sector were overcrowded and undesirably close together—as were all the Army's base installations. But there were enough to have all 83 Group and two wings of 84 Group stationed in Normandy, and it is impossible to show that at this stage of the fighting air operations were seriously curtailed or their effectiveness impeded by shortage of airfields.

None of the discomfort at home and in America would have arisen if the American attack in the west could have started on the day after Goodwood as originally intended. At the time it seemed to the public that the capture of St. Lô and the Goodwood attack had done nothing to quicken the slow pace of Allied progress; the public still knew nothing of the coming American attack near St. Lô which was only held up by weather. The truth is that at this time the unaccommodating behaviour of the weather provided the only real grounds for complaint.

---

[13] *Report by the Supreme Commander* . . . , pp. 41, 45. (Author's italics.)

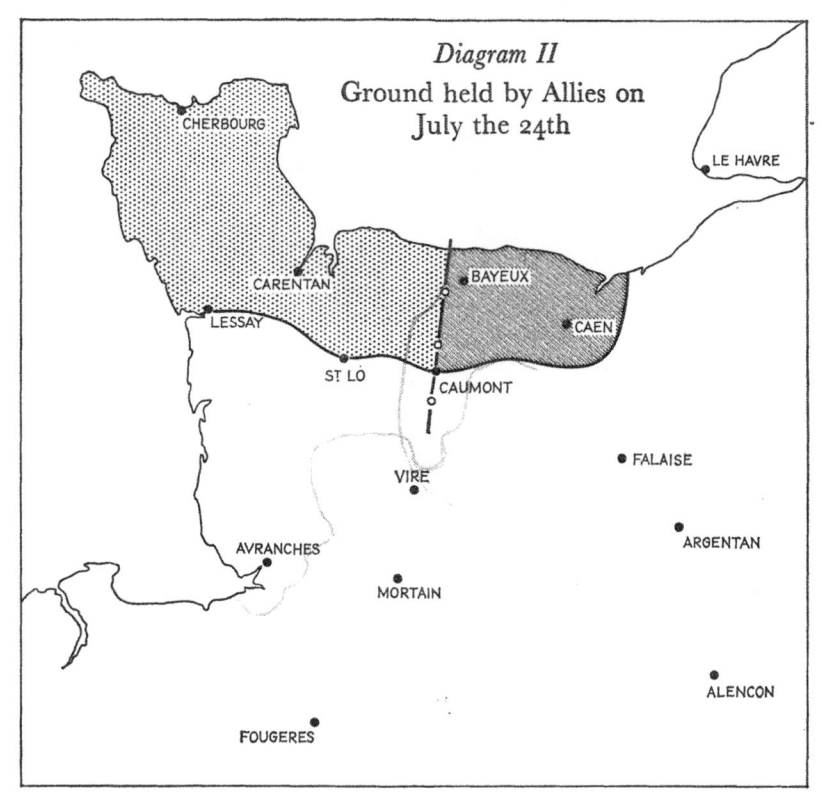

Diagram II
Ground held by Allies on July the 24th

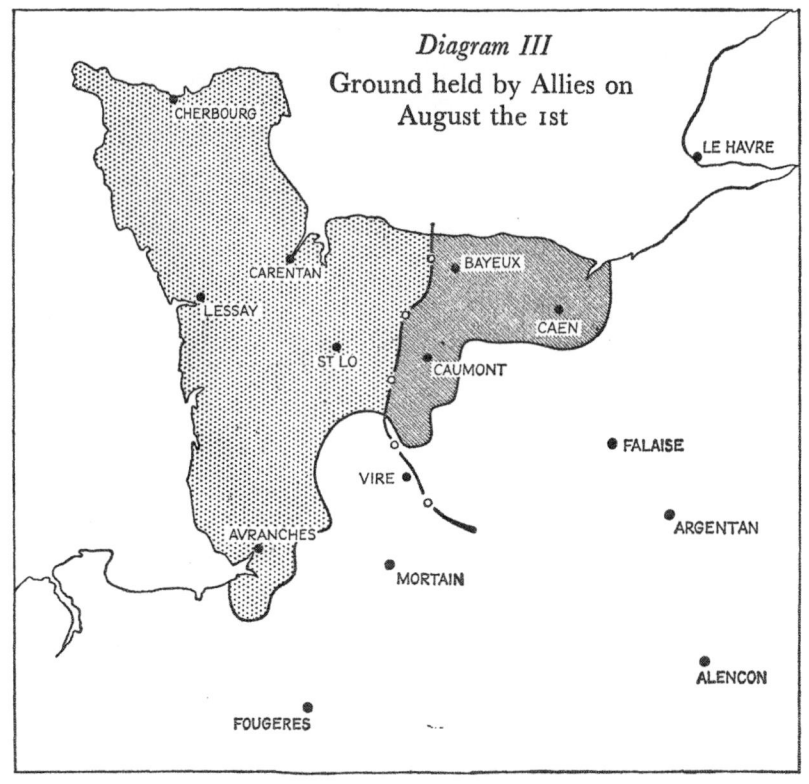

Diagram III
Ground held by Allies on August the 1st

CHAPTER XVI

THE PLOT TO MURDER HITLER

'If a government is using its apparatus of power to lead a nation to destruction, rebellion is not merely the right, but the duty of each and every citizen.' Adolf Hitler in 1925[1]

THE British armoured attack south-east of Caen had continued during the 19th of July and that day American troops had occupied St. Lô. On the German side, von Kluge had taken personal command of Army Group B after Rommel's incapacitation and was now confirmed in his dual command. He had moved to Rommel's old headquarters at la Roche Guyon and had retained Speidel as his chief of staff for the army group; his headquarters as Commander-in-Chief, West, remained in Paris at St. Germain with Blumentritt in charge. On July the 20th the British attack on the front of Panzer Group West had not been renewed and no serious operations had yet developed from the American capture of St. Lô. On that morning the position was thus easier. Starting early, von Kluge drove to Panzer Group West headquarters at Mittois (some thirteen miles north-east of Falaise) for a conference with Eberbach, Hausser and other commanders which lasted into the afternoon. It was a sultry day and the violent rainstorm in the afternoon turned much of the country into a quagmire. Von Kluge did not get back to his headquarters at la Roche Guyon till a quarter past six. Two messages were waiting for him. The first, telephoned by Blumentritt at about five o'clock, said that Hitler was dead and revolt had broken out in Berlin; the second, received only a few minutes before his return, was from a broadcast statement to the effect that an attempt to kill the Führer had failed and that Hitler would himself broadcast later in the evening.

The plot to murder Hitler is not only important for its immediate bearing on the campaign in the West but because it determined the manner in which the war would end. Its failure, underlined by Hitler's bloody revenge, killed the last flicker of military resistance to his rule and to the Nazi régime and killed any chance of early surrender; the war would go on now to the bitter end. Some account of the plot, its military implications and the consequences of its

---

[1] 'Wenn durch die Hilfsmittel der Regierungsgewalt ein Volkstum dem Untergang entgegengeführt wird, dann ist die Rebellion eines jeden Angehörigen eines solchen Volkes nicht nur Recht, sondern Pflicht.'—*Mein Kampf.*

failure is therefore pertinent here, though it involves a digression from the Normandy battle and a brief excursion into German history.

The leadership and skill of General Hans von Seeckt had made possible the illicit rebirth of the German Army after its defeat in 1918 and by 1925 had enabled it to win a dominant position in the German Republic; holding aloof from party faction it had become the recognised guardian of the Reich. But the death of President Ebert in 1925 and the appointment of Field-Marshal von Hindenburg as president and supreme commander led to von Seeckt's retirement and initiated the régime of General Kurt von Schleicher. Under him the Army descended into 'the arena of political intrigue, with a consequent besmirching of its reputation and the ultimate destruction of its authority'.[2] It is not necessary here to follow the details of its tortuous course but only to note a few outstanding events that marked the progress of its decline.

In 1933 the Army condoned the dissolution of the Republic and furthered the rise to power of Hitler and his National Socialist party. In 1934 it was guilty of complicity in the bloody purge of those whom Hitler distrusted, including Schleicher. In that year it accepted Hitler as Head of the State and Supreme Commander of the Armed Forces and every soldier from field-marshal to private declared:

> 'I swear by God this sacred oath, that I will yield unconditional obedience to the Führer of the German Reich and *Volk*, Adolf Hitler, the Supreme Commander of the Wehrmacht, and, as a brave soldier, will be ready at any time to lay down my life for this oath.'[3]

This marked the irrevocable abrogation of the Army's integrity. No longer could it oppose even the foulest brutalities of the Nazi régime without being in conflict with legitimate and constituted authority. No longer was the Army even master of its own house. In its lust for political power it had sacrificed moral principles to the temptations of political opportunism. And it had been hopelessly outwitted by Hitler's political acumen, firmness of purpose and amoral ruthlessness. It had now to watch Heinrich Himmler and his fellow sadists complete the means by which it and the German people would be held in intellectual servitude, and to see the development of rival military formations, fanatically obsessed by Nazi doctrine, trained in Nazi brutality and commanded by Nazi officers. Its further humiliation came in 1938 when Hitler's establishment of a new 'High Command of the Armed Forces' (OKW) relegated the

---

[2] J. W. Wheeler-Bennett, *The Nemesis of Power* (1953), p. 153.

[3] 'Ich schwöre bei Gott diesen heiligen Eid, dass ich dem Führer des deutschen Reiches u. Volkes Adolf Hitler, dem Obersten Befehlshaber der Wehrmacht, unbedingten Gehorsam leisten u. als tapferer Soldat bereit sein will, jederzeit für diesen Eid mein Leben einzusetzen.'—(Text in Lieut-Colonel Stuhlmann, *Wehrlexikon*, 1936.)

Army's proud and once-famous General Staff to a subordinate position and so further 'humbled their pride and hobbled their power'.[4] With effect from the 28th of February 1938 thirteen army and air force generals were retired and twenty-two were transferred to other positions. From then on such civilian opposition to Hitler's dictatorship as had survived his use of murder and concentration camps to suppress it, and such opposition to his military policy as existed in the Army, moved slowly towards active resistance and finally crystallised in conspiracy. Of the disgruntled army leaders in 1938, only General Ludwig Beck, Chief of the General Staff, had the courage to voice his conviction that Hitler's policy in regard to Czechoslovakia would lead to general war and, when his criticism was not accepted, to resign. He had already been a leader of army opposition: from now on he was the recognised head of military conspiracy. Dr. Carl Goerdeler, who had resigned his post as Hitler's Price Controller in 1935 and his office of *Oberbürgermeister* of Leipzig in the following year, in protest at the persecution of the Jews, was his most active fellow-conspirator among civilians. Civilian groups in opposition to the Nazi régime had been systematically broken up by the Gestapo as they were discovered; many of their members had been murdered and many more imprisoned in concentration camps. The surviving groups with which Goerdeler was associated included the so-called 'Kreisau Circle' whose members had diverse views and came from many walks of life but were united in their desire to see the overthrow of Nazidom and to prepare for the day of its accomplishment. Recognising that this could only be achieved by the Army they accepted Beck's leadership of the conspiracy but were chiefly involved, through Goerdeler, in plans and preparations for what should follow Hitler's downfall.

Though the plotters were more active after 1938 little progress was made while Hitler's military policy appeared successful up to 1940. Then the war with Russia rekindled the mood of active resistance and in 1943, after the disasters of Stalingrad and the Allied victory in North Africa, smouldering dissatisfaction showed fresh signs of breaking into flame. Even then it was difficult to win any considerable support from army leaders. Many who professed a desire to get rid of Hitler hesitated to join the conspiracy and the explanation of their unwillingness to commit themselves is not hard to understand. They justified their continued loyalty to the Führer first by the oath of unconditional obedience they had sworn, observance of which, it may be noted, offered the chance of promotion, military distinction and personal gain. Von Kluge, for instance, was promoted Field-Marshal in 1940, and later accepted a personal

---

[4] Wheeler-Bennett, op. cit., p. 694.

'birthday present' of some £20,000 from Hitler.[5] Moreover, to reinforce these inducements to loyalty and discouragements to revolt stood Himmler with thousands of secret police and trained thugs and with all the apparatus of murder, torture and concentration camps. On the other hand, revolt against Hitler and his régime offered them—what? It was difficult for them to foresee clearly anything but the very obvious personal risk. In the early talk of opposition it had been proposed to seize Hitler and bring him to trial for his crimes, to set up a new Government based on law and justice and to court friendship with—but here the opposition was divided, some wishing for alliance with the Western Powers and others with Russia. By 1943 it was generally recognised by the leading conspirators that the first and essential thing to achieve was the death of Hitler and his chief henchmen. The Army would then seize power, suppress the Nazi régime, appoint a provisional Government and, while continuing the war with Russia, would open negotiations for an armistice on the western front—though the Allies had meanwhile announced that they would only accept unconditional surrender of all armed forces. How an armistice with the Western Allies alone was to be obtained was not clear, and it is easy to see why a majority of the army leaders hesitated to join a conspiracy whose aims could only be stated in such unconvincing terms.

It is also easy to understand that the uncertain measure of army support (as well as the need for absolute secrecy) made it very difficult for the conspirators to work out detailed plans, or to predict with assurance the reactions of the German people and of the Allies. Nevertheless, active planning was given fresh impetus by the arrival of a new conspirator in the summer of 1943. The central group led by Beck and Goerdeler had long included General Friedrich Olbricht, deputy to Colonel-General Fromm, Commander-in-Chief of the Home Army.[6] Olbricht's principal staff officer, Major-General Oster, had been one of the more active organisers of revolt in the military districts through which the German Home Army and the garrisons of occupied countries were administered. In August, Oster was superseded by Colonel Claus von Stauffenberg. An aristocrat, a fervent Catholic, an officer of a crack regiment, he had distinguished himself in the Polish, French and North African campaigns where he received wounds that would have put an end to the military career of any ordinary man. In his case the loss of his right forearm, his left eye and two fingers of his left hand, with other

---

[5] Hitler subsequently stated: 'I promoted him twice, gave him the highest decorations, gave him a large endowment settlement so that he could have a permanent home, and gave him a large supplement to his pay as Field-Marshal.'

[6] This abbreviation is used as a convenient reference to 'the Chief of Army Equipment and Commander of the Replacement Army'.

injuries to his left arm and knee, had not stopped his reporting for duty as soon as his wounds were healed, and his outstanding reputation as an organiser led to his appointment to Olbricht's staff. In his own regiment he was known as an outspoken critic of the Nazi régime; he now threw himself with enthusiasm into the conspiracy to end it. With his arrival the plotting was brought to a head.

'But the Führer's evil guardian angel was working overtime.'[7] Six times in the last half of 1943 the murder of Hitler was carefully planned but on each occasion circumstances prevented its accomplishment. In the first months of 1944, disagreements and uncertainty still delayed action. None of the serving field-marshals had been willing to commit himself,[8] though there were conspirators among their staffs; the personnel of the proposed provisional government to be set up after Hitler had been removed was not agreed with the leading civilians in the conspiracy until June. By then von Stauffenberg had decided to take the killing into his own hands and had devised the method he would adopt, and the conspirators had agreed on the action that should follow in so far as this could be fore-ordained while the reactions of the Army, the German people and the Allies were still unpredictable. In outline the intention was as follows:

The Murder of Hitler, Göring and Himmler. When next von Stauffenberg had to attend a meeting at which these three with their staff officers would be present, in Hitler's concrete and heavily guarded headquarters at Berchtesgaden, he would carry in his despatch case a time-bomb, powerful enough to kill all present if it were exploded in so confined a space; he would himself have left the room after setting the fuse. As soon as the bomb exploded Olbricht would be informed by telephone; then all communications between Hitler's headquarters and the outside world would be blocked and von Stauffenberg would fly to Berlin to join the conspirators' headquarters.

The Seizure of Power. In each major command and each military district of Germany and the occupied territories key people 'in the know' would be told by codeword ('Valkyrie') that Hitler was dead, that the Army had been empowered to form a new government with Beck as its head and von Witzleben as commander-in-chief of all armed forces; and that, under the latter, executive powers with the right of delegation were transferred to territorial commanders-in-chief of the Home Front and of all occupied territories. To them

---

[7] Wheeler-Bennett, op. cit., p. 589.

[8] In 1942 Field-Marshal Erwin von Witzleben, then commanding in the West, had been willing to head a conspiracy and had undergone a minor operation in order to be fully fit for the task. But when he was thus temporarily incapacitated he was relieved of his command and was not again employed.

were subordinated all army units, Waffen SS, civil servants and police in their districts and they were to relieve from office forthwith and place in secure military confinement all *Gauleiters, Reichstatthalters,* ministers, provincial governors, police presidents, senior SS and police chiefs, heads of Gestapo and Nazi district leaders. All Waffen SS units were to be incorporated in the Army. Any resistance to military power was to be relentlessly suppressed.[9]

The Setting up of a Provisional Government. A provisional government was then to be set up under Beck as soon as possible; it would include Dr. Goerdeler as Chancellor, Olbricht as Minister for War, von Stauffenberg as Secretary of State for War, von Witzleben as Commander-in-Chief Armed Forces. The military conspirators with the armed forces under their control would thus hold a master position in the government. What was intended with regard to the war was of necessity uncertain but it was proposed to bring hostilities in the West to a speedy conclusion. Clearly all would depend in the first place on the promptitude and efficiency with which the army leaders acted when Hitler was dead—on whether they accepted without cavil or hesitation the assumed authority of Beck, von Witzleben and their associates.

What then was the position of the principal commanders in the West? To what extent were the field-marshals involved in the conspiracy and how far were they prepared to act without hesitation on Hitler's death?

Field-Marshal von Rundstedt had known of the conspiracy's existence a long time and had consistently refused to have anything to do with it. But while his oath of loyalty prevented him from taking part, it did not prevent him from keeping to himself his knowledge that treason was brewing. Field-Marshal von Kluge too had long known of the conspiracy and, in spite of his oath and of his personal obligation to Hitler, he had given wavering and non-committal encouragement to proposals to overthrow him; and in the autumn of 1943, while holding a command on the weakening Russian front, he had at last categorically declared that he was ready to act once Hitler was dead. Shortly afterwards he was incapacitated by a motor-car accident and after his recovery, as already told, he was appointed to replace von Rundstedt as Commander-in-Chief, West. On taking up his new command he had soon realised that the military situation in Normandy was hopeless and he sent a message to Beck reaffirming his readiness to support a putsch once Hitler was dead.[10] The officer who took this message was a trusted conspirator on the staff

---

[9] See Wheeler-Bennett, op. cit., Appendix C, pp. 724–725.

[10] See H. B. Gisevius. *To the Bitter End* (London, 1948), pp. 458–468; F. von Schlabrendorff, *Revolt against Hitler* (London, 1948), pp. 113, 124–125, 132; A. W. Dulles, *Germany's Underground* (New York, 1947), p. 176.

of General von Stülpnagel, Military Governor of France, himself a staunch and active supporter of the plot and subject to von Kluge's authority. Field-Marshal Rommel was away in hospital, badly wounded. He had begun by being an enthusiastic admirer of Hitler, to whose support he owed quick promotion and the command in North Africa which won him military fame. He was not interested in politics, being wholly devoted to military affairs. But since his recall from Africa he had gradually realised that under Hitler's rule Germany was suffering grievously and was in grave danger; by 1944 he was consumed by the desire to save her and the armies he commanded—to stop a sanguinary war which could have but one end before the Allies' devastating bombs reduced Germany to ruins. He first learnt of the plot in February 1944. After the Allies' landings he realised the futility of Hitler's policy and when his advice was consistently rejected he began to contemplate an independent approach to the Allies. According to Speidel he regarded the warning he had addressed to Hitler on July the 15th, 'the unequal struggle is nearing its end' (page 326) as giving the Führer 'his last chance'. If Hitler did not act on this warning he, Rommel, would take independent action to bring hostilities in France to an end. He was opposed to the plan to murder Hitler, not on moral grounds but because it would make the Führer appear as a martyr; exactly what alternative course he intended to take is not clear. Speidel, his chief of staff, was in personal touch with the leading conspirators and not opposed to the killing of Hitler. Late in May he had a meeting in his own flat with two of the conspirators to discuss Rommel's likely reaction if the plot succeeded.[11] But Speidel himself, though thus furthering the conspiracy and trying to win Rommel's adherence, was careful not to commit himself to any incriminating part in the plot, and retained freedom to follow 'whichever way the cat jumped'.

> 'Treason doth never prosper: what's the reason?
> For if it prosper, none dare call it treason.' [12]

The Military Governor of France, General von Stülpnagel, was thus the only commander in the West who was wholeheartedly pledged, the only one ready on Hitler's death to carry out previously arranged plans immediately and with firmness. Within the area of his command preparations for the military *coup d'état* were secretly completed.

Two considerations impelled von Stauffenberg to act in July without further delay. In the first place there were indications that

---

[11] See Speidel, *Invasion 1944*, pp. 85–87, 137–139; D. Young, *Rommel* (1950), p. 221.

[12] Sir John Harrington, 1561–1612. *Epigrams*. Bk. IV, No. 5.

Himmler had for some time been aware that a conspiracy was afoot, and as the months passed a number of civilians more or less closely associated through the Kreisau Circle had been arrested on various pretexts. There were now indications that the Gestapo were closing in, and the arrest of Julius Leber (designated for the office of Minister of the Interior in the Provisional Government) on July the 4th convinced the conspirators of the extreme peril in which they stood. But the second, even more obvious reason to act without further delay, was the success of the Allies' landings in Normandy and the threat of an early break in the German defence. Hesitations and disagreements had already lost the plotters the chance to act, as they had intended, *before* the invasion was launched so that the danger of an Allied attack in the West would be avoided; the Allies, it was thought, would welcome a chance to recover France without a fight and would be ready to treat with the proposed provisional government once Hitler and his Nazi régime had been overthrown; but having lost this opportunity it was important to act before, rather than after, the defeat which threatened in Normandy.

Accordingly von Stauffenberg decided to carry out the planned murder on July 11th when he was to attend a meeting at Hitler's headquarters at Berchtesgaden. He went with a time-bomb in his despatch case but when he arrived he found that neither Himmler nor Göring was present and decided to hold his hand. On the 14th Hitler transferred his headquarters to the alternative 'Wolf's Lair' near Rastenburg in East Prussia (which the Russian armies were rapidly approaching), and a meeting there was called on the 15th. Again von Stauffenberg attended with his bomb. This time all the coveted victims were present but before he could set the time-fuse Hitler was called from the room and did not return. Yet again von Stauffenberg had to carry his bomb away; yet again Hitler had escaped destruction.

On July the 20th von Stauffenberg was required to attend another meeting in the Wolf's Lair in order to report progress in the creation of front-line divisions from the troops of the Home Army. This was a question of urgent importance, for the Central Army Group on the eastern front had lost heavily while trying to stem the advancing Russian armies, now only about fifty miles away from Hitler's headquarters.

Once again von Stauffenberg arrived with a time-bomb in his brief case. Once again he learned on arrival that neither Göring nor Himmler was there. This time he decided to act.

The Wolf's Lair was hidden among the trees of a dark forest. It consisted of a deep concrete bunker for Hitler's use and, on the surface, a group of one-storey buildings containing signals and other offices and rooms for various uses. The whole was surrounded by barbed wire and blockhouse defences. In Jodl's phrase, 'it was a cross between a monastery and a concentration camp'.[13] July the 20th was a very hot day; the bunker was undergoing reconstruction so the meeting was held above ground in an airy room (about forty feet long by sixteen feet wide) with all its windows wide open. There was a long table, resting on solid cross-supports near either end instead of the usual legs. Those present stood round the table.

Von Stauffenberg, having set the fuse of his bomb, put his despatch case under the table and left the room 'to use the telephone'. Almost immediately the bomb exploded.

There were three detonations. Clouds of smoke split by yellow flames filled the wrecked room and shouts of alarm mingled with cries of the wounded and dying. A few minutes later a little procession of blackened, bleeding and bedraggled men emerged. Hitler had not been murdered after all. His right arm was temporarily paralysed, his leg burned and his back bruised; his ear-drums were damaged, his hair singed and a livid scarlet burn marked his pallid face. 'The Führer's trousers had also been torn to bits'! But he was outwardly calm as he was led by Keitel to his quarters in the bunker.

Without stopping to learn the result von Stauffenberg had set out for Berlin as soon as the bomb exploded, leaving General Fellgiebel, Hitler's chief signals officer and a conspirator, to play his vitally important rôle. This was to telephone the news to Olbricht in Berlin and then immediately put out of action the whole of the Wolf's Lair system of communication with the outside world.

But already the conspirators' plans had begun to miscarry. The explosion's effectiveness had been reduced by the fact that the meeting was held in an airy room instead of in a close concrete bunker, for which the bomb was intended. General Warlimont, who was in the room when the bomb exploded, gave this explanation next day:

> 'As the Führer's *Bunker* is under reconstruction at present, the situation conferences are being held in a building nearby. Although protected on the outside by concrete walls, it is constructed inside of wood, and in particular, is not set firmly on the ground. This fact was decisive for the murder attempt, as the atmospheric pressure did not therefore meet the resistance it would have done in a normal *Bunker*.'

It was able to escape through a row of open windows as well as through the door; and the floor gave way which also reduced atmospheric pressure. Also the solid wooden table-support had partially shielded Hitler from the blast of the explosion. General Fellgiebel had neither telephoned to Olbricht in Berlin nor cut off communications when he saw Hitler and the other survivors emerge

---

[13] *Nuremberg Record*, XV, 295 (quoted by Wheeler-Bennett, op. cit., p. 636).

from the ruined meeting place—with the disastrous result that Olbricht and the other conspirators waiting to issue Valkyrie orders did not know that the bomb had been exploded till hours later. When von Stauffenberg got back to Berlin with (mistaken) news that Hitler was dead, Keitel and others were already telephoning from the Wolf's Lair that Hitler was alive. While the conspirators were issuing Valkyrie orders Himmler and others were countering them with more authoritative orders for the suppression of revolt and the arrest of all who were involved in it. Troops who had been ordered to Berlin by the conspirators to arrest Nazi leaders were on arrival ordered to arrest the conspirators. General Fromm was released but superseded by Himmler as Commander-in-Chief of the Home Army, and others whom the conspirators had taken prisoner were freed. Beck, Olbricht, von Stauffenberg and their associates were, in turn, arrested and their immediate execution ordered. Beck was allowed to take his own life; von Stauffenberg, Olbricht and two others were shot by a firing squad before Himmler intervened. Everyone involved in the plot would certainly die too, but not so quickly or so painlessly, not before interrogation and torture had revealed information which might incriminate others. By midnight the revolt in Berlin had in effect been crushed. The day which was to have ended Nazi tyranny saw the beginning of a new and horrible era of Nazi persecution.

To this brief summary of what happened at the Wolf's Lair and in Berlin must be added the account of its effects in France, at von Kluge's army group headquarters at la Roche Guyon, in C-in-C West headquarters at St. Germain and at the headquarters of the Military Governor of France, General von Stülpnagel, in Paris.

After von Kluge got back to his army group headquarters and found waiting for him a telephone message that Hitler was dead and a broadcast report that he was alive, he summoned Blumentritt from St. Germain and von Stülpnagel from Paris. They arrived about seven o'clock or soon after. In the meantime Beck had rung up von Kluge from Berlin (before he was arrested) to say that Hitler was dead and to ask whether he accepted his (Beck's) authority as acting Head of the Reich (Reichsverweser). Von Kluge temporised, promising to reply in half an hour. Instead he rang up Keitel at the Wolf's Lair and having been told the state of affairs there he rang up Warlimont. The following extract is from Army Group B war diary's record of the conversation:

'On being asked, the Deputy Chief of the OKW Operations Staff [Warlimont] gives the following information:

(1) At noon today a contemptible attempt was made to murder the Führer. The Führer is in full health.

(2) Perjured officers have formed a new régime and declared a state of emergency.
(3) Apart from Colonel-General Fromm, Field-Marshal von Witzleben and Colonel-General Hoepner are involved in the affair. Colonel Count Stauffenberg, Chief of Staff to Commander of the Replacement Army, seems to be one of the main participants.
(4) The Führer has appointed Reichsführer SS Himmler Commander of the Replacement Army.'

This seemed to confirm the fact that Hitler was both alive and in control; but about the same time a teleprint order was received at St. Germain purporting to come from General Fromm in Berlin. This stated that the official broadcast announcement was false—the Führer *was* dead. 'All pertinent measures will be carried out rapidly.' The authority of this order being questioned, the Operations Officer at St. Germain consulted OKW. There he was told that 'there was nothing to be added to the broadcast announcement'. The 'Fromm' order was therefore ignored and von Kluge left Beck's question unanswered.

Von Kluge was still undecided and did nothing. With an interval for dinner von Stülpnagel spent most of the evening trying to persuade him that whether Hitler was dead or alive he should head the revolt in the West (as Rommel had been prepared to do) and at least bring operations in France to an end before they finished in catastrophe. But von Kluge was not to be moved. He had said he would act if Hitler was dead, but Hitler was not dead and von Kluge was not the man to risk independent action while the result of the revolt in Berlin was still uncertain. General Speidel, who had been in personal association with the conspirators and knew of the planned action to be taken in Paris and elsewhere once the signal 'Valkyrie' was issued, was present at much of these discussions but neither his post-war account of the evening nor the Army Group B war diary reveal his part in them. He does describe the dinner party at which von Kluge tried to be jocular and the rest ate in gloomy silence.

Only after dinner, in a final attempt to commit von Kluge, did von Stülpnagel tell him that as previously arranged with the conspirators in Berlin the Valkyrie signal had been acted upon as soon as it was received. The first task was to arrest and imprison all the Nazi administrators and Gestapo in Paris and by now this should have been done. This frightening news at last stung von Kluge into action. Realising the risk of implication he at once ordered von Stülpnagel to return to Paris and undo what had been done without his, von Kluge's, authority. This was the only order von Kluge gave that night on his own initiative. Shortly afterwards Admiral Krancke and Field-Marshal Sperrle, both '200% Nazi', telephoned von Kluge to say that something was wrong in Paris for the commander of the Gestapo and his men had been arrested.

Soon after midnight Blumentritt had returned to C-in-C West headquarters in St. Germain. C-in-C West's war diary record of subsequent events gives the following information:

> 'At 0145 hrs a further teleprint is received "signed Fromm, Colonel-General", to the effect that the putsch is defeated and he has re-assumed command. As the contents of this teleprint contradict various orders and announcements, its text is reported verbatim to the OKW Operations Staff (by telephone, first). [Himmler already had been appointed to succeed Fromm.] Then the Chief of Staff, C-in-C. West [Blumentritt] reported by telephone to Field-Marshal von Kluge, suggesting he should immediately suspend the Military Governor, France, General v. Stülpnagel, from his duties for the time being; and the Chief of Staff, C-in-C West should temporarily take over the affairs of the Military Governor. Field-Marshal von Kluge agreed and gave [him] the necessary powers.'

Before leaving for Paris Blumentritt telephoned von Kluge:

> '... I would propose that the Herr Field-Marshal should, as C-in-C West, send the Führer a letter of congratulations and loyalty. ...'

Von Kluge having agreed, Blumentritt asked shortly afterwards:

> 'May .I now, Herr Field-Marshal, read out the letter to the Führer: "The *coup* against your life, undertaken by the hands of ruthless murderers, has, my Führer, failed, thanks to a gracious dispensation of Providence. At this time, I, in the name of the three Services subordinate to me as C-in-C West, congratulate you and assure you, my Führer, of our unchangeable loyalty, come what may." '

Again von Kluge agreed and gave his assent to Blumentritt's further proposal to send a second letter of 'congratulations and the most respectful and loyal greetings' on behalf of 'all the General Staff officers of the Western Army'.[14]

Blumentritt then left for Paris, which was in fact the only place where the first orders of the conspirators had been effectively carried out before von Kluge rescinded them. The first moves had been planned well ahead by von Stülpnagel and the Commandant of Paris with Speidel abetting. Complete secrecy had been maintained,

---

[14] General Speidel, writing after the war, does not mention this but gives an account, not recorded in the war diary, of how two officers sent by Goebbels and Keitel demanded that a telegram be sent to Hitler; 'they had already prepared the text', a modified version of which von Kluge 'had to sign'.

notwithstanding the presence in Paris of strong Nazi elements in the naval and air headquarters and a force of many hundred Gestapo. On the receipt of Valkyrie orders the head of the Gestapo and all his men had been arrested and imprisoned without the firing of a shot; with equal smoothness they were already released by the time that Blumentritt reached Paris. There he told von Stülpnagel that he was relieved of his command and proceeded to arrange matters with the released SS Lieut-General Oberg so as to 'save face' for both the Army and the Gestapo. The C-in-C West war diary record reads:

> 'In the ensuing discussion it was decided that the whole affair should be publicly described as an alarm exercise carried out by two parties.'

General von Stülpnagel being thus himself 'undone' and subsequently summoned to report to Keitel tried to shoot himself on the way, but was found in a canal and taken to hospital. Nursed back to health, blind and helpless, he was tried by the People's Court and hanged a month later.

The plot and its failure had no immediate effect on the conduct of the campaign in France. Away from Hitler's headquarters the armies in the field knew only of the broadcast announcement that an attempt to kill Hitler had failed; they were too busy to do more than speculate about what lay behind the news. Von Kluge's command was apparently unaffected and his orders were unchanged. And it is not necessary in this campaign history to pursue the full knowledge of what had been happening elsewhere or to recount at length the nauseating story of Hitler's revenge. The results to be noted here were as follows:

(1) Himmler, already in control of all Nazi security forces, was now also Commander-in-Chief of the Home Army on which all commanders in the field depended for reinforcements.

(2) Himmler's Waffen SS were promoted to equal status with the Army, Navy and Air Force.

(3) The Army was no longer allowed to use its traditional salute but was ordered to adopt the Nazi salute on all occasions 'as a sign of its unshakeable allegiance to the Führer and of the close unity between the Army and the Party'.

(4) General Guderian had been appointed acting Chief of the General Staff of the Army. He was a pioneer in the development of armoured forces before the war and had proved himself a skilled commander. Like von Rundstedt he had known of the plot and like him had refused to have anything to do with it. And, again like von Rundstedt, he had the curious sense of 'honour' which forbade his joining the conspiracy but

excused him from exposing a treacherous plot against the Führer he had sworn to serve 'even at peril of his life'. His conscience having avoided that difficult hurdle he now 'ran straight' for Hitler's favour. On July the 29th he ordered that 'every General Staff officer must be a National Socialist Political Officer [Nationalsozialistischer Fuhrungsoffizier] ... actively co-operating in the political indoctrination of younger commanders in accordance with the tenets of the Führer'. To such cringing abasement was the once proud Officer Corps reduced.

(5) As already told (page 370), the execution of leading conspirators taken *in flagrante delicto* was quickly stopped by Himmler so that everyone traced as even distantly connected with the conspiracy might be arrested, exhaustively questioned and if need be tortured in the hope that they would incriminate others who might be hunted down.

After long drawn-out torture the physically broken Goerdeler was hanged in the most cruel way but not until February the 2nd, 1945, and General Oster not until April the 9th. Hitler had ordered that all in the conspiracy *and their families* were to be exterminated: they were to perish as though they had never been born, and their children after them. The hunt went on till the very end; twenty-five were shot on the night of April the 21st, 1945, when Russian troops were already in the suburbs of Berlin. Some who had been arrested because of their kinship with conspirators were found imprisoned when Allied troops advanced through Germany; at one time there were ten members of the von Stauffenberg family and eight Goerdelers in Buchenwald—to name only two families. There is no complete record of those who suffered through Hitler's desire for revenge and Himmler's love of cruelty; the number ran into thousands. The cumulative effect of these measures was to extinguish for ever the last flame of opposition and so to consolidate Hitler's domination that the war would go on till both he and the German Army were destroyed.

Von Kluge did not let his sympathy with Hitler distract attention from his own troubles. He had been quick to send his congratulations on the Führer's escape from 'ruthless murderers'; later he wrote a personal letter on the dangers in the West, enclosing the letter from Rommel that he had received over a week before. After the attempt to murder Hitler, while the abortive putsch in Paris had hardly been quelled and von Kluge's Military Governor there had proved a traitor; while Hitler had yet to learn which army leaders were involved in the conspiracy and whether von Kluge and Rommel were implicated, von Kluge chose this most unpropitious time to send forward Rommel's opinion that 'the unequal struggle is nearing its end'. Endorsing this unpalatable prophecy, von Kluge now wrote that 'discussion with the commanders of the formations at Caen' after recent fighting had afforded 'grievous proof that ..., in view of the enemy's complete air supremacy, there is no way of finding a battle technique which will neutralise the positively annihilating effects of their air attacks short of giving up the battle area ... The moment has drawn near when this front already so severely strained will break. And once the enemy is in open country orderly control of the battle will hardly be practicable owing to our lack of mobility.' He delayed sending forward this letter till he had discussed it with Jodl and it did not reach Hitler in person till the 23rd (or later). There is evidence that by then the Führer was beginning to contemplate the loss of Normandy, and that OKW planners were considering alternative defence lines based on the Seine, the Somme and the Vosges. Jodl told Warlimont on July the 23rd that he had reported to Hitler on 'the main defence line' and that 'thereupon the work [of planning for withdrawal] was started'.

CHAPTER XVII

THE AMERICAN BREAK-OUT

Now that Goodwood had secured more room for movement east of the Orne, the headquarters of Lieut-General Crerar's First Canadian Army which had been waiting in England (page 304) was brought forward and made operational on July the 23rd. He would take under command, at the outset, the British I Corps and responsibility for the east flank sector; for the present II Canadian Corps would remain in Second Army and General Dempsey would extend his front westwards to Caumont in order to relieve the American division there. American forces were about to be formed into two armies, together making the United States Twelfth Army Group[1] under General Bradley; this would comprise the First Army, to be commanded by Lieut-General C. H. Hodges, and the Third Army under Lieut-General Patton. It was left to General Bradley to decide when this reorganisation should become effective and, in fact, it did so on the 1st of August. Until General Eisenhower decided to take direct command, General Montgomery would continue in operational control of both army groups in Normandy.

With the capture of St. Lô on the 19th the American First Army had reached a position from which Cobra could be launched, and General Bradley had flown to England to concert with air commanders final co-ordination of the air bombardment and the ground assault. Because the two were inseparably related the decision to launch the attack must depend on good flying weather and at that time the forecast was unpromising. Meanwhile on the British front, in furtherance of Montgomery's orders to buttress German belief that we contemplated a major advance towards Falaise and Argentan, and encourage the Germans to keep on building up strength in the east rather than against the Americans, Lieut-General G. G. Simonds' II Canadian Corps issued orders on the 23rd for a limited attack down the Falaise road. Irrespective of a decision when Cobra could begin and whatever the state of the weather the Canadian attack would start at dawn on the 25th. For three days bad weather had made large-scale air operations impossible, but signs of improvement on the 23rd and a forecast of

---

[1] To persuade the enemy that there was still an American army group in eastern England, the army group forming on the Continent was named the Twelfth, the 'First Army Group' continuing to exist only on paper.

clearing skies encouraged Leigh-Mallory to agree with General Bradley that the American attack should begin late on the morning of the 24th. When morning came, however, visibility did not improve as quickly as was expected and the attack was postponed for twenty-four hours. Unfortunately a number of the American bombers which had already left England failed to get the cancellation order and dropped their bombs, but visibility was still bad and some fell among American troops. With improving conditions in the afternoon the order to restart the attack on the 25th was confirmed.

Meanwhile the enemy had been able to observe much movement behind the British front and (as Montgomery hoped) Eberbach was convinced that the British would renew their main attack as soon as an improvement of the weather favoured the use of Allied air forces; he expected that the British aimed at breaking through to Mézidon and Falaise. While bad weather still held up Allied operations Eberbach used the pause to strengthen his forces in the east. By the evening of the 24th he had moved 9th SS Panzer Division across the Orne from Evrecy into the woods west of Bretteville sur Laize, where it would be well placed to strike at the flank of a British southward thrust; 2nd Panzer Division, having just been relieved in the Caumont sector by 326th Infantry Division, was being moved southeast across the Orne to be near 9th SS Panzer Division; 116th Panzer Division, newly arrived from the Fifteenth Army, was assembled east of St. Sylvain. Eberbach also intended to move 10th SS Panzer Division to the Bretteville area as soon as it could be disengaged. (Situation map opposite.)

At half past three on the morning of the 25th II Canadian Corps, strengthened by the 7th Armoured and Guards Armoured Divisions, began to attack southwards down either side of the Caen–Falaise road. It was still dark and as the leading infantry moved forward they had the unusual experience of being attacked by fragmentation bombs dropped by a few German aircraft. East of the Falaise road 3rd Canadian Infantry Division started from Bourguébus and advanced on Tilly la Campagne. (Map page 352.) Supported by tanks of the 2nd Canadian Armoured Brigade they reached the village, but it and the neighbourhood were strongly garrisoned by the 1st SS Panzer Division, with reinforcements in the woods behind la Hogue, and before it was light the Germans began counterattacking. Sixty medium bombers of the Second Tactical Air Force had bombed their positions late on the previous evening, but poor visibility and intense flak had reduced the value of the strike in which twenty aircraft were damaged. The Canadian fight went on all day. The attacking infantry brigade lost heavily and the tank squadron supporting them was practically wiped out; the attack was overwhelmed and by nightfall the survivors had been forced back to

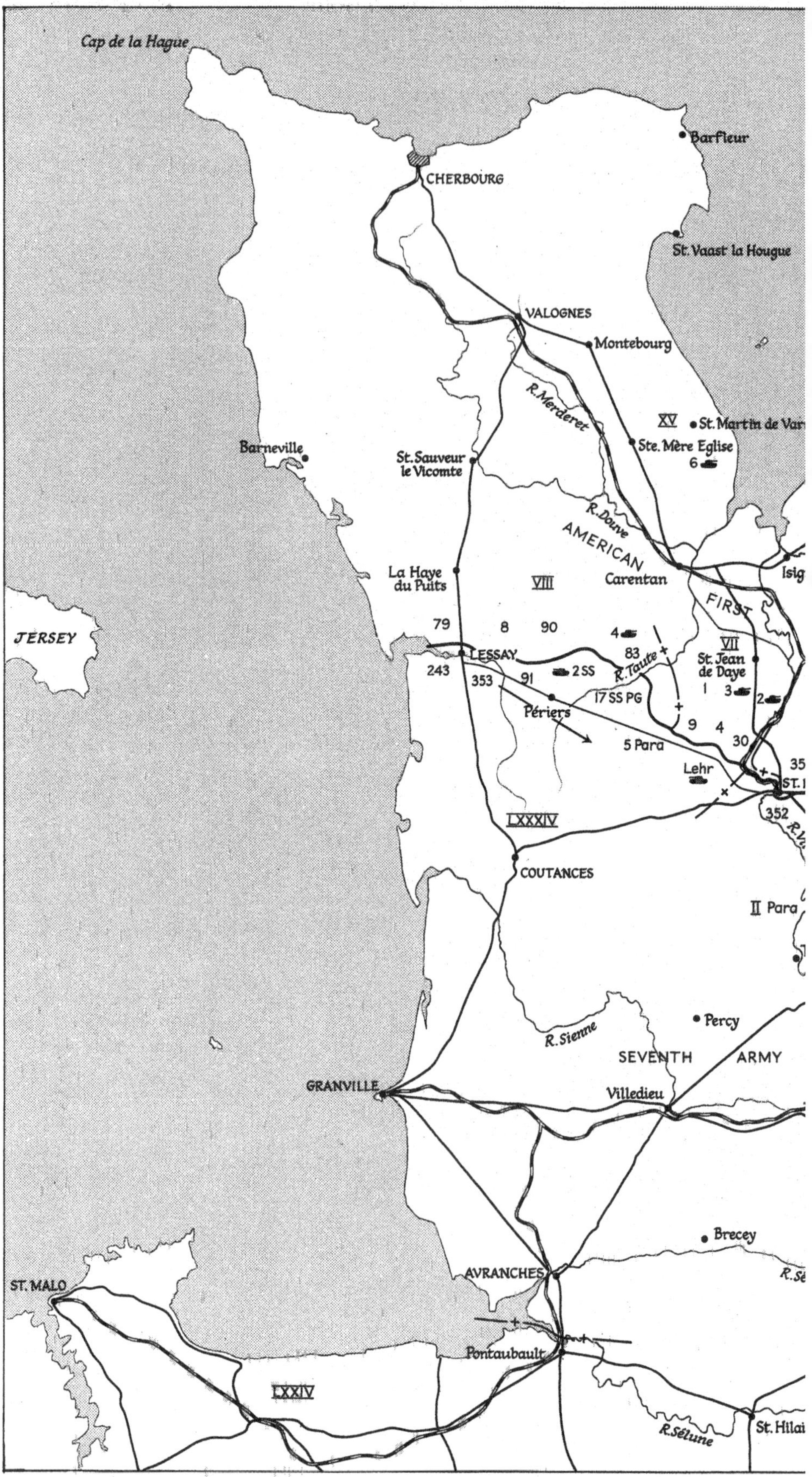

Cap de la Hague
Barfleur
CHERBOURG
St. Vaast la Hougue
VALOGNES
Montebourg
R. Merderet
XV
St. Martin de Var
Ste. Mère Eglise
6
Barneville
St. Sauveur le Vicomte
R. Douve
AMERICAN
Carentan
La Haye du Puits
VIII
FIRST
JERSEY
79
8
90
4
VII
83
LESSAY
St. Jean de Daye
243
353
91
2 SS
R. Taute
1
3
2
17 SS PG
Périers
9
4
30
5 Para
Lehr
ST. L
352
LXXXIV
COUTANCES
II Para
Percy
R. Sienne
SEVENTH
ARMY
GRANVILLE
Villedieu
Brecey
AVRANCHES
ST. MALO
Pontaubault
LXXIV
R. Sélune
St. Hilai

SITUATION MIDNIGHT 24th JULY 1944

Allied Front	～～～
Army Boundary	―o―
Corps Boundary	―+―
Corps	XXX
Infantry Division	50
Armoured Division	7 🛡
Airborne Division	6 ⛵

Allied troops are shown in Red and German troops in Blue.

Bourguébus. West of the Falaise road the 2nd Canadian Infantry Division had started to attack at the same early hour with two brigades abreast. On the left, Verrières was captured and was held against all counter-attacks but the attempt to follow on to Rocquancourt was defeated by numerous anti-tank guns covering the next rise and got little further. On the right the attack ran into great difficulties from the start. St. Martin and St. André sur Orne were never wholly freed from the enemy, and although twice during the morning a footing was gained in May sur Orne it could not be maintained. The battalion attacking Fontenay le Marmion had over three hundred casualties and found the place and its nearby iron-ore workings too strongly held by troops in well-camouflaged defences and by 'tanks disguised as haystacks'.

Throughout the day our aircraft were active, flying over 1,700 sorties in order to support the attack and to limit the power of the enemy's counter-attacks. Rocket-firing Typhoons alone flew over fifty missions in response to the Army's calls for their help during the action, and fighters continually searched far and wide for any movement of reinforcements or any signs of enemy aircraft.

The armoured divisions had been ready to push forward down the Falaise road but, since the infantry had failed to pierce the enemy's defences, armour had no opening to exploit. 7th Armoured Division's tanks and those of 2nd Canadian Armoured Brigade helped to stem enemy counter-attacks and had sharp engagements with 1st and 9th SS Panzer Divisions all along the corps front; they claimed a heavy toll of German tanks but lost fifty-six themselves. The Guards Armoured Division waiting behind them was not called on. The Canadians had lost some fifteen hundred casualties in this day's bloody and abortive fight. They had been butting against a wall which had not given way; with General Dempsey's agreement it was decided late in the day not to pursue the attempt at a point where the defences were so strong. By maintaining the threat to Falaise and so holding the main armoured strength away from the Americans, the immediate object had been achieved. Miles away in the west, the long-delayed American attack had begun and, against a weak defence, was making promising headway.

The American front, at this time, ran from Caumont on the left to St. Lô and from there to Lessay on the west coast of the Cotentin. The road from St. Lô to Lessay was held by the Germans with a considerable salient which included the town of Périers; the American positions faced them from the north of the road. Cobra was to begin to the west of St. Lô near Hebécrevon with an intense aerial bombardment by fighter-bombers, medium and heavy bombers, supported by strong artillery fire; the area to be bombed was a rectangle six thousand yards wide and two thousand four hundred

THE BREAKOUT

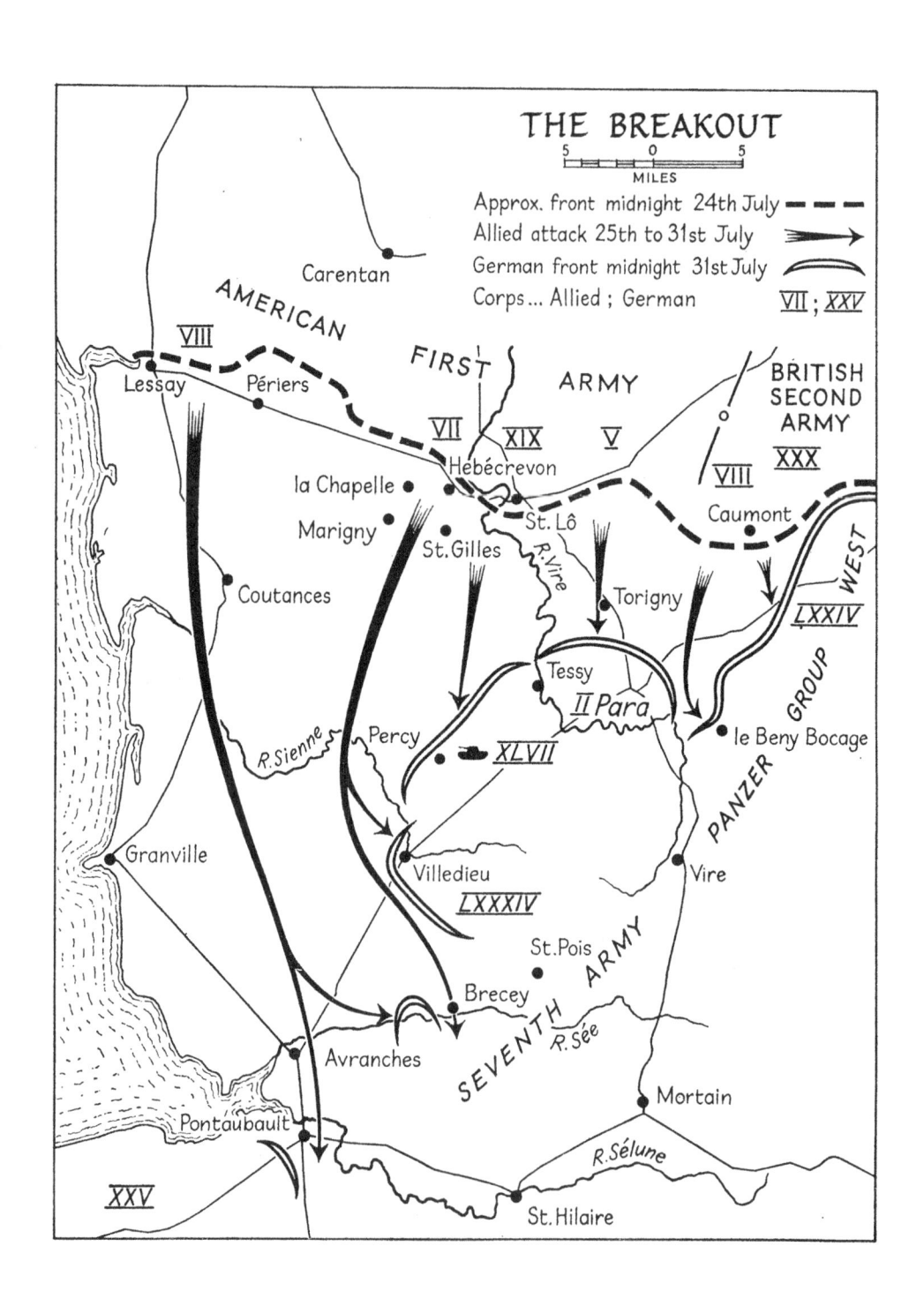

yards deep, with its northern boundary on the St. Lô–Lessay road. As soon as the bombardment ceased the American VII Corps under Lieut-General J. L. Collins was to attack with three infantry divisions abreast across the devastated area, in order to open a gap and to secure its flanks. Through this gap two armoured divisions and one motorised infantry division were to follow as quickly as possible to exploit the opening; two of these divisions would drive south and south-east, while the third would swing west towards Coutances. Meanwhile troops on the rest of the American front would exert strong pressure on the enemy—V and XIX Corps in the Caumont–St. Lô sector on the east and VIII Corps in the western, coastal sector.

The morning of the 25th was fine, with adequate visibility, and at 9.40 a.m. the air bombardment of the opening battle-ground began, American front-line troops having been drawn back 1,200 yards for safety. First, 600 fighter-bombers of the Ninth Air Force attacked for thirty minutes a 300-yard northern strip of the designated rectangle, covering the enemy's forward defences along and beyond the St. Lô–Lessay road; the 300 tons which they dropped included a large amount of napalm bombs—incendiaries filled with jellied petrol. As they completed their task over 1,500 heavy bombers of the Eighth Air Force flew in wave after wave for an hour, dropping over 3,400 tons of explosive and fragmentation bombs over the rest of the rectangle. Finally, medium bombers of the Ninth Air Force continued for a further hour to attack three target areas just south of the main bombed areas, dropping over 130 tons of high explosive and more than 4,000 fragmentation bombs. Altogether nearly 3,000 aircraft had joined in carpeting the battle-ground with bombs in preparation for the infantry attack. Most of the bombs were well placed but unfortunately some again fell in the American lines north of the St. Lô road, killing over a hundred and wounding six hundred of the troops waiting to go forward in the attack.

Nevertheless, recovering quickly from this 'short' bombing, VII Corps infantry began their advance at eleven o'clock as the heavy bombers drew off. Their objectives were St. Gilles on the left and Marigny on the right; they had strict orders to leave the roads clear and to make the flanks secure for the armoured troops who were to follow them.

The infantry on the left had first to capture Hebécrevon, a strong German position covering the junction of the road to St. Gilles. It had survived the bombardment and after hard fighting all day it was only conquered finally at midnight. On the right of the bombed area less troublesome centres of resistance that remained alive were overcome more quickly, and the enemy defences were pierced for about a thousand yards beyond the St. Lô road and southwards toward Marigny. In the centre the lateral road was also crossed and la Chapelle en Juger was reached but not yet taken. Throughout the afternoon medium and fighter-bombers of the Ninth Air Force in great strength attacked road and rail targets south of the battle zone while fighters gave close support and, with fighters of 83 Group, maintained armed reconnaissance over a wide area.

On this first day the air bombardment had assisted VII Corps to cross the St. Lô road and to advance a mile or two beyond it but had apparently not done more; those who had imagined that it would obliterate all opposition were disappointed. But in fact it had done far better than was yet realised. VII Corps infantry were already almost through the enemy's thin defence of this sector, for the troops of Panzer Lehr Division who had been holding it had been nearly destroyed—only isolated groups of resistance that had been missed by the bombing still fought on, with shattered communications and no hope of reinforcement. Their commander, General Bayerlein, when taken prisoner some months later, described his front after the air bombardment that morning as looking like a *mondlandschaft*—a landscape on the moon, 'all craters and death'. At least seventy per cent of personnel, he said, were out of action, either dead, wounded, crazed or stupefied; the thirty or forty tanks he had in the front line were all knocked out. In one farm he found the whole command post of his 902nd Panzer Grenadier Regiment completely destroyed in the very centre of a bomb carpet.

General Collins could not know all this on the evening of the 25th, but he knew enough to believe that his VII Corps had practically broken the forward German defence, and in order to deny the enemy time to regroup he ordered his armoured exploiting force to advance early next morning in the hope of completing a breakthrough. His enterprise was fully justified. At the close of the second day's fighting both flanks were deeper and more firmly held; St. Gilles was captured and Marigny reached and the infantry had moved off the roads running southwards to leave them clear for the armour. The advance had gained on average a further four miles and against weakening opposition the corps pushed on through the night.

The close support of the Ninth Air Force continued to play an active part in the battle. The use of a Visual Control Post mounted in a tank, which was referred to in the account of Goodwood (page 338), had been extensively developed by the Americans. Known to them as 'Air Support Parties', every armoured column had one in verbal touch with its supporting aircraft; four of these flew in armed reconnaissance over the leading tanks, ready to attack instantly targets seen ahead and, if need be, to call up other aircraft standing by on 'ground alert'. The resulting close co-operation was most effective on this day and in the days that were to follow.

GERMAN LEFT BROKEN

The third day's fighting, on July the 27th, was decisive. On the left flank XIX Corps had advanced southward almost to Tessy sur Vire; VII Corps in the centre were nearly half way to Villedieu and further to the right were within two miles of Coutances. There they met stubborn resistance from troops trying to keep open a way of escape for the German forces in the coastal sector, now being driven before the approaching American VIII Corps. The latter captured Coutances next day and from then on the German Seventh Army's withdrawal in the coastal sector began to degenerate into a disorderly retreat. Four thousand five hundred prisoners were taken on the 28th and on the 29th an enemy column was trapped a few miles south-east of the town; fighter-bombers attacked while it was jammed on the road and destroyed many tanks, armoured cars, troop carriers, guns, lorries and other vehicles.

On the 30th Avranches was entered and next day a bridgehead was secured embracing crossings over the Sienne, the Sée and the Sélune rivers. The break-out in the west was virtually achieved. The battered Seventh Army defence had been broken through and what remained had been forced back to precariously held positions stretching roughly from near Torigny, east of the Vire, to Tessy and Percy, with only scattered and crumbling opposition through which American forces were steadily penetrating; the way to open country in the south was practically clear. (Map at page 386.)

Though the American success was due first and foremost to the skill with which the attack had been planned and prepared and the strength and vigour with which it was being carried out, the comparative weakness of the German Seventh Army, faulty dispositions and conflicting orders contributed to the enemy's failure. As already told (page 354), the recurrent attacks of the British forces in the east had led von Kluge to give almost all the additional troops which arrived in July to Panzer Group West, leaving the Seventh Army to make the most of the forces it had. Of these the Seventh Army commander reported on July the 19th that, through losses in the previous two and a half weeks' fighting in west Normandy, the 'infantry holding the main defensive line has become so thin in many places that in further thrusts and attacks . . . penetrations inevitably occur. . . . As army reserve there are at present only three battalions of the 275th (Infantry) Division available.' He added, '. . . the newly brought up battle group, 275th Infantry Division and 5th Parachute Division, cannot appreciably relieve the strain on the Seventh Army. This force is lacking in field or collective training. In two regiments of 5th Parachute Division, except for the commanding officers there are no unit commanders or cadres with battle experience.' Many of the divisions holding the front were in little better case.

The main American attack fell on LXXXIV Corps, responsible for eighteen miles from Hebécrevon, near St. Lô, to Lessay on the west coast. This front was divided into seven divisional sectors. For one sector the 5th Parachute Division was responsible; the other six were held by two armoured and four infantry divisions, all below strength and all made up of a veritable hotch-potch of battalions which had been pushed about to plug holes as they occurred in the previous weeks' fighting.[2] Apart from the 2nd SS Panzer and Panzer Lehr Divisions and the 5th Parachute Division (whose weakness has already been described above), there were nominally twenty-three infantry battalions defending the corps front. Details of these are given in an enemy report made on July the 23rd which classified only one as 'strong' and five as 'medium' or 'average'; nine were 'weak' and eight were 'exhausted'. The two armoured divisions had between them 109 tanks, most of which were being used to hold the front line. Of supporting arms, and particularly of artillery, Seventh Army had a considerable amount with each division holding the corps front but nothing comparable with the weight of army and corps artillery behind the American divisions; and of course there was no air force to match with the Allied air forces.

It was with this uneven, patched-up defence that the Germans met the American attack, with no reserves worth speaking of and no plans for any possible withdrawal. Even so, the Seventh Army's first response to the attack is not impressive. Hampered by the destruction of communications in the battle area, out-paced by the speed of American movement, with neither authority nor preparation for any possible withdrawal, confusion quickly grew. It was made worse by contradictory orders from the army commander (Hausser) and the corps commander (von Choltitz), while some of von Kluge's orders never reached the troops. On the 26th von Kluge ordered the 2nd Panzer Division, then east of the Orne, to be made ready to move westwards if there was further 'deterioration in 7th Army's grave situation' and summoned Hausser to confer with him next day. During the 27th and 28th von Kluge ordered both the 2nd and 116th Panzer Divisions to be transferred from Panzer Group West to the Seventh Army and, with remnants of Panzer Lehr and the 352nd Infantry Division, to be put under XLVII Panzer Corps headquarters, which at that time was also being transferred from the Caumont sector. On the 28th, angered by the reports he had received on the conduct of operations by Seventh Army and LXXXIV Corps, he dismissed the chief of staff of the army and the commander of the corps. On the 30th he went to Seventh Army command post

---

[2] It may be noted that a German infantry division would normally contain either six or nine battalions, according to its type, and an armoured division four or six battalions of infantry and from ninety to over two hundred tanks.

and took personal command of operations. Telephoning from there early on the 31st he told Blumentritt at C-in-C West's headquarters: 'The situation here is completely farcical ... Yesterday I took charge of the corps and the army ... Things are in a gigantic mess here.' The situation 'is critical in the extreme ... the infantry have completely disintegrated and the troops are no longer fighting properly. They are putting up a wretched show.'

In fact, by that time (July 31st) the coastal area had been lost to the Americans and the remnant of the German front was bent back almost to the Vire. Something of what had happened is told in a 'Most Secret' report from Seventh Army commander to the C-in-C West a week later.

> 'Owing to the enemy armoured break-through on the Army's left wing, a large proportion of the divisions which had been fighting continuously since the invasion began and had not rested or received any considerable reinforcement, i.e. the 77th, 91st, 243rd, 275th, elements of 265th and 352nd and 353rd, 5th Parachute Division, 2nd SS Pz Division and 17th SS Pz Grenadier Division, disintegrated into [small] groups, which fought their way back through the enemy lines on their own. Whether acting on proper rallying orders, or on unconfirmed verbal instructions, most of these groups were without officers or NCOs and roamed at random through the countryside, heading east or south-east. Objectives of these movements: Bagnoles and le Mans.
>
> The stragglers are for the most part in a very bad state. They only bring some weapons with them—rifles, pistols and sub-machine guns. Motorised and horse-drawn units still have the odd machine gun or heavy infantry weapon, but these are largely in need of repair. Condition of clothing is appalling. Many men are without headgear or belts and their footwear is worn out. Many go barefoot. When they cannot obtain rations from supply depots, they live off the country, regardless of property rights, thus stirring up hatred amongst the population and intensifying terrorist activity. A not inconsiderable number disappear at the hands of terrorists. The paratroops are particularly unpopular with the local inhabitants. The morale of most of these stragglers is badly shaken.'

XLVII Panzer Corps was now fighting on the flank of the breakthrough. Three infantry divisions had also been ordered up from the Pas de Calais and the Atlantic coast but Hitler had refused to allow a fourth to be brought up from the south of France. The 9th Panzer Division was on the way to replace 116th Panzer Division on the British front but could not arrive for some days, and LXXIV Corps had come from Brittany and taken over responsibility for holding the Caumont sector. There, on the 30th, the British opened a new attack.

On July the 27th General Montgomery had met his army commanders and after reviewing the position had issued new instructions (M.515). The main blow of the whole Allied plan, he said, had now been delivered by the First United States Army. It was making excellent progress and the object of everything done elsewhere must be to further American operations. British attacks on the Orne front had compelled the enemy to bring such strong forces to oppose them that any further large-scale effort in that area was 'definitely unlikely to succeed'. At that time all six of the German armoured divisions on the British front were located *east* of Noyers. We must now take advantage of this situation and deal a very heavy blow *west* of Noyers where there was no armour at all. Second Army was therefore to regroup and to launch a new attack with not less than six divisions from the area of Caumont, and the sooner it began the better. Early next day, when he learnt how well the Americans were doing, he told General Dempsey to start the attack on the 30th and to 'step on the gas for Vire'. On the same day (the 28th) he received a message from General Eisenhower. He, too, realised the urgency of the moment and, while expressing his approval of General Montgomery's directive and urging that his assignments to British and Canadian armies should be carried out with vigour and determination, he also suggested the advisability of speeding up the main blow of Second Army in the Caumont area. 'I feel very strongly that a three-division attack now on Second Army's right flank will be worth more than six-division attack in five days' time ... now as never before opportunity is staring us in the face. Let us go all out on the lines you have laid down in your M.515 and let us not waste an hour in getting the whole affair started.'

But already Twenty-First Army Group had begun to shift its weight towards the Allied centre. Hardly a formation in the British and Canadian armies but had to adjust its positions or 'up sticks' and move at once. Some of VIII Corps' formations who did not receive their orders till near midday on the 28th had to pull out from the other side of the Orne and drive forty or fifty miles along roundabout and crowded routes through the back areas, always mindful of the need for secrecy. Thanks to good staff work, good march discipline and, above all things, air superiority, all needed for opening the attack on the 30th were able to cross their start lines (hastily briefed and a little breathless, perhaps) on time.

When the battle opened on the 30th the reorganised British front was held as follows. The eastern flank, stretching from the Channel coast to the Orne south of Caen, was held by the First Canadian Army's I Corps and the Second Army's II Canadian Corps,

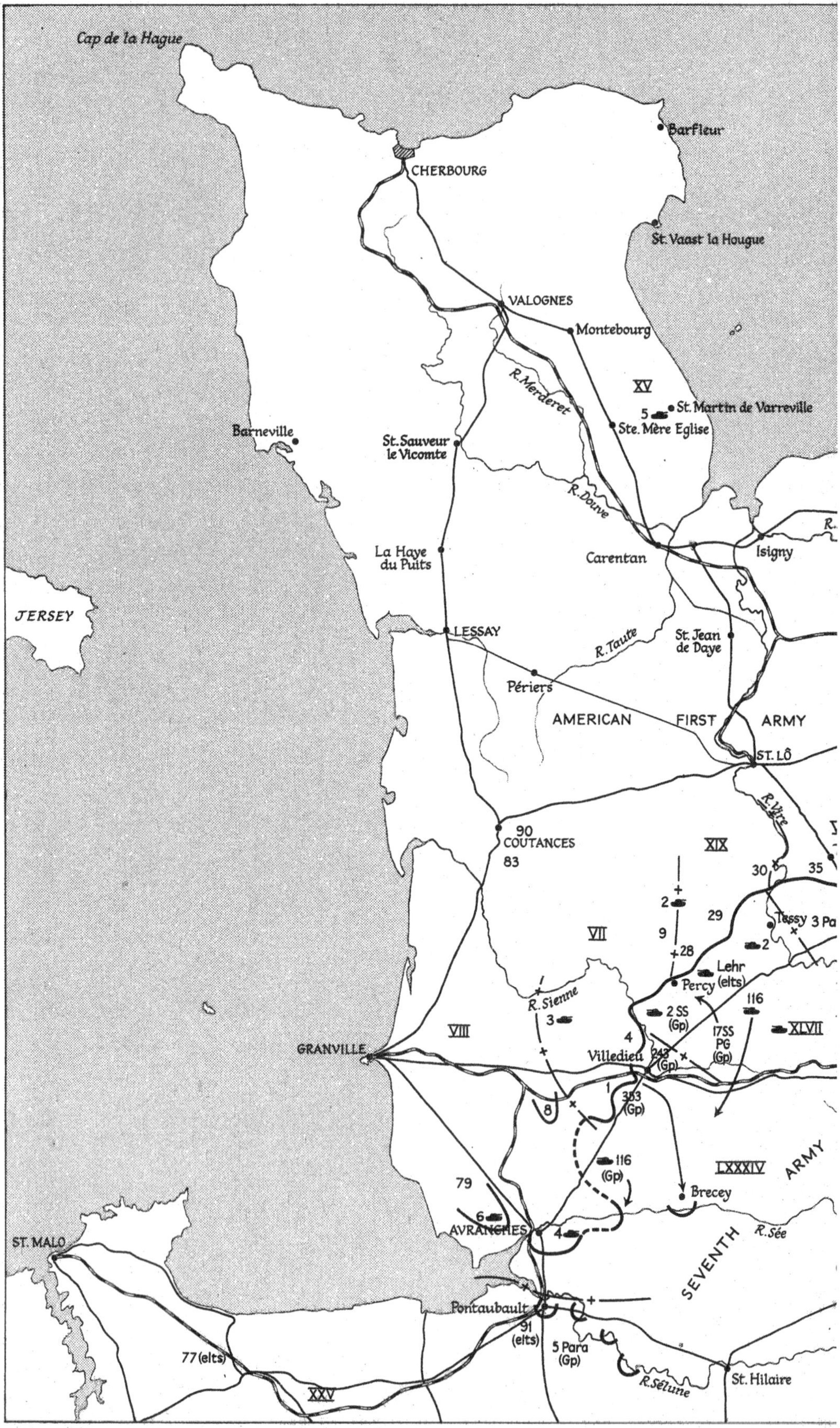
Cap de la Hague
CHERBOURG
Barfleur
St. Vaast la Hougue
VALOGNES
Montebourg
R. Merderet
XV
5
St. Martin de Varreville
Ste. Mère Eglise
Barneville
St. Sauveur le Vicomte
R. Douve
La Haye du Puits
Carentan
Isigny
JERSEY
LESSAY
R. Taute
St. Jean de Daye
Périers
AMERICAN FIRST ARMY
ST. LÔ
R. Vire
90
COUTANCES
83
XIX
30
35
2
29
Tessy
VII
9
28
2
Lehr
Percy (elts)
R. Sienne
116
3
2 SS (Gp)
VIII
17 SS PG (Gp)
XLVII
GRANVILLE
4
Villedieu
243 (Gp)
1
353 (Gp)
8
116 (Gp)
LXXXIV
ARMY
79
Brecey
6
AVRANCHES
4
R. Sée
SEVENTH
ST. MALO
Pontaubault
91 (elts)
77 (elts)
5 Para (Gp)
R. Sélune
St. Hilaire
XXV

SITUATION MIDNIGHT 31st JULY 1944

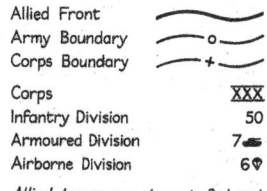

Allied Front
Army Boundary
Corps Boundary
Corps   XXX
Infantry Division   50
Armoured Division   7
Airborne Division   6

Allied troops are shown in Red and German troops in Blue.

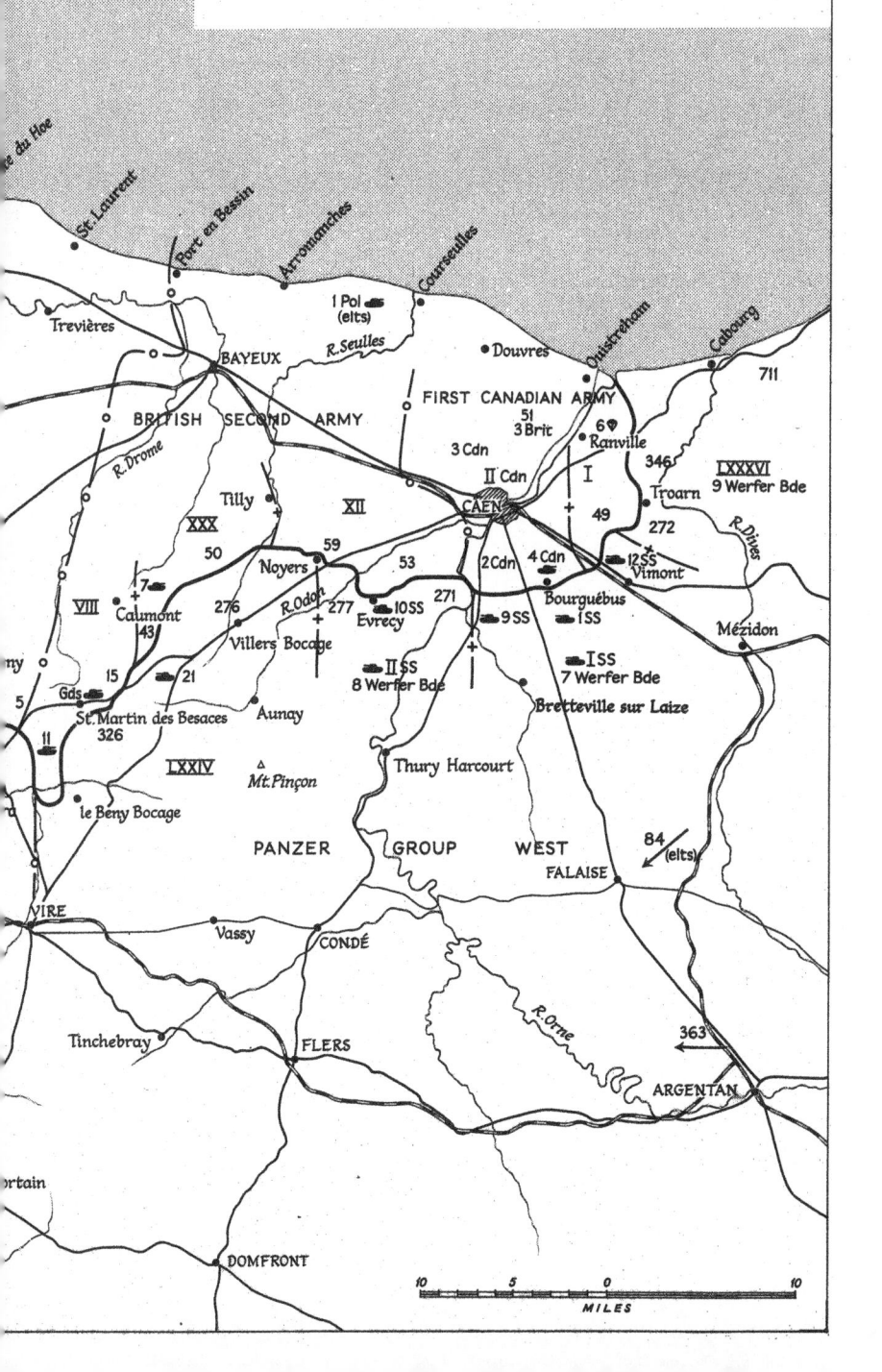

together comprising one airborne and three infantry divisions, two commando brigades, one armoured division and three armoured brigades, supported by three army groups of artillery. Opposed to them were three German armoured divisions and a heavy tank battalion (with a fourth armoured division and another heavy tank battalion in reserve), three infantry divisions (one very weak), and two *werfer* brigades.

Stretching westwards from the Orne the British front was now held by Second Army's XII, XXX and VIII Corps, comprising together five infantry divisions, three armoured divisions and four armoured brigades, with three army groups of artillery. Confronting these the enemy had four infantry divisions, one armoured division and one heavy tank battalion, one Panther anti-tank battalion and a *werfer* brigade. Two fresh infantry divisions and an armoured division were moving up to strengthen the defence.

Thus, counting by divisions, the Germans had about twice as many armoured divisions as the British east of the Orne though about a third less infantry; but west of the Orne, while we had no great preponderance of infantry divisions Second Army had more than three times the German strength in armour. Moreover, it must be recognised that several of the enemy divisions were below strength, unlike the British divisions, and across the whole front the Allies had overwhelming superiority of artillery and air power. It is a measure of the German soldier's fighting quality that, notwithstanding these disadvantages, he continued to offer effective opposition and to make skilful use of country that is, in itself, an obstacle to rapid movement.

For the country into which Second Army was now to thrust was even more difficult than any it had yet encountered—*bocage* at its very worst, a jumble of tree-clad hills and valleys. Metalled roads were few and far between; from Caumont there was only one in the right direction that was wide enough for two-way traffic. The rest were mostly tortuous one-way by-roads or farm tracks, with little ditches on either side and enclosed by the usual high banks and hedges. There were few towns of any size and most of the sparse population lived in small villages or farmsteads. Streams ran in all directions, through steep or marshy borders, their bridges too fragile to carry tanks or heavy vehicles. The Souleuvre river which crossed the front about ten miles south of Caumont, and the Vire on its west flank, ran through deep valleys and were formidable obstacles. (See map facing page 410.)

While pressure was being maintained all along the British front, Second Army's immediate intention was for XXX and VIII Corp to strike southwards from Caumont into the country between the Orne and the Vire and to prevent the Germans from using the Mont Pinçon hills as a hinge for methodical withdrawal from in front of the Americans. Looking southwards from the high ground on which Caumont stands reconnoitring parties could discern no identifiable place or feature in the succession of ill-defined, wooded ridges except two prominent hills on the sky-line. The one on the left is Point 361 at the western end of the Mont Pinçon ridge; it rises to about 1,200 feet above sea level and is crowned by trees. This was to be the first day's objective of XXX Corps' 43rd Division while the 50th Division secured the Amaye sur Seulles feature near Villers-Bocage on its left flank. The other prominent hill on the sky-line two miles away to the west of Point 361 is Point 309. It is marked by a quarry showing just below the summit and was the first day's objective of VIII Corps' 15th Division. On its right flank 11th Armoured Division was meanwhile to make good the area round St. Martin des Besaces. The 7th Armoured Division in XXX Corps and the Guards Armoured Division in VIII Corps would be in reserve, ready to exploit progress when the time came.

Because of the speed with which the operation had been mounted, artillery and air support could not be on so large a scale as on some recent occasions; in the interests of secrecy and surprise no preparatory counter-battery or air bombardments were allowed. To cover the opening advance concentrations would be fired by the artillery on the enemy's known forward defences and against entrenched positions in thick *bocage*; three-quarters of the 25-pounder shells were fused to give air bursts. The subsequent advance would be preceded by barrages or concentrations as required.

Heavy bombers of Bomber Command would attack four areas, four to six thousand yards ahead of XXX Corps, while the Ninth Air Force medium bombers similarly attacked three areas ahead of VIII Corps. Six of these bombing attacks were to be made an hour or so after the attack had started; the seventh, on the 15th Division's final objective, would be made some time during the afternoon. A few fighter-bomber strikes against nearby targets would be made as the advance began but, in the main, the fighters were to be held in reserve to meet calls for immediate support. The day began with a grey and sultry morning; low dense clouds prevented fighter or fighter-bomber attacks till after midday and the early bombers were much handicapped. Of the seven hundred aircraft from Bomber Command on the front of XXX Corps more than half were recalled because their targets could not be distinguished, while the rest bombed Amaye sur Seulles and Cahagnes from below 2,000 feet; all but sixty of the Ninth Air Force mediums bombed les Loges and Dampierre in front of VIII Corps through thick cloud.

The battle was opened by each corps on a three-brigade front. On the left XXX Corps led off at about six o'clock in the morning with the 231st and 56th Brigade Groups from the 50th Division and the 130th from the 43rd Division; on the right VIII Corps began about an hour later with 227th Brigade Group from the 15th Division and 29th Armoured and 159th Infantry Brigade Groups from the 11th Armoured Division. Almost everywhere the troops were met by heavy fire as they began moving forward, but their biggest trouble at the outset was with minefields. All night the Royal Engineers had been clearing and marking routes up to the start lines and detachments of flail tanks from the 79th Armoured Division were included in the forward brigades, but all along the front the task of mine-clearing was to prove more formidable than had been expected. The front lines abreast of Caumont had hardly altered since the middle of June. On the Allied side the sector had been held by different American or British divisions; until a few days before, when infantry took over, the 2nd Panzer Division had defended it for nearly six weeks. Americans, British and Germans had all laid mines, the Allies mainly to block the most likely enemy approaches; the 2nd Panzer Division, apparently having a plentiful supply, had scattered them in large numbers all over their forward area and among reserve positions prepared for use in emergency.

On the eastern flank two brigades of the 50th Division began to cross the main Caen–Caumont road about six in the morning, each accompanied by a squadron of Sherman tanks from the 8th Armoured Brigade; they struck the junction of the German 276th and 326th Infantry Divisions. The 231st Brigade on the left slowly but steadily fought its way through the woods between Orbois and St. Germain d'Ectot and threw back a weak counter-attack by elements of three battalions from the enemy's 276th Division. By dark they had secured a shallow footing across a stream about 2,000 yards from the original starting line. On their right the 56th Brigade made less headway. The St. Germain d'Ectot ridge, a short distance from the starting point, held several German platoon localities and when they were cleared all attempts to advance down the forward slopes in front were stopped by the enemy, strongly posted on another ridge less than a mile away.

To their right the 43rd Division attack opened at eight o'clock when the 130th Brigade, with an extra infantry battalion and an armoured regiment under command, set out to take Briquessard village and the Cahagnes area about two miles further south. Briquessard was captured soon after midday, its garrison having been thoroughly shaken by a load of bombs from a Bomber Command aircraft. A crossing was secured over the stream behind the village but a mile to the right, around le Repas, the advance made little progress. The fields were full of German anti-personnel mines, and on quite a short stretch of one lateral road the engineers dug up forty-nine anti-tank mines, laid by the Americans while they were

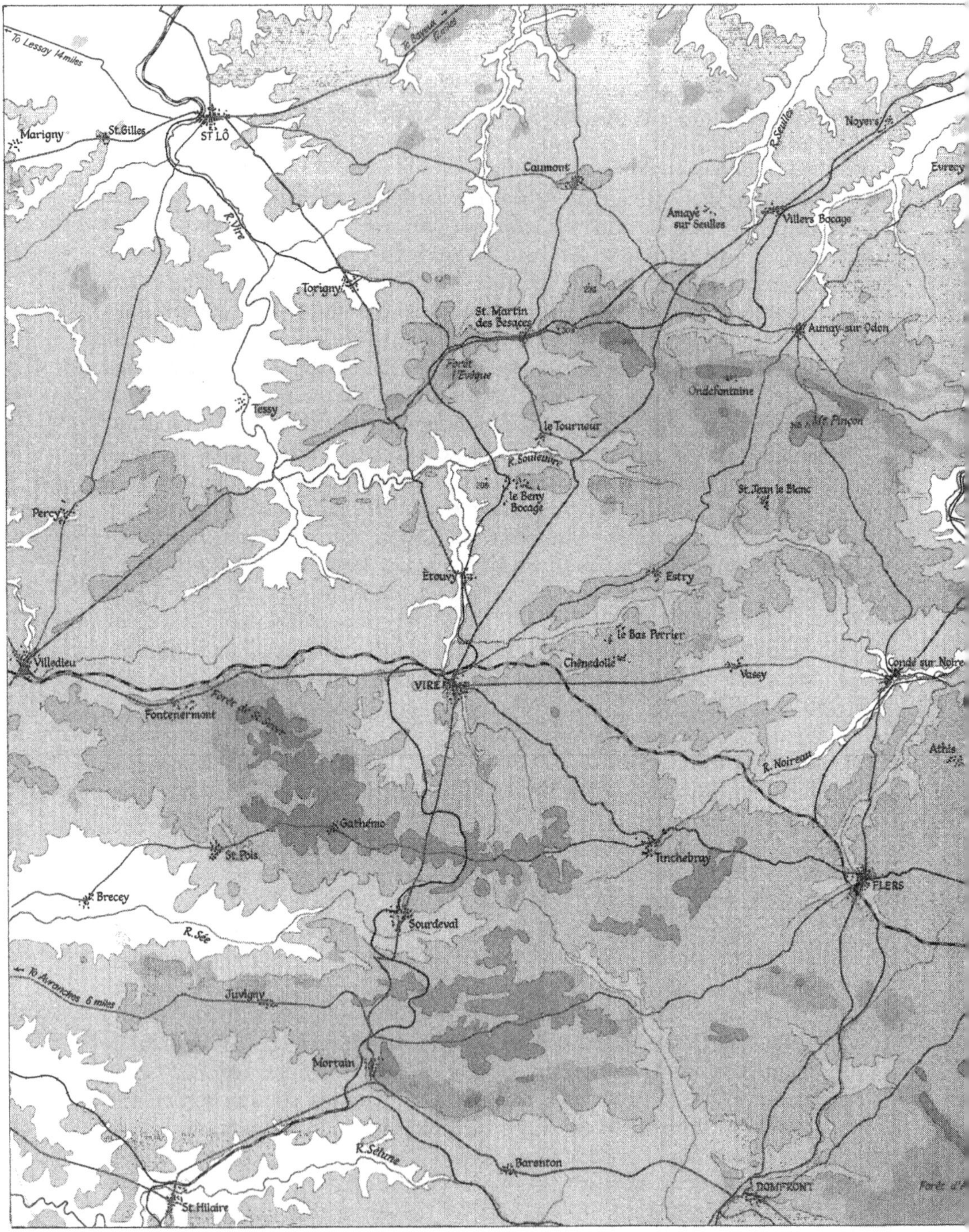
To Lessay 14 miles
Marigny
St.Gilles
St LÔ
Caumont
Noyers
Evrecy
R.Seulles
Amayé sur Seulles
Villers Bocage
R.Vire
Torigny
St. Martin des Besaces
Forêt l'Evêque
Aunay sur Odon
Ondefontaine
Mt Pinçon
Tessy
le Tourneur
R.Souleuvre
le Beny Bocage
St.Jean le Blanc
Percy
Etouvy
Estry
le Bas Perrier
Villedieu
Chênedollé
Vassy
Condé sur Noireau
VIRE
Fontenermont
Forêt de St Sever
R. Noireau
Athis
Gathémo
St.Pois
Tinchebray
FLERS
Brecey
Sourdeval
R. Sée
To Avranches 6 miles
Juvigny
Mortain
R. Sélune
Barenton
DOMFRONT
St.Hilaire

ST LÔ TO FALAISE

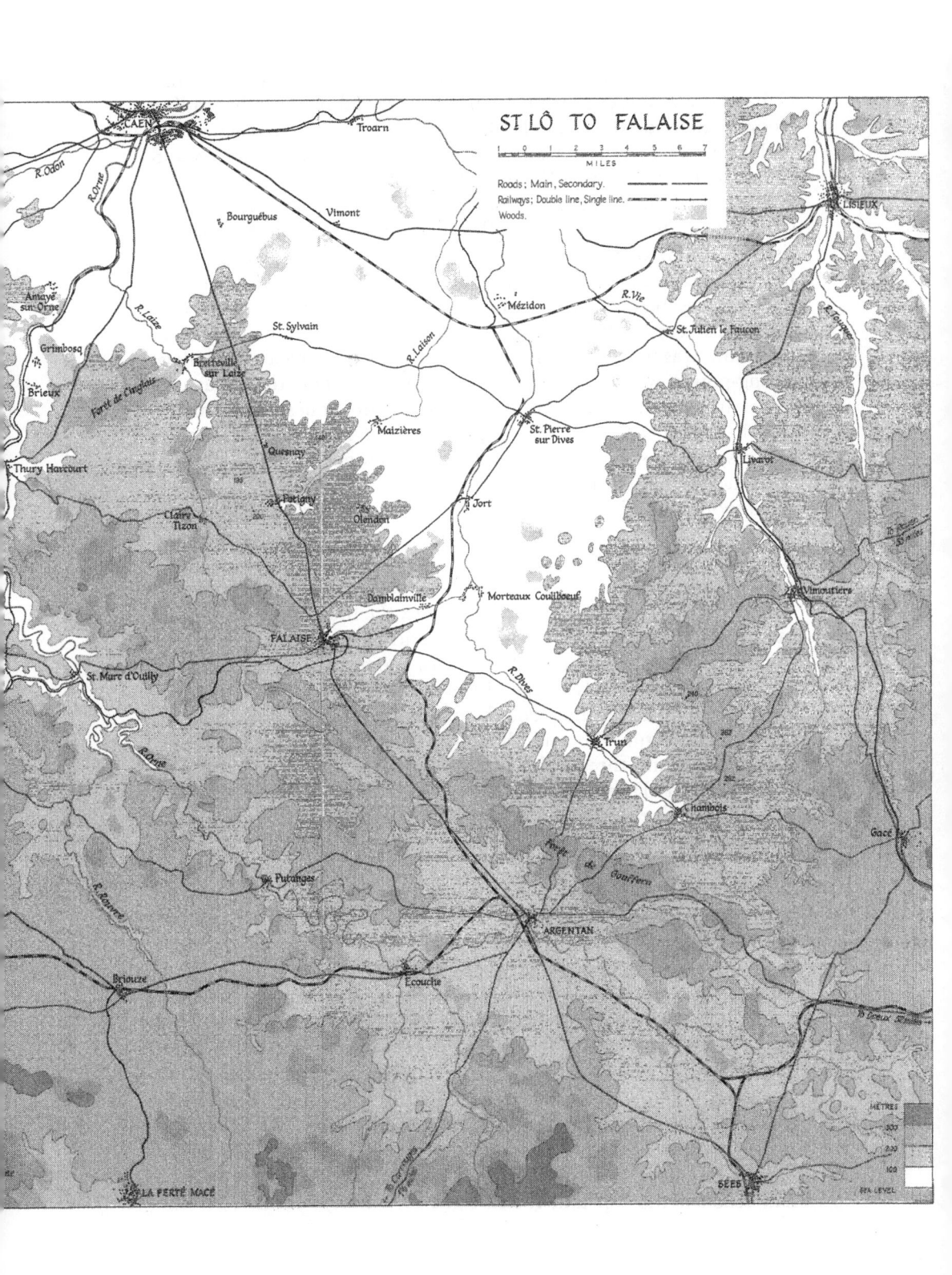

holding the front. At seven in the evening a new attack against Cahagnes was launched from the north-west and by dark the leading troops had cleared la Londe; by midnight they had reached the high ground just outside Cahagnes. It had been an unrewarding and rather baffling day for XXX Corps.

VIII Corps had better fortune and their spearheads were five or six miles south of Caumont by the end of the day. The 15th (Scottish) Division, with the 6th Guards Tank Brigade in support, and the 11th Armoured Division on their right began their advance a few minutes before seven. Attacking on a one-brigade front 15th Division's 227th Brigade, reinforced by an additional infantry battalion, was in the lead on the left. First it had to clear two village strong-points within a mile of Caumont and then to capture les Loges and a nearby hill—Point 226 two or three miles further south. One battalion of Churchill tanks, the 4th Tank Battalion Grenadier Guards, was in support at the start and two more would go forward with the brigade in the second phase.

As soon as the leading troops showed themselves on the forward slopes of the Caumont ridge they ran into heavy defensive fire, and seven of the Churchills and two flail tanks were put out of action by mines. Passages, however, were quickly flailed; the tanks caught up with the infantry and by about ten o'clock the first objectives were in our hands. The mopping-up of snipers and bazooka teams remained to be done, and the infantry detailed for the next phase were slowed up. Not to lose the advantage of the artillery programme the tanks went ahead as fast as they could, spraying the hedges and orchards with machine-gun fire and shelling any buildings they could see. Between two and three o'clock they had reached Point 226, near les Loges, and the Hervieux cross-roads about a mile to the west. They had had a very rough ride, '. . . we were all black and blue from the jumps we had been over and quite a number of men, including my signal officer in my own tank, had been knocked senseless'. Others complained rather bitterly about the cider apples which poured down through open turrets, for the driver could see little and the tank commander had to stand up to guide him while struggling with the branches to keep his other tanks in view.

Since the 43rd Division had been unable to make further headway in XXX Corps' sector the Scottish division's left flank was open but the tanks which were at Hervieux were told to seize the hill at Point 309 without waiting for the infantry, while others carried up an infantry battalion to reinforce them. Finding the village of la Morichesse les Mares held by German tanks and infantry, the Churchills turned to the left and drove straight at the hill. Several became bogged or turned over but by seven o'clock the leading squadron had reached the top and found signs of a hasty German retreat.

There was some sniping from the undergrowth but the position was held without difficulty till the infantry arrived just before dark.

Meanwhile there had been trouble further back about les Loges which 6th Guards Tank Brigade, with one squadron disposed about Point 226, had been told to hold at all costs. About six o'clock, by which time a company of infantry had joined the tanks, accurate shelling and mortaring started from woods to the left rear. Eight Churchills were in flames within a minute or two and shortly afterwards three Jagdpanthers[3] drove over the hill and knocked out others. They were engaged by the other squadrons and two of them were later found abandoned down in the valley with their tracks shot away. Their attack was not followed up and, with the arrival of more infantry, the Point 226 area was reorganised. No ground had been lost and infantry went on steadily mopping up the divisional area until after midnight. By then the 15th Division's 46th Brigade was strongly posted about Point 309, having manhandled its anti-tank guns up the hill, and the other brigades were echeloned behind them keeping a watchful eye on the exposed left flank.

The tank battalions stayed for the night of the 30th in the forward areas alongside the infantry with whom they had lived and trained for well over a year. This was their first time in action together and they had had a successful day.

The 11th Armoured Division, on the right, had also made good progress. Mindful of their earlier experience of the *bocage* during the Odon battle, Epsom, both the 11th and the Guards Armoured Divisions had reorganised their two brigades so as to provide each with an equal number of tank and infantry units. The 11th Armoured Division advanced in two columns—29th Armoured Brigade on the left with two armoured regiments, one infantry battalion and the motor battalion; 159th Infantry Brigade on the right with one armoured regiment and two infantry battalions; and the armoured reconnaissance regiment under divisional command followed behind for the moment. While protecting the right flank of the Scottish division the 11th Armoured's task was to take St. Martin des Besaces and the ridge to its west, and exploit south-westwards past the Forêt l'Evêque.

Troops in the opening phase of the attack from the outskirts of Caumont had much the same experience as the other divisions. By midday the 29th Armoured Brigade had skirted the fighting around Sept Vents and was making progress, though further to the right, among the woods near Cussy, there were sharp engagements which continued into the late afternoon. The 159th Brigade fared better

---

[3] The Jagdpanther (literally, 'hunter-panther') was an 88-mm anti-tank gun mounted on a Mark V tank chassis, and weighed altogether about 45 tons. In this particular case they belonged to the 654th G.H.Q. Anti-tank Battalion.

and, having pushed across the Caumont–Torigny road, the leading troops were about a mile past Dampierre by dusk. The 29th Brigade on their left had by then gained St. Jean des Essartiers, two miles short of St. Martin. The division was still in contact with the enemy at several points on its front; further west the adjacent division of the American V Corps had been able to make little progress beyond the Caumont–St. Lô road. But 11th Armoured Division had orders to continue the advance into the night, and the armoured car regiment was brought forward to exploit the situation at dawn the next day.

As reports of British progress reached von Kluge's headquarters during the 30th he ordered the 21st Panzer Division (then in Panzer Group West reserve, east of the Orne) to move at once to LXXIV Corps' defence of the Caumont sector. It left its bivouacs in the Forêt de Cinglais at about five o'clock but by ten at night the foremost armour was still two or three miles short of Cahagnes, having taken five hours to cover some twenty miles, for it had moved in daylight, shadowed and harried by a hostile air force overhead.

The British advance exposed the flank of II Parachute Corps, facing the Americans in the next sector, for all touch had been lost with the 326th Division on its right. An air attack appeared to have put the division's headquarters out of action and two of its regimental headquarters were surrounded by British tanks. The right flank of II Parachute Corps was now in the air and von Kluge had no choice but to authorise the corps to withdraw during the night to positions running westwards from St. Martin. On the whole battle front there was indeed much activity that night on both sides.

On the left, Royal Engineers worked unceasingly to clear or breach the minefields which had delayed XXX Corps' progress and by first light on the morning of the 31st troops of its 43rd Division, developing a 'right hook' against Cahagnes, had pushed forward to within striking distance when the enemy met them with a sharp counter-attack. The fight got to close quarters but the enemy were driven off with heavy loss. Cahagnes was taken during the afternoon, ground south of the Briquessard stream was cleared of scattered opposition and late that night St. Pierre du Fresne was entered. Soon after daybreak on August the 1st the enemy again attacked with tanks and infantry, but they were driven off and the advance continued southwards to Point 361—the hill at the eastern corner of the Bois du Homme. As the leading troops reached it they were attacked by three heavy tanks but two ditched themselves and the third was knocked out by an anti-tank gun.

Less progress towards Amaye sur Seulles had been made by 50th Division, and 7th Armoured Division was ordered to move forward through 43rd Division's area and capture Aunay sur Odon from the west. But the armoured division made very slow progress. The absence of roads running southwards on XXX Corps front and the nature of country which kept them largely road-bound led them to seek a route through the outskirts of Caumont. The town, however, was crowded by rear elements of other divisions and on all roads leading into and out of it there was appalling congestion. The 43rd Division was not yet clear of the roads and the 7th Armoured Division could only move at a snail's pace. Its leading troops had only reached Breuil by nightfall; though they had met but little opposition they were still five miles short of Aunay. XXX Corps had made disappointing progress but was at least in a better position to achieve General Dempsey's aim which was to continue the attack south-eastwards across the Odon and over the Mont Pinçon ridge.

During these two days VIII Corps on the British right and the Americans beyond them had thrust further southwards. It will be remembered that on the night of the 30th the 15th Scottish Division was extending the position it had won at Point 309. Next morning the 21st Panzer Division made several attempts to assemble for counter-attack in and about the Bois du Homme but all were frustrated by gun-fire and air attacks; five squadrons of Typhoons of 83 Group rocketed the wood while two more bombed targets outside it. Afterwards the army calculated that during the morning the air force and artillery had between them destroyed some thirty tanks. However, 21st Panzer Division was ordered 'to continue to counter-attack with all resources at its disposal. Point 300 [a misprint for 309] . . . must be taken.' But the division was still being delayed by fighter-bomber attacks and artillery fire and as a result its main counter-attack did not develop till next day—August the 1st. Then infantry and tanks (including some Tigers) attacked 15th Division's position from Bois du Homme, from la Ferrière au Doyen to the north and from Galet to the south, but all attacks were broken up by fire of the Scottish infantry and tanks of the 6th Guards Tank Brigade, augmented by mortars and artillery fire. Throughout the rest of the day the enemy continued probing attacks, and when they withdrew they were followed up by infantry and tanks. By nightfall on the 1st of August not only was the main position based on Hill 309 firmly held but la Ferrière and Galet were cleared and in Scottish hands.

On their right the armoured divisions had also had two successful days' fighting. On the night of the 30th, leading troops of the 11th Armoured were working round St. Martin des Besaces. On the 31st they launched a two-pronged attack and by eleven o'clock had broken through a screen of anti-tank guns and were clearing the village. Meanwhile reconnaissance troops had been probing southwards. About 10.30 a.m. a squadron of the Household Cavalry armoured cars sent back a wireless message which, half blanketed by hills, could not at first be read. Ordered to repeat it the squadron leader replied, 'I say again, at 1035 hours, the bridge at 637436 is clear of enemy and still intact'.[4] A patrol had found a way through the enemy's front and reached the Souleuvre bridge five miles behind it. They had moved through l'Evêque forest, raced through la Ferrière and reached the river about two miles west of le Bény-Bocage. On receipt of their message another troop of armoured cars and some tanks were ordered to the bridge. The tanks got through and made it secure; the armoured cars were held up on emerging from l'Evêque forest and seeking a detour ran into an ambush and were destroyed.

The opening of a route through l'Evêque forest and the capture of the Souleuvre bridge enabled 11th Armoured Division to push troops across the river that night and reach the hills west of le Bény-Bocage; a good bridgehead was formed and the slopes of Point 205 occupied. South of l'Evêque forest American troops were met and arrangements were concerted with them for defence of the right flank.

Early that afternoon, on learning of the 11th Armoured's success at the Souleuvre, General O'Connor ordered the Guards Armoured Division (then waiting north of Caumont) to come up on the 11th's left and secure additional routes over the river in the neighbourhood of le Tourneur. By evening the leading troops of the division had reached the hills south-east of St. Martin to find them strongly held by tanks and infantry of the 21st Panzer Division. First attempts to take Point 192 that night were beaten back. At an early hour on the 1st the attack was resumed, and by midday both Points 192 and 238 were captured by the 5th Guards Brigade. It had been a stiff fight and, as patrols and air reconnaissance showed 21st Panzer Division's tanks to be in some strength ahead, the 32nd Guards Infantry Brigade was passed through to take the final objective. Despite some heavy fire in the early stages the advance went well; le Tourneur was entered in the late evening and a fresh infantry attack made after dark quickly gained the nearby bridge over the Souleuvre.

Meanwhile, during the course of the day the 11th Armoured Division had captured le Bény-Bocage. While some of its troops then turned left on to the high ground opposite le Tourneur, armoured cars explored the country well to the south. They got to within two miles of Vire but found the enemy building up strong resistance around the town and further progress was not attempted that day;

---

[4] R. Orde, *The Household Cavalry at War* (1953), p. 101.

GERMAN WITHDRAWAL DEBATED

moreover, an agreed modification of boundaries had left the capture of Vire to the Americans and Second Army was now to wheel eastwards—XXX Corps to the Orne and VIII Corps on the outer flank towards Condé sur Noireau and Flers. (Map, page 389.)

With 21st Panzer Division tied to the British front, the German 84th Infantry Division which was being hurried across the Seine to the restless Canadian sector was now directed instead to reinforce their Seventh Army, while 89th Infantry Division from the Fifteenth Army was warned to be ready to take the place of 84th Division in Panzer Group West. The 21st Panzer Division's attempts to capture Point 309 had been finally abandoned as offering no prospect of success, and Eberbach told Army Group B that whatever might be the state of the Caen front the LXXIV Corps sector of the Caumont front was at the moment the decisive one. Should not 9th SS or 12th SS Panzer Division be moved across at once? After considerable discussion of possibilities von Kluge ordered Eberbach to move II SS Panzer Corps with 9th SS and 10th SS Panzer Divisions, the 8th Werfer Brigade, Corps Troops, and the 668th Heavy Anti-tank Battalion when it arrived; the armoured corps would also take over 21st Panzer Division. On arrival, 10th SS Panzer Division was to halt the British thrust towards Aunay and 9th SS Panzer Division to gain the line from le Tourneur to Point 205 at le Bény-Bocage and link up with II Parachute Corps at Carville. Thus, at a crucial moment for the whole German front in the West, the British Caumont offensive was drawing to itself two more armoured divisions which now might otherwise have been sent to the American front. Yet Eberbach was not content. He told Speidel that the three armoured divisions which he was using on his left front might indeed be able to check the enemy but could never effectively halt him. He believed that the only sound thing to do was to pull everything back to the Seine. Speidel replied that he would report this to von Kluge.

Almost at the same time the question of withdrawal was being discussed at Hitler's headquarters. It will be remembered that on July the 23rd, before Cobra had started, the British gains on the Caen front and the growing American threat to St. Lô had already convinced Jodl that withdrawal in the West might soon become necessary (page 375), and planning for such an eventuality had begun at OKW. On July the 30th Jodl handed to Hitler 'a draft order for possible withdrawal from the coastal fronts' and a conference with him was held on July the 31st. The meeting began a few minutes before midnight and lasted a little more than an hour. There were present besides the Führer only Jodl, Warlimont (Jodl's deputy), the SS representative and the Luftwaffe adjutant on Hitler's staff, and three minor staff officers. Except for one or two comments by Jodl and a few short answers to questions from others, Hitler spoke uninterruptedly throughout the whole meeting. It is one of the comparatively few of Hitler's meetings of which there remains a full verbatim report and it is therefore of particular interest. From Hitler's shapeless, hour-long monologue it is possible not only to gain insight into his views on general policy but to see the effect on his mind and mood, and on his physical condition, of the attempt to murder him eleven days before.

Of the physical effects he said:

> 'I wanted so much to get across to the West, but I cannot do it now with the best will in the world; I shall not be able to climb into an aeroplane, on account of my ears [*sic*], for at least the next week ... Now if I climb into an aeroplane with its roaring engines and varying pressures it would, in certain circumstances, be catastrophic; and what would happen if I suddenly got inflammation of the middle ear! ... The danger of infection is there as long as the wound is open ... I stand naturally, and can also speak for a certain time, but then suddenly I have to sit down again. I would not trust myself today to speak in front of 10,000 people ... because in certain circumstances I suddenly get an attack of giddiness and collapse. Even when I am walking I may suddenly, at a moment's notice, have to take a tight grip on myself to keep going straight ... Otherwise a miracle has happened to me—my nervous trouble has almost disappeared on account of the coup. My left leg still keeps trembling a bit when the conferences are too long, but it used to tremble before in bed. Because of the coup this trouble has suddenly almost completely disappeared, but I should not like to say that I consider it the proper cure.'

The most noticeable effect on Hitler's mind was, not unnaturally, to aggravate his deep-seated distrust of Army generals and the General Staff. Speaking of the Russian threat in the East, he declared that Germany would weather this crisis if the 'crisis in morale' were overcome.

> 'This cannot be considered separately from the act perpetrated here; for this act is not to be regarded as an isolated one' but as a kind of 'internal blood-poisoning which we have suffered. After all, what do you expect of an entire front, if, in the rear, as we see now, the most important positions in its supreme command are filled by absolute wreckers—not defeatists, but wreckers and traitors to their country. For it is so: if our signals channels and Quartermaster's Office are filled by people who are downright traitors—and we don't know at all how long they have already been conspiring with the enemy or the people over there—we cannot expect the spirit required to stop such an affair to be forthcoming from that quarter: for the Russians' morale has surely not become so much better in one or two years ... but

we have undoubtedly grown worse, morally speaking—grown worse because we have had that set-up over there which has been continually spreading poison through the channels of the General Staff organisation, the organisation of the Quartermaster General, of the Signals Chief, etc., so that today we only need to ask, or no longer *need* to ask: how does the enemy learn our thoughts from us? Why is so much checkmated? . . . It is probably not all due to the discernment of the Russians but to permanent treason which has been continually practised by a small, accursed clique . . . Even if the position cannot be explained so precisely it would be quite enough that influential positions are here filled by people who, instead of constantly radiating energy and spreading confidence and, above all things, increasingly realising the historically decisive nature of this battle of destiny which cannot in any way be resolved, or its end negotiated, by any clever sort of political or tactical skill . . . essentially a Hunnish sort of battle in which one must either stand or fall and die—one of the two . . . It must be stopped. It will not do. We must remove and expel these basest of creatures in all history who have ever worn the soldier's uniform, this rabble who have survived from a former régime. That is the supreme duty.'

There was further scathing condemnation of army leaders (especially of Beck and von Stülpnagel) on whose misconduct he blamed Germany's serious situation. Mixed up with this diatribe were some indications of his views on strategy. The first concern, he said, was to stabilise the eastern front, where a break-through would threaten the German homeland. The attitude of Turkey and the Balkan countries depended in great measure on whether the eastern front could be held. Possession of Hungary was essential to German defence because of its vital food supplies, raw materials and communications with south-east Europe. 'Any English attempt, therefore, to land in the Balkans or Istria, or the Dalmatian Islands, would be highly dangerous because it might have immediate effects on Hungary . . . An English landing might naturally lead to catastrophic results.' He did not wish to keep his armies in Italy yet felt that their withdrawal would free Allied forces to fight elsewhere.

Coming to the real purpose of the meeting, the discussion of Jodl's plan for withdrawal, Hitler's fear of treachery came out strongly. 'If we lose France as a war zone, we shall lose the starting point of the U-boat war . . .' Landings at various points or a break-through in France would raise questions too big for von Kluge to solve. 'I cannot leave the Western campaign to Kluge.' Von Kluge must be told only what was immediately required of him; broad plans should be withheld for if orders were issued as formerly 'the enemy would be apprised immediately of all we are doing . . . C-in-C West has to know no more than is necessary.' In fact, he need only know that no withdrawal would be tolerated. 'He must know, first, that he must fight here in all circumstances, secondly, that this battle is decisive, thirdly, that the idea of operating freely in the open is nonsense.'

But while von Kluge was thus to be held fighting blindly for the existing front, a special staff should be formed by OKW to prepare for the withdrawal which even Hitler now realised might soon be necessary. The special staff would determine the lines in France to which the troops would withdraw and arrange for the work on them, which must not be left to the army in the West. 'We can only offer serious resistance at those points where we either have the West Wall, or at least ground conditions which permit this, that is, in the Vosges—there we can organise resistance.' And, without being told why, von Kluge must be ordered to make some of his formations 'absolutely mobile'.

While 'we ourselves shall determine the various eventualities from the very start by means of the [special] staff', it was essential to delay the enemy's advance by two measures. 'The only thing which can act as a brake on the enemy when he is throwing in unlimited equipment, troops and formations, is the number of landing places at his disposal. If he does not obtain . . . ports which are workable, that is the only brake on his otherwise boundless possibilities of movement.' These ports should be turned into fortresses and resolute commanders should be appointed to hold them. The second check was to be made by destroying all essential bridges and all railway equipment in the course of withdrawal. 'I shall present him [the enemy] with a war . . . of scorched earth, on other than German soil.'

In a written statement made by General Warlimont after the war it is said that after others had left the meeting it was agreed that Warlimont should go to the West front in order to size up the situation and to convey Hitler's instructions to von Kluge. On being pressed by Warlimont for clear instructions as to *what* von Kluge was to be told, Hitler said brusquely, 'Tell Field-Marshal von Kluge that he should keep his eyes riveted to the front and on the enemy without ever looking backward. If and when precautionary measures have to be taken in the rear of the theatre of operations in the West everything necessary will be done by OKW and OKW alone.'[5] But several hours *before* the midnight meeting with Hitler, Jodl, noting that Hitler 'accepts the order for a possible withdrawal in France', told von Kluge's Chief of Staff that such an order was to be expected, and that 'it was now necessary to begin preliminary staff work and planning'. On July the 24th von Kluge considered that '15th Army's sector from north of the Somme down to the Seine continues to be

---

[5] Pogue, *The Supreme Command*, p. 203.

particularly endangered' though 'a widely separated landing operation becomes less probable'. On the 27th he sought permission to transfer two infantry divisions from the 15th Army to Normandy 'as no immediate signs are discernible of a second assault landing'. But if von Kluge no longer expected it Hitler was less sure. Though he consented to the proposed transfers yet 'in order to replace the reserves withdrawn from 15th Army, worn-out infantry or panzer divisions will be transferred behind 15th Army as soon as possible'.

Throughout July Bomber Command had continued the attack on flying-bomb sites and strategic targets when not required to give direct assistance to the Army in the capture of Caen, the Goodwood battle and the advance from Caumont at the end of the month. The flying-bomb counter-offensive took a large measure of its strength, for on average it employed over two hundred bombers each day except on three occasions during the whole month. Many of these attacks were made by day, for Bomber Command had developed a high standard of accuracy in daylight bombing, but throughout July bad flying weather greatly increased the difficulty of hitting targets that were small and hard to distinguish. In continuance of Bomber Command's attack on communications, important main-line railway centres on the lines converging on Paris were constantly attacked; two fuel storage-depots were bombed, over three hundred Mosquito 'intruder' sorties were flown against airfields and mine-laying was continued almost daily. During the first half of July these and other operations allowed only small-scale Mosquito attacks against German cities, designed to keep the inhabitants on edge rather than to effect much material damage, but each of these elusive little aircraft could carry a 4,000-pound bomb so their sting was not to be despised. Berlin was attacked nine times in July and other cities 'stung' included Hanover, Cologne, Bremen, Aachen, Frankfurt and Mannheim. Then, in the last weeks of the month, Bomber Command was able to renew the heavy attacks on German industrial cities which had been interrupted since D-day to give more direct support to Overlord and deal with the flying-bomb attack on England. Attacks on synthetic oil plants and factories in the Ruhr were resumed, and on the 23rd Kiel was struck by 629 bombers which dropped nearly 3,000 tons on the city. On the 24th a prolonged attack on Stuttgart began; that night 614 bombers dropped over 1,700 tons; on the following night 550 bombers dropped over 1,400 tons; and three nights later nearly 500 bombers added a further 1,600 tons. On that night also 300 bombers attacked Hamburg with over 1,100 tons of bombs. Such raids left a trail of material damage and interfered with industrial production.

Throughout July the Eighth Air Force had carried out some attacks on flying-bomb launching sites but, apart from the direct assistance given to army operations, had been mainly concerned in its share in the disruption of communications, the weakening of the enemy air force and the curtailment of oil supplies. In the attack on communications it had concentrated largely on the destruction of road and rail bridges of importance to the enemy and on railway marshalling yards. In its effort to reduce the enemy air strength, airfields and aerodromes had been attacked in France and the Low Countries and aircraft production works and industrial areas in Germany. And German synthetic oil plants and oil depots had been attacked on a rising scale. The bearing on Overlord of the operations of Bomber Command and the American Eighth Air Force will be discussed when the story of the battle of Normandy has been concluded and what was done in August can be brought into the account.

In this connection two further maps, reproduced from the German railway engineers' report mentioned on page 111, show the enemy's record of damage done to railway communications by Allied bombing and sabotage in June and July. The maps show how the enemy's movement of reinforcements and supplies was effectively restricted by the attacks of Allied air forces and how well the latter succeeded in isolating the Normandy battle area from railway communication with Germany.

It will also be convenient to sum up later the part played by the German Air Force in the battle of Normandy. During July there had been changes in the grouping and command of units of the Third Air Fleet and it had had some reinforcements. But the *Luftwaffe* had never been able to interfere with Allied operations. Thirty or forty aircraft at a time made offensive sweeps over the battle area fairly frequently but did little damage; usually when enemy aircraft appeared they were on defensive patrol, trying to protect their own troops. According to their records, an average of about 500 sorties was flown daily on all types of operations including reconnaissance and mining at sea.

Zerstörungskarte – Juni 1944 (Railway destruction)

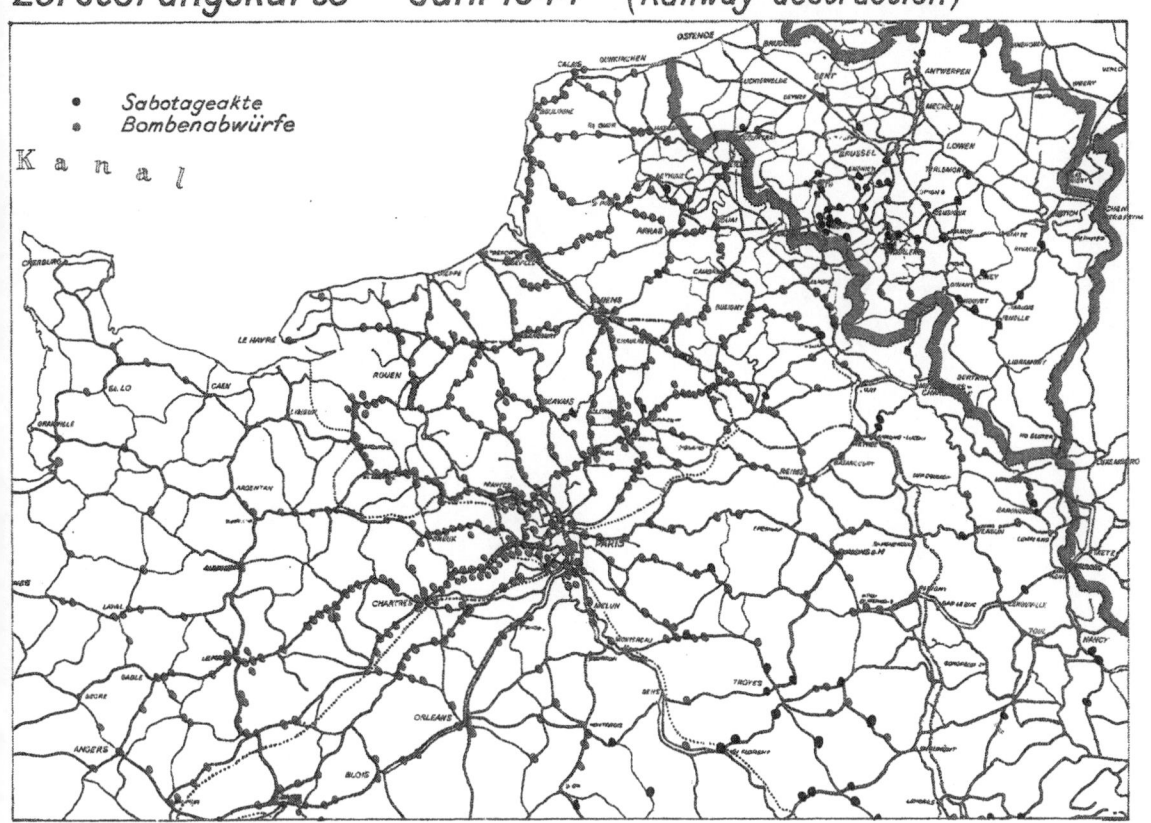

- Sabotageakte
- Bombenabwürfe

Zerstörungskarte – Juli 1944

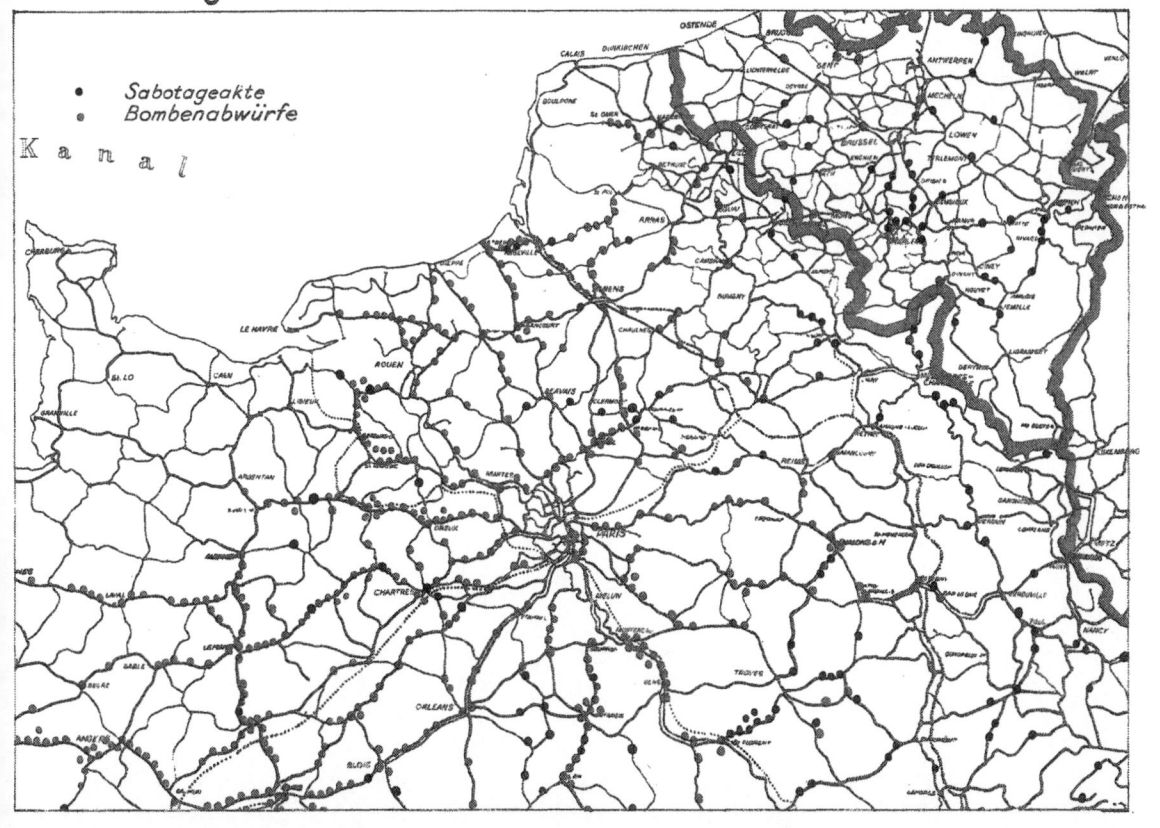

- Sabotageakte
- Bombenabwürfe

CHAPTER XVIII

BEGINNING OF THE ENVELOPMENT

THE Second Army's attack was continued on the 2nd of August. VIII Corps renewed its advance with 11th Armoured Division starting from le Bény-Bocage in the direction of Tinchebray and the Guards Armoured Division on its left aiming at Estry and Vassy. Opposition by infantry detachments and tanks was met and overcome at many points but increased as the day wore on; nevertheless, Etouvy on the right flank was occupied by 11th Armoured Division and its leading troops were established on the Perrier ridge, overlooking much of the Vire–Vassy road between Vire and Chênedolle. On the same day the reconnaissance battalion of the Guards Armoured Division reached the high ground above Estry, by-passing positions held by 21st Panzer Division on their left at Arclais, Montcharivel and Montchamp which the following infantry were to attack. The armoured divisions had made a deep penetration but some of the ground they had overrun still needed clearing of enemy troops and there were recurrent outbreaks of fighting in the intervening country till mopping up was completed and the flanks made secure. The newly-arriving 9th SS Panzer Division tried desperately hard to regain both the le Tourneur bridge over the Souleuvre and the Perrier ridge to the east of Vire, but was thrown back with heavy losses.

Vire is the meeting place of seven major roads and, though much damaged by bombing, was of key importance to the German defence. East of Vire, Eberbach's Panzer Group West was responsible for the front; west of the town the loose flank of Hausser's Seventh Army was bent back to prevent the enlargement of the American breakthrough. At the beginning of August the two were inadequately joined; there was virtually a gap in the defences to the east of Vire which Eberbach was ordered to fill, for a further Allied breakthrough there might well cut off the Seventh Army. It was to stop this that II SS Panzer Corps was being brought up on the left of LXXIV Corps. Vire itself had been only lightly held when British patrols first reached the vicinity but the agreed boundary between the British and American armies had been drawn east of Vire and now its defences were being strengthened. In the next few days, while the armoured divisions of VIII Corps held their ground on the

Perrier and Estry ridges and fought off attempts to break in behind them, infantry were ordered forward to clear the ground overrun and to strengthen the outer flanks of the salient: on the right, the 185th Brigade of the 3rd Division (newly moved from Caen) and on the left, the 44th Brigade of the 15th Division. Subsequently the 3rd Division and the 15th Division were to come forward on the flanks of the two armoured divisions so that VIII Corps could then continue its advance on a four-division front.

Meanwhile XXX Corps on the left had made less progress. In the early hours of August the 2nd the 43rd Division had started from the Bois du Homme and, overcoming a number of attacks by small battle groups, had advanced some three miles through difficult country, driving 21st Panzer Division troops out of Jurques and capturing Hill 301, two miles to the south. Next day their progress was held up in stubborn fighting with newly-arrived troops of the 10th SS Panzer Division. On their left 7th Armoured Division had made no progress towards the capture of Aunay. Attacking with its armoured brigade on August the 2nd and its infantry brigade on the 3rd, it had been counter-attacked by 10th SS Panzer Division and forced back almost to Breuil, whence it had started forty-eight hours earlier. The third division of XXX Corps—the 50th—had taken the high ground two miles west of Villers-Bocage, the Amaye sur Seulles feature, capturing a regimental commander and his headquarters from the enemy's 326th Division. On the 4th of August, Lieut-General B. G. Horrocks (from England) succeeded Lieut-General G. C. Bucknall in command of XXX Corps, and Brigadier G. L. Verney (from 6th Guards Tank Brigade) succeeded Major-General G. W. E. J. Erskine in command of 7th Armoured Division.

Meanwhile, in the American sector the projected reorganisation of their forces had become operative on August the 1st. General Bradley became commander of the U.S. Twelfth Army Group and there was a corresponding rearrangement of air force commands. Matched with the army group was the Ninth Air Force now commanded by Major-General H. S. Vandenberg.[1] Under him were IX Tactical Air Command (Major-General E. R. Quesada), associated with General Hodges' First Army, and XIX Tactical Air Command (Brigadier-General O. P. Weyland), associated with General Patton's Third Army; the rest of the Ninth Air Force continued for the present to be based in England. About the same time the temporary appointment of Commander, Advanced Allied Expeditionary Air Force was abolished and Air Marshal Coningham, commanding the British Second Tactical Air Force, moved to

---

[1] General Brereton was to command the First Allied Airborne Army, now being formed in England.

France and set up his main headquarters adjacent to the main headquarters of Twenty-First Army Group, which had moved from England on August the 4th and was established at le Tronquay (six miles south-west of Bayeux). Under Air Marshal Coningham in France were 83 Group (Air Vice-Marshal Broadhurst), associated with Dempsey's Second Army, and most of 84 Group (Air Vice-Marshal L. O. Brown), associated with the First Canadian Army; by this time much of 85 Group (Air Vice-Marshal C. R. Steele), with night and day fighters, concerned mainly with base defence and maintenance, was also in France. By August the 7th there was a total of thirty-eight squadrons of the Second Tactical Air Force in France operating from eleven airfields; the rest of the Second Tactical Air Force, including 2 Group (Air Vice-Marshal B. E. Embry), was for the time being still operating from England.

By August the 1st the American VIII Corps was consolidating its advance in the Cotentin coastal zone and, having reached Pontaubault, south of Avranches, was about to turn westwards into Brittany. General Bradley's 'Letter of Instruction No. 1' dated July the 29th (effective at noon of August the 1st) had directed First Army 'to drive south in its zone and seize area Mortain–Vire', while Third Army was 'to drive south in its zone and seize the area Rennes–Fougères' and then turn 'west into Brittany with the mission of securing St. Malo, Quiberon Bay and Brest, and of clearing the rest of the peninsula'. Up to this point Bradley's intention was to use Third Army for the early capture of Brittany and the ports to which such great importance had always been attached. But by August the 1st two things were already clear. There was a gap between the west coast and the loose end of the German front which was steadily widening under the American attacks; and enemy forces in Brittany had been so robbed to bolster up the German Seventh Army's defence that apart from those retained to hold the ports there were few troops left to oppose the Americans. On July the 29th Twenty-First Army Group planners estimated that one American corps would now suffice to secure Brittany. The situation was discussed by General Montgomery with General Bradley and General Dempsey on August the 1st, and on the 3rd General Bradley issued his second 'Letter of Instruction'. This ordered the First Army to advance in the Vire–Mortain zone to secure the Mayenne–Domfront area, prepared for further action eastwards, and ordered a change in the task of General Patton's Third Army on the lines adumbrated in General Montgomery's directive of July the 10th (page 327). This was to have momentous consequences. To complete the clearance of the Brittany peninsula and secure its ports General Patton was now to use only 'minimum forces'; with the rest of his army he was to clear the country southwards to the Loire and be prepared for further action 'with strong armoured forces' towards the east and south-east—that is in the open, largely undefended country south of the *bocage*.

The American First Army had meanwhile been driving back the enemy's broken-ended front. Progress had been slowed down by determined opposition of the German II Parachute Corps, LXXXIV and XLVII Panzer Corps; nevertheless, while the British advanced through le Bény-Bocage and towards the Condé sur Noireau–Vire road as has already been described, the First Army began to outflank the German defence. Though Vire and St. Pois were still in enemy hands they had captured Juvigny and Mortain, and between Mortain and the Loire there was no consecutive front but only disjointed opposition at various points. Into that more open country the Third Army's main forces were to drive—XV Corps going south-eastwards towards Laval and le Mans, XX Corps southwards to Angers near the Loire to protect the river flank from the area of the German First Army. Only General Patton's VIII Corps continued its advance westwards into Brittany.

General Montgomery's April forecast of the way in which he

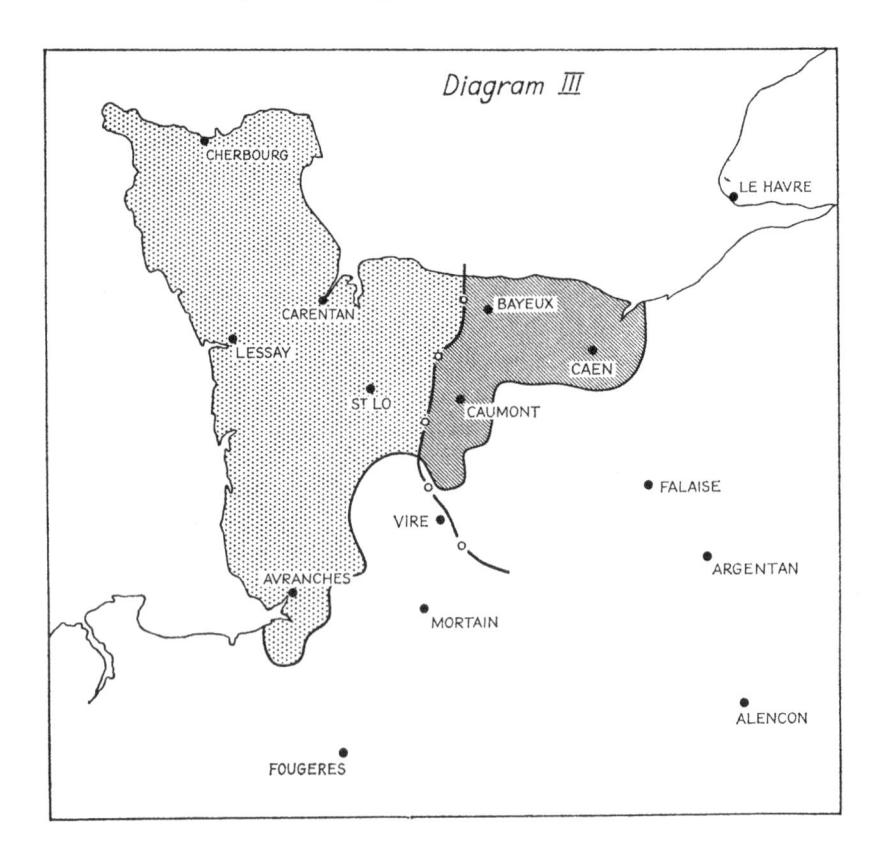

Diagram III

HITLER'S ORDERS

thought that Overlord would be developed (see Diagram I, page 357 above) was nearly realised; Diagram III (here repeated) shows that apart from Brittany the Allied position on August the 1st closely approximated to the position in the forecast from which a wheel eastwards would begin. It will be remembered that at the end of June (page 309) General Montgomery had said that when the base of the Cotentin peninsula was reached near Avranches, the right-hand corps should be turned westwards into Brittany but that plans should be prepared for the rest of General Bradley's command to 'direct a strong right wing in a wide sweep south of the bocage country' to successive objectives Laval–Mayenne, le Mans–Alençon. The 'wide sweep' had now begun.

As already mentioned, II SS Panzer Corps had been ordered westwards to contest the British advance in the Caumont area. For in spite of the overriding importance of preventing a British breakthrough towards Falaise on the eastern flank, the attack in the Caumont sector threatened a break in the centre near Vire, the hinge which linked the front of Panzer Group West and the bent-back defence of the Seventh Army. Though von Kluge had managed to find additional infantry divisions he realised that the front could only be stabilised by the use of armoured divisions at its most threatened points, even though this increased the risk on the eastern flank.

He had reached this conclusion when his thoughts were rudely upset. At about one o'clock in the morning of August the 3rd he received orders from Hitler.[2]

> 'The front between the Orne and the Vire will mainly be held by infantry divisions. To this end the infantry divisions which are approaching will be wheeled to the north, and, if necessary, the front line will be taken back, so that a new main defence line will be formed and held on the general line: Thury-Harcourt–Vire–Fontenermont.
>
> The armoured formations which have up to now been employed on that front must be released and moved complete to the left wing. The enemy's armoured forces which have pressed forward to the east, south-east and south will be annihilated by an attack which these armoured formations—numbering at least four—will make, and contact will be restored with the west coast of the Cotentin at Avranches—or north of that—without regard to the enemy penetrations in Brittany.'

Whatever von Kluge thought about the wisdom of this order he

---

[2] Sent by OKW at 2315 hrs. on August 2nd and repeated to Army Group B HQ at 0020 hrs. on the 3rd.

immediately took steps to carry it out. That afternoon he informed OKW of the consequent instructions he had issued. 'In order to close [the gap] in the front and form a strong armoured assault' the front of Panzer Group West and Seventh Army would that night begin withdrawing to a new main defence line (described in detail) based on Thury-Harcourt and Vire. Using the newly arrived 84th and 363rd Infantry Divisions, Seventh Army would release the battle groups of 2nd SS Panzer Division and 17th SS Panzer Grenadier Division, and Panzer Group West would assemble 1st SS Panzer Division north of Falaise with a further unspecified armoured division. With the armoured forces thus made available,

> '7th Army will prepare a panzer group attack on both sides of Sourdeval, so that the enemy between Mortain and Avranches will be annihilated by a thrust from east to west and the Cotentin front will be closed again. For this attack there will probably be available XLVII Panzer Corps and LXXXI Corps with 2, 9, and 116 Panzer Divisions, a battle group of 2 SS Panzer Division and a battle group of 17 SS Panzer Grenadier Division.'

The attack was to be conducted by the commander of XLVII Panzer Corps—General Funck.

At that time Headquarters LXXXI Corps and 9th Panzer Division were *not* 'available' for they had not yet reached the battle area;[3] the other divisions named were actively engaged in vainly trying to hold the western end of the German front and arrest the Allied advance. Von Kluge can hardly have believed his ingenuous pretence that if relieved by infantry they could then annihilate the enemy between Mortain and Avranches and close the Cotentin front again.

Next day, August the 4th, at Seventh Army battle headquarters, von Kluge and Hausser discussed plans for the armoured attack and decided that it would not be launched before the night of the 6th/7th. C-in-C West war diary noted their decision and added:

> 'The attack planned represents the decisive attempt to restore the situation in the Normandy battle area. If the enemy who have penetrated the Rennes area and Brittany can be successfully cut off from their rearward communications, the clarification of the situation in that area will have to be dealt with later. If, on the other hand, the thrust does not succeed, further developments will have to be expected. OKW . . . therefore orders the construction of further positions in the West under the responsible military direction of the Military Governor in France,

---

[3] The corps headquarters was on the way from Rouen: 9th Panzer Division coming from Avignon and 708th Infantry Division from Royan, near the mouth of the Garonne, were to be commanded by LXXXI Corps.

who is for this purpose placed directly under the command of the OKW Operations Staff.'[4]

The last paragraph refers to a further order which von Kluge had received from OKW when he got back from his meeting with Hausser. While he had been planning to annihilate the enemy's armoured forces and restore contact with the coast at Avranches, his Military Governor had been ordered to proceed independently to direct the construction of defensive positions far away in the east on the line of the Somme, Marne, Saône and Jura (clearly as insurance against failure). It was von Kluge's first official indication that Hitler at last contemplated the possibility of failure to prevent a complete collapse in Normandy.

While von Kluge was giving effect to Hitler's order to thrust with four divisions twenty miles westwards to Avranches, General Montgomery was issuing to the four Allied armies orders for a hundred-mile advance in the opposite direction. The Allied armies would swing the right flank towards Paris, forcing the enemy back against the Seine over which all the bridges had been destroyed between Paris and the sea. The immediate tasks of Twenty-First Army Group were for Second Army to continue thrusting southwards and eastwards, while First Canadian Army attacked strongly towards Falaise, starting if possible on the 7th. Two days later he amplified this order in view of the developments in the meantime. His general plan remained unchanged; to pivot on the left and swing hard with the right. The boundary between the British and American army groups he now carried on to the Seine, drawing the line through Tinchebray, Argentan and Dreux to Mantes-Gassicourt. After securing Falaise, First Canadian Army would hand the town over to Second Army and advance eastwards to Lisieux and Rouen. Second Army would advance through Argentan and Laigle, make for the Seine downstream of Mantes-Gassicourt, and be ready to force a crossing of the river between there and les Andelys. The American army group, advancing on a broad front, would arrange for 'the right flank to swing rapidly eastwards, and then north-eastwards towards Paris; speed in this movement is the basis of the whole plan of operations'. A strong airborne force (including two British divisions) would be used ahead of the Americans to secure the Chartres area and prevent the enemy escaping between Orléans and Paris. The Air Commander-in-Chief had been asked to direct the main air power to help the swing of the right flank and ensure that all enemy movement across the Seine, between Paris and the sea, would be stopped as far as this was possible. (Map, page 27.)

---

[4] After the abortive plot to murder Hitler, General Kitzinger had been appointed to succeed General von Stülpnagel as the Military Governor in France.

On the night of the 3rd the Panzer Group West began the withdrawal which von Kluge had ordered to a line to run roughly from Thury-Harcourt on the Orne to Vire. (Map, page 389.)

Its first effect was on Second Army's left wing where XII Corps followed the withdrawal closely with 53rd and 59th Divisions. At the outset they met little opposition but were hindered by a profusion of mines and booby traps on all the likely routes and defiles. By the evening of the 4th the left was at the Orne near Amaye, the centre had reached Evrecy and the right, in company with troops of XXX Corps, had occupied the shattered ruins of Villers-Bocage. On the 5th they met fewer mines and obstacles and only weak detachments of infantry, and some columns covered six or seven miles during the day. By nightfall the 53rd Division (on the left) had cleared the east bank of the Orne almost as far as Grimbosq, and on their right the 59th Division (with 34th Tank Brigade and 56th Infantry Brigade under command) had reached the river further upstream. From the loop in the Orne near Thury-Harcourt the British line then bent back westwards for three or four miles to where it faced the Mont Pinçon heights.

On 59th Division's front the Orne runs through a deep and narrow valley, the slopes on the western side being in many places so steep and heavily wooded that vehicles can only get down to the river where roads lead to bridges—all of which were broken. On the eastern bank the slopes are gentler, with orchards, farmhouses and small villages running up to the Forêt de Grimbosq—a useful 'hide' for assembling a counter-attack. Though there were several places where infantry could ford the river, the heavy weapons and tanks might have to wait until a bridge was built. The enemy could be seen digging busily on the far bank and on the hills beyond.

In the early evening of August the 6th the leading infantry of the 59th Division began wading the river near Brieux and before daylight next morning three battalions were across. They quickly freed a stretch of the river from small-arms fire and the engineers began their bridging. As it grew light the site was heavily mortared and shelled but the work went on; a bridge to carry up to nine tons was ready by seven-thirty, and a squadron of tanks had found a place where they too could ford the river. The infantry were glad to see them for, in the meantime, there had been two or three counter-attacks by local reserves of the 271st Infantry Division and Tiger tanks had been sighted. The fighting gradually died down, however, and the division set about improving and expanding its holding.

In the evening of the 7th the attacks were renewed in greater strength. A tank and infantry battle group of the 12th SS Panzer Division, hurried across from the Canadian sector, fought with determination but could not turn the scale. For twenty-four hours there was bitter close-quarter fighting, in which Captain David Jamieson of the Royal Norfolk Regiment gained the Victoria Cross; but the fire of infantry weapons and artillery broke up all attacks, and though a little ground was lost the bridgehead was firmly held.

XXX Corps, further west, was left on August the 3rd facing south-east from Villers-Bocage to the outskirts of Ondefontaine. After occupying Villers-Bocage its 50th Division went into reserve; for the first time since the landing on D-Day it was temporarily relieved of responsibility for holding any part of the front. The 7th Armoured Division was then holding the left of the corps front. Moving forward it occupied the now empty Aunay sur Odon and the high ground east of the village and prepared to continue southwards towards Condé sur Noireau. But first Mont Pinçon which stood in the way must be captured, a task which was given to the 43rd Division.

After a night and day of hard fighting, the 43rd Division finally secured Ondefontaine on the 5th and fanning out southwards made a firm junction with the 15th Division of VIII Corps. For the assault on Mont Pinçon a brigade group (129th Brigade and 13th/18th Hussars) was moved to le Mesnil-Auzouf to lead the six-mile advance eastwards. The intention was to make the final approach on a broad front, on the left via Duval and on the right by a turning movement through St. Jean le Blanc. As the columns approached in the evening the stream which flows a mile or so short of Mont Pinçon, it soon became clear that the enemy was determined to prevent this being crossed, and desperate fighting ensued between Duval and la Varinière and around St. Jean. The latter was in fact a key position in Panzer Group West's new defence line and, according to Eberbach, there were eight battalions of the 276th and 326th Infantry Divisions disposed on a four-mile front in its vicinity. Abandoning the attempt to advance through St. Jean, the divisional commander decided to concentrate the main attack on the west face of the hill but to reinforce this by bringing up another brigade (the 130th) from the direction of Ondefontaine to assault the north face. Mont Pinçon is an outstanding tactical feature towering over the surrounding countryside; it is about 1,200 feet high and on the western side the slopes are steep and rough. Its approaches were covered by guns, mortars and automatics of the defenders on its heights.

The attack began at half past two on the 6th. It was a very hot afternoon. The leading troops came under heavy fire as they approached the stream; one battalion, already weakened by losses on the previous day, was soon reduced to an effective strength of only sixty rifles. But while a reserve battalion was moving to pass through, the Hussars got some tanks across the stream and sent two troops on ahead to try to reach the crest. One tank overturned in a quarry and another had its tracks blown off but, with great determination and using the cover of a smoke screen, seven climbed to the top and by eight o'clock the rest of the squadron had joined them. Shortly afterwards thick fog came down and two infantry battalions of the 129th Brigade reached the hill. They dug in among the bracken and scrub and shared the flat hill-top with the Germans for the rest of the night. When the fog cleared in the early morning the garrison was eliminated and two hundred prisoners were taken.

Meanwhile the 130th Brigade from Ondefontaine had fought its way to the slopes on the north side, and the 214th was on the way to assist mopping-up and to clear le Plessis-Grimoult, a long straggling village south of the hill on the road to Condé. The Germans at le Plessis were still resisting strongly and it was nearly midnight before they were overwhelmed in more hand-to-hand fighting. About thirty dead were counted and another hundred and twenty prisoners were taken; among a varied collection of captured equipment was a 'Royal Tiger'—a brute of a tank weighing 68 tons. In the early hours of the 8th tanks were heard approaching which proved to be the 7th Armoured Division making for Condé.

To the right of XXX Corps the armoured divisions of VIII Corps were having to fight hard to hold their positions on the Perrier ridge for the enemy was equally determined not to give more ground. The German defence of Chênedolle had indeed been strengthened and the 15th Division had been unable to oust them from the Estry ridge or make any substantial advance towards Vassy. Estry itself had been developed as a well organised strong-point, manned by the 9th SS Panzer Division with dug-in tanks, '88's and *werfers*. On the other flank of VIII Corps the 3rd Division had taken Montisanger and la Houdenguerie, was across the Allière and on the high ground north of the railway running into Vire. It had kept touch with the American troops, who had first penetrated into Vire on the night of the 6th. At about five o'clock that night VIII Corps positions on the Perrier ridge were strongly attacked by 10th SS Panzer Division hurriedly moved from the Aunay front. The latter were strengthened by Tiger tanks from the corps and though they got between some of our forward positions at the outset all were thrown back before nightfall, having lost heavily and gained no ground.[5] Attacks by our aircraft added to their discomfort as they withdrew.

During this week Bomber Command (while continuing attacks on strategic targets and flying-bomb sites[6]) was not asked to give direct

---

[5] In this fighting Corporal S. Bates, of the 1st Battalion, Royal Norfolk Regiment, was mortally wounded, after showing outstanding gallantry for which he was awarded posthumously the Victoria Cross.

[6] For an attack on flying-bomb sites on August the 4th, Squadron Leader I. W. Bazalgette, D.F.C., of 635 Squadron R.A.F., was awarded posthumously the Victoria Cross. His 'courage and devotion to duty were beyond praise'.

LEGEND

Allied front midnight 29th July 1944	– – – –
Allied front midnight 31st July 1944	⌣
Allied front midnight 6th August 1944	⌣
Army Group boundary	— oo —
Army boundary	— o —
Corps boundary	— + —
Corps	V , LXXIV
Divisions	15 , 326 (Armd)

Allied troops are shown in red, German troops in blue.

CAUMONT AND MT PINÇON

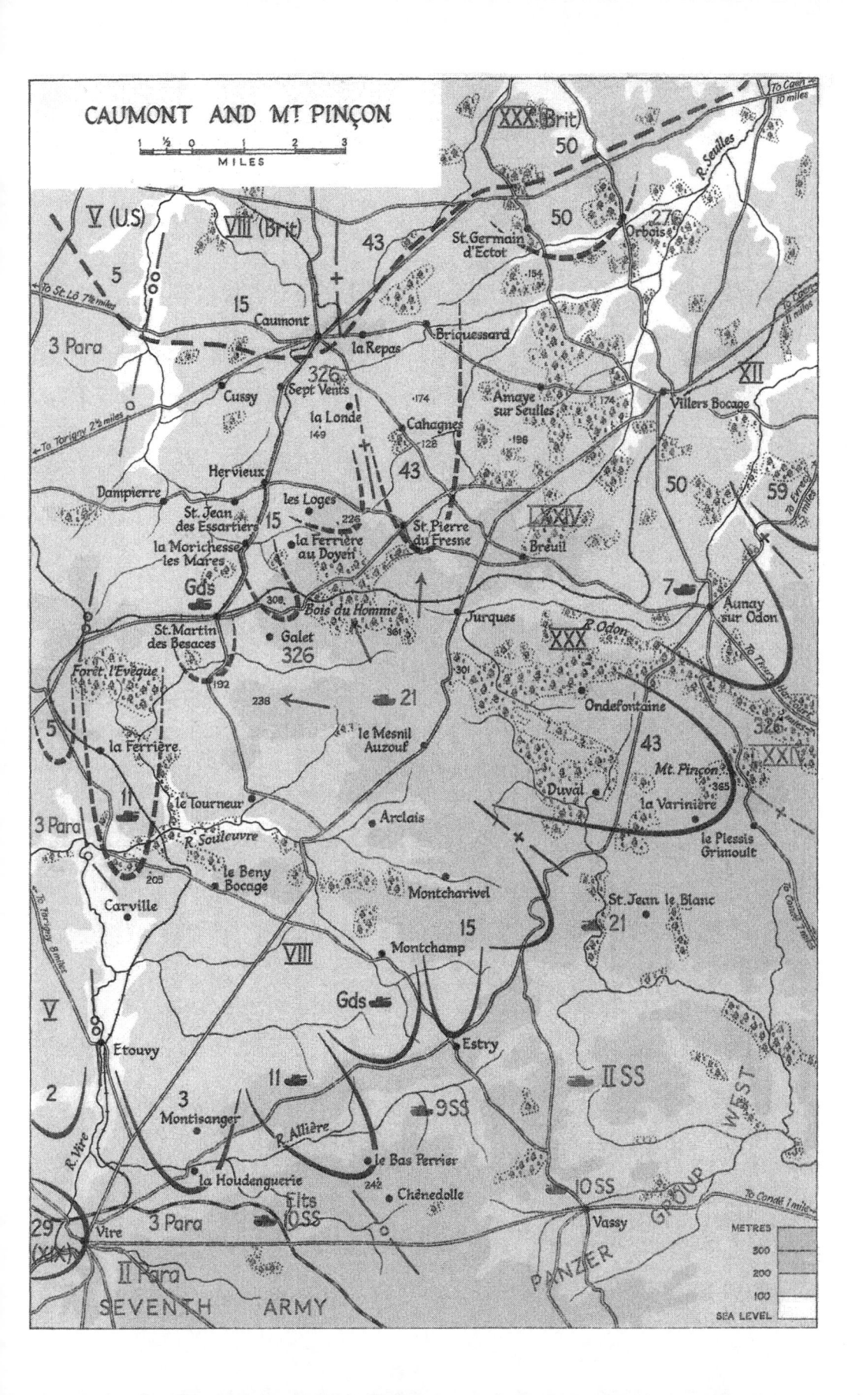

support to ground operations but the Second Tactical Air Force was continuously busy. Reconnaissance and attacks by bomb, rocket, cannon and machine gun were essential factors in the armies' advance. XII Corps near Grimbosq and Thury-Harcourt, XXX Corps at Ondefontaine and Mont Pinçon and VIII Corps on the Estry and Perrier ridges were strongly supported; moreover ground operations were everywhere protected from interference by German aircraft.

The enemy, on the other hand, found movement to be growing more dangerous than ever as their area of defence was progressively constricted. Allied penetrations did not allow troop movements to wait for darkness and by day they were constantly hindered by air attacks. For example, on the 2nd bad weather had kept the Royal Air Force on the ground till the early afternoon, but as it cleared a large amount of armour and motor transport was reported heading for Vire. Within an hour over two hundred Typhoons and fighter-bombers went into the attack, and a Canadian reconnaissance pilot took some photographs which showed sixty tanks, and as many lorries, on the short stretch of road between Condé sur Noireau and Vassy. More sorties followed in the next few hours (as well as a further six hundred on more distant tasks) and a considerable number of tanks were destroyed or damaged. When II SS Panzer Corps had been ordered urgently to move westwards and to close the gap north-east of Vire (page 401), 9th SS Panzer Division took the whole night and most of the next day, the 2nd of August, to cover barely thirty miles. The corps was due to attack that afternoon between Bois du Homme and le Bény-Bocage, but conditions overhead prevented all but disjointed and ineffective attacks late in the day.

Further afield, increasing attention was given by medium bombers and fighters to movement across and on the Seine (where much barge traffic was now in evidence), through the Orléans gap, or over the Loire. It must not be supposed that the absence of enemy aircraft made the work of the air forces easy, for the Germans sought to counter-balance their weakness in the air by strengthening anti-aircraft defence. Usable river crossings and major headquarters were strongly covered by anti-aircraft fire and aircraft attacking inevitably suffered loss and damage. In the battle area all German formations, halted or on the move, were also strongly protected by flak. In one attack by medium bombers on tanks and transport between Argentan and Flers six aircraft out of twenty-eight were lost, and in a daylight attack on tanks collecting near the XII Corps bridgehead at Grimbosq thirty-six Mitchell bombers out of fifty-four were damaged, some of them too badly to fly back to England.

South of the widening gap in the German western flank American progress was everywhere rapid—see map facing page 428. By August the 6th Mayenne and Laval had been captured; in Brittany, Rennes was in American hands, Loudéac had been reached, Vannes taken and St. Malo, Brest and Lorient were about to be invested. French Resistance, particularly in Brittany, was playing an active and well-organised rôle both in harrying the German forces and in protecting installations and positions which would facilitate the American advance. But the depleted German Seventh Army's stubborn defence of their loose-ended front was maintained and the Americans had to fight hard to win St. Pois on the 5th and Vire on the night of the 6th. By then they had also taken Chérence le Roussel, Juvigny, St. Barthélémy and Mortain, but Sourdeval and the westward bulge of rugged country round Gathémo was still held by the enemy. Defending it was the 116th Panzer Division with the 84th Infantry Division moving in to relieve it. This enemy salient north of Chérence was virtually the end of the enemy's coherent front; the counter-attack towards Avranches, which Hitler had ordered on August the 2nd, was to be made through the country immediately south of it. (Map, page 414.)

It would be difficult to give a clear and coherent account of the incessant telephoning that went on during the two days before the attack (i.e. the 5th and 6th), backwards and forwards between the various German headquarters concerned—OKW, C-in-C West, Army Group B, Seventh Army and Panzer Group West—the last renamed on the 6th as the 'Fifth Panzer Army'. By the afternoon of the 6th the west flank of the front was already 'turned' by the American Third Army, whose advanced troops at Laval and Mayenne would soon be threatening Hausser's headquarters at le Mans. Von Kluge had agreed with Eberbach that neither 21st, 9th SS nor 10th SS Panzer Division could be taken from the British front, where all three were fighting to stem the British attacks. By then it was also clear that only part of 116th Panzer Division and none of 2nd Panzer Division's promised reinforcements would be in position to start the counter-attack till after midnight, and 1st SS Panzer Division would hardly be ready to follow up their opening attack quickly and in strength. The first arrivals of 9th Panzer and 708th Infantry Divisions were already involved further south with the American Third Army, though their orders were now not only to cover the flank of XLVII Panzer Corps but also 'if necessary to press on the attack to Avranches'. To make things more difficult that afternoon OKW sent orders that von Kluge should report his plans and order of battle for the attack. He was also told that Hitler wished Eberbach to command it instead of Funck and wanted a stronger armoured force to be employed. Von Kluge was almost in despair. The attack as planned was due to start in a few hours; to change the command and assemble more armour would involve dangerous delay. He told OKW, 'I am pressed for time and have no guarantee that the infantry will hold the position for long against the English and American tanks. I must, therefore, attack as soon as possible.' The launching of the operation as planned was authorised, but although it was put back for two hours not all the formations expected had arrived when, protesting that he was short of troops he had been promised, Funck launched the attack after midnight on the 6th/7th.

On the right flank of the attack the 116th Panzer Division was to attack north of the river Sée without previous assembly. The division had been fighting hard for several days to resist strong American pressure, and the newly-arrived 84th Infantry Division had not yet wholly taken over the sector from which the 116th was due to advance. On its left the 2nd Panzer Division was to advance in two columns. One was to drive westwards along the south bank of the Sée; the other was to capture St. Barthélémy and advance through Juvigny. The 2nd SS Panzer Division was to capture Mortain and advance westwards. The 1st SS Panzer Division was to follow up the attack towards Juvigny in order to exploit initial success and 'recapture Avranches'. Such was the German intention. The accomplishment was very different.

North of the Sée, the 116th Panzer Division did not move. Starting while it was dark, one column of the 2nd Panzer Division pushed along the south bank of the river, meeting little opposition till American outposts detected the movement of approaching enemy and called down artillery fire as they fell back on Chérence. Soon after daybreak leading enemy troops having passed through le Mesnil Tôve were approaching le Mesnil Adelée when they ran into resistance which stopped their progress. The German tanks sought for cover and their infantry began to dig in. The other column of the 2nd Panzer Division, including a tank battalion of the 1st SS Panzer Division, overran the American troops in St. Barthélémy, but after heavy fighting were held up a few miles westwards on the road towards Juvigny. The remainder of the 1st SS Panzer Division, which was intended to exploit initial success, passed through St. Barthélémy at about eleven o'clock but had not gone two miles along the road to Juvigny when they too were stopped about midday. Meanwhile the 2nd SS Panzer Division, starting shortly after midnight without preliminary bombardment, had encircled and overrun Mortain in darkness and in the morning mist some moved westwards by Romagny and south-west down the road to St. Hilaire. On that route there were few American troops to stop them and, meeting no significant opposition, reconnaissance troops reached la Bazoge, Fontenay, Chèvreville and Milly. But fighting round Mortain continued all day, for the Americans held doggedly the high ground —Hill 317—which overlooked the village and surrounding country from the east, and from that vantage ground directed artillery fire on the Germans.

Until nearly midday (by which time the advance had already been arrested) the attackers had been favoured by a cover of cloud and mist which prevented flying. While it lasted Air Marshal Broadhurst and Major-General Quesada arranged that as soon as it cleared the former's rocket-firing Typhoons of 83 Group would concentrate their attack on enemy tanks and troop concentrations, while Thunderbolts and Mustangs of the Ninth Air Force would prevent interference by enemy aircraft and attack transport and communications leading to the battle area. The mist cleared about midday and from then on German tanks and formations stretched out along high roads and by-ways leading westwards were mercilessly attacked. On the road just westwards of St. Barthélemy, for instance, some 60 tanks and about 200 vehicles of the 1st SS Panzer Division were heavily attacked. Not only was much material damage inflicted there and elsewhere in the battle area, but the morale of Funck's troops was severely shaken. Their anti-aircraft defence was slight. The Typhoons, operating at short notice and flying low over unfamiliar country, could see men abandoning their tanks to run for cover. That afternoon the German Seventh Army reported: 'The actual attack has been at a standstill since 1300 hours, owing to the employment by the enemy of a great number of fighter-bombers and the absence of our own aircraft . . .' but it would continue '*as soon as the situation in the air allows this*'.[7] The war diary of Army Group B recorded that day: 'Early morning fog favoured the attack . . . when the weather cleared the spearheads came under continuous attack by many hundreds of aircraft; as a result the attack came to a standstill in the afternoon and heavy losses were sustained in men and material. Our own fighter protection failed to operate, since our squadrons were unable to reach the battle area owing to the very strong enemy counter-action.' The Chief of Staff of XLVII Panzer Corps told Seventh Army that 'the activity of the fighter-bombers is said to have been well-nigh unendurable . . .' and 1st SS Panzer Division 'has no previous experience of fighter-bomber attacks on this scale'. The truth is that seldom had so many vehicles been caught 'at a standstill'.

Thus by one o'clock the German counter-attack which was meant to reach Avranches had been stopped a few miles from where it started. Except in the surprise capture of Mortain and St. Barthélemy the German troops had advanced through practically

---

[7] Author's italics.

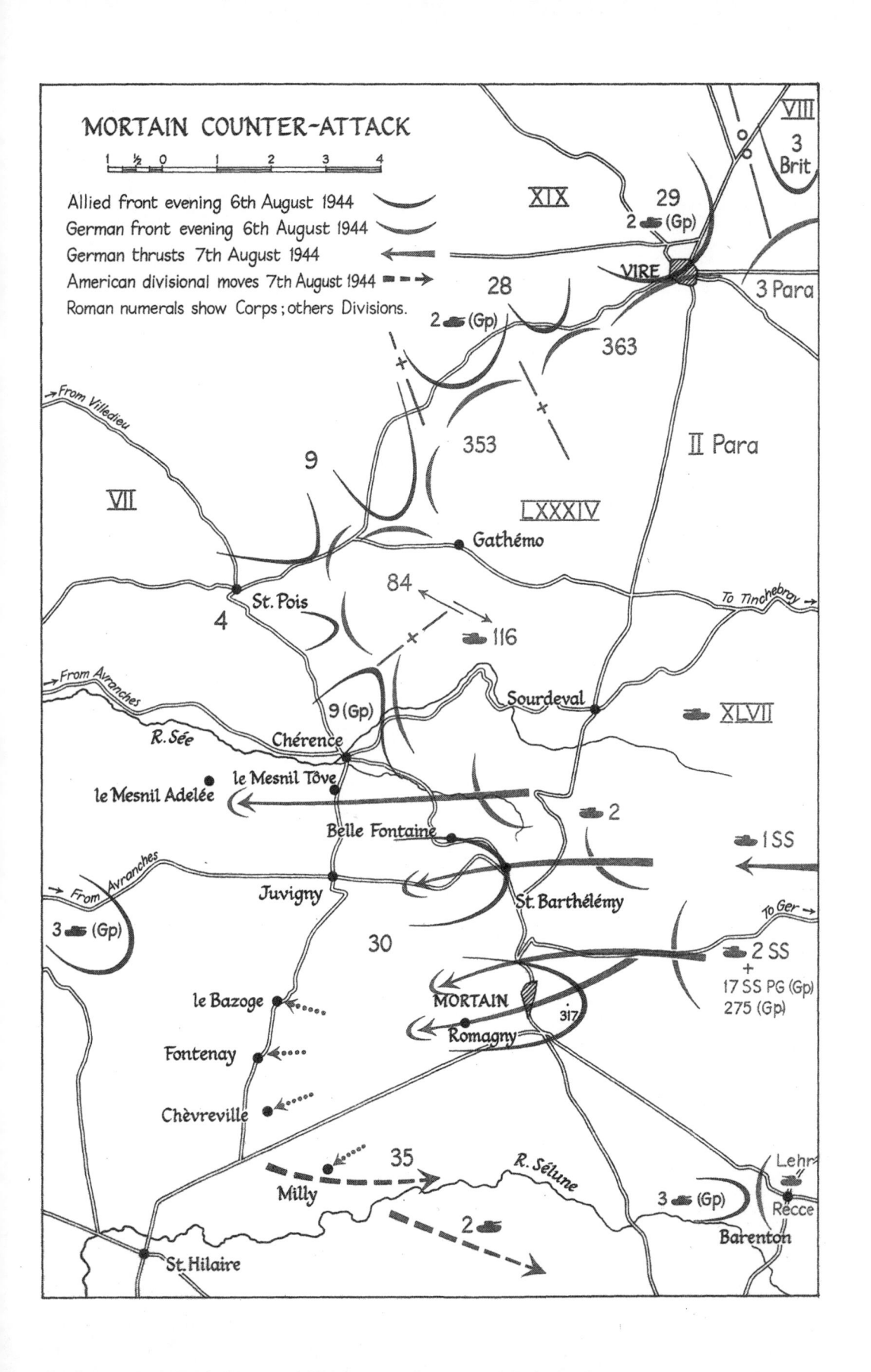

MORTAIN COUNTER-ATTACK

Scale: 1 ½ 0 1 2 3 4

- Allied front evening 6th August 1944
- German front evening 6th August 1944
- German thrusts 7th August 1944
- American divisional moves 7th August 1944
- Roman numerals show Corps; others Divisions.

undefended country until they encountered American resistance. In the face of opposition and under the devastating attack of Allied air forces they went to ground. The German operation on August the 7th was a parody of Hitler's intention to 'annihilate' the Allied forces between Mortain and Avranches.

As planned the attack was obviously inadequate to compass the object in view but even so it was not fully carried out. Of the four armoured divisions ordered to attack that morning the 116th, already engaged by an American attack, made no advance. The 2nd Panzer Division was to have been reinforced by a tank battalion of the 116th but this reinforcement did not materialise. The 1st SS Panzer Division was short of an infantry regiment and assault guns, which had been held back by the Fifth Panzer Army when the division was given to Seventh Army for the counter-attack. Colonel von Kluge (the field-marshal's son) had visited the formations and had reported that 145 tanks in all would attack that day. If those of the 116th Panzer Division which did not move be subtracted, there may have been some seventy to eighty tanks in action in the country between Chérence on the right and Mortain on the left—not an impressive number for the object in view. The Avranches counter-attack, so called by the Germans, petered out once for all half way through the first day.

But if the ineffectiveness of German action is obvious so too is the efficiency of the American counter-action. The sudden opening of a formidable-looking armoured attack on the most dangerous region in their tenuous lines of communication obviously threatened very ugly possibilities. The firm resistance on the spot and the speed with which overwhelming artillery and anti-tank fire and air attacks were focused on the attacking columns stopped the enemy; and the quick and confident way in which reinforcements were moved prevented any further nibbling at their flank. By the end of the day General Collins, Commanding VII Corps, had five infantry and two armoured divisions holding the front and in position to thwart any further attempt of the enemy to break through to Avranches. The fact that elsewhere the American advance was continued without pause shows how well the Allied ascendency was rooted. In this and the next few days American troops had some stiff and costly fighting, for the enemy tried hard to maintain the small gains they had made, but the fighting was due to the American determination to oust them rather than to any German effort to advance further. At that point in their front American progress was delayed for a few days and considerable casualties were incurred but, beyond that, the Germans gained no advantage from the action; indeed, as will be seen later, ultimately it contributed to their defeat in Normandy.

That night General Montgomery sent a telegram to the C.I.G.S.

giving a short account of what had been happening and including the statement: 'Enemy attack in Mortain area has been well held by Americans . . .'; he had 'no fear whatever for the security of this part of the front and [am] proceeding with my offensive plans elsewhere without change'. He followed this with a report of American progress towards le Mans, adding: 'If only the Germans will go on attacking at Mortain for a few more days it seems that they might not (repeat not) be able to get away'.

Owing to the progress southwards the armies' most active fighting during this first week of August was beyond the reach of the naval guns. The most notable event in the Channel was a determined renewal of the enemy's attack by special craft on the night of the 2nd/3rd of August. This time both 'human torpedoes' (*marders*) and explosive motor boats were used. The latter were known to the Germans as *linsen*. *Linsen* units operated as a group of three—a control boat, in which was a coxswain and two radio controllers, and two explosive boats acting as satellites, each carrying a pilot and about six hundredweight of explosive which was fired by impact with the vessel attacked. A group would approach slowly in single line ahead to escape detection; when committed to an attack the two explosive boats would draw ahead at speed till they reached striking distance, their pilots would then jump overboard and their boats would be finally directed on to the targets by radio from the control boat; the control boat was then to retrieve the pilots from the water and withdraw. It sounds a simple plan but, if *linsen* were to attack effectively through an alert defence, technical skill, great determination and more than average good fortune would be needed.

On this occasion the attack began with *marders* shortly before three o'clock in the morning, when an old cruiser, the *Durban*, which had been scuttled as an extension to the Sword Gooseberry, was torpedoed and ten minutes later the destroyer *Quorn* on patrol further north was torpedoed and sunk without warning; shortly afterwards a minesweeper in the area was also torpedoed and sunk. While attention was thus focused on what was happening in the north the nature of the attack changed. About four o'clock an enemy motor boat approached the 'Trout' defence line and during the next two hours successive waves of *linsen* tried to break through the double line of defence patrols while *marders* made their single-handed attempts to do so. Neither succeeded. One Landing Craft (Gun) was sunk and two transports were damaged, but forty of the fifty-eight *marders* were destroyed by gunfire or Spitfires of 83 Group, and of thirty-two *linsen* and control boats only fifteen survived the action.

Their next attack took place on the night of the 8th/9th when sixteen *linsen* and their control boats sailed from Honfleur. They were no more successful. Hunted by ships and aircraft, all the explosive boats and all but one of the control boats were sunk without doing any damage.

On two successive nights the enemy used another weapon which they called *dackel*. This was a long-range torpedo which could keep a straight course for about fourteen miles and then go on circling at slow speed for about two hours. If it did not hit anything before its motive power ran out it remained alive as a drifting mine: it was thus very difficult to distinguish. On two nights, a 5,000-ton transport, the old cruiser *Frobisher*, the repair ship *Albatross*, and a minesweeper were damaged either by these or by mines.

On the 16th and 17th further attempts to pierce the defences were made by human torpedoes. Bad weather interfered with the first of these: on the second, forty-two set out to attack. One landing craft was blown up and a Gooseberry blockship was harmlessly hit. Twenty-six of the *marders* were sunk and five more accounted for by aircraft of Coastal Command and the Fleet Air Arm who shared in harassing their withdrawal. Never again in the Bay of the Seine did the enemy challenge Commander Sellar's Support Squadron with their special weapons before the Allied operations moved eastwards.

An amusing feature of the actions described was the fascination exercised on the Germans by the old French battleship *Courbet*. This veteran had been sunk as part of the Gooseberry breakwater off Sword shortly after D-day. Though abandoned in shallow water her brave appearance, flaunting a large tricolour and the flag of the *Croix de Lorraine*, attracted many bombs, shells and torpedoes of the enemy who failed to recognise her true purpose for several weeks. The illusion of her activity was fostered by the Support Squadron who frequently carried out bombardments from behind her. On the night of the 17th she was torpedoed twice without in any way impairing her efficiency as a blockship.

But before the Bay of the Seine was finally cleared of all danger U-boats had had their last fling. While those in the Bay of Biscay were trying to escape from the operations described on page 290 a number had penetrated the Channel with some success. They torpedoed six merchantmen totalling nearly 25,000 tons, the Canadian corvette *Regina*, an infantry landing ship and a minesweeper. Three U-boats (U.413, 736 and 984) were sunk by warships escorting convoys or on patrol.

CHAPTER XIX

FALAISE

As the day on which the Germans counter-attacked towards Avranches came to an end, General Crerar's First Canadian Army on the British eastern flank renewed the attack southwards towards Falaise. Preparations for a renewed advance were already being made when General Montgomery ordered it on the 4th (page 407) and great care had been taken in its planning. The German forward positions included la Hogue, Tilly la Campagne and May sur Orne. Preliminary attempts to capture la Hogue and Tilly had been made on August 5th but neither had succeeded and earlier attacks on Tilly had similarly failed. The open country over which attacking troops must move afforded full scope to the enemy's well concealed long-range anti-tank guns and mortars and this was equally true of his second line of defence. The latter lay about four miles back, based on St. Sylvain on the east and Bretteville sur Laize on the west. The main road from Caen to Falaise ran through both these strongly held, defensive positions. (See map facing page 432.)

Since the direction and objectives of the Canadian attack could not be disguised General Simonds, who was to command it, planned to counter this disadvantage by starting the operation at an unexpected time and by employing unusual methods. The attack would be led by the infantry and the armour used to exploit initial gains. The advance would begin at the fall of darkness and continue through the night; at the same time a heavy bomber night attack would be made on the enemy's defences on the flanks and an artillery barrage would open across the front of the main attack as the troops began to move forward. These would consist of two infantry divisions and two armoured brigades and, in order to facilitate the capture of his forward positions before the defence had recovered from the heavy bombers' attack, the leading infantry would be carried through the enemy's forward fire-zone in bullet-proof vehicles. They would then dismount and attack their various objectives. As there were two belts of defences only a part of the available bomber force would be used on the first; the remainder would be used later to support the attack on the second which, by that time, would be out of range of most of the artillery.

The use of heavy bombers at night in close support of advancing troops had never been attempted before; to assist the Master Bombers in their assessment of the positions of the target indicators dropped by radio-directed pathfinders, artillery would emphasise the targets by firing coloured marker-shells. The use of bullet-proof vehicles to carry attacking infantry forward into battle was also new and the vehicles had been largely improvised for the occasion. Most of them were American self-propelled field guns known as 'priests', which had been used in the assault landings on D-day but subsequently replaced by British 25-pounders. Their guns were dismantled, seats and ammunition bins were removed, and steel sheets were welded across the openings in front; they were soon nicknamed 'unfrocked priests' or 'holy rollers'. To help the armoured columns to keep direction a variety of aids were to be used, including radio direction beams, anti-aircraft guns firing tracer shells along the axis of advance, and coloured smoke to mark identifiable features.

General Simonds' II Canadian Corps (2nd and 3rd Infantry and 4th Armoured Divisions and 2nd Armoured Brigade) was reinforced for the attack by the British 51st Division and 33rd Armoured Brigade (from I Corps) and the recently arrived 1st Polish Armoured Division. The opening attack would be made by the 51st Division and 33rd Armoured Brigade to the east of the Falaise road, and by the 2nd Canadian Division with the 2nd Canadian Armoured Brigade west of it. Crossing a line between Soliers and St. André sur Orne at 11.30 p.m. on August the 7th, their task was to capture la Hogue on the left, St. Aignan de Cramesnil and Gaumesnil in the centre, and Caillouet near the river Laize on the right, together with the intervening country. About 2.0 p.m. on the 8th the 1st Polish and 4th Canadian Armoured Divisions should pass through the leading troops to attack the second belt of defences, the Poles to seize the high ground east of the main road between Potigny and Falaise, the Canadians to take the hills between Potigny and the Laize valley. Meanwhile the 3rd Canadian Infantry Division would be ready to occupy the ground between the armoured and infantry divisions.

I Corps on the left flank was not at first to be directly involved. Its primary rôle was to hold its own front against any counter-attack from the direction of Vimont or Mézidon. But as the operation developed and the Canadian corps widened its penetration, I Corps might well be required to take over part of its front as far south as St. Sylvain.

The front to be attacked, from la Hogue to the Orne, was held by I SS Panzer Corps with the 89th Infantry Division, newly arrived from the Fifteenth Army, and the 12th SS Panzer Division (with some forty-eight tanks) disposed behind it. The bulk of the 'eighty-eights' of III Flak Corps and the mortars of two werfer brigades were still east of the Orne and the corps commander also had a battalion of about twenty-one Tiger tanks at his disposal. On the front east of la Hogue was the 272nd Division of LXXXVI Corps.

At eleven o'clock on the night of the 7th the leading aircraft of over a thousand from Bomber Command began raining down high-explosive bombs from la Hogue to Mare de Magne on the left, and on Fontenay le Marmion and May sur Orne on the right. Half an hour later the assaulting columns of tanks and infantry crossed the start-line towards the roar of bursting bombs. Each closely packed column covered a front of some sixteen yards which held four vehicles abreast. Navigating tanks with 'gapping teams' of flail tanks and AVREs from the 79th Armoured Division led each column, whose successive ranks were separated by only a yard or two. Directly behind the leaders came the main body or 'assault force', with Sherman tanks followed by the armoured troop carriers. Then came the infantry's supporting weapons, the armoured recovery vehicles, bulldozers and half-track ambulances, etc. A few more tanks brought up the column's rear. On the left of the Falaise road were two parallel columns, each with tanks of the 33rd Armoured Brigade, and an infantry brigade of the 51st Division in armoured vehicles; on the right, an infantry brigade of the 2nd Canadian Division, also in armoured troop carriers, led by tanks of the 2nd Canadian Armoured Brigade, moved in four parallel columns. As they advanced a barrage fired by 360 medium and field guns opened ahead of them. It stretched across a front of 4,000 yards astride the Falaise road and lifted two hundred yards every two minutes to keep pace with the assault columns.

The blinding cloud of dust raised by exploding bombs was increased by that churned up by hundreds of oncoming vehicles and by bursting shells. The bombers' targets were soon so obscured by dust and smoke that shortly before midnight the Master Bombers intervened and ordered the aircraft to return to base without releasing more bombs. About two-thirds of their programme had been carried out; ten of their aircraft had been brought down by the enemy.

Driving through unseen country in the dust-laden darkness there were inevitably crashes, collisions and 'strays', and as the enemy's gun and mortar crews gradually recovered from their original confusion they began to increase defensive fire. Yet the 'break-in' tactics that had been adopted were proving a marked success. Before daybreak the infantry of the 51st Division had dismounted. By first light Garcelles-Secqueville, Cramesnil and St. Aignan were captured with a hundred and forty prisoners. The Canadians had more difficulty in keeping direction and some time had been lost, but by seven o'clock in the morning they had captured the important hill on the main road near Cramesnil, Point 122, and the ridge running westwards, and later in the morning they reached the Caillouet area. Marching infantry following up the attack had much stiff fighting, particularly on the flanks. Lorguichon and Rocquancourt were taken, but May sur Orne and Fontenay le Marmion had been largely missed by the bombers and minefields delayed their capture; and the stubborn garrison of Tilly la Campagne was still unconquered. When dust settled and the morning mist cleared, bitter fighting developed as the enemy sought to recover lost ground. Scottish troops at St. Aignan and Canadians at Point 122 were repeatedly attacked with great determination. In one fight twenty Canadian tanks were lost while the Germans lost eleven—but all gains were held.

Throughout the fighting the infantry divisions were greatly helped by the Second Tactical Air Force, whose fighters were out in strength and answered many calls from the forward troops. Typhoon squadrons attacked gun positions, tanks and infantry at various points between Vimont and the woods to the west of the Laize, or made concentrated attacks on enemy headquarters. At the same time squadrons of Spitfires and Mustangs were flying on armed reconnaissance along likely approach routes, in particular those converging on Mézidon and Falaise, on which incoming transport was shot up.

During the morning the Polish and Canadian armoured divisions closed up on the fighting. Behind a second bombing attack, this time by the United States Eighth Air Force,[1] and a new artillery programme, they were to force their way through the enemy's second line of defence between St. Sylvain and Bretteville sur Laize and to drive for the high ground a few miles short of Falaise.

Soon after twelve-thirty the leading Fortresses flew in from the west and began bombing St. Sylvain and Bretteville; in the next hour they were followed by other formations making for Cauvicourt and Gouvix. During their approach heavy flak had caused some loss of cohesion and, though the sky was clear, many of them could not distinguish their targets despite the coloured markers fired by artillery. Less than 500 of the 678 despatched released their bombs, roughly half of which were high explosive and half fragmentation. A large proportion were wide of the target; a few fell west of the Orne in Second Army's area and others among the gun positions and units moving up to the battle; over 300 casualties were suffered by Canadian, British and Polish troops. Ten Fortresses were brought down by flak, but escorting American Mustangs kept German fighters at a distance and shot down or damaged about as many of a large formation caught near the Seine.

---

[1] Originally this attack was to have been a repeat operation by Bomber Command but, on the morning of the 7th, there were indications that the aircraft returning from the night attack would probably be prevented by bad weather from landing at their proper airfields, and would not have enough time to refuel and 'bomb up' for a second operation twelve hours later. The Eighth therefore took their place at rather short notice.

Both the Polish and Canadian armoured divisions had gone into battle that morning for the first time and they had difficulty in working their way forward through the fighting; they were not in a position to launch their own attack till late afternoon and had thus lost much of the advantage of air and artillery bombardments. When the Poles debouched near St. Aignan they were at once involved with German tanks and infantry trying to recapture the area. The Poles fought their way forward a mile or so to Robertmesnil, but when they emerged from the wood beyond the village they were heavily engaged by Tiger tanks, well hidden on the outskirts of St. Sylvain. They claimed six but could make little progress that night. The Canadian armour, meanwhile, deployed on either side of the Falaise road while infantry cleared Gaumesnil, captured Cintheaux and took Hautmesnil by the end of the day.

Both flanks of the advance had meanwhile been strengthened. On the left flank Scottish infantry had occupied la Hogue and ground to the south after a stiff fight. On the right the Canadians had captured Fontenay le Marmion and May sur Orne and, further forward, had reached the outskirts of Bretteville sur Laize.

Later that night—the 8th—it was reported to OKW that in von Kluge's view,

> 'the idea of the thrust to Avranches is now scarcely feasible. In the north the English have achieved a very deep penetration astride the Caen–Falaise road . . . 89th Division have been destroyed by several bomb carpets . . . 12th SS Pz Division, who were operating a strong battle group, have been . . . destroyed by the bomb carpet . . . This absolute and unmistakable air supremacy, with our forces bombed to bits, was again decisive today; Field-Marshal Sperrle told us again today . . . that he cannot even get his 110 fighters into the area where the 1,000 fighter-bombers are drumming down on us. The cover provided by enemy fighters is such that our fighters cannot get into the danger zone at all . . . for the most part his few aircraft were caught on the airfields as they were taking off.'

Von Kluge added that he would of course carry out orders but he pointed out that a continued thrust towards Avranches 'would be welcome to the English' as it would help their push from Caen to Falaise.

Unfortunately, though he rightly judged the results of the air attacks as a whole he exaggerated the achievement of the heavy bombers. Allied troops soon realised that neither the 89th Division nor 12th SS Panzer Division had been 'destroyed'; the commander of the Fifth Panzer Army himself said that they had lost fifty per cent of their effectives, which may well have been truer.

In this first day of the battle—called 'Totalize'—II Canadian

Corps had won six or seven miles of strongly defended country, but its leading troops were still about twelve miles from Falaise. The fight was to continue without pause and two Canadian battle groups set out in the night to capture Bretteville le Rabet and high ground west of the Falaise road round Point 195, three miles further south.

During August the 9th the 1st Polish Armoured Division on the left of the corps front started from Robertmesnil and during the day took St. Sylvain, Cauvicourt, Soignolles and reached the hills at Point 111, about a mile further on to the south-east. There they were held up by a strong anti-tank screen. The enemy was determined to prevent the capture of Falaise and was building up a new line of defence covering the Laison stream and through the Quesnay woods. Though fierce fighting ensued till nightfall no further progress was made. On their right the 4th Canadian Armoured Division's two battle groups had moved forward during darkness from Hautmesnil to take Bretteville le Rabet and Point 195. One attacked Bretteville while the other set off southwards but, moving round Bretteville on the east, it lost direction and without realising this pushed on and established itself, not on Point 195 to the west of the Falaise road, but at Point 140 some three miles away to the east of the road. There they too were heavily engaged by '88' guns and repeatedly counter-attacked by infantry and tanks. Fighting continued all day, and when darkness was falling and they had lost forty-seven of their sixty tanks, what remained of the infantry was forced back by the enemy's final attack.

Meanwhile Bretteville le Rabet had been cleared but a further attempt to reach Point 195 had made little progress. The 3rd Canadian Infantry Division moved up to relieve the armour and during darkness troops of the 4th Canadian Division passed undetected between the German defences at Grainville Langannerie and Quesnay and by the morning of the 10th had established a brigade on Point 195 and high ground near the Laize. Further attempts to push on to Point 206 near Potigny were, however, defeated though a number of determined German counter-attacks were beaten off. During this fighting the enemy directed about twenty radio-controlled tanks against the Canadian positions on Point 195 which exploded with much noise but did no harm; it was some twenty-four '88' guns covering their front which held up movement.

At eight o'clock on the evening of the 10th the 3rd Canadian Division made a double attack on what was now practically a redoubt in the Quesnay woods, but after a night of confused and costly fighting the troops were withdrawn in the early morning of the 11th. By then the German defence had been augmented by the arrival of the 85th Infantry Division from the Fifteenth Army and it was clear

52. German dual-purpose 88-mm gun

53. Knocked-out German Tiger tank

54. British medium (5·5-in.) gun

55. Shermans in the Caumont country

56. Rocket-firing Typhoons over the Falaise 'pocket'   *Painting by Frank Wootton*

57. German transport destroyed by air attack

58. Knocked-out German Panther tank

59. Six-barrelled German mortar ('*nebelwerfer*')

that a full-scale attack must be organised to break through to Falaise.

During the course of the day the inter-corps boundary had been swung to the south and I Corps had taken the 51st Division and 33rd Armoured Brigade under command again. Scottish troops had already reached Poussy la Campagne and, as they relieved the Poles in St. Sylvain after dark, the 49th Division began to move forward towards Vimont on the northern flank.

While the First Canadian Army was thus occupied on these four days the British Second Army had maintained pressure on the German front between the Orne and the Vire. XII Corps on the left, fighting in difficult country, had gradually cleared the Grimbosq forest, gaining contact with Canadian patrols near the Laize, and on the Orne had reached Thury-Harcourt. Reconnaissance parties entered the town on the 11th but found it strongly held. Further west XXX Corps, battling their way from the Mont Pinçon watershed towards Condé sur Noireau, were still five miles away from the town; VIII Corps on their right had not yet reached Tinchebray and Estry was still an enemy strong-point.

Meanwhile, after heavy fighting the American First Army had been steadily obliterating the enemy salient west of Mortain, and the leading corps (XV) of the American Third Army, pushing eastwards, captured le Mans on the 8th. Sensing an opportunity to cut off a large part of the German armies, and with General Montgomery's approval, General Bradley turned the American spearhead sharply northwards towards Alençon to meet the Canadians attacking southwards towards Falaise. General Eisenhower was with General Bradley at the time and assured him that if need be his advanced troops could be supplied by air.[2]

The German commanders in the field should have been free to concentrate on a reorganisation of their defence in order to meet these encircling dangers; instead they were distracted by the receipt of fresh orders from Hitler every other day, describing how and where they were to renew the attack westwards with forces which, in the rapidly worsening situation, were urgently needed for defence. Throughout these four days, the 7th to the 11th of August, the pretence that they could renew the attack westwards largely dominated German operations—in so far as they were not dictated by Allied progress. On the 7th Hitler ordered a renewal of the attack towards Avranches from the existing salient. On the 9th his order was to attack suddenly from the Domfront area south-westwards, later veering to the north-west, with the help of divisions disengaged by withdrawing Seventh Army front to a shorter and more favourable

---

[2] See Eisenhower, *Crusade in Europe*, p. 302; and Chester Wilmot, *The Struggle for Europe*, p. 415 n.

line. The attack was to be commanded by General Eberbach, with Colonel von Kluge as his chief of staff. Eberbach was to be subordinated to the Seventh Army commander.[3] Not until the 11th would the Führer recognise that the American thrust must first be defeated and, following a recommendation from von Kluge, order an attack in the Alençon–le Mans area.

It is not necessary here to trace the movements of German divisions in efforts to conform to these changing orders and simultaneously to provide for defence against Allied progress, but two significant statements recorded during that time throw useful light on conditions in the battle area. Commenting on objectives given in Hitler's order of the 9th, Eberbach wrote:

> 'This fact must be taken into account, that with the moon in its present phase there are, generally speaking, *only six hours each day in which* it is possible *to attack* (from 0300 hrs to 0900 hrs in the morning, subject to the presence of ground mist after it has become light). An attack by forces of any size during the day is not possible, owing to the enemy's supremacy in the air. Equally, supply can only take place at night; this makes the time available for attack still shorter.'

And on the 10th von Kluge wrote that,

> 'owing to the favourable weather conditions for the enemy and to the time required in bringing up troops, it is not expected that the attack on Avranches can be launched before August 20'.

By the evening of the 11th St. Barthélémy and Mortain were already under close attack and the rest of the salient had been lost; both places were in American hands next morning, and from the east of Mortain the German front swung behind Barenton; their communications were seriously threatened by the Canadian attack towards Falaise and the American advance towards Alençon. The German Seventh and Fifth Panzer Armies were fast becoming sandwiched between Allied forces, with only a narrowing way eastwards still open.

After conferring with his chief commanders and a discussion with Jodl over the telephone, von Kluge began to extract armoured divisions from the Mortain front and to move them back on Alençon, to counter the rapidly increasing threat of the oncoming American XV Corps; the first to move were to be the 1st SS, 2nd and 116th Panzer Divisions. In doing this von Kluge had anticipated an order from Hitler which reached him later that evening. It stated that in order to eliminate the dangerous threat to the southern flank of Army Group B, the American XV Corps between le Mans and

---

[3] While Eberbach was in charge of this operation, General Sepp Dietrich was to command Fifth Panzer Army.

ALTERNATIVE PLANS

Alençon must be eliminated by an armoured attack under Eberbach; to free the required armour Seventh Army was authorised to make a 'minor withdrawal' between Sourdeval and Mortain. So far, this only endorsed von Kluge's action, but Hitler made two additions which showed how little he appreciated the seriousness of the situation in Normandy. First, he ordered that three infantry divisions, to be collected round Chartres in order to cover Paris and the rear of Army Group B, were to be ready *to move forward in the direction of le Mans* as soon as possible so as to mop up after Eberbach's counter-attack; and, second, he ordered that the intention *to resume the offensive westwards, towards the sea* must be firmly adhered to. Both of these orders were quite unrealistic.

On the same day (the 11th) General Montgomery issued a further directive confirming the American thrust northwards from le Mans, which he had agreed verbally with General Bradley on the 8th. The general intention to destroy enemy forces between the Loire, Paris and the sea, set out in the directive which he had issued on the 6th (page 407), was not changed but, seeing that the bulk of the enemy's forces were west of the general line Caen–le Mans and that the gap through which all their supplies must come from the east was narrowing, his immediate intention was to concentrate on closing that gap. Twenty-First Army Group would thrust southwards and eastwards to secure Falaise and Argentan; while Twelfth Army Group would swing its right wing northwards from le Mans up to Alençon and then on to the general line from Carrouges to Sées—which is about twelve miles south of Argentan. It might be possible to destroy the enemy's main forces where they were but, if it appeared likely that they might escape, the Allied armies must be ready to execute the fuller plan, issued on the 6th, for operations up to the Seine.

In the next three days both the First Canadian Army's II Corps and the British Second Army's XII Corps fought their way southwards between the Laize and the Orne. On the 12th XII Corps cleared the forest of Cinglais (making contact with the Canadians on their left); on the 13th they finally cleared the Thury-Harcourt area and were soon astride the road which runs from there to Falaise. Meanwhile the 2nd Canadian Infantry Division, starting from Bretteville sur Laize on the 12th, had taken Barbéry and Moulines; next day they captured Tournebu (and several hundred prisoners from the enemy's 271st Division) and wading the Laize secured a foothold over the river near Clair Tizon, which was enlarged to a substantial lodgement by early morning of the 14th. There they were within six miles of Falaise, while the leading troops of XII Corps were about seven miles from the town, athwart the Thury-Harcourt road.

By then the leading troops of the American Third Army's XV

Corps coming up towards them from the south were only about eighteen miles away. Two armoured divisions were leading their advance—the 5th U.S. Armoured Division and the 2nd French Armoured Division; the latter, commanded by General Leclerc of North African fame, was the first French division to engage in fighting the Germans in France under Allied command. Since leaving le Mans neither division had encountered any serious opposition till they met elements of the 9th Panzer and 708th Infantry Divisions which had been meant to join in the counter-attack towards Avranches but had become involved with American troops before they could reach the western battle area.

On the capture of Sées and Alençon on the 12th, the 5th Armoured Division was ordered to take Argentan while the 2nd French Armoured Division took Carrouges and established a front from there towards Argentan. Between the divisions directed to Carrouges and Argentan lay the forest of Ecouves and the French, whose more direct line of approach lay on the west, sent one column round the east of the forest, thereby preventing the use of the road by the Americans' petrol convoy for six hours. While American progress towards Argentan was thus delayed the headquarters of the German XLVII Panzer Corps, with units of 116th Panzer Division, reached Argentan and quickly took control of the remnants of 9th Panzer Division and other troops in the area. During the French and American mix-up the Germans sent a blocking force post-haste towards Sées and strengthened their hold on Argentan. When the American advanced troops got on the move again in the late afternoon they were strongly opposed and brought to a halt ten to twelve miles south of Argentan. During the 13th of August XV Corps, by then clear of the forest of Ecouves, built up a front between Carrouges and Ecouché (five miles west of Argentan), but all nearer approach to the town that day was defeated by the enemy's stiffening opposition.

Von Kluge asked permission on the 13th to withdraw Seventh Army to a line astride Flers and to reinforce Eberbach with all available armour. At about five o'clock in the morning of the 14th he received Hitler's reply. In this the Führer named some armoured divisions to be given to Eberbach for the attack which was to destroy a large part of the American XV Corps in the Alençon–Carrouges area, and he agreed that this would entail a shortening of what was now described as 'the salient west of Flers'; but this was only to be carried out to the extent and at the speed imposed by Allied actions. Had von Kluge known, his immediate anxiety for the safety of Argentan would have been unexpectedly relieved, for General Bradley had ordered XV Corps not to continue their advance northwards. Their advanced troops were already beyond

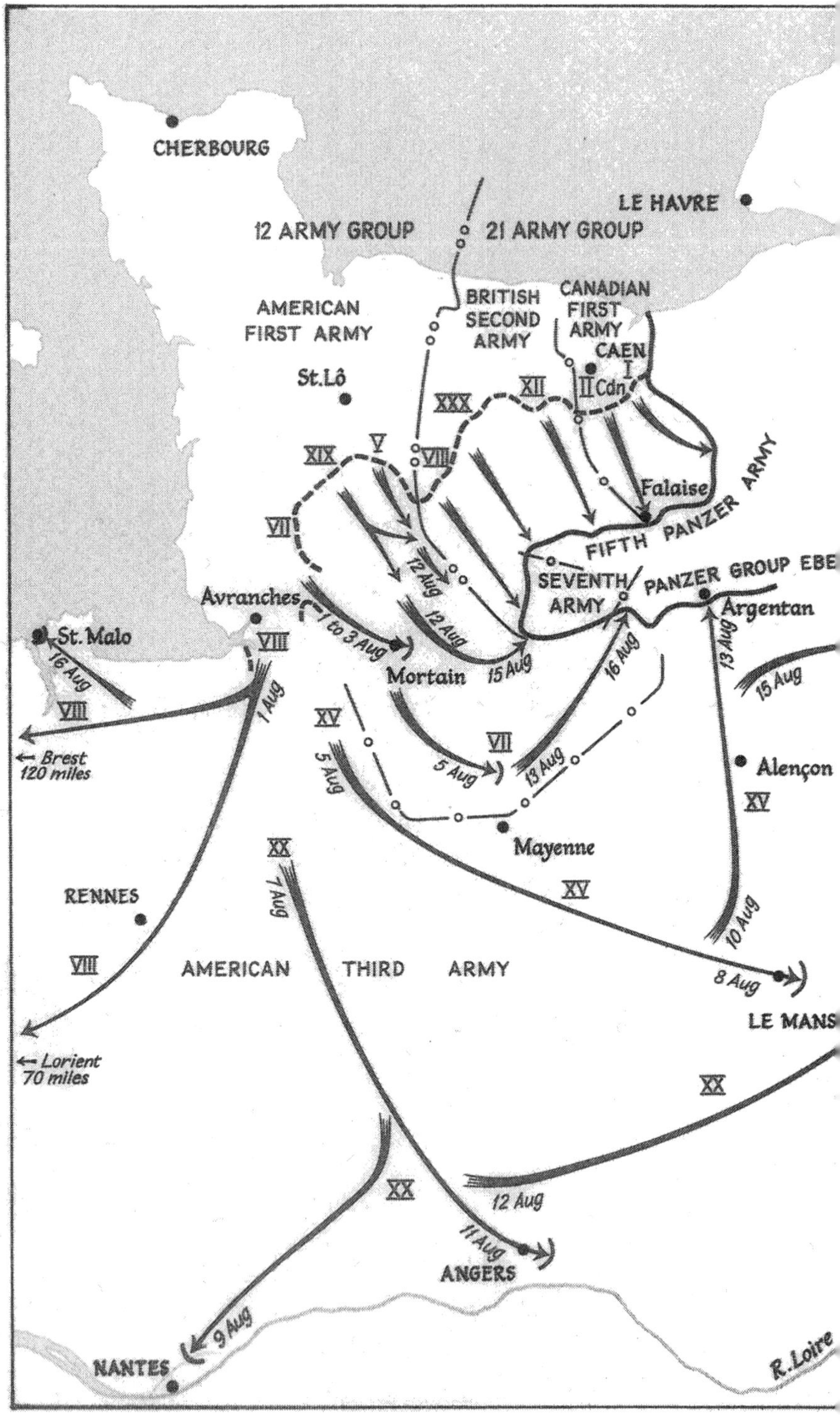

CHERBOURG
LE HAVRE
12 ARMY GROUP
21 ARMY GROUP
AMERICAN FIRST ARMY
BRITISH SECOND ARMY
CANADIAN FIRST ARMY
CAEN
I
II Cdn
St.Lô
XXX
XII
XIX
V
VIII
VII
Falaise
FIFTH PANZER ARMY
SEVENTH ARMY
PANZER GROUP EBE
Argentan
Avranches
St. Malo
16 Aug
VIII
1 to 3 Aug
12 Aug
15 Aug
16 Aug
13 Aug
Mortain
1 Aug
VIII
← Brest 120 miles
XV
5 Aug
VII
5 Aug
13 Aug
15 Aug
Alençon
XV
Mayenne
XX
7 Aug
XV
RENNES
VIII
AMERICAN THIRD ARMY
10 Aug
8 Aug
LE MANS
← Lorient 70 miles
XX
XX
12 Aug
11 Aug
ANGERS
9 Aug
NANTES
R. Loire

THE ENVELOPMENT
1st to 16th August 1944

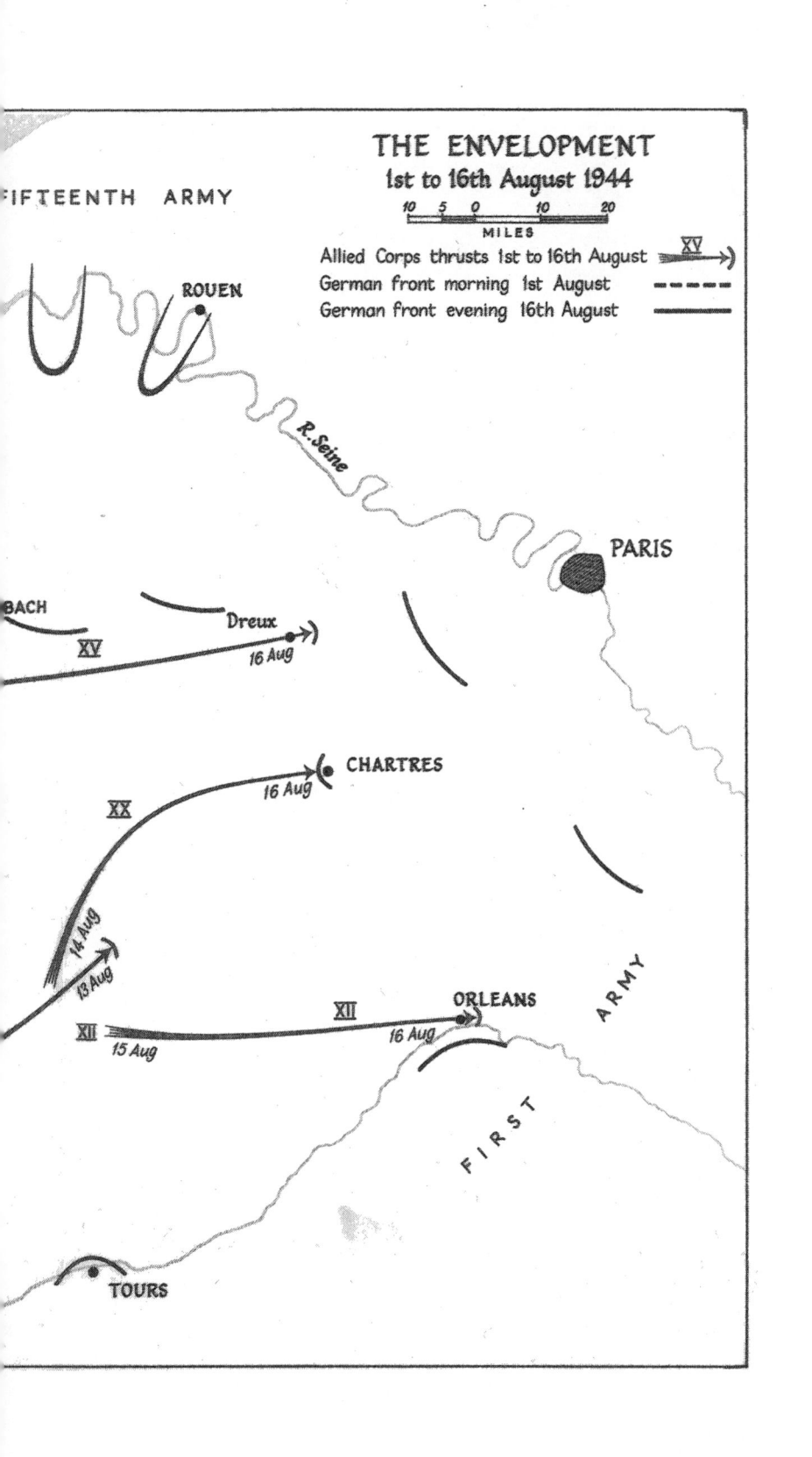

FIFTEENTH ARMY

ROUEN

R. Seine

PARIS

BACH

Dreux
XV
16 Aug

CHARTRES
XX
16 Aug

14 Aug
13 Aug

XII
15 Aug

XII
16 Aug
ORLEANS

FIRST ARMY

TOURS

Allied Corps thrusts 1st to 16th August
German front morning 1st August
German front evening 16th August

the Carrouges–Sées line named by General Montgomery in his directive of the 11th (page 427).

The decision of General Bradley not to proceed with the attempt to meet the Canadians with the aim of cutting off the major German forces has long been a matter for argument and criticism. General Bradley has maintained that '... the decision to stop Patton was mine alone ... Monty had never prohibited and I never proposed that U.S. forces close the gap from Argentan to Falaise'. He says he believed at the time that 'already the vanguard of panzers and SS troops were sluicing back through it toward the Seine' and that nineteen German divisions were 'stampeding to escape the trap'. 'Although Patton might have spun a line across that narrow neck, I doubted his ability to hold it ... The enemy could not only have broken through, but he might have trampled Patton's position in the onrush. I much preferred a solid shoulder at Argentan to the possibility of a broken neck at Falaise.' In the second place, he did not wish to risk a potentially dangerous head-on meeting between two converging Allied armies.[4]

When he gave this explanation after the war either his memory of dates was at fault or he must have been seriously misinformed when he decided not to proceed with the attack on Argentan. For on August the 13th the 'panzer and SS troops' were not 'sluicing back' towards the Seine but were moving back to defend Argentan and counter the American threat to close the gap between that place and Falaise; and no German divisions were 'stampeding to escape the trap'—they were fighting strongly to prevent the reduction of the pocket in which the Allies' converging attacks were enclosing them.

However, the fact is that when the two leading divisions of XV Corps which had turned northwards were held up by the German defence south of Argentan, General Bradley decided not to persist with his attack northwards and, leaving the French 2nd Armoured Division and an American infantry division to hold the positions at Carrouges and to the south and east of Argentan, he ordered Patton to pursue Montgomery's earlier plan to drive eastwards to the Seine with a view to cutting off the German forces there. The rest of XV Corps, XX Corps and XII Corps of the Third Army were directed to move with all speed on Dreux, Chartres and Orléans respectively. As they set off at full pace through largely undefended country the First Canadian Army resumed its main attack southwards on the 14th, in an operation called 'Tractable', with orders to envelop Falaise and to dominate the roads running north, east and south. The town itself was to be taken by troops of the Second British Army

---

[4] Bradley, *A Soldier's Story*, p. 377.

coming in from the west and as soon as it was secured the Canadians were to exploit to Trun, about twelve miles away to the south-east.

As the German opposition was strongest near the Caen–Falaise road, where commanding ground and numerous villages had been organised for defence, General Simonds decided to ask for this area to be neutralised by bombing and to attack through more open country three or four miles to the east. When the two attacking divisions had crossed the Laison stream they would swing south-westwards towards Falaise.

At half past eleven, medium bombers of the Second Tactical Air Force began dropping fragmentation bombs on enemy positions in the Laison valley in the line of the attack and rocket fighters attacked guns and other strong-points on the higher ground in the enemy rear. At noon the leading infantry and tanks of the 3rd and 4th Divisions (the infantry of each division in a solid phalanx of bullet-proof vehicles) crossed the start-line on either side of Soignolles and drove for the Laison behind a thick smoke screen and a heavy counter-battery bombardment from all the corps artillery. At the same time the 51st Division of I Corps, on their left, also attacked towards the Laison to protect the Canadian flank. The opening attack soon reached the Laison, where a number of bewildered Germans hastened to give themselves up. While fascine-carrying tanks of the 79th Armoured Division improvised crossing places, reconnaissance parties searched for others; a good proportion of the armour was across by about three o'clock and the infantry had dismounted and begun clearing the valley positions between Montboint and Ernes. As usual the Germans soon recovered. Their defensive fire from machine guns, mortars, artillery and heavy anti-tank weapons came down very quickly, and as our tanks manœuvred to gain the higher ground their losses increased very considerably. Later in the afternoon more infantry reached the Laison and as some joined the tanks on the far side the attack regained its momentum.

Meanwhile, at two o'clock, aircraft of Bomber Command began to bomb six points selected in the enemy positions astride the Falaise road between Quesnay and Bons-Tassilly. The majority of the eight hundred heavy bombers concentrated accurately on the German redoubts and tank harbours, but owing to a mistake in navigation seventy-seven dropped their loads before reaching their true targets, hitting many of our own troops. Their original mistake was accentuated by the fact that, unknown to Bomber Command, the standard colour used by the Army to show their positions to friendly aircraft was yellow, and yellow was used by Bomber Command to indicate targets; so the more the troops burnt yellow flares to show their positions the more the errant aircraft bombed them. Every effort was made to correct the mistake but by the time that the Master Bombers were able to halt the attack nearly four hundred casualties had been caused, of whom sixty-five were killed.

Despite some resulting disorganisation, the 2nd Canadian Division from Clair Tizon and the Polish Armoured Division, mopping up the bombed areas, had got nearer to Falaise by nightfall; the corps steadily built up strength beyond the Laison and I Corps on its left made corresponding progress. The newly won territory east of the Falaise road included both Sassy and Olendon and high ground nearby.

During the evening the Canadians were now ordered to capture Falaise as quickly as possible but not to let this interfere with their move on Trun. Fighting patrols reached the road between Falaise and St. Pierre sur Dives in the night and the infantry brigades made some ground. Next day the attack was continued but progress was slow, for as the Germans were forced back on to their last defences of Falaise they contested every yard. Converging attacks were made by three Canadian divisions and a division of XII Corps, but when night fell the attackers were still held by commanding positions two or three miles from the outskirts of the town. The Polish division had meantime been switched across to the left flank and there it forced a way over the Dives at Jort (eight miles from Falaise) and set out for Trun. It had again been a gruelling day for the First Canadian Army.

Hitler is reported as saying, a fortnight later: 'The 15th of August was the worst day of my life'.[5] A flood of ugly reports was coming in from the West. Falaise was almost lost and between it and the sea LXXXVI Corps (under attack by the British I Corps) was being withdrawn behind the river Dives. I SS Panzer Corps at Falaise was exhausted; the 85th Division had been almost wiped out, 12th SS Panzer Division had only fifteen tanks left. The '88's of III Flak Corps were too busy with British planes to give much help with the ground fighting and none of the promised reinforcements had yet arrived. LXXIV Corps near Condé had so little ammunition left that it could not hold on without further supplies. At Ecouché (south-west of Argentan) the French were surging forward and were only eleven miles from the British north of the gap. Eberbach had found it impossible to launch an attack from Alençon and his troops were now on the defensive. A map captured outside the gap showed that a newly-identified American armoured division had orders to drive northwards from Dreux. Early that morning Allied forces had begun an assault-landing on the French Mediterranean Coast, as had been expected for some days. To increase Hitler's worries on

---

[5] *Hitler Directs His War*, ed. F. Gilbert (O.U.P., New York, 1950), p. 102.

that day, when immediate counter-measures to the Allied threat were urgently needed, von Kluge was missing. He had left his headquarters to visit Hausser and Eberbach at 5.30 in the morning and nothing had been heard of him since. After what had happened in Paris at the time of the attempted murder, Hitler had had doubts about the loyalty of the C-in-C West; now he strongly suspected that the missing von Kluge was meeting the enemy to discuss a German surrender. He reacted to all this disturbing news by ordering the commander of Seventh Army (Hausser) to act temporarily as C-in-C West and attack the enemy spearhead near Sées immediately, using Eberbach's armoured group and LXXXI Corps. And he sent for Field-Marshals Walter Model and Albert Kesselring in order to choose a successor for von Kluge.

On the 16th, the 3rd Canadian Division reached the two road junctions on the northern outskirts of Falaise and the 2nd Canadian Division broke in from the west, to face a night and morning of mopping up among the ruins of the old market town. Early that morning General Simonds, seeing that Falaise and its exits would be captured by his two infantry divisions, had decided that the 4th Armoured Division should be directed on Trun. Later, General Crerar gave Trun as first priority for General Simonds and Lisieux for General Crocker, whose I Corps would be reinforced during the day by the 7th Armoured Division from Second Army. That afternoon General Montgomery, telephoning General Crerar, said he believed the panzer divisions then west of Argentan would try to break out between there and Falaise and would then go north-east. It was vital therefore that Trun, situated in the middle of the gap at the junction of several roads, should be captured quickly and strongly held.

By dark both the armoured divisions of II Corps had gained two or three miles through wooded and hilly country where the Germans fought hard. The 4th Division closed on Damblainville and seized a small bridge over the Dives at Morteaux Coulibœuf which the Poles had now almost reached from across the river. Further north I Corps had taken St. Pierre sur Dives and its leading troops were heading for Lisieux, opening a gap between LXXXVI Corps in the coastal sector and I SS Panzer Corps around Falaise.

At Hitler's headquarters on this August the 16th it was reported that the missing von Kluge had returned, explaining that he had first been caught in a succession of Allied air attacks which put all his wireless sets out of action, and then by the chaotic congestion on the roads; he had certainly not been in touch with the enemy, as Hitler believed.

On his return he learnt that the Canadians were practically in Falaise, the British Second Army at Condé sur Noireau and Flers,

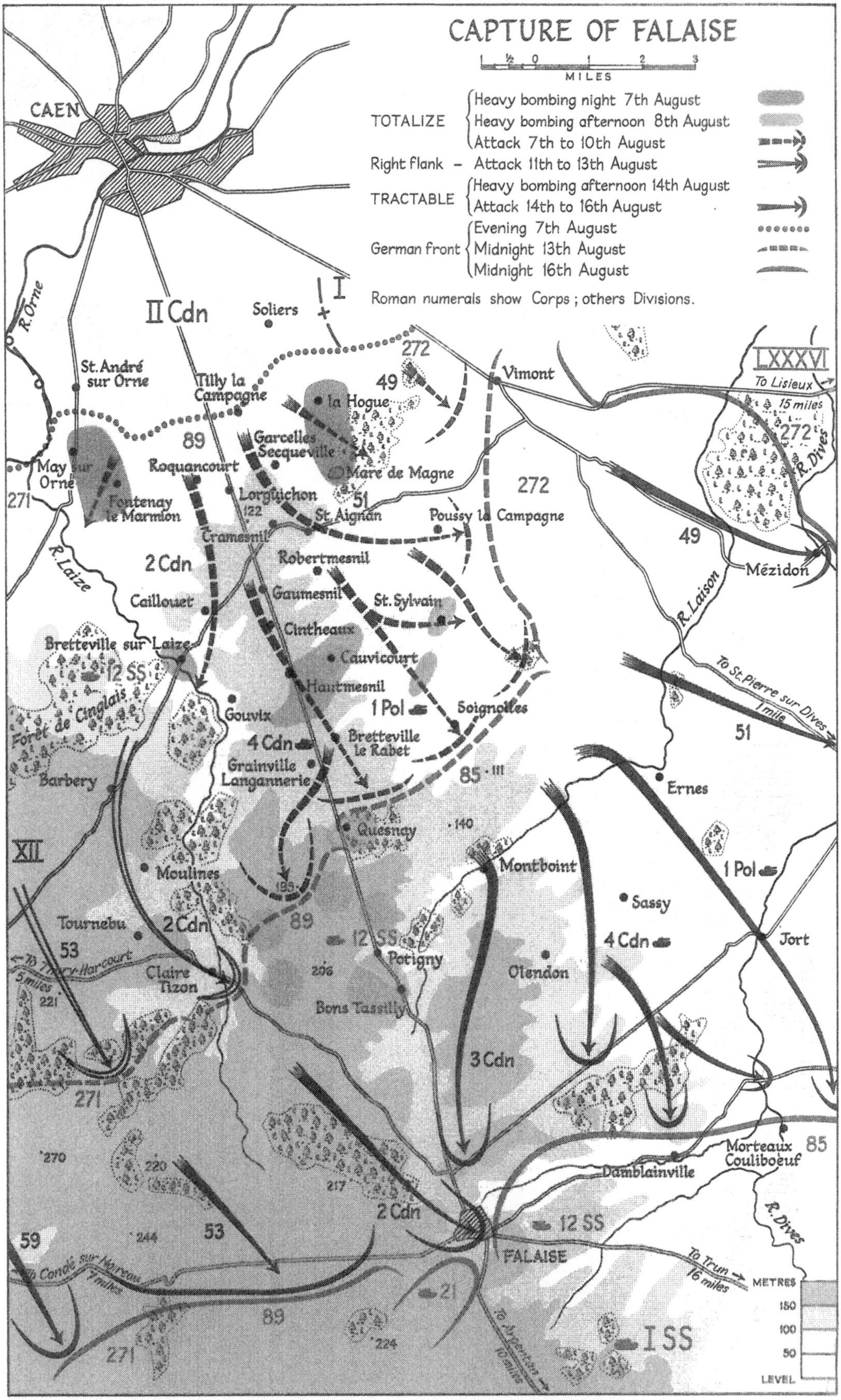
CAPTURE OF FALAISE
MILES
TOTALIZE
Heavy bombing night 7th August
Heavy bombing afternoon 8th August
Attack 7th to 10th August
Right flank – Attack 11th to 13th August
TRACTABLE
Heavy bombing afternoon 14th August
Attack 14th to 16th August
German front
Evening 7th August
Midnight 13th August
Midnight 16th August
Roman numerals show Corps; others Divisions.
CAEN
R. Orne
II Cdn
I
Soliers
St. André sur Orne
Tilly la Campagne
272
49
la Hogue
Vimont
LXXXVI
To Lisieux 15 miles
R. Dives
89
Garcelles Secqueville
May sur Orne
Roquancourt
Mare de Magne
272
271
Fontenay le Marmion
Lorguichon
51
St. Aignan
Poussy la Campagne
Tramesnil
R. Laize
2 Cdn
Robertmesnil
49
Mézidon
R. Laison
Caillouet
Gaumesnil
St. Sylvain
Cintheaux
Bretteville sur Laize
Cauvicourt
To St. Pierre sur Dives 1 mile
12 SS
Hautmesnil
Forêt de Cinglais
Gouvix
1 Pol
Soignolles
51
4 Cdn
Bretteville le Rabet
Grainville Langannerie
85
Barbery
Ernes
Quesnay
XII
Montboint
1 Pol
Moulines
Sassy
Tournebu
2 Cdn
89
12 SS
53
Potigny
4 Cdn
Jort
To Thury-Harcourt 5 miles
Claire Tizon
Olendon
Bons Tassilly
3 Cdn
271
Morteaux Couliboeuf
85
Damblainville
2 Cdn
12 SS
59
53
FALAISE
To Condé sur Noireau 7 miles
To Trun 16 miles
R. Dives
21
89
271
To Argentan 10 miles
I SS
METRES
150
100
50
LEVEL

and the American First Army pushing forward from Domfront to several places on the road between Flers and Argentan; Patton's leading troops were at Dreux and other Third Army spearheads were closing on Chartres and Orléans. Telephoning Jodl he told him quite plainly that it was impossible to comply with Hitler's order to attack through Argentan and Sées. All the available armoured forces would together be insufficient to restore the increasingly critical situation on the southern flank and in the army group's rear areas; moreover, the tanks were short of petrol. His advice was that the troops in the western salient must be evacuated immediately through the gap which still existed between Argentan and Falaise; any hesitation in accepting this recommendation must inevitably result in 'unforeseeable developments'. 'These forces can no longer be expected to attack . . . It would be a disastrous mistake to entertain hopes which cannot be fulfilled. No power in the world can realise them, nor will any orders which are issued. That is the situation.'

Jodl gave him to understand that a new directive would be sent him and he could assume 'a certain freedom of action', and on this he began ordering the withdrawal of Army Group B.

How much of all that he had said to Jodl was reported to Hitler is not on record. What is known is that that afternoon the Führer made two orders which mark the virtual admission that his attempt to hold Normandy and the whole of France was being defeated. The first was the following:

'1. Army Group B will withdraw the forces situated west of the Argentan gap behind the Orne and then behind the Dives, where they will seek to establish contact with LXXXI Corps at Gacé.
    Falaise will be held tenaciously as a bastion for this purpose and the area of attack will be extended by Group Eberbach who will attack south-eastward.
    Further orders for the general conduct of operations will follow.
2. Field-Marshal von Kluge will move immediately out of the threatened area to 5th Panzer Army's battle H.Q. and will conduct the withdrawal from there.

[signed] Adolf Hitler'

The second gave orders for the withdrawal of Army Group G from central and southern France 'as owing to development of the situation at Army Group B it appears possible that the 19th Army [responsible for southern France where the Allied landings had begun] will be cut off within the foreseeable future . . . Army Group G will disengage from the enemy, with the exception of those forces remaining in Toulon and Marseilles, and will establish contact with the southern wing of Army Group B . . .'

The first order reached von Kluge on the 16th and did not involve much modification of orders he had already given. The second was not issued till late on the 17th and before it had arrived von Kluge had been relieved of his command. For on the 16th Model had reported to Hitler's headquarters and, without previous warning to von Kluge, had been appointed C-in-C West and commander of Army Group B. He arrived at von Kluge's headquarters on the evening of the 17th and took over command. Von Kluge left by road for Germany, having written a long personal letter to Hitler justifying his own conduct of operations and declaring his loyalty and his unshaken admiration of the Führer. On his way back he committed suicide.

Though the Twenty-First Army Group was not directly concerned in the Allied landings on the Mediterranean coast their place in the history of Overlord must be appreciated; for when once these landings had been made and a 'back-door' had been opened in the south, the American and French armies passing through it were to join General Eisenhower's command in the attack on Germany—a fact which he was to take into account in subsequent decisions on future strategy.

It has already been noted earlier (page 36) that this operation—first known as Anvil—was the subject of prolonged Anglo-American controversy because of its bearing on high strategy and on the planning of Overlord. First considered at the Quebec Conference (Quadrant) in August 1943 (page 18) as an operation 'to create a diversion in connection with Overlord', it was subsequently agreed on as a means to hold in the south of France German forces which would otherwise be free to increase opposition to the Allied landings in Normandy. It had had to be postponed, however (page 37), and the landings had been successfully achieved without such aid.

Mr. Churchill and the British Chiefs of Staff had contended that forces available for Anvil could be used more effectively in conjunction with the Allies' Mediterranean campaign, but they had failed to convince President Roosevelt and the American Chiefs of Staff and at the end of June the British had reluctantly given way 'in the broadest interests of Anglo-American co-operation'; on July the 2nd orders had been given that Anvil, as originally conceived, should be launched on August the 15th.

Long drawn-out arguments and counter-arguments for and against Anvil somewhat disturbed Anglo-American unity of outlook on strategy at this time. They are described fully in John Ehrman's

British history of *Grand Strategy* and in the American history of *The Supreme Command* by Forrest C. Pogue. It was characteristic of British strategy that although it had been decided in 1943 that a subsidiary attack in the Mediterranean should be launched simultaneously with Overlord, the British had expressed their view that the exact nature of such a diversionary operation should depend on the military situation at the time; as the European situation changed they matched such changes by proposals designed, as they believed, to meet them most effectively. It is equally characteristic of American strategy in Europe that, having once accepted the policy, and with the Russians agreeing, they were thereafter unwilling to let subsequent events influence the decision.

At the end of June when the final decision was taken, Mr. Churchill had written to President Roosevelt that he regarded the decision 'as the first major strategical and political error for which we two have to be responsible'. By then a firm foothold in Normandy had already been gained; he therefore considered that the use of Anvil forces for what he had once described as a forlorn march up the Rhône valley would have little value compared with the political and strategic consequences which would follow if, instead, they were used in conjunction with the Allied Italian campaign to capture Trieste. He argued that Hungary, Yugoslavia, Albania, Greece, the Aegean, Turkey, Bulgaria and Rumania would all be violently and probably decisively affected. The fact that Hitler realised this, too, and dreaded what would be the effect of a further Allied landing in that area is shown by his recorded statements on July the 31st which were quoted on page 397 above.

The President had replied, opposing such a change: 'I am compelled by the logic of not dispersing our main efforts to a new theatre, to agree with my Chiefs of Staff . . . I always think of my early geometry: "a straight line is the shortest distance between two points".' At that time, very naturally, both the President and the American Chiefs of Staff were concerned to give all support possible to General Eisenhower, who strongly urged adherence to the original Anvil plan. That he did so is also understandable; for at the end of June progress in Normandy was proving disappointingly slow and as he had always maintained that the projected landings in the south would be of great positive assistance to his campaign in the north, he could not easily agree to forgo help on which he was counting while the Allied forces were still contained in a small bridgehead. As to whether Anvil forces would be of greater value elsewhere General Eisenhower's view at the end of June could not be unbiased for he was quite clear about the value they would have for him. In a letter to the Combined Chiefs of Staff he set out the purpose of Anvil as he saw it.

'To contain and destroy enemy forces which might otherwise directly oppose Overlord.

To secure a major port in South France for the entry of additional Allied forces.

By advancing to the north, to threaten the south flank and rear communications of enemy forces opposing Overlord.

To develop Lines of Communication for the support of the advancing Anvil forces and of the additional forces which will be introduced through the port to support the Allied Expeditionary Force.'

His desire to secure a southern port had been fortified by the effects of the mid-June storms on the Mulberry harbours and the knowledge that there would be inevitable delay in recovering the full use of Cherbourg. He knew that large additional forces were waiting for him in America but he could not yet know when the lodgement area would be big enough to receive them. The early capture of a large port in southern France thus seemed important. Commenting on details of shipping required for Anvil, General Eisenhower recognised that this would entail certain sacrifices by Overlord, but they would be made gladly because he was convinced of the transcendent importance of Anvil. This being the Supreme Commander's opinion the American Chiefs of Staff could hardly take an unbiased view of any alternative proposal; and with a strongly held desire to avoid further commitments in the Mediterranean and General Eisenhower claiming that Anvil was necessary to ensure success of Overlord, it would hardly have been possible for them to do other than support him. So the decision on Anvil had been finally agreed and when the Chiefs of Staff suggested that for security's sake it should be given a new name, Mr. Churchill ordered that in future it should be called 'Dragoon'!

Nevertheless, in the first week of August, when the break-out in Normandy had changed the Overlord situation and silenced critics, the Prime Minister returned to the charge, urging this time that the Dragoon attack should now be switched to St. Nazaire or other ports in the Bay of Biscay as offering nearer access to the Overlord battlefield for reinforcements coming direct from America. Not only were General Eisenhower and the American Chiefs of Staff strongly opposed to this change, but General Sir Henry Maitland Wilson who, as Supreme Allied Commander, Mediterranean Theatre, had been made responsible for the planning and launching of Dragoon, pointed out that it would involve serious difficulties. All preparations for the assault were practically complete, the assaulting forces were already assembled in Mediterranean and North African harbours, landing craft were loading, and the assault was due to start in little more than a week; to change the plans at the last minute would lead to such disorganisation and delay as would evidently defeat the object of the switch. So the Dragoon plan was adhered to and, as already noted, landings had begun on August the 15th.

The opening assault was made by three American infantry divisions and a combat command of a French armoured division, preceded by heavy air and naval bombardments, the landing of an airborne division containing a British brigade, and a Canadian-American Special Service Force and French Commandos. Enemy opposition to the landings was ineffective and in the first three days' fighting ashore Allied troops secured a bridgehead over forty miles wide and about twenty miles deep, and took over 2,800 German prisoners. Eventually the Allied forces (under command of Lieut-General A. M. Patch, United States Seventh Army) were to be built up to ten divisions. They were to capture Toulon and Marseilles and strike northwards up the Rhône valley and the mountainous route through Grenoble. Only when they had cleared the Germans out of southern France and joined up with the Allied armies in the north would they come under General Eisenhower's command. Till that date (September the 15th) their operations belong to the history of Allied operations in the Mediterranean theatre rather than to this account of Overlord.

CHAPTER XX

ADVANCE TO THE SEINE

THE Normandy battle was reaching its climax. The Allies had almost surrounded the whole of the German Seventh Army and nearly half of the Fifth Panzer Army in a shrinking pocket lying west of the Falaise–Argentan road. The gap between those two places was the only way of escape eastwards, but that fifteen-mile mouth of the pocket was still kept open by troops of the Fifth Panzer Army facing Falaise on the north and by divisions of Eberbach's armoured group holding the Argentan area on the south. (See map facing page 448.)

On August the 16th von Kluge placed Hausser in charge of all troops within the pocket and ordered their withdrawal eastwards, starting to cross the Orne that night with a view to a reorganisation of defence behind the Dives. General Montgomery purposed to stop them at the Dives. He gave orders to the Canadian Army to seize Trun as quickly as possible, while General Bradley was asked to order the American force near Argentan to push on north-eastwards and join forces with the Canadians in the neighbourhood of Chambois, a village four miles south-east of Trun. If von Kluge's intention were realised the Seventh Army would escape from the pocket; if Montgomery's plan were carried out promptly Seventh Army would be trapped, for with the Trun–Chambois area held by the Allies, the only way of escape would be closed. It will be seen as the story unfolds that neither commander's intention was fully realised.

When Falaise was captured on the 16th four divisions of the Fifth Panzer Army[1] held a front which started at Cabourg on the Channel coast and was pushed back across the Dives, where I Corps had a bridgehead at St. Pierre sur Dives and II Canadian Corps had forced the river near Jort (page 431). The front then ran south-westwards to Falaise. From there, in the compressed pocket, the remaining six divisions of the Panzer Army[2] continued the front westwards, from the vicinity of Falaise to that of Condé sur Noireau, facing the British Second Army. From Condé the base of the pocket hung southwards to about five miles beyond Flers and then turned eastwards. Up to that point the enemy was facing the Second British Army: from there he faced the American First Army. On the sector

---

[1] 346th, 272nd, 85th Infantry and 12th SS Panzer Divisions.
[2] 21st Panzer, 89th, 271st, 277th, 276th and 326th Infantry Divisions.

of the front which ran south of Briouze and la Ferté Macé to the river Rouvre was what remained of Hausser's Seventh Army, consisting of four divisions and five divisional battle groups;[3] to the east of the Rouvre Eberbach's Panzer Group still held Argentan, with a curving front on either side of it from the Rouvre to the upper Dives. His XLVII Panzer Corps, with four armoured divisions, two battle groups and most of the heavy mortars in Normandy,[4] faced the right wing of the American First Army and the divisions of General Patton's Third Army which had been left in the Argentan area when the rest of the Third Army was ordered eastwards to Dreux, Chartres and Orléans (page 429). In addition, the headquarters of II SS Panzer Corps had just joined Eberbach's command from Seventh Army, bringing with it the 9th SS Panzer Division and two heavy tank battalions.

Between the Dives and the Touques near Gacé neither side had more than a few patrols. Beyond the Touques the Fifth Panzer Army's LXXXI Corps, with bits and pieces of three new divisions[5] from north of the Seine, was trying to organise some sort of front for the fifty miles back to Dreux, where it hoped to join up with the hotch-potch of the German First Army units hurrying to cover Paris. But driving eastwards, across or through LXXXI Corps' fragmentary defence, Patton's troops had already reached Dreux on the 16th and, further south, other Third Army columns were outside Chartres and in Orléans. The contemplated airborne operation between the Seine and the Loire was now unnecessary and was cancelled.

The Seventh Army's withdrawal on the 16th began after dark as an orderly movement with careful traffic control. It was unmolested by Allied planes for the Mosquitos of 2 Group were busy attacking railways and river crossings nearer the Seine during darkness.

Second Army's troops soon realised that on their front a major withdrawal had begun. Pushing forward to compress the pocket had involved them in severe fighting on the 16th[6] but on the 17th opposition was negligible until the German rearguards were encountered during the afternoon. Then, as Dempsey's divisions fought their way forward to the Rouvre they found an abundance of mines and demolitions and all the bridges blown. Following up the enemy's withdrawal further south the American First Army, in touch with the British, were attacking Briouze. The retreating enemy had

---

[3] 3rd Parachute, 353rd, 84th Infantry and 10th SS Panzer Divisions; and battle groups of 363rd, 331st, 243rd, 275th Infantry, and 9th Panzer Divisions.

[4] 1st SS, 2nd SS Panzer, 2nd and 116th Panzer Divisions; two battle groups of 9th Panzer Division and 17th SS Panzer Grenadier Division and 8th and 9th Werfer Brigades.

[5] 331st, 344th and 17th (GAF) Infantry Divisions, and a battle group of 6th Parachute Division.

[6] Lieutenant Tasker Watkins, 1/5th The Welch Regiment, 53rd Division, was awarded the Victoria Cross for outstanding gallantry in the fighting about five miles west of Falaise.

covered four to eight miles during the night and was waiting to move back another stage as soon as it was again dark. The rearmost divisions were still twelve to fifteen miles west of the Argentan–Falaise road, but a great deal of traffic had been moving out all day across the Dives and passing through Chambois and Trun in the direction of Vimoutiers. This traffic included II SS Panzer Corps which was ordered back to act as army group reserve in the Vimoutiers area where it would be well outside the pocket.

Allied attempts during the day to close the escape route in the Trun–Chambois area had made general but not spectacular progress. The Germans could still use the two good roads running northeast through those places for Allied troops had not yet got to either of them. The two armoured divisions of II Canadian Corps (4th Canadian and 1st Polish Armoured Divisions) had begun the day with orders to secure Trun, and in the afternoon Montgomery told Canadian Army that the Poles were to push on past Trun to Chambois, as quickly as possible and regardless of cost; it was absolutely essential, he said, that the armoured divisions should close the gap between themselves and the Americans.[7] But I SS Panzer Corps had put up so stout a resistance in the broken, hilly country north of Trun (and had been reinforced by the 21st Panzer Division coming from within the pocket) that by nightfall Canadian tanks were still three to four miles north of Trun, with one regiment about a mile short of the road to Vimoutiers; and the leading squadrons of Poles on their left were also stopped by anti-tank guns short of that vital road.

Meanwhile the American assault on Chambois had not yet begun, for headquarters of V Corps was being brought forward from the First Army to organise it and its commander was not yet ready to launch the attack. The Trun–Chambois gap was still open.

Bad flying weather had saved the enemy during the morning and at noon the Allies had to set a new bombline which stopped any more air attacks nearer than Vimoutiers; the fluid situation made it too dangerous to fix it nearer. When the weather cleared in the afternoon Second Tactical Air Force Spitfires and Typhoons, operating outside the bombline, soon found large concentrations of transport beyond Vimoutiers and near Lisieux, '. . . just the sort of targets the pilots had been waiting for since D-day'. About five hundred fighters scoured the country, leaving a large number of vehicles in flames and destroying several barges on the Seine. Their attacks continued until dark when the aircraft returned to their fields with ammunition exhausted. Later that night some two hundred bombers of 2 Group took up the attack on the roads and river crossings beyond Lisieux.

---

[7] See C. P. Stacey, *The Victory Campaign* (The Queen's Printer, Ottawa, 1960), p. 252; see also K. Jamar, *With the Tanks of the 1st Polish Armoured Division* (Hengelo, Holland, 1946).

At two o'clock in the early morning of the 18th a Polish column from the Canadian left wing moved on again. In the darkness they headed too far to the east and ran unexpectedly into an enemy column on the move. Spotlights were switched on and the Poles had some good shooting before the enemy got away; then the Poles reached les Champeaux on the Trun–Vimoutiers road. There they were turned southwards for Chambois and the 4th Canadian Armoured Division was also ordered to push on to Chambois via Trun. All attempts to do so were fiercely resisted by troops of I SS Panzer Corps but by nightfall the Canadians had taken Trun and some of the Polish armour had reached the broken hill country near Coudehard. South-east of Trun the leading troops of the Canadian armoured division were held up fighting for St. Lambert sur Dives, as were the Poles in the Coudehard country. Both were still three or four miles away from Chambois.

Meanwhile equally strong enemy resistance by Eberbach's XLVII Panzer Corps had also brought the American attack on Chambois to a halt about three miles short of the village. The gap had thus been reduced to about six miles—but it had not been closed by the end of the 18th.

The air forces were almost closing it. For as soon as the morning mist had cleared the Second Tactical Air Force had gone out in strength searching for targets beyond the bombline between Vimoutiers and Rouen. At first their reports were mostly of 'scattered motor transport', but shortly after midday reconnaissance showed large concentrations of vehicles to the south-west of Trun and in the Forêt de Gouffern. As this was well inside the bombline special arrangements were speedily made with the armies and by mid-afternoon a large part of the Second Tactical Air Force, followed later by a proportion of the Ninth, had been turned on to these exceptional targets. For the rest of the day relays of Spitfires, Typhoons, Mustangs, Lightnings and Thunderbolts were striking at targets both inside and outside the bombline. In contrast to these earlier reports pilots now referred to 'considerable motor transport', 'congested M.T.', 'concentration of 400 vehicles', and so on. One Canadian officer, who was captured by the enemy but escaped two days later, described what he saw in the gap on the 18th in these words:

> 'All roads, and particularly the byways, were crowded with transport two abreast, grinding forward. Everywhere there were vehicle trains, tanks and vehicles towing what they could. And everywhere there was the menace of the air . . . On many vehicles an air sentry rode on the mudguard. At the sound of a plane every vehicle went into the side of the road and all personnel ran for their lives. The damage was immense and flaming

transport and dead horses were left in the road while the occupants pressed on, afoot . . .'[8]

A shuttle service of fighters continued attacking until pilots were reporting 'little movement seen; most vehicles already destroyed' or 'too dark to operate successfully'. When the 18th had ended the Second Tactical Air Force alone had flown 1,471 sorties against the retreating armies. It claimed 1,100 vehicles and 90 tanks destroyed, with another 1,500 vehicles and 100 tanks damaged; but one pilot had reported 'no results observed owing to the number of aircraft in the area' and figures given inevitably included many duplicated claims.

But there had been one unfortunate result of the air operations which took place after arrangements had been made with the Army that aircraft should attack the congested German troops south-west of Trun and in the Forêt de Gouffern—an area well within the general bombline then in force. To the north of II Canadian Corps, I Corps had begun advancing eastwards and by errors which were not satisfactorily explained Allied aircraft attacked not only the retreating German troops in the closing pocket, but also some of the advancing troops of I Corps to the north of it. Over forty air attacks on our own forces were reported, mostly between the Dives and the Vie, seven or eight miles away; the greatest sufferers were the 51st Division. After full enquiry a Canadian Army report was immediately sent to Twenty-First Army Group. At this time all—Allies and enemy alike—were making eastwards for the Seine and there was no easily recognisable front. For aircraft in flight to distinguish between retreating Germans and pursuing Allies needed careful briefing, accurate map-reading and skilled observation. Failure in one or other of these respects by some less experienced pilots or Army air liaison officers would probably account for these mistaken attacks. On behalf of General Crerar the Canadian report concluded:

> 'It is considered essential that all possible steps are taken by both Services on a high priority to ensure that possibility of further attacks by Allied aircraft on our own troops are reduced to a minimum. If this is NOT effected, this powerful weapon in support of the Army will constitute a deterrent to ground operations rather than the stimulant of which it is potentially capable.'

General Crerar also pointed out to his own commanders the particular difficulties of the air forces when they were giving close support to three armies all converging on the same objective.

The German Air Force had been powerless to ease the situation of their troops in the critical area, being kept well to the rear by Air

---

[8] Quoted in Stacey, op. cit., p. 257.

Defence of Great Britain patrols along the Seine. There a considerable force of FW 190s from the Beauvais airfields was encountered, but sixteen were claimed to be shot down and the rest turned away.

On the morning of the 18th the new C-in-C West—Field-Marshal Model—held a conference of senior officers near Lisieux and agreed that Seventh Army and Fifth Panzer Army could not now organise any defence behind the Dives but must continue the withdrawal to the Touques; Eberbach's XLVII Panzer Corps must shore up the southern wall of the escape route and II SS Panzer Corps (now behind Vimoutiers) would take over the armour of I SS Panzer Corps and would be responsible for the northern wall. But later that evening it was realised that Seventh Army was now encircled though it was still a 'loose' encirclement, 'probably only by light forces'. At the end of the day, therefore, II SS Panzer Corps was ordered to restore contact with the Seventh Army by immediately attacking southwards towards Trun.

That day Model reported to OKW his plans and requirements. Put shortly, he said that Seventh Army would be responsible for the front from the sea to Laigle, and Fifth Panzer Army from Laigle to Paris: General von Choltitz would be responsible for the defence of Paris, which would be covered by an outlying 'switch line' on the west and south-west. In saying this he was adopting von Kluge's earlier plan but by now much of this was impracticable, for Seventh Army was nearly surrounded in the pocket and was unlikely to be capable of holding the named front; and Paris could not be defended. Moreover, any 'switch line' on the west and south-west of Paris was in danger of being broken through before its defence could be organised. Model's immediate 'requirements' are summarised in C-in-C West war diary for that day. These were:

> 'Restriction of enemy air superiority, reinforcement with twenty draft battalions, five G.H.Q. engineer battalions, 270 tanks, nine batteries of artillery and 180 light field howitzers and transport of 9,000 tons gross capacity. C-in-C West further asks to be sent the six armoured brigades being formed [in Germany].'

Hitler must have been tired of being told by his commanders in the West that the Allies' air supremacy must be restricted. He had heard this so often. Now Model stated that 'the very difficult withdrawal from the neck of the pocket and the entire system of supply depend on this'. He told Jodl that the troops had been decimated and if the requirements he named were not met nothing could be expected of them in battle.[9]

---

[9] Two notes made by Jodl after a Hitler Conference on August 19th read: 'Make plans for going over to the offensive in November when the enemy cannot operate in the air'—which seems to foreshadow the Ardennes counter-attack; and 'about *25 divisions must* go to the West in 1–2 months'.

During the night of the 18th Seventh Army resumed its withdrawal from the Orne, making for the general line of the Argentan–Falaise road. Pressure from behind by Second Army, now compressed to a three-division front,[10] and by the equally constricted First United States Army, had failed to overwhelm the German rearguards and, though weak and short of petrol and ammunition, Seventh Army's fighting formations had so far maintained their discipline and good order. Their move that night was undisturbed from the air, for strong forces of 2 Group's Mosquitos were again employed between Lisieux and the Seine, adding to the havoc on roads and among the ferries, pontoons and landing stages on the river.

During most of the following day (the 19th) the right of 4th Canadian Armoured Division, reinforced with infantry, continued their effort to reach St. Lambert where their advanced troops were fighting desperately against the enemy's determined attempt to dislodge them. A flood of enemy troops trying to escape from the pocket swirled round the village but the Canadian field guns had moved to within range and, as one forward observation officer reported, '. . . targets appeared one after another . . . It was an O.P. officer's dream . . . roads and fields were full . . . the resulting carnage was terrible'.[11] The Canadians beat off every enemy attack but in the end still held only about half of the village. The left of the 4th Division got across the Trun–Vimoutiers road to the high ground about Hordouseaux but did not reach the Poles who were engaged in a series of bloody dog-fights four or five miles away in the Coudehard hill country. Isolated and short of petrol (for a good deal had unfortunately been destroyed by one of our own air attacks on the previous day) the Poles were maintaining a most courageous fight. About seven o'clock in the evening a group at last fought their way through into Chambois—and met there troops of the American 90th Division who had arrived just before.

By the capture of Trun and Chambois on the 19th roads running north-eastwards out of the pocket had at last been cut though, as Model realised, the Allied encirclement of Seventh Army was a loose one. The enemy formations retiring each night had inevitably kept on or near the roads. The Allied troops closing in on them had cut off and captured a bag of prisoners that grew larger each day, and Allied shelling and traffic break-downs led to the wholesale abandonment of destroyed and damaged vehicles and guns. Until the main forces reached the Falaise–Argentan road cohesion had been maintained. Now, it was largely lost.

---

[10] XII Corps, 53rd and 59th Infantry Divisions. XXX Corps, 11th Armoured Division. VIII Corps had been pinched out.

[11] Stacey, op. cit., p. 260.

East of the Falaise–Argentan road lies a range of broken, wooded country across the enemy's way of retreat which contributed to the difficulties of control. The loss of Trun and Chambois on the 19th made Hausser realise that there could be no further orderly retreat. Led by what remained of II Parachute Corps and Panzer Group Eberbach, the troops must try to break out north-eastwards through the still hardly consolidated Allied encirclement. Apart from its few tanks, Seventh Army would have no fire support for by now it had lost all its guns and heavy weapons. The two armoured divisions of II SS Panzer Corps, assembled behind Vimoutiers, had been unable to make an immediate move to meet the Seventh Army for during the day fighter attacks, renewed in great strength, had forced them under cover and deprived them of their petrol. Large numbers of their lorries and armoured vehicles had also been destroyed.

The critical attempt to break out got under way early on the 20th. About eight o'clock that morning it came up against the Canadian positions around St. Lambert and an American regiment on the fringe of Chambois. After a slow start with no fire support, the example of the 3rd Parachute Division in particular and the sheer weight of the movement carried the retreating troops forward on both sides of St. Lambert, where the small Canadian detachment was still grimly holding on to one part of the village and enemy troops to the other. Heavy artillery fire now split the mass into smaller groups and control was lost, for all wireless vehicles had long since been destroyed. Some pushed 'past the enemy front line', as Seventh Army's chief of staff described it to Speidel that evening, and others ran into the Poles and were killed or driven off to seek a fresh way of escape; many, including a corps commander, were taken prisoner. During the battle one Polish regiment near Chambois was able to hand over its own wounded and German prisoners it had taken to the Americans, who provided needed ammunition and rations. The rest of the division held grimly to the Coudehard positions still under enemy attack. For now it was being hard pressed in the rear and from the east by the divisions of II SS Panzer Corps who had at last received petrol. A change of weather kept Allied aircraft away and the belated counter-attack by the panzer corps began about ten in the morning. It did not get very far. One main thrust was eventually halted by the Poles north of Coudehard and the other became involved with the Canadians. Nevertheless, it held apart the two Allied divisions and thus offered a way of escape to German soldiers, many without arms, trudging back from the Dives.

In the evening General Simonds ordered the 4th Canadian Armoured Division to attack south-eastwards in order to seal escape routes and to reach the Poles. There were then five armoured regiments near Hordouseaux, but the fighting became confused and the

Polish positions were not known. In the event, little progress was made that night.

Next morning, August the 21st, II Canadian Corps still had a number of sharp fights; moving south-eastwards the 4th Division's armoured brigade met and destroyed a number of tanks and self-propelled guns, and never stopped firing its machine guns at parties of retreating Germans until the Poles were reached around Coudehard. The scenes which they saw were described in one regimental diary.

> 'The road, as were all the roads in the area, was lined and in places practically blocked by destroyed German vehicles of every description. Horses and men lay rotting in every ditch ... Most of the destruction must have been caused by the air force, but the Poles had done their share ... The picture at [Point] 262 was the grimmest the regiment has so far come up against. The Poles had had no supplies for three days; they had several hundred wounded who had not been evacuated, about 700 prisoners of war lay loosely guarded in a field ... Unburied dead ... were strewn about by the score ... The Poles cried with joy when we arrived ...'[12]

Isolated for three days, and short of supplies until a small quantity was dropped to them by parachute early on the 21st, the Polish Armoured Division had fought with the greatest gallantry and stood its ground to a man.

Back at the Dives, near Trun, some German infantry and a few armoured vehicles had made a last desperate effort to get away early in the morning, but the Canadian machine guns caught them in the open and completely disposed of the attempt. As troops of the British 53rd Division pushing in from the west met the Canadians near Trun, battle groups of the 3rd and 4th Canadian Divisions joined up with the stout-hearted troops at St. Lambert[13] and thrust on to Chambois. The gap was at last closed in strength.

Army Group B estimated at the time that forty to fifty per cent of those who attempted the break-out on the 20th succeeded in reaching II SS Panzer Corps. What the total losses were in the six-day withdrawal, from the 16th to the 21st, is impossible to say. British daily returns of prisoners taken over this period, *by those divisions actually engaged around the 'pocket'*, come to some 20,000—7,500 in Second Army and 12,000 in II Canadian Corps. United States First Army's figures for prisoners captured in the fighting round the pocket are not shown separately in American records but were

---

[12] Quoted in Stacey, op. cit., p. 264.
[13] Major D. V. Currie, 29th Canadian Armoured Reconnaissance Regiment (South Alberta Regiment), in command at St. Lambert sur Dives, was awarded the Victoria Cross—the first Canadian V.C. of the campaign.

probably on a similar scale; they recorded 9,000 prisoners on the peak day, the 21st, which was about the same total as our own.

As soon as the battle ended, No. 2 Operational Research Section, Twenty-First Army Group, examined the whole area. Within that portion bounded by Pierrefitte (on the main road, half-way between Argentan and Falaise), Argentan, Chambois, Vimoutiers, Trun and Pierrefitte, they counted 344 tanks, self-propelled guns and other armoured vehicles, 2,447 lorries and cars and 252 towed guns—3,043 items in all. Much of the German transport was horse-drawn, the proportion being as high as three-fourths in an infantry division. Of this no account could be made, for the investigators found '... the stench of dead horses was so overpowering that where there was any number of horse-drawn vehicles that area had to be passed with all speed'.

The armies on which Hitler had counted for defence in Normandy had been dramatically beaten. Yet the reader of this chapter may well question whether the narrow gap between Trun and Chambois could not have been closed more quickly and more thoroughly and the victory have been even more complete. The conduct of the battle by II Canadian Corps is chiefly involved. On this the Canadian official historian is perhaps the best judge. He writes: 'Had our troops been more experienced, the Germans would hardly have been able to escape a worse disaster. They were especially fortunate in that the two armoured divisions available to the First Canadian Army—the 4th Canadian Armoured Division and the 1st Polish Armoured Division—had never fought before they were committed to battle in Normandy at one of the highest and fiercest crises of the war. Less raw formations would probably have obtained larger and earlier results.'[14] On August the 21st the command of the 4th Canadian Armoured Division was changed.

While the Trun–Chambois gap was being closed much had been happening on either side of it. To the north, between II Canadian Corps and the sea, I Corps (with four divisions) had been working eastwards. In the coastal sector the 6th Airborne Division (reinforced by 1st and 4th Special Service Brigades and Belgian and Dutch contingents newly arrived from England[15]) had taken Troarn without any difficulty. After two naval bombardments by the monitor *Erebus* the persistent battery at Houlgate which had remained a thorn in our side since D-day was overrun but inundations, together with the long-established concrete defences at Cabourg and the overlooking positions around Dozule, made the advance across the Dives delta a very slow one.

---

[14] Stacey, op. cit., p. 276.
[15] 1st Belgian Infantry Brigade and Royal Netherlands Brigade (Princess Irene's).

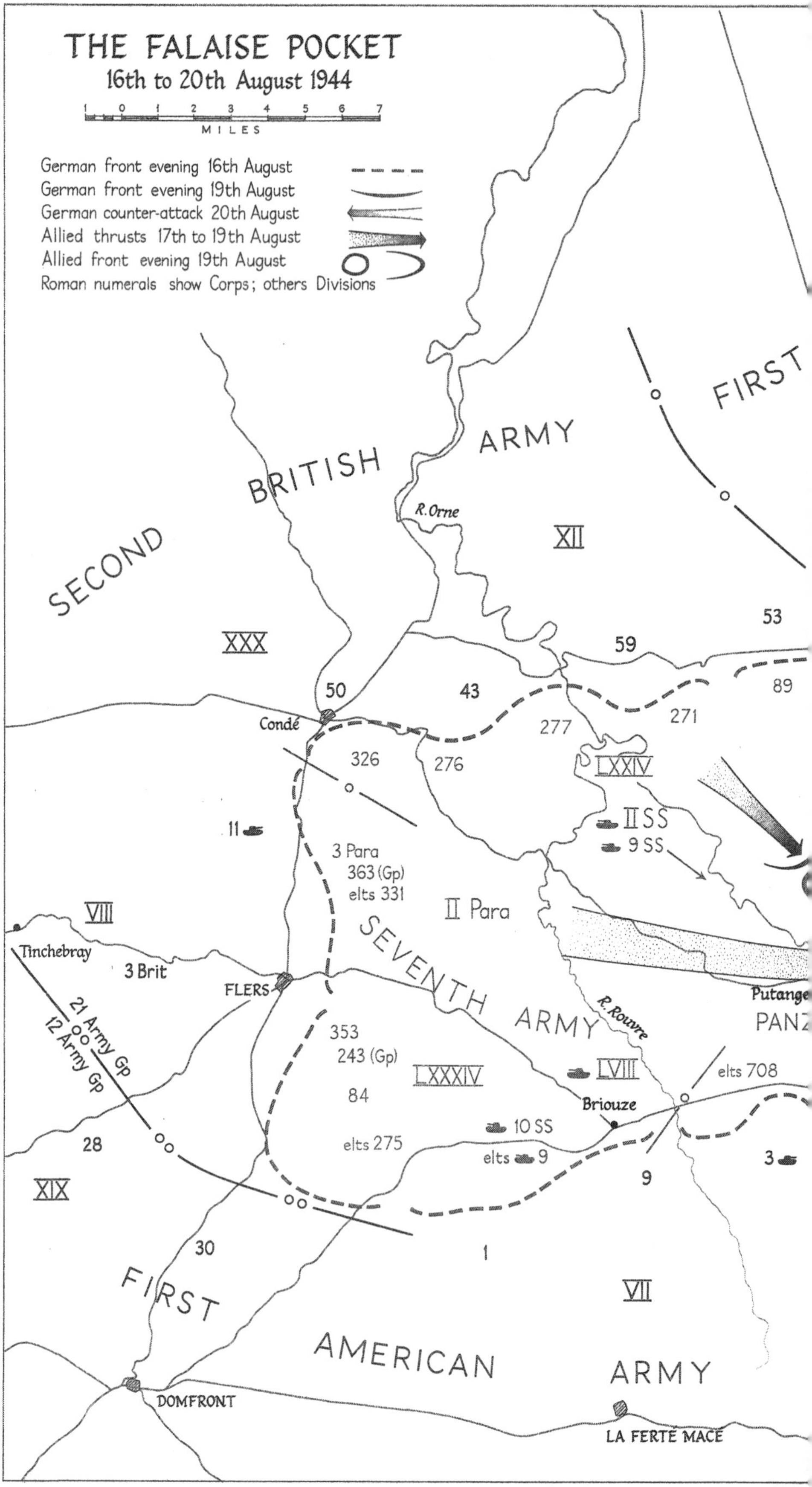
THE FALAISE POCKET
16th to 20th August 1944
MILES
German front evening 16th August
German front evening 19th August
German counter-attack 20th August
Allied thrusts 17th to 19th August
Allied front evening 19th August
Roman numerals show Corps; others Divisions
SECOND BRITISH ARMY
FIRST
R. Orne
XII
XXX
53
59
89
50
43
271
277
Condé
326
276
LXXIV
II SS
9 SS
11
3 Para
363 (Gp)
elts 331
II Para
VIII
Tinchebray
3 Brit
FLERS
SEVENTH ARMY
R. Rouvre
Putange
PANZ
21 Army Gp
12 Army Gp
353
243 (Gp)
LXXXIV
84
LVIII
elts 708
Briouze
10 SS
elts 275
elts 9
9
3
28
XIX
1
30
VII
FIRST AMERICAN ARMY
DOMFRONT
LA FERTÉ MACÉ

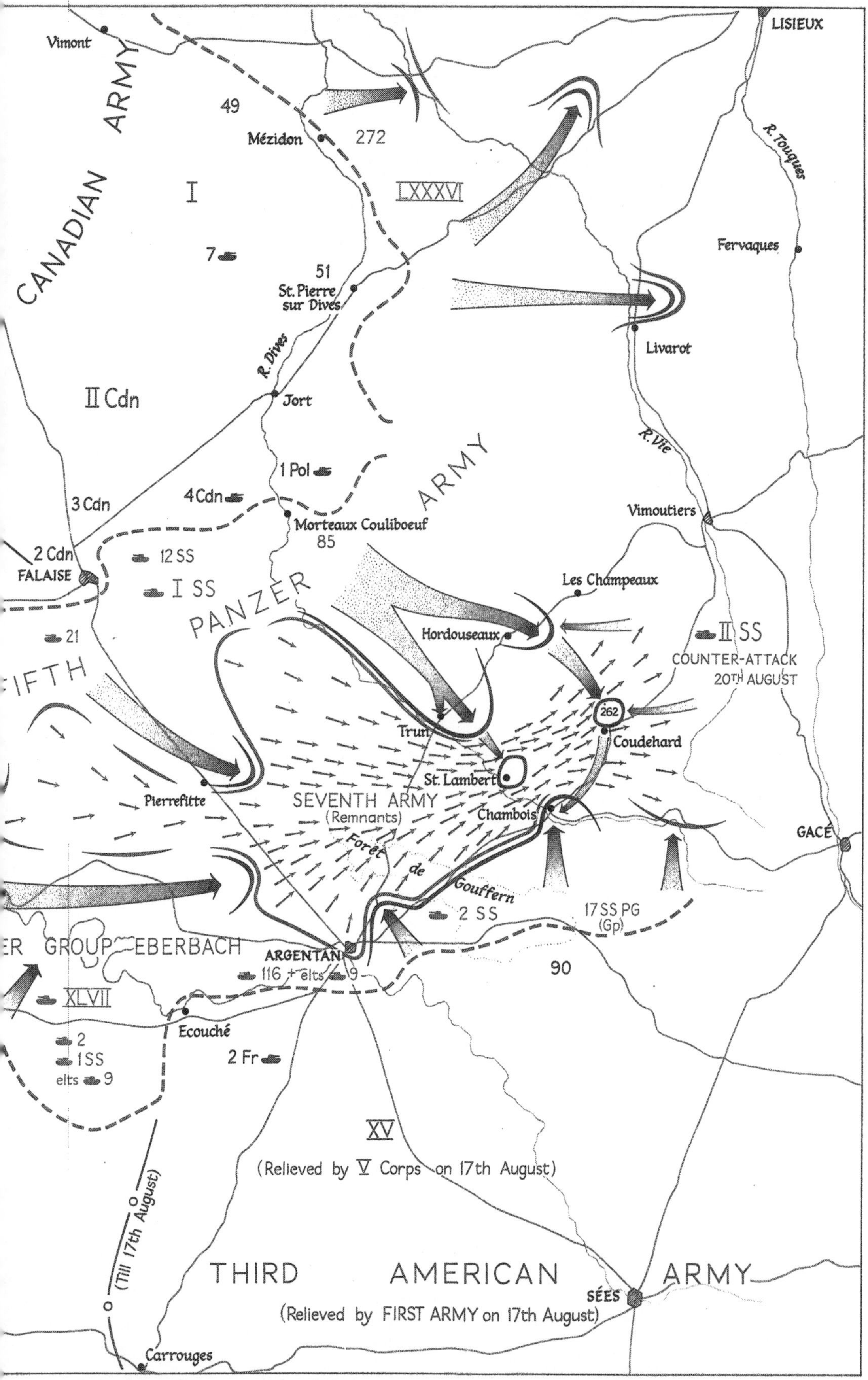
LISIEUX
Vimont
CANADIAN ARMY
49
Mézidon
272
LXXXVI
R. Touques
I
7
51
St. Pierre sur Dives
Fervaques
Livarot
R. Dives
II Cdn
Jort
R. Vie
1 Pol
ARMY
4 Cdn
3 Cdn
Morteaux Couliboeuf
85
Vimoutiers
2 Cdn
FALAISE
12 SS
I SS
Les Champeaux
PANZER
Hordouseaux
II SS
21
COUNTER-ATTACK 20TH AUGUST
FIFTH
262
Trun
Coudehard
St. Lambert
Pierrefitte
SEVENTH ARMY (Remnants)
Chambois
Forêt de Gouffern
GACÉ
2 SS
17 SS PG (Gp)
ER GROUP EBERBACH
ARGENTAN
116 + elts
9
90
XLVII
Ecouché
2
1 SS
elts 9
2 Fr
XV
(Relieved by V Corps on 17th August)
(Till 17th August)
THIRD AMERICAN ARMY
SÉES
(Relieved by FIRST ARMY on 17th August)
Carrouges

AMERICANS CROSS THE SEINE

The 49th Division in the centre had crossed the Dives and the Vie near their junction, and by the 20th was up on high ground again, about six miles south-west of Pont l'Evêque on the Touques. On its right 51st Division was nearing Lisieux from the west, and further to the right again 7th Armoured Division's infantry had taken Livarot while its tanks went on to capture Fervaques on the Touques and there turned northwards for Lisieux. German troops of LXXXVI Corps had been on this flank since D-day and knew the difficult country well. They were imposing the maximum of delay by stubbornly fighting at key localities such as Cabourg, Dozule and Lisieux, by timing with skill the blowing of bridges and by other demolitions.

On the American front the situation was more open and General Bradley decided that the long Third Army flank on the Loire could now safely be guarded by the Ninth Air Force. The advance of Patton's three corps in the country between the Loire and the Seine (the 'Orléans gap') had occasioned some anxiety lest they might run short of supplies, but the cancellation of the projected airborne operation on the 16th (page 440) meant that further air supply would be available if need be; the railway would be open to le Mans at any minute and available road transport was increased by the loan of four British truck companies. With this in mind on the 17th General Bradley ordered Patton to send his XV Corps forward from Dreux to the Seine. (See map facing page 470.) Its task was to seize the communications centre of Mantes-Gassicourt on the left bank, barely thirty miles below Paris, and to prevent any Germans from escaping to the south-east. At the same time he set XIX Corps moving eastwards to occupy the ground which XV Corps would leave open between Gacé and Dreux. Advancing against very little opposition XV Corps was soon at the Seine. The ferry sites and Army Group B headquarters across the river at la Roche Guyon were shelled and all the roads were blocked. On the 19th General Montgomery conferred with Generals Dempsey and Bradley and it was agreed that two corps of the U.S. First Army should turn northwards towards Rouen and the coast, in order to quicken the capture of the Seine ferries by which German troops were still escaping and secure bridgeheads across the river where possible. Starting from the general line Mantes-Gassicourt–Dreux–Verneuil, they would make for Louviers and Elbeuf, with light forces pushing ahead to the mouth of the Seine. They would hold the positions won till Twenty-First Army Group troops arrived to relieve them. That day a task force of the American 79th Division occupied Mantes-Gassicourt and found the Germans had gone. The division received orders to cross and bridge the Seine that night. In torrential rain one infantry regiment got across an undamaged weir in single file, and another followed in assault boats and rafts; before dawn engineers began building a light bridge. Within twenty-four hours most of the division was over and had a good bridgehead, dealing adequately with a newly arrived German division and some desultory air raids.

Other decisions taken on the 19th were confirmed in writing by General Montgomery next day. He had gathered from Bradley something of General Eisenhower's intentions on future strategy and his directive recognised that, as the situation developed, the Supreme Commander would be issuing orders about the general direction of the land armies. In the meantime the policy must be for the armies so to dispose themselves beyond the Seine, both tactically and administratively, that they could comply with General Eisenhower's requirements without delay.

With that in mind General Montgomery gave as his intention: 'To complete the destruction of the enemy forces in north-west France. Then to advance northwards, with a view to the eventual destruction of all enemy forces in north-east France.' The eventual boundary between the Twelfth Army Group and Twenty-First Army Group up to the Seine was given as Argentan–Dreux–Mantes and, beyond that, to Amiens–Ghent–Antwerp.

Twenty-First Army Group (once all the Germans still in the 'pocket' had been killed or captured) would advance to the Seine with all speed, Second Army to cross between Mantes and Louviers, First Canadian Army in the neighbourhood of Rouen. From the Seine Second Army would drive north to cross the Somme between Amiens and the sea, and then be prepared to go on and clear the Pas de Calais with the help of the Allied airborne army. From Rouen the Canadian army was to wheel left and quickly secure the whole of the le Havre peninsula and the important railway system connecting with the port.

Meanwhile Twelfth Army Group's right wing was to assemble to the west and south-west of Paris but was not to take the city until the Supreme Commander decided that it was a sound military proposition to do so. Having secured or passed to the south of Paris, the army group would then advance to the general line Orléans–Troyes–Reims–Amiens and be so disposed in that general area that it could operate north-eastwards towards Brussels and Aachen, with or without a portion directed due east to the Saar.

As the Allied commanders received Montgomery's instructions, C-in-C West had a Hitler directive dated the 20th. The enemy, it declared, intended to destroy all forces of Army Group B between the lower Seine, the sea and the Argentan area. The most important task of C-in-C West was therefore to maintain a bridgehead west of Paris and to prevent the enemy, south of Paris, from pushing through between the Seine and the Loire towards Dijon. The severely

GERMAN PLANS

battered forces of Fifth Panzer Army and Seventh Army were first to fight their way back behind 'the Touques sector' and reorganise, putting armoured formations on the southern flank. Should it prove impossible to make a stand in front of the Seine, a defended line was to be organised and held along the river with a bridgehead west and south-west of Paris, and thence along the Yonne and through Dijon to the Swiss border. Seventh Army could not be expected to remain for long in front of the Seine without bridges behind it, and while it was being ferried across Fifth Panzer Army was to prevent the enemy from advancing northwards down the Seine valley. 'If the state of the 5th Panzer Army's forces and the supply situation permit' it should use its main strength to keep open communications with the Paris bridgehead: this would be based on the numerous Seine bridges, behind which a defence line would be held right through the city along the course of the river. 'If need be the battle in and about Paris will be fought regardless of the city's destruction.' While formations from south and south-west France were retiring behind the Dijon line they would be covered by First Army holding the canal running north and south of Montargis, about forty miles east of Orléans; and if Nineteenth Army troops moving up the Rhône valley could not reach the Dijon line in time, they would be diverted through mountain passes into northern Italy. Finally Model was told that *no* additional transport could be supplied and that orders in regard to the supply of reinforcements and material would follow.

After receiving this directive Model reported to OKW next day (21st) the steps he was taking to implement it. Hausser had been badly wounded on the 20th, Seventh Army was no longer fit to operate effectively, and Dietrich with the Fifth Panzer Army was now in charge of the whole front from the Channel to the junction with the German First Army west of Paris. Armoured formations that could still function were being sent to Evreux with orders to fight their way into Paris. The Paris bridgehead was being strengthened with another division and two were hurrying to the lower Seine.

But clearly the keystone of Hitler's plan was the defence of Paris and of this Model wrote:

> 'The establishment and defence of a chord position right through Paris would necessitate the bringing in of more troops: at the present time none are available for this purpose. This city of $3\frac{1}{2}$ million inhabitants has insufficient power supplies to maintain adequate working or living conditions... Signs of insurrection, limited to local outbreaks, have everywhere been suppressed by force, but the alarm units will be inadequate to deal with larger uprisings... Nevertheless Paris remains a big military problem;

if, with fighting going on all round it, a major uprising occurs simultaneously, it will not be possible to keep the upper hand with the 20,000 troops at our disposal ... To provide for all contingencies I have already given instructions for an emergency rallying position to be reconnoitred to the north and east of Paris.'

Not only did this show no sign of compliance with Hitler's orders, it was an ingenuous understatement of the conditions in Paris. For while a line of outlying field defences covering the principal approaches to the city from the west and south-west was manned by forces that were but lightly armed, no steps were being taken—no steps could be taken—to organise or prepare an adequate defence of Paris. Naval, Air Force and SS personnel of their headquarters in Paris had been leaving the endangered city for some days and when Model's report was made there were nothing like 20,000 troops at his disposal.[16]

Meanwhile General Dempsey could not readily deploy his forces coming from the crowded pocket with all their supplies and equipment, until the Canadians on his left veered northwards and the Americans on the right gave him passage. Moreover, he would soon meet the American corps wheeling at right angles across his front to Rouen. This criss-crossing of boundaries involved complicated arrangements and inevitably affected the Allied air forces. For the time being it was arranged that 83 and 84 Groups of Second Tactical Air Force would operate only as far forward as the river Risle, and the American Ninth Air Force between there and the Seine. As it happened, however, the bad weather which had returned on the 20th was destined to continue and restrict flying for another four days.

Twenty-First Army Group's two armies were to advance to the Seine on a front of four corps, VIII Corps being 'grounded' near Vire in army group reserve and its transport added to the general pool. Second Army set XXX Corps to lead along the army group boundary, and directed it to make the right-hand crossing at Vernon. XII Corps, being compelled to wait until the Canadians had cleared its front, was to come up on the left and cross the Seine near Louviers. First Canadian Army was sending II Canadian Corps through Vimoutiers and Bernay to Elbeuf, while I Corps made its main thrust to the Risle at Pont Audemer. From now on, any German garrisons in the seaside towns which showed fight were to be sealed off as economically as possible.

---

[16] Von Choltitz has since written that his troops consisted of a security regiment of low grade and badly equipped troops, only fit to keep order or guard military depots; a battalion of 17 tanks (later reduced to 4); a 'mobile' battalion which had 17 French armoured cars of 1917 vintage, two cyclist companies with light machine guns, and one French gun from the First War with 68 rounds of ammunition. There were also a 'largish' number of flak batteries with 17-year-old crews.

As advanced troops of the American XIX Corps moved northwards from Verneuil, General Horrocks' XXX Corps started eastwards from the Chambois area; its 11th Armoured Division reached the Touques near Gacé on the evening of the 21st. There some stiffish opposition was outflanked and Laigle was occupied the following day. On the 23rd XXX Corps was able to deploy a second division and this quickly cleared the large Forêt de Breteuil lying just behind the river Risle. By the 24th the third division (the 43rd), which General Horrocks had detailed to force the Seine at Vernon and held in reserve while it made its preparations, began to advance. Just ahead was the left of the First American Army; catching up on the left was XII Corps.

As had been anticipated, XII Corps had had to wait for the Canadians to move before getting off the mark. It had to shed the 59th Division, unhappily selected for disbandment,[17] and received in its place the 15th which was to seize the corps bridgehead near Louviers. By the 24th the corps was well on its way and its armoured cars would soon meet American patrols on the river Risle south-east of Bernay.

That evening Bernay itself had been reached by the First Canadian Army's II Corps heading for Elbeuf. Next day all three Canadian divisions bridged and crossed the Risle and linked up near Elbeuf with the Americans who, with the arrival of the Canadians, finally cleared the place that night and then prepared to withdraw.

Simultaneously I Corps had continued its advance near the coast. The Touques was crossed on the 22nd, both Pont l'Evêque and Deauville being occupied the same day. Two days later Lisieux fell and the rest of the corps closed to the Risle. By early morning on the 26th the line of the Risle, from Montfort to the sea, was in its hands, including Pont Audemer where the 6th Airborne Division completed its final Normandy task. On the 27th of August the airborne men rested.

To appreciate the significance of that sentence it is necessary to realise that their division had never been out of the front line since their first landings on June the 6th. In their positions on the extreme left of the British front they had been in many fights. They had originally expected to be taken home after a week or two in order to prepare for the next airborne operation. Instead they had remained there week after week until I Corps began to advance towards the Seine. They were indeed due for a rest.

Within this last week the Americans who had turned northwards

---

[17] It was realised before D-day that because of the manpower situation some formations in Twenty-First Army Group would have to be disbanded sooner or later. Owing to the acute shortage of trained infantry reserves and because it was the junior division, formed during the war, the 59th Division was the first to be broken up.

across the British front had done well. The armoured spearheads of XIX Corps, driving north from Verneuil and Dreux, had easily scattered the infantry detachments of LXXXI Corps, vainly struggling to stop them in the excellent tank country. Their advanced guards, thrusting through Evreux, were in fact almost at Elbeuf as the Canadians approached. Thereabouts they ran into more stubborn resistance from various groups of armour collected by Dietrich to stop the rot. Further east, between the river Eure and the Seine, the broken and wooded country lent itself to ambushes and delaying tactics. There XV Corps, having driven in some panzer grenadier battle groups, got within reach of Louviers on the 24th. Though Fifth Panzer Army recorded that they and Seventh Army had moved thousands of vehicles across the Seine between the 20th and the evening of the 24th (when the weather was too bad for flying) the American thrusts had now deprived them of more than half the ferries they had been using, and consequently the two big loops made by the Seine south and south-west of Rouen became packed with transport. Now the American XV Corps was ordered to pull out, leaving XIX Corps to complete its tasks on the following day—the 25th. XIX Corps did this by securing both Louviers and Elbeuf.

While the British and Canadian corps were advancing to the Seine preparations were completed for bridging the river. From Rouen to the sea it widens and the tides flow strongly; the French had never attempted to bridge it there. Between Rouen and Paris it is about 250 yards wide or more and all the bridges had been broken by air attacks. It channels its course between many small islands, winding its way between steep cliffs on one bank and long, low approaches on the other. As far up as Louviers it is tidal and subject to sudden bores or tide-waves. Though bridgeheads should be gained fairly easily, the building of new crossings to maintain a large force must take some time.

The available engineer troops and equipment of Twenty-First Army Group were divided between XXX, XII, and II Canadian Corps, with GHQ and Army engineers, so that each corps had twenty-one field companies.

In XXX Corps the 43rd Division which was to cross at Vernon was organised in three groups. The first, with the troops and equipment for bridging the Eure river and assaulting the Seine, contained 1,500 vehicles; most of the artillery, and material for one bridge, were in the second group with 1,900 vehicles; the remainder of the division and about 1,000 vehicles formed the third. The leading group harboured in the forest of Breteuil for the night of the 24th and sent forward its reconnaissances, together with some engineers to repair the bridge over the Eure at Pacy. Two four-hour timings through the American XIX Corps area (along only one route) were now given to the division for the 25th, and by four in the afternoon the first group was assembled under cover behind Vernon and would assault that evening. The second group, however, proved much too large for its timing; about 700 vehicles were shut out and had to be filtered through during the night. On the 26th, the American corps began to withdraw southwards and XXX Corps moving eastwards was given one six-hour period to pass through them in the morning on two routes. But this again was insufficient for 50th Division and for the 43rd's last group which only managed to reach the river late that night. XXX Corps had another six-hour timing on the 27th and the Americans were finally clear of the British sector early the next morning.

XII Corps had had few difficulties of this nature, being a little later in arriving on the scene. The commander of the 15th Division planned to assault on the 27th. II Canadian Corps would also be ready to launch two divisions east of Elbeuf early on the 27th. North of the town, however, the situation was different, for between the Forêt de la Londe and the mouth of the Seine stood the last of Fifth Panzer Army, with 'chord' lines across the three loops which are marked by Rouen, Duclair and Caudebec en Caux. These had still to be cleared, the first by 2nd Canadian Division and the other two by I Corps.

On the morning of the 25th the weather improved and fighters of the Second Tactical Air Force began a day of ceaseless attacks on Seine traffic and vehicles collecting on the left bank. Great destruction was done which culminated in an attack on a German convoy observed by reconnaissance planes early in the evening. A number of 2 Group's medium bombers on their way to the Seine were re-briefed in the air and thirty attacked. The Germans reported that they were unable to complete a new floating bridge at Rouen and that ferries downstream at both Caudebec and Quillebeuf had been destroyed by direct hits.

On the same day the Ninth Air Force prevented enemy aircraft from making an all-out effort to cover the Seine and the remaining ferries. A large number were caught over Beauvais and Soissons, and at their new bases east of Paris, and many were destroyed. The Third Air Fleet record shows that they lost 78 that day.

Similar operations by both tactical air forces continued throughout the 26th in spite of intense German flak round Rouen which made them difficult and expensive.

On August the 20th, as the two American corps wheeled down the Seine two others—XII and XX—had begun a new advance from Orléans and Chartres. As they moved eastwards, affairs in Paris came to a head. Knowing that the Allies were approaching and seeing German forces leaving Paris, thousands of the Resistance movement were soon in a state of near-revolt. The majority were grouped in the F.F.I., recognising General de Gaulle's leadership and willing to obey orders from General Koenig, in so far as these could reach them. Though held back from a general rising against the occupying German forces, they had already seized most of the public and administrative buildings and if they did not yet control the city they at least prevented the enemy from doing so. But the Resistance movement also contained a large and vigorous minority of groups with Communist ambitions and affiliations. These did not recognise de Gaulle's leadership or Koenig's authority. They and the members of the F.F.I., though united in their common hatred of the German enemy, were so sharply divided by political antagonism that they hated each other hardly less intensely. In the absence of any unified control clashes with parties of German troops and with each other had grown more serious daily, and on August the 19th large numbers of the excited population were involved with them in local conflicts and street rioting. The city was on the verge of a general uprising and revolution. By the 19th there were perhaps only 5,000 or 6,000 miscellaneous German troops left in the city, holding local positions, isolated from each other and able to do little to keep the Resistance in check; they could not prevent them from barricading streets and seizing public buildings. With the disappearance of SS security personnel the French police were assisting the Resistance; the Metropolitan Railway men had stopped work and traffic was almost at a standstill. That evening Mr. Raoul Nordling, the Swedish Consul-General, persuaded von Choltitz to agree to a truce (or as Choltitz preferred to call it an 'understanding') with the Resistance (Choltitz called them 'the insurgents'). Both were anxious to avoid the loss of life and the damage and destruction that must result from widespread fighting in the city. This uneasy agreement of mutual non-interference had been reached late on the 19th only a few hours before Hitler's directive of the 20th arrived, ordering that if need be the battle in and around Paris was to be fought 'regardless of the city's destruction'. Fortunately von Choltitz observed the 'understanding' he had agreed to and ignored Hitler's order. But though he was merely marking time, leaders of the Resistance feared that he was preparing some form of 'frightfulness' and sent envoys to the American armies begging them to march on Paris without delay. They described the 'truce' made with von Choltitz as due to expire at midday on the 23rd (though no termination had been fixed when Mr. Nordling arranged it) and drew a grim picture of what was then likely to happen. On August the 22nd, therefore, General Eisenhower ordered that Allied troops should move on Paris and be ready to enter the city next day. The Allies had agreed before the campaign opened that for the sake of national prestige French troops would be employed in the final liberation of their capital, and General Bradley now ordered that the First U.S. Army's V Corps would include the 2nd French Armoured Division in the force detailed to enter Paris. Its commander, General Leclerc, had already been designated by General de Gaulle as Military Governor of Paris on the city's liberation.

As the Allied troops fought their way in through the outlying defences on the 23rd, Hitler issued a further order.

> 'The defence of the Paris bridgehead is of decisive military and political importance. Its loss would expose the entire coastal front north of the Seine and deny us the base for V-weapon attacks against England. In history the loss of Paris has always meant the loss of France. Therefore the Führer repeats his order to hold the defence zone in advance of the city and points to the reinforcements that have been promised to the C-in-C West.
>
> Within the city the first signs of incipient revolt must be countered by the severest measures (e.g. demolition of blocks of houses, public execution of ringleaders, evacuation of districts concerned) as by this means a spread of revolt may be prevented. The Seine bridges will be prepared for demolition. Paris must not fall into the hands of the enemy except as a field of ruins.'

On the 25th this was elaborated:

> 'As operations develop the centre of the rebellion will be narrowed down by moving up security formations from outside and using special weapons (heavy assault-howitzers and assault tanks). The rebellious districts will then be annihilated with the aid of the Luftwaffe (dropping high explosive and incendiary bombs).'

But late on the 24th the first French and American troops had reached the city and on August the 25th von Choltitz surrendered to General Leclerc and ordered German resistance to cease.

By that time the American advance south of Paris had already secured five bridgeheads along the Yonne–Seine line between Sens and Melun. Next day Patton's Third Army swept on for another 40 miles to Troyes and First Army moved up another Corps—VII—to broaden the advance to the north-east. The Germans' ragged First Army was being driven towards the Marne. Headquarters of C-in-C West had moved from Paris to somewhere near Reims; Army Group B was now in Hitler's old bunker at Soissons; Fifth Panzer Army Staff left Rouen on the 26th for the neighbourhood of Amiens. The maps of that day and the next show two new armoured brigades from Denmark in action against Patton, and two panzer grenadier divisions nearing Troyes by train from Italy—the first fruits of

Hitler's effort to prop up the western front—while new divisions and fighting units were being created in Germany on a large scale.

The full story of the liberation of Paris belongs to American and French history rather than to this volume, for British troops had no direct hand in it and General Montgomery declined an invitation that he and a British contingent should take part in the military parade by which it was celebrated. But the British nation may derive satisfaction from the knowledge that though London suffered grievously from German bombing while France was no longer an ally, there was no retaliation on German-occupied Paris and the city when liberated was virtually undamaged. In the provision of food and other relief to its people during the critical ten days immediately following liberation the British shared equally with the Americans, some 5,000 tons of supplies being carried into the capital by each. Although the Civil Affairs team responsible for establishing liaison with the French authorities in Paris at the local administrative level was predominantly American, it included a British element. And in the Shaef Mission to France, which was to perform these functions at the Governmental level, the British played their full part.[18]

Von Choltitz has since claimed credit for preventing the city's destruction because, he says, he realised its historic and political significance. What he certainly realised was his own inability to act on Hitler's orders while his depleted forces were virtually prisoners of the Resistance and the Allied armies were approaching the city. If he had tried to do what was ordered the Resistance would probably have triumphed but victory would have been a bloody affair and might well have involved much loss of life and damage to property. As it was, Paris was saved by the restraint of the Resistance, by the inactivity of von Choltitz and by the timing and method of the Allied entry.

Rather surprisingly (in view of the emphasis Hitler had placed on the importance of holding Paris) the loss of the French capital is hardly noticed in the C-in-C West war diary and if von Choltitz' surrender was known it is not mentioned in the various messages sent to OKW on the 25th. The C-in-C West's daily report that night merely said: 'At Paris the enemy penetrated the perimeter defence between Versailles and Route Nationale 20 with two or three armoured and infantry divisions, including the 2nd French Armoured Division . . . and penetrated to the inner town . . .' A day later their report said that the Paris situation was still not clear.

Hitler's other orders during the last week of August were largely concerned with future operations which have yet to be described or with preparations for the development of various rearward

---

[18] See Donnison, *Civil Affairs and Military Government in North-West Europe*, pp. 89–93.

defensive positions, and they need not be noted here: they concern operations that will be described in the second volume of this history. On August the 31st he ordered that no further troops of the Fifteenth and Fifth Panzer Armies were to be moved forward across (i.e. west of) the Somme as they would only be destroyed there and thus jeopardise the establishment of secure defence on the river itself. 'The Führer is in agreement with a step-by-step withdrawal to the Somme.'

With the end of the battle of Normandy in sight General Montgomery meanwhile had first disclosed his view of future policy in a telegram to the C.I.G.S. on August the 18th:

> 'Have been thinking ahead about future plans but have not (repeat not) discussed subject with Ike. My views are as follows. After crossing Seine 12 and 21 Army Groups should keep together as a solid mass of some 40 divisions which would be so strong that it need fear nothing. The force should move northwards. 21st Army Group should be on Western flank and should clear the channel coast and the Pas de Calais and West Flanders and secure Antwerp. The American armies should move with right flank on Ardennes directed on Brussels, Aachen and Cologne. The movement of American armies would cut the communications of enemy forces on channel coast and thus facilitate the task of British Army Group. The initial objects of movement would be to destroy German forces on coast and to establish a powerful air force in Belgium. A further object would be to get enemy out of V-1 or V-2 range of England. Bradley agrees entirely with above conception. Would be glad to know if you agree generally. When I have got your reply will discuss matter with Ike.'

He had discussed future policy with General Bradley the day before he wrote this, but apparently he was mistaken in his belief that Bradley agreed entirely with him. For Bradley wrote afterwards that he and Patton had been thinking of a quite different plan for future action. 'The first or predominantly American plan called for emphasis on a thrust to the Reich straight through the middle of France to the Saar and beyond the Saar to the Rhine in the vicinity of Frankfurt . . . Both the First and Third American Armies . . . would be required for this major effort.'[19]

Montgomery saw Bradley again on the 19th and learned from him then that 'Ike wants to split the force and send half of it eastwards towards Nancy'. Knowing this when he issued his directive on the 20th (page 450 above) he told the C.I.G.S.: 'I have so worded my directive that we shall retain the ability to act in any direction.'

---

[19] Bradley, *A Soldier's Story*, p. 398.

On the 22nd the V.C.I.G.S.[20] (Lieut-General Sir Archibald Nye) flew over to France and Montgomery gave him the following summary of his views concerning both the strategy to be followed and the organisation of command.

> '1. The quickest way to win this war is for the great mass of the Allied armies to advance northwards, clear the coast as far as Antwerp, establish a powerful air force in Belgium, and advance into the Ruhr.
> 2. The force must operate as one whole, with great cohesion and so strong that it can do the job quickly.
> 3. Single control and direction of the land operations is vital for success. This is a *whole time* job for one man.
> 4. The great victory in N.W. France has been won by personal command. Only in this way will future victories be won. If staff control of operations is allowed to creep in, then quick success becomes endangered.
> 5. To change the system of command now, after having won a great victory, would be to prolong the war.'

General Eisenhower, however, was holding to the concept of policy for the advance into Germany on two axes which he had approved on May the 27th (page 82) and the command arrangements foreshadowed in his directive of June the 1st (page 83). Reporting to the Combined Chiefs of Staff, he gave September the 1st as the target date on which the final system of command, as foreseen from the beginning of the campaign, would be put into operation and General Montgomery's responsibility 'for coordinating actions between 21st and 12th Army Groups' would terminate. The final stage in command was becoming necessary because of somewhat diverging lines of operation and because on *each of the main fronts* there must be a commander who could handle, with a reasonable degree of independence, the day by day detailed operations of troops, guided by the overall directives prescribed by Shaef. The Army Group of the North (hitherto Twenty-First Army Group commanded by General Montgomery) would operate north-eastward, securing successive bases along the coast with the final base possibly at Antwerp. Eventually it would be directed to advance eastwards generally north of the Ardennes. It would probably be reinforced by the entire airborne command and by other units to enable it to accomplish its first and immediately important mission, which would be to destroy forces lying between the Seine and Pas de Calais and to occupy that area. The Army Group of the Centre (hitherto Twelfth Army Group) commanded by General Bradley, less portions necessarily employed elsewhere, would advance to the east and north-east of Paris, from which area it could either strike north-eastward, thus assisting the

---

[20] The C.I.G.S. was visiting the Italian front with the Prime Minister.

rapid fall of the Calais area and the later advance through the Low Countries, or, if the enemy strength in that region was not greater than he now believed, it could alternatively strike directly eastwards, passing south of the Ardennes. The speed of advance would be governed by the supply situation and depending on this it might prove possible for General Bradley to thrust a mobile column southeast to create an additional threat, and to speed up the rate of advance of Dragoon.

Thus, General Eisenhower envisaged that two groups of armies, each with its separate Commander-in-Chief acting directly under orders of the Supreme Commander, might, if conditions allowed, advance north and south of the Ardennes, the Central group giving such assistance as might be needed to the Northern group in its advance through northern France and the Low Countries. General Montgomery, on the other hand, held that both groups of armies should advance together north of the Ardennes, and both remain under the control and direction of a single commander. It will be found, as the story of the campaign develops, that this difference of opinion persisted and had effect on the conduct of operations—and indeed on the final outcome of the Allied campaign in the West.

On the 23rd General Eisenhower, accompanied by his chief of staff, visited General Montgomery and in discussing future plans told him that the changes of command that had been forecast in his directive of June the 1st would take effect on September the 1st. Afterwards, Montgomery sent an account of their meeting to the C.I.G.S.:

> 'Ike came to see me today. After a long and weary discussion he agreed on our left flank we must clear the channel coast and establish a powerful Air Force in Belgium and invade Ruhr. He also considers it necessary to invade Saar and would like to split the force. After further discussion he agreed that left flank movement must be strong enough to achieve quick success and it was then suggested there would not (repeat not) be enough left over for Saar operations at present. The problem of Command and control was then discussed. It seems public opinion in America demands Bradley shall hold his command directly under Ike and shall not be (repeat not be) subordinated to me. I said that left flank operations into Belgium and beyond would require careful coordination and control and that one Commander must do this. This was finally agreed. Bedell came with Ike but I insisted that Ike must settle big points with me alone and Bedell was excluded. They have now both gone off to draft a directive as a result of our conversation. I think discussion was valuable and cleared the air and there is a good hope that directive will be what is wanted. The draft is to be shown to me before it is issued. It has been a very exhausting day.'

Next day (24th), when a directive notifying the changes of command was issued from Shaef, Eisenhower wrote to Montgomery:

> 'Confirming our conversation of yesterday, the necessary directive will soon be issued to outline the general missions of the two Army Groups. It will be very brief, giving the Army Group of the North the task of operating north-east, in the area generally to the westward of Amiens–Lille, destroying the enemy forces on its front, seizing the Pas de Calais area and airfields in Belgium, and pushing forward to get a secure base at Antwerp. Its eventual mission will be to advance eastwards on the Ruhr. By the time Antwerp is reached the general strength and composition of the forces needed for the later task will have been determined.
>
> Bradley's Army Group will be directed to thrust forward on its left, with its principal offensive mission, for the moment, to support the Army Group of the North in the attainment of the objectives noted above. He will likewise be directed to clean up the Brittany Peninsula as rapidly as possible, protect against any threat against our communications from the general area of Paris, and to begin building up, out of incoming forces, the necessary strength to advance eastward from Paris towards Metz.
>
> You, as Commanding General of the Army Group of the North, will be given the authority to effect the necessary operational co-ordination between your advancing forces and Bradley's left wing. Mechanical details for effecting this will be left to you and Bradley.
>
> We must immediately prepare definite plans for the employment of the entire airborne force so as to speed up the accomplishment of the missions that you must attain rapidly in the northeast. Unless we use the Airborne Army, assuming it is practicable to do so, we will not be using all available assets and there would be no excuse for insisting upon the deployment of the major part of Bradley's strength on his extreme left.
>
> Bradley is coming to see you this morning with instructions to bend every effort toward speeding up the deployment of his forces in that direction. The faster we do it the more certain will be our success and the earlier will come our opportunity to advance eastward from the Paris area.
>
> All of us having agreed upon the general plan, the principal thing we must now strive for is speed in execution. All of the Supply people have assured us they can support the move, beginning this minute—let us assume that they know exactly what they are talking about and get about it vigorously and without delay.'

If the policy adumbrated in this letter was clear to the writer it was open to a variety of interpretations. To General Eisenhower it meant (as he is reported to have written to General Marshall that day) that he had temporarily changed his basic plan for attacking both to the north-east and the east in order to help General Montgomery seize tremendously important objectives in the north-east. He considered the change necessary even though it interfered with his desire to push eastward through Metz, because Twenty-First Army Group lacked sufficient strength to do the job. He did not doubt Twelfth Army Group's ability to reach the Franco-German border, but 'saw no point in getting there until we are in a position to do something about it'.[21]

To General Montgomery, however, the letter meant that, though the prime importance of his objectives in the north-east had been recognised by the welcome decision that Twelfth Army Group's principal offensive mission for the moment was to assist in their attainment, General Eisenhower's basic plan was not changed; the intention also 'to push eastwards towards Metz' might be temporarily interfered with but was to be pursued as the necessary strength was built up.

After receiving General Eisenhower's letter, General Montgomery wrote that day to the C.I.G.S.:

> 'Ike has now decided on his line of action. His directive to me is about all that I think I can get him to do at present. Ike has agreed that we must occupy the Pas de Calais and get possession of Belgian airfields and then prepare to move eastwards into Ruhr and he has given this mission to 21st Army Group. He has ordered 12 Army Group to thrust forward its left with what it can spare to assist 21st Army Group in carrying out its tasks and for this some six to eight U.S. divisions will possibly be available. The remainder 12th Army Group is to clear up Brittany and then assemble east of Paris. Eventually the whole 12th Army Group is to move eastwards from Paris towards Metz and the Saar. Ike is taking command himself of 12th and 21st Army Groups on 1st Sep. He has given me power to co-ordinate action of forces being used for northward drive to the Pas de Calais and Belgium including those divisions 12th Army Group which (? word omitted) taking part in this movement.
>
> You will see that instead of moving combined might of two army groups northwards into Belgium and then eastwards into Germany via the Ruhr Ike proposes to split the force and to move American portion eastwards from Paris and into Germany via the Saar. I do not (repeat not) myself agree what he proposes to do and have said so quite plainly. I consider that directive which is being issued by Ike is the best that I can do myself in matter and I do not (repeat not) propose to continue argument with Ike. The great point is that I have been given

---

[21] See Pogue, *The Supreme Command*, p. 251.

power to co-ordinate and control movement of left wing northward towards Antwerp and Belgium.'

General Bradley had also understood General Eisenhower's letter of the 24th to mean that though Twelfth Army Group's principal offensive mission 'for the moment' was to thrust forward on his left to support Twenty-First Army Group's advance north-eastwards, this did *not* mean that Twelfth Army Group should not also start to advance eastwards. Indeed, he issued a Letter of Instruction next day (the 25th) in which he ordered Third Army to:

> '1. Cross the line of Seine and Yonne rivers in zone. Advance to the line Troyes–Chalons sur Marne–Reims. Protect the right flank eastwards from Orléans (inclusive) with at least one division.
>
> 2. Be prepared to continue the advance rapidly in order to seize crossings of the Rhine river from Mannheim to Koblenz.' It was also to complete the reduction of the Brittany peninsula and 'protect south flank along the Loire river'.

CHAPTER XXI

THE SEINE TO THE SOMME

On August the 26th, Montgomery issued a new directive. So far as Twenty-First Army Group was concerned the intention was 'To destroy all enemy forces in the Pas de Calais and Flanders, and to capture Antwerp'; its eventual mission would then be '... to advance eastwards on the Ruhr'. Having crossed the Seine, the First Canadian Army must secure Dieppe and le Havre with the minimum forces and quickly clear the coastal belt as far as Bruges. The First Allied Airborne Army would be dropped in the Pas de Calais well ahead of the Canadian columns, which should operate with their main weight on the right and deal with resistance by outflanking movements and 'right hooks'. Second Army was to cross the Seine with all speed and, quite irrespective of the progress by other armies on its flanks, secure the area Amiens–St. Pol–Arras, with a strong force of armour making a dash for Amiens. Swift and relentless action by Second Army would thus cut across the communications of the enemy opposing the Canadians. When these objectives had been gained Second Army must be prepared to drive forward through north-eastern France and into Belgium, and possibly a portion of it might have to be diverted to back up the airborne operation.

He had arranged with General Bradley that the boundary between the army groups should run generally on the line Mantes-Gassicourt, Beauvais, Albert, Douai and Antwerp. Twelfth Army Group had been ordered 'to thrust forward on its left, its principal offensive mission being, for the present, to support Twenty-First Army Group in the attainment of the objectives' that Montgomery had named. 'The Army Group is employing First U.S. Army for this task.' It 'is to advance north-east on the general axis Paris–Brussels and establish itself in the general area Brussels–Maastricht–Liège–Namur–Charleroi'. Nothing was said of the Third Army.[1]

Montgomery considered that the enemy had not the troops to hold any strong position. Speed of action and movement was now vital; he relied on commanders of every rank and grade to drive ahead with the utmost urgency.

In the evening of the day when the Germans surrendered Paris,

---

[1] On August the 29th Brussels was included within Second Army's boundary.

August the 25th, guns and mortars of XXX Corps opened fire on the enemy positions across the Seine from Vernon. In a flash the excited townspeople vanished from the streets and riverside where they had been offering advice and encouragement to the newly arrived soldiers of the 43rd Division, while men of the German division who had been sunbathing on the cliffs opposite leapt to their feet and disappeared to their action stations.

Fifteen minutes later, as the guns changed to smoke shell, the first British troops began to cross the river in stormboats,[2] for the road bridge which joined Vernon to Vernonnet on the opposite bank was extensively damaged and the railway bridge four hundred yards downstream had a large gap in it. On the right the two leading boats grounded on a submerged island and they and most of the men they bore were destroyed by enemy fire from the opposite bank. Others turned upstream and landed about half a company of infantry, but seven of the eight boats that had started originally had by then been lost and further crossings there were postponed till after dark. Two companies of the left battalion had been landed on what also proved to be an island but were re-embarked and crossed near by. In spite of these mishaps a battalion and a half crossed during the night. They fought off a number of enemy attacks and wiped out troublesome mortar and machine-gun posts. Sappers meanwhile were busy bridging the river, though held up for a time by enemy fire. Meanwhile Vernonnet was cleared, and by late afternoon of the 26th a light bridge was completed and armoured cars, carriers and anti-tank guns were also being rafted across. Infantry pushed out to the high ground beyond Vernonnet and the 43rd Division's second brigade began moving over to strengthen and enlarge the bridgehead. Some tanks of the 8th Armoured Brigade were ferried across early on the 27th and helped to beat off determined efforts by infantry and some Tiger tanks, rushed up from Beauvais to drive in the bridgehead. After stiff fighting all were repulsed and that evening the division's third brigade began crossing. Next day (28th) the division and its attached troops beat through the large Forêt de Vernon and established a perimeter four miles east of the Seine. Completion of their task had cost some 550 casualties; the enemy had lost to them about as many prisoners. Meanwhile other formations of XXX Corps were moving forward to carry on the advance: 11th Armoured Division was crossing and, from Condé 120 miles back, the Guards Armoured Division in tank transporters was on the way and expected to reach the river on the 29th.

XII Corps, on XXX Corps' left, had also won bridgeheads east

---

[2] Stormboat. Made of wood. Length 20 ft. Weight 1,500 lb. Powered by 50-h.p. outboard motor. Normal capacity: 12 soldiers plus crew of two, or one jeep or one 6-pdr. anti-tank gun. Maximum speeds: laden—6 knots, empty—20 knots.

of the Seine by the 27th. One brigade of the 15th (Scottish) Division had crossed in stormboats followed by Dukws near St. Pierre du Vauvray, about two miles from Louviers (losing three boats to machine-gun fire, with heavy casualties) and a second near Portejoie, a few miles further downstream, where little opposition was met. By eleven o'clock in the morning of the 28th the two bridgeheads were joined and extended eastwards enabling the third brigade to cross unmolested at Muids, below les Andelys. Engineers had been hard at work rafting carriers and anti-tank guns across and bridging the river; before midnight on the 28th a light bridge was open for traffic at Muids and a heavier one for tanks at St. Pierre. By the 29th les Andelys was included in their bridgehead and they were holding the high ground above it; their patrols were in touch with the 43rd Division on their right. The 53rd Division and the 4th Armoured Brigade were moving up to pass through the Scottish bridgehead; the 7th Armoured Division was coming across from I Corps but was still thirty miles or so from Louviers.

The First Canadian Army, and especially II Corps at Elbeuf, south of Rouen, had had a tougher task. For all that remained of the German Fifth Panzer Army's troops west of the Seine were crowded ahead of them in a bridgehead formed by the Rouen, Duclair and Caudebec loops of the river and were holding the Forêt de la Londe, to the north-west of Elbeuf, which covered most of the enemy's remaining escape routes. Owing to the expenditure of bridging material at the Touques and the Risle and some delay in the arrival of what was needed at the Seine, the crossing could not begin till the morning of the 27th, though on the night before a few men of the 4th Armoured Division had crossed the Seine in a small boat about three miles above Elbeuf and made a little bridgehead. In the morning infantry of the 4th Division crossed in stormboats at that point and men of the 3rd Division at Elbeuf, meeting little opposition; but they found that the enemy's 17th G.A.F. Division was holding the high ground ahead, determined to block approaches to Rouen from that side of the river. The infantry had heavy fighting so the 4th Division moved its armoured brigade to the other bridgehead at Elbeuf, where the engineers had tank-carrying rafts in operation by midnight. Early on the 28th a Bailey pontoon bridge was also open there and by nightfall the two divisions were strongly established on the low hills north of Igoville. On the 29th the Canadian advance continued. From the bridgehead east of the Seine their tanks reached Boos and, nearer the river, their infantry got to within five miles of Rouen. West of the Seine in the Fôret de la Londe a fresh German division from the Pas de Calais and sundry battle groups and tanks had been ordered to stand fast whatever the circumstances. Despite attacks by 500 light and medium bombers on the crossings behind them, the enemy fought a skilful delaying action in which the depleted Canadian 2nd Infantry Division had a further 600 casualties.

With the news of British crossings above Rouen and of the American spearheads at Soissons, Model decided that his army group must give up the lower Seine and withdraw to the 'Dieppe line'—Fifteenth Army holding from Dieppe to Neufchâtel and Seventh Army (under Eberbach) from there to the Oise. The rest of the front would be held by the Fifth Panzer and First Armies. These positions were to be occupied on the 31st, but by then his orders were overtaken by events and that morning Hitler was compelled to agree to Model's withdrawal behind the Somme. The 29th therefore saw the last of the German resistance west of the Seine. Heavy rain and the nearness of our troops prevented air attacks on their final evacuation. On the 30th Canadians entered a nearly deserted Rouen, while the rest of II Canadian Corps started crossing the Seine in strength and I Corps on its left hurried to get over the river by any means it could find.[3]

With the Seine crossed the pace of Twenty-First Army Group's advance quickened. General Montgomery's statement that speed of action and movement was now vital was in everyone's mind. Accordingly, while the First Canadian Army fanned out to capture le Havre and Dieppe and to clear the coastal belt northwards to Bruges, General Dempsey's Second Army set out on the first stage of their drive through north-eastern France and on into Belgium.

At first light on the 29th two armoured brigade groups, screened by armoured cars, started out from the Vernon bridgehead in heavy rain and thick mist; they were spearheads of XXX Corps whose task was to force a way over the Somme on both sides of Amiens and establish two armoured divisions in the Amiens–St. Pol–Arras area with the utmost speed. On the right 8th Armoured Brigade (under command of 11th Armoured Division) started along the route which the Guards Armoured Division would take as soon as it caught up; on the left 29th Armoured Brigade led on the other route of 11th Armoured Division.

At long last the British armour would have a chance to show its paces, for the country between the Seine and the Somme is almost wholly cultivated in wide hedgeless fields, very different from the close *bocage* which had so hampered movement; apart from several large forests only the villages are clad in trees and orchards. And beyond the Somme lie the still more open plains of Picardy. Small parties of German infantry with a few tanks and anti-tank guns delayed 11th Armoured Division at times in defiles or at cross-roads, but by nightfall its leading columns had covered twenty miles and

---

[3] See Stacey, *The Victory Campaign*, chap. XII.

taken a thousand prisoners. The 50th Infantry Division was moving up behind it, ready to support the armour and to protect the flanks; the Guards were crossing the Seine and would take over from the 8th Armoured Brigade on the 30th. Good contact had been made on the right with leading detachments of the Americans advancing from their bridgehead at Mantes-Gassicourt. On the left XII Corps was to start from les Andelys in the morning.

The 30th of August was the first of many dramatic days that were to follow, as people who had been in thrall for four years suddenly awoke to the fact that they were being freed. When the advance was resumed church bells were ringing and French crowds were on the roads waving tricolours, throwing flowers and pressing gifts on the troops. Men wearing F.F.I. armbands and with all kinds of weapons hissed warnings that 'mitrailleuses', 'quatre-vingt huits' and 'soixante-quinze canons' were out in front and willingly relieved the tank crews of prisoners they captured. The armour was in Gisors by the middle of the morning, searching for unbroken bridges over the Epte between Gisors and Gournay. By five in the afternoon the leaders had driven the Germans from the streets of Beauvais and were clearing the country to the north-west. The 8th Armoured Brigade had completed its task and was freeing the roads for the Guards. General Horrocks ordered the 11th Armoured Division to drive through that night to Amiens, still thirty miles ahead of the leading tanks. The columns would have to pause for refuelling after dark and continue their advance when the moon came up. But the moon was not visible when the march was resumed in pouring rain.

A night march through enemy territory is a tense affair at the best of times;[4] on a very dark night like this it had many hazards, though the enemy did not count for much as the few who were met were far too bewildered to fight. It was the armoured car and tank crews who found the night most testing—drivers, peering out of their visors, intent only on avoiding the ditch by the side of the road; commanders staring ahead for signs of the enemy or landmarks by which to check the route; gunners seeing almost nothing and holding to the trigger mechanism simply for support; wireless operators at the bottom of the turret, in a strange world of their own and with stranger noises in their ears. All were encumbered by headphones, microphones and lengths of cable and all were sleepy at the end of a long day. But discipline, training and excitement carried them along.

At four in the morning of the 31st leading tanks of the 29th Armoured Brigade, with infantry close behind them, were three miles south of Amiens; at five they reached the outskirts; half an hour later they were over the first railway bridge and by six were in the

---

[4] Well described in Orde, *The Household Cavalry at War*, p. 203.

centre of the town. Some German troops, not realising who they were, drove along amongst them. 'Dawn found divisional headquarters alongside an enemy field bakery defended, or rather accompanied, by one Mark IV tank which was destroyed before it could fire a shot.'[5]

Soon after eight General Eberbach was captured. He had arrived to take over from the Fifth Panzer Army and was examining the Somme positions for himself. General Sepp Dietrich, however, got away.

Shortly before eleven the two main bridges at Amiens were captured and positions were secured on the far bank. Meanwhile, the German garrison was being mopped up, together with much disorganised transport which continued to drive in from the west. At six in the evening a brigade of the 50th Division arrived to take over the town and the 11th Armoured Division prepared for another long day's advance.

The Guards Armoured Division was also across the Somme, seven or eight miles further east. After numerous brushes with the enemy, armoured cars had reached the river about midday, just in time to prevent the bridges they were making for ('Faith', 'Hope' and 'Charity') from being blown in their faces. The Germans made several attempts to retrieve their failure but the arrival of tanks and infantry soon settled the issue. By dark the Guards held a substantial bridgehead, some ninety miles from where they had started at two o'clock that morning.

By then XII Corps was coming up on XXX Corps' left; its leading columns, driving through the night, would be at the Somme in the morning. The corps had had a difficult day. Its 53rd Division, going forward on the left with an open flank, had run into a lot of scattered opposition; and the 7th Armoured Division, due to join in the lead, was delayed for several hours in the morning by the collapse of a bridge on its way to the Seine. The 4th Armoured Brigade had made better progress and by nightfall was north of Poix and about twelve miles short of the Somme. The 7th Armoured was by then catching up quickly and arrangements were made for it to pass through, nonstop, to seize the bridges at Picquigny and Longpré before the Germans could destroy them.

By hard fighting and skilled use of ground the Germans had held up the Canadian advance until the great body of their surviving troops had got across the Seine, but they had still to make good their escape northwards. General Crerar now ordered that those Canadian Army formations not immediately required to capture le Havre, St. Valéry and Dieppe, would thrust forward through Neufchâtel to

---

[5] *Taurus Pursuant: History of 11th Armoured Division* (published privately), p. 51.

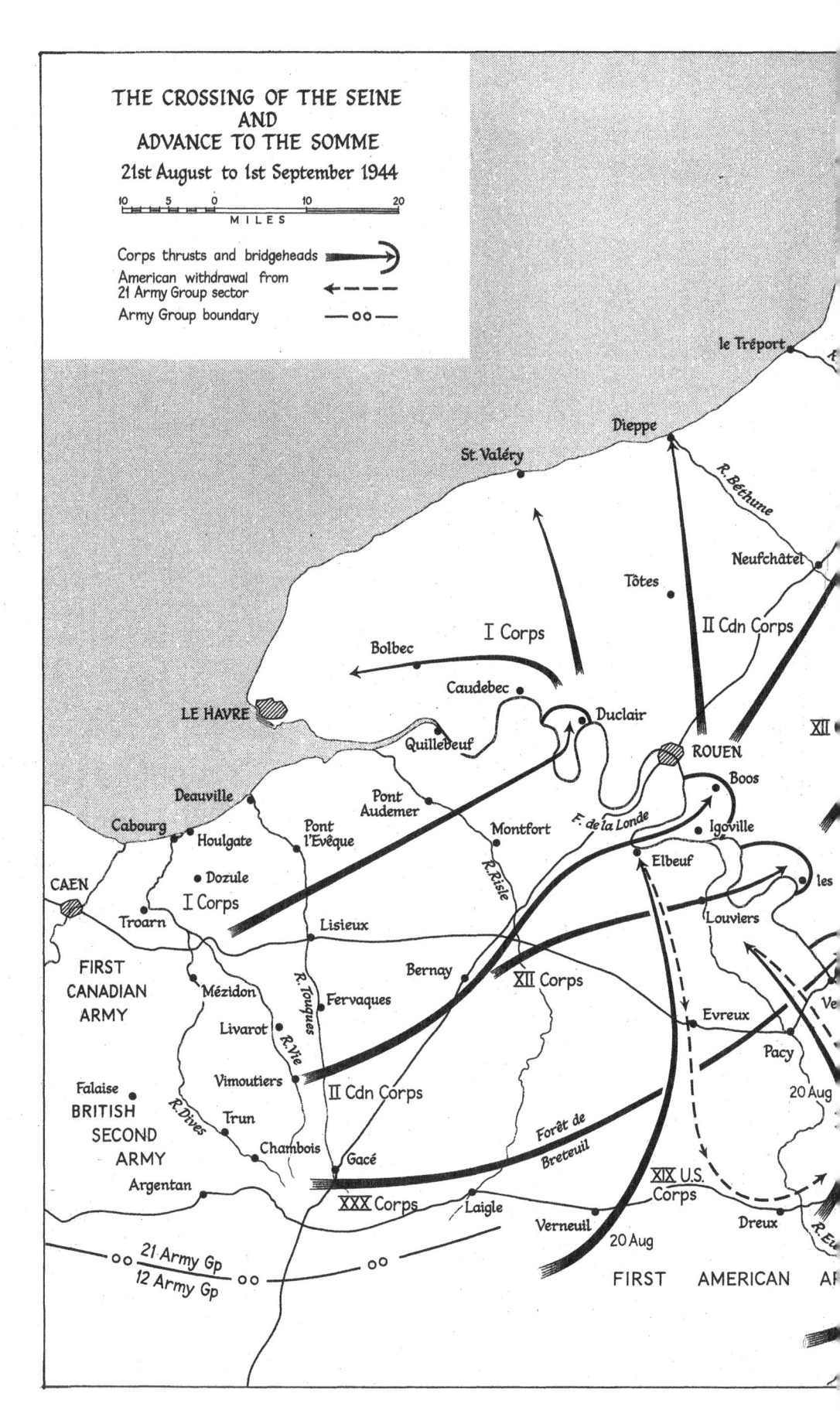

THE CROSSING OF THE SEINE
AND
ADVANCE TO THE SOMME
21st August to 1st September 1944

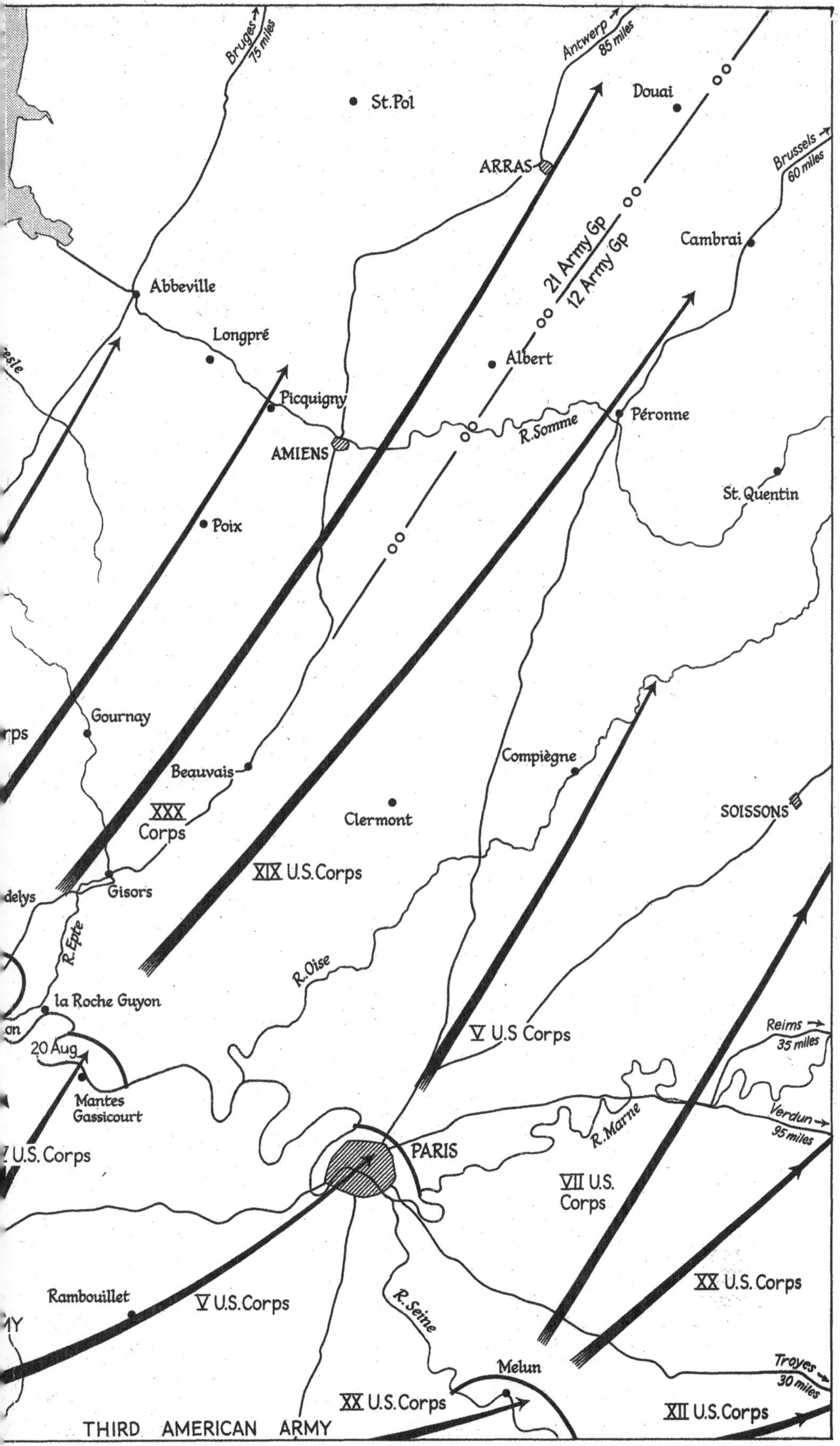

Bruges 75 miles
Antwerp 85 miles
St. Pol
Douai
ARRAS
Brussels 60 miles
21 Army Gp
12 Army Gp
Cambrai
Abbeville
Longpré
Albert
Picquigny
Péronne
R. Somme
AMIENS
St. Quentin
Poix
Gournay
rps
Beauvais
Compiègne
Clermont
SOISSONS
XXX Corps
XIX U.S. Corps
delys
Gisors
R. Epte
R. Oise
la Roche Guyon
V U.S Corps
Reims 35 miles
20 Aug
Mantes Gassicourt
Verdun 95 miles
R. Marne
U.S. Corps
PARIS
VII U.S. Corps
XX U.S. Corps
Rambouillet
V U.S. Corps
R. Seine
Melun
Troyes 30 miles
XX U.S. Corps
XII U.S. Corps
THIRD AMERICAN ARMY

Abbeville. The Canadian Army was hungry to avenge men lost in the 1942 raid on Dieppe and the 51st Highland Division to obliterate the 1940 memories of St. Valéry. On the last day of August 1944 they were well on the way to both of these objectives.

Second Army's advance and, in particular, XXX Corps' dash to Amiens had shattered any hope that Model may have had of holding the Somme. And with neighbouring American columns coming up fast on Second Army's right, a large gap in the middle of his Somme–Oise front was clearly imminent. If, as informed gossip in Allied circles had it, Model was a man who liked nothing better than to be asked to do the impossible, then here was a situation to offer him full scope.

During these last weeks of August the Navy's defeat of the German midget submarines, explosive motorboats and circling torpedoes had not meant that the Channel and Bay of Biscay were free from danger; indeed, August was the U-boats' most successful month. When the campaign opened there had been two on patrol north of the assault area, another was just starting back to Brest, and two more were off the north of Brittany on their way to the Channel. By mid-August U-boat crews were becoming more proficient in the practice of schnorkelling and more aggressive. On the 14th nine were or had been operating in the Channel. Between them they sank six merchantmen totalling 24,800 tons, a corvette, a minesweeper and an infantry landing ship, and damaged a 7,000-ton merchantman. But they paid dearly. In the Channel, seven U-boats were sunk by the Navy, one jointly by the Navy and Air Force, and a ninth by an air-laid mine. Meanwhile in the Bay of Biscay one was sunk by the Navy, two jointly by the Navy and Air Force, three by the Air Force and another by an air-laid mine. Of these sixteen U-boats that were sunk in August ten were schnorkel boats. The evacuation of U-boats from Brest had begun as early as the 7th of August and after the 15th, on Hitler's orders, they were being withdrawn to Norway. About the end of the month those not seaworthy, six in number, were scuttled by the Germans themselves in Biscay ports.

Meanwhile, as the Canadian Army cleared the Channel coast up to the Seine mouth and prepared to attack le Havre from landward as soon as the river was crossed, the Navy instituted a close blockade of the approaches to the port. It was the most westerly harbour left to the enemy and the Germans were trying to reinforce the garrison with supplies and to withdraw their remaining shipping. The naval blockade began on August the 26th when existing patrols by fast coastal craft were doubled and stiffened by frigates and destroyers. Thereafter, on four successive nights escorted German convoys trying to leave le Havre were strongly engaged. Some enemy vessels slipped through in the darkness but captured German records confirm their loss of nine and by the 30th the port was empty; no enemy shipping ever attempted to enter le Havre again.

The German air force had also suffered badly in the Allied progress eastwards during the latter half of August. The *Luftwaffe* were unable to prevent the Allies' continuous air attack on their retreating troops for their efforts were hamstrung by loss of forward airfields and lack of petrol (page 569). The Third Air Fleet headquarters had been compelled to move back, first to Reims and then to Arlon, west of Luxembourg; and after the air battle with the Ninth Air Force on the 25th (page 455) the airfields near Beauvais and Soissons were abandoned and others occupied further east in France and Belgium. They were to find no safety there. Already, on the 15th, Bomber Command and the Eighth Air Force had attacked airfields in Belgium, Holland and West Germany with nearly 2,000 bombers, covered by over 1,600 fighters; and these were followed by repeated Mosquito attacks on airfields in eastern France and Belgium.

The Second Tactical Air Force had similarly begun moving eastwards, in their case to facilitate pursuit of the enemy. On August the 27th 83 Group headquarters moved to the neighbourhood of Gacé with Second Army headquarters and during the next three days its squadrons began using airfields near Evreux. There they were in a better position to harry the German withdrawal on every opportunity and by all available means; road junctions, key railway centres and forward supply dumps were persistently under attack.

It is not possible to determine the full tale of damage and destruction inflicted by the Allied air forces before the last of the German troops escaped across the Seine. Shortly afterwards the Operational Research Group of Twenty-First Army Group made a detailed examination of three areas: the 'pocket', the Trun–Chambois–Vimoutiers neighbourhood (which they named 'the shambles') and the approach and crossings of the Seine. They counted over 12,000 enemy tanks, guns and vehicles but could not always tell which had been destroyed by air attack and which by artillery fire. Again, no attempt was made to measure the destruction of thickly congested horse-drawn transport, on which the German infantry divisions largely depended, for in many places the stench of death was overpowering. But if the total count was not complete it was at least proof of the huge loss inflicted by aircraft and artillery fire, especially in 'the shambles' and in the loops of the Seine near Rouen.

Bomber Command and the U.S. Eighth Air Force meanwhile continued the strategic offensive against Germany, concentrating mainly on centres affecting aircraft and other war production, oil, communications and industrial morale. In particular, Bomber Command twice made heavy night attacks on Kiel, Königsberg, Rüsselsheim and Stettin and others on Brunswick, Bremen, Sterkrade and Darmstadt.[6]

There was accumulating evidence that the Allies' air offensive had not only won for them virtual mastery of the air but, by its attacks on industrial areas, oil plants and communications, was seriously affecting the enemy's war-making capacity. On the Allies' side, however, signs of possible embarrassment were not caused by any shortage of supplies but by the pace at which their advance was extending the lines of communication. Administrative plans had been based on an assumption that the enlargement of the lodgement area in the early stage would be comparatively rapid, but that the subsequent advance to the Seine was likely to be slower and the river crossing strongly opposed. As things had worked out the lodgement area had not been substantially enlarged till the American break-out at the end of July, but once the break-out was made the enemy had been outflanked and defeated so effectively that the Seine had been reached and crossed with hardly a pause. After the slow, hard-fought progress of June and July, August had seen a leap forward. During much of June and July the Allied armies were thinking in terms of a hundred yards in three minutes and hoping for enough ammunition; by the end of August their thoughts were of a hundred miles in three days and hopes rested on petrol.

Early in August, Twenty-First Army Group brought its Rear Headquarters to France and assumed responsibility for the control and maintenance of the principal routes eastwards. Six further general transport companies, two tank transporter and four bulk petrol companies were brought in and the army group took control of the allocation of all road transport in order to ensure that every available lorry was mobilised and given to the armies. Only a bare minimum of general transport was retained for port and beach clearance; many Lines of Communication units were grounded and their transport diverted to support the advance. By the end of the month large stocks of supplies had been accumulated in the Rear Maintenance Area so daily imports were reduced from some 16,000 to 7,000 tons to provide still more transport for long-distance runs. Already, before the end of August, further roadheads had been opened, No. 3 at Lisieux for the First Canadian Army and No. 4 near Laigle for the British Second Army. The railway had been re-opened through Caen and Mézidon to Argentan by the end of the month and in the American area reached Paris via Chartres at the same time.

Air supply was already being used extensively by the Americans in

---

[6] See Webster and Frankland, *The Strategic Air Offensive*, vol. III, pp. 176–77.

the delivery of supplies to the more extended advance of their Third Army, and air transport had played a useful if less conspicuous part in British operations, flying backwards and forwards on daily missions between England and France carrying equipment, people and papers for special purposes. Two typical days' work of this nature may be quoted from the record of the Royal Air Force 46 Group:

> '*August 3rd.* Carried 264 passengers to France and brought home 482, including 435 casualties, 12 German p.o.w. and 2 V.I.Ps. Delivered 10,063 lbs of mail and 4,500 lbs of newspapers; 49,475 lbs of equipment, including blood plasma, signals equipment, ammunition, tractor, M.T. and A.F.V. spares. Brought home 8,280 lbs of mail and a German midget tank, captured intact.'

> '*August 27th.* Carried 80 passengers to France, and brought home 255 casualties and 35 other passengers. Delivered 9,868 lbs of mail and 9,640 lbs of newspapers, and 2,000 maps; 83,517 lbs of stores and equipment, including M.T. stores and blood plasma, 8 barrels of beer and 375,123 lbs of biscuits. Brought home 8,635 lbs of mail, and the salvaged parts of an aircraft which had force-landed in France.'

But air lift for the forward supply of Twenty-First Army Group had not yet been necessary though it was about to become of paramount importance.

For the Americans the supply position was more difficult. With Brest still in enemy hands[7] and other Brittany ports and harbours unusable they had organised 'through freight' convoys between St. Lô and Chartres which they called the 'Red Ball Express'. Using some 6,000 vehicles it made a peak delivery of 12,000 tons at Chartres on August the 29th, but their armies at the Seine were by then facing serious supply problems.[8] If General Eisenhower maintained his decision to develop attacks on Germany on a broad front the question of priorities must soon become acute. They were soon to have a direct effect on the pace of the Allied advance.

On August the 29th Generals Montgomery and Bradley received from General Eisenhower a letter which is the fullest indication of his policy.

> 'The German Army in the West has suffered a signal defeat in the campaign of the Seine and the Loire at the hands of the combined Allied Forces. The enemy is being defeated in the East, in

---

[7] The Third U.S. Army's VIII Corps had opened an attack on Brest on August the 25th supported by H.M.S. *Warspite's* 15-inch guns and Bomber Command's heavy bombers and, next day, by the heavies of Eighth Air Force. But the garrison defied their combined efforts and siege warfare continued. Brest was not captured till the 19th of September.

[8] See Ruppenthal, *Logistical Support of the Armies*, vol. I, p. 560.

the South and in the North; he has experienced internal dissension and signs are not wanting that he is nearing collapse. His forces are scattered throughout Europe and he has given the Allied Nations the opportunity of dealing a decisive blow before he can concentrate them in the defence of his vital areas. We, in the West, must seize this opportunity by acting swiftly and relentlessly and by accepting risks in our determination to close with the German wherever met. By means of future directives the Seventh Army, rapidly advancing on Dijon from the South, will have its action co-ordinated with that of our other Armies. It is my intention to complete the destruction of the enemy forces in the West and then advance against the heart of the enemy homeland.

The Northern Group of Armies will operate in a zone of action generally west of the line Amiens–Lille. It will cross the Seine, and, in conjunction with the left wing of the Central Group of Armies, destroy the enemy forces south of the Somme. It will then advance rapidly across the Somme, and be prepared to continue the advance to the north and north-east in order to seize the Pas de Calais area, the airfields in Belgium, and secure a base at Antwerp. The Commander-in-Chief Northern Group of Armies is authorised to effect, through the Commander-in-Chief Central Group of Armies, any necessary co-ordination between his own forces and the left wing of the Central Group of Armies. Details for effecting this day-to-day co-ordination are left to the Commanders concerned. The Commander-in-Chief Northern Group of Armies, in conjunction with the Commanding General First Allied Airborne Army, will plan and direct the employment of the entire Airborne force which is made available to the Northern Group of Armies to expedite the accomplishment of its assigned missions.

The Central Group of Armies will operate generally east of the line Amiens–Lille in conjunction with the Northern Group of Armies. On its right it will eventually gain contact with the Seventh Army advancing from the south. Initially, it will cross the Seine and thrust rapidly north with the principal offensive mission of assisting the Northern Group of Armies in the destruction of the enemy forces west of the Oise and south of the Somme. It will then advance rapidly across the Somme, prepared to continue the advance to the north-east. Necessary co-ordination with the Northern Group of Armies will be effected by the Commander-in-Chief Northern Group of Armies as indicated in the preceding paragraph. In addition to its principal offensive mission, the Central Group of Armies will complete the elimination of enemy resistance in the Brittany Peninsula, and protect our right and southern flanks. The Commander-in-Chief Central Group of Armies will build up our incoming forces generally east of Paris, prepare to strike rapidly eastwards towards the Saar Valley to reinforce the Allied advance north and west of the

Ardennes, and to assist the advance of the Seventh Army to and beyond Dijon.

The First Allied Airborne Army, in conjunction with the Northern Group of Armies, will plan and prepare for launching an airborne assault to insure the destruction of the retreating enemy forces. Planning and initial employment, in co-ordination with the Allied Naval and Air Commanders concerned, will be as directed by the Commander-in-Chief Northern Group of Armies. After their employment as indicated above, the airborne troops must be rapidly assembled in preparation for future operations to the north.

In addition to continuing to furnish close support to the Allied Armies and Navies and the reduction of enemy mobility by attacks on his communications, the Allied Expeditionary Air Force will deny to the enemy the crossings of the Somme, the Oise and the Marne, in that order of priority. The U.S. Strategic Air Force and Bomber Command, in addition to carrying out their primary missions against strategic targets, will always be prepared to support the effort of the Ground Forces.

The Commander-in-Chief, French Forces of the Interior will continue to provide direct support to the operations of the Army Groups by harassing, sabotage, counter-scorching (and mopping up action), and by protecting important installations of value to Allied lines of communication.

The Allied Naval Commander, Expeditionary Force will continue his support of the Armies' operations.'

On September the 1st General Montgomery was promoted Field-Marshal and General Eisenhower assumed direct command of the Allied armies in Northern France. On that day or in a matter of hours the forward troops were in Verdun, Reims, Cambrai, Douai, Dieppe, St. Valéry and other places whose names recall memories of other battles and earlier wars. Tactical air forces were leaving their Normandy airfields and moving eastwards and the Navy was ready to open the Channel ports as soon as they were recaptured. Flying-bomb sites were being overrun and after a few more days the noise of approaching bombs would cease to trouble England's peace.

60. Mosquito of Coastal Command

61. Seine bridges, old and new

62. Trail of a beaten army at the Seine

63. Advance of a victorious army from the Somme

CHAPTER XXII

THE WINNING OF OVERLORD

THE campaign in Normandy had been won. It had been won not only by the valour of the fighting forces but also by the thought and toil of those behind them. Earlier chapters have described the long drawn-out planning and preparation of Neptune and Overlord, inevitably made difficult by conditions which changed while plans were developing and by the need to reconcile the views of two nations and the demands of three Services. By the light of experience gained in other campaigns the Services could judge with considerable assurance what they should provide; without the lessons of North Africa, Sicily and Italy the planning of Overlord would have been a far more 'chancy' business. And though final preparations were so handicapped by delay in the appointment of a Supreme Commander and the consequent hold-up of final plans that the opening of the campaign had to be postponed for a month, and in the last hectic weeks some training was incomplete and some staffs almost exhausted by overwork, yet all the forethought and devoted labour was abundantly justified by subsequent achievements. Those who have followed the course of the campaign from the Normandy beaches to beyond the banks of the Somme will do well to look back, at this point, to see more clearly *how* it had been done and to realise more fully what had been involved in human effort and human life.

In retrospect 'Operation Neptune' may not figure in naval history as a great victory but it must surely hold an outstanding place as at once the largest, most complicated, carefully planned, efficiently organised and well conducted operation, and as a triumphant success. Complex arrangements for the due integration and marshalling of vast and various forces had worked smoothly, and much of the success of D-day was attributable to this and to combined training in the use of amphibious techniques and special equipment which had been developed by Combined Operations Headquarters and tested in assault landings in the Mediterranean. Neither difficulties encountered in its execution, nor adverse weather, nor the enemy's contrivance prevented the full realisation of its purpose. The sea was seldom kind and often angrily hostile, and although the German Navy could produce no substantial opposition to the heavy sea-traffic which plied continuously between England and France, German U-boats, E-boats, explosive boats, human torpedoes and mine laying aircraft buzzed about its flanks intermittently like venomous flies, able to bite though seldom to kill. The vigilant counter-action of naval and air forces defeated their purpose. Naval and air bombardment before and on the day of the assault left little of importance of the enemy's fortifications on shore, and although beach obstacles caused initial loss of life and landing craft they did not even delay the assault.

There is no need to repeat here what has been written in previous chapters of the Allied navies' distinctive and fundamental part in the assault on which the whole campaign depended, of their subsequent assistance to the land fighting and the continuous maritime operations in surrounding waters; but looking back over the weeks that had passed since D-day it is now easier to realise how much of the success of British operations had also depended on the Royal Navy's never-failing though less conspicuous ally, the Merchant Navy. Beween June the 6th and the end of August, a span of 87 days, there were landed in Normandy approximately two million men, nearly half a million vehicles and three million tons of stores and supplies. The analysis of these huge totals is as follows:

	British	American[1]	Total
Men	829,640	1,222,659	2,052,299
Vehicles . . .	202,789	235,682	438,471
Stores (tons) . .	1,245,625	1,852,634	3,098,259

Though much of the British total was carried to France by ships and landing craft of the Royal Navy, the greater proportion of men and material was borne in merchant shipping, sailing daily in convoys organised, controlled and guarded by the Royal Navy under the cover provided by the Allied air forces. Little mention has been made, so far, of these merchant seamen and their ships; they carried out their hard and dangerous duties with such unostentatious efficiency and determination that their courageous performance tends to be taken for granted. Yet without them the whole enterprise would have been impossible, and throughout the long months of fighting in France and Germany till the day of ultimate victory the armies were never embarrassed for want of supplies through any cause attributable to the merchant ships which brought them in. In the words of Admiral Vian: 'From D-day onwards the Merchant Navy proved its staunchness and fidelity in whatever circumstances.'

The all-important build-up of Allied strength in Normandy depended on the organisation and protection of shipping and,

---

[1] The story of how the high American totals were achieved is told in the American histories; and in particular in R. G. Ruppenthal's *Logistical Support of the Armies*.

although the landings in Normandy were somewhat behind the programme that had been prepared before the assault was launched, there was never any shortage that was more than a temporary inconvenience; setbacks through bad weather, which was a continuing cause of anxiety, never seriously threatened the success of build-up arrangements which had been made with such care.

The build-up of such great strength, without access to any considerable port, triumphantly vindicated the measures taken to provide sheltered water off the assault beaches by the Mulberry harbours and the Gooseberry breakwaters. Earlier chapters have described how the Gooseberries were made by the Navy's age-old method of sinking blockships and how, in the Mulberry harbours, blockships were reinforced and extended by huge concrete caissons. Within the sheltered water, the harbours were equipped with steel piers to facilitate landings. The potential value of the American harbour, practically destroyed by the June storm, cannot be judged, but the British harbour at Arromanches was completed and in full use and was to continue in service for several months. Certainly it was justifying tributes subsequently paid to 'the imagination, resource, resolution and courage of those who planned and carried it out'.

To construct its massive components in England, transfer them to the far shore and there build them up into a harbour which withstood the fury of the June storm was indeed a notable feat. Inevitably it was very costly in labour and materials and took many weeks to complete; on the other hand, the Gooseberry breakwaters were comparatively trifling in cost and were completed in a few days. It is therefore natural to compare the value of the shelter provided by the harbour and by the Gooseberries.

Of the total British stores landed up to the end of August about thirty-five per cent was landed through the harbour; about fifty per cent on beaches, sheltered by Gooseberry breakwaters off Juno and Sword (during the three weeks when Sword was used) and on the unsheltered beach outside the harbour in Gold area; the remaining fifteen per cent of the British total was landed in the little French harbours of Port en Bessin and Courseulles.

These percentages do not, however, tell the whole story; other factors must be taken into account. In the first place, the harbour was ordered in 1943 when a three-division assault was contemplated and was intended to land 7,000 tons a day. That designed capacity was fully realised when the harbour was completed. Secondly, its piers made possible, among other things, the landing of heavy machinery and other 'awkward loads' which would have been very difficult to get ashore directly on to an open beach. Thirdly, the piers greatly helped the embarkation of casualties and the back-loading of damaged vehicles. Finally, the shelter given to hundreds of ships and craft during the June storm should be remembered when assessing the contribution of the harbour to the success of the build-up.

The feature most open to question was the harbour's equipment of piers, strongly built of integrated steel roadway with complicated pierheads which rose and fell with the tide. Only about nine per cent of the total British stores were off-loaded on to the piers and it is arguable that they were needlessly elaborate; the steel roadway used was difficult to tow across the Channel and forty per cent of what was made was lost at sea. The first pier was not working till June the 29th and the long L.S.T. pier not until July the 19th. They had been developed by the War Office for use on an exposed shore, before it was decided to provide sheltered water for Overlord landings. They might have been differently designed had it been known earlier that they would be used within the shelter of a harbour.

It is, in fact, difficult to know whom to admire most—those who were responsible for the creation of the Mulberry harbours or those, sheltered only by Gooseberry breakwaters, who managed to do so well without the harbours' help. And here high tribute must be paid to the enterprise and energy of the American Army beach organisation. In spite of the storm's virtual destruction of their harbour the figures given above show that they landed even larger quantities of stores with only the advantage of their additional mechanical appliances on shore.

Among the most important stores was petrol—the very life blood of a fully mechanised army and of all air forces—in the French phrase *le sang rouge de la guerre*. The plan to supply petrol to the forces in France by pipe lines under the ocean (Pluto) had not yet been realised and the account of its ultimate achievement belongs to the next volume. Till then the two means of supply were by normal shipments of cased petrol, landed over the beaches or through the Mulberry harbour or the small ports, and by the method described on page 302 of buoyed pipes leading from tankers moored off-shore to the joint Anglo-American system of storage tanks at Port en Bessin and Ste. Honorine. Although these 'Tombola' pipelines reached their theoretical daily capacity of 8,000 tons only once in July and once in August, and although deliveries were seriously interrupted by storms in August which put one line out of action for over a week and badly damaged another, by the end of August over 175,000 tons had been delivered through this system; of this, about 88,000 tons were earmarked for British use. In the same period the total British stores landed (page 478) included 181,000 tons of cased petrol. So long as the fighting was comparatively circumscribed these supplies had proved sufficient, but since the break-out from the lodgement area and the development of a moving battle a very different situation was beginning to obtain.

Petrol in particular and supply in general were soon to have a strong influence on the campaign. Supply is a controlling factor in all military operations and it has been aptly said that a rapid advance is paradise for the tactician but hell for the quartermaster.

The supply of petrol to the army and air forces was but one item involved in the whole complex programme of supply. If the reader will think of two cities like Birmingham and Glasgow, or any other area with a total population of some two millions (much of it frequently moving), he may picture more easily the magnitude of the work required in organising the storage and systematic distribution of supplies, stores, equipment, petrol and ammunition to meet the manifold needs of a similar number of men. At the end of August the men of the British and Canadian forces alone exceeded the total population of Liverpool.

The lay-out of the British Rear Maintenance Area in August is indicated on the plan overleaf. It shows where the vast amounts of equipment and stores were accumulated for subsequent distribution to the troops. It also shows the miles of pipeline which had been laid to carry petrol and aviation spirit from the storage tanks that had been constructed at Port en Bessin to selected filling points for the army at Blary and Bronay and for the air force at Coulombs. By the end of August twenty-three airfields had been constructed or repaired by the Airfield Construction Wing of the Royal Air Force and the five Royal Engineers' Airfield Construction Groups, and were in use by the squadrons of 83 and 84 Groups: the position of airfields adjacent to the Rear Maintenance Area is shown on the plan.

On the plan of the maintenance area only the principal roads are shown; it was in reality intersected by numerous by-roads, and until the lodgement area was enlarged after the break-out every by-road and lane there and throughout the lodgement area had had to be utilised. During a traffic census, 17,000 vehicles were counted past one check-point in a single day—one in every five seconds. With roads in such constant use the Engineers were hard-pressed to carry out their necessary repair and improvement. Few roads were well metalled and their edges soon collapsed under heavy military convoys. Among other things the Engineers were obliged to develop a number of stone quarries in order to get the road material not only for maintenance but also for the construction of a dozen or more new by-pass roads at particularly congested places.

The wide range of duties traditionally undertaken by the Royal Engineers in addition to roads and bridges included port reconstruction and operation, railways, water supply, building construction, mining and general field engineering. Their scope had been increased by the development of assault Engineers with their varied mechanical equipment in armoured vehicles—AVREs. The great value of these in the landings and in subsequent fighting has been indicated in previous chapters.

If petrol is the life-blood of mechanised armies and air forces, signals are the nerves by which all movement at sea, on land or in the air is controlled; without efficient communications at every level no military operation can be conducted. The Navy, Army and Air Force have their own distinctive signal systems and, with the development of wireless communication, equipment has become far more efficient—and much more complicated; considerable scientific knowledge and mechanical skill are involved in the use of modern signalling apparatus. The exercise of inter-Service command in the initial phase of the assault, from headquarters ships with combined signal staffs of all three Services, showed, however, the acceptance of common doctrine and the high standard of team work that had been developed in recent years. Moreover, British and American forces, though 'divided by a common language', were united by the adoption of a common signals jargon.

The Royal Corps of Signals who, in association with regimental signallers, are responsible for the Army's system of communications, had the further task in Overlord of maintaining communications between the theatre of operations and England. In the field and in such long-distance work transmission by both wireless and cable was employed. In co-operation with the Royal Navy and the General Post Office four submarine cables had been laid across the Channel, and by the end of August twenty-seven speech and thirty-nine telegraph circuits were available for communication with England. The Corps also provided and operated through its Air Formation Signals all the land-line communications required in the field by the Royal Air Force, except the internal communications within R.A.F. units.[2]

In a modern army, fighting troops depend on essential services provided by such specialised units as the Royal Army Service Corps, the Royal Army Ordnance Corps, the Royal Electrical and Mechanical Engineers and the Pioneer Corps. An appendix (IV) to this volume describes the composition of the British personnel in Twenty-First Army Group and shows the balance of its various components. It will be seen that in August 1944 armour, artillery, engineers, signals and infantry, the arms normally regarded as 'fighting troops', numbered fifty-six per cent of the Army's total strength; the 'services' accounted for forty-four per cent.

In addition to the feeding, clothing and equipment of the armies, the maintenance of good health, the care of the sick and wounded and the revival of those temporarily exhausted by the strain of continuous warfare had also to be provided for.

---

[2] See R. F. H. Nalder, *The Royal Corps of Signals* (1958), p. 429.

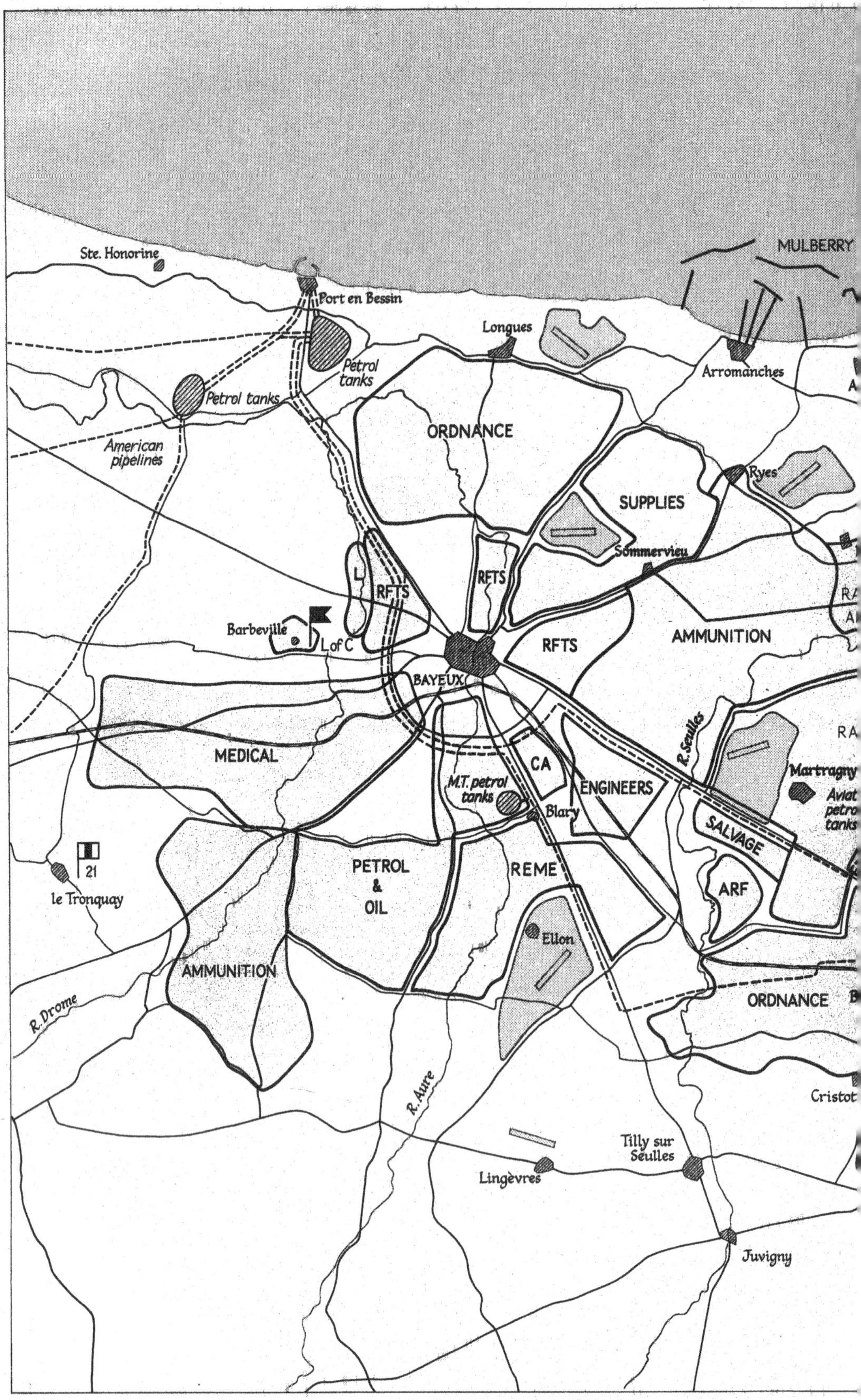

MULBERRY
Ste. Honorine
Port en Bessin
Petrol tanks
Petrol tanks
Longues
Arromanches
American pipelines
ORDNANCE
Ryes
SUPPLIES
Sommervieu
RFTS
RFTS
RFTS
L
Barbeville
L of C
AMMUNITION
BAYEUX
R. Seulles
MEDICAL
CA
M.T. petrol tanks
ENGINEERS
Martragny
Blary
SALVAGE
ARF
21
le Tronquay
PETROL & OIL
REME
Ellon
AMMUNITION
ORDNANCE
R. Drome
R. Aure
Cristot
Tilly sur Seulles
Lingèvres
Juvigny

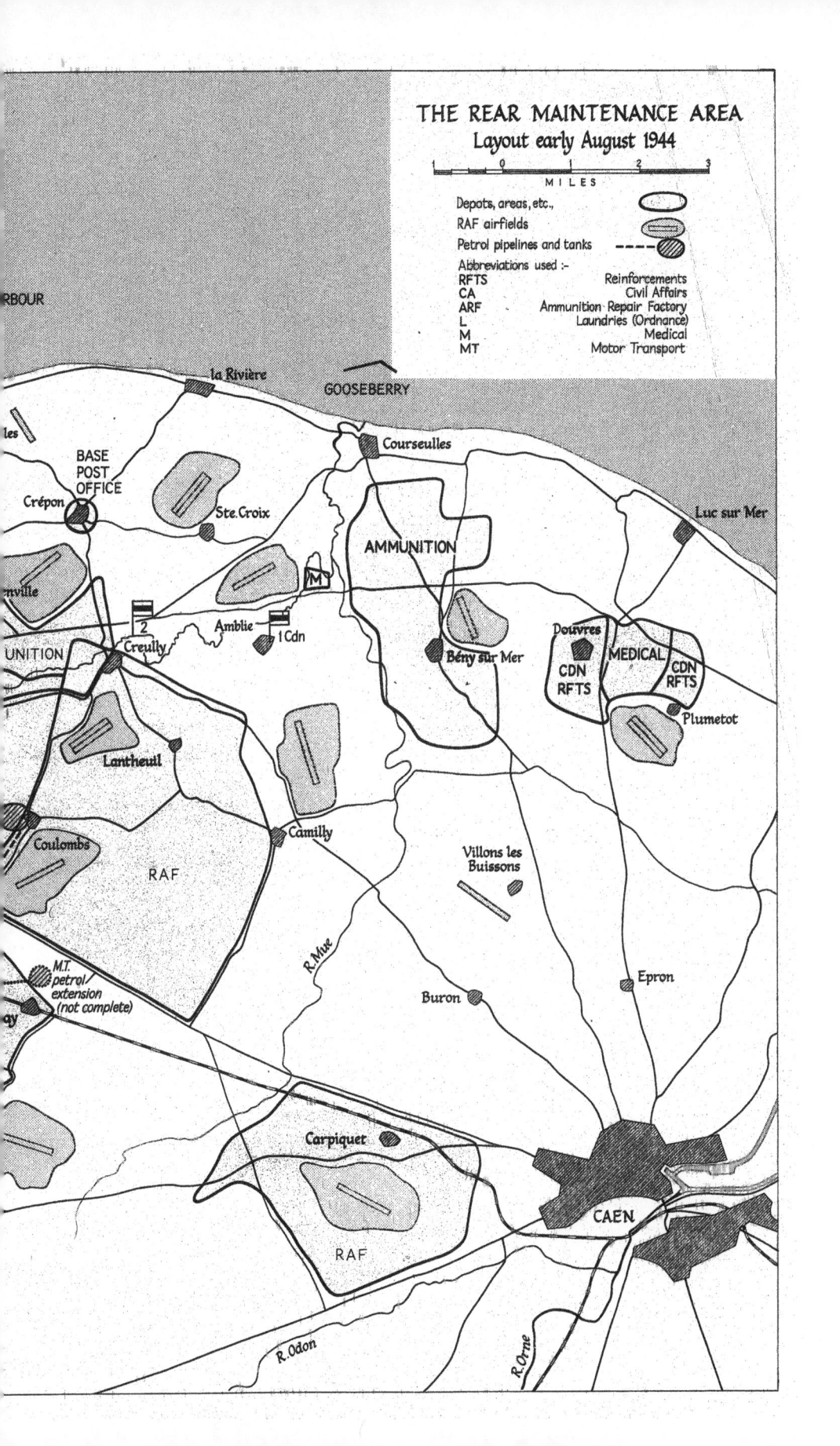

THE REAR MAINTENANCE AREA
Layout early August 1944

MILES

Depots, areas, etc.,
RAF airfields
Petrol pipelines and tanks

Abbreviations used:—
RFTS — Reinforcements
CA — Civil Affairs
ARF — Ammunition Repair Factory
L — Laundries (Ordnance)
M — Medical
MT — Motor Transport

GOOSEBERRY

la Rivière
Courseulles
Luc sur Mer
BASE POST OFFICE
Crépon
Ste. Croix
AMMUNITION
Amblie
1 Cdn
Creully
Douvres
MEDICAL
Bény sur Mer
CDN RFTS
CDN RFTS
Plumetot
Lantheuil
Coulombs
RAF
Camilly
Villons les Buissons
M.T. petrol/extension (not complete)
R. Mue
Buron
Epron
Carpiquet
RAF
CAEN
R. Odon
R. Orne

It had been planned that until hospitals could be established in the bridgehead all casualties would be evacuated to the United Kingdom, but each beach group that landed on D-day included a self-contained medical organisation. Field ambulances were landed with brigades and battalions; field dressing stations were open and surgeons working, in all beach-heads but one, only an hour and a half after the first wave of the assault hit the shore. In the next few days casualty clearing stations were set up in the assault area. The first General Hospital arrived on June the 10th and was followed swiftly by six others; thereafter the period for which sick or wounded were treated overseas was gradually extended as accommodation increased and the army group commander decided.

At first all evacuated casualties were carried home by sea, either in hospital carriers or specially equipped L.S.T.s, but evacuation by air began on June the 13th, a week *sooner* than planned. There are obviously advantages of speed and comfort in air travel; its comparative safety is shown by the fact that during the whole campaign 82,000 British and Canadian casualties were evacuated by aircraft without a single accident. From the beginning of the campaign till the end of August 57,426 casualties, including some personnel of the Royal Navy and Royal Air Force, had been evacuated by sea and 22,646 by air. Latterly more were being carried by air than by sea.

While the majority of men wounded in battle or seriously ill were brought home, those suffering from exhaustion or 'battle fatigue' were, as a matter of policy, treated in the theatre of operations. As the July fighting continued an increasing number of men succumbed to the exhausting strains of the battlefield, but the incidence of 'battle-fatigue' during that period was quickly reversed during the fighting in August. In the latter half of that month divisional centres for the treatment of men suffering from exhaustion were discontinued or almost emptied and the convalescent depot closed down. At the end of August several hospitals had also been closed and were ready to move forward behind the armies; of the remaining 29,000 beds in British and Canadian hospitals only 15,000 were maintained and only 9,700 were occupied.

An outbreak of enteritis in late July and the early days of August was attributed to the large fly population caused by crowded conditions in the bridgehead and hundreds of unburied carcasses of horses and cattle in the battle area; a soon-localised appearance of typhoid in one unit headquarters was the only real epidemic of the campaign so far. In general the health of the troops was continuously good. Throughout the war, as in this campaign, no corps can have won more gratitude than the Royal Army Medical Corps—from the medical officers with units in the battle to the surgeons and staffs of every rank who cared for those men who were sick or wounded and helped to restore health to so many. And with them will be remembered thankfully the Sisters of Queen Alexandra's Imperial Military Nursing Service and their gentle ministrations.

In addition to the well-known work of the Naval, Army and Air Force Institutes (Naafi) in providing for the troops' personal needs in stores and canteens, a number of voluntary agencies, e.g. the Y.M.C.A. and Entertainments National Service Association (Ensa), had begun work for the comfort and entertainment of the troops as soon as the military situation allowed it.

Foremost among services contributing to the well-being of the troops was that of the Army Postal Service, a special branch of the Royal Engineers. A regular air-mail service was instituted on July the 6th and something like 20,000 letters a day were being dealt with that month by one corps postal depot alone. Such delays in their delivery at home as occurred were at that time due as much to disorganisation there by flying bombs as to the situation in Normandy.

The only aspect of the German long-range weapon attack on England which directly concerns this campaign history is its bearing on the conduct of Allied operations on the Continent. General Eisenhower's ruling in June (page 267) that air attacks on V-bomb launching sites and storage depots ('Crossbow' targets) must take precedence over 'everything except the urgent requirements of the battle' had had no adverse effect on the direct air support of army operations. The counter-measures were of two sorts, namely, attack by bombers of sites thought to be in use for the storage or launching of either flying bombs or rockets, and the destruction by fighters of flying bombs *in flight* near or over England. Not unnaturally the Royal Air Force played the major part in both types of 'Crossbow' operations, since the defence of England was involved. Measured by sorties the Second Tactical Air Force and the Air Defence of Great Britain flew 22,776 sorties and Bomber Command 16,605 in attacks on launching sites, supply depots and flying bombs in flight, while the American bombers contributed something over 9,000.[3] The preliminary bombing of these targets secured a valuable advantage to Overlord during a most critical stage, for it prevented the enemy from launching the flying-bomb attack until after the Allied armies had landed and were firmly established in Normandy.

Nevertheless this effort had not prevented the Allied air forces from giving full support to army operations; both tactical and strategic air forces had done all and more than all they had been asked to do. But the use of strategic bombers to counter the V-bomb

---

[3] The advance of the Allies towards the end of August brought the main flying-bomb offensive to a close on September the 5th. By then over 9,000 V.1 bombs had been launched against England. Of these our defences had observed over 7,000 and about half of them had been brought down—some 1,800 by fighter aircraft, the rest by gun-fire or balloons. The German V.2 long-range rocket attack had not yet begun.

attack and for participation in army operations had reduced correspondingly the strength they could devote to their attacks on enemy communications and on targets in Germany. Measured by the number of sorties flown from D-day till the end of August, Bomber Command had devoted about fifty per cent to support, in various forms, of Overlord operations; about thirty per cent to Crossbow attacks and about twenty per cent to the strategic air offensive on Germany. The corresponding percentages of sorties flown by the American Eighth Air Force in the same period had been approximately fifty-six per cent for the support of Overlord, less than four per cent on Crossbow and some forty per cent on the strategic air offensive. It is easy to see how important was the direct assistance of the heavy bombers to the Army operations which have been described in previous chapters; it is less easy to measure the assistance to Overlord of the more distant and diffuse air offensive on Germany. Yet it can be said without any fear of contradiction that it was of fundamental importance and that without its assistance Overlord would hardly have been possible; to substantiate that claim it is only necessary to be reminded of its objects and of what it had achieved.

When General Eisenhower was given authority to direct the operations of the strategic air forces, their air offensive against Germany had been conducted in the previous year with mounting strength and improved effectiveness under the Pointblank directive (page 21). In the new directive given by Sir Arthur Tedder on behalf of the Supreme Commander on April the 17th, 1944, the over-all mission of the Strategic Air Forces remained as it had been stated in the Pointblank directive: 'the progressive destruction and dislocation of the German military, industrial and economic system' with the addition of 'the destruction of vital elements of lines of communication'. In execution of this purpose the particular missions named were the destruction of the enemy's air-combat strength and of his rail communications system, and the disorganisation of German industry; by verbal authorisation oil production and storage was subsequently added. In effect the new directive made no substantial departure from Pointblank objectives (varied from time to time with changing circumstances) but named targets which were of immediate importance to Overlord.

In this account of Overlord it is not necessary to trace the long and complicated story of how the heavy bomber forces of the Allies had increased in strength, technical efficiency and operational skill till they constituted a most powerful offensive instrument. Within the wide terms of their directives the Commander-in-Chief of Bomber Command and the Commanding General of the Eighth Air Force were largely free to select targets which they favoured and to frustrate attempts to divert them to others which they regarded as less rewarding. These are matters which belong to the separate history of the strategic air offensive[4] but it is desirable to realise how that offensive affected Overlord. It had begun years before; what then did Overlord gain from its achievements?

First, and of first importance to Overlord, it had enabled the Allies to win complete mastery of the air, over their home base in England, over their communications across the western seas and over the battlefields of France, and a very large measure of air superiority over Germany. This advantage to Overlord was so outstanding that, apart from the Navy's essential mastery at sea, no other is comparable and it would be idle to speculate on what might have happened without it. Of course it is true that tactical air forces had a very large share in winning air mastery but the foundations of air victory were laid by the strategic air forces. It was the growing danger of their attacks on Germany—devastating cities, destroying and damaging industrial plants and disrupting communications—that led to the German concentration on air *defence* and concomitant neglect to develop a strong *offensive* bomber force. This failure alone ensured a precious advantage to Overlord. When Allied troops were crowding into southern England, when the country was thickly dotted with fully occupied airfields and many harbours filled with assault craft and shipping, the bombers which Germany possessed did not attempt to disturb the training and assembly of the Overlord forces; even the landings in Normandy were left almost unmolested by heavy bomber attacks.

By August the 31st, apart from fighter-bombers and dive-bombers designed for ground attack, the *total* number of bombers shown in the German air strength returns for the eastern and western fronts and the defence of the Reich amounted only to 881, of which only 649, including many classed as non-operational, were serviceable; but there were 2,492 fighters of which 422 were in the Third Air Fleet and 1,192 in the Reich defence forces.

Not only had the air offensive against Germany led to this concentration on defence but it had also helped to reduce the effectiveness of the defensive fighter force which Germany had increased at the expense of heavy bombers. The Eighth Air Force daylight bombing attacks on German aircraft production plants had drawn the enemy's protecting fighters into a losing battle with the long-range fighters which were an essential part of the Eighth Air Force. Bomber Command's night attacks on German industry similarly attracted the enemy's fighters and destroyed many, but the German *night* fighter was never completely mastered.[5]

Thus a two-fold result of strategic operations was, first, to make

---

[4] Webster and Frankland: *History of the Strategic Air Offensive against Germany, 1939–1945.*
[5] On the 31st of August there were 648 night fighters in the Reich defence force.

the enemy air force concentrate mainly on home defence and thereby weaken the Third Air Fleet opposing the Allies in the West until it was almost completely ineffective when matched by the over-powering strength of the Allies.

A second outstanding contribution of the strategic bombers to the success of Overlord was their sustained attack on enemy communications, intensified near the battlefield by the tactical air forces. Before D-day this had severely handicapped the movement of material needed to fortify the coast. Since D-day it had made the movement of reinforcements and supplies a slow, unreliable and dangerous affair and thus had increased greatly the difficulties of the German armies in France. The thoroughness of the sustained Allied air attack on enemy railway communications has been shown by the photographically reproduced sections of German maps on pages 112 and 400.

In other and less closely related operations the strategic air offensive on Germany contributed much to the success of Overlord. The destruction it wrought on industrial towns, economic resources and communications had caused the absorption of much manpower and material for the work of repair and reconstruction that might otherwise have been used to strengthen the German fighting forces. The reductions of the enemy's oil supply had already begun a strangulation of German military and industrial power that was tightening its grip daily. Yet when this volume ends *it still remained for German territory to receive in the succeeding eight months twice the tonnage of bombs it had received in the first five years of the war.*

Previous chapters have described the ubiquitous and effective manner in which both tactical and strategic air forces filled their momentous rôle in preparatory operations, in the landings and throughout the subsequent fighting. It is no more possible to assess separately their contribution to Overlord than it is to value the parts played in combined operations by each of the three Services. But in so far as the air attack on Germany was distinct from Overlord it should be recognised as largely contributing to conditions in which the Overlord campaign was being fought with success.

Measured by the number of individual sorties, aircraft of the Allied air forces had flown over 480,000 sorties from June the 6th to August the 31st, made up as follows:

By Second Tactical Air Force and Air Defence of Great Britain	151,370	
By Bomber Command	54,687	224,889
By Coastal Command	18,832	
By United States Eighth Air Force	133,146	255,428
By United States Ninth Air Force	122,282	
Total Allied Sorties		480,317

This huge total includes continuous attacks on German forces wherever they were found at sea, in the air, or on land; on their bases, depots, headquarters and airfields; on German war production and industrial strength in material resources, manpower and organisation; on communications and means of transportation and on V-weapon sites and bombs in flight. The provision of fighter protection at all times over the battle area, shipping routes and home bases and the air reconnaissance which never ceased are also included.

The cost in lives and in Allied aircraft was as follows:

Force	Pilots and aircrew killed or missing	Aircraft lost
Royal Air Force Second Tactical Air Force and Air Defence of Great Britain Bomber Command Coastal Command	1,035 ⎫ 6,761 ⎬ 8,178 382 ⎭	829 ⎫ 983 ⎬ 2,036 224 ⎭
U.S. Army Air Force Eighth Air Force Ninth Air Force	7,167 ⎫ 8,536 1,369 ⎭	1,168 ⎫ 2,065 897 ⎭
	Total aircrew 16,714[6]	Total aircraft 4,101

If the total number of sorties of all sorts is taken into account, it is calculated that on average some thirty-six men and nine aircraft were lost for every thousand sorties flown by the Royal Air Force, and that the United States Air Forces lost some thirty-four men and eight aircraft for every thousand sorties. It must however be remembered, when counting the cost, that before Overlord was launched the Allied air forces had lost some 12,000 men and over 2,000 aircraft in preparatory operations, during April and May, which are described in Chapter V.

The German conduct of the campaign in Normandy was conditioned by the fact that their armies had not only been outgeneralled but had fought against forces which soon grew stronger than their own. When the battle opened their coastal defence had already been severely weakened and their communications largely disrupted by Allied air attacks. They had neither naval nor air forces that could effectively oppose the Allies' command at sea and in the air, and once they had failed to prevent the assaulting armies from

---

[6] In the same period the Air/Sea Rescue Services of Coastal Command and the Air Defence of Great Britain, using patrolling aircraft and high-speed launches, saved 1,245 airmen and airborne troops from the sea.

gaining a firm footing on shore they fought with waning strength against an enemy who waxed stronger day by day.

But their conduct of the campaign suffered even more from the absence of effective command. Their absolute commander, Adolf Hitler, was lacking in both military training and reliable information, for which self-assurance and intuition are inadequate substitutes. Handicapped by Hitler's close control, the two experienced field-marshals (von Rundstedt and Rommel) who commanded in the West during the most critical phase had complete confidence neither in Hitler nor in each other; they were only agreed that no victory could be gained from a battle fought as Hitler was directing it and, once the Allies were established in strength, they were soon convinced that the battle in Normandy could not be won at all. There is no evidence on record that either Hitler or his commanders in the West had made any plan for dealing with the invasion should the Allies succeed in securing a firm lodgement. When Rommel was wounded and von Rundstedt was dismissed, von Kluge's decline of confidence in Hitler's leadership was soon only equalled by Hitler's distrust of von Kluge's loyalty. Matched against the Allies' unity of command and confident leadership, the German disunity and mistrust was bound to be beaten.

It is arguable that the German 'delaying action'—which was what the battle in Normandy amounted to—was not worth fighting to a finish when once the Allies were firmly ashore and could build up strength unhindered. Hitler's attempt to hold them stalemated in their bridgehead was bound to involve a continuing expenditure which could lead to nothing but bankruptcy, and its ultimate failure was made more certain by keeping the bulk of Fifteenth Army's forces east of the Seine until the Seventh Army was beaten further west. As described in an earlier chapter (page 103), the Allied deception plan, Fortitude, had been designed to mislead the enemy into a belief 'that the Normandy assault was but a diversionary attack'; that 'the main attack would come in the Pas de Calais' and be launched 'about the third week in July'. How well the deception plan had succeeded! Only as July passed with no sign of the expected attack in the Pas de Calais did Hitler conclude that the Fifteenth Army could no longer be kept out of battle in readiness to repel a second landing. That expensive mistake is in part explained by the failure of the German Intelligence to see through the Allies' bluff and in part by Hitler's conviction that he could foresee what the Allies would do. German knowledge of affairs in Britain, admittedly handicapped by lack of air reconnaissance, was nevertheless inaccurate and incomplete so far as it went and the deductions drawn from it were false. German Intelligence was unable to pierce Allied security and failed to question Hitler's 'hunches'. OKW and Army leaders found it easy to accept his belief that the proximity of the Pas de Calais would attract the main Allied assault. Yet Hitler's attempt to keep the Allies penned in a small corner of France, while he assumed that they would make a second landing, was not altogether unreasonable. By clinging to the highly defensible *bocage* he kept the Allies' mobile armies from the less easily defensible country further south.

Apart from the fatal defects in their command, German operations were fought under the insuperable handicap of the Allies' mastery in the air. No single factor did so much to assist the Allied armies' victory as the sustained air attack which seldom ceased and which rose at times to almost unbearable intensity. In this branch of warfare the German air force could neither hit back with comparable blows nor defend itself effectively. Yet in spite of this appalling handicap and others that have been recognised, the German armies in Normandy deserve credit for the tenacity and discipline with which they fought and the manner in which they held up the Allies' progress. That their fight ended in defeat was partly due to factors which soldiers in the field could not control. It is true that a significant number surrendered or were taken prisoner but many fought their way back and were to fight another day. The battle of Normandy was not only lost by the German Army's heavy defeat in the field but by Hitler's way of fighting it.

Comparatively little has been said about the part played by the German Air Force in the Normandy campaign. In fact there is little to say. Greatly outnumbered by the Allied air forces they had, perhaps, been as active as their strength and the supremacy of Allied air forces allowed, but their resulting effort was of little account to the Allied armies. Their most effective operations were the dropping of mines in the shipping-infested waters of the assault area. The commander of the Third Air Fleet, Field-Marshal Hugo Sperrle, had held that appointment during the whole of the German occupation of France, 'living soft' in Paris. He does not seem to have had any lively reaction when the Allies landed and none of his subordinates is distinguishable in the air fighting in Normandy. The war diaries of the army commands in the West have few references to the *Luftwaffe* that are not critical and they give no indication that Sperrle had any voice in shaping the conduct of operations. He was, in fact, relieved of his command at the end of August and placed on the retired list.

The air forces defending the Reich from the Allied strategic offensive were also suffering from lack of effective control. Göring had also been 'living soft' and there was no dominant figure in the air command to give reality to the figurehead he had become. Speer had greatly increased the production of aircraft—even during

1944; what Speer could not do was to increase correspondingly the supply of skilled instructors or the proficiency of the training programme. The flying hours allowed to trainees, at this time, were far less than those of the Allies and perhaps this accounts for the fact that, according to German records, between D-day and the end of August 644 aircraft of the Third Air Fleet and the Reich Defence Force were destroyed and 1,485 damaged *not* by Allied action and *while not on operations*. The German returns also show that in this period these two air forces lost *on operations* 3,656 aircraft, all but 513 of which were destroyed by Allied action; 2,127 of the Third Air Fleet and 1,016 of the Reich Defence Force.

In virtually abandoning reliance on bombers as an offensive weapon it must be assumed that the flying bomb and long-range rocket were expected by Hitler to be an effective alternative, but when this, like so many of his calculations, was not realised it was too late to make up for lost time.

The conduct of the Twenty-First Army Group's operations during the battle of Normandy gives little occasion for adverse criticism. Its troops had been consistently well led. They had fought without pause for nearly three gruelling months, never losing the initiative and mastering, step by step, the enemy's strongest opposition. As in every prolonged campaign there were at times some formations or some units which fought with less determination or less success than others. It is easy to point to delay in the capture of Caen or complain that slow progress was made in extending the British bridgehead southwards, but such criticism fails to recognise the strength of the enemy's determination to hold his ground and the skill and tenacity with which the German troops fought.

It may be held that the plan to capture Caen and exploit with armour towards the Evrecy ridge and Villers-Bocage on D-day was over-ambitious. The troops available had been at sea all night, had known the strain and excitement of landing in the face of the enemy and had fought their way inland. In some, the desire to hold a position gained acted as a brake on enterprise. The tanks ashore had inevitably become widely distributed with the infantry and when the advance was held up by increased enemy opposition there was no reserve of armour available to add the weight needed to reach the long-distance objectives.

If the possibility of capturing the more distant objectives on D-day had been over-estimated, the difficulty of subsequent advances through the *bocage* had certainly been under-estimated. Its closely cultivated jumble of steep hills and deep valleys, clothed in woods and patterned by a lacework of hedge and orchard, offers endless cover for defence and terrible hindrances to advance. At times, too, mist and fog or heavy rain made progress almost impossible.

It was the highly efficient German mortars which caused most of the casualties to our own infantry, and their strong contingents of long-range anti-tank guns, particularly '88's, which were responsible for knocking out most of our tanks. Their conventional artillery, field and heavier, was neither numerous nor efficient; British artillery on the other hand was plentiful, flexible and had improved out of all recognition during the four years of war. Twenty-First Army Group's persistent pressure had compelled Rommel to make good a shortage of infantry by using his armour defensively. The strongest armoured divisions were clustered round that eastern flank until the American army had reached a position from which it was ready to break through the less heavily guarded western front. But while that was a designed result of Montgomery's tactics it had a less desirable effect on British operations. For until the middle of August the strength of the German armour-supported defences in the east prevented the British armoured divisions from reaching country in which they could be used with full effect. Twenty-First Army Group was in much the same position as the Germans in that the proportion of infantry was low and General Montgomery was anxious to avoid heavy casualties. He therefore had to support the infantry closely with tanks and was compelled on occasion to use armoured divisions in the van of the attack instead of being able to hold them in reserve for a break-through. But though the battle, as conducted, did progress more slowly at first than had been hoped, it moved more quickly than was expected towards the end and gained then a resounding victory.

In that victory the American armies had played a most distinguished part. They had shown their skill and valour in the exhausting fight which they knew as 'the battle of the hedgerows', in their break through the German defence near St. Lô and the immediate exploitation of the opening it created, in their repulse of the Mortain counter-attack and subsequent share in the formation and eventual closing of the pocket, and in their vigorous pursuit of the retreating enemy. In all this they owed a great deal to General Bradley's leadership. He had accepted with complete loyalty General Montgomery's over-all control while he commanded the United States First Army when in Twenty-First Army Group; during August, when he commanded the American Twelfth Army Group, he showed initiative and willing collaboration in the planned operations. How far his own opinions were reflected in General Montgomery's directives it is difficult to tell, for these were always issued after discussions with General Bradley and General Dempsey (and latterly with General Crerar) and no record of such discussions was taken.

For the same reason contributions made by General Dempsey or General Crerar to the shaping of General Montgomery's directives cannot be known. General Dempsey, like General Montgomery, put very little on paper but the paucity of written records is no indication of the part he played in the campaign. He was always in firm control of all that was done by Second Army. Much of his day was usually spent in visits to formations chiefly involved, to confer with commanders on their problems and progress and to give them clear and concise verbal orders. The directives he received left him little scope for any conspicuous initiative but his understanding of Montgomery's purpose, his own knowledge of the troops he commanded and his quiet and steady personality continued to give both his superior and his subordinates confidence in his judgment and in his leadership.

Measured by the casualties of the Allied armies the cost of their success up to the end of August was as follows:

	Killed	Wounded	Missing	Total
Of Twenty-First Army Group . . .	16,138	58,594	9,093	83,825
Of the American Armies	20,838	94,881	10,128	125,847
Total	36,976	153,475	19,221	209,672

Happily these totals are appreciably smaller than those that had been forecast before the campaign was launched.

General Montgomery had kept firmly to the general plan he intended to follow, undeterred by incidental disappointments and unperturbed by ill-informed criticism. He can fairly be criticised for what at times he said or wrote, but not easily for what he did. By the day on which he handed over to General Eisenhower his direction of the armies that had been fighting in Normandy, the liberation of France was virtually accomplished. It had been hoped to reach the Seine in some ninety days but assumed that heavy fighting might well be needed then to win river crossings; as the battle had been fought the enemy had been too badly beaten to make any strong stand on the Seine and Allied troops had begun crossing the river almost unopposed days ahead of the forecast time-table. The view may be held that if greater strength had been brought forward to cover the mouth of the Falaise pocket more quickly and more effectively, and if the American drive down the left bank of the Seine had not been stopped at Elbeuf, fewer of the enemy would have escaped. But the direction of four Allied armies, so as to use their power to the full in a situation that changed hour by hour, was very difficult.

The underlying strategy which General Montgomery had determined to adopt, his prescient realisation of the enemy's likely reactions and his patient adherence to tactics that would, he believed, achieve his purpose, were alike justified by results. Only personal prejudice would deny this, for it is the verdict of events that is conclusive.

It is also characteristic of his command during the battle of Normandy that he used tactfully the authority which General Eisenhower had given him to direct the operations of both British and American armies throughout the most critical phase of Overlord. There had been no Anglo-American friction, no divergence of opinion with General Bradley who wrote afterwards:

> 'During these operations in the lodgement where Montgomery bossed the U.S. First Army as part of his 21st Army Group, he exercised his Allied authority with wisdom, forbearance and restraint ... I could not have wanted a more tolerant or judicious commander.' [7]

Similarly, General Montgomery's relations with the Supreme Commander had exposed no differences which affected the conduct of the campaign. Montgomery had been given authority to control operations; in conformity with American tradition, General Eisenhower left him to do so without interference and without expecting him to wait for the Supreme Commander's approval. General Eisenhower's knowledge of what was being done in Normandy was provided by the information, Intelligence and orders issuing from Twenty-First Army Group, by direct correspondence with General Montgomery and by visits to the lodgement area for personal conference with him and with General Bradley at least once a week; very naturally he maintained close personal touch with Bradley and the American troops. Most of the letters he wrote to Montgomery were to express approval and encouragement; they never openly criticised his orders or disapproved his actions. Only when slow progress and mounting American casualties were provoking public criticism (especially in the American Press) did he show some impatience and advocate a more wholesale attack on the British front. Beyond this he said little to show that he misunderstood General Montgomery's conduct of the battle. That he *did* misunderstand it is revealed in his report to the Combined Chiefs of Staff after the war was ended.

In the last weeks of August, however, questions involving both strategy and command had begun to reveal divergent views on future policy which affected the conduct of subsequent operations and would prove difficult to reconcile; they relate to the latter part of the Overlord campaign and so belong to the second volume of this history. Meanwhile it would be wrong to conclude the present volume on a note of controversy. For the conduct of the Normandy battle

---

[7] Bradley, *A Soldier's Story*, pp. 319–320.

EUROPE
5th June 1944

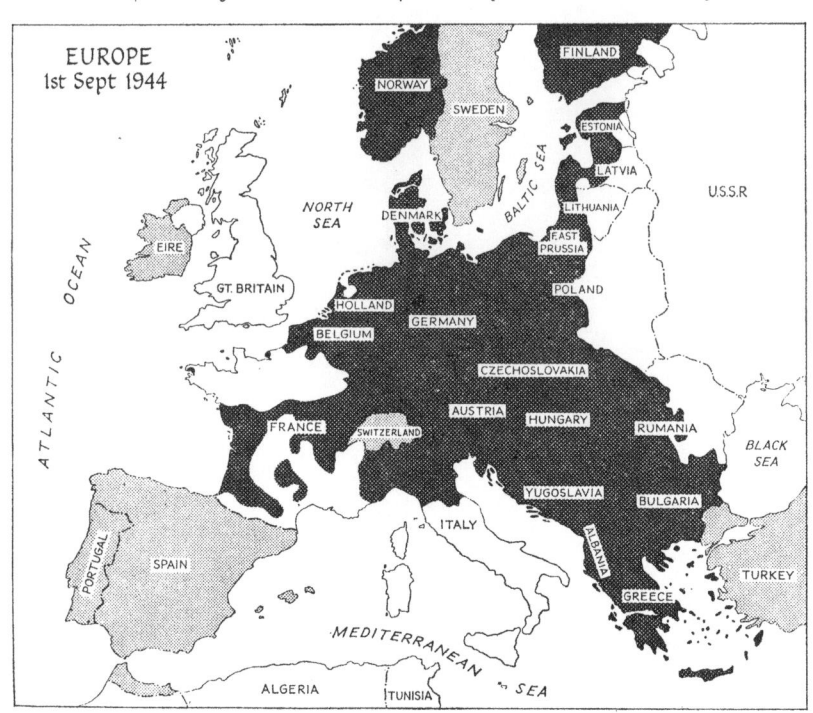

German occupied territory ■   Allied occupied territory □   Neutral territory ▨

EUROPE
1st Sept 1944

had been blessedly free from any conflict of opinions or clash of personalities.

On the eastern front the Russians had opened their offensive on June the 23rd—seventeen days after the Western Allies had begun landing; by that time the latter had already won a firm footing in France. By the end of August Russian forces had reached the border of East Prussia in the north; in the centre they were outside Warsaw, little more than three hundred miles from Berlin; in the south they had driven into Rumania and the vital Ploesti oil wells were already in their possession.

Meanwhile on the Italian front the Allied armies under General Alexander, which had taken Rome two days before the Overlord landings began, had driven the German forces northwards beyond Florence by the end of August. The map on page 495 shows the Allied gains in Europe while Overlord was being fought. From now on the shrinkage of Nazi domination in Europe would be more rapid: the next volume will describe its obliteration by the Allies' triumphant advance to victory. But there was to be much heavy fighting on the way.

Appendices

APPENDIX I

Directive to Supreme Commander, Allied Expeditionary Force

(Issued February the 12th, 1944)

1. You are hereby designated as Supreme Allied Commander of the forces placed under your orders for operations for the liberation of Europe from the Germans. Your title will be Supreme Commander, Allied Expeditionary Force.

2. *Task*. You will enter the Continent of Europe and, in conjunction with the other United Nations, undertake operations aimed at the heart of Germany and the destruction of her armed forces. The date for entering the Continent is the month of May, 1944. After adequate Channel ports have been secured, exploitation will be directed towards securing an area that will facilitate both ground and air operations against the enemy.

3. Notwithstanding the target date above, you will be prepared at any time to take immediate advantage of favorable circumstances, such as withdrawal by the enemy on your front, to effect a re-entry into the Continent with such forces as you have available at the time; a general plan for this operation when approved will be furnished for your assistance.

4. *Command*. You are responsible to the Combined Chiefs of Staff and will exercise command generally in accordance with the diagram at Appendix A [reproduced below]. Direct communication with the United States and British Chiefs of Staff is authorized in the interest of facilitating your operations and for arranging necessary logistic support.

5. *Logistics*. In the United Kingdom the responsibility for logistics organization, concentration, movement and supply of forces to meet the requirements of your plan will rest with British Service Ministries so far as British Forces are concerned. So far as United States Forces are concerned, this responsibility will rest with the United States War and Navy Departments. You will be responsible for the co-ordination of logistical arrangements on the Continent. You will also be responsible for co-ordinating the requirements of British and United States Forces under your command.

6. *Co-ordination of operations of other Forces and Agencies*. In preparation for your assault on enemy occupied Europe, Sea and Air Forces, agencies of sabotage, subversion, and propaganda, acting under a variety of authorities, are now in action. You may recommend any variation in these activities which may seem to you desirable.

7. *Relationship to United Nations Forces in other areas*. Responsibility will rest with the Combined Chiefs of Staff for supplying information relating to operations of the forces of the U.S.S.R. for your guidance in timing your operations. It is understood that the Soviet forces will launch an offensive at about the same time as OVERLORD with the object of

preventing the German forces from transferring from the Eastern to the Western front. The Allied Commander-in-Chief, Mediterranean Theatre, will conduct operations designed to assist your operation, including the launching of an attack against the south of France at about the same time as OVERLORD. The scope and timing of his operations will be decided by the Combined Chiefs of Staff. You will establish contact with him and submit to the Combined Chiefs of Staff your views and recommendations regarding operations from the Mediterranean in support of your attack from the United Kingdom. A copy of his directive is furnished for your guidance. The Combined Chiefs of Staff will place under your command the forces operating in Southern France as soon as you are in a position to assume such command. You will submit timely recommendations compatible with this regard.

8. *Relationship with Allied Governments—the re-establishment of Civil Governments and Liberated Allied Territories and the administration of enemy territories.* Further instructions will be issued to you on these subjects at a later date.

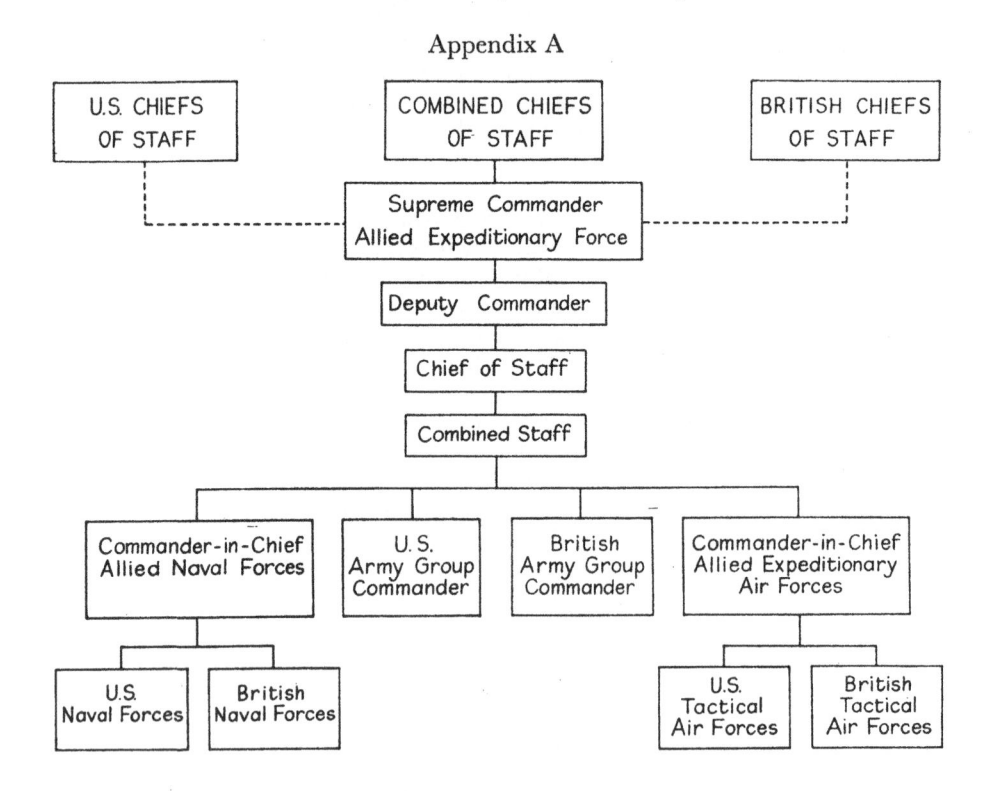

Appendix A

```
┌──────────────┐      ┌──────────────────┐      ┌──────────────┐
│ U.S. CHIEFS  │      │ COMBINED CHIEFS  │      │BRITISH CHIEFS│
│   OF STAFF   │      │    OF STAFF      │      │   OF STAFF   │
└──────┬───────┘      └────────┬─────────┘      └──────┬───────┘
       │               ┌───────┴────────┐               │
       └───────────────┤Supreme Commander├──────────────┘
                       │Allied Expeditionary Force│
                       └───────┬────────┘
                       │Deputy Commander│
                       └───────┬────────┘
                       │ Chief of Staff │
                       └───────┬────────┘
                       │ Combined Staff │
                       └───────┬────────┘
    ┌──────────────┬───────────┴──────────┬──────────────┐
Commander-in-Chief  U.S.        British   Commander-in-Chief
Allied Naval Forces Army Group  Army Group Allied Expeditionary
                    Commander   Commander  Air Forces
    ┌────┬────┐                              ┌────┬────┐
  U.S.  British                            U.S.  British
  Naval Naval                            Tactical Tactical
  Forces Forces                          Air Forces Air Forces
```

Liaison shown thus - - - - - - - - - -

APPENDIX II

Allied Naval Forces in Operation Neptune

Part I
COMMAND

Allied Naval Commander-in-Chief Expeditionary Force (ANCXF)
Admiral Sir Bertram H. Ramsay, R.N.

Chief of Staff
Rear-Admiral G. E. Creasy, R.N.

*Chief Naval Administrative Officer
and Flag Officer British Assault Area (designate)*
Rear-Admiral J. W. Rivett-Carnac, R.N.

Rear-Admiral Mulberry/Pluto
Rear-Admiral W. G. Tennant, R.N.

WESTERN NAVAL TASK FORCE	EASTERN NAVAL TASK FORCE
Rear-Admiral A. G. Kirk, U.S.N.	Rear-Admiral Sir Philip Vian, R.N.
U.S.S. *Augusta* (Cruiser)	H.M.S. *Scylla* (Cruiser)

ASSAULT FORCES

FORCE U	FORCE G
Rear-Admiral D. P. Moon, U.S.N.	Commodore (1st Class)
U.S.S. *Bayfield* (H.Q. Ship)	C. E. Douglas-Pennant, R.N.
	H.M.S. *Bulolo* (H.Q. Ship)

FORCE O	FORCE J
Rear-Admiral J. L. Hall Jr., U.S.N.	Commodore (1st Class)
U.S.S. *Ancon* (H.Q. Ship)	G. N. Oliver, R.N.
	H.M.S. *Hilary* (H.Q. Ship)

FORCE S
Rear-Admiral A. G. Talbot, R.N.
H.M.S. *Largs* (H.Q. Ship)

APPENDIX II

BOMBARDING FORCES

FORCE A (Supporting FORCE U)
Rear-Admiral M. L. Deyo, U.S.N.
U.S.S. *Tuscaloosa* (Cruiser)

FORCE C (Supporting FORCE O)
Rear-Admiral C. F. Bryant, U.S.N.
U.S.S. *Texas* (Battleship)

FORCE K (Supporting FORCE G)
Captain E. W. L. Longley-Cook, R.N.
H.M.S. *Argonaut* (Cruiser)

FORCE E (Supporting FORCE J)
Rear-Admiral F. H. G. Dalrymple-Hamilton, R.N.
H.M.S. *Belfast* (Cruiser)

FORCE D (Supporting FORCE S)
Rear-Admiral W. R. Patterson, R.N.
H.M.S. *Mauritius* (Cruiser)

FOLLOW-UP FORCES

FORCE B
Commodore C. D. Edgar, U.S.N.
U.S.S. *Maloy* (Destroyer)

FORCE L
Rear-Admiral W. E. Parry, R.N.

ADMINISTRATION

Flag Officer West
Rear-Admiral J. Wilkes, U.S.N.

Commodore Depot Ships
Commodore (2nd Class)
H. T. England, R.N.
H.M.S. *Hawkins* (Cruiser)

Naval Officers-in-Charge (ashore)

Utah Area
Captain J. E. Arnold, U.S.N.R.

Omaha Area
Captain Camp, U.S.N.

Gold Area
Captain G. V. M. Dolphin, R.N.

Juno Area
Captain C. D. Maud, R.N.

Sword Area
Captain W. R. C. Leggatt, R.N.

APPENDIX II

Part II

ORGANISATION OF TASK FORCES

(showing associated Army formations; leading groups marked *)

WESTERN NAVAL TASK FORCE
(U.S.)
United States First Army

FORCE U
4 Inf Div (VII Corps)

Assault Groups
Green and Red
   8 R.C.T.*
  22 R.C.T.
  12 R.C.T.

Bombarding Force A
Support Group

FORCE O
1 Inf Div (V Corps)

Assault Groups
O1 116 R.C.T.*
O2 16* and 115 R.C.Ts.
O3 18 R.C.T.
O4 2* and 5 Ranger Bns

Bombarding Force C
Support Group

FORCE B
29 Inf Div

Naval Groups in Divisions of
Landing Ships and Craft
26 R.C.T. (1 Inf Div)
175 R.C.T. (29 Inf Div)
359 R.C.T. (90 Inf Div)
Overheads 82 Airborne Div

EASTERN NAVAL TASK FORCE
(British)
British Second Army

FORCE G
50 Inf Div (XXX Corps)

Assault Groups
G1 231 Inf Bde Group*
G2 69 Inf Bde Group*
G3 56 Inf Bde Group
     151 Inf Bde Group

Bombarding Force K
Support Squadrons (two)

FORCE J
3 Cdn Inf Div (I Corps)

Assault Groups
J1 7 Cdn Inf Bde Group*
J2 8 Cdn Inf Bde Group*
J3 9 Cdn Inf Bde Group
J4 1 and 4 S.S. Bdes

Bombarding Force E
Support Squadrons (two)

FORCE S
3 Brit Inf Div (I Corps)

Assault Groups
S1 9 Inf Bde Group
S2 185 Inf Bde Group
S3 8 Inf Bde Group*

Bombarding Force D
Support Squadron

FORCE L
7 Armd Div

Assault Groups
L1 22 Armd Bde Group
L2 22 Armd Bde Group
L3 153 Inf Bde Group
    (51 Inf Div)
Overheads 7 Armd Div

Note. A representative of the Air Commander-in-Chief embarked in the headquarter ship of each task and assault force.

APPENDIX II

Part III

BOMBARDING FORCES

General Reserve

Battleship	H.M.S. *Nelson*	9 16-in / 12 6-in

WESTERN TASK FORCE

Cruiser	U.S.S. *Augusta* (Task Force Flagship)	9 8-in / 8 5-in

Reserve

Cruiser	H.M.S. *Bellona*	8 5·25-in
Destroyers	As required from those engaged in escort duty	

Bombarding Force A — UTAH

Battleship
U.S.S. *Nevada* — 10 14-in / 16 5-in

Monitor
H.M.S. *Erebus* — 2 15-in

Cruisers
U.S.S. *Tuscaloosa* (Flagship) — 9 8-in / 8 5-in
U.S.S. *Quincy* — 9 8-in / 12 5-in
H.M.S. *Hawkins* — 7 7·5-in
H.M.S. *Enterprise* — 6 6-in
H.M.S. *Black Prince* — 8 5·25-in

Gunboat
H.N.M.S. *Soemba* (Dutch) — 3 5·9-in

Destroyers
U.S.S. *Fitch*
U.S.S. *Corry*
U.S.S. *Hobson*
U.S.S. *Shubrick* — 4 or 6 5-in
U.S.S. *Herndon*
U.S.S. *Forrest*
U.S.S. *Butler*
U.S.S. *Gheradi*

Bombarding Force C — OMAHA

Battleships
U.S.S. *Texas* (Flagship) — 10 14-in / 6 5-in
U.S.S. *Arkansas* — 12 12-in / 6 5-in

Cruisers
H.M.S. *Glasgow* — 12 6-in
F.F.S. *Montcalm* (French) — 9 6-in
F.F.S. *Georges Leygues* (French) — 9 6-in

Destroyers
U.S.S. *McCook*
U.S.S. *Carmick*
U.S.S. *Doyle*
U.S.S. *Baldwin* — 4 or 6 5-in
U.S.S. *Harding*
U.S.S. *Frankford*
U.S.S. *Thompson*
U.S.S. *Emmons*
H.M.S. *Melbreak*
H.M.S. *Tanatside* — 4 or 6 4-in
H.M.S. *Talybont*

APPENDIX II

EASTERN TASK FORCE

Cruiser	H.M.S. *Scylla* (Task Force Flagship)	8	4·5-in

Reserve

Battleship	H.M.S. *Rodney*	9	16-in
		12	6-in
Cruiser	H.M.S. *Sirius*	10	5·25-in
Destroyers	As required from those engaged in escort duty		

Bombarding Force K — GOLD

Cruisers
- H.M.S. *Orion* — 8 6-in
- H.M.S. *Ajax* — 8 6-in
- H.M.S. *Argonaut* — 10 5·25-in
- H.M.S. *Emerald* — 7 6-in

Gunboat
- H.N.M.S. *Flores* (Dutch) — 3 5·9-in

Destroyers — 4 or 8 4·7-in
- H.M.S. *Grenville*
- H.M.S. *Jervis*
- H.M.S. *Ulster*
- H.M.S. *Ulysses*
- H.M.S. *Undaunted*
- H.M.S. *Undine*
- H.M.S. *Urania*
- H.M.S. *Urchin*
- H.M.S. *Ursa*

Destroyers — 4 or 6 4-in
- H.M.S. *Cattistock*
- H.M.S. *Cottesmore*
- H.M.S. *Pytchley*
- O.R.P. *Krakowiak* (Polish)

Bombarding Force E — JUNO

Cruisers
- H.M.S. *Belfast* (Flagship) — 12 6-in
- H.M.S. *Diadem* — 8 5·25-in

Destroyers — 4 or 8 4·7-in
- H.M.S. *Faulknor*
- H.M.S. *Fury*
- H.M.S. *Kempenfeldt*
- H.M.S. *Venus*
- H.M.S. *Vigilant*
- H.M.C.S. *Algonquin*
- H.M.C.S. *Sioux*

Destroyers — 4 or 6 4-in
- H.M.S. *Bleasdale*
- H.M.S. *Stevenstone*
- H.N.M.S. *Glaisdale* (Norwegian)
- F.F.S. *La Combattante* (French)

APPENDIX II

Bombarding Force D

SWORD

Battleships				Destroyers		
H.M.S.	Warspite	4	15-in	H.M.S.	Kelvin	
		8	6-in	H.M.S.	Saumarez	
H.M.S.	Ramillies	4	15-in	H.M.S.	Scorpion	
		12	6-in	H.M.S.	Scourge	
				H.M.S.	Serapis	
Monitor				H.M.S.	Swift	
H.M.S.	Roberts	2	15-in	H.M.S.	Verulam	4 or 8
				H.M.S.	Virago	4·7-in
Cruisers				O.R.P.	Slazak	
H.M.S.	Mauritius	12	6-in		(Polish)	
(Flagship)				H.N.M.S.	Stord	
H.M.S.	Arethusa	6	6-in		(Norwegian)	
H.M.S.	Frobisher	7	7·5-in	H.N.M.S.	Svenner	
H.M.S.	Danae	5	6-in		(Norwegian)	
O.R.P.	Dragon	6	6-in	H.M.S.	Middleton	4 or 6
	(Polish)			H.M.S.	Eglinton	4-in

In addition to the bombarding forces listed above each naval assault force included landing craft equipped with various weapons to give additional close support to the assaulting troops. The type of craft and the nature of their armament were as follows:

Type	Western Task Force	Eastern Task Force	Armament
Landing Craft Gun (Large) . .	9	16	2 4·7-in (naval) guns, 2 to 7 20-mm Oerlikons (AA)
Landing Craft Tank (Rocket) .	14	22	800 to 1000 5-in high explosive rockets
Landing Craft Support (Large) .	—	14	1 6-pdr or 2-pdr in tank turret, 2 ·5-in machine guns, 2 20-mm Oerlikons (AA), 1 4-in smoke mortar
Landing Craft Support (Medium)	2	24	2 ·5-in machine guns, 1 4-in smoke mortar
Landing Craft Support (Small) .	36(a)	—	24 rockets, 2 ·5-in machine guns
Landing Craft Flak	11	18	4 2-pdrs and 8 Oerlikons, or 8 2-pdrs and 4 Oerlikons
Landing Craft Assault (Hedgerow)	—	45	24 60-lb Spigot bombs
Landing Craft Tank	26	103(b)	temporarily mounting army weapons

Notes. (a) All except these small American landing craft were British.
(b) On the British front the following weapons were mounted in L.C.T.s to give close fire support: 80 Centaur tanks mounting 95-mm howitzers; 20 Sherman tanks mounting 75-mm guns; 240 self-propelled 25-pdr or 105-mm field guns. Three craft carried 17-pdr high velocity guns for destroying concrete defences.

APPENDIX II

Part IV

SUMMARY OF FORCES ASSIGNED TO OPERATION NEPTUNE

The figures shown in the following tables are the gross numbers as planned. They will not necessarily agree exactly with the numbers recorded in actual operations on D-day owing to last-minute changes, but the variations are negligible.

Pooled reserves of landing craft, etc., and new craft which became available as the operation proceeded are not shown.

The total number of vessels assigned to the operation was:

Naval Combatant Vessels	1,213	Table A
Landing Ships and Craft.	4,126	„ B
Ancillary Ships and Craft	736	„ C
Merchant Ships	864	„ D
Total	6,939	

The nationalities of the combatant vessels in Table A were:

British and Canadian.	79	per cent
United States	$16\frac{1}{2}$	„ „
Other Allies[1]	$4\frac{1}{2}$	„ „

---

[1] European Allied vessels normally operated under British control and here include French, Norwegian, Dutch, Polish and Greek units.

APPENDIX II

Table A. Naval Combatant Vessels

Type	Western Task Force	Eastern Task Force	In reserve under A.N.C.X.F.	Home Commands (a)	Total
BOMBARDING SHIPS (137)					
Battleships	3	3	1		7
Monitors	1	1			2
Cruisers	10	13			23
Gunboats	1	1			2
Destroyers (Fleet Class)	30	28		20	78
Destroyers (Hunt Class)	5	14		6	25
ESCORTS (221)					
Destroyers (Escort)	10	6		13	29
Sloops		4		10	14
Frigates	2	8		19	29
Corvettes	4	17		50	71
Patrol Craft (U.S.)	18				18
Anti-Submarine Trawlers	9	21		30	60
MINESWEEPERS (287)					
Fleet Minesweepers	56	42			98
Auxiliary Minesweepers	26	30			56
Motor Minesweepers	20	30	20		70
Magnetic Minesweepers (Trawlers)			20		20
Danlayers	16	27			43
MINELAYERS (4) . . . . . (b)		2		2	4
SEAPLANE CARRIER (1) . . . (b)		1			1
LANDING SHIPS HEADQUARTERS (8) (Warships)					
Destroyers		2			2
Frigates		5			5
Gunboat		1			1
MIDGET SUBMARINES (2)		2			2
COASTAL FORCES (495)					
All types, British and U.S. including Rescue Launches	113	90		292(c)	495
ANTI-SUBMARINE ESCORT GROUPS (58)					
Escort Carriers				3	3
Destroyers				14	14
Sloops				3	3
Frigates				38	38
				TOTAL	1,213

Notes

(a) *Home Commands* includes (i) vessels engaged in covering operations under Cs.-in-C. Portsmouth, Plymouth, the Nore, Western Approaches, or Flag Officer, Dover, and

APPENDIX II

Table B. Landing Ships and Craft

Type	Western Task Force	Eastern Task Force	Total
ASSAULT			
LANDING SHIPS			
Headquarters (other than warships)	2	4	6
Infantry	18	37	55
Tank	106	130	236
Emergency Repair	2	2	4
Dock	1	1	2
MAJOR LANDING CRAFT			
Headquarters	15	11	26
Infantry (Large)	93	116	209
Infantry (Small)		39	39
Tank (load-carrying)	350	487	837
Support (all types)[1]	34	66	100
MINOR LANDING CRAFT			
Assault	94	408	502
Vehicle and Personnel	189		189
Support (all types)[1]	38	73	111
Personnel (Smoke)	54	90	144
Personnel (Survey)		10	10
SHIP TO SHORE FERRY SERVICE			
LANDING BARGES			
Vehicle	108	120	228
Rhino Ferries	31	41	72
Flak		15	15
Ancillary Services	81	135	216
MINOR LANDING CRAFT			
Vehicle and Personnel	260	396	656
Mechanised	206	240	446
Ancillary Services	18	5	23
TOTAL			**4,126**

[1] For details of Support Craft see page 506.

    (ii) others available for supplementary duty under the Allied Naval Commander-in-Chief (A.N.C.X.F.) as required by him.

 (b) Two minelayers, H.M.S. *Apollo* and H.M.S. *Plover*, with twenty-two motor launches and thirty-six motor torpedo-boats shown in this table under Coastal Forces, were used in Operation 'Maple'. Two other minelayers and the seaplane carrier were employed, one as a headquarter ship and the others as repair ships.

 (c) Seventy-two motor launches within this total were attached to the fleet minesweeping flotillas for the assault. Thirty-six of these were fitted as minesweepers.

APPENDIX II

Table C. Ancillary Ships and Craft

Depot and Repair Ships[1]	6
Fighter Direction Tenders	3
'Eagle' Ships (A.A.)	9
Smoke-making Trawlers	62
Force 'Pluto'	34
Control Ships (Mulberries)	9
Miscellaneous small craft	295
Tugs	216
Rescue Tugs	14
Buoy Laying Ships	5
Salvage and Wreck Dispersal	42
Surveying Ships	4
Telephone Cable Ships	6
Mooring Force	31
Total	736

[1] In addition, eight warships and three landing ships listed in Tables A and B.

Table D. Merchant Ships

(Other than Landing and Headquarters Ships)

Personnel	18
Motor Transport Ships	224
Motor Transport Coasters	64
Stores Coasters	122
Tankers and Colliers	49
Cased Petrol Carriers	136
Ocean-going Store Ships	78
Blockships[1]	59
Accommodation Ships	10
Hospital Ships and Carriers	10
Ammunition Carriers	76
Ammunition Supply Issuing Ships	18
Total	864

[1] Four of these were obsolete warships.

Note. Fleet Air Arm squadrons which took part in Overlord were under the control of the Air Officer Commanding-in-Chief, Coastal Command, and are therefore included in Appendix VI.

APPENDIX II

Part V

LANDING SHIPS AND CRAFT

Development and Production

WITHOUT specialised landing ships and craft an invasion of France from the sea against German opposition would have been impossible.

Between the wars the conduct of amphibious warfare had been studied at the Staff Colleges and in 1938 a *Manual of Combined Operations* was issued on planning and execution, but did not deal with the question of special equipment or landing craft. Recent weapon developments and the growth of air power were thought by many to make an opposed landing from the sea virtually impossible. But although no immediate need for such operations was foreseen and financial stringency severely limited all preparations for war, an Inter-Service Technical Development Committee had been set up by the Chiefs of Staff in 1937 to examine the practical needs of a landing operation in terms of special equipment, with a handful of officers and men to conduct trials and experiments. Under its auspices the first modern landing craft were designed and a few were built which later proved their value. On the outbreak of war Britain thus possessed a few assault landing craft and a nucleus of officers who had made a study of amphibious operations and of the special equipment they require. The development of the amphibious tank and many devices which came to fruition in later years received initial impetus from the work of this committee.

With the collapse of France in 1940 and the enemy's seizure of the European seaboard from the North Cape to the Pyrenees we were forced to recognise that, unless and until we could master the problems involved in an opposed landing from the sea across open beaches, British armies would not again be able to fight in western Europe. It was then, during the grim struggle for survival, that the foundations of our modern amphibious fleet were laid; even while anti-invasion preparations were at their height the newly-formed Combined Operations organisation began to assess the requirements first for offensive raids and, later, for an eventual return to the Continent in strength. Both required provision of suitable ships and craft. Passenger ships could be adapted as troop carriers, but operations across the English Channel would require not only small landing craft which could be carried in the transports but larger craft able to make the crossing under their own power and to land tanks and fighting vehicles on defended beaches. The first new development called for was therefore a landing craft tank (L.C.T.). This was evolved in Combined Operations Headquarters in consultation with the Admiralty and the first was afloat before the end of 1940. It was a flat-bottomed vessel designed to carry three 40-ton tanks in an open hold, with a hinged ramp door in the bow to enable the vehicles to embark and disembark. It was followed by larger types carrying five of the biggest tanks or a mixed load of ten to twelve vehicles.

But the L.C.T. was not designed for extended voyages in the open sea, and the abortive expedition to Dakar in August 1940 proved that in an operation involving an ocean passage other means must be devised for landing armour and artillery in large numbers to support an infantry attack. On the Prime Minister's direction the Admiralty undertook to design a ship for this purpose, and in the meantime three shallow-draught tankers were converted and saw service in 1942. The landing ship tank (L.S.T.), like its more humble relative the L.C.T., was provided with a ramp door in the bow for the discharge of vehicles. It could accommodate about fifty in a capacious hold and on the upper deck, as well as a hundred and fifty soldiers.

In the autumn of 1941 the first attempt was made to measure the resources needed for an invasion of France. The assault by a well balanced force would have to be followed by a swift and continuous build-up of all arms across the beaches won, including the landing of the heavy equipment of a modern army.[1] These early calculations suggested that apart from merchant shipping about 2,250 L.C.T.s or their equivalent would be needed, whereas at that time fewer than ninety had been completed and little more than another hundred could be expected in 1942. Our continuing shortage of essential resources was thus exposed and it was obvious that some fresh source of supply must be found if we were ever to reach the minimum target necessary to mount an invasion. The embryo L.S.T. offered no immediate remedy; the prototype was not yet complete and, as for each one built in Britain we should have to forego a destroyer or three corvettes, we could not then produce large numbers ourselves.

In November 1941 the United States agreed to build small landing craft for our use and a British mission visited Washington with designs of several vessels for which no production facilities could be spared in Britain. While these designs were being examined the Japanese struck at Pearl Harbour and America was at war. This event marks amongst many other things the opening of the period of effective progress in landing ship and craft production, but many difficulties still lay ahead. The United States Navy were not yet convinced of the need for such vessels but, with the vigorous support of General Marshall, the President intervened and in January 1942 it was agreed that the United States should mass-produce landing ships and craft for both nations. In February British orders were placed in America for two hundred L.S.T.s and an equal number of a small type of L.C.T. which could be carried on the upper deck of the parent L.S.T. across the Atlantic. By now the American Navy had come to recognise the need for specially designed assault vessels and ordered large quantities for use both in the European theatre and more particularly for their own operations against Japan in the Pacific. Orders were also placed jointly for other types of craft large and small, some account of whose characteristics is given below.

The L.S.T. as it finally emerged from American yards was the product of both American and British initiative. The original Admiralty design was modified to simplify mass production and this vessel eventually

---

[1] Planning calculations assumed an initial landing by thirteen battalions with four army tank brigades, followed by perhaps six armoured divisions and other formations on an appropriate scale.

APPENDIX II

proved to be a war-winning equipment of outstanding importance. Before the end of the war more than a thousand had been built, but only 115 were made available to Britain and operated under the White Ensign.

In retrospect it is possible to see that these arrangements for the production of craft mark a turning point in the Allied conduct of the war, making possible amphibious operations which would otherwise have been impossible, but this was not apparent at the beginning of 1942.

By the beginning of 1943 the new L.S.T.s and other craft were being delivered in good quantity, but then a set-back occurred which had an adverse effect on the later planning of Overlord. At the Allied conference at Casablanca in January 1943, when strategic plans for the future were discussed, it was decided that requirements for the Battle of the Atlantic, then at a crucial stage, should hold first priority with chief emphasis laid on the building of destroyers and escort vessels. Landing craft programmes were cut back and by July of that year deliveries of L.S.T.s had fallen to less than half what they had been in February.

Meanwhile in Britain production was necessarily confined to L.C.T.s and smaller craft but even these fell far short of our requirements. Experience at Dieppe in 1942 had shown that in an opposed landing in daylight a much heavier scale of fire support for the infantry than hitherto provided was essential. To supplement the heavy guns of warships every landing should be supported by close-range weapons mounted in shallow-draught vessels and means must be found to enable the Army's field artillery to fire while still afloat. This led to an extensive development of support craft by the conversion of a number of L.C.T.s for the new rôle. Their advent was important though the resulting depletion of the number of L.C.T.s available for load carrying added to our difficulties.

The Americans were not convinced of the need for such support craft, preferring to rely only on the fire of warships; thus all the special vessels, numbering over a hundred, which took part in the invasion of France were provided from British resources, leaving aside those which were only temporarily converted to serve as field artillery carriers. Some authorities in Washington also believed that greater use should be made of improvised vessels, but in the British view there could be no substitute for specially designed landing craft in an attack on the most heavily defended coast in the world where strong tidal streams, a wide range of tides, flat beaches and the notorious fickleness of the Channel weather had to be taken into account. As time passed the chances of mounting a successful invasion seemed to recede. The Combined Commanders had estimated craft requirements on the assumption that the landing force would be two-thirds British; on that basis invasion would only be possible if American output were expanded to meet British deficiencies as well as their own requirements.

In May 1943, at a further Allied conference in Washington, an arbitrary allocation of craft for the invasion of France was made by the Combined Chiefs of Staff; it was based on what *might* be made available on May the 1st 1944, but was unrelated to any tactical plan. The rigidity of these decisions, which stemmed in part at least from the large but unspecified needs of Pacific operations, lay at the root of many of the

APPENDIX II

difficulties which later afflicted General Morgan and his staff and which are referred to in Chapters I and II.

As this volume shows, the difficulties of supply were at length resolved after causing acute anxiety and delay during months of planning. The solution was made possible by supreme exertions in Britain and by a favourable turn, during 1943, in the Battle of the Atlantic which enabled greater resources to be allotted to the production of landing craft in the United States. The overall figures for the production of craft during the war for use in all theatres are shown in the following table. It will be realised that only a proportion of these were available for Overlord.

Landing Ships and Craft

Overall war production for use in all theatres

	1939/42	1943	1944	1945 (six months)	Totals
British					
Landing Ships	—	3	—	21	24
Major Landing Craft . .	281	442	418	123	1,264
Minor Landing Craft . .	644	1,017	887	319	2,867
Totals	925	1,462	1,305	463	4,155
United States					
Landing Ships	62	344	862	305	1,573
Major Landing Craft . .	620	479	1,356	31	2,486
Minor Landing Craft . .	6,276	13,898	15,988	6,362	42,524
Totals	6,958	14,721	18,206	6,698	46,583

The above figures show that more than fifty thousand landing ships and craft were built during the war for amphibious operations, the great majority of them in the United States. This total leaves out of account the merchant ships built or converted for use as troop carriers, headquarters ships and various other duties. In addition, America built amphibious vehicles in large numbers, of which many were transferred to the British for Overlord and other operations.

Over 2,500 vessels of American production listed above were transferred to Britain under Lend-Lease arrangements and served under the British flag until the end of the war.

Characteristics of Landing Ships and Craft used in the Normandy landings

(Vessels designed or used by British forces)

LANDING SHIPS

Landing Ship Headquarters (L.S.H.)

The function of these ships was to serve as joint command posts accommodating the appropriate naval and military commanders with their

APPENDIX II

staffs and, in divisional command, a representative of the air commander. These ships were the nerve centres from which the battle was fought until the military commanders landed. Passenger liners were used for corps and divisional commands; the most successful, H.M.S. *Bulolo*, was a ship of 6,200 gross tons carrying over four hundred personnel of the three Services in addition to her normal crew. Lower formations (brigade groups) used specially equipped frigates or other warships. The best possible lay-out of operations rooms, staff accommodation, internal communications and radio services on a lavish scale were the chief features of these ships.

Landing Ship Infantry (L.S.I.)

Passenger ships and cargo liners of varying capacity were adapted to carry troops for an assault landing. A particular requirement was the ability to land all, or nearly all, the assault troops at one time. Large liners were therefore unsuitable though, in default of available alternatives, they were often used in Mediterranean operations. Assault landing craft were carried in place of lifeboats. Many of these ships were manned by their normal Merchant Navy crews and wore the Red Ensign. Others were taken over and manned by the Royal Navy and some were drawn from Allied nations.

Landing Ship Tank (L.S.T.)

These ships were able to cross the ocean, at a convoy speed of 10 knots, loaded with heavy vehicles and their crews and to land them over fairly steep beaches without assistance, with their bow grounded in about 3 feet 6 inches of water. On very flat beaches such as those in Normandy other measures had to be adopted. The ship could either dry out on the beach and discharge at low water or she could anchor in deep water and discharge into craft placed under the ramp. Rhino ferries (see page 517) and shallow-draught L.C.T.s were extensively used for discharging L.S.T.s at anchor.

Three L.S.T.s were converted to act as *Fighter Direction Tenders* in Neptune and performed useful service. They carried R.A.F. radar equipment (which could be put ashore as soon as suitable sites became available) and all necessary naval radio. They were placed in outlying positions to provide information by radio to the headquarters ships and to control fighter operations in their own area.

During later operations in France certain L.S.T.s were fitted with rails in the tank deck to accommodate railway trucks, and when ports became available in France extensive use was made of this method of transporting rolling stock.

Landing Ship Carrier

From an early stage in amphibious developments there arose a need for ships which could ferry landing craft and their crews to the scene of operations in any part of the world. Varieties built were—Landing Ship Dock (L.S.D.), Landing Ship Gantry (L.S.G.), Landing Ship Sternchute (L.S.S.). These vessels, though comparatively few in number, played an important part in transporting craft from building yards and bases to assembly and operational areas, and without them the concentration of sufficient craft in the assembly areas for Neptune could not have been accomplished in time. Five train ferries were later used to transport locomotives to France.

Major Landing Craft

This term covers all types of landing craft which proceed to an operation under their own power.

Landing Craft Infantry (Large) (L.C.I.(L))

This craft, capable of carrying up to 200 soldiers in covered accommodation for periods not exceeding 24 hours, was initiated in Britain and mass-produced in the United States. It had a sea speed of 15 knots and took part in all major operations from Sicily onwards, making the passage of the Atlantic under its own power. Over 200 took part in Neptune. It landed troops in the later phases by means of ramps carried by the craft but was too vulnerable for use by the first waves of the assault. Some were converted to serve as headquarters craft.

A smaller version, the *Landing Craft Infantry (Small)*, capable of carrying 100 soldiers, was built in Britain and used in Neptune to land some of the Commandos. A wooden vessel with petrol engines, it was very vulnerable and suffered heavy casualties.

Landing Craft Tank (L.C.T.)

The origin of this type and its chief characteristics have been described above. Although first intended for landing tanks in support of an infantry assault, its use for transporting vehicles of all kinds during the build-up phase of a large operation became, later, a factor of at least equal importance.

In October 1941, when the requirements for an invasion of France were first closely studied, it was realised that operations would have to be carried out over very flat beaches for which existing designs of L.C.T.s were not well suited owing to excessive draught. A new type was therefore evolved in which other qualities were sacrificed to obtain the shallowest possible beaching draught and a somewhat similar type was adopted later in the United States. All types were used in Normandy with success but the inevitably weak structure of the very shallow types led to heavy losses in action.

About fifty craft were specially armoured for the assault but the armour affected their seaworthiness and they were not a success.

Support Craft

A number of L.C.T.s and other landing craft were converted to provide close fire support; their armament is shown in the table on page 506.

Of these the *Landing Craft Gun* was the most successful both during and after the assault, but special mention should also be made of the craft equipped with rockets. The drenching effect of a pattern of these rockets in a relatively small area was much greater than could be achieved by any other means and helped to demoralise enemy troops in the open at the crucial moment of the assault.

APPENDIX II

Minor Landing Craft

This term covers all types of craft normally embarked in seagoing ships for a landing operation. It includes the following varieties used in Neptune:

Landing Craft Assault (L.C.A.)

An armoured craft of about 10 tons unloaded weight capable of carrying 36 soldiers with their personal weapons and landing them over a ramp in the bow. It had a low silhouette and silent engines to satisfy the requirements for night raiding. It could be carried at the davits of an ordinary passenger ship. Designed before the war, this type first saw service in the Norway operations and later in the assault phase of nearly every British landing operation.

Landing Craft Vehicle and Personnel (L.C.V.P.)

The American equivalent of the L.C.A. and used in most of their assault landings. It could carry a small vehicle, if required, in place of an equivalent load of men. It was faster than the L.C.A. but had no protection.

Landing Craft Personnel (L.C.P.)

This craft, originally designed in the United States, was the parent of the L.C.V.P. It was of similar dimensions to the L.C.A., but faster, unarmoured and without a ramp.

Landing Craft Mechanised (L.C.M.)

The first British type was a craft with an unloaded weight of 22 tons, capable of carrying an 18-ton tank or other vehicle and landing it over a ramp in the bow. It could be hoisted by the heavy derrick in most large merchant ships.

A later improved design was produced in the United States which could carry a load of 30 tons. Both were extensively used in British operations as ship to shore ferries.

Landing Barges and Rhino Ferries

About 550 barges were adapted in Britain to supplement landing craft for ship to shore ferrying and as ancillaries for naval services in the assault area; most of them were used by the Navy but 120 were equipped and manned by the Army. When the battle moved out of Normandy the landing barge fleet followed eastwards along the coast and continued to operate from bases in France and Belgium.

For unloading L.S.T.s in deep water a self-propelled raft known as a *Rhino Ferry* was built of steel pontoons assembled in sections, with a detachable portion carrying the propulsion unit. The largest of these rafts weighing 400 tons measured 175 feet by 45 feet. Rhino ferries were very difficult to handle except in the finest weather. Some were lost at sea and many were destroyed during the gale in June 1944.

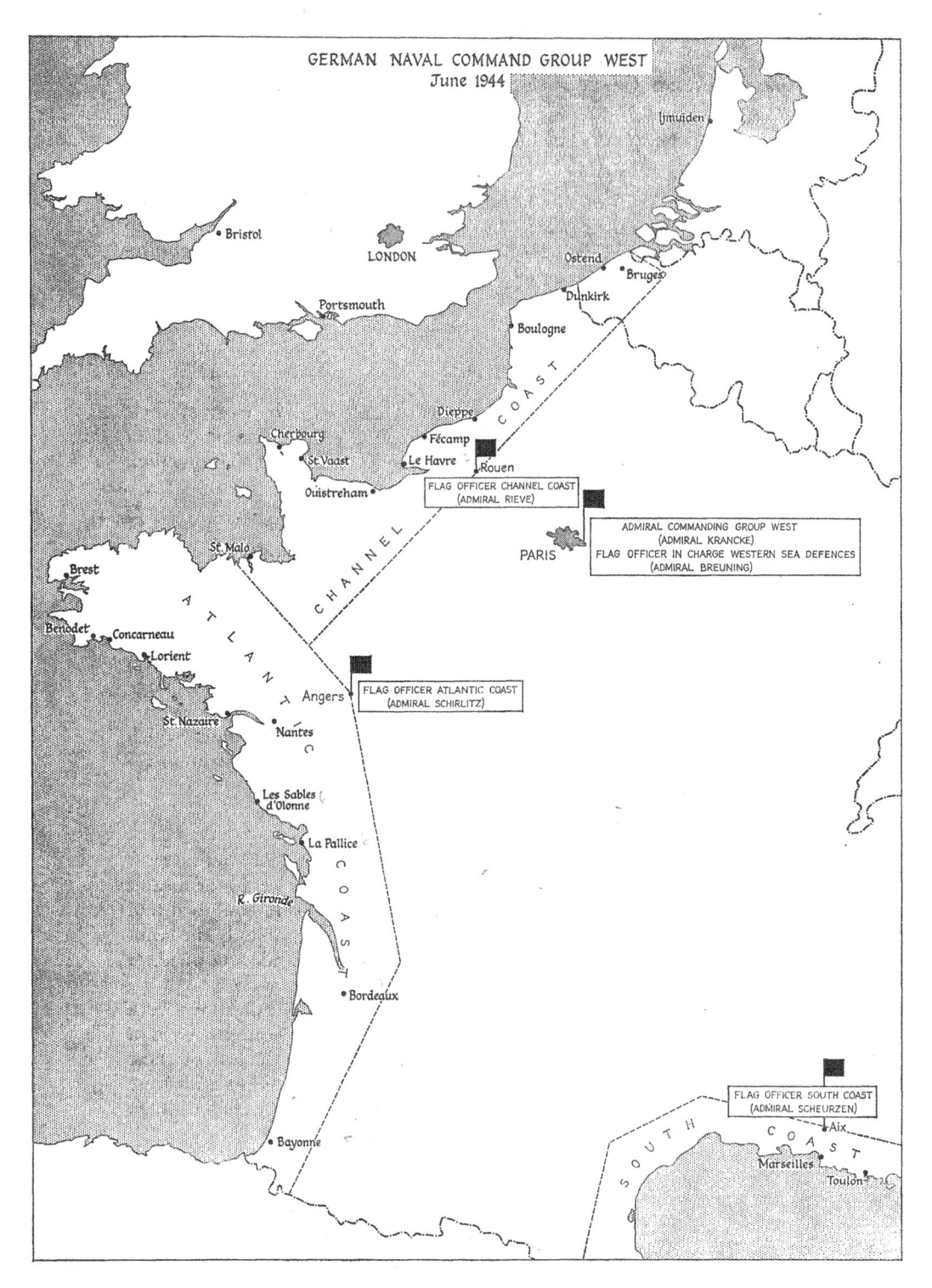

GERMAN NAVAL COMMAND GROUP WEST
June 1944

FLAG OFFICER CHANNEL COAST
(ADMIRAL RIEVE)

ADMIRAL COMMANDING GROUP WEST
(ADMIRAL KRANCKE)
FLAG OFFICER IN CHARGE WESTERN SEA DEFENCES
(ADMIRAL BREUNING)

FLAG OFFICER ATLANTIC COAST
(ADMIRAL SCHIRLITZ)

FLAG OFFICER SOUTH COAST
(ADMIRAL SCHEURZEN)

APPENDIX III

German Naval Forces in the West, June 1944

1. *German Naval Command Group West*
   The map opposite shows the command sectors in France and Belgium.

2. *Distribution of German Naval Forces in the West*

Surface vessels—Channel coast

Base	Torpedo-boats	Motor torpedo-boats	Mine-sweepers	Patrol vessels	Artillery barges
Ijmuiden	—	6	—	—	—
Bruges	—	—	12	13	—
Ostend	—	5	35	—	—
Dunkirk	—	—	11	—	—
Boulogne	—	8	11	—	16
Dieppe	—	—	12	—	—
Fécamp	—	—	—	—	15
Le Havre	5	—	50	21	—
Ouistreham to St. Vaast	—	—	12	—	11
Cherbourg	—	15	—	—	—
St. Malo	—	—	20	23	—
Total	5	34	163	57	42

Surface vessels—Atlantic coast

Base	Destroyers	Torpedo-boats	Mine-sweepers all types	Patrol vessels
Brest	—	1	36	16
Benodet	—	—	6	—
Concarneau	—	—	19	—
Lorient	—	—	—	16
St. Nazaire, Nantes	—	—	16	15
Les Sables d'Olonne	—	—	20	—
La Pallice	1	—	—	—
Gironde	4	—	49	—
Bayonne	—	—	—	12
Total	5	1	146	59

U-boats—Group Landwirt—for anti-invasion duty

Base	Normal strength	Number fitted with Schnorkel	Not immediately ready for sea	Sailed before midnight 6th June
Brest	24	8	9	15
Lorient	2	1	—	2
St. Nazaire	19	—	5	14
La Pallice	4	—	—	4
Total	49	9	14	35

Large U-boats

Large long-range U-boats for overseas operations were also based at Lorient and Bordeaux but none of them took any part in anti-invasion operations.

APPENDIX IV

The Allied Armies

Part I

FORCES ENGAGED ON THE CONTINENT

THE lists which follow show the main formations and units employed between June the 6th and August the 31st, 1944, the period covered by this volume.[1] They are not a complete order of battle, for many essential specialist and administrative units have been omitted owing to limitations of space and the great variety of their tasks.

For those who are not familiar with the structure of a British expeditionary force in the later stages of the war, it may be well to explain that an *army group* was composed of GHQ Troops and two or more armies, with Lines of Communication Troops and base installations. An *army* consisted of Army Troops and two or more corps, and a *corps* of Corps Troops and two or more divisions. Corps might be transferred from one army to another and are therefore listed in sequence without reference to the army or armies they served in during this period. Similarly, *divisions* are listed without reference to particular corps since all except one moved from one corps to another as operations required; having a fixed composition, however, they are shown with their own brigades and units.

TWENTY-FIRST ARMY GROUP

General Sir Bernard L. Montgomery
Commander-in-Chief

Major-General Sir Francis W. de Guingand
Chief of Staff

G.H.Q. AND ARMY TROOPS

79th Armoured Division

Major-General Sir Percy C. S. Hobart

30th Armoured Brigade	*1st Tank Brigade*
22nd Dragoons	11th, 42nd and 49th Battalions
1st Lothians and Border Horse	R.T.R.
2nd County of London Yeomanry (Westminster Dragoons)	
	1st Assault Brigade R.E.
141st Regiment R.A.C.	5th, 6th and 42nd Assault Regiments R.E.

79th Armoured Divisional Signals
1st Canadian Armoured Personnel Carrier Regiment

---

[1] See (i) H. F. Joslen, *Orders of Battle Second World War, 1939–45* (H.M.S.O., 1960)
(ii) C. P. Stacey, *The Victory Campaign*, Appendices F and G.

APPENDIX IV

Independent Brigades

4th Armoured Brigade
The Royal Scots Greys
3rd County of London Yeomanry (Sharpshooters) (to 28.7.44)
3rd/4th County of London Yeomanry (Sharpshooters) (from 29.7.44)
44th Battalion R.T.R.
2nd Battalion The King's Royal Rifle Corps (Motor)

6th Guards Tank Brigade
4th Tank Battalion Grenadier Guards
4th Tank Battalion Coldstream Guards
3rd Tank Battalion Scots Guards

8th Armoured Brigade
4th/7th Royal Dragoon Guards
24th Lancers (to 29.7.44)
The Nottinghamshire Yeomanry
13th/18th Royal Hussars (from 29.7.44)
12th Battalion The King's Royal Rifle Corps (Motor)

27th Armoured Brigade (to 29.7.44)
13th/18th Royal Hussars
1st East Riding Yeomanry
The Staffordshire Yeomanry

31st Tank Brigade
7th Battalion R.T.R. (to 17.8.44)
9th Battalion R.T.R. (to 31.8.44)
144th Regiment R.A.C. (23–31.8.44)

33rd Armoured Brigade
1st Northamptonshire Yeomanry
144th Regiment R.A.C. (to 22.8.44)
148th Regiment R.A.C. (to 16.8.44)
1st East Riding Yeomanry (from 16.8.44)

34th Tank Brigade
107th and 147th Regiments R.A.C.
153rd Regiment R.A.C. (to 24.8.44)

2nd Canadian Armoured Brigade
6th Armoured Regiment (1st Hussars)
10th Armoured Regiment (The Fort Garry Horse)
27th Armoured Regiment (The Sherbrooke Fusiliers Regiment)

H.Q. Anti-Aircraft Brigades
74th, 76th, 80th, 100th, 101st, 105th, 106th and 107th

Heavy Anti-Aircraft Regiments
60th, 86th, 90th, 99th, 103rd, 105th, 107th, 108th, 109th, 112th, 113th, 115th, 116th, 121st, 146th, 165th and 174th; 2nd Canadian

Light Anti-Aircraft Regiments
20th, 27th, 32nd, 54th, 71st, 73rd, 93rd, 109th, 112th, 113th, 114th, 120th, 121st, 123rd, 124th, 125th, 126th, 127th, 133rd, 139th and 149th

Searchlight Regiments
41st

APPENDIX IV

56th Infantry Brigade
(Became integral part of the 49th Division from 20.8.44)
2nd Battalion The South Wales Borderers
2nd Battalion The Gloucestershire Regiment
2nd Battalion The Essex Regiment

1st Special Service Brigade
Nos. 3, 4 and 6 Commandos
No. 45 (Royal Marine) Commando

4th Special Service Brigade
Nos. 41, 46, 47 and 48 (Royal Marine) Commandos.

Other Formations and Units

Armoured

G.H.Q. Liaison Regiment R.A.C. ('Phantom')
2nd Armoured Replacement Group
2nd Armoured Delivery Regiment
25th Canadian Armoured Delivery Regiment (The Elgin Regiment)

Artillery

H.Q. Army Groups Royal Artillery: 3rd, 4th, 5th, 8th and 9th; 2nd Canadian

Heavy Regiments: 1st, 51st, 52nd, 53rd and 59th

Medium Regiments: 7th, 9th, 10th, 11th, 13th, 15th, 53rd, 59th, 61st, 63rd, 64th, 65th, 67th, 68th, 72nd, 77th, 79th, 84th, 107th, 121st and 146th; 3rd, 4th and 7th Canadian

Field Regiments: 4th R.H.A., 6th, 25th, 86th, 147th, 150th and 191st; 19th Canadian

Engineer

H.Q. Army Groups Royal Engineers: 10th, 11th, 12th, 13th and 14th; 1st Canadian

G.H.Q. Troops Engineers: 4th, 7th, 8th, 13th, 15th, 18th, 48th and 59th

Airfield Construction Groups: 13th, 16th, 23rd, 24th and 25th

Army Troops Engineers: 2nd, 6th and 7th; 1st and 2nd Canadian

2nd and 3rd Battalions Royal Canadian Engineers

Signal

Twenty-First Army Group Headquarters Signals
Second Army Headquarters Signals
First Canadian Army Headquarters Signals
Air Formation Signals, Nos. 11, 12, 13, 16, 17 and 18
1st Special Wireless Group

Infantry

4th Battalion The Royal Northumberland Fusiliers (Machine Gun)
First Canadian Army Headquarters Defence Battalion (Royal Montreal Regiment)

Royal Marine

Armoured Support Group: 1st and 2nd Royal Marine Armoured Support Regiments

Army Air Corps

Glider Pilot Regiment: 1st and 2nd Glider Pilot Wings

APPENDIX IV

Special Air Service
1st and 2nd Special Air Service Regiments
3rd and 4th French Parachute Battalions

European Allies
1st Belgian Infantry Brigade
Royal Netherlands Brigade (Princess Irene's)

ARMIES, CORPS AND DIVISIONS

Second Army
Lieutenant-General Sir Miles C. Dempsey
General Officer Commanding-in-Chief
Brigadier M. S. Chilton
Chief of Staff

First Canadian Army
Lieutenant-General H. D. G. Crerar
General Officer Commanding-in-Chief
Brigadier C. C. Mann
Chief of Staff

I Corps
Lieutenant-General J. T. Crocker

The Inns of Court Regiment R.A.C. (Armoured Car)
62nd Anti-Tank, 102nd Light Anti-Aircraft, 9th Survey Regiments R.A.
I Corps Troops Engineers   I Corps Signals

VIII Corps
Lieutenant-General Sir Richard N. O'Connor

2nd Household Cavalry Regiment (Armoured Car)
91st Anti-Tank, 121st Light Anti-Aircraft, 10th Survey Regiments R.A.
VIII Corps Troops Engineers   VIII Corps Signals

XII Corps
Lieutenant-General N. M. Ritchie

1st The Royal Dragoons (Armoured Car)
86th Anti-Tank, 112th Light Anti-Aircraft, 7th Survey Regiments R.A.
XII Corps Troops Engineers   XII Corps Signals

XXX Corps
Lieutenant-General G. C. Bucknall (to 3.8.44)
Lieutenant-General B. G. Horrocks (from 4.8.44)

11th Hussars (Armoured Car)
73rd Anti-Tank, 27th Light Anti-Aircraft, 4th Survey Regiments R.A.
XXX Corps Troops Engineers.   XXX Corps Signals

II Canadian Corps
Lieutenant-General G. G. Simonds

18th Armoured Car Regiment (12th Manitoba Dragoons)
6th Anti-Tank, 6th Light Anti-Aircraft, 2nd Survey Regiments R.C.A.
II Canadian Corps Troops Engineers   II Canadian Corps Signals

APPENDIX IV

Guards Armoured Division
Major-General A. H. S. Adair

5th Guards Armoured Brigade
2nd (Armoured) Battalion Grenadier Guards
1st (Armoured) Battalion Coldstream Guards
2nd (Armoured) Battalion Irish Guards
1st (Motor) Battalion Grenadier Guards

32nd Guards Brigade
5th Battalion Coldstream Guards
3rd Battalion Irish Guards
1st Battalion Welsh Guards

Divisional Troops

2nd Armoured Reconnaissance Battalion Welsh Guards
Guards Armoured Divisional Engineers

55th and 153rd Field, 21st Anti-Tank and 94th Light Anti-Aircraft Regiments R.A.
Guards Armoured Divisional Signals

7th Armoured Division
Major-General G. W. E. J. Erskine (to 3.8.44)
Major-General G. L. Verney (from 4.8.44)

22nd Armoured Brigade
4th County of London Yeomanry (Sharpshooters) (to 29.7.44)
1st and 5th Battalions R.T.R.
5th Royal Inniskilling Dragoon Guards (from 29.7.44)
1st Battalion The Rifle Brigade (Motor)

131st Infantry Brigade
1/5th, 1/6th and 1/7th Battalions The Queen's Royal Regiment

Divisional Troops

8th King's Royal Irish Hussars
7th Armoured Divisional Engineers
7th Armoured Divisional Signals

3rd and 5th Regiments R.H.A.; 65th Anti-Tank and 15th Light Anti-Aircraft Regiments R.A.

11th Armoured Division
Major-General G. P. B. Roberts

29th Armoured Brigade
23rd Hussars
2nd Fife and Forfar Yeomanry
3rd Battalion R.T.R.
8th Battalion The Rifle Brigade (Motor)

159th Infantry Brigade
3rd Battalion The Monmouthshire Regiment
4th Battalion The King's Shropshire Light Infantry
1st Battalion The Herefordshire Regiment

APPENDIX IV

Divisional Troops

2nd Northamptonshire Yeomanry (to 17.8.44)
15th/19th The King's Royal Hussars (from 17.8.44)
11th Armoured Divisional Engineers

13th Regiment R.H.A.; 151st Field, 75th Anti-Tank and 58th Light Anti-Aircraft Regiments R.A.
11th Armoured Divisional Signals

3rd Division

Major-General T. G. Rennie (to 13.6.44)
Brigadier E. E. E. Cass (acting)
Major-General L. G. Whistler (from 23.6.44)

8th Brigade

1st Battalion The Suffolk Regiment
2nd Battalion The East Yorkshire Regiment
1st Battalion The South Lancashire Regiment

9th Brigade

2nd Battalion The Lincolnshire Regiment
1st Battalion The King's Own Scottish Borderers
2nd Battalion The Royal Ulster Rifles

185th Brigade

2nd Battalion The Royal Warwickshire Regiment
1st Battalion The Royal Norfolk Regiment
2nd Battalion The King's Shropshire Light Infantry

Divisional Troops

3rd Reconnaissance Regiment R.A.C.
3rd Divisional Engineers
3rd Divisional Signals

7th, 33rd and 76th Field, 20th Anti-Tank and 92nd Light Anti-Aircraft Regiments R.A.
2nd Battalion The Middlesex Regiment (Machine Gun)

6th Airborne Division

Major-General R. N. Gale

3rd Parachute Brigade

8th and 9th Battalions The Parachute Regiment
1st Canadian Parachute Battalion

5th Parachute Brigade

7th, 12th and 13th Battalions The Parachute Regiment

6th Airlanding Brigade

12th Battalion The Devonshire Regiment
2nd Battalion The Oxfordshire and Buckinghamshire Light Infantry
1st Battalion The Royal Ulster Rifles

APPENDIX IV

Divisional Troops

6th Airborne Armoured Reconnaissance Regiment R.A.C.
6th Airborne Divisional Engineers
53rd Airlanding Light Regiment R.A.
6th Airborne Divisional Signals

15th (Scottish) Division
Major-General G. H. A. MacMillan (to 2.8.44)
Major-General C. M. Barber (from 3.8.44)

44th (Lowland) Brigade
8th Battalion The Royal Scots
6th Battalion The Royal Scots Fusiliers
7th Battalion The King's Own Scottish Borderers

46th (Highland) Brigade
9th Battalion The Cameronians
2nd Battalion The Glasgow Highlanders
7th Battalion The Seaforth Highlanders

227th (Highland) Brigade
10th Battalion The Highland Light Infantry
2nd Battalion The Gordon Highlanders
2nd Battalion The Argyll and Sutherland Highlanders

Divisional Troops

15th Reconnaissance Regiment R.A.C.
15th Divisional Engineers
15th Divisional Signals

131st, 181st and 190th Field, 97th Anti-Tank and 119th Light Anti-Aircraft Regiments R.A.
1st Battalion The Middlesex Regiment (Machine Gun)

43rd (Wessex) Division
Major-General G. I. Thomas

129th Brigade
4th Battalion The Somerset Light Infantry
4th and 5th Battalions The Wiltshire Regiment

130th Brigade
7th Battalion The Hampshire Regiment
4th and 5th Battalions The Dorsetshire Regiment

214th Brigade
7th Battalion The Somerset Light Infantry
1st Battalion The Worcestershire Regiment
5th Battalion The Duke of Cornwall's Light Infantry

Divisional Troops

43rd Reconnaissance Regiment R.A.C.
43rd Divisional Engineers
43rd Divisional Signals

94th, 112th and 179th Field, 59th Anti-Tank and 110th Light Anti-Aircraft Regiments R.A.
8th Battalion The Middlesex Regiment (Machine Gun)

APPENDIX IV

49th (West Riding) Division
Major-General E. H. Barker

70th Brigade (to 20.8.44)
- 10th and 11th Battalions The Durham Light Infantry
- 1st Battalion The Tyneside Scottish

146th Brigade
- 4th Battalion The Lincolnshire Regiment
- 1/4th Battalion The King's Own Yorkshire Light Infantry
- Hallamshire Battalion The York and Lancaster Regiment

147th Brigade
- 11th Battalion The Royal Scots Fusiliers
- 6th Battalion The Duke of Wellington's Regiment (to 6.7.44)
- 7th Battalion The Duke of Wellington's Regiment
- 1st Battalion The Leicestershire Regiment (from 6.7.44)

56th Brigade (from 20.8.44)
See under GHQ Troops (page 523)

Divisional Troops
- 49th Reconnaissance Regiment R.A.C.
- 49th Divisional Engineers
- 49th Divisional Signals
- 69th, 143rd and 185th Field, 55th Anti-Tank and 89th Light Anti-Aircraft Regiments R.A.
- 2nd Princess Louise's Kensington Regiment (Machine Gun)

50th (Northumbrian) Division
Major-General D. A. H. Graham

69th Brigade
- 5th Battalion The East Yorkshire Regiment
- 6th and 7th Battalions The Green Howards

151st Brigade
- 6th, 8th and 9th Battalions The Durham Light Infantry

231st Brigade
- 2nd Battalion The Devonshire Regiment
- 1st Battalion The Hampshire Regiment
- 1st Battalion The Dorsetshire Regiment

Divisional Troops
- 61st Reconnaissance Regiment R.A.C.
- 50th Divisional Engineers
- 50th Divisional Signals
- 74th, 90th and 124th Field, 102nd Anti-Tank and 25th Light Anti-Aircraft Regiments R.A.
- 2nd Battalion The Cheshire Regiment (Machine Gun)

APPENDIX IV

51st (Highland) Division
Major-General D. C. Bullen-Smith (to 26.7.44)
Major-General T. G. Rennie (from 27.7.44)

152nd Brigade
2nd and 5th Battalions The Seaforth Highlanders
5th Battalion The Queen's Own Cameron Highlanders

153rd Brigade
5th Battalion The Black Watch
1st and 5th/7th Battalions The Gordon Highlanders

154th Brigade
1st and 7th Battalions The Black Watch
7th Battalion The Argyll and Sutherland Highlanders

Divisional Troops
2nd Derbyshire Yeomanry R.A.C.
51st Divisional Engineers
51st Divisional Signals
126th, 127th and 128th Field, 61st Anti-Tank and 40th Light Anti-Aircraft Regiments R.A.
1/7th Battalion The Middlesex Regiment (Machine Gun)

53rd (Welsh) Division
Major-General R. K. Ross

71st Brigade
1st Battalion The East Lancashire Regiment (to 3.8.44)
1st Battalion The Oxfordshire and Buckinghamshire Light Infantry
1st Battalion The Highland Light Infantry
4th Battalion The Royal Welch Fusiliers (from 5.8.44)

158th Brigade
4th and 6th Battalions The Royal Welch Fusiliers (to 3.8.44)
7th Battalion The Royal Welch Fusiliers
1st Battalion The East Lancashire Regiment (from 4.8.44)
1/5th Battalion The Welch Regiment (from 4.8.44)

160th Brigade
2nd Battalion The Monmouthshire Regiment
4th Battalion The Welch Regiment
1/5th Battalion The Welch Regiment (to 3.8.44)
6th Battalion The Royal Welch Fusiliers (from 4.8.44)

Divisional Troops
53rd Reconnaissance Regiment R.A.C.
53rd Divisional Engineers
53rd Divisional Signals
81st, 83rd and 133rd Field, 71st Anti-Tank and 116th Light Anti-Aircraft Regiments R.A.
1st Battalion The Manchester Regiment (Machine Gun)

APPENDIX IV

59th (Staffordshire) Division
Major-General L. O. Lyne

176th Brigade (to 26.8.44)
7th Battalion The Royal Norfolk Regiment
7th Battalion The South Staffordshire Regiment
6th Battalion The North Staffordshire Regiment

177th Brigade (to 26.8.44)
5th, 1/6th and 2/6th Battalions The South Staffordshire Regiment

197th Brigade (to 26.8.44)
1/7th Battalion The Royal Warwickshire Regiment
2/5th Battalion The Lancashire Fusiliers
5th Battalion The East Lancashire Regiment

Divisional Troops

59th Reconnaissance Regiment R.A.C. (to 31.8.44)
59th Divisional Engineers
59th Divisional Signals

61st, 110th and 116th Field (to 31.8.44), 68th Anti-Tank (to 26.8.44) and 68th Light Anti-Aircraft (to 22.8.44) Regiments R.A.
7th Battalion The Royal Northumberland Fusiliers (Machine Gun) (to 24.8.44)

4th Canadian Armoured Division
Major-General G. Kitching (to 21.8.44)
Major-General H. W. Foster (from 22.8.44)

4th Armoured Brigade
21st Armoured Regiment (The Governor General's Foot Guards)
22nd Armoured Regiment (The Canadian Grenadier Guards)
28th Armoured Regiment (The British Columbia Regiment)
The Lake Superior Regiment (Motor)

10th Infantry Brigade
The Lincoln and Welland Regiment
The Algonquin Regiment
The Argyll and Sutherland Highlanders of Canada (Princess Louise's)

Divisional Troops

29th Reconnaissance Regiment (The South Alberta Regiment)
4th Canadian Armoured Divisional Engineers

15th and 23rd Field, 5th Anti-Tank and 8th Light Anti-Aircraft Regiments R.C.A.
4th Canadian Armoured Divisional Signals

APPENDIX IV

2nd Canadian Division
Major-General C. Foulkes

4th Brigade

The Royal Regiment of Canada
The Royal Hamilton Light Infantry
The Essex Scottish Regiment

5th Brigade

The Black Watch (Royal Highland Regiment) of Canada
Le Régiment de Maisonneuve
The Calgary Highlanders

6th Brigade

Les Fusiliers Mont-Royal
The Queen's Own Cameron Highlanders of Canada
The South Saskatchewan Regiment

Divisional Troops

8th Reconnaissance Regiment (14th Canadian Hussars)
2nd Canadian Divisional Engineers
2nd Canadian Divisional Signals

4th, 5th and 6th Field, 2nd Anti-Tank and 3rd Light Anti-Aircraft Regiments R.C.A.
The Toronto Scottish Regiment (Machine Gun)

3rd Canadian Division
Major-General R. F. L. Keller (to 8.8.44)
Major-General D. C. Spry (from 18.8.44)

7th Brigade

The Royal Winnipeg Rifles
The Regina Rifle Regiment
1st Battalion The Canadian Scottish Regiment

8th Brigade

The Queen's Own Rifles of Canada
Le Régiment de la Chaudière
The North Shore (New Brunswick) Regiment

9th Brigade

The Highland Light Infantry of Canada
The Stormont, Dundas and Glengarry Highlanders
The North Nova Scotia Highlanders

Divisional Troops

7th Reconnaissance Regiment (17th Duke of York's Royal Canadian Hussars)
3rd Canadian Divisional Engineers
3rd Canadian Divisional Signals

12th, 13th and 14th Field, 3rd Anti-Tank and 4th Light Anti-Aircraft Regiments R.C.A.
The Cameron Highlanders of Ottawa (Machine Gun)

APPENDIX IV

1st Polish Armoured Division
Major-General S. Maczek

10th Polish Armoured Brigade
1st Polish Armoured Regiment
2nd Polish Armoured Regiment
24th Polish Armoured (Lancer) Regiment
10th Polish Motor Battalion

3rd Polish Infantry Brigade
1st Polish (Highland) Battalion
8th Polish Battalion
9th Polish Battalion

Divisional Troops
10th Polish Mounted Rifle Regiment
1st Polish Armoured Divisional Engineers
1st and 2nd Polish Field, 1st Polish Anti-Tank and 1st Polish Light Anti-Aircraft Regiments
1st Polish Armoured Divisional Signals

LINES OF COMMUNICATION AND REAR MAINTENANCE AREA

Headquarters Lines of Communication
Major-General R. F. B. Naylor

Nos. 11 and 12 Lines of Communication Areas
Nos. 4, 5 and 6 Lines of Communication Sub-Areas
Nos. 7 and 8 Base Sub-Areas
Nos. 101, 102 and 104 Beach Sub-Areas
Nos. 10 and 11 Garrisons

Engineers

Nos. 2, 3, 5 and 6 Railway Construction and Maintenance Groups
No. 3 Railway Operating Group
No. 1 Canadian Railway Operating Group
No. 1 Railway Workshop Group
Nos. 2, 6, 8, 9, 10 and 11 Port Operating Groups
Nos. 1, 2, 4 and 5 Port Construction and Repair Groups
Nos. 3 and 4 Inland Water Transport Groups
No. 2 Mechanical Equipment (Transportation) Unit

Signals

Nos. 2 and 12 Lines of Communication Headquarters Signals
No. 1 Canadian Lines of Communication Headquarters Signals

Infantry

5th and 8th Battalions The King's Regiment
7th Battalion The East Yorkshire Regiment
2nd Battalion The Hertfordshire Regiment
6th Battalion The Border Regiment
1st Buckinghamshire Battalion The Oxfordshire and Buckinghamshire Light Infantry
5th Battalion The Royal Berkshire Regiment
18th Battalion The Durham Light Infantry

APPENDIX IV

UNITED STATES TWELFTH ARMY GROUP

Lieutenant-General Omar N. Bradley
Commanding General
Major-General Leven C. Allen
Chief of Staff

First Army

Lieutenant-General Courtney H. Hodges
Commanding General
(Succeeded General Bradley from 1.8.44)
Major-General William B. Keen
Chief of Staff

Third Army

Lieutenant-General George S. Patton, Jr.
Commanding General
Major-General Hugh J. Gaffey
Chief of Staff

Corps

V. Major-General Leonard T. Gerow
VII. Major-General J. Lawton Collins
VIII. Major-General Troy H. Middleton
XII. Major-General Gilbert R. Cook (to 18.8.44)
    Major-General Manton S. Eddy (from 19.8.44)
XV. Major-General Wade H. Haislip
XIX. Major-General Charles H. Corlett
XX. Major-General Walton H. Walker

Divisions

Armoured: 2nd, 3rd, 4th, 5th, 6th and 7th; 2nd French
Infantry: 1st, 2nd, 4th, 5th, 8th, 9th, 28th, 29th, 30th, 35th, 79th, 80th, 83rd and 90th
Airborne: 82nd and 101st

Part II

NOTES ON BRITISH ARMY ORGANISATION

THOUGH the main structure of the British Army remained much as it was in 1940, four years of fighting in different parts of the world had altered the balance of its components and produced many changes in organisation and equipment. Not only did Twenty-First Army Group reap the fruits of this experience but, unlike so many less fortunate expeditions, it was able to enter on this campaign fully up to strength both in men and material.

Divisional Organisation

The composition of British and Canadian divisions is set out below. To save space the various headquarters, defence and employment platoons, field security sections and postal units have been omitted.

	ARMOURED DIVISION		INFANTRY DIVISION		AIRBORNE DIVISION	
Brigades and their Main Units	Armoured Brigade	1	Infantry Brigades	3	Parachute Brigades	2
	Armoured Regiments	3	Infantry Battalions	9	Parachute Battalions	6
	Motor Battalion	1			Airlanding Brigade	1
	Infantry Brigade	1			Airlanding Battalions	3
	Infantry Battalions	3				
Reconnaissance	Armoured Reconnaissance Regiment	1	Reconnaissance Regiment	1	Airborne Armoured Reconnaissance Regiment	1
Artillery	Field Regiments	2	Field Regiments	3	Airlanding Light Regiment	1
	Anti-Tank Regiment	1	Anti-Tank Regiment	1	Airlanding Anti-Tank Batteries	2
	Light Anti-Aircraft Regiment	1	Light Anti-Aircraft Regiment	1	Airlanding Light Anti-Aircraft Battery	1
Engineers	Field Squadrons	2	Field Companies	3	Parachute Squadrons	2
	Field Park Squadron	1	Field Park Company	1	Airborne Field Company	1
	Bridging Troop	1	Bridging Platoon	1	Airborne Field Park Company	1
Signals	Armoured Divisional Signals	1	Infantry Divisional Signals	1	Airborne Divisional Signals	1
Machine Guns	Independent Machine-Gun Company	1	Machine-Gun Battalion	1		
Special Units					Independent Parachute Company (Pathfinders)	1
Supply and Transport	Brigade Companies	2	Brigade Companies	3	Composite Companies	2
	Divisional Troops Company	1	Divisional Troops Company	1	Light Composite Company	1
	Divisional Transport Company	1				

		(Infantry Division)		(Airborne Division)	
Medical Services	.	Field Ambulance	1	Field Ambulances	3	Parachute Field Ambulances . .	2
		Light Field Ambulance . . .	1	Field Dressing Stations . . .	2	Airlanding Field Ambulance . .	1
		Field Dressing Station . . .	1	Field Hygiene Section . . .	1		
		Field Hygiene Section . . .	1				
Ordnance . .	.	Ordnance Field Park . . .	1	Ordnance Field Park . . .	1	Ordnance Field Park . . .	1
Workshops . .	.	Brigade Workshops . . .	2	Brigade Workshops . . .	3	Divisional Workshop . . .	1
		Light Anti-Aircraft Regiment Workshop	1	Light Anti-Aircraft Regiment Workshop	1	Airlanding Light Aid Detachments (with units)	7
		Light Aid Detachments (with units)	12	Light Aid Detachments (with units)	11		
Provost . .	.	Divisional Provost Company . .	1	Divisional Provost Company . .	1	Divisional Provost Company . .	1
Strength . .	.	Officers 724, Other Ranks 14,240		Officers 870, Other Ranks 17,477		Officers 702, Other Ranks 11,446	
TOTAL STRENGTH	.	14,964 All Ranks		18,347 All Ranks		12,148 All Ranks	
Vehicles . .	.	3,414 vehicles including: cruiser tanks 246; light tanks 44; tracked carriers, armoured 261; scout cars, armoured 100; trucks and lorries 2,098.		3,347 vehicles including: tracked carriers, armoured 595; armoured cars 63; trucks and lorries 1,937.		1,708 vehicles including: light tanks 16; cars 5-cwt ('Jeeps') 904; trucks and lorries 567.	
Weapons . .	.	Rifles and pistols 9,013; machine carbines 6,204; light machine guns 1,376; medium machine guns 22; mortars, 2-, 3- and 4·2-in, 160; anti-tank projectors (PIATs) 302; field guns, 25-pdr, 48; anti-tank guns, 6- and 17-pdr, 78; anti-aircraft guns, 20- and 40-mm, 141.		Rifles and pistols 12,265; machine carbines 6,525; light machine guns 1,262; medium machine guns 40; mortars, 2-, 3- and 4·2-in, 359; anti-tank projectors (PIATs) 436; field guns, 25-pdr, 72; anti-tank guns, 6- and 17-pdr, 110; anti-aircraft guns, 20- and 40-mm, 125.		Rifles and pistols 10,113; machine carbines 6,504; light machine guns 966; medium machine guns 46; mortars, 2-, 3- and 4·2-in, 535; anti-tank projectors (PIATs) 392; pack howitzers, 75-mm, 24; anti-tank guns, 6- and 17-pdr, 68; anti-aircraft guns, 20-mm, 23.	

Note: (i) Although fully mechanised the infantry division required three transport companies (approximately 270 lorries) from corps if it was to move all its infantry battalions in one lift.

(ii) The airborne division had 4,502 cycles and motor cycles.

APPENDIX IV

Analysis of British Army's Composition

As was stated on page 482, of the British[1] personnel in Twenty-First Army Group in August 1944 some 56 per cent were what are usually termed 'fighting troops' and 44 per cent were 'services'. The detailed percentages for the 660,000 personnel concerned were as follows:

Fighting Troops

    Royal Artillery (including anti-aircraft regiments of the Royal Marines) 18; Infantry (rifle, machine-gun, motor, parachute and airlanding battalions; commandos and glider pilot wings) 14; Royal Engineers 13; Royal Armoured Corps 6 and Royal Corps of Signals 5 ... total 56 per cent.

Services

    Royal Army Service Corps 15; Pioneer Corps 10; Royal Electrical and Mechanical Engineers 5; Royal Army Medical Corps, Army Dental Corps and Queen Alexandra's Imperial Military Nursing Service 4; Royal Army Chaplains' Department, Royal Army Ordnance Corps, Royal Army Pay Corps, Royal Army Veterinary Corps, Army Educational Corps, Intelligence Corps, Army Physical Training Corps, Army Catering Corps, Auxiliary Territorial Service, Corps of Military Police, Military Provost Staff Corps and a number of 'unspecified', 10 ... total 44 per cent.

The Divisional Slice

Before D-day it was estimated that for every division ashore (averaging about 16,000 men) there would ultimately be an additional 25,000 men present in the theatre in Corps, Army, GHQ and Lines of Communication Troops. The combined figure was known as the 'divisional slice' or 'gross division'. For Twenty-First Army Group it was calculated that the 'slice' would amount to approximately 41,000 men and 8,000 vehicles and that it would be accompanied to the Continent by 4,000 Royal Air Force personnel.

Organisation of Divisions, Brigades and Units including GHQ, Army and Corps Troops

79TH ARMOURED DIVISION

Since early 1943 all specialised armour in the United Kingdom had been concentrated in the 79th Armoured Division so that one commander would be responsible for developing the equipment, advising on its use and training the units. The same principle obtained during the campaign. While the division remained under direct command of Twenty-First Army Group, portions of it were placed in support of the armies as operations required.

As far as possible each type of equipment had its own brigade, whose headquarters acted as 'parent' to the units, but in battle brigade and unit

---

[1] If Canadian personnel were included in the analysis the overall percentages for the army group would show a small rise in the proportion of 'fighting troops', as the Canadians were unable to provide their full share of 'services', the deficiency being made good from British resources.

APPENDIX IV 537

commanders usually administered a mixed team and, at the same time, acted as advisers to the formation commanders with whom they were associated.

The composition of the division varied during the course of the campaign but for the assault and the phase covered by this volume the emphasis lay on amphibious, mine-clearing and flame-throwing tanks and on engineer assault vehicles. These are described below, page 543.

During August the Canadian army improvised some armoured personnel carriers from their own resources. One brigade of searchlight tanks was also landed in Normandy but had not yet been in action.

Brigades and Army Groups Royal Artillery

Independent Armoured and Tank Brigades

Contained three regiments or battalions of tanks, with a proportion of Signals and Services; strength approximately 3,400 all ranks. The 1,200 vehicles included some 190 medium or infantry tanks and 33 light tanks. In the five armoured brigades the basic tank was the Sherman; in the three tank brigades the Churchill. All light tanks were Stuarts (or 'Honeys'). Two armoured brigades also included a motor battalion.

These independent brigades were primarily intended and trained for close co-operation with the infantry divisions, but Twenty-First Army Group policy, as prescribed by the C-in-C, required that they should be equally capable of working with the armoured divisions.

Anti-Aircraft Brigades

Each contained two or more heavy and three or more light anti-aircraft regiments, together with at least one battery of searchlights.

Army Groups Royal Artillery

Generally contained one heavy and three medium regiments. Some groups also had one or more field regiments. Average strength was about 4,400 all ranks. AGRAs were provided on the scale of one per corps plus one spare.

As the campaign developed it became common practice to reinforce a group with regiments from the anti-aircraft brigades for use against ground targets.

Units

ARMOURED

Armoured and Armoured Reconnaissance Regiments and Tank Battalions

Except in some minor details all were organised alike and capable of performing the same rôle.

Headquarters: four cruiser or infantry tanks.

Headquarter squadron: four troops; anti-aircraft (four tanks fitted with 20-mm guns), reconnaissance (11 light tanks), intercommunication (eight scout cars) and administrative.

Three tank squadrons: each a headquarters of four, and five troops of three tanks, total 19. This was the organisation with standard tanks, but as units began to receive the scarce 17-pdr Sherman shortly before or after D-day, their squadrons were re-organised into four troops of four tanks, one of which had the new 17-pdr.

Total tanks: cruiser (Shermans and Cromwells) or infantry (Churchills) 61; light (Stuarts) 11.

Strength: 36 Officers and 630 Other Ranks.

Armoured Car Regiments

Headquarters: three armoured cars.

Headquarter squadron: three troops; anti-aircraft (five armoured cars fitted with 20-mm guns), intercommunication (13 scout cars) and administrative.

Four armoured car squadrons: each a headquarters with four armoured cars, five troops with two armoured cars and two scout cars, a heavy troop with two armoured cars and a support troop of riflemen in armoured half-track carriers.

Total armoured cars: Daimlers (the basic troop car), A.E.C. (in the heavy troops) and U.S. Staghounds (headquarters car) 67. Total scout cars (each with a wireless set): Daimlers and Humbers 67.

Strength: 55 Officers and 680 Other Ranks.

Reconnaissance Regiments (in the infantry division only)

Headquarters: one armoured car.

Headquarter squadron: anti-tank battery (eight 6-pdr guns); mortar troop (six 3-in mortars); signals and administrative troops.

Three reconnaissance squadrons: each a headquarters, three scout troops with armoured cars, light reconnaissance cars and Bren carriers, and one assault troop of riflemen in armoured half-track carriers.

Total armoured fighting vehicles: armoured cars (Humbers) 28; light reconnaissance cars (Humbers) 24; Bren carriers 63.

Strength: 41 Officers and 755 Other Ranks.

ARTILLERY (headquarters omitted)

Field Regiments

Three batteries: each two troops of four 25-pdr guns, total 24 guns per regiment; tractor-towed or self-propelled. Ammunition carried in 1st Line: HE 144, smoke 16, armour-piercing 12 rounds per gun.

Medium Regiments

Two batteries: each two troops of four 5·5-in guns, total 16 guns per regiment; tractor-towed. Ammunition carried in 1st Line: HE 100 rounds per gun.

Heavy Regiments

Two batteries of four 7·2-in howitzers and two batteries of four U.S. 155-mm guns, total 16 howitzers and guns per regiment.

Light Anti-Aircraft Regiments

Three batteries: each three troops of six 40-mm guns, total 54 guns per regiment.

Heavy Anti-Aircraft Regiments

Three batteries: each two troops of four 3·7-in guns, total 24 guns per regiment.

APPENDIX IV

Anti-Tank Regiments
Four batteries: each one troop of 6-pdr and two troops of 17-pdr guns in the infantry division's regiment; three troops of 17-pdrs in all other cases. Total: 48 guns per regiment.

Survey Regiments
Two batteries: each one observation, one sound-ranging and one survey troop.

Air Observation Post Squadrons
Although the Royal Air Force owned and maintained the aircraft, the flying personnel were all Royal Artillery. Squadrons were provided on the scale of one per corps, plus one spare per army. They contained three flights, each of four aircraft.

INFANTRY (including the Army Air Corps)

Rifle Battalions
Support company: four platoons; mortar (six 3-in mortars), carrier (13 Bren carriers), anti-tank (six 6-pdr guns) and assault pioneer.
Four rifle companies: each three platoons of three sections. The section contained 10 men with one light machine gun; the platoon one officer and 36 men with one 2-in mortar, and the company five officers and 122 men with three PIATs at company headquarters.
Battalion transport included 38 carriers of all kinds and 55 cars, trucks and lorries.
Strength: 35 Officers and 786 Other Ranks.

Machine-Gun Battalions
Heavy mortar company: four platoons; total 16 4·2-in mortars.
Three machine-gun companies: each three platoons with total of 12 medium machine guns (Vickers, ·303-in).
Strength: 35 Officers and 662 Other Ranks.

Motor Battalions
Support company: five platoons; three anti-tank (total 12 6-pdr guns) and two medium machine-gun (total eight guns).
Three motor companies: each three platoons of riflemen in 15-cwt trucks and one platoon in Bren carriers.
Strength: 37 Officers and 782 Other Ranks.

Commandos (Royal Marines and Army)
Not organised in companies but in troops of three officers and 60 men.
Lightly armed and equipped, with a minimum of wheeled transport.
Strength: 24 Officers and 440 Other Ranks.

Airlanding Battalions (glider-borne)
Support company: six platoons which included one with four 3-in mortars.
Anti-Aircraft/Anti-Tank company: four platoons; two anti-aircraft (total 12 20-mm guns) and two anti-tank (total eight 6-pdr guns).
Four rifle companies: each four platoons.
Strength: 47 Officers and 817 Other Ranks.

Parachute Battalions (Army Air Corps)
Headquarter company: five platoons which included two mortar (each four 3-in mortars) and one anti-tank (ten PIATs).
Three rifle companies: each three platoons.
Strength: 29 Officers and 584 Other Ranks.

Glider Pilot Wings (Army Air Corps)
Contained a variable number of squadrons, and squadrons a variable number of flights. A flight had 20 gliders, each with two pilots who were trained to fight alongside their passengers on reaching their destination. Gliders were Royal Air Force equipment.

ENGINEER UNITS

Field companies (or squadrons) on the establishment of divisions had three identical platoons (or troops) and a strength of seven officers and some 250 other ranks.

The field park company (or squadron) contained one workshop and one stores platoon (or troop), its task being to act as a base for the field companies and hold specialist and bulky equipment such as dozers. The divisional bridging platoon, now separated from the field park company, carried the materials for 80 feet of Bailey bridging capable of taking loads of 40 tons.

SIGNAL UNITS

Divisional Signals contained three or four companies (or squadrons) depending on the type of division, the total strength being in the neighbourhood of 28 officers and 700 other ranks. One company (or squadron) provided the communications for divisional headquarters, a second supplied sections to the divisional artillery units and a third to the headquarters of infantry brigades, the reconnaissance regiment, the machine gunners and the engineers. Additionally, in the armoured division, a fourth squadron performed the same function for the armoured brigade and its units. In the case of the airborne division the duties included the maintenance of communication with the home base.

Part III

NOTES ON AMERICAN ARMY ORGANISATION

As with Twenty-First Army Group the composition of corps and armies varied with operational requirements. The most notable difference between the American organisation and our own lay in the divisions.

The infantry division contained three infantry regiments, each of three battalions, but the regiment also included one company of six 105-mm howitzers and one company of 57-mm anti-tank guns. The infantry battalion had three rifle companies (190 strong), and one 'heavy weapons company' with mortars and machine guns. The smallest infantry subunit was the 'squad' of twelve men with one light automatic. Divisional field artillery consisted of three battalions of 105-mm howitzers (total 36 guns) and one battalion of twelve 155-mm howitzers.

Except in two cases, the armoured division contained three tank and three infantry battalions and normally operated as two mixed groups,

APPENDIX IV

termed 'Combat Commands' ('A' and 'B'). Tanks amounted to 186 mediums (Shermans) and 83 lights (Stuarts). There were three battalions of self-propelled 105-mm howitzers, totalling 36 guns.

Airborne divisions were authorised parachute and glider infantry regiments but, in practice, their numbers varied from division to division at this time.

In all cases the authorised strengths were lower than in the corresponding British formations, being in the neighbourhood of 14,000 for infantry, 11,000 for armoured and under 9,000 for airborne divisions, due mainly to a smaller establishment of administrative units. Each division, however, was backed by something like 30,000 more fighting troops and services, making the American 'divisional slice' in this campaign in the neighbourhood of 42,000 men which was approximately the same as the British.

Part IV

BRITISH ARMY WEAPONS, VEHICLES AND EQUIPMENT[1]

SMALL ARMS

Rifle: the 'No. 4'; ·303-in with a tapered nine-inch bayonet. Aperture backsight of new pattern incorporating a battle-sight for use up to 400 yards.

Pistol: the 'Revolver No. 2'; ·38-in, six-chambered.

Machine Carbines: the 'Sten'; 9-mm, $6\frac{1}{2}$ lbs, magazine 32 rounds. The 'Thompson'; ·45-in, 10 lbs, magazine 20 rounds.

Grenades: various; weights $1\frac{1}{4}$ to 4 lbs. Percussion; HE or smoke, thrown by hand or discharged from rifle. Anti-tank; 'sticky' for fixing to armoured vehicles or mine type for breaking tracks.

Light Machine Gun: the 'Bren'; ·303-in, air-cooled. Effective range 1,000 yards. 30-round magazine. Weight with bipod 23 lbs. Fired either from the shoulder or the bipod; single shot or in short bursts.

Medium Machine Gun: the 'Vickers'; ·303-in, water cooled, belt fed. Weights; gun 40 lbs, tripod 50 lbs. Normal rate of fire, one belt (250 rounds) in two minutes; rapid, one belt in one minute.

Mortars: 2-in; weight $23\frac{1}{2}$ lbs, bomb $2\frac{1}{2}$ lbs, range 100–500 yards. 3-in; weight with mounting 148 lbs, bomb 10 lbs, range 500–1,500 yards (charge I) or 950–2,800 yards (charge II). 4·2-in; bomb 20 lbs, range 1,050–2,800 yards (charge I) or 1,500–4,100 yards (charge II).

Projector Infantry Anti-Tank: the 'PIAT'; weight $34\frac{1}{2}$ lbs, bomb $2\frac{1}{2}$ lbs. Maximum effective range against tanks 115 yards, against houses 350 yards.

20-mm Anti-Aircraft/Anti-Tank Equipments: the 'Polsten/Oerlikon'; rate of fire 450–480. The 'Hispano'; 650 rounds per minute. Round $8\frac{1}{2}$ ozs, magazine 60 rounds. Effective ceiling 3,000 feet, horizontal range 1,000 yards.

---

[1] See Part V for Tanks and Anti-Tank Guns.

ARTILLERY

	Weight of shell	Maximum range	Normal rate of fire	Remarks
Field				
75-mm pack howitzer (US)[1]	14 lbs	9,500 yds	3 rds per min	Airborne divisions only.
25-pdr gun/howitzer	25 lbs	13,400 yds	3 rds per min	Standard field gun.
25-pdr SP ('Sexton')	25 lbs	13,400 yds	3 rds per min	One regiment per armoured division.
105-mm SP ('Priest') (US)[1]	33 lbs	12,150 yds	3 rds per min	In two assault divisions for initial landing.
Medium				
4·5-in gun	55 lbs	20,500 yds	1 rd per min	Two batteries only in 21 Army Group.
5·5-in gun	80 lbs	18,100 yds	1 rd per min	Standard medium gun.
	100 lbs	16,200 yds	1 rd per min	
Heavy				
155-mm gun (US)[1]	95 lbs	Mk. I, 16,500 yds; Mk. II, 19,600 yds	1 rd in two mins	In equal numbers in each regiment.
7·2-in howitzer	200 lbs	25,400 yds	1 rd in two mins	
			1 rd in two mins	
Anti-Aircraft				
40-mm Bofors	2 lbs	Maximum ceiling, 23,000 ft.	60 rds per min, single shot; 120, automatic	Standard light gun. Maximum horizontal range, 10,800 yds.
3·7-in	28 lbs	Maximum ceiling, 48,000 ft.	10–25 rds per min (with mechanical fuse-setter)	Standard heavy gun. Maximum horizontal range, 15,800–18,000 yds.

[1] American equipment made available to the British Army.

APPENDIX IV

SPECIALISED ARMOUR OF THE 79TH ARMOURED DIVISION

Amphibious, DD (Duplex Drive) Tank. An ordinary, waterproofed Sherman tank with a tall, collapsible canvas screen around the top of its hull to make it float, and provided with propellers to drive and steer it in the water.

Mine-clearing, Flail (or 'Crab') Tank. A Sherman tank, retaining its main armament and fitted with a rotary chain flail actuated by the tank engine. The rotor carried a wire-cutting device.

Flame-thrower (or 'Crocodile') Tank. A Churchill tank with a flame gun in place of the bow machine gun. The tank towed a two-wheeled armoured trailer, weighing nine tons, which contained the flame fuel and gas bottles to give the necessary pressure. Approximately 100 one-second shots were possible before replenishment. Maximum range 100 yards.

AVRE (Assault Vehicle Royal Engineers) Tank. A Churchill tank in which the gun had been replaced by a mortar (or 'petard') for use against concrete. The 40-lb HE projectile could be thrown 80 yards with accuracy. Among a variety of other rôles the AVRE was used for carrying either a short bridge, a fascine for craters and ditches, or a carpet for laying over mud and boggy ground.

CARRIERS TRACKED

These were of two main types: the Universal (or 'Bren') and the Loyd, both weighing $4-4\frac{1}{2}$ tons.

The Universal, with 10-mm of armour, a maximum speed of 30 miles an hour and an open top, was primarily used as a mobile fire unit and carried three men with one Bren light machine gun. It was also in general use as an armoured observation post. Other versions carried the 3-in mortar, the medium machine gun or a flame-thrower.

The Loyd, with less speed, lighter armour and a canvas canopy was used either for towing the 6-pdr anti-tank gun or for carrying the 4·2-in mortar.

ARMOURED CARS (Wheeled)

The types in most general use were the Daimler and the Humber Mark IV. Each weighed about seven tons, had a crew of three, a maximum speed of 45–50 miles an hour and 14–16-mm of armour. The Daimler carried a 2-pdr gun and the Humber a 37-mm, each supplemented by a co-axial 7·92-mm Besa machine gun.

The AEC ($12\frac{3}{4}$ tons) had a 75-mm gun and the Staghound ($13\frac{1}{2}$ tons) a 37-mm.

SCOUT CARS

These were small, two-seater Daimlers and Humbers, capable of 55–60 miles an hour. They had 14–30-mm of armour and carried a Bren light machine gun.

The larger, more lightly armoured American 'White Scout Car' and its half-tracked version, the M.14, carried the rifle sections of reconnaissance and armoured car regiments. They were also frequently used as command vehicles.

UNARMOURED VEHICLES

In August 1944 there were some 55 different types of unarmoured vehicles within the infantry division and several hundreds in the Army as a whole. When it is realised that this multiplicity of types was composed essentially of ordinary load-carrying chassis, with special bodies of one kind or another, the situation may well be regarded as surprising. But there it was and it is clearly impracticable to attempt any detailed description here. Suffice to say that the load-carrying vehicles ranged from the American 5-cwt 'Jeep', through the 15-cwt truck, the 3-, 6- and 10-ton lorries to the 40-ton transporter with its 24 wheels; and many of them also towed trailers.

An outstanding vehicle was the American amphibious, six-wheeled DUKW, or 'duck', a number of which were made available to the British under Lend-Lease. It carried a load of $2\frac{1}{2}$ tons and was mainly used for ferrying stores from ships in the anchorage to dumps in the beachhead. Some were employed in the Seine crossings.

ENGINEER AND BRIDGING EQUIPMENT

Having done their share of breaching the coastal defences the Engineers and their associated Pioneers had to contend with a tightly congested bridgehead where airfields were non-existent, roads had been completely neglected for four years and all the bridges were down. These were tasks calling for a wealth of resources and at this stage of the war they were available. To the meagre mechanical aids of 1939—compressors and water pumps—had been added the earth-moving and road-making equipment used by civil engineers in America, Britain and the Dominions. Angledozers, bulldozers, excavators, ploughs, scrapers, graders, rollers, stone crushers and other mechanical devices were now employed on a large scale.

Apart from the three bridge-laying tanks included in each armoured brigade and the special devices in the 79th Armoured Division, the two types of British bridging equipment in everyday use were the F.B.E. (Folding Boat Equipment) which was limited to nine-ton loads, and the Bailey which could be built to take loads of up to 70 tons. The light, quickly-built F.B.E. bridge was usually the first to be constructed after the assault crossing of a river and could take most of the vehicles on charge of the infantry division. As soon as practicable this was supplemented by a 40-ton Bailey so that the main routes in a divisional area could be developed for 40-ton loads. This would cover all tanks and vehicles except loaded transporters which required 70-ton routes and, normally, one of these was developed in each army area. The Bailey equipment was very versatile. Its maximum standard single-span capacity was 190 feet for 40-ton loads and 150 feet for 70-ton. With the addition of pontoons and a few extra parts, robust floating bridges, capable of operating without interruption throughout wide fluctuations in the water level, could be constructed across the broadest river. From D-day to the break-out, 10,000 feet of equipment bridges were built in Twenty-First Army Group's area. The greatest obstacle was the river Orne, over which three Bailey pontoon bridges were built across tidal gaps of 250 to 300 feet, and

APPENDIX IV

14 fixed bridges over the river as a whole. Between the Orne and the Seine, where the main problem was enemy demolitions rather than major rivers, some 3,000 feet were built. Across the Seine three F.B.E. and eight Bailey pontoon bridges were constructed over gaps ranging between 450 and 750 feet, four of them being in tidal water. Each Bailey was built by two or three field companies in time varying between 14 and 34 hours.

SIGNAL EQUIPMENT

The course of the war had clearly shown that the speed with which a wireless set could get into action made it the primary means of communication for mobile operations, and especially so where troops on the ground must combine with ships at sea and aircraft in the sky. For long-distance links in more static circumstances wireless also served as an invaluable standby until lines, with their greater traffic capacity, could be built or remade.

In the forward areas the main sets were the Nos. 18 and 38, generally carried on the man, and the Nos. 19 and 22 which were fitted into vehicles. The first two were infantry sets. The No. 18, weighing 30 lbs complete with a 'battle battery', had a maximum range under good conditions of about five miles, and was the normal means of communication between the company and battalion headquarters. The No. 38, a few pounds lighter, had a range of up to two miles and was the set used within the company, and between the company and its close support tanks who also carried one. The No. 19 had been developed for use by armour. It embodied three sets in one; the 'A' for ranges up to about 10 miles on speech and 15 on key, the 'B' for speech between the tanks of a troop and the 'C' to enable the tank commander to speak to his crew. The No. 22 was basically the same type as the No. 19 but had a longer range of 15 miles on speech and up to perhaps 30 on key. It was chiefly to be found at brigade and divisional headquarters and among artillery units.

Part V

TANKS AND ANTI-TANK GUNS

British Development

Between the two wars the British had allowed the design and supply of tanks—their own invention—to dwindle almost to nothing. When events compelled them to rearm, progress was handicapped by conflicting ideas about the rôle that tanks would play in battle. While the relative priorities fluctuated disconcertingly, policy, such as it was, called for two types of tank; one, with heavy protective armour, to give close support to the infantry; the other, possessing high mobility, to exploit success. But in neither case did gun power appear to have been of major importance. 1940 saw almost our whole tank strength lost in France and from then onwards the fear of a shortage was so dominant that it was virtually a case of any tank being better than no tank at all. Output increased considerably and soon caught up with the Germans. In the three and a half years between September 1939 and March 1943 the United Kingdom produced

3,000 more tanks than did Germany. Yet the North Africa battles made it painfully obvious that, judging by results, the German tanks were superior. Our latest infantry tank showed promise but it still had many teething troubles, and the new series of cruisers was not yet ready. When the American Sherman became available in quantity at the end of 1942 we were very glad to accept it.

During the first three months of the Normandy campaign two-thirds of the basic tanks in the armoured divisions and independent brigades of Twenty-First Army Group were Shermans, the remaining third being our own Cromwells (cruisers) and Churchills (infantry). All the light reconnaissance tanks were American Stuarts. In the specialist 79th Armoured Division Churchills and Shermans were about equal, and a number of obsolete British types gave good service as bridge-layers and anti-tank gun tractors.

By 1944 our anti-tank guns were the 6-pdr and 17-pdr, the latter being a really hard-hitting weapon which had seen action in the Middle East since early 1943. The ammunition had also been improved from 'armour-piercing' (AP) to 'armour-piercing capped' (APC) and then to 'armour-piercing capped ballistic capped' (APCBC), the last type having a second cap which gave better penetration beyond 500 yards. Further research had led to the development of 'discarding sabot' (DS) ammunition. In this a tungsten core was enclosed in a light metal casing or 'sabot' which was discarded as the projectile left the gun and resulted in greatly increased velocity and penetration. A small quantity of this ammunition for the 6-pdr became available for D-day but it was late in August before there was any for the 17-pdr. In Normandy the infantry and reconnaissance units were equipped with the 6-pdr, and the anti-tank regiments with both 6- and 17-pdrs roughly in the proportion of 1 to 2. All these guns were towed except for some American 'tank destroyers' (M 10s with 3-in guns) obtained for the initial landings. A proportion of the latter were converted to take 17-pdrs, but no British self-propelled anti-tank gun was available until the 17-pdr on a Valentine tank chassis arrived in October 1944.

The Sherman tank had been built with a 75-mm gun firing both high-explosive and armour-piercing ammunition, and the British intended to have the same gun eventually in their Cromwells and Churchills. But its armour-piercing power was only about half that of the 17-pdr and it was soon recognised that the 17-pdr must be got into a tank. The Cromwell was selected and redesigned under the name of 'Challenger', but production troubles developed and in the summer of 1943 it was obvious that this tank could not be ready in time for Normandy. Experiments to mount the gun in the Sherman proved successful and a 'rush' conversion programme by the Royal Ordnance Factories provided every British Sherman unit with twelve 17-pdr tanks by D-day or shortly afterwards. At the same time the Americans, also searching for better penetration, had fitted a few Shermans with a new 76-mm gun, but this proved to be unsatisfactory with high-explosive shell. They also had a 90-mm 'tank destroyer' almost ready in mid-1944 and tests showed this to be not far short of the 17-pdr in performance.

APPENDIX IV

German Development

The Germans had lost little time before acting on their experiences in Russia during 1941 and 1942. They stopped production of their two lightest tank models which had served them well in Poland and France and, while further improving the heavier types, particularly the Mark IV, concentrated on producing two entirely new and more powerful vehicles—the Mark V (Panther) and Mark VI (Tiger). At D-day they had a harder-hitting gun—the 88-mm KwK 43 in the Tiger—than anything in Allied hands, while their 75-mm KwK 42 in the Panther was not far behind our 17-pdr. Both tanks were also more heavily armoured than ours except for the Mark VII Churchill; but of this model Twenty-First Army Group had barely a hundred. In armour and armament, at any rate, the Germans were maintaining their lead and, moreover, reached their peak of tank production in June 1944. They had also used their newest tank chassis to provide two very formidable self-propelled anti-tank weapons—the Jagdpanther and Jagdtiger. These were manufactured in increasing numbers right to the end of 1944, the Jagdtiger being the most powerful armoured fighting vehicle of the Second World War.

At pages 548–9 are tables giving certain data about the tanks and anti-tank guns used by each side in the first three months of the campaign. Such tables, however, cannot give the complete picture. Reliability, manœuvrability, numbers and tactics are also factors of great importance. But, above all, the weapon must hold the confidence of those who have to use it in battle.

Test by Battle

After the first ten days' fighting doubts began to be raised about the adequacy of our tanks, particularly in the minds of some British tank commanders recently in the Middle East, the chief concern being the ineffectiveness of the 75-mm gun against the German Panther and Tiger. Before long the Americans (including General Eisenhower) were similarly worried and also somewhat dubious about their new 76-mm.

This led General Montgomery to send a 'Memorandum on British Armour' to the War Office in early July. He began by expressing the view that '. . . we have had no difficulty in dealing with German armour once we had grasped the problem. In this connection British armour has played a notable part. I cannot emphasise too strongly', he said, 'that victory in battle depends, not on tank action alone, but on the intimate co-operation of all arms; the tank by itself can achieve little.' He then went on to compare Allied and German tanks in some detail, and on the subject of firepower ('it is the firepower that chiefly matters') stated that the 17-pdr gun compared favourably with any of the German weapons and '. . . will penetrate *any known German tank*, frontally or anywhere else'. The 6-pdr with 'sabot' ammunition was very good and would pierce the Panther anywhere except on the sloping front plate. He did not, however, mention any distances. In armour the Tiger was superior to anything we had, the Panther was superior in front though not on the sides, but the Mark IV was in no way superior. In mechanical efficiency the Sherman was the best tank in the field and the Cromwell also promised well,

Tanks—armour, armament, speed and weight, June to August 1944

Type	Maximum armour		Main gun	Maximum speed	Weight	Remarks
	Front	Side				
British and American						
Stuart	44 mm	25 mm	37 mm	40 mph	12½–15 tons	Reconnaissance. Several versions.
Sherman	76 mm	51 mm	75 mm	24 mph	30–32 tons	Some with 17-pdr in British units and some with 76-mm in American formations.
Churchill, Marks I to VI	90 mm	76 mm	75 mm	15 mph	37 tons	Some with 6-pdr gun.
Churchill, Mark VII	150 mm	95 mm	75 mm	12 mph	41 tons	In one (flame-thrower) regiment of 79th Armoured Division; a few in 34th Tank Brigade.
Cromwell	75 mm	63 mm	75 mm	40 mph	27 tons	
German						
Mark IV	80 mm	30 mm	75 mm KwK 40	25 mph	25 tons	Half the tanks in the armoured division were of this type in most cases.
Mark V (Panther)	100 mm	45 mm	75 mm KwK 42	34 mph	45 tons	Half the tanks in the armoured division were of this type in most cases. Jagdpanther on this chassis with maximum front armour 80 mm.
Mark VI, E (Tiger)	100 mm	80 mm	88 mm KwK 36	23 mph	54 tons	
Mark VI, B (Tiger)	180 mm	80 mm	88 mm KwK 43	25 mph	68 tons	Jagdtiger on this chassis with maximum front armour 250 mm.

All British and American tanks had a secondary armament of two light machine guns, one of which was co-axial in the turret. German tanks had up to three machine guns according to type.

[25 mm = ·985 of an inch; 100 mm = 3·94 inches]

Tank and anti-tank guns—performance against armour, June to August 1944

Gun	Projectile	Penetration against homogeneous armour plate at 30° angle of attack:				Remarks
		At 100 yards	At 500 yards	At 1,000 yards	At 2,000 yards	
British and American						
75-mm, Mark V	APCBC (US and Brit)	74 mm	68 mm	60 mm	47 mm	In Sherman, Churchill and Cromwell tanks. Muzzle velocity 2,050 feet per second.
57-mm	APC (US)	—	81 mm	64 mm	50 mm	Towed American anti-tank gun.
6-pdr, Mark V	APCBC (Brit)	93 mm	87 mm	80 mm	67 mm	Towed British anti-tank gun and in some Churchill tanks.
3-in	APC (US)	109 mm	99 mm	89 mm	73 mm	In American self-propelled tank destroyer (M 10).
76-mm	APC (US)	109 mm	99 mm	89 mm	73 mm	In American self-propelled tank destroyer (M 18) and in some of their Sherman tanks. Muzzle velocity 2,600 feet per second.
90-mm	APC (US)	123 mm	113 mm	104 mm	87 mm	Later in American self-propelled tank destroyer (M 36) and towed anti-tank gun.
6-pdr, Mark V	DS ('Sabot') (Brit)	143 mm	131 mm	117 mm	90 mm	Towed British anti-tank gun. Later in some Churchill tanks. Muzzle velocity 3,800 feet per second.
17-pdr, Mark II	APCBC (Brit)	149 mm	140 mm	130 mm	111 mm	Towed British anti-tank gun and in some British Shermans.
17-pdr, Mark II	DS ('Sabot') (Brit)	221 mm	208 mm	192 mm	161 mm	Small quantity available August 1944. Muzzle velocity 3,950 feet per second.
German						
75-mm KwK 40	APCBC	99 mm	92 mm	84 mm	66 mm	In Mark IV tanks. Muzzle velocity 2,460 feet per second.
75-mm PaK 40	APCBC	99 mm	92 mm	84 mm	66 mm	Anti-tank gun, towed and self-propelled.
88-mm KwK 36	APCBC	120 mm	112 mm	102 mm	88 mm	In Mark VI, E (Tiger) tanks.
75-mm KwK 42	APCBC	138 mm	128 mm	118 mm	100 mm	In Mark V (Panther) tanks. Muzzle velocity 3,060 feet per second.
88-mm KwK 43	APCBC	202 mm	187 mm	168 mm	137 mm	In Mark VI, B (Tig**e**r) tanks, Jagdpanthers and towed anti-tank guns. Muzzle velocity 3,280 feet per second.
128-mm PaK 44	APCBC	—	212 mm	202 mm	182 mm	In Jagdtigers.

[25 mm = ·985 of an inch; 100 mm = 3·94 inches]

whereas the Tiger and the Panther both had a short life and were often in workshops. We needed a better telescope for the 17-pdr, a more powerful engine in the Churchill, thicker armour and a greater use made of sloping plates. The 75-mm gun was rapidly becoming out of date and he did not want the 76-mm for Twenty-First Army Group. His main recommendation was that eventually every tank ought to mount the 17-pdr gun with high-explosive as well as armour-piercing shell, and as more of these guns became available the British should share them with the Americans.

The Commander-in-Chief was writing after a month in which most of the armour's experience had been in enclosed *bocage* country which discounted the enemy's advantage at the longer ranges. It was before we were aware of the capabilities of the newest version of the German Tiger, and before the battles in the more open country south of Caen where we took our highest tank casualties. It was also, of course, before the Allied armour could show its paces as it did after the break-out.

Part VI

MEASURES TO DEAL WITH THE GERMAN MORTAR

'THE casualties in the present campaign from mortars have been very heavy, heavier in fact than from all the other weapons put together, at least as far as the Infantry are concerned . . . A number of infantry battalion Medical Officers, from four different divisions, all agreed in placing the proportion of mortar casualties to total casualties among their own troops as above 70 per cent. This figure is widely accepted among infantrymen, and it is thought if anything to be an underestimate.' The above are extracts from a report of July the 30th by No. 2 Operational Research Section, Twenty-First Army Group, then attached to Second Army.

In the later stages of the war German interest in conventional field and medium artillery seems to have been on the wane. Instead they were setting more store by mortars and *nebelwerfers*,[1] of which they had large numbers in Normandy. In their infantry division (and on a comparable scale in the other types) there were nearly 60 81-mm mortars throwing a 7½-lb bomb for 2,600 yards, and up to 20 larger ones of 120-mm which fired a 35-lb bomb to a distance of 6,000 yards. Also among their GHQ Troops were five regiments of nebelwerfers, most of which were permanently located opposite the British sector. A regiment contained 60 to 70 of these mortars (or projectors) which were multi-barrelled and had a high rate of fire. They were of three sizes: 150-mm calibre, 75-lb projectile, range 7,300 yards; 210-mm calibre, 248-lb projectile, range 8,600 yards, and 300-mm calibre, 277-lb projectile, range 5,000 yards.

The German mortar had been recognised as a major problem for some time. Its small flash, ease of concealment and high rate of fire, coupled with the silent approach of the bomb and its capacity for bursting in the

---

[1] The '*Nebelwerfer*' was a mortar or projector, with five to ten barrels, firing a rocket-type projectile. Originally designed for smoke-making, the projectile now contained high explosive.

APPENDIX IV

top of a tree, made it unpleasantly effective. Our army in Italy had evolved special counter-mortar teams and at home there had been much research and experiment. Nevertheless, when Overlord opened the British Army contained no official organisation specifically designed to provide the counter. Divisions were therefore told to create their own organisation. From their own resources they each produced a 'Counter-Mortar Officer' (usually a Gunner) and a small team of 'spotters' and signallers, whose task was to provide the guns with a quick succession of enemy mortar locations. All the existing aids were pressed into service—air photographs, sound ranging, flash spotting and so on, and in some cases the newly developed 'four pen recorder' and 'radar' equipment as they became available. But the task proved too big for makeshift arrangements and in August the problem was tackled anew and on the highest level. As a result steps were taken to provide the additional personnel, communications and equipment for each brigade and division to have its counter-mortar team, for the corps artillery survey regiment to have a 'four pen recorder troop', and for each army to have its own 'radar battery'. This was a great advance, but the system would remain in a continuous state of development until the end of the campaign.

APPENDIX V

The Enemy

Part I

GERMAN COMMAND IN THE WEST

Midnight 5th/6th June, 1944

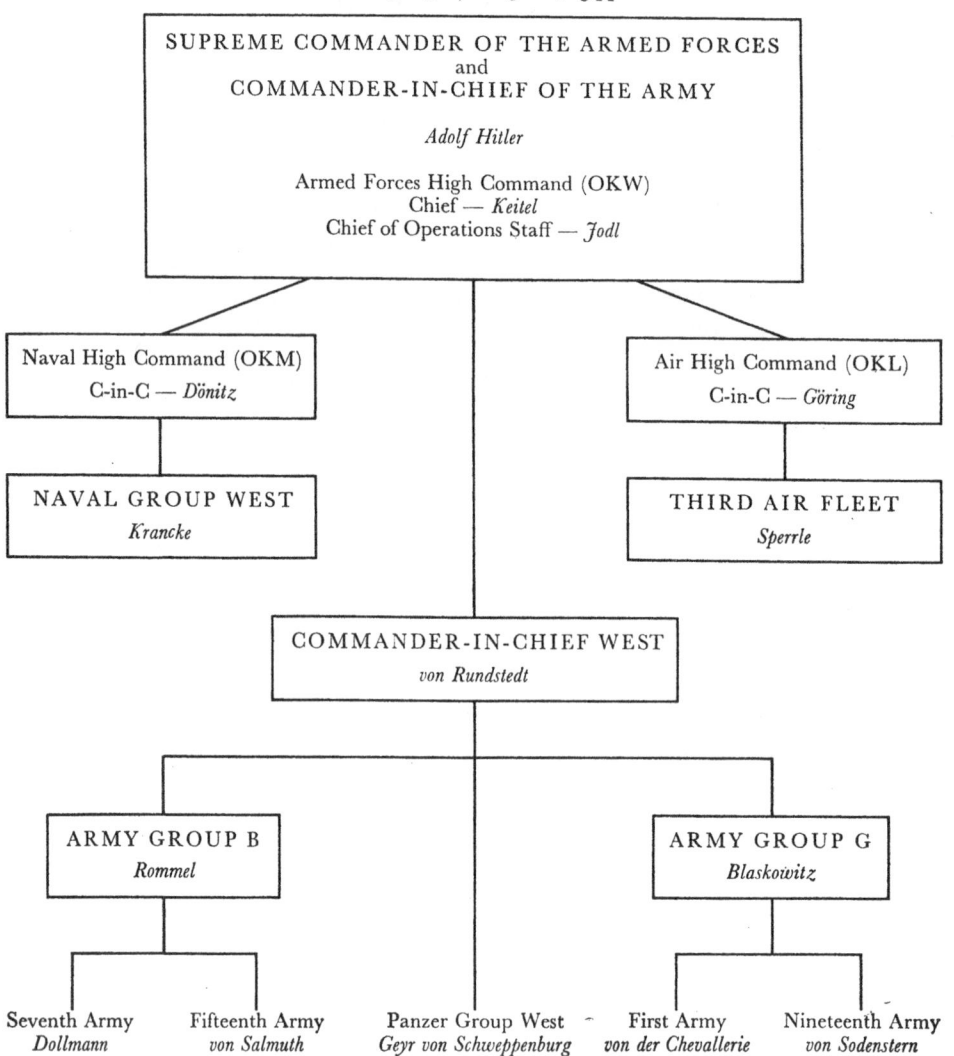

```
┌─────────────────────────────────────────────────┐
│ SUPREME COMMANDER OF THE ARMED FORCES           │
│                    and                          │
│      COMMANDER-IN-CHIEF OF THE ARMY             │
│                                                 │
│                 Adolf Hitler                    │
│                                                 │
│         Armed Forces High Command (OKW)         │
│               Chief — Keitel                    │
│         Chief of Operations Staff — Jodl        │
└─────────────────────────────────────────────────┘
```

- **Naval High Command (OKM)** — C-in-C — *Dönitz*
  - **NAVAL GROUP WEST** — *Krancke*
- **Air High Command (OKL)** — C-in-C — *Göring*
  - **THIRD AIR FLEET** — *Sperrle*

COMMANDER-IN-CHIEF WEST — *von Rundstedt*

- **ARMY GROUP B** — *Rommel*
  - Seventh Army — *Dollmann*
  - Fifteenth Army — *von Salmuth*
  - Panzer Group West — *Geyr von Schweppenburg*
- **ARMY GROUP G** — *Blaskowitz*
  - First Army — *von der Chevallerie*
  - Nineteenth Army — *von Sodenstern*

Note:
  (i) OKH, the Army High Command, was concerned with operations on the Russian front only.
  (ii) Armed Forces Command Netherlands (*Christiansen*) was under Army Group B, but not involved in operations during the period of this volume.
  (iii) Military Governors (France, *von Stülpnagel*; Belgium and N. France, *von Falkenhausen*) working in connection with C-in-C West, were responsible for internal security but not concerned with normal military operations.
  (iv) Locations of German formations, down to divisions, are shown on the map at page 120.

APPENDIX V

Part II

GERMAN LAND FORCES ENCOUNTERED BY THE ALLIES

BETWEEN June the 6th and August the 31st, the Allied forces in northern France were engaged with the German Seventh, Fifteenth, Fifth Panzer (formerly Panzer Group West) and First Armies, and with the following thirteen corps and fifty-one divisions:

Armoured (Panzer) Corps: I SS, II SS, XLVII and LVIII.
Infantry Corps: II Parachute, XXV, LXVII, LXXIV, LXXX, LXXXI, LXXXII, LXXXIV and LXXXVI.
Armoured (Panzer) Divisions: 1st SS, 2nd, 2nd SS, 9th, 9th SS, 10th SS, 12th SS, 21st, 116th and Lehr.
Motorised (Panzer Grenadier) Divisions: 3rd, 15th and 17th SS.
Infantry Divisions: 2nd, 3rd, 5th and 6th[2] Parachute; 16th, 17th and 18th Luftwaffe Field; 47th, 48th, 49th, 77th, 84th, 85th, 89th, 91st Airlanding, 226th, 243rd, 245th, 265th, 266th, 271st, 272nd, 275th, 276th, 277th, 326th, 331st, 343rd, 344th, 346th, 348th, 352nd, 353rd, 363rd, 708th, 709th, 711th and 716th.

Notes on German Army organisation and weapons

Armoured (Panzer) Divisions. These were fully motorised and generally conformed to a '1944 Establishment'. So far as armour and personnel were concerned, however, each had its own organisation. This particularly applied to the *Waffen-SS*[3] divisions (prefixed 'SS') which were much stronger in fire power and numbers than the comparable Army divisions. All the armoured divisions contained an armoured regiment of two battalions—one with Mark IV, the other with Mark V (or Mark IV) tanks—and two regiments of infantry. For the Army divisions this meant four infantry battalions, for the SS divisions six. In all cases the divisional troops included armoured reconnaissance, anti-tank, anti-aircraft, engineer and signal battalions, plus three or four battalions of field and medium artillery, a fair proportion of the guns being self-propelled. Altogether, the division's weapons comprised some 160 tanks (on an average), 700 machine guns, 70 mortars, 37 infantry guns and howitzers, 40 field and medium guns, 33 anti-tank guns and over 100 various pieces of anti-aircraft artillery. Motor vehicles, armoured troop carriers and tractors totalled about 2,950.

Strength of the Army division was approximately 14,750 officers and men but some SS divisions were found to have as many as 20,000 of all ranks.

Motorised (Panzer Grenadier) Divisions. These resembled the armoured divisions and had four or six infantry battalions depending on whether they were Army or SS divisions. They did not contain tanks but had an

---

[2] Battle group only.

[3] SS = Schutzstaffel, the *corps d'élite* of the Nazi Party. 'Waffen' indicated its militarised elements.

assault-gun battalion of 45 guns on tank chassis. Vehicles totalled about 2,900; strength was approximately 14,750 officers and men.

Infantry Divisions. In all types the transport was mostly horsedrawn. Of the 38 divisions encountered, five had been allotted a static rôle and contained nine battalions of infantry, as did the three parachute divisions. The remaining thirty were on a '1944 Establishment' which gave them six infantry battalions, organised in most cases as three regiments each with some infantry howitzers and towed anti-tank guns of its own. The divisional troops comprised a fusilier battalion for reconnaissance, mostly mounted on bicycles, an anti-tank battalion which also included some anti-aircraft guns, three battalions of field and one of medium artillery, engineer and signal battalions and services. A division's weapons included 650 light and heavy machine guns, 76 mortars, 24 infantry guns and howitzers, 31 anti-tank guns, 48 field and medium guns. Motor vehicles and tractors totalled 615 and horsedrawn vehicles about 1,450.

Strength was approximately 12,500 officers and men.

GHQ and Army Troops. The most formidable of these was III Flak Corps,[4] practically the whole of which was deployed on the British front in a dual-purpose rôle—air and ground. Maximum strength appears to have been between 120 and 160 88-mm guns and about double that number of light guns. Other units identified by Twenty-First Army Group were three heavy tank battalions with 45 Tigers each, two battalions of Jagdpanthers (45 each), several anti-tank battalions with towed 88s and several assault-gun battalions mounting 75s. Field and medium artillery was relatively scarce and only one heavy regiment, with 170-mm guns, was met.

Tank and anti-tank guns have been described in Appendix IV, together with mortars and nebelwerfers.

Infantry Weapons. The rifle and light machine gun were of 7·92-mm calibre, the latter having a noticeably higher rate of fire than our Bren. Many German soldiers carried a 9-mm machine carbine. Corresponding to the British PIAT and the American 'bazooka' were two handy anti-tank weapons, the *Panzerfaust* and the *Panzerschreck*. These could penetrate 200-mm of armour within a hundred yards or so but were rather of a 'do-or-die' nature. The heavy weapons were the quick-firing 75-mm gun, with a shell of 13 lbs and a range of 3,780 yards, and the 150-mm howitzer with a 85-lb shell and a range of 5,140 yards.

Artillery. The standard field gun in the German division was the 105-mm with a maximum range of about 12,000 yards; the shell, appreciably heavier than the corresponding British one, weighed 34 lbs. The medium gun was of 150-mm calibre, shell 96 lbs and range about 14,500 yards. The 170-mm heavy gun fired a shell of 150 lbs to a range of 32,000 yards. Chief anti-aircraft guns were the light 20-mm, which had a maximum ceiling of 12,000 feet, and the heavy 88-mm. The latter threw a 22-lb shell to a height of 35,000 feet, though some models claimed a maximum ceiling of 49,000 feet.

---

[4] Strictly speaking, this was a German Air Force formation.

APPENDIX V

Captured Equipment. The Germans made good use of the equipment which fell into their hands in the early years of the war, particularly guns and tank chassis. Much of it was issued to the static, coast defence divisions, but most of the armoured divisions obtained a share of it and this they adapted in their own workshops to increase their number of self-propelled guns, and even of tanks.

APPENDIX VI

Allied Air Forces

Part I

FORCES ENGAGED

ALLIED EXPEDITIONARY AIR FORCE

Air Chief Marshal Sir Trafford L. Leigh-Mallory
Air Commander-in-Chief
Major-General Hoyt S. Vandenberg, USAAF (to 6.8.44)
Major-General Ralph Royce, USAAF (from 7.8.44)
Deputy Air Commander-in-Chief
Air Vice-Marshal H. E. P. Wigglesworth
Senior Air Staff Officer

Royal Air Force. Second Tactical Air Force

Air Marshal Sir Arthur Coningham
Air Marshal Commanding
Air Vice-Marshal A. V. Groom
Senior Air Staff Officer

34 Reconnaissance Wing	16, 69, 140 Squadrons	Spitfire Wellington Mosquito
3 Naval Fighter Wing	808 (FAA), 885 (FAA), 886 (FAA), 897 (FAA) Squadrons	Seafire
(Air Spotting Pool)	26, 63 Squadrons 1320 Special Duty Flight	Spitfire Typhoon

No. 2 Group—Air Vice-Marshal B. E. Embry

137 Wing	88, 226, 342 (Fr) Squadrons	Boston Mitchell
138 Wing	107, 305 (Pol), 613 Squadrons	Mosquito
139 Wing	98, 180, 320 (Dutch) Squadrons	Mitchell
140 Wing	21, 464 (RAAF), 487 (RNZAF) Squadrons	Mosquito

No. 83 Group—Air Vice-Marshal H. Broadhurst

39 (RCAF) Reconnaissance Wing	168, 400 (RCAF), 414 (RCAF) Squadrons	Mustang
	430 (RCAF) Squadron	Spitfire

FAA = Fleet Air Arm; Fr = French; Pol = Polish; RAAF = Royal Australian Air Force; RNZAF = Royal New Zealand Air Force; RCAF = Royal Canadian Air Force.

APPENDIX VI

121 Wing	174, 175, 245 Squadrons	Typhoon
122 Wing	19, 65, 122 Squadrons	Mustang
124 Wing	181, 182, 247 Squadrons	Typhoon
125 Wing	132, 453 (RAAF), 602 Squadrons	Spitfire
126 (RCAF) Wing	401 (RCAF), 411 (RCAF), 412 (RCAF) Squadrons	Spitfire
127 (RCAF) Wing	403 (RCAF), 416 (RCAF), 421 (RCAF) Squadrons	Spitfire
129 (RCAF) Wing	184 Squadron	Typhoon
143 (RCAF) Wing	438 (RCAF), 439 (RCAF), 440 (RCAF) Squadrons	Typhoon
144 (RCAF) Wing	441 (RCAF), 442 (RCAF), 443 (RCAF) Squadrons	Spitfire
Air Observation Posts	652, 653, 658, 659, 662 Squadrons	Auster

No. 84 Group—Air Vice-Marshal L. O. Brown

35 Reconnaissance Wing	2, 4, 268 Squadrons	Mustang Spitfire
123 Wing	198, 609 Squadrons	Typhoon
131 (Pol) Wing	302 (Pol), 308 (Pol), 317 (Pol) Squadrons	Spitfire
132 (Nor) Wing	66, 331 (Nor), 332 (Nor) Squadrons	Spitfire
133 (Pol) Wing	129, 306 (Pol), 315 (Pol) Squadrons	Mustang
134 (Cz) Wing	310 (Cz), 312 (Cz), 313 (Cz) Squadrons	Spitfire
135 Wing	222, 349 (Belgian), 485 (RNZAF) Squadrons	Spitfire
136 Wing	164, 183 Squadrons	Typhoon
145 (Fr) Wing	329 (Fr), 340 (Fr), 341 (Fr) Squadrons	Spitfire
146 Wing	193, 197, 257, 266 Squadrons	Typhoon
Air Observation Posts	660, 661 Squadrons	Auster

No. 85 (Base) Group—Air Vice-Marshal J. B. Cole-Hamilton (to 9.7.44)
Air Vice-Marshal C. R. Steele (from 10.7.44)

141 Wing	91, 124, 322 (Dutch) Squadrons	Spitfire
142 Wing	264, 604 Squadrons	Mosquito (N/F)
147 Wing	29 Squadron	Mosquito (N/F)
148 Wing	409 (RCAF) Squadron	Mosquito (N/F)
149 Wing	410 (RCAF), 488 (RNZAF) Squadrons	Mosquito (N/F)
150 Wing	56[1] Squadron	Spitfire
	3, 486 (RNZAF) Squadrons	Tempest

Nor = Norwegian; Cz = Czech; N/F = Night Fighter.

[1] Changed to Tempest 6.7.44.

APPENDIX VI

Airfield Construction Wing	5022, 5023, 5357 Squadrons
Beach Squadrons	1, 2, 4
Balloon Squadrons	974, 976, 980, 991
Port Balloon Flight	104

Royal Air Force Regiment Group—Colonel R. L. Preston

Mobile Wings	1300, 1301, 1302, 1303, 1304, 1305, 1306, 1307, 1308, 1309, 1310, 1311, 1312, 1314, 1315, 1316, 1317, 1318
Armoured Squadrons	2742, 2757, 2777, 2781, 2806, 2817
Light Anti-Aircraft Squadrons	2701, 2703, 2734, 2736, 2773, 2794, 2800, 2809, 2819, 2834, 2843, 2872, 2873, 2874, 2875, 2876, 2880, 2881
Rifle Squadrons	2713, 2717, 2726, 2729, 2798, 2816, 2827
Special Duty Squadron	2739

Royal Air Force. Air Defence of Great Britain
Air Marshal Sir Roderic M. Hill
Air Marshal Commanding
Air Vice-Marshal W. B. Callaway
Senior Air Staff Officer

No. 10 Group—Air Vice-Marshal C. R. Steele (to 9.7.44)
Air Vice-Marshal J. B. Cole-Hamilton (from 10.7.44)

1, 41, 126, 131, 165, 610, 616[2] Squadrons	Spitfire
263 Squadron	Typhoon
151 Squadron	Mosquito (N/F)
68, 406 (RCAF) Squadrons	Beaufighter (N/F)
276 (A/SR) Squadron	Spitfire, Warwick, Walrus
1449 Flight	Hurricane

No. 11 Group—Air Vice-Marshal H. W. L. Saunders

33, 64, 74, 80, 127, 130, 229, 234, 274, 303 (Pol), 345 (Fr) 350 (Belgian), 402 (RCAF), 501, 611 Squadrons	Spitfire
137 Squadron	Typhoon
96, 125 (Newfoundland), 219, 456 (RAAF) Squadrons	Mosquito (N/F)
418 (RCAF), 605 Squadrons	Mosquito Intruder
275 (A/SR), 277 (A/SR), 278 (A/SR) Squadrons	Spitfire, Warwick, Walrus

No. 12 Group—Air Vice-Marshal M. Henderson

316 (Pol) Squadron	Mustang
504 Squadron	Spitfire

A/SR = Air/Sea Rescue.
[2] Re-equipped with Meteor (jet) between 12.7.44 and 15.8.44.

APPENDIX VI 559

25, 307 (Pol) Squadrons	Mosquito (N/F)
Fighter Interception Unit	Beaufighter, Mosquito, Mustang, Tempest

No. 13 Group—Air Commodore J. A. Boret

118 Squadron	Spitfire
309 (Pol) Squadron	Hurricane

Royal Air Force. Airborne and Transport Forces
Air Vice-Marshal L. N. Hollinghurst
Commander
Air Commodore F. M. Bladin
Senior Air Staff Officer

No. 38 Group (Airborne Forces)—Air Vice-Marshal L. N. Hollinghurst

295, 296, 297, 570 Squadrons	Albemarle
190, 196, 299, 620 Squadrons	Stirling
298, 644 Squadrons	Halifax

No. 46 Group (Transport Command)—Air Commodore A. L. Fiddament

48, 233, 271, 512, 575 Squadrons	Dakota

United States Ninth Air Force[3]
Lieutenant-General Lewis H. Brereton (to 6.8.44)
Major-General Hoyt S. Vandenberg (from 7.8.44)
Commanding General
Brigadier-General Victor H. Strahm
Chief of Staff

10 Photographic Reconnaissance Group (5 Squadrons)	Lightning, Black Widow

U.S. IX Tactical Air Command—Major-General Elwood R. Quesada

70 Wing	48, 367, 371, 474 Groups (12 Squadrons)	Lightning, Thunderbolt
71 Wing	366, 368, 370 Groups (9 Squadrons)	Lightning, Thunderbolt
84 Wing	50, 365, 404, 405 Groups (12 Squadrons)	Thunderbolt
	67 Tactical Reconnaissance Group (4 Squadrons)	Mustang

U.S. XIX Tactical Air Command—Brigadier-General Otto P. Weyland

100 Wing	354, 358, 362, 363 Groups (12 Squadrons)	Mustang, Thunderbolt
303 Wing	36, 373, 406 Groups (9 Squadrons)	Thunderbolt
	422, 425 Night Fighter Squadrons	Black Widow

---

[3] In the United States Army Air Force, wings correspond to the Royal Air Force groups and groups to the Royal Air Force wings.

APPENDIX VI

U.S. IX Bomber Command—Brigadier-General Samuel E. Anderson

97 Wing	409, 410, 416 Groups (12 Squadrons)	Havoc
98 Wing	323, 387, 394, 397 Groups (16 Squadrons)	Marauder
99 Wing	322, 344, 386, 391 Groups (16 Squadrons)	Marauder
	One Pathfinder Squadron	Marauder

U.S. IX Troop Carrier Command—Brigadier-General Paul L. Williams

50 Wing	439, 440, 441, 442 Groups (16 Squadrons)	Dakota
52 Wing	61, 313, 314, 315, 316 Groups (20 Squadrons)	Dakota
53 Wing	434, 435, 436, 437, 438 Groups (20 Squadrons)	Dakota
	One Pathfinder Group	Dakota

ALLIED STRATEGIC AIR FORCE

Royal Air Force. Bomber Command

Air Chief Marshal Sir Arthur T. Harris
Air Officer Commanding-in-Chief
Air Marshal Sir Robert Saundby
Deputy Air Officer Commanding-in-Chief
Air Vice-Marshal H. S. P. Walmsley
Senior Air Staff Officer

No. 1 Group—Air Vice-Marshal E. A. B. Rice

12, 100, 101, 103, 166, 300 (Pol), 460 (RAAF), 550, 576, 625, 626 Squadrons — Lancaster

No. 3 Group—Air Vice-Marshal R. Harrison

15, 75, 115, 514, 622 Squadrons	Lancaster
90 Squadron	Lancaster, Stirling
149, 218[4] Squadrons	Stirling
138 Special Duty Squadron	Halifax, Stirling
161 Special Duty Squadron	Halifax, Hudson, Lysander

No. 4 Group—Air Vice-Marshal C. R. Carr

10, 51, 76, 77, 78, 102, 158, 346 (Fr), 347 (Fr), 462 (RAAF), 466 (RAAF), 578, 640 Squadrons — Halifax

---

[4] Re-equipped with Lancaster, August 1944.

APPENDIX VI

No. 5 Group—Air Vice-Marshal The Hon R. A. Cochrane

9, 44 (Rhodesian), 49, 50, 57, 61, 106, 207, 463 (RAAF), 467 (RAAF), 619, 630 Squadrons	Lancaster
617 Squadron	Lancaster, Mosquito

No. 6 (RCAF) Group—Air Vice-Marshal C. M. McEwen, RCAF

415 (RCAF),[5] 420 (RCAF), 424 (RCAF), 425 (RCAF), 426 (RCAF), 427 (RCAF), 429 (RCAF), 431 (RCAF), 432 (RCAF), 433 (RCAF), 434 (RCAF) Squadrons	Halifax
408 (RCAF), 419 (RCAF) Squadrons	Lancaster
428 (RCAF) Squadron	Halifax, Lancaster

No. 8 Pathfinder Group—Air Vice-Marshal D. C. T. Bennett

7, 35, 83, 97, 156, 405 (RCAF), 582, 635 Squadrons	Lancaster
105, 109, 139, 571, 608, 627, 692 Squadrons	Mosquito

No. 100 (BS) Group—Air Commodore E. B. Addison

85 (BS), 141 (BS), 157 (BS), 169 (BS), 239 (BS) Squadrons	Mosquito
23, 515 (BS) Squadrons	Mosquito Intruder
214 (BS) Squadron	Fortress
192 (BS) Squadron	Halifax, Mosquito, Wellington
199 Squadron	Stirling
223 (BS)[6] Squadron	Liberator

United States Eighth Air Force

Lieutenant-General James H. Doolittle
Commanding General
Major-General Earle E. Partridge
Deputy Commander
Brigadier-General John H. Samford
Chief of Staff

7 Photographic Reconnaissance Group (4 Squadrons)	Lightning, Spitfire

1st Bomb Division—Major-General Robert B. Williams

91, 92, 303, 305, 306, 351, 379, 381, 384, 398, 401, 457 Groups (48 Squadrons)	Fortress

2nd Bomb Division—Major-General James P. Hodges

44, 93, 389, 392, 445, 446, 448, 453, 458, 466, 467, 489, 491, 492 Groups (56 Squadrons)	Liberator

---

BS = Bomber Support.

[5] From Coastal Command 27.7.44.

[6] Forming August 1944.

APPENDIX VI

3rd Bomb Division—Major-General Curtis E. Le May

94, 95, 96, 100, 385, 388, 390, 447, 452 Groups (36 Squadrons)	Fortress
34, 486, 487, 490, 493 Groups[7] (20 Squadrons)	Liberator

VIII Fighter Command—Major-General William E. Kepner

65 Wing	4, 56, 355, 356, 479 Groups (15 Squadrons)	⎫ Lightning
66 Wing	55, 78, 339, 353, 357 Groups (15 Squadrons)	⎬ Mustang ⎭ Thunderbolt
67 Wing	20, 352, 359, 361, 364 Groups (15 Squadrons)	Lightning, Mustang

ROYAL AIR FORCE. COASTAL COMMAND
Air Chief Marshal Sir W. Sholto Douglas
Air Officer Commanding-in-Chief
Air Vice-Marshal A. B. Ellwood
Senior Air Staff Officer

No. 15 Group—Air Vice-Marshal Sir Leonard H. Slatter

59 Squadron	Liberator (VLR)
120 Squadron	Liberator (VLR, L/L)
422 (RCAF), 423 (RCAF) Squadrons	Sunderland
811 (FAA) Squadron	Avenger, Wild Cat

No. 16 Group—Air Vice-Marshal F. L. Hopps

119 Squadron	Albacore
143, 236, 254, 455 (RAAF), 489 (RNZAF) Squadrons	Beaufighter
415 (RCAF)[8] Squadron	Wellington, Albacore
819 (FAA), 848 (FAA), 854 (FAA), 855 (FAA) Squadrons	Avenger, Swordfish

No. 18 Group—Air Vice-Marshal S. P. Simpson

86 Squadron	Liberator (VLR)
210 Squadron	Catalina
330 (Nor), 333 (Nor) Squadrons	Catalina, Mosquito, Sunderland
1693 Flight	Anson

No. 19 Group—Air Vice-Marshal B. E. Baker

144, 235,[9] 404 (RCAF) Squadrons	Beaufighter
58, 502 Squadrons	Halifax

VLR = Very Long Range; L/L = Leigh Light.

[7] Three groups changed to Fortress, August 1944.
[8] To Bomber Command 27.7.44.
[9] Re-equipped with Mosquito, July 1944.

APPENDIX VI

53, 224 Squadrons	Liberator (L/L)
206, 311 (Cz), 547 Squadrons	Liberator
248 Squadron	Mosquito
10 (RAAF), 201, 228, 461 (RAAF) Squadrons	Sunderland
172, 179, 304 (Pol), 407 (RCAF), 612 Squadrons	Wellington (L/L)
524 Squadron	Wellington
816 (FAA), 838 (FAA), 849 (FAA), 850 (FAA) Squadrons	Avenger, Swordfish
Attached—103 (USN), 105 (USN), 110 (USN) and (det) 114 (USN) Squadrons	Liberator

Part II

NOTES ON ALLIED AIRCRAFT EMPLOYED
Royal Air Force

Heavy Bombers. Bomber Command was equipped with the Lancaster and Halifax four-engined bombers. The Lancaster had a top speed of 287 miles an hour at 11,500 feet and a service ceiling of 20,000 feet; the Halifax a top speed of 280 miles an hour at 13,500 feet with a similar service ceiling. The bomb load varied with the range; the Lancaster could carry 10,000 lbs for 2,250 miles, or 14,000 lbs for 1,660 miles, while the Halifax could carry 6,250 lbs for 2,000 miles, or 13,000 lbs for 980 miles. Both types had a crew of seven. Armament consisted of eight ·303-in machine guns in the Lancaster and nine in the Halifax.

Medium and Light Bombers. No. 2 Group was equipped with three types of twin-engined aircraft, Mitchell—a medium bomber, Boston and Mosquito—light bombers. The Mitchell and Boston were built in the U.S.A. The Mitchell had a top speed of 292 miles an hour at 15,000 feet with a service ceiling of 20,000 feet and could carry 4,000 lbs of bombs for a range of 1,660 miles or 6,000 lbs of bombs for 965 miles; it had a crew of five and an armament of seven ·5-in machine guns. The Boston had a top speed of 320 miles an hour at 11,000 feet with a service ceiling of 24,500 feet and could carry 2,000 lbs of bombs for a range of 1,570 miles or 4,000 lbs of bombs for 710 miles; it had a crew of four and an armament of five ·5-in guns. The Mosquito's maximum speed was 370 miles an hour at 13,000 feet with a service ceiling of 32,000 feet. Its bomb load was 2,000 lbs for a range of 1,270 miles or 1,000 lbs for 1,650 miles. It had a crew of two and was armed with four ·303-in and four 20-mm guns. In addition to its rôle in No. 2 Group it was also used in some squadrons of Bomber Command. This type of Mosquito had a top speed of 397 miles an hour at 26,000 feet with a service ceiling of 36,000 feet and could carry 3,000 lbs of bombs for 1,485 miles, or 5,000 lbs for 1,370 miles. It was unarmed.

Fighters and Fighter-Bombers. The aircraft used as day fighters and fighter-bombers were the Spitfire, Mustang and Typhoon. Their speeds were between 400 and 450 miles an hour with service ceilings of 32,000 to 43,000 feet. The armament varied according to the allocated duty—high cover or ground attack—and consisted of four to six guns of three calibres—·303-in, 20-mm and ·5-in. The normal Spitfire load, when employed as a fighter-bomber, was three bombs of a total weight of 1,000 lbs. The Typhoon could be armed with eight 60-lb rocket projectiles, or with 2,000 lbs of bombs. All day fighters and fighter-bombers were single-seater aircraft. Two squadrons of Spitfires were specially equipped and trained in spotting for naval gun fire.

The night fighter and night intruder aircraft was another type of Mosquito, armed with four 20-mm guns.

Photographic Reconnaissance Aircraft. Long-range strategic photographic reconnaissance was carried out by specially modified and unarmed Mosquitos and Spitfires which normally operated at heights up to 40,000 feet. For tactical reconnaissance, both photographic and visual, Spitfire and Mustang fighters were used.

Transport Aircraft. There were two groups of transport aircraft. No. 38 Group had the twin-engined Albemarle for glider-towing and parachute troops, and the four-engined Halifax and Stirling for glider-towing only. No. 46 Group had the twin-engined American Dakota for parachute troops and transport duties.

The gliders were the Horsa and the Hamilcar, the Horsas representing about 90 per cent of all those used. The Horsa had a military load of 3·1 tons and could carry twenty-nine passengers or a jeep with trailer. The Hamilcar's military load was 7·8 tons. It could take forty passengers, two Bren carriers or a field gun with its tractor.

Air Observation Post Aircraft. The Air Observation Post squadrons in Nos. 83 and 84 Groups were equipped with Auster aircraft—a small light machine for artillery observation, close reconnaissance and rapid communication, which could be operated from a limited and unprepared space.

Coastal Command Aircraft. The majority of squadrons were modified for anti-U-boat operations and were equipped with ASV (Air to Surface-Vessel), a radar device for airborne search and homing on enemy submarines. Depth charges replaced the normal load of bombs in nine squadrons equipped with the four-engined Halifax and Liberator, and in five squadrons of the twin-engined Wellington. Eight of these squadrons were also equipped with the Leigh Light, a powerful searchlight which gave the attacking aircrew, homing on ASV, visual detection at night of an enemy vessel on the surface.

The flying boats were the four-engined Sunderland and the twin-engined Catalina. The Sunderland had a cruising speed of 110 knots, an operational range of 1,500 nautical miles, a bomb load of eight depth charges, an armament of seven ·303-in guns and a crew of ten. The Catalina cruised at 106 knots, had an operational range of 1,650 nautical miles, a bomb load of four depth charges, an armament of two ·5-in and two ·303-in guns and a crew of nine.

APPENDIX VI

For anti-shipping operations in Home waters twin-engined Beaufighter, Mosquito and Wellington aircraft were used; the Beaufighter and Wellington were equipped with ASV.

Fleet Air Arm Aircraft. The nine Fleet Air Arm squadrons on loan to Coastal Command for anti-U-boat and anti-shipping operations were equipped with single-engined Swordfish and Avenger. The former, with a crew of two and armed with one ·303-in gun, carried three depth charges or four 250-lb bombs. The Avenger had a crew of three, armament of three ·5-in and one ·303-in guns and bomb load of four depth charges. Four other squadrons on loan to Second Tactical Air Force for directing the fire of naval guns on enemy shore batteries were equipped with the single-seater Seafire; a single-engined fighter armed with four ·303-in and two 20-mm guns, it had a cruising speed of approximately 200 miles an hour, a service ceiling of 33,000 feet with maximum range of 500 miles and maximum speed of 340 miles an hour.

United States Army Air Forces[10]

Heavy Bombers. The strategic bombers of the Eighth Air Force were of two types, the B.17 (Fortress) and the B.24 (Liberator). Both aircraft carried a crew of ten and had a top speed of 300 miles an hour with a service ceiling of over 30,000 feet. The Fortress was armed with twelve ·5-in machine guns and could carry 4,000 lbs of bombs for over 2,000 miles; the Liberator had ten ·5-in machine guns and carried 2,500 lbs of bombs for 2,850 miles.

Medium Bombers. The B.26 (Marauder) was the medium bomber of the Ninth Air Force. It had a top speed of 285 miles an hour, a crew of six, twelve ·5-in machine guns and could carry 4,000 lbs of bombs for 1,100 miles.

Light Bombers. The light bomber of the Ninth Air Force was the A.20 (Havoc). It had a top speed of 325 miles an hour and carried a crew of three. It was armed with nine ·5-in machine guns, or five ·5-in machine guns and twelve rocket projectiles, and could carry 2,000 lbs of bombs for 250 miles.

Fighters and Fighter-Bombers. The fighters and fighter-bombers in both the Eighth and the Ninth Air Forces were the P.38 (Lightning), the P.47 (Thunderbolt) and the P.51 (Mustang). Their maximum speeds were between 410 and 480 miles an hour with service ceilings of 35,000 to 41,500 feet. Armament was four, eight and six ·5-in machine guns respectively and the P.38 had in addition one 20-mm gun. The P.47, when used as a fighter-bomber, carried two 1,000-lb bombs or could be armed with rocket projectiles. With the Eighth Air Force the main rôle of these fighters was to escort large formations of the heavy bombers in daylight raids over Europe. The P.47 and the P.51, by increasing their fuel capacity, proved capable of operating as far as Berlin, and were also adapted to carry out long range photographic reconnaissance.

---

[10] See Craven and Cate, *The Army Air Forces in World War II*, vol. VI, chap. VI, pp. 199–225.

Transport Aircraft. All airborne and transport operations were done by C.47/53 (Dakota) aircraft of the Ninth Air Force.

The glider in general use was the C.G.-4A (Waco) with a military load of 1·7 tons. It could carry fifteen passengers, a jeep or a light howitzer.

United States Naval Aircraft. Three squadrons of Liberators of the United States Navy were lent to Coastal Command and operated under No. 19 Group.

APPENDIX VII

German Air Force in the West

Part I

ORGANISATION AND STRENGTH

THIRD Air Fleet on May the 31st 1944 was organised as follows, with headquarters as shown on the map overleaf.

Formation	Aircraft		
	Types	Strength	Serviceable
Third Air Fleet			
Units of No. 5 Group . .	Night fighters	33	17
Nos. 5 and 123 Groups .	Long-range reconnaissance	59	30
No. 13 Group	Short-range reconnaissance	30	16
Transport Units . . .	Transport	64	31
Fighter Corps II.	(Main fighter defence)		
Fighter Division 4 . . .	Day fighters	104	71
	Night fighters	57	29
Fighter Division 5 . . .	Day fighters	69	48
Air Corps II	Close-support fighters	73	55
Air Corps IX	Long-range bombers	326	150
Air Corps X.	Anti-shipping	23	20
Air Division 2	Torpedo bombers	53	30
Summary			
	Fighters (all types)	425	266
	Bombers (including anti-shipping and torpedo)	402	200
	Transport aircraft	64	31
	TOTAL	891	497

On D-day only 319 aircraft were able to operate but plans had been made in advance to transfer all single-engined fighter units in Germany to Air Corps II in the West as soon as the Allied assault began. The transfer was at first delayed because the Commander-in-Chief West expected the main landing in the Pas de Calais, but the move was soon ordered and by June the 10th some 300 fighters, 45 torpedo-carrying and 90 long-range bombers had reinforced Air Corps II: a week after D-day German aircraft in the West amounted to about 1,000 of all types. But nearly all the airfields previously prepared for the new arrivals had been heavily bombed by the Allied air forces and often hastily arranged landing grounds had to be made ready for them. Advance parties had been flown in but the main strength of the new units had to come by rail and, owing

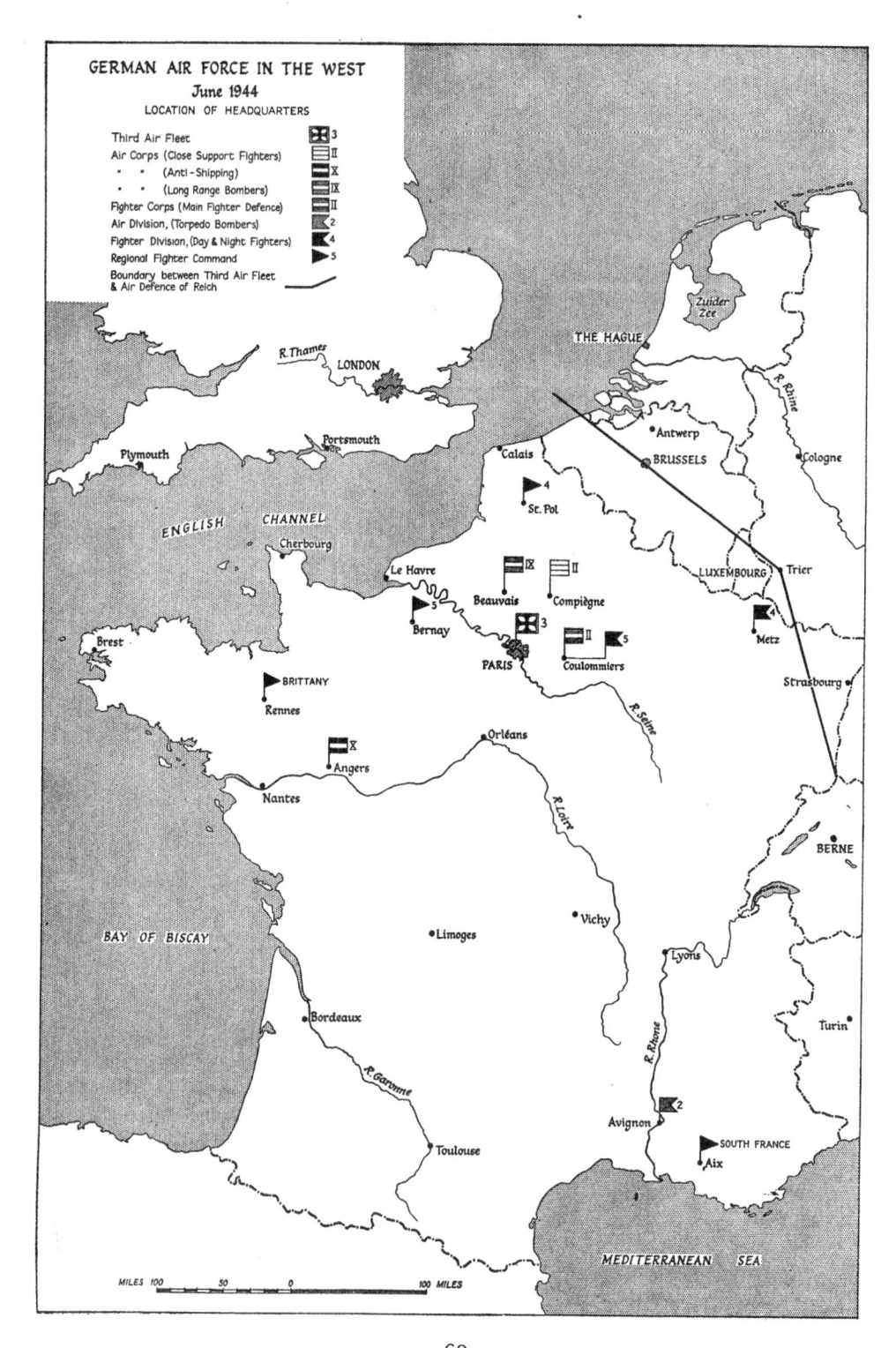

GERMAN AIR FORCE IN THE WEST
June 1944
LOCATION OF HEADQUARTERS

to the disruption of the railways by Allied air attacks, they were days or even weeks late in arriving. The signals network broke down and made communication between units and their headquarters slow and difficult; confusion and lack of facilities severely limited the number of missions flown. The number of fighter sorties was gradually increased but losses steadily ate into the German fighter strength.

In the first few days the long-distance bombers of Air Corps IX found that they could not operate effectively over the Allied assault area for anti-aircraft, balloon and searchlight defences compelled them to fly at so great a height that small targets could not be distinguished. From the 12th of June onwards the whole of the bomber force was used for the dropping of mines or circling torpedoes—a much more effective nuisance to Allied shipping. Early in July the anti-shipping aircraft of Air Corps X were withdrawn to Norway and Germany and in August the corps headquarters was disbanded.

Then came a worse blow. On August the 11th the Third Air Fleet, acting on instructions from Berlin, issued orders to all subordinate commands and units imposing severe restrictions on flying activity of all kinds. Fighters were only to undertake unrestricted operations in defence against attacks by heavy bombers; reconnaissance (though very necessary at this time) could only be carried out when essential for the general conduct of operations; fighter-bombers for ground attack were specifically limited to action considered decisive after close scrutiny; four-engined bombers were grounded unless special permission to fly them was first obtained. This dire limitation of air power just as the battle approached its crisis was ordered because of an alarming decline in fuel supplies. Allied air attacks on the German oil industry were drastically reducing the production of synthetic oil, and petrol in hand was being used up or destroyed by their attacks on storage dumps and depots.

About August the 20th two fighter units were sent to France from Germany in order to provide increased protection for the retreating armies, but about the same time all forward air forces were compelled by the Allied advance to move back towards the Belgian frontier. In the last week of August fighter forces, about 420 strong, were precariously disposed in Belgium and north-eastern France; the long-range bombers and night fighters were moved back to bases in Holland and north-west Germany.

The German Air Force provided the anti-aircraft (flak) defence in the theatre.

Part II

NOTES ON GERMAN AIRCRAFT EMPLOYED

The main aircraft in the Third Air Fleet were—

Junkers 88. A twin-engined aircraft it was used as a bomber, on long-range reconnaissance and as a day and night fighter. As a bomber and long-range reconnaissance aircraft it carried a crew of four; with a normal bomb load of 2,200 lbs it had a cruising speed of about 250 miles an hour at 16,400 feet, a service ceiling of approximately 24,000 feet and a maximum range of 1,300 miles; it was armed with six 7·9-mm guns and one

20-mm gun. When used as a day and night fighter it carried a crew of two or three; the speed varied from approximately 310 to 340 miles an hour with a service ceiling of 30,200 feet and a maximum range of 800 miles; it was armed with six 7·9-mm and three 20-mm guns.

Junkers 188. A twin-engined aircraft it was used as a bomber and on long-range reconnaissance. With a crew of four or five and a normal bomb load of 2,200 lbs it had a cruising speed of approximately 250 miles an hour, a service ceiling of 33,000 feet and a maximum range of 670 miles. It was armed with two 7·9-mm, two 13-mm and one 20-mm guns.

Focke-Wulf 190. A single-engined, single-seater aircraft used for ground attack, as a day fighter and on close and long-range reconnaissance. On ground attack it carried a normal bomb load of 550 lbs and was armed with two 7·9-mm and two 20-mm guns; its speed varied between 300 and 360 miles an hour, with a service ceiling of approximately 31,000 feet and a maximum range of about 460 miles. As a day fighter and on close and long-range reconnaissance its speed was between 330 and 380 miles an hour, with a service ceiling of 36,000 feet and maximum range of approximately 520 miles. It was armed with two 7·9-mm and two 20-mm guns.

Messerschmitt 109. A single-engined, single-seater aircraft used mainly as a day fighter, or as a night fighter and on close and long-range reconnaissance. The speed varied between 330 and 400 miles an hour; it had a service ceiling of 38,500 feet, a maximum range of approximately 600 miles and was armed with two 7·9-mm and three 20-mm guns.

Messerschmitt 110. A twin-engined night fighter with a crew of two. Its speed varied between 300 and 360 miles an hour, with a service ceiling of 34,800 feet and a maximum range of about 900 miles. It was armed with five 7·9-mm and two 20-mm guns.

Dornier 217. A twin-engined aircraft used as a bomber or night fighter. As a bomber it carried a crew of four; with a normal bomb load of 4,400 lbs it had a cruising speed of 240 miles an hour at 15,000 feet, a service ceiling of 21,500 feet and maximum range of approximately 1,100 miles. It was armed with four 7·9-mm, four 13-mm, one 15-mm and one 20-mm guns. As a fighter it had a crew of three, a speed between 280 and 320 miles an hour, a service ceiling of 29,000 feet and a maximum range of about 1,200 miles. It was armed with four 7·9-mm, two 13-mm and four 20-mm guns.

Messerschmitt 410. A twin-engined aircraft, with a crew of two, employed as a bomber and on long-range reconnaissance. With a normal bomb load of 1,100 lbs it had a cruising speed of 330 miles an hour at 19,000 feet, a service ceiling of 30,000 feet and maximum range of 1,190 miles. It was armed with two 7·9-mm, two 13-mm and two 20-mm guns.

Junkers 52. This was the main transport aircraft. Three-engined with a crew of three or four, it had a cruising speed of about 130 miles an hour with a service ceiling of 16,000 feet, a load of 5,000 lbs and a maximum range of 530 miles. It was armed with five 7·9-mm guns.

APPENDIX VIII

Civil Affairs in France[1]

THE Allies had foreseen the inevitability of an interim régime between the expulsion of German forces from countries they had occupied and the re-establishment of national governments with full sovereignty. However quickly national governments could resume their functions the Allies must retain the right to control such territory, communications and resources as they needed for the continued prosecution of the war against Germany; in so far as the military situation required it there must be a temporary surrender of sovereignty to the Allies' Supreme Commander.

Before Overlord was launched the refugee Governments of Norway, Holland, Belgium and Luxembourg had concluded mutually acceptable agreements with the Allies, under which General Eisenhower was endowed with supreme authority but would use local administrators as far as possible and would transfer his authority to the national government as soon as the military situation permitted. It had not proved possible to conclude any similar agreement with France. There was no French government to treat with and although General de Gaulle claimed that he spoke for France, and that his *Comité Français de la Libération Nationale* should be accepted as the provisional government of France, both the British and American Governments felt unable to accept his claims without clearer evidence that they were justified. The Allies were determined to preserve for the people of France the right and opportunity to decide for themselves what form of government they would have and needed further assurance that General de Gaulle and the authority of the National Committee which he had formed in Algiers would be generally acceptable in Metropolitan France.

In default of any agreement the first Civil Affairs officers who landed with the Allied troops found the French suspicious of their concern with local administration, but confidence on both sides soon increased. The French realised that the Allied Civil Affairs officers were sincere in their desire to interfere as little as possible with French domestic administration; the Allies found that French civil administration was able generally to assume more responsibility than had been expected. Leading men of the Resistance stepped into the shoes of deposed or fugitive Vichy officials and Civil Affairs detachments at corps and divisional levels were able to work indirectly through such men and to a lesser extent through General de Gaulle's liaison officers—once he allowed them to co-operate. The Resistance has hardly been given sufficient credit for this less romantic side of its work. It did in fact produce local administration in the period covered by this volume.

---

[1] See Donnison, *Civil Affairs and Military Government in North-West Europe*, chap. III.

Politically as well as practically the growth of mutual confidence was important. Early in June, General de Gaulle had visited Normandy and his reception had done much to modify the Allies' uncertainty concerning his status in Metropolitan France. A Second Army report describes the welcome that he received. 'All shades of political opinion in Bayeux were in varying degrees enthusiastic and emphatic that de Gaulle and no one else could solve the deadlock.' In July the National Committee was recognised by the British and American Governments as the *de facto* authority for the civil administration of France and in the last week of August agreements between the United Kingdom and France, and between the United States and France, were concluded, embodying the principles which had been acted on in practice since the Allied landings.

Liberated France was to be divided into a 'Forward Zone' and an 'Interior Zone'. The Delegate of the French National Committee was given power to determine from time to time the Forward Zone, the area 'affected by active military operations', but he was to do so 'in such a manner as to meet the requirements stated by the Supreme Commander'. Military areas, lines of communication, airfields and bases, wherever they were, were to be treated if necessary in the same way as the Forward Zone, and the Delegate was required to take all measures in the Forward Zone which the Supreme Commander regarded as essential for the successful conduct of his operations. Military necessities were thus guaranteed, though the overriding authority of the Supreme Commander was implied rather than stated. In the Interior Zone the control of administration was left entirely in the hands of French authorities.

APPENDIX IX

Overlord and French Resistance

THE Resistance movement in France was not only an invaluable factor in the national revival but was of immediate assistance to the Allies. Its existence depended on personal initiative, courage and self-sacrifice but its effectiveness depended mainly on the Allies' supply of arms and other equipment and on guidance which related its actions to the Overlord campaign. Without arms and explosives it could have done little damage to the enemy; without military direction it would have been of much less help to the Allies.

The British Government had been doing all in its power to foster French Resistance ever since the German victory in 1940 but the story of the movement's triumphs and tragedies in the intervening years lies outside the scope of this volume. Experience had shown that attempts to develop any large-scale organisation increased the risk of discovery by the Gestapo and the danger of dispersal with savage reprisals. Instead it proved more helpful to drop specially trained, able and resolute men with radio sets in areas where they could make touch with Resistance groups, advise on activities which would have the greatest military effect, and arrange reception committees to receive arms and equipment for sabotage, when dropped at night. These Allied representatives worked with no defined boundaries, ignored political affiliations and did not attempt to form disciplined relationships of command and subordination; among them were French volunteers who had been flown out from France and trained in England. Some of these brave men, working clandestinely in German-held country, had been betrayed to the Gestapo; 64 were known to have been killed, 297 had disappeared, others had been brought back to England after a tour of duty; at the time of Overlord nearly 300 were working in France. As D-day approached the supply of both personnel and material aid was increased and a mounting tale of sabotage followed—duly noted in the German weekly reports from the western front. Sabotage of railways had made a valuable addition to the major damage and disruption of enemy communications inflicted by the Allied air forces. Enemy movement by rail was made slow and difficult and in the French interior ambushes and obstructions made transport by road dangerous. Some notable sabotage was also done to electrical and other industrial plants, and by threats of a heavy bombing attack some managements were induced to sabotage their own machinery in order to avoid greater destruction by the bombers.

With the launching of Overlord Resistance activities increased. In the three months which had preceded it nearly 150 men and some 1,500 tons of arms and supplies had been dropped in France; between D-day and the end of August over 400 men and more than 6,500 tons of supplies were dropped, requiring nearly 4,500 sorties by Allied aircraft. Two of these operations, involving over 500 sorties, were carried out in daylight by the U.S. Eighth Air Force, but all the other deliveries had been made in darkness by British aircraft of No. 38 Group.

Two further forms of assistance were introduced during Overlord. First, small specially trained 'Jedburgh' teams, of British, American and French officers and men with wireless equipment, were dropped to help Resistance groups, especially in Brittany where the movement was extensive but needed better organisation and more arms and where there were good opportunities to damage the enemy. Second, and of a different nature, were detachments of Special Air Service troops.[1] These were British and French soldiers who were dropped to carry out particular tasks behind the German lines. Sometimes they formed a stiffening for operations in which the Resistance were associated; at others they acted independently in parties which varied in size from an officer and a few men to as many as 18 officers and 126 men. From D-day to the end of August, 1,873 S.A.S. troops had been flown in with over 8,000 containers of supplies, two 6-pdr guns and sixty jeeps.

By these various measures Resistance activities were assisted and augmented, and their multiple operations were related to the single purpose of Overlord. By their damage and disruption of rail, road and telephone communications they helped to hamper the movement of German troops against the Allied lodgement, enemy re-grouping after the Allied break-out and the German retreat from France; they facilitated the Allies' rapid advance by enabling them to dispense with many normal military precautions for flank protection and mopping-up; by furnishing military intelligence; and by providing in liberated areas organised groups ready to undertake static guard duties at short notice without further training. Some illustrations have been given in earlier pages. Meanwhile in the south, guerilla operations of the Maquis so weakened the German control of central and southern France that the Allies' landings in the Mediterranean were materially eased and their advance northwards to join General Eisenhower's command greatly assisted.

The contribution of Resistance movements to Overlord in France, Belgium and Holland was to continue during further operations which, however, belong to the second volume of this history.

---

[1] For their composition see page 524.

APPENDIX X

Code Names Mentioned in Text

ANVIL	First name for Allied landing in the south of France, August 1944.
ARCADIA	The Washington Conference, December 1941–January 1942.
BODYGUARD	Cover and deception plan for Allied strategy in Europe.
BOLERO	Build-up of United States forces and supplies in United Kingdom for cross-Channel operations.
BOMBARDON	Floating steel component of breakwaters to seaward of Mulberry harbours.
COBRA	American break-out near St. Lô, July 25th–29th.
CORNCOB	Blockship component of Gooseberry breakwaters.
CROSSBOW	Allied measures against attacks by flying bombs and rockets.
DAUNTLESS	XXX Corps operation in 'Epsom' battle, June 25th.
DRAGOON	Final name for 'Anvil'—see above.
EPSOM	Second Army's operation to cross the Odon and Orne rivers south-west of Caen, June 26th–July 1st.
EUREKA	The Teheran Conference, November 1943.
FORTITUDE	Cover plan for 'Overlord'.
GOODWOOD	Second Army's attack south-east of Caen, July 18th–21st.
GOOSEBERRY	Artificial breakwater for the offshore anchorages and Mulberry harbours.
JUPITER	VIII Corps attack towards upper Orne, July 10th.
MAPLE	Mine laying programme in 'Neptune' operations.
MULBERRY	Artificial harbour off the Normandy coast.
NEPTUNE	Naval assault phase of 'Overlord'.
OVERLORD	Allied campaign in north-west Europe, 1944–45.
PHOENIX	Concrete caisson for Mulberry breakwaters.
PLUTO	Scheme to supply petrol from England to the Continent by submarine pipeline.
POINTBLANK	Combined Bomber Offensive against Germany.
QUADRANT	The Quebec Conference, August 1943.
RANKIN	Plan to return to Continent in event of sudden German collapse or surrender prior to 'Overlord'.
ROUNDUP	Plan for a major Allied landing in France in 1943, replaced by Overlord.
SEXTANT	The Cairo Conference, November–December 1943.
SLEDGEHAMMER	Provisional plan for Allied landing in France in 1942.
SYMBOL	The Casablanca Conference, January 1943.

TOMBOLA	Supply of petrol by pipeline from tankers to shore storage depots in Normandy.
TOTALIZE	First Canadian Army's attack towards Falaise: Phase I, August 8th–11th.
TRACTABLE	First Canadian Army's attack towards Falaise; Phase II, August 14th–16th.
TRIDENT	The Washington Conference, May 1943.
WHALE	Floating steel roadways and pierheads for the Mulberry harbours.

Index

INDEX

Only those forces and individuals mentioned in the text are included in this index. Other names will be found in the appendices

Aachen: 399, 450, 459

Administration and Logistics: concentration and marshalling, 83, 136; supply and maintenance system, 83-6; ports and harbours, 87, 263, 479; cross-Channel convoys, 90; build-up, 217, 239, 263-5; beach organisation, 218; effect of storm, 274; progress of supply and maintenance, 302-4, 473, 478-482

Airborne Operations: 16, 33; invasion plan, 64, 80; arguments over, 138; D-day assault, 149-58, 199, 204-6, 215; First Allied Airborne Army becomes available for, 402n, 460, 462, 465, 475

Aircraft: numbers available for 'Overlord', 28, 72; jet types, 61. *See also* Appendices VI and VII *passim*

Airfields: built in U.K., 29; attacks on enemy —, 96, 110, 399, 472; construction in France, 77, 305, 358, 481

Air Forces, Allied: preparatory operations, 22-4, 94-113 *passim*; command and organisation, 40-3, 73-5, Appendix VI; Overall Air Plan, 71-7; cover for 'Neptune', 145, 161; June operations, 306; operations and losses summarised, 487. *See also* Allied Expeditionary Air Force, Royal Air Force, United States Army Air Force, Air Mastery

Air/Ground Co-operation: in assault, 161-4, 170, 211; in bridgehead, 233-5, 251; in 'Epsom', 280-7; at Caen, 311-13; in 'Goodwood', 335, 337-9; use of Visual Control Posts, 338, 382; in 'Cobra', 379-82; at Caumont, 388, 393; in 'Totalize', 421; in 'Tractable', 430; in Falaise 'pocket', 442

Air Mastery, Allied: vital for 'Overlord', 93-5; German commanders' views on, 110, 120, 375, 423, 426, 444; reviewed, 490

Air Reconnaissance:
Allied: pre-D-day, 104-6, 130; in assault and lodgement, 211, 234, 251, 287, 306; in 'Goodwood', 338; in 'Cobra', 382; in Falaise 'pocket', 442
German: failure of, 130, 212, 307, 489

Air Supply and Transport: to Resistance, 123, 288, Appendix IX; on D-day, 205, 221; in August, 473; evacuation of wounded, 483

Ajax, H.M.S.: 163, 231

Albatross: 417

Alençon: in Allied plans, 81, 303, 308, 405; air attacks on, 235; U.S. Third Army directed on, 425-7; Germans at, 426, 431; captured, 428

Alert, buoy-layer: 245

Alexander, General the Hon. Sir Harold: 18, 126, 496

Algiers: 123, 125

Allied Expeditionary Air Force (A.E.A.F.): command and organisation, 73-5, Appendix VI; pre-D-day operations, 94, 96; and 'Transportation Plan', 97, 101; 'Crossbow' operations, 106; June operations summarised, 109. *See also* Royal Air Force *and* United States Army Air Force

Amaye sur Orne: and XII Corps, 331, 334, 337, 408

Amaye sur Seulles: and XXX Corps, 255, 388, 392, 402

Amfreville: 248

Amiens: in Allied plans, 82, 450, 462, 475; Second Army directed on, 465, 468; captured, 470

Amphibious Vehicles: in assault, 165, 169, 174, 181, 191; at Cherbourg, 292

Amphibious Warfare: *see* Combined Operations

Anchorage, defence of: plans for, 71; during 'Neptune', 221, 240

Ancon, U.S.S.: 145

Andrews, Lieut-General F. M.: 15

Anglo-American Co-operation: in planning, 3-6, 9, 20, 29, 85; in command, 30-2, 37-40, 492, 494

Antwerp: Allied armies directed on, 450, 459, 462, 464, 475

'Anvil' operation: planning for, 18, 24; Anglo-American arguments over, 36, 293, 434-6; launched, 431, 437. *See also* 'Dragoon'

'Arcadia' Conference (Washington): 3-6

Ardennes, The: 82, 444n, 459-61

Arethusa, H.M.S.: 162, 227, 248, 271

Argentan: in Allied plans, 81, 351, 377, 407, 450; air attacks on, 234, 307; U.S. Third Army directed on, 427; Germans at, 428, 433, 439, 450; railway re-opened to, 473

Argonaut, H.M.S.: 163, 210

Armies: *see* British and Canadian, German, United States Armies

Arnold, Lieut-General H. H.: 5

Arromanches: in the assault, 175, 199, 209; 'Mulberry' harbour at, 90, 263, 273, 301, 479

Artificial Harbours: origins and plans, 87-90; construction, 263, 272, 301; storm damage to, 272, 301; assessed, 479

Ashanti, H.M.S.: 241

Asnelles sur Mer: in the assault, 171, 175, 201, 211

Assault Shipping: *see* Landing Craft

Assembly and Briefing: of shipping and units, 135-7, 144

Atlantic, Battle of: 9, 60

579

Atlantic Charter: 3
Atlantic Wall: construction of, 52–5; air attacks on, 102, 159; arguments over, 118–120; failure of, 194, 213, 223, 268
Audrieu: 231, 252
Aunay sur Odon: Bomber Command on, 256; 334, 393, 402; captured, 409
Aure R.: 210, 254, 261
Authie: Canadians at, 229, 314
Avranches: 234, 238, 327; captured, 383; Germans fail to recapture, 405–7, 412–15, 423, 425
Avres: see Tanks
Azalea, H.M.S.: 133

Baie de la Seine: described, 78; 199
Banneville la Campagne: in 'Goodwood', 337, 343, 346
Barker, Major-General R. W.: 10
Baron: and 'Epsom' operation, 281–5; and Hitler's counter-attack orders, 319, 325
Barton, Sergeant J. H.: 113
Base in Normandy: plans for, 85–7; established, 303; development, 473, 481
Basset ('Marie'): 122
Bates, Corporal S.: 410n
Bavent Woods: in British airborne assault, 152, 205; 343
Bayerlein, Lieut-General F.: 234, 382
Bayeux: in Allied plans, 86, 171; and the assault, 209–12, 225; captured, 231, 265; de Gaulle visits, 280 (photograph) and Appendix VIII
Bayfield, U.S.S.: 145
Bazalgette, Squadron Leader I. W.: 410n
Beaches and Assault Areas: suitable for landings and build-up, 115
  'Band': 66
  'Gold': in plans, 66, 79, 143; 'Mulberry' at, 88; in assault, 163, 170 et seq., 209; beach obstacles at, 217
  'Jig': 171–5
  'Juno': in plans, 66, 79, 143; in assault, 164, 170, 173, 178 et seq.; mentioned, 141, 160, 263, 271
  'King': 176–8
  'Mike': 178–82
  'Nan': 182
  'Omaha': in plans, 66, 78; 'Mulberry' at, 88, 263, 273, 301; operations at, 165–8, 187, 190–3, 213–15, 232, 235; 'Tombola' pipelines at, 303
  'Queen': 184–7
  'Sword': in plans, 66, 79, 143; in assault, 164, 170, 183 et seq.; mentioned, 141, 160, 273, 293
  'Utah': in plans, 66, 79, 138; operations at, 165–8, 187–90, 215, 232; storm damage at, 273
Beach Organisation: plans, 64, 66; in the assault, 177, 194, 217–19; post D-day, 303
Beauvais: German airfields at, 444, 455, 472; captured, 469
Beck, General L.: 363–6, 370
Belfast, H.M.S.: 176, 311, 314
Belgian Armed Forces: 1st Belgian Infantry Brigade, 448n

Belgium: Resistance in, 51, Appendix IX; Allied bombing of, 100–3, 111, 279, 472; airfields in, 459–63, 475; Second Army directed on, 465, 468; and Civil Affairs, Appendix VIII
Bénerville: German batteries, 162, 293
Bénouville: 150, 200, 203; and 'Goodwood', 338
Bény sur Mer: 208
Berchtesgaden: 296, 319, 365, 368
Berlin: 82; Bomber Command on, 95, 399
Bernières sur Mer: 179, 182, 206–8
Beuville: 202–4
Biéville: 202–4
'Big Week' bomber operation: 94
Biscay, Bay of: U-boats in, 107, 199, 240, 290, 471
Blackwood, H.M.S.: 242
Blaskowitz, Colonel-General J.: 120
Blumentritt, General G.: 268, 361; and Hitler plot, 370, 372
Boadicea, H.M.S.: 244
Bocage: described, 78, 276, 387
'Bodyguard' (deception): 103
Bois du Homme: 392, 402, 411
'Bolero' build-up: 9, 17, 85
Borgmann, Lieut-Colonel: 321
Boulogne: Allied minelaying off, 108; E-boats at, 240, 290; bombed, 243
Bourgébus: in 'Goodwood' plan, 331, 335, 337, 348; fighting at, 341, 346, 349, 378
Bourne, General A. G. B.: 11
Bradley, Lieut-General Omar N.: to command U.S. First Army Group, 65, 78; advocates airborne landings in Cotentin, 138; consults with Montgomery, 225, 327, 403, 427, 449, 459; aims to cut Cotentin, 257; directs U.S. First Army on St. Lô, 318; directs U.S. VIII Corps on Coutances, 327; orders 'Cobra', 330, 377; on Montgomery's policy, 357; commands U.S. Twelfth Army Group, 377, 402; Letters of Instruction—Nos. 1 and 2, 403, No. 6, 464; directs U.S. XV Corps northwards on Alençon, 425; halts XV Corps, 428; directs XV Corps to the Seine, 449; his generalship, 492; on Montgomery, 494
Bras: in 'Goodwood', 342, 344–9
Brauchitsch, Field-Marshal W. von: 52
Breakwaters: see Artificial Harbours
Brécy: 211, 230
Bremen: bombed, 399, 473
Brereton, Major-General L. H.: 75, 402n
Brest: U-boats at, 59, 70, 121, 241, 289, 471; Allied minelaying off, 108; German fears for, 128; German destroyers at, 240; and U.S. Third Army, 403, 412, 474n
Bretteville l'Orgueilleuse: 209, 229
Bretteville sur Laize: in 'Epsom' plan, 271, 276; in 'Goodwood', 331, 351; 378; in 'Totalize', 419, 422, 427
Breuil: 393, 402
Bréville: and British airborne bridgehead, 205, 248
Brewer, Sergeant J. V.: 113
Bridging: in assault, 116, 169, 182; in river crossings, 226, 344, 454, 467. See also Appendix IV, Part IV

INDEX

BRITISH AND CANADIAN ARMY:
Total allotted for 'Overlord' campaign, 28; numbers landed on D-day, 223; and by 30 June, 294, 308; and by 31 August, 478; total casualties by 31 August, 493; morale, 131, 159

Forces Engaged: see also Appendix IV

Twenty-First Army Group: command, 31, 40, 460; composition, 65, 79, 116n, 132, 482; to become Northern Group of Armies, 83; and 'Transportation Plan', 97; and air support, 103, 170, 279, 443; location of H.Q., 139, 304, 403; and manpower situation, 308; in break-out to Seine, 386, 403-7, 427, 449-52; bridging Seine, 454; beyond Seine, 459-68, 475 (Northern Group); administration, 473; achievements reviewed, 491-4

Northern Group of Armies: *see* Twenty-First Army Group

British Second Army: in invasion plans, 64, 77-81; in assault, 168-70, 197, 217, 265; and air support, 256, 281, 403, 422; drawing main enemy effort, 260, 309; and administration, 264, 303, 473; in expansion of lodgement area, 271, 299, 315; build-up, 274; in 'Goodwood', 327-37, 352; in break-out to Seine, 377-408, 425-50; beyond Seine, 465-72

First Canadian Army: in invasion plans, 77-81; H.Q. operational, 304, 377; in attack on Falaise, 407, 419, 429-31; directed on Trun, 439; Seine, 452-68

Corps:
I: 79; in assault, 170-212; 228-86; at Caen, 310-16; in 'Goodwood', 333-48; 377-86, 420-68 *passim*
VIII: 79; in 'Epsom', 271-96; 310-15; in 'Goodwood', 328-48; 386-452 *passim*
XII: 79; in 'Goodwood', 331-49; 387, 408-70 *passim*
XXX: 79, 132n; in assault, 170-212; 230-65; in 'Epsom', 271-87; in 'Goodwood', 333-49; 387-471 *passim*
II Canadian: in 'Goodwood', 331-50; 377-386; in 'Totalize'/'Tractable', 420-432; at Falaise 'pocket', 441-8; 452-68

Armoured Divisions:
Guards: 281, 311; in 'Goodwood', 333-52; 378-401, 466-70
7th: 79, 132n, 219, 247-64; in 'Goodwood', 333-49; 378-410, 432-70
11th: in 'Epsom', 275-85; in 'Goodwood', 333-52; 388-401, 445n-70
79th: 116n, 309-11, 389, 421, 430
4th Canadian: in 'Totalize'/'Tractable', 420-32;'at Falaise 'pocket', 441-8; 467
1st Polish: in 'Totalize'/'Tractable', 420-32; at Falaise 'pocket', 441-8

Infantry Divisions:
3rd: 79, 154; in assault, 170-206; 227, 286; at Caen, 309-15; in 'Goodwood', 333-46; 402-10
15th: in 'Epsom', 275-85, 334, 388-410, 453-67
43rd: in 'Epsom', 275-85; 309-18, 388-410, 453-67

49th: 79, 261-4; in 'Epsom', 276-85; 333-348, 425, 449
50th: 79, 132n; in assault, 170-212; 230-261, 334, 388-409, 455-70
51st: 79, 132n, 247-50, 274, 343; in 'Totalize', 420-5; 430, 443, 449, 471
53rd: 334, 408, 440n, 470
59th: at Caen, 309-15; 334, 408, 445n-53
2nd Canadian: in 'Goodwood', 333-50; 379; in 'Totalize'/'Tractable', 420-432, 455-68
3rd Canadian: 79; in assault, 170-218; 228, 252; at Caen, 311-17; in 'Goodwood', 333-47; 378; in 'Totalize'/'Tractable', 420-32; 447, 467

Airborne Divisions:
1st: 132n, 247
6th: 79; in assault, 138, 149-58, 200-16; 265, 448-53

Armoured Brigades:
4th: 132n, 228, 247, 265-83, 317, 348, 467-70
5th Guards: 394
6th Guards: 390-4, 402
8th: 132n, 230, 250, 277, 389, 466-9
22nd: 251-4
27th: 311, 343
29th: 278-85, 338-42, 389-92, 468
31st Tank: 275-80, 317
33rd: 255-64, 314, 348, 420-5
34th Tank: 408
2nd Canadian: 252, 311, 333-43, 378, 420

Infantry Brigades:
8th: 184-206
9th: 184-206, 228
32nd Guards: 281-6, 309, 342-9, 394
44th: 277, 402
46th: 277, 317, 391
56th: 178, 209, 231, 252-4, 388, 408
69th: 171-8, 209-11, 230, 250-3
70th: 277
129th: 309, 409
130th: 389, 409
131st: 254
146th: 277
147th: 277
151st: 178, 209-11, 231, 255
152nd: 250, 274, 343
153rd: 219, 247-50
159th: 280-6, 338-40, 389-91
185th: 184-206, 228, 402
214th: 309, 317, 410
227th: 278-80, 389
231st: 171-5, 209, 230, 255, 388
3rd Parachute: 149-55, 226, 248
5th Parachute: 149-52, 226
6th Airlanding: 227
1st Special Service: 187-205, 226, 448
4th Special Service: 183, 448
4th Canadian: 344-9
5th Canadian: 344
6th Canadian: 349
7th Canadian: 179-218, 229-35, 344
8th Canadian: 179-218, 309, 343
9th Canadian: 183-208, 229, 344
1st Belgian: 448n
Royal Netherlands: 448n
1st Polish Parachute: 138

British Armoured and Infantry Regiments:
  2nd Bn. Argyll and Sutherland Highlanders: 280–4
  5th Bn. Black Watch: 248
  6th Bn. Border Regt.: 218
  5th Bn. Cameron Highlanders: 275
  1st (Armoured) Bn. Coldstream Guards: 341
  Commandos: No. 3, 205; No. 4, 186; No. 6, 205; No. 10 Inter-Allied, 186. *See also under* Royal Marines
  County of London Yeomanry: 2nd (Westminster Dragoons), 175–7, 202; 4th (Sharpshooters), 254
  2nd Bn. Devonshire Regt.: 175
  1st Bn. Dorsetshire Regt.: 171–5, 230
  22nd Dragoons: 182
  Durham Light Infantry: 6th Bn., 210; 8th Bn., 230; 9th Bn., 210; 18th Bn., 218
  5th Bn. Duke of Cornwall's Light Infantry: 317
  1st East Riding Yeomanry: 228
  East Yorkshire Regiment: 2nd Bn., 186, 201–6; 5th Bn., 169–76
  2nd Bn. Essex Regt.: 210, 252
  2nd Fife and Forfar Yeomanry: 340
  2nd Bn. Glasgow Highlanders: 278
  Glider Pilot Regiment: 156
  2nd Bn. Gloucestershire Regt.: 210
  Green Howards: 6th Bn., 176, 252; 7th Bn., 176
  Grenadier Guards: 2nd (Armoured) Bn., 341; 4th Tank Bn., 390
  1st Bn. Hampshire Regt.: 171–5
  2nd Bn. Hertfordshire Regt.: 218
  2nd Household Cavalry Regt.: 394
  8th Hussars: 254
  11th Hussars: 254
  13th/18th Hussars: 184, 202, 249, 275, 409
  23rd Hussars: 280, 340
  2nd (Armoured) Bn. Irish Guards: 343
  King's Regt.: 5th Bn., 218; 8th Bn., 218
  2nd Bn. King's Shropshire Light Infantry: 202–4
  1st Bn. King's Own Scottish Borderers: 228
  24th Lancers: 217, 230
  2nd Northamptonshire Yeomanry: 342
  Nottinghamshire Yeomanry: 177, 230
  Oxfordshire and Buckinghamshire Light Infantry: 2nd Bn., 150, 200–5, 227; 1st Buckinghamshire Bn., 218
  Parachute Regt.: 7th Bn., 151, 200, 205; 8th Bn., 152, 206; 9th Bn., 152–5, 249; 12th Bn., 151, 200, 249; 13th Bn., 151, 200; Independent Coy., 249
  Queen's Royal Regt.: 1/5th Bn., 254; 1/7th Bn., 254
  Reconnaissance Regts. R.A.C.: 43rd, 275n; 61st, 230
  Rifle Brigade: 1st Bn., 254; 8th Bn., 282–4, 340
  5th Bn. Royal Berkshire Regt.: 218
  4th/7th Royal Dragoon Guards: 177, 210, 230, 252
  1st Bn. Royal Norfolk Regt.: 203, 228, 409–410n
  Royal Tank Regt.: 3rd Bn., 282, 340; 5th Bn., 254, 343; 7th Bn., 317
  Royal Ulster Rifles: 1st Bn., 205, 227; 2nd Bn., 206, 228
  2nd Bn. Royal Warwickshire Regt.: 202–5, 228
  5th Bn. Seaforth Highlanders: 275
  1st Bn. South Lancashire Regt.: 186, 201
  2nd Bn. South Wales Borderers: 210
  Staffordshire Yeomanry: 202–4
  1st Bn. Suffolk Regt.: 187, 201–6
  1/5th Bn. Welch Regt.: 440n
  2nd Armoured Reconnaissance Bn. Welsh Guards: 341
Canadian Armoured and Infantry Regiments:
  6th Armoured Regt. (1st Hussars): 181–209, 253
  10th Armoured Regt. (Fort Garry Horse): 182, 208
  27th Armoured Regt. (Sherbrook Fusiliers Regt.): 183, 208, 229
  29th Reconnaissance Regt. (South Alberta Regt.): 447n
  1st Bn. Canadian Scottish Regt.: 181, 207, 230
  Essex Scottish Regt.: 349
  North Nova Scotia Highlanders: 208, 229
  North Shore (New Brunswick) Regt.: 182, 208
  1st Parachute Bn.: 152–5, 249
  Queen's Own Cameron Highlanders of Canada: 349
  Queen's Own Rifles of Canada: 182, 208, 253
  Régiment de la Chaudière: 208
  Regina Rifle Regt.: 181, 207, 229
  Royal Winnipeg Rifles: 181, 207, 229
  South Saskatchewan Regt.: 349
Royal Artillery:
  A.G.R.A.s: 3rd, 311, 317; 4th, 311; 8th, 317
  4th Airlanding Anti-Tank Bty.: 152
  20th Anti-Tank Regt.: 203
  Field Regts.: 7th, 185, 202; 33rd, 185; 76th, 185; 86th, 177; 90th, 177, 210; 147th, 177, 209
  F.O.B. (Forward Officer Bombardment): 164, 248
Royal Canadian Artillery:
  12th, 13th, 14th and 19th Field Regts.: 183
Royal Engineers: 481
  Airfield Construction Groups: 77, 481
  Air Survey Liaison Section: 137
  Army Postal Service: 484
  Assault Regts.: 5th, 202; 6th, 177
  Assault Sqns.: 26th, 181; 79th, 202
  A.V.R.E.s: 169–82, 340, 421, 481
  Field Coys.: 17th, 205; 71st, 205; 249th, 150
  286th Field Park Coy.: 151
  Parachute Sqns.: 3rd, 152; 591st, 151
Royal Corps of Signals: 482
Royal Army Service Corps: 482
  106th Bridging Coy.: 205
Royal Army Medical Corps: 483
Royal Army Ordnance Corps: 482
Royal Electrical and Mechanical Engineers: 482
Pioneer Corps: 482
Lines of Communication H.Q.s:
  11 L. of C. Area: 303

INDEX

4 L. of C. Sub-Area: 264, 303
101, 102 and 104 Beach Sub-Areas: 218, 303

British Broadcasting Corporation (B.B.C.): 51, 198
British Expeditionary Force (B.E.F.): withdrawn from France, 1, 11; command arrangements, 37-9
Brittany: in Allied plans, 63, 78, 81, 87, 328, 331; German fears for, 128; and U.S. Third Army, 403, 412, 464; state of ports in, 474
Broad, Group Captain H. P.: 83
Broadhurst, Air Vice-Marshal H.: 304, 403, 414
Bronay: 230, 252, 276; petrol storage at, 481
Brooke, Field-Marshal Sir Alan, C.I.G.S.: in touch with Montgomery, 267, 328, 344, 415, 459, 463
Brown, Air Vice-Marshal L. O.: 403
Brunswick: bombed, 96, 473
Brussels: in future plans, 450, 459, 465
Bucknall, Lieut-General G. C.: commands XXX Corps, 171, 212, 253; relinquishes command, 402
Build-up in Normandy: organisation for (BUCO), 90; behind schedule at first, 217-219, 239, 263-5; effect of storm on, 274; recovery, 302-4; position at 31 August, 478 et seq.
Bulolo, H.M.S.: 163, 212, 244
Bures: 152, 155, 336
Buron: Canadian attacks at, 229, 314
Buttlar, Major-General H. von: 117

Cabourg les Bains: 63, 299; and I Corps, 439, 448
Caen: in Allied plans, 15, 78, 138, 228; Allies aim to capture on D-day, 171, 184; D-day advance on, 202-4; not captured on D-day, 212, 491; bombed, 212, 313; out-flanking moves on, 247; not captured by 16 June, 265; and 'Epsom' attack, 271, 276 et seq.; Germans concentrate defence of, 296, 308, 311, 348; direct British attack, 309-16; Germans disagree about Caen flank, 320 et seq.; 'Goodwood' plans to push southeast from, 327 et seq., 336; Canadians cross Orne at, 344; railway through re-opened, 473
Caen Canal: airborne assault on bridges, 150 et seq., 200; Bailey bridges built, 205
Cagny: I Corps directed on, 247; in 'Goodwood', 337-52 *passim*
Cahagnes: 388-90, 392
Cairo Conference ('Sextant'): 21-4, 32, 36
Calais: 106, 108, 461
Cambes: and I Corps, 205, 228, 311
Canadian Army: *see* British and Canadian Army
Carentan: and U.S. airborne landings, 156, 210, 215; not captured on D-day, 225; 232, 235; Germans reinforce, 238; Americans capture, 247, 257, 262
Carpiquet: and the I Corps assault, 171, 208, 229; 276; airfield bombed during 'Epsom', 280, 284; attack and capture by I Corps, 283, 309, 316

Carrouges: 427-9
Casablanca Conference ('Symbol'): 9, 19, 21, 41
Casualties: in U.K. from air raids and flying bombs, 29, 266; War Cabinet fears for civilians in Europe, 100
Battle Casualties
Allied: in bombing of Nuremberg, 95; in pre-D-day air operations, 95, 112; on D-day, 156, 186, 214, 222; total to end of June, 307; in I Corps at Caen, 316; in 'Goodwood', 334, 343, 345; total for air forces, 488; total for armies, 493
German: to end of June, 308n; at Caen, 316; to 16 July, 323; in 'Cobra', 382; in Falaise 'pocket', 447
Caumont: captured by U.S. First Army, 247, 253, 257; 377, 379, 381, 384; Second Army launch attack from, 386 et seq.
Chambois: Allied armies directed on, 439, 441; captured, 445, 447; destruction in area around, 472
Chartres: German divisions near, 128, 198, 236, 427; bombed, 279; airborne attack planned, 407; U.S. Third Army directed to, 429, 433, 440; railway through re-opened, 473
Cherbourg: plans to capture, 15-17, 32, 63, 78, 87, 225, 247, 271; German naval forces at, 70, 199, 240, 242, 290; minelaying off, 108; coastal defences at, 115; German fears for, 128, 237, 258, 262; captured, 288-91; clearance of harbour, 291; Hitler's order to recapture, 295
Chérence le Roussel: 412, 415
Cheux: in 'Epsom', 276, 278, 280, 283
Chiang Kai-shek, General: 21
Chief of the Imperial General Staff (C.I.G.S.): *see* Brooke, Field-Marshal Sir Alan
Chiefs of Staff:
British: responsibilities, 4; membership, 5, 11; and Cossac plan, 17; on overall strategy for Europe, 18; and assault craft, 34; on 'Anvil', 36, 293, 434-6
American: membership, 5; and Cossac plan, 17; on strategy for Europe, 18; and assault craft, 34; on 'Anvil', 36, 434-6
Combined: institution of, 4; and Cossac plan, 16-19; successful working of, 20; and postponement of 'Overlord', 36; directive to Supreme Allied Commander, 39
Choltitz, General D. von: and defence of Paris, 444, 452n, 456-8
Churchill, Rt. Hon. W. S.: meets President Roosevelt, 3, 17, 21; constitutional position, 4; institutes Combined Operations Headquarters, 11; on landing craft shortage, 14; urges stronger invasion force, 17, 33; on 'Anvil', 37, 293, 434-6; urges use of artificial harbours, 87; fears for French civilian air raid casualties, 100; visits France, 358
Civil Affairs: 126, 458, Appendix VIII
Clair Tizon: 427, 431
Coastal Defences, Enemy: described, 27; Atlantic Wall concept, 52-5; strengthened by Rommel, 58, 118; air attacks on, 102, 153, 158, 166, 170, 174; beach obstacles, 115; German arguments over, 118-20; at

INDEX

Coastal Defences, Enemy—*cont.*
  Merville, 154; naval bombardment of, 161-8, 187, 448; on D-day in British sector, 174-85 *passim*; in U.S. sector, 187-93; failure of, 194, 223, 268
'Cobra' operation: plans, 330, 348, 377; delays, 332, 351, 354; launched, 379 *et seq.*
Cocks, Lieut-Colonel A. D. B.: 185
Colleville: in 'Epsom', 278, 280, 282
Colleville sur Mer: in 'Omaha' assault, 192, 199, 214
Colleville sur Orne: in I Corps assault, 201, 203
Collins, Lieut-General J. L.: 381, 415
Cologne: bombed, 23, 399; 459
Colombelles: 201; in 'Goodwood', 337, 341, 343
Combined Bomber Offensive: *see* Strategic Bombing
Combined Commanders: 14-16
Combined Operations Headquarters: 11-13, 132, 477
Combined Staff Planners: 7
Command Arrangements:
  Allied: Combined Chiefs of Staff, 4; Cossac, 10; Combined Commanders, 14; Eisenhower appointed Supreme Allied Commander, 24; Overlord appointments, 30-2; Shaef organisation, 37-9; chain of command, 39; control of strategic air forces, 40-3; command of land forces, 40, 65, 304, 377; naval command, 67, 293, 299; air command, 73-5; reorganisation of land and air commands 1 August, 402; Montgomery and Eisenhower differ on future policy, 460-4; Eisenhower assumes direct command, 476
  German: army command in West, 53, 56, 117-21; air command, 58, 490; naval command, 59, 120; Hitler's close control, 249; von Rundstedt superseded, 321-5; von Kluge dismissed, 434
Commandos: *see* British and Canadian Army, Royal Marines
Communications: arrangements in assault, 77; air/ground links, 338, 382; signals organisation, 482. *See also* Appendix IV
Condé sur Noireau: 395, 409, 425, 432
Conferences: Cairo, 21-4, 32, 36; Casablanca, 9, 19, 21, 41; Quebec, 17, 434; Teheran, 21, 36; Washington 1941, 3-6; Washington 1943, 10
Coningham, Air Marshal Sir Arthur: 73-5, 328, 402
Convoys: cross-Channel, 90
Cormelles: 331, 336, 347
Corry, U.S.S.: 188, 215
Cossac: set up, 10; plans, 14-17, 25, 33, 77, 138; Eisenhower praises, 25; absorbed into Shaef, 37; views on Resistance, 52. *See also* Morgan, Lieut-General F. E.
Contentin Peninsula: included in assault area, 15, 33; described, 78; airborne landings in, 138, 156-8, 200; coastal defences of, 160, 166; D-day assault on, 187-90, 198-201, 215; minefield off, 188, 245; operations after D-day, 232, 237, 258-62, 288, 403
Coudehard: 442, 445

Coulombs: 211, 230; petrol supply point, 481
Courbet, F.F.S.: 417
Courseulles: and the initial assault, 78, 115, 170, 178-82, 206; harbour opened, 263, 479
Coutances: an American objective, 318, 327, 330; captured, 381-3
Cover Plans: *see* Deception
Crerar, Lieut-General H. D. G.: commands First Canadian Army, 304, 377, 432, 470, 492; on bombing of own troops, 443
Creully: on D-day, 207, 209, 211; 304
Cristot: 252, 261
Crocker, Lieut-General J. T.: commands I Corps, 171, 212, 314, 432
'Crossbow' operations: 106. *See also* V-Weapons
Cruikshank, Flying Officer J. A.: 300n
Cunningham, Admiral of the Fleet Sir Andrew: 5, 271
Currie, Major D. V.: 447n
Cussy: in Caen operations, 311, 315
Cuverville: 250; in 'Goodwood', 337, 340, 352

'Daimler' battery position: 203, 206
Danae, H.M.S.: 162
Darlan, Admiral J. F.: 46
'Dauntless' operation: 275
Dawnay, Lieut-Colonel C.: 329
D-day, choice of: provisional date, 91, 139; postponed, 141; decided, 143
Deception: early plans and measures, 10, 53, 83, 97; 'Fortitude' and 'Bodyguard', 103, 127-9, 323, 377n, 489; on D-day, 158-60
De Guingand, Major-General Sir Francis: 81, 267
Démouville: 250; in 'Goodwood', 337, 340-4
Dempsey, Lieut-General Sir Miles: commands Second Army, 78; on D-day, 203, 212; consultations with Montgomery, 225, 327, 403, 449; 253; and 'Epsom', 284; 304; and 'Goodwood', 328, 330, 336, 348, 354; 377, 379, 393, 452; his leadership, 493
Deyo, Admiral M. L.: 291
Diadem, H.M.S.: 208
Dieppe: lessons of the 1942 raid, 12, 28, 53; 'sabotage' in, 122; Canadians directed on, 465, 468, 470, 476
Dietrich, General Sepp: 426n, 451, 454, 470
Dill, Field-Marshal Sir John: 5, 20
Dives R.: airborne assault at, 149, 152 *et seq.*; 225, 265, 293; air attacks, 338; Germans forced across, 431, 439-41, 446
Dollmann, General F.: 236, 296
Domfront: 103; and the American envelopment, 403, 425, 433
Dönitz, Admiral K.: 60, 268, 289, 297
Douglas, Air Marshal Sir Sholto: 14
Douglas-Pennant, Commodore C. E.: 164, 293
Dozule: 448
Dragon, O.R.P.: 162, 301
'Dragoon' operation: 436, 461. *See also* 'Anvil'
Dreux: 279, 407; and the American envelopment, 429-49 *passim*
Drome R.: 209, 231
Duisburg: 23, 111
Dukws: 191, 292
Dunkirk: 1940 evacuation from, 11, 32, 193

INDEX

Durban, H.M.S.: 416
Düsseldorf: 23, 96
Dutch Armed Forces: Royal Netherlands Brigade (Princess Irene's), 448n

Eaker, Lieut-General I. C.: 23
Eberbach, General H.: on defence tactics, 318, 325; commands Panzer Group West, 322; in 'Goodwood', 336, 345–7; 361, 378; and Caumont–Vire sector, 395, 401, 409, 412; and Hitler's counter-attack orders, 426–8, 431; holds Argentan area, 440, 442, 446; takes over Seventh Army, 468; captured, 470
Ebert, President: 362
E-boats: dispositions, 240; anti-Neptune operations, 242–5, 290, 299
Edward III, King: in an earlier landing, 291n
Eire: 125
Eisenhower, General Dwight D.: 1, 15; appointed Supreme Allied Commander, 24; high reputation, 30; and plan for 'Overlord', 32 *et seq*.; his directive from C.C.S., 39, Appendix I; directive to his Commanders-in-Chief, 40; control of strategic air forces, 41–3, 73, 94, 96, 98–101, 485; on future strategy, 82, 460–4; on ground forces' command, 83; on air mastery, 112; 134; and U.S. airborne assault, 139; and fixing of D-day, 139–44; on 'Crossbow', 267; on damaged 'Mulberry' harbours, 301; consultations with Montgomery and Bradley in the field, 304, 425, 461–3, 494; and 'Goodwood', 328, 332, 353–8; urges speed in Caumont sector, 386; supports 'Anvil', 434–7; orders Allied troops to Paris, 456; directive of 29 August, 474–6; assumes direct command in France, 476
Elbeuf: and crossing of the Seine, 449, 452–5, 467
Embry, Air Vice-Marshal B. E.: 403
Emerald, H.M.S.: 209, 231, 311
Emiéville: and 'Goodwood', 336, 340–3, 346
Enterprise, H.M.S.: 339
Entertainments National Service Association (E.N.S.A.): 484
Epron: 311, 314
'Epsom' operation: 271, 274–86 *passim*
Erebus, H.M.S.: 448
Erskine, Major-General G. W. E. J.: 251, 255, 402
Escoville: and British airborne bridgehead, 152, 205, 227; 340
Esquay: 284, 286; XII Corps at, 334
Essen: 23, 96
Estry: 401, 410, 425
Eterville: 317, 336
'Eureka' Conference (Teheran): 21, 36
Evrecy: 247, 256, 261; and 'Goodwood', 329, 334; captured, 408
Evreux: 451, 454, 472

Falaise: in Allied plans, 81, 327, 329–31, 351; 225, 234, 307, 348; in Canadian attacks, 377–9, 407, 419 *et seq*.; captured, 432
Fame, H.M.S.: 242

PP*

Fellgiebel, General E.: 369
Feuchtinger, Major-General E.: 203
Fleet Air Arm: *see* Royal Navy *and* Appendix VI
Flers: 234, 395, 428, 432
Fleury sur Orne: 331, 336, 347
Flores, H.N.M.S.: 250
Flying Bombs: *see* V-Weapons
Fontaine-Henry: 207, 209
Fontenay le Marmion: II Canadian Corps at, 379, 421–3
Fontenay le Pesnel: XXX Corps at, 276
Forêt de Cerisy: 235, 256, 262
Forêt de la Londe: 455, 467
Forêt l'Evêque: 391, 394
'Fortitude' (deception): 103, 127, 323, 489
Fougères: 235, 309, 403
Four: 342, 346
France: German occupation and Vichy régime, 45–8; Free French movement and General de Gaulle, 49, 123–6; resistance and sabotage, 49–51, 121–4, 323, 412, 456; civilian casualties, 126; Civil Affairs, 126, 458. *See also* Appendices VIII and IX
Franceville Plage: 154, 197, 227
Frankfurt: 95, 399, 459
French Armed Forces:
 2nd French Armoured Division in England, 126; with U.S. Third Army, 428; enters Paris, 457
See also Appendices II, IV and VI
French Forces of the Interior (F.F.I.): 123, 469, 476
Frénouville: in 'Goodwood', 337, 343, 346, 349
Frobisher, H.M.S.: 162, 417
Fromm, Colonel-General F.: 364, 370–2
Funck, General H. von.: 406, 412

Gacé: 433, 440, 453, 472
Gale, Major-General R. N.: and the British airborne bridgehead, 152, 249
Galmanche: and battle for Caen, 229, 311, 313
Garcelles-Secqueville: in 'Goodwood', 335–51 *passim*; captured, 421
Gaulle, General Charles de: in 1940, 49; relations with Resistance, 49, 123, 456; relations with Allies, 50, 125–7; visits Normandy, 280 (photograph), Appendix VIII
Gaumesnil: in 'Totalize', 420, 423
Gavrus: in 'Epsom', 278, 282, 284–6; captured, 334
'Gee', bombing aid: 23
George VI, King: attends Shaef conference, 134; visits Normandy, 271

GERMAN AIR FORCE:
 command in West, 58; losses in Allied pre-D-day attacks, 110; losses in June, 306; operations reviewed, 400, 486, 490
Forces Engaged: *see also* Appendix VII
Reich Air Fleet: 110, 306, 486, 491
Third Air Fleet: pre-D-day effectiveness, 58, 110, 121, 130; reactions on D-day, 193, 198, 212; post-D-day action, 233, 244, 262, 306, 443, 455, 472; H.Q. withdraws east, 472; 486, 491
III Flak Corps: *see* German Army

GERMAN ARMY:
High Command of the Armed Forces (OKW): and the Atlantic Wall, 52; controls reserves, 117–20, 198; D-day reactions, 200, 216; and Hitler, 362, 370; contemplates withdrawal, 375, 395, 398, 406; and Mortain counter-attack, 412
Headquarters of the German Army (OKH): 118
Army in the West:
command, 53–7, 117–21; pre-D-day strength, 3, 41, 53–9, 117; forces facing allied assault, 197; operations reviewed, 488–90
Forces Engaged: see also Appendix V
Commander-in-Chief West H.Q. (OB West): von Rundstedt in command, 56, 117–20; Normandy reinforced, 128; initial D-day reaction, 199; armoured reserves ordered to move, 200; and situation 10 June, 258; and expected second landing, 258, 323, 398, 489; von Kluge relieves von Rundstedt, 321; and Mortain counter-attack, 412; Model relieves von Kluge, 434; Model's first orders, 444; and Paris, 450, 457
Army Group B: Rommel in command, 56, 118–20; and likelihood of invasion, 129; initial D-day reaction, 198; reserves move up, 237; von Kluge takes command, 361; and Mortain counter-attack, 412–14; Model in command, 434; 449, 457
Army Group G: 120, 433
First Army: to Army Group G, 120; on Loire, 404; in defence of Paris, 440, 451, 457, 468
Seventh Army: in Army Group B, 56, 118; D-day dispositions and reactions, 197–200, 204; command, 238; situation 10 June, 258; Hausser assumes command, 323; Americans outflank, 383–5; reinforced, 395; British attack threatens, 401; and Mortain, 405, 412–15; withdrawal and Falaise 'pocket', 426, 428, 439, 444–6; at Seine, 451, 454; 468
Fifteenth Army: in Army Group B, 56, 118; D-day dispositions and reactions, 197–200; and defence east of Orne, 227; and expected second landing, 258, 322, 398, 489; 459, 468
Nineteenth Army: to Army Group G, 120; withdrawal from southern France, 433, 451
Panzer Group West: operational, 238; H.Q. destroyed, 258; at Carpiquet, 310; Eberbach assumes command, 322; new directive, 325; in 'Goodwood', 332 *et seq.*; and front east of Vire, 401, 405–9; renamed, 412
Fifth Panzer Army: succeeds Panzer Group West, 412; and 'Totalize', 423; command, 426n; withdrawal and Falaise 'pocket', 426, 439, 444–6; at Seine, 451, 454, 467; 459, 468
Netherlands Command: 56
Corps:
I SS Pz: on D-day, 216; against bridgehead, 230, 236, 238, 258; in 'Epsom', 279, 284; 310; at Caen, 315, 320; in 'Goodwood', 333, 347; in 'Totalize'/'Tractable', 420, 431; at Falaise 'pocket', 441
II SS Pz: to Normandy, 259; in 'Epsom', 279, 282–5; at Caen, 311, 315, 320; 318; in 'Goodwood', 333, 349; in Vire sector, 395, 401, 405, 411; at Falaise 'pocket', 444–7
XLVII Pz: to Normandy, 262; and 'Cobra', 384, 404; at Mortain, 406, 412, 414; in withdrawal and Falaise 'pocket', 428, 440–4
LXXIV: to Normandy, 385; 392, 395, 431
LXXXI: on D-day, 197; 227; at Mortain, 406; in 'Totalize'/'Tractable', 432; 440, 454
LXXXIV: H.Q. attacked from air, 170; on D-day, 197–201; command, 237; in 'Cobra', 384, 404
LXXXVI: to Normandy, 274; at Caen, 315; in 'Goodwood', 333, 341; 431, 449
II Parachute: delayed in reaching Cotentin, 237, 262; strengthened, 274; in Vire sector, 392, 395, 404; in Falaise 'pocket', 446
III Flak: control of, 120; against bridgehead, 265; in 'Epsom', 277; at Caen, 311; in 'Goodwood', 332; in 'Totalize'/'Tractable', 420, 431
Armoured Divisions:
1st SS Pz: 119, 237, 261; arrival delayed by air attacks, 279; in 'Epsom', 282; at Caen, 311, 316; 318, 320; in 'Goodwood', 332–49; 378; at Mortain, 406, 412–15; 426, 440n
2nd SS Pz: 237, 262; in 'Epsom', 282, 286; 319; and 'Cobra', 384; at Mortain, 406, 413; 440n
9th SS Pz: 259; in 'Epsom', 282–6; 333, 378; in Vire sector, 395, 410–12; 440
10th SS Pz: 259; in 'Epsom', 282–6; 318, 333, 378; in Vire sector, 395, 402, 410–12; 440n
12th SS Pz: D-day position, 119, 198; arrival delayed, 200, 206, 216, 225, 236; against bridgehead, 229, 261; in 'Epsom', 276–80, 286; at Caen, 309–20; in 'Goodwood', 333, 336–8, 346–9; 408; in 'Totalize'/'Tractable', 420, 423, 431; 439n
2nd Pz: D-day position, 119, 225; against bridgehead, 237, 254, 261, 274; in 'Epsom', 279–82; in 'Goodwood', 333, 349; 378; in Vire sector, 384, 389; at Mortain, 406, 412, 415; 426, 440n
9th Pz: 385; not at Mortain, 406, 412; 428, 440n
21st Pz: 119, 128; on D-day, 198–208, 213, 216, 236; against bridgehead, 227, 250, 261, 275; in 'Epsom', 276–81; at Caen, 311, 320; in 'Goodwood', 333–47; in Vire sector, 392–5, 401, 412; 439n, 441
116th Pz: 119, 346, 348, 354, 378, 384; at Mortain, 406, 412–15; 426, 428, 440n
Pz Lehr: D-day position, 119, 128, 198, 200, 206, 216, 225, 236; against bridgehead, 231, 234, 253; in 'Epsom', 276–9; 319, 327, 354; in 'Cobra', 382–4
Infantry Divisions:
17th SS Pz Grenadier: 225, 237; at Carentan, 262, 319; in 'Cobra', 385; at Mortain, 406; 440n
77th: 216, 237; in 'Cobra', 385

84th: 395, 406, 412, 440n
85th: in 'Totalize'/'Tractable', 424, 431; 439n
89th: 395, 420; in 'Totalize', 423; 439n
91st Airlanding: on D-day, 128, 199, 215; in 'Cobra', 385
243rd: in 'Cobra', 385; 440n
265th: 216, 262; in 'Cobra', 385
266th: 216, 274
271st: 333, 354, 408; in 'Totalize', 427; 439n
272nd: in 'Goodwood', 333–49; 354
275th: 216, 234, 262; in 'Cobra', 383–5; 440n
276th: 319, 333, 389, 409, 439n
277th: 334, 439n
326th: 333, 378, 392, 402, 409, 439n
331st: 440n
344th: 440n
346th: 216, 227, 248, 260; in 'Goodwood', 333–6, 343; 439n
352nd: on D-day, 197, 201, 210–14; 232, 238, 253; in 'Cobra', 384
353rd: 262, 274; in 'Cobra', 385; 440n
363rd: 406, 440n
708th: 406n, 412, 428
709th: on D-day, 199
711th: on D-day, 198, 200, 216, 227; in 'Goodwood', 333, 343
716th: on D-day, 151, 197–201, 207, 216, 227; 238
16th G.A.F.: at Caen, 311, 316; in 'Goodwood', 333–6, 343–7
17th G.A.F.: 440n, 467
3rd Parachute: 237, 274, 440n; in Falaise 'pocket', 446
5th Parachute: 354; in 'Cobra', 383–5
6th Parachute: 440n
Brigades:
7th Werfer: 260, 265, 311, 333
8th Werfer: 237, 279, 333, 395, 440n
9th Werfer: 333, 440n
Regiments:
6th Parachute: 128, 216
26th SS Pz. Grenadier: 229, 309
125th Pz. Grenadier: 151, 200
192nd Pz. Grenadier: 200
726th Infantry: 207, 211
736th Grenadier: on D-day, 151, 200, 202, 208
858th Infantry: 248
902nd Pz. Grenadier: 382
915th Infantry: 200, 210
1057th Infantry: 215
1716th Artillery: 208
Battalions:
101st SS Heavy Tank: 333
102nd SS Heavy Tank: 318, 333
352nd Anti-Tank: 210
352nd Fusiliers: 210
503rd Heavy Tank: 333, 341
654th Heavy Anti-Tank: 333
668th Heavy Anti-Tank: 395

GERMAN NAVY:
Vessels available to meet 'Overlord' campaign, Appendix III; losses in Allied pre-D-day attacks, 108; D-day dispositions, 121, 240; special craft (*dackel, linsen, marder*), 300, 416. See also Maritime Operations
Forces Engaged: see also Appendix III
Naval Group West: command, 59, 120; D-day dispositions, 121, 240; D-day reactions, 162, 198, 240
8th Destroyer Flotilla: 199
5th Torpedo-Boat Flotilla: 199, 242
9th Torpedo-Boat Flotilla: 242
See also E-boats and U-boats

Germany: the 'prime enemy', 3, 6; bombing of prior to D-day, 21–3, 94–6, 109–13; industrial war output, 59–61; air attacks on after D-day, 306, 399, 472, 485–8; military resistance to Hitler in, 361–74 *passim*
Gerow, Lieut-General L. T.: 256
Giberville: 336–8, 344
Glasgow, H.M.S.: 291
Gliders: numbers available, 28, 138; in D-day operations, 149 *et seq.*, 204, 215. See also Appendix VI, Part II
Goebbels, Dr.: 372n
Goerdeler, Dr. Carl: 363–6, 374
Goodson, H.M.S.: 289
'Goodwood' operation: 327–58 *passim*
'Gooseberries': *see* Artificial Harbours
Göring, Field-Marshal H.: refuses Rommel control of III Flak Corps, 120; 297, 365, 368; ineffective, 490
Grainville sur Odon: 253; in 'Epsom', 280, 282
Grandcamp les Bains: 199, 201, 304
Graye sur Mer: 179, 181
Great Britain: 2; as base for 'Overlord', 28–30; under air and flying-bomb attack, 29, 266, 307
Gruchy: 311, 314
Guderian, General H.: 373
Guillerville: 337, 343, 346

Hable de Heurtot: 171, 176, 178
Haida, H.M.C.S.: 241
Hall, Rear-Admiral J. L.: 145, 187, 191
Hambledon, H.M.S.: 242
Hamburg: 399
Hanover: 399
Harbours: *see* Artificial Harbours, Courseulles, Port en Bessin
Harris, Air Marshal Sir Arthur: member of Joint Staff Mission to U.S.A., 5; C.-in-C. Bomber Command, 23; on command of Allied strategic air forces, 42; on 'Transportation Plan' and area bombing, 98
Hausser, SS General P.: and 'Epsom', 284; commands Seventh Army, 320; urges give up Caen, 320; 361; and American breakout, 384; and Mortain counter-attack, 406, 412, 432; and withdrawal from Falaise 'pocket', 439, 446; severely wounded, 451
Havelock, H.M.S.: 242
Headquarters:
Allied: organisation and location pre-D-day, 37, 73–5, 139; on D-day, 164, 212; naval reorganisation, 293; Army arrange-

Headquarters—*cont.*
    ments, 304; Canadian Army H.Q. operational, 377; air and army reorganisation, 402; Twenty-First Army Group Rear H.Q. moved to France, 473
    German: organisation and location at D-day, 57; Panzer Group West H.Q. destroyed, 258; von Kluge's arrangements, 361; air H.Q. moved eastwards, 472
Health: of Allied troops in France, 482–4
Hebécrevon: in 'Cobra', 379–81, 384
Hermanville sur Mer: D-day fighting at, 170, 186, 201, 203, 206
Hérouville: and capture of Caen, 311–13, 315
Hérouvillette: and British airborne bridgehead, 150, 205, 227
Hilary, H.M.S.: 164, 212, 291
Hill, Air Marshal R. M.: 266
Hill 112: in 'Epsom', 280–5; captured, 317, 349
'Hillman' strongpoint: 201–6
Himmler, Heinrich: and plot against Hitler, 362–74 *passim*
Hindenburg, Field-Marshal von: 362
Hitler, Adolf: 1–3; and Atlantic Wall, 52, 119; on probable sites of Allied invasion, 54, 128, 489; directive of Nov. 1943, 55; directives after D-day, 259, 295, 322, 405, 433, 450, 457–9; and German command in the West, 56, 117–20, 321–4, 432, 434, 489; D-day reactions, 200, 206, 236; no withdrawal to Cherbourg, 262; conferences, 268, 296, 395–8, 444n; on German naval tasks, 289; plot against, 361–74 *passim*; on German strategy, 375, 397, 435
Hodges, Lieut-General C. H.: and U.S. First Army, 377, 402
Hoepner, General E.: 371
Holland: 52, 322, 472. *See also* Low Countries and Dutch Armed Forces
Hollis, Sergeant-Major S. E.: 176n
Hopkins, Harry: 7
Hornell, Flight-Lieutenant D. E.: 290
Horrocks, Lieut-General B. G.: and XXX Corps, 402, 453, 469
Horton, Admiral Sir Max: 71
Hottot: XXX Corps attack, 250, 261, 287; captured, 334
Houlgate: battery at shelled, 159, 162, 293; 301; captured, 448
Hubert-Folie: in 'Goodwood', 336, 342, 346–9
Hungary: 128, 397, 435
Huron, H.M.C.S.: 241

Ifs: 314, 347, 350
Inconstant, H.M.S.: 242
Intelligence: Allied, 51, 103, 106, 123, 127, 176; failure of German, 53, 128, 489; key enemy H.Q. destroyed by R.A.F., 97. *See also* Deception
Isigny: and American progress from 'Omaha' bridgehead, 225, 232, 235, 247
Italy: campaign in, 2, 18, 41, 496

Jamieson, Captain D.: 409
Japan: 2, 6

Jarrot ('Goujon'): 122
'Jedburghs': and Allied aid to Resistance, 124
Jodl, General A.: Chief of OKW Operations Staff, 120; 128; on D-day, 216; at Hitler conferences, 268, 296, 395, 398; 369, 375, 426, 433, 444n
Jort, 431, 439
'Jupiter' operation: 315
Juvigny (near Mortain): 404, 412
Juvigny (near Tilly sur Seulles): 250, 276

Keitel, Field-Marshal W.: 296, 369–73
Kesselring, Field-Marshal A.: 432
Keyes, Admiral of the Fleet Sir Roger: 11
Kiel: 399, 473
King, Admiral E. J.: 5, 8, 34
Kirk, Rear-Admiral D. P.: commanding Western Naval Task Force, 68, 187, 292, 294
Kitzinger, General: 407n
Kluge, Field-Marshal G. von: succeeds von Rundstedt, 322; appraises situation in West, 324–6; and 'Goodwood' attack, 345; and plot against Hitler, 361, 363, 366, 370–5; and American break-out, 384; and Caumont offensive, 392, 395, 397; and Mortain counter-attack, 405–7, 412, 423, 426; and withdrawal from Falaise, 428, 439; dismissal and suicide, 432–4; relations with Hitler, 489
Kluge, Colonel von: 415, 426
Koenig, General: C.-in-C. of F.F.I., 123, 126, 456
Krancke, Vice-Admiral: commands Naval Group West, 59, 120; on Allied command of the Channel, 107, 162; on Allied air mastery, 110; doubts imminence of invasion, 129; reactions to assault, 198, 240; on bombing of le Havre, 243; and plot against Hitler, 371

La Bijude: captured, 311–15
La Brèche: D-day landing at, 183, 186
La Hogue: and 'Goodwood', 342, 344; 378; in 'Totalize', 419–23
Laigle: bombed, 234, 307; in advance to the Seine, 407, 444, 453, 473
Laison R.: 424, 430
Laize R.: 420, 427
Landing Craft and Assault Shipping: defined, 14; supply problems, 9, 13, 17, 20, 24, 33–6; rôle in 'Neptune' assault, 65–7; training and exercises, 132–4; assembly and passage, 136, 141 *et seq.*, 164–6; in assault, 169–93 *passim*; losses, 179–81, 184, 191, 214, 217, 245. *See also* Appendix II
Langrune sur Mer: 183, 208
Largs, H.M.S.: 163
La Rivière: and D-day landings, 170, 176, 207
La Roche Guyon: H.Q. of Army Group B at, 361, 370, 449
La Rosière: 209
Laval: 234; and American envelopment, 309, 412
Laval, Pierre: 46, 48
Lawford, H.M.S.: 244

INDEX 589

Laycock, Major-General R. E.: 271
Leahy, Admiral W. D.: 5
Leatham, Admiral Sir Ralph: 70
Le Bas de Ranville: and British airborne assault, 151, 200, 205
Le Bény-Bocage: and the Vire sector, 394, 401, 411
Leber, Julius: 368
Lebisey: and the Caen attacks, 204, 228, 311–15
Leclerc, General: 126, 428, 457
Le Fresne-Camilly: 207, 209
Le Hamel: and D-day landings, 170–5, 178, 197, 209
Le Haut du Bosq: in 'Epsom', 276, 278–80
Le Havre: in Allied plans, 81; 108, 129; German naval forces in, 199, 240, 242–4, 290, 299, 301; attacked by Bomber Command, 243; Canadians directed on, 450, 465, 468; naval blockade of, 471
Leigh-Mallory, Air Marshal Sir Trafford: and Combined Commanders, 14; Air Commander-in-Chief for 'Overlord', 19, 23, 32; and expanded assault plans, 33; and Neptune Initial Joint Plan and Overall Air Plan, 43, 63, 71 et seq., 80; and 'Transportation Plan', 97, 99; 134; on rôle of airborne troops, 138, 247; and 'Crossbow', 266; 378
Le Mans: 235; in Montgomery's plans, 308; and American envelopment, 404, 412, 416, 425; Germans speak of counter-attacking at, 426; 449
Le Mariquet: 200, 205
Le Mesnil: 154, 206
Le Mesnil-Frémental: in 'Goodwood', 340–2
Le Plein: and British airborne bridgehead, 155, 206, 227, 249
Le Port: 151, 204
Les Andelys: and crossing of the Seine, 407, 467, 469
Les Loges: and VIII Corps' attack from Caumont, 388, 390
Les Roquettes: 171, 174
Lessay: and 'Cobra', 379–81, 384
Le Tourneur: 394, 401
Le Valtru: in 'Epsom', 278, 282, 284
Lingèvres: in advance from Bayeux, 250, 252, 255
Lion sur Mer: and D-day landings, 183, 186, 202, 205
Lisieux: under Allied air attack, 212, 234, 441, 445; 303; German forces at, 336, 346; in First Canadian Army's advance to the Seine, 407, 432, 449, 453, 473
Little, Admiral Sir Charles: 5, 19, 70
Locust, H.M.S.: 293
Logistics: *see* Administration and Logistics
Loire R.: in Allied plans, 63, 80, 87; bridges bombed, 102, 288, 411; U.S. Third Army directed on, 403; 449, 464
London: 136; flying-bomb attacks on, 266, 307, 322
Longues: on D-day, 159, 163, 209; captured, 231
Longueval: and British airborne bridgehead, 205, 227, 250
Lorient: 216, 412

Loughrey, Sergeant R.: 113
Louviers: and crossing of the Seine, 449, 452–4, 467
Low Countries, The: German forces in, 3, 16, 41; in Allied plans, 82, 461; Allied air operations over, 94, 97, 400. *See also* Holland
Luftwaffe: see German Air Force

McKenzie, Commodore T.: 291
McLean, Brigadier K. G.: 83
Maltot: 159; and XII Corps, 317, 346, 349
Manneville: 'Goodwood', 337, 343, 346
Mannheim: 399, 464
Manpower: 131–3, 308, 453n
Mantes-Gassicourt: 407; Americans capture, 449; 465, 469
'Maple' operation: 108
Maps: 136, 144
Maquis, The: 50, 123. *See also* Resistance
Marcelet: 283, 309
Marcks, General E.: 238
Marigny: 159, 318, 381
Maritime Operations: Battle of Atlantic, 9, 59; pre-assault, 64, 70; 'Neptune' crossing, 144–8; coastal bombardment, 161–8; cover for seaborne landings, Chapters IX and X *passim*; June, 240–5, 289–95; July, 299–301; August, 416, 471; reviewed, 477
Marne R.: 407, 457, 476
Marriot, Flight Sergeant C. R.: 112
Marseilles: 434, 437
Marshall, General G. C.: 5, 7–9, 20
Mauritius, H.M.S.: 162, 227, 339
Mayenne: 235, 309, 403, 405, 412
May sur Orne: and II Canadian Corps, 379, 419, 421–3
Medical Services: 482–4
Meersch, Ganshof van der: 52
Merchant Navy: 2, 478
Merderet R.: and First American Army, 156, 215, 232, 257, 261
Merville: and British airborne assault, 149, 153–5, 158, 205, 227
Meteorological Reports: 139–44
Meuvaines: 175, 201, 210
Mézidon: 234, 345, 378, 420, 422, 473
Middleton, Major-General T. H.: 327
Minelaying at sea: British, 71, 108, 287; German, 244
Minesweeping: 68, 146; at Cherbourg, 292
Model, Field-Marshal W.: succeeds von Kluge, 432–4; 444, 451, 468, 471
Mondrainville: 280, 282
Montebourg: 232, 235, 257
Mont Fleury: on D-day, 159, 171, 176, 210
Montgomery, General Sir Bernard L.: appointed C.-in-C. Twenty-First Army Group, 31–3; overall ground forces commander for assault, 40; 43, 63, 85; forecasts of progress, 80, 134, 356–9, 404; and U.S. airborne assault, 138; consultations with Bradley and Dempsey, 225, 327, 386, 403, 449, 459; draws German armour to British flank, 239, 260, 265–8; plans to outflank Caen, 247, 250; directives, 16 June 271, 30 June 308, 10 July 327, 21 July 350, 27 July 386, 4 & 6 August 407, 11 August 427, 20 August 450,

26 August 465; and development of 'Goodwood', 328–32, 344; criticisms of, 352–8; in operational control of both Allied army groups, 377; Mortain counter-attack, 415; plans to prevent German escape, 432, 439, 441; views on future strategy, 459–64; promoted Field-Marshal, 476; his conduct of campaign reviewed, 491–4
Mont Pinçon: 387, 408–11
Moon, Rear-Admiral D. P.: 145
Morale: 131, 145, 159
Morgan, Lieut-General F. E.: appointed C.O.S.S.A.C., 10; his outline plan approved, 17; presses for more assault craft, 20; Eisenhower's tribute to, 25; to Shaef staff, 31. *See also* Cossac
Mortain: U.S. First Army directed on, 309, 403, 412; Germans counter-attack at, 406–16; Americans recapture, 425–7
Mortars, German: see Appendix IV, Part VI
Mouen: 281, 283
Moulin, Jean Pierre: 50
Mountbatten, Vice-Admiral Lord Louis: 11, 15, 88
Mourne, H.M.S.: 242
Mue R.: and Canadians, 181, 207, 229, 252, 276
'Mulberries': *see* Artificial Harbours
Mynarski, Pilot Officer A. C.: 305n

National Committee of Liberation: 50, 123, 125
Naval Forces, Allied: command, 19, 293; assault organisation, 66–71, 135, 140; German craft attacked, 240–5, 289–91; and Cherbourg, 291; 'Neptune' ends, 294; post-'Neptune', 299
Naval Operations: *see* Maritime Operations
Navy, Army and Air Force Institutes (N.A.A.F.I.): 484
Nelson, H.M.S.: 140, 250
'Neptune' operation: plans, 43, Chapter IV *passim*, 134–6; assembly of forces, 136; fixing of D-day, 140–4; invasion fleet sails, 144–8; airborne landings, 149–58, 204; opening bombardment and approach, 158–68; the assault and bridgehead won, Chapters IX and X *passim*; D-day's statistics, 222; 'Neptune' officially ended, 294; reviewed, 294, 477–9
Nordling, Raoul: 456
Normandy: as site of invasion, 15; coast described, 78, 171, 187; the *bocage* country, 79, 276, 387
North Africa: Allied landings, 8
Norway: 1940 campaign, 17; rôle in Allied deception plans, 104, 127; German naval craft based on, 107, 471; forces serving with the Allies, Appendices II and VI
Noyers: 247, 250, 283; attacked, 334
Nuremberg: 95
Nye, General Sir Archibald: 460

Oberg, SS Lieut-General C. A.: 373
Obstacles, anti-invasion: on beaches, 27, 91, 115; against gliders, 156; effectiveness on D-day, 169–94 *passim*, 213–17

O'Connor, Lieut-General Sir Richard: and VIII Corps in 'Epsom', 282–4; in 'Goodwood', 346; 394
Odon R.: in 'Epsom', 276–83; German counter-attacks, 285; 317, 344
Office of Strategic Services (O.S.S.): 51, 123
Oil, German: strategic bombing of, 99, 400, 472, 485; Rumanian wells captured by Russians, 496
Oise R.: 102, 129, 468, 471
Olbricht, General F.: 364–6, 369
Oliver, Commodore G. N.: 164, 293
Ondefontaine: 409–11
Operational Research Section: examination of German losses, 448, 472
Orion, H.M.S.: 176, 211, 250
Orléans: Allied air attacks on Orléans gap, 235, 279, 411; and U.S. Third Army, 429, 433, 440
Orne R.: 64, 66, 78; in assault operations, 149–249 *passim*; bridgehead east of extended, 274; and 'Epsom', 276–81; 310–18; and 'Goodwood', 331–45; 408; Germans withdraw beyond, 433, 439, 445
Osprey, U.S.S.: 146
Oster, Major-General H.: 364, 374
Ouistreham: 78, 115; bombed, 159, 161; D-day fighting, 183, 186, 201
Overall Air Plan: 71–7

Paget, General Sir Bernard: 14, 31, 40
Palmer, Sergeant W. A.: 113
Paris: 81; railways around bombed, 235, 279, 399; 358; and plot against Hitler, 370–3; 407; German defence of, 440, 444, 450–2; Resistance in and liberation, 455–8; railway re-opened, 473
Pas de Calais: as site of invasion, 15; German defences in, 54, 102, 119; Germans expect invasion in, 102–4, 127–9, 305, 323, 489; Twenty-First Army Group to clear, 450, 459–63, 465, 475
Patch, Lieut-General A. M.: 437
Pathfinders: 23, 149–54 *passim*, 339, 419
Patton, Lieut-General George S.: 304, 377, 428
Peenemünde: 105
Pemsel, Major-General M · 198, 216
Périers (in Cotentin): 318, 379
Périers sur le Dan: and German tank attack, 201, 204–6; 228
Perrier: 401, 410
Pétain, Marshal Phillipe: 45–9
Petrol: 87; stocks and importance of, 265, 302, 473, 480
Photographic Reconnaissance: 104, 116, 234
Plans: of Combined Commanders, 14–16; of Cossac, 14–17, 25; further development of, 33–7; Initial Joint Plan, 43, 63–6; 'Neptune' naval plan, 66–71; Overall Air Plan, 71–7; army plan, 77–80; reviewed, 80, 134–6; administrative and logistical, 83–91; deception, 103; Joint Fire Plan, 167; for future strategy, 459–64
Ploesti (oil wells): 496
'Pluto': 302, 480
Point 64: 311, 314

INDEX

Point 122: 421
Point 213: 254
Point 309: 388–95 *passim*
'Pointblank' operation: 21, 42, 94–7
Pointe du Hoe: 159, 190, 193, 214
Polish Armed Forces: 138 and Appendices II, IV and VI; 1st Polish Armoured Division in Falaise area, 420–5, 431, 441, 445–8
Pontaubault: 235, 403
Portal, Air Chief Marshal Sir Charles: 5, 99, 271
Port en Bessin: 66, 78, 87, 115, 171; its capture by Royal Marine Commandos, 176, 209, 231; 263; petrol depot at, 303, 479–481
Pound, Admiral of the Fleet Sir Dudley: 5
Pridham-Wippell, Vice-Admiral Sir H.: 70
Pugsley, Captain A. F.: 299
Putot en Bessin: 229, 235, 252

Quebec Conference ('Quadrant'): 17, 434
Queen Alexandra's Imperial Military Nursing Service: 484
Queen Elizabeth, S.S.: 29
Queen Mary, S.S.: 29
Quesada, Major-General E. R.: 402, 414
Quorn, H.M.S.: 416

Radar: attacks on German stations, 96, 102, 109; deception measures against, 158–60
Railways: Allied bombing of, 97–102, 235, 281, 287, 399; lines re-opened, 473
Ramillies, H.M.S.: 162
Ramsay, Admiral Sir Bertram: and Combined Commanders, 15; Naval C.-in-C. for 'Overlord', 19, 32; and development of plans, 33, 43, 63, 66, 80; 134; directing 'Neptune' operations, 140, 143, 147, 164, 243, 263, 271, 292; post-'Neptune', 299
'Rankin' operation: 39
Ranville: airborne landings at, 150, 200, 204, 226; German attacks on bridgehead at, 227, 248, 250, 261, 346
Rauray: XXX Corps capture, 276–80; German counter-attack repulsed, 285
Rear Maintenance Area: 85–7, 473, 481
Regina, H.M.C.S.: 417
Rennes: and Allied plans, 81n, 303, 309, 403; in American hands, 412
Rennie, Major-General T. G.: 206
Resistance: in France, 49–51, 121–4, 323, 412, 456; in Belgium and Holland, 51; Allied relations with, 51, 123–5; air support for, 123, 288. *See also* Appendices VIII and IX
Reviers: 181, 207
Risle R.: 452, 467
Rivett-Carnac, Rear-Admiral J. W.: 293, 299
Roads, construction and maintenance: 473, 481
Robehomme: 154
Roberts, H.M.S.: 162, 275, 311, 339
Rocquancourt: 340, 379, 422
Rodney, H.M.S.: 141, 309, 311, 314
Rommel, Field-Marshal E.: 7, 31; commands Army Group B, 56; on defence in the West, 115, 118; relations with von Rundstedt, 118–20, 237; reactions on D-day, 216; view on campaign policy, 258, 323; at Hitler conferences, 268, 296; attitude towards Hitler, 294, 367, 489; 315, 320; relations with von Kluge, 324; injured, 326
Roosevelt, President F. D.: 3, 8; meetings at Quebec and Cairo, 17, 21, 24; on French civilian casualties, 101; on 'Anvil', 434
Roseveare, Major J. C. A.: 152
Rouen: 122, 407, 450, 467; German withdrawal, 457
'Roundup' operation: 7

ROYAL AIR FORCE:
Aircraft available for 'Overlord' campaign, 72; losses in pre-D-day operations, 95–7, 112; and in airborne assault, 156, and on D-day, 223; and in maritime operations, 244; and summarised, 488; morale, 133
Forces Engaged: see also Appendix VI
Air Defence of Great Britain: organisation, 73–5; pre-D-day operations, 109; on D-day, 146, 158, 161; 'Crossbow' operations, 266, 484; post-D-day operations, 287, 338, 443; summary to 30 June, 306; and to 31 August, 487
Air/Sea Rescue Service: 290, 488n
Bomber Command: new techniques adopted, 22; control of in 'Overlord', 42; pre-D-day operations, 94 ('Big Week'), 95–7, 98–103 ('Transportation Plan'), 105, 108, 109–13 (summary); and Resistance, 123, 288; D-day operations, 153, 158–60; army support 7 to 30 June, 225, 235, 256, 281, 285, 287, 306 (summary); maritime support, 243, 287; 'Crossbow' operations, 281, 287, 399, 484; at Caen, 313; in 'Goodwood', 337–41, 351; at Caumont, 388; operations in Germany, 399, 472; in 'Totalize'/'Tractable', 421, 430; summary to 31 August, 484–8
Coastal Command: anti-U-boat patrols, 107, 109, 241, 289, 300; attacks on surface craft, 109, 240; on D-day, 145; summary to 30 June, 306; and to 31 August, 487
Fleet Air Arm: *see* Royal Navy
Second Tactical Air Force: organisation and command, 73–5, 133; pre-D-day operations, 96, 102, 109 (summary); on D-day, 158, 162, 170, 204, 211; army support 7 to 30 June, 225, 235, 251, 258, 283, 287, 306 (summary); 'Crossbow' operations, 266, 484; at Caen, 313, 315; in 'Goodwood', 342; 378, 411, 422, 430; H.Q. moves to Normandy, 402; at Falaise 'pocket', 441–3; at Seine, 455; moves east, 472; summary to 31 August, 484–8
Groups:
No. 2: D-day operations, 158, 170; attacks Panzer Group West H.Q., 258; at Caen, 313; still based in U.K., 403; at Seine, 440, 445, 455
No. 3: 124
No. 12: 32
No. 15: 107
No. 16: 107, 241n
No. 18: 107

Groups—*cont.*
  No. 19: 107, 241
  No. 38: and Resistance, 124, Appendix IX; in airborne assault, 138, 149, 204
  No. 46: in airborne assault, 138, 149, 204, 221; in air transport operations, 474
  No. 83: on D-day, 170, 219; 255; attacks Panzer Group West H.Q., 258; in 'Epsom', 277, 279–81; all in Normandy, 305, 358, 403; at Caen, 310; in 'Goodwood', 338, 349; in 'Cobra', 382, 393; at Mortain, 414; H.Q. moved eastwards, 472
  No. 84: on D-day, 170; 255; in 'Goodwood', 338; part in Normandy, 358, 403
  No. 85: 403
  No. 100: 159
Commonwealth and Allied Units: *see* Appendix VI
Royal Air Force Regiment: 228n, 307
Airfield Construction Wing: 481
Photographic Reconnaissance Unit: 104

Royal Marines:
  Armoured Support Group: 132
  Armoured Support Regiments: 164; 1st, 174, 177; 2nd, 180, 202, 208; 5th Independent Battery, 184
  Commandos: No. 41, 186, 202; No. 45, 205; No. 47, 175, 209, 231; No. 48, 183, 208

ROYAL NAVY:
  Vessels and craft allotted to 'Overlord' campaign, Appendix II, Part IV; Allied losses to 30 June, 295. *See also* Maritime Operations
Forces Engaged: see also Appendix II
Eastern Task Force: 66; sailed, 144–7; on D-day, 161–8, 221
  Force G: 67, 133; sailed, 146; on D-day, 164
  Force J: 67, 133; sailed, 146; on D-day, 164
  Force L: 67, 219
  Force S: 67, 133; sailed, 144–7; on D-day, 164
Fleet Air Arm: 71; on D-day, 146, 163; 241n, 251

Ruhr, The: bombing of, 23, 148, 399; in Allied strategic plans, 82, 460–3, 465
Rundstedt, Field-Marshal G. von: appointed C.-in-C. West, 53; reports on defence in West, 54; relations with Rommel, 56, 118–20, 237; on likelihood of Allied invasion, 128; reactions on D-day, 198–200, 206, 216; 237, 239; views on campaign policy, 258, 323; at Hitler conferences, 268, 296; attitude towards Hitler, 294–6, 366; superseded, 320–2
Russia: attacked by Germany and counter-offensives, 2, 7, 39; opens 1944 offensive, 496
Ryes: 175, 209

Saar, The: 459, 461, 463
Sabotage: 51, 112, 121–3, 323, 400

St. Aignan de Cramesnil: 420–3
St. Aubin d'Arquenay: 203, 206
St. Aubin sur Mer: and Canadian assault, 66, 179, 183, 206, 208
St. Barthélémy: 412–14, 426
St. Contest: 229, 314
St. Gilles: 381
St. Lambert sur Dives: 442, 445–7
St. Laurent: 193, 214; 'Mulberry' harbour at, 273
St. Lô: 78, 212, 235, 257; American drive on, 316, 318, 327, 330; captured, 348
St. Malo: 290, 304, 309, 403, 412
St. Martin de Fontenay: 350, 379
St. Martin des Besaces: 388, 391–4
St. Mauvieu: 253, 278
St. Nazaire: 53, 436
Saint Pierre: 231, 251, 261
St. Pierre sur Dives: 431, 439
St. Pois: 404, 412
St. Sauveur le Vicomte: 261, 318
St. Sylvain: 419, 422–5
St. Valéry: 470, 476
Ste. Croix sur Mer: 181, 207
Ste. Honorine: 303, 480
Ste. Honorine la Chardonnerette: and I Corps, 227, 250, 274; 340
Ste. Mère Eglise: 156, 215, 232
Sannerville: 152, 337, 343
Satterlee, U.S.S.: 193
Scharnhorst: 59
Schleicher, General K. von: 362
Schweinfurt: 95
Schweppenburg, General Geyr von: and the armoured reserve, 119, 238, 295; advocates withdrawal from Caen, 320; superseded, 322
Scimitar, H.M.S.: 133
Scylla, H.M.S.: 146, 162, 221, 290
Security: 52, 83, 125–7, 136, 489
Seeckt, General H. von: 362
Sées: 427, 432
Seine R.: 78, 81; bridges bombed, 102, 129, 288, 308; in strategic plans, 356, 358; German plans to defend, 375, 395, 450; 407, 429; Allied armies cross, 449, 452–5, 466–9
Sellar, Commander K. A.: 299
Serapis, H.M.S.: 205
Seulles R.: 207, 209, 231
'Sextant' Conference (Cairo): 21–4, 32, 36
Shaef (Supreme Headquarters Allied Expeditionary Force): organisation, 37–40; 139; and 'Goodwood', 328, 332, 353–6
Sheltered Waters: *see* Artificial Harbours
Shipping: Allied merchant losses, 7, 18; supply of assault and landing craft, 13, 17, 33–6; available for 'Neptune', 67–70; assembly and sailing, 136, 140–8
  Losses: on passage, 164; in assault, 179–81, 184, 191, 214, 217; to 16 June, 245; total in 'Neptune', 295; in July, 300; in August, 416, 471
  See also Appendix II
Simonds, Lieut-General G. G.: commands II Canadian Corps, 377; 419, 430, 432, 446
Site of Invasion: choice and description of, 15,

INDEX

78, 171, 187; Allied deception and German estimates, 54, 102-4, 127-9, 305, 323, 489
'Sledgehammer' operation: 7, 19
Smith, Lieut-General W. Bedell: 30, 32, 461
Smuts, Field-Marshal J.: 134
Soignolles: 424, 430
Soissons: 455, 457, 468, 472
Soliers: 337, 342, 346
Somme R.: Germans plan defence of, 375, 407, 459; Allied armies directed on, 450, 468; crossed, 470
Souleuvre R.: and VIII Corps, 387, 394, 401
Sourdeval: 406, 412, 427
Spaatz, General Carl: 42, 99
Special Air Service Troops: 124, 138. *See also* Appendix IX
Special Force Headquarters: 51, 123
Special Operations Executive (S.O.E.): 51, 122
Speer, Albert: 60, 490
Speidel, Lieut-General H.: 117, 198; and Hitler conference, 268; 285, 324; attitude to plot against Hitler, 367, 371
Sperrle, Field-Marshal H.: commands Third Air Fleet, 58; 297, 371, 490
'Spout', The: in naval assault plans, 69-71; 146, 241-3, 289
Stagg, Group Captain J. M.: 143
Stalin, Marshal J.: 21, 24
Stark, Admiral H. R.: 5
'Starkey' operation: 54
Stauffenberg, Colonel C. von: 364-71
Steele, Air Vice-Marshal C. R.: 403
Storm: effects of, 271-4, 301-3
Strategic Bombing: Combined Bomber Offensive, 9, 21-3; relation to 'Overlord', 40-3; 'Big Week', 94; 'Pointblank', 94-7; 'Transportation Plan', 97-102, 109-12; in June, 306; in July, 399; in August, 472; reviewed, 484-8
Strategy, Allied: and Combined Chiefs of Staff, 4; Germany the principal enemy, 5; arguments for a North African landing, 7-9; birth of 'Overlord' plan, 10-17; 'Overlord'-'Anvil' arguments, 18-21, 36, 293, 434-6; Montgomery's views on strategy of campaign, 81, 356-9, 404; Eisenhower's long-term plans, 82; Eisenhower and Montgomery differ, 459-64
Strengths and Replacements: Allied build-up in United Kingdom, 28; German armies in West before D-day, 3, 41, 53, 55, 57-9, 117; Allied landings on D-day, 223; strengths at 1 July, 294, 308; and at end of August, 478
Stülpnagel, General H. von: 367, 370-3
Stuttgart: 95, 112, 399
Sullivan, Commodore W. A.: 291
Sully: 231
Supplies: *see* Administration and Logistics
Svenner, H.N.M.S.: 163, 199
'Symbol' Conference (Casablanca): 9, 19, 21, 41

Tailleville: 183, 208
Talbot, Rear-Admiral A. G.: 145, 164, 219
Talybont, H.M.S.: 193

Tanks and anti-tank guns:
  Allied: special assault types, 116, 481; in D-day assault, 169, 178-84 *passim*, 188-91
  German: numbers in France before D-day, 117; losses—in 'Cobra', 382; at Mortain, 414; in Trun–Chambois gap, 448
  See also Appendix IV, Part V
Tartar, H.M.S.: 241
Tedder, Air Chief Marshal Sir Arthur W.: Deputy Supreme Commander, 30, 43, 73; on 'Transportation Plan', 99; and use of airborne troops, 139; criticises Montgomery's conduct of campaign, 265, 353-6
Teheran Conference ('Eureka'): 21, 36
Temple, Commander J. B. G.: 292
Texas, U.S.S.: 291
Thorne, Lieut-General Sir A. F. A. N.: 127
Thury-Harcourt: 405-8, 425, 427
Tilly la Campagne: in 'Goodwood'/'Totalize', 342-5, 378, 419, 422
Tilly sur Seulles: and XXX Corps, 231, 234, 250-2, 255, 261
Todd, Sergeant C. R.: 113
'Tombola': 302, 480
'Totalize' operation: 419-25
Touffreville: in airborne assault, 150, 152; 250; in 'Goodwood', 337, 343
Toulon: 434, 437
Touques R.: 81, 444, 451, 453
Tourmauville: 278, 280
'Tractable' operation: 429-32
Tracy-Bocage: 254
Training: 12; and final exercises, 131-4
'Transportation Plan': 97-100; operations under, 101, 110-12. *See also* under the various Allied air forces
'Trident' Conference (Washington): 10
Troarn: in airborne assault, 152-6, 206; and 'Goodwood', 335-7, 343-6; 448
'Trout' Line: 221, 299
Trun: 430-2, 439-42; Trun–Chambois gap closed, 447; effect of air attacks on, 472

U-boats: 2; new types, 60; 70, 107; dispositions, 121; D-day alert, 199, 240; in Channel, 241, 289, 300, 417; August operations, 471

UNITED STATES ARMY:
  Total allotted for 'Overlord' campaign, 28; numbers landed on D-day, 223; and by 30 June, 308; and by 31 August, 478; total casualties by 31 August, 493
Forces Engaged: see also Appendix IV
First Army Group: in preliminary plans, 40, 65, 78, 83; in deception plan, 377n
Twelfth Army Group: formed, 377, 402; force for Brittany reduced, 403; and main thrust to east, 404, 429, 449; and advance beyond Seine, 450, 460-5, 475; renamed Central Group of Armies, 460
First Army: in invasion plans, 64, 77-81; in assault, 187, 213; in Cotentin, 261, 271, 304, 309; in advance to St. Lô, 318, 327, 330; in 'Cobra', 377 *et seq.*; and Mortain, 403, 413; and Elbeuf, 449; and Paris, 457; beyond Seine, 465

Third Army: in invasion plans, 65, 77–81; Patton to Normandy, 304; operational, 377, 402; main thrust to east (Brittany one corps), 403; in envelopment, 425, 429; at Seine, 449; beyond Seine, 457

Seventh Army: 437, 475

Corps:
V: 79; on D-day, 187, 190, 213; 232, 247, 256, 288; in 'Cobra', 381; at Falaise 'pocket', 441; Paris, 457
VII: 79; on D-day, 187, 215; 232, 247, 257; cuts Cotentin, 261; captures Cherbourg, 288; 318; in 'Cobra', 381–3; at Mortain, 415; 457
VIII: 79, 288, 318, 327; in 'Cobra', 381–3; into Brittany, 403; attacks Brest, 474n
XII: 429, 455
XV: in envelopment, 404, 425, 428; Seine, 449; 454
XIX: 79, 257, 288; attack towards St. Lô, 318; in 'Cobra', 381, 383; north to Elbeuf, 449, 453
XX: 404, 429, 455

Divisions:
1st: 67, 79; on D-day, 190; 232, 256
2nd: 79, 256
4th: 67, 79; on D-day, 188, 215; 232
9th: 79
29th: 79; on D-day, 190; 232, 235, 257
79th: 79; Seine, 449
90th: 79; at Falaise 'pocket', 445
2nd Armoured: 79
3rd Armoured: 319
5th Armoured: in envelopment, 428
82nd Airborne: 80; arguments over use, 138; on D-day, 156–8, 215; 232
101st Airborne: 80; arguments over use, 138; on D-day, 156–8, 215; 232
2nd French Armoured: 126; in envelopment, 428; Paris, 457

Regimental Combat Teams:
8th: 188, 215
12th: 188, 215
16th: 190, 214
18th: 190, 213
22nd: 188, 215
26th: 214
115th: 190, 214
116th: 190, 192, 214
Rangers: 190, 193, 214

UNITED STATES ARMY AIR FORCE:
Aircraft available for 'Overlord' campaign, 72; losses in pre-D-day operations, 95, 112; and from 6 June to 31 August, 488
Forces Engaged: see also Appendix VI
Eighth Air Force: a daylight bombing force, 23; control of in 'Overlord', 42; pre-D-day operations, 94 ('Big Week'), 96, 98–103 ('Transportation Plan'), 105 ('Crossbow'), 109 (summary); on D-day, 146, 166, 174, 211; army support 7 to 30 June, 234, 306 (summary); in 'Goodwood', 337–9, 342, 351; in 'Cobra', 381; July operations, 399; in 'Totalize', 422; August operations, 472; summary to 31 August, 484–8
Ninth Air Force: pre-D-day operations, 94 ('Big Week'), 96, 98–103 ('Transportation Plan'), 109 (summary); on D-day, 138, 146, 166, 170, 211; army support 7 to 30 June, 234–6, 288, 306 (summary); nine groups based in Normandy, 305; at Caen, 313; in 'Goodwood', 337–9; in 'Cobra', 381; at Caumont, 388; command alterations, 402; at Mortain, 414; at Falaise 'pocket', 442; to guard Loire flank, 449; at Seine, 455; summary to 31 August, 484–8
IX Tactical Air Command: 402
IX Troop Carrier Command: on D-day, 158, 216
XIX Tactical Air Command: 402
Fifteenth Air Force: in 'Big Week', 95

UNITED STATES NAVY:
Vessels and craft allotted to 'Overlord' campaign, Appendix II, Part IV; Allied losses to 30 June, 295
Forces Engaged: see also Appendix II
Western Task Force: 66; sailed, 141–6; on D-day, 161–8
Force O: 67, 133; sailed, 145; on D-day, 187, 191
Force U: 67, 133; sailed, 141–6; on D-day, 160, 187, 215

Urville-Hague: signal station destroyed, 97

Vandenberg, Major-General H. S.: 73, 402
Varaville: 150, 153–5
Vassy: 401, 410
Vaucelles: and 'Goodwood', 331, 336, 344, 347
Vendes: 276, 334
Ver sur Mer: 171, 176
Verney, Brigadier G. L.: 402
Vernon: 102; Seine crossed at, 452–5, 466
Verrières: and 'Goodwood', 336, 340, 349, 379
Verson: 281, 309
Vian, Rear-Admiral Sir Philip: on 'Neptune' crossings, 145; D-day, 221; 294; on Merchant Navy, 478
Vichy Government: 45–51
Vie R.: 443, 449
Vierville: 193, 214
Villers-Bocage: bombed, 225, 234, 285; sharp action at, 230, 247, 252–5; captured, 408
Villons les Buissons: 208, 229
Vimont: in 'Goodwood', 331, 336, 341, 345, 349; in 'Totalize', 420, 422, 425
Vimoutiers: 441, 446, 452, 472
Virago, H.M.S.: 163
Vire: 234; Second Army and, 386, 394; German defence of, 401, 405; First U.S. Army and, 403, 410, 412
Vire R.: in assault area, 66, 187, 247; fighting around, 256–60; 318, 387
V-Weapons: 54; Hitler's belief in, 61, 106; development and Allied counter-measures, 105–7; flying-bomb attacks on England, 266, 307; air attacks on sites, 281, 287, 306, 399, 484; sites overrun, 476

Walter, Captain P. N.: 83
Warlimont, General W.: and plot against

INDEX

Hitler, 369; at Hitler conference 31 July, 395, 398
Warspite, H.M.S.: 162, 474n
Washington Conferences: 1941 'Arcadia', 3–6; 1943 'Trident', 10
Waterproofing: of assault equipment, 137
Watkins, Lieut. T.: 440n
Weapons and Equipment: *see* Appendix IV (Parts IV, V and VI) and Appendix V (Part II)
Welfare: arrangements for troops, 482–4
Wemyss, General Sir Colville: 5
Weyland, Brigadier-General O. P.: 402
Wilkes, Rear-Admiral J.: 293

Willday, Sergeant W. A. E. J.: 113
Wilson, General Sir Henry Maitland: 31, 436
'Window': 158, 160
Witzleben, Field-Marshal E. von: 365, 371
'Wolf's Lair': 368–70
Wrestler, H.M.S.: 147

Yonne R.: 451, 457, 464
Young Men's Christian Association (Y.M.C.A.): 484

Zuckerman, Professor S.: 97

HISTORY OF THE SECOND WORLD WAR
UNITED KINGDOM MILITARY SERIES

Reprinted by the Naval & Military Press in twenty two volumes with the permission of the Controller of HMSO and Queen's Printer for Scotland.

THE DEFENCE OF THE UNITED KINGDOM

Basil Collier

Official history of Britain's home front in the Second World War, from the Phoney War, through the Battle of Britain and the Blitz to victory in Europe.
ISBN: 1845740556
Price £22.00

THE CAMPAIGN IN NORWAY

T. H. Derry

The catastrophic 1940 campaign which caused the downfall of Neville Chamberlain and brought Winston Churchill to power.
ISBN: 1845740572
Price: £22.00

THE WAR IN FRANCE AND FLANDERS 1939-1940

Major L. F. Ellis

The role of the BEF in the fall of France and the retreat to Dunkirk.
ISBN: 1845740564
Price £22.00

VICTORY IN THE WEST

Volume I: The Battle of Normandy

Major L. F. Ellis

The build-up, execution and consequences of D-Day in 1944.
ISBN: 1845740580
Price: £22.00

Volume II: The Defeat of Germany

Major L. F. Ellis

The final stages of the liberation of western Europe in 1944-45.
ISBN: 1845740599
Price £22.00

www.naval-military-press.com

THE MEDITERRANEAN AND MIDDLE EAST

Volume I: The Early Successes against Italy (to May 1941)

Major-General I. S. O. Playfair

Britain defeats Italy on land and sea in Africa and the Mediterranean in 1940.
ISBN: 1845740653
Price: £22.00

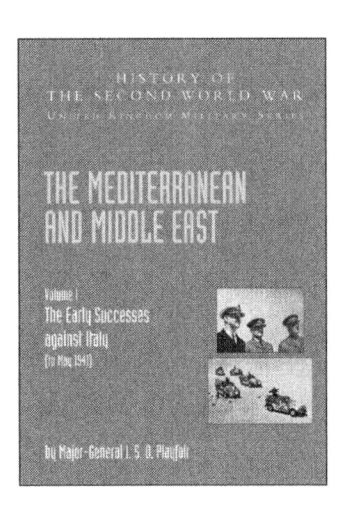

Volume II: The Germans Come to the Help of their Ally (1941)

Major-General I. S. O. Playfair

Rommel rides to Italy's rescue, Malta is bombarded, Yugoslavia, Greece and Crete are lost, and Iraq and Syria are secured for the Allies.
ISBN: 1845740661
Price: £22.00

Volume III: (September 1941 to September 1942) British Fortunes reach their Lowest Ebb

Major-General I. S. O. Playfair

Britain's darkest hour in North Africa and the Mediterranean, 1941-42.
ISBN: 184574067X
Price: £22.00

Volume IV: The Destruction of the Axis Forces in Africa

Major-General I. S. O. Playfair

The battle of El Alamein and 'Operation Torch' bring the Allies victory in North Africa, 1942-43.
ISBN: 1845740688
Price: £22.00

Volume V: The Campaign in Sicily 1943 and the Campaign in Italy — 3rd Sepember 1943 to 31st March 1944

Major-General I. S. O. Playfair

The Allies invade Sicily and Italy, but encounter determined German defence in 1943-44.
ISBN: 1845740696
Price: £22.00

Volume VI: Victory in the Mediterranean Part I: 1st April to 4th June 1944

Brigadier C. J. C. Molony

The Allies breach the Gustav, Hitler and Caesar Lines and occupy Rome.
ISBN: 184574070X
Price: £22.00

Volume VI: Victory in the Mediterranean Part II: June to October 1944

General Sir William Jackson

The 1944 Italian summer campaign breaches the Gothic Line but then bogs down again.
ISBN: 1845740718
Price: £22.00

Volume VI: Victory in the Mediterranean Part III: November 1944 to May 1945

General Sir William Jackson

The messy end of the war in Italy, Greece, and Yugoslavia.
ISBN: 1845740726
Price: £22.00

THE WAR AGAINST JAPAN

Volume I: The Loss of Singapore
Major-General S. Woodburn Kirby
The fall of Hong Kong, Malaya and Singapore in 1941-42.
ISBN: 1845740602
Price: £22.00

Volume II: India's Most Dangerous Hour
Major-General S. Woodburn Kirby
The loss of Burma and Japan's threat to India in 1941-42.
ISBN: 1845740610
Price: £22.00

Volume III: The Decisive Battles
Major-General S. Woodburn Kirby
Turning the tide in the war against Japan at the battles of Kohima, Imphal and the Chindit campaigns.
ISBN: 1845740629
Price: £22.00

Volume IV: The Reconquest of Burma
Major-General S. Woodburn Kirby
The reconquest of Burma by Bill Slim's 'forgotten' 14th Army.
ISBN: 1845740637
Price: £22.00

Volume V: The Surrender of Japan
Major-General S. Woodburn Kirby
Victory in South-East Asia in 1945 - from Rangoon to Nagasaki.
ISBN: 1845740645
Price: £22.00

www.naval-military-press.com

THE WAR AT SEA - 1939–1945

Captain Roskill has long been recognised as the leading authority on The Royal Navy's part in the Second World War. His official History is unlikely ever to be superceded. His narrative is highly readable and the analysis is clear. Roskill describes sea battles, convoy actions and the contribution made by technology in the shape of Asdic & Radar.

Volume I: The Defensive

Captain S. W. Roskill, D.S.C., R.N.

2004 N&MP reprint (original pub 1954).
SB. xxii + 664pp with 43 maps and numerous contemporary photos.
ISBN: 1843428032
Price: £32.00

Volume II: The Period of Balance

Captain S. W. Roskill, D.S.C., R.N.

2004 N&MP reprint (original pub 1956).
SB. xvi + 523pp with 42 maps and numerous contemporary photos.
ISBN: 1843428040
Price: £32.00

Volume III: Part I The Offensive
1st June 1943-31 May 1944

Captain S. W. Roskill, D.S.C., R.N.

2004 N&MP reprint (original pub 1960).
SB. xv + 413pp with 21 maps and numerous contemporary photos.
ISBN: 1843428059
Price: £32.00

Volume III: Part 2 The Offensive
1st June 1944-14th August 1945

Captain S. W. Roskill, D.S.C., R.N.

2004 N&MP reprint (original pub 1961).
SB. xvi + 502pp with 46 maps and numerous contemporary photos.
ISBN: 1843428067
Price: £32.00

www.naval-military-press.com